普通高等教育"十一五"国家级规划教材

跨文化交际学选读

Selected Readings in Intercultural Communication Studies

（第3版）

李本现　田德新　文晓莉 编

 西安交通大学出版社　国家一级出版社
XI'AN JIAOTONG UNIVERSITY PRESS　全国百佳图书出版单位

内容简介

本书包括12个单元24篇课文,每篇课文前后均有导言、注释和思考题,书后另附有跨文化交际学相关的术语解释。本书的主要内容涉及跨文化交际学概述、语言与文化的相互关系、语言与非语言交际、东西方思维模式与价值观念差异、文化与感知模式、跨文化交际障碍与文化适应,以及日常生活与商贸洽谈跨文化交际实践等诸多方面。本书适合英语专业本科高年级学生和硕士研究生的教学使用,也是具有中级以上水平的广大英语学习者和各类涉外工作人员的必备参考读本。

图书在版编目(CIP)数据

跨文化交际学选读:英文/李本现,田德新,文晓莉编.—3版.—西安:西安交通大学出版社,2022.9
 ISBN 978-7-5693-2623-9

Ⅰ.①跨⋯ Ⅱ.①李⋯ ②田⋯ ③文⋯ Ⅲ.①文化交流-英文 Ⅳ.①G115

中国版本图书馆 CIP 数据核字(2022)第 088925 号

跨文化交际学选读(第3版)
KUAWENHUA JIAOJIXUE XUANDU(DI 3 BAN)

主　　编	李本现　田德新　文晓莉	
责任编辑	李　蕊	
责任校对	蔡乐芊	

出版发行	西安交通大学出版社	
	(西安市兴庆南路1号　邮政编码 710048)	
网　　址	http://www.xjtupress.com	
电　　话	(029)82668357　82667874(市场营销中心)	
	(029)82668315(总编办)	
传　　真	(029)82668280	
印　　刷	西安日报社印务中心	
开　　本	710mm×1000mm　1/16　　印张　33.5　　字数　850千字	
版次印次	2022年9月第3版　　2022年9月第1次印刷	
书　　号	ISBN 978-7-5693-2623-9	
定　　价	85.00元	

如发现印装质量问题,请与本社市场营销中心联系。
订购热线:(029)82665248　(029)82667874
投稿热线:(029)82668531　(029)82665371

版权所有　侵权必究

第3版前言

《跨文化交际学选读》出版至今已逾15年,2004年修订再版后,本书依然受到使用者的喜爱,并成功遴选为普通高等教育"十一五"国家级规划教材,这给予了我们更多的鼓舞和激励。提到修订,其实西安交通大学出版社早在去年就给出了指导意见,后来还分享了多篇有关文献供我们学习领会;西安外国语大学的校、院级领导在繁忙的工作中也分别抽时间专门讨论修订方案,并给予大力支持,对此我们编者团队表示由衷的感谢。

经过一年多的资料收集和对使用者的反馈调研,《跨文化交际学选读》的再版修订工作终于在丹桂飘香的金秋十月正式启动。编者们经过认真讨论,坚持恩师杜瑞清先生初版时制定的编写框架的大原则不变,同时采纳了圈内许多专家的建议和使用者(尤其是西安外国语大学英文学院拔尖班同学们)的反馈,新选多篇更为合适的阅读文本进入教材,以弘扬习近平总书记倡导的"文明交流互鉴是推动人类文明进步和世界和平发展的重要动力"的思想,充分体现"文化多元共存、文明互学互鉴"的原则,争取为读者"国际视野的开阔、跨文化交际能力的提升"贡献力量,进而为"向世界讲好中国故事"提供一本富有价值的跨文化交际学读本。

此次具体修订及分工如下。

一、调换了第1单元和第7单元的四篇阅读(文晓莉承担)、第3单元的第2篇阅读(李本现承担)、第6单元的第2篇阅读和第12单元的第2篇阅读(田德新承担)。

二、各单元阅读后讨论题的5个题目中,原则上至少有一道题增补了新的思考点或增设了中国文化视角练习(由各单元编者完成)。

三、新增了练习"微型案例网上研究与朋友圈分享"(由各单元编者完成)。该部分设计的初衷,一是顺应大学生读者偏爱利用朋友圈学习和互动的习惯,二是采纳了其他读者提出的阅读中穿插若干鲜活实例的建议。据此,我们在选取微型案例时兼顾了学术价值和趣味性的有机结合。

四、增补了一些较新的术语解释(田德新承担)。

我们真切希望新版《跨文化交际学选读》能进一步满足新时代对我国高等院校跨文化交际学和跨文化对比研究等课程的教学需要,尤其能成为众多研习跨文化交际学的同学们喜爱的读物。同时,在使用本书的过程中,如有好的想法或建议,敬请广大读者一如既往地不吝赐教。

最后,我们向修订出版过程中支持和关心《跨文化交际学选读》(第3版)的师长、出版社编辑、同仁及广大读者再次致以诚挚的谢意。

编 者

2021年12月

前　言

　　日新月异的现代化交通工具和全球联网的高科技通信手段,使得整个世界缩小,让全人类似乎生活在一个地球村里。不同国家、不同文化、不同种族之间的交往日益频繁。欲实现顺畅、有效和得体的交流与沟通,我们需要培养大量具有跨文化交际能力的各类人才。为适应跨文化交际学在国内外的发展态势,并结合我国英语专业本科与研究生教学的实际需求,在多年教学实践的基础上,我们编写了《跨文化交际学选读》一书。

　　本书10个单元共20篇文章,每篇文章前后设有导言、注释和思考题,书后附有跨文化交际学术语解释与参考书目。书中主要内容涉及跨文化交际学概述、语言与文化的相互关系、语言与非语言交际、东西方思维模式与价值观念差异、文化与感知模式、跨文化交际障碍与文化适应,以及日常生活与商贸洽谈跨文化交际实践等诸多方面。课前导言提纲挈领,旨在激发读者求知欲的同时,将其导入正文赏析;文中术语和文化背景注释尽可能简明扼要;思考题紧扣文章主旨,并力求发人深省;书后术语解释与参考书目可为读者理解原文和进一步研修提供方便。

　　读者通过本书的学习,一方面能够熟悉各种跨文化交际规则,另一方面能够提高在不同场合的跨文化交际能力。本书适于英语专业本科高年级学生和硕士研究生的教学使用,同时,也是具有中级以上水平的广大英语学习者和各类涉外工作人员的必备参考读本。

　　本书由杜瑞清教授规划统筹。编选工作分工如下:

　　田德新　第四、五、六、八单元、术语解释、参考书目;

　　李本现　第二、三、九、十单元;

　　杜瑞清　第一、七单元。

　　在本书编写过程中,承蒙曾萍和刘颖勤两位同事协助搜集、提供材料,谨在此致谢。

　　限于编者的水平及其他客观原因,本书难免有疏漏之处,敬请英语界各位前辈、同行和广大读者不吝赐教,予以指正。

编　者
2004 年 7 月

再版前言

《跨文化交际学选读》于2004年出版后受到了广大读者的欢迎和肯定,被全国许多高校列为教材使用,并被遴选为普通高等教育"十一五"国家级规划教材。为了更全面、更及时地反映全球范围内跨文化交际学研究成果,更有效地保证和提高我国高等院校跨文化交际学课程的教学质量,进一步促进跨文化交际学研究,我们广泛征求了意见,在西安交通大学出版社和西安外国语大学的大力支持下,对该书内容进行了修订和增补。

第2版在保持原书基本框架和体系的前提下,采纳了许多专家和读者的建议,增加了4篇有关跨文化交际理论探讨的文章,构成本书的第11单元和第12单元,调换了第8单元的第1篇和第9单元的第2篇选文,补充和调整了部分注释,增补和更新了附录中的术语和参考书目。

我们殷切希望《跨文化交际学选读》(第2版)能更好地适应我国高等院校跨文化交际课程的教学需要,满足广大读者的要求。对修订版中仍然存在的缺憾或不足,我们期待着各位专家和读者的建议和批评。

值此《跨文化交际学选读》(第2版)出版之际,我们再一次向关心、支持本书的各位专家和广大读者表示衷心的谢意。

编　者
2009年12月

Contents

Unit One　Intercultural Communication: An Overview ……………… (1)
　Studying Intercultural Communication ……………………………… (1)
　Notes in the History of Intercultural Communication ……………… (31)

Unit Two　Language and Culture ……………………………………… (51)
　Communicative Codes: Linguistic Aspects …………………………… (52)
　Language and Culture: Sounds and Actions ………………………… (74)

Unit Three　Cultural Identity and Intercultural Communication …… (98)
　Intercultural Dilemma in Multicultural Setting: Doing vs. Being ……… (98)
　Identity and Interpersonal Bonding …………………………………… (117)

Unit Four　Verbal Communication …………………………………… (132)
　Verbal Intercultural Communication ………………………………… (132)
　Relationships in Face-to-Face Communication ……………………… (156)

Unit Five　Nonverbal Communication ………………………………… (177)
　Nonverbal Intercultural Communication ……………………………… (178)
　Nonverbal Codes and Cultural Space ………………………………… (204)

Unit Six　Cultural Patterns and Perception …………………………… (226)
　Cultural Patterns and Communication: Taxonomies ………………… (226)
　The Allegory of the Cave ……………………………………………… (252)

Unit Seven　Intercultural Communication—East and West ………… (260)
　Individualism – Collectivism and Personality ………………………… (261)
　Intercultural Conflict Styles: A Face-Negotiation Theory …………… (275)

1

Unit Eight   Intercultural Barriers ……………………………………… (297)
   Attitudes toward the Culturally Different: The Role of Intercultural
      Communication Barriers, Affective Responses, Consensual Stereotypes,
      and Perceived Threat …………………………………………… (298)
   Stumbling Blocks in Intercultural Communication …………………… (321)

Unit Nine   Intercultural Communication in Business, Management and
              Negotiation ……………………………………………… (337)
   Negotiating Across Cultures …………………………………………… (338)
   Reconciling Cultural Dilemmas ………………………………………… (355)

Unit Ten   Cultural Adaptation and Intercultural Competence ……… (373)
   Cross-Cultural Adaptation: Axioms …………………………………… (374)
   The Potential for Intercultural Competence …………………………… (392)

Unit Eleven   Theories of Intercultural Communication ……………… (409)
   Theorizing about Intercultural Communication: An Introduction ……… (410)
   Measuring Culture: The Utility of Verifying Hofstede's Cultural Dimensions
      ………………………………………………………………………… (444)

Unit Twelve   Scholarship on Chinese Communication ……………… (460)
   Chinese Communication Scholarship as an Expansion of the Communication
      and Culture Paradigm …………………………………………… (461)
   Construction of a Water and Game Theory for Intercultural Communication
      ………………………………………………………………………… (485)

Glossary ……………………………………………………………………… (510)

Unit One

Intercultural Communication: An Overview

Reading One

Introductory Remarks

We are now living in a rapidly changing world with larger forces driving us to interact with people from different cultural backgrounds. Technology, business, educational opportunities, and political turmoil are some of the many forces that lead to the active and/or passive intercultural communication/interaction. Intercultural communication is a form of communication aiming to share information across different cultures and social groups. It describes the wide range of communication processes and problems that naturally appear within an organization, made up of individuals from different religious, social, ethnic, and educational backgrounds. Intercultural communication as a human activity dates back to ancient, however, it is relatively new as an academic discipline.

In terms of the reasons to study intercultural communication, they are wide and varied. Martin and Nakayama (2017) believe that all the varied reasons can fall into six categories that they call imperatives, that is, the important or compelling reasons. Martin and Nakayama (2017) identify the six imperative categories as peace, demographic, economic, technological, self-awareness, and ethical. These imperatives are not mutually exclusive, instead, they are interwoven with one another in the covert and/or overt relationship, which could be perceived as sparking a brainstorm or creativity. What is your reason for studying intercultural communication?

Studying Intercultural Communication[1]

Judith N. Martin and Thomas K. Nakayama

A child born today will be faced as an adult, almost daily, with problems of a global interdependent nature, be it peace, food, the quality of life, inflation, or scarcity of resources. He/she will be both an actor and a beneficiary or a victim in the total world fabric, and may rightly ask: "Why was I not warned? Why was I not better educated? Why did my teachers not tell me about these problems and indicate my behavior as a member of an interdependent human race?"

—Robert Muller[2]

This quote from Robert Muller, known as "the father of global education" is as relevant today as it was 30 years ago and underscores the importance of learning about our interdependent world. In addition to peace, food, the economy, and the quality of life identified by Muller, climate change, terrorism, conflicts around the globe require working across cultural differences to find solutions to these complex problems. For example, religious and ethnic conflicts in the Middle East and Africa, territorial tensions in Asia over strategic island claimed by more than one country as well as the worldwide refugee problem with millions of migrants streaming into Europe into already fragile economies, for example, Greece and Eastern European countries. In addition, the once powerful Chinese economy is now struggling, leading to nervousness of U.S. investors and a volatile stock market. On the more positive side, global interconnectedness also brings us the World Cup, the Olympics, as well as global cooperation in dealing with health challenges like the Ebola and Zika outbreaks.

The personal impact of this global interconnectedness has been extensive. Although the recession in the United States is technically over, wages here are stagnant and the promises of the American Dream seem illusive for many—particularly for minority households whose financial resources remain at a fraction of White households. Perhaps your parents or someone you know lost their jobs, or their houses in the economic down-town. Perhaps you worry about how you'll pay off your college debt or whether you'll ever be able to own a home or achieve economic independence. Let's consider how the economic conditions and world tensions are affecting intercultural relations. In the United States where some adult children, many saddled with large college debt, are still living at home and according to a recent report, even though there have been positive economic trends, there has been no increase in the number of young adults establishing their own households. In fact, the number is no higher in 2015 than it was before the recession. As one 20—something said "I can't foresee a future where we're going to buy a house ... It'll be 10 to 15 years, and by that time, we'll be too old to have children. I don't know how people afford to have children these days".

This intergenerational living arrangement, common in many parts of the world, presents challenges to independent-minded children (and parents) in the United States and requires (intercultural) communication skills—listening to each other openly and respectfully. Some even say it's a good thing—that parents and children get to spend extra time with each other that they wouldn't be able to do in other circumstances.

The global economic slowdown has had enormous consequences for intercultural relations in the fledging European Union (EU). As you probably know, European countries have experienced the crisis differently but are economically inter dependent. The northern countries like Germany, Finland, Sweden, and Denmark have implemented austerity measures and have relatively healthy economies, which are being dragged down by the economically weak southern countries like Greece, Spain, and Italy. The resulting tensions over economic issues and the recent refugee crisis are fueling old stereotypes. Germans (even some politicians) are calling Greeks work-shy, rule-bending, and recklessly extravagant while they see themselves as hard-working, law-abiding people who live within their means. On the other hand, Greeks make fun of German frugality and some are even invoking the old "Germans as Nazis" stereotype.

The challenges of increased immigration and economic tensions in Europe and the resulting fears of security are present in the United States as well. After the devastating terror attacks in Paris and San Bernardino in 2015, security concerns translated to anti-immigrant/refugee attitudes and legislation. One poll found that 53 percent of U.S. Americans didn't want to accept any Syrian refugees at all and about 50 percent said "immigrants are a burden because they take jobs, housing, and health care". While some feel that these are reasonable attitudes and policies, others feel that it paves the way for increased prejudice and discrimination against foreigners, particularly those from the Middle East and Latin America.

So what does all this mean for intercultural communication? While these close economic connections highlight our global economy, these relationships also point to the large numbers of people who communicate every day with people from around the world. Some of this communication is face-to-face with international students, business travelers, tourists, migrants, and others. Some of this communication is online through the Internet, texting, or other communication media.

Economics are one important force, but there are many other reasons that people come into intercultural contact. Wars or other violent conflicts drive some people to leave their homelands to seek a safer place to live. Natural disasters can drive people to other areas where they can rebuild their lives. Some people seek a better life somewhere else, or are driven by their own curiosity to seek out and visit other parts of the world. People often fall in love and build families in another country. Can you think of other reasons that drive people to interact across cultural differences?

What do you as a student of intercultural communication need to learn to understand the complexities of intercultural interaction? And how can learning about intercultural communication benefit you?

It is easy to become overwhelmed by that complexity. However, not knowing everything that you would like to know is very much a part of the learning process, and this inability to know everything is what makes intercultural communication experiences so exciting. Rather than being discouraged by everything that you cannot know, think of all the things you can learn from intercultural communication experiences. This book will introduce you to some of the basic concepts and guidelines for thinking about intercultural interaction. You can also learn a lot of intercultural communication by listening to other people's experiences, but intercultural communication is a lifelong project and hope you will continue your journey after you read this book.

Why is it important to focus on intercultural communication and to strive to become better at this complex form of interaction? There are many reasons why you might want to learn more about intercultural communication. Perhaps you want to better serve a diverse clientele in your chosen occupation; perhaps members of your extended family are from different races or religions, or have physical abilities that you would like to understand better. Perhaps you want to better understand the culturally diverse colleagues in your workplace. Or perhaps you want to learn more about the people you come into contact with through the Internet, or to learn more about the countries and cultures that are in the daily news. In this article we discuss the following imperatives—reasons to study intercultural communication. Perhaps one or more will apply to your situation.

THE PEACE IMPERATIVE

The key issue is this: Can individuals of different genders, ages, ethnicities, races, languages, and religions peacefully coexist on the planet? According to the Center for Systemic Peace, while conflict between national powers has decreased, societal wars (conflict between groups within a country) have increased. The current trend is toward longer, more intranational protracted conflicts where military or material support is supplied by foreign powers—fighting "proxy wars"[3]—to warring groups. For example, consider the strife between Kurds and government forces in Iraq and Turkey, the conflict between insurgent rebel groups and the government in Syria, the various groups in Libya where there is no central government at the moment, and woven throughout this region. There are also the conflicts between the government and various drug cartels in Mexico, and the Boko Haram in Nigeria.

Some of the conflicts have roots in the past foreign policies. The strength of the Taliban related to the U.S. policies in twice promising to help Afghanistan people and both times withdrawing military and infrastructure building support, both times leaving Afghanistan people at the mercy of the Taliban. Still other conflicts are tied to the tremendous influence of U.S. technology and media which may be celebrated by some and as a cause of resistance by others. For example, the massive influence of U.S. pop culture is seen by some as inhibiting the development of other nations' indigenous popular culture products and forcing U.S. values on them, which sometimes leads to resentment and conflict.

Some conflicts have to do with economic disparities and legacies of oppression, seen in the racial and ethnic tensions in U.S. neighborhoods and recent conflicts between law enforcement and some Black communities. There are also tensions regarding what some people perceive as racist symbolism of the Cleveland Indians, a U.S. major league baseball team, and the Washington Redskins, a U.S. professional football team.

Communication scholar Benjamin Broome has worked with many conflict areas, including in Cyprus with Greeks and Turk Cypriots (once the most heavily fortified border in the world) and also Native American groups in the United States. He emphasizes that one cannot focus only on the interpersonal level or the societal level, but all levels. He proposes an approach of peacebuilding which is not just the absence of conflict, but an effort to stop all forms of violence and promote transformative ways to deal with conflict, including strategies that address personal, relational, and structural (organizational, economic conditions, etc.) elements of conflict. According to Broome, communication, especially facilitated dialogue, plays a key role in the peacebuilding process. We need to remember that individuals often are born into and are caught up in conflicts that they neither started nor chose and are impacted by larger societal forces.

THE ECONOMIC IMPERATIVE

You may want to know more about intercultural communication because you foresee tremendous changes in the workplace in the coming years. This is one important reason to know about other cultures and communication patterns. In addition, knowing about intercultural communication is strategically important for U.S. businesses in the emerging transnational economy. As noted by writer Carol

Hymowitz of the *Wall Street Journal*, "If companies are going to sell products and services globally, then they will need a rich mix of employees with varied perspectives and experiences. They will need top executives who understand different countries and cultures."

The Workplace
Given the growing cultural diversity in the United States, businesses necessarily must be more attentive to diversity issues. As the workforce becomes more diverse, many businesses are seeking to capitalize on these differences: "Once organizations learn to adopt an inclusive orientation in dealing with their members, this will also have a positive impact on how they look at their customer base, how they develop products and assess business opportunities, and how they relate to their communities." Benefiting from cultural differences in the workplace involves not only working with diverse employees and employers but also seeing new business markets, developing new products for differing cultural contexts, and marketing products in culturally appropriate and effective ways. From this perspective, diversity is a potentially powerful economic tool for business organizations.

The Global Economy
Businesses all around the world are continually expanding into overseas markets in a process of globalization. This recent trend is shown dramatically in the report of a journalist who asked a Dell computer manager where his laptop is made. The answer? It was codesigned by engineers in Texas and Taiwan; the microprocessor was made in one of Intel's factories in Philippines, Costa Rica, Malaysia, or China; the memory came from factories in the Republic of Korea, Germany, China, or Japan. Other components (keyboard, hard-disk drive, batteries, etc.) were made by Japanese, Chinese, Irish, Israeli, or British firms with factories mainly in Asia; and finally, the laptop was assembled in China. What is the ultimate impact of globalization on the average person? Some economists defend it, saying that the losses are always offset by the gains in consumer prices but many workers who have lost jobs in the recent past and seen wages stagnate are not so sure. There are many blue collar industrial jobs that have been lost to overseas in the past 10 years but one recent study concludes that as many as 14 million white-collar jobs are also vulnerable to being outsourced offshore—jobs in information technology, accounting, architecture, advanced engineering design, news reporting, stock analysis, and medical and legal services—jobs that generate

the bulk of tax revenues that fund our education, health, infrastructure, and social security systems. In fact, the Department of Labor reminds us that the track record for the re-employment of displaced U.S. workers is not good, that more than one in three workers who are displaced remains unemployed, and many of those who are lucky enough to find jobs take major pay cuts.

The world economy has been volatile and seemingly shrinking in recent years. The economic powerhouse, China, has seen disastrous economic trends with a plummeting stock market, housing crises, and a manufacturing slowdown, and its slowest growth since 1990. The worry now and the evidence seems to support it that a slowing China also lowers growth in other countries.

The point is that to compete effectively in this shrinking global market, Americans must understand how business is conducted in other countries and how to negotiate deals that are advantageous to the U.S. economy. However, they are not always willing to take the time and effort to do this. For example, eBay, the successful American Ecommerce giant copied its American model to China and got completely destroyed by local competitor *Taobao*. Why? Because *Taobao* understood that in China, shopping was a social experience and people like talking and even haggling with sellers and building relationships with them. *Taobao* had a chat feature that allowed customers to easily talk to sellers. Stories abound of U.S. marketing slogans that were inaccurately translated, like Pepsi's "Come alive with Pepsi Generation" (which was translated into Chinese as "Pepsi brings your ancestors back from the grave"), or General Motors marketing the Nova in South America (*no va* is Spanish for "no go"). In contrast, Starbucks' recent decision to change its logo when it enter the Asian markets seems to be successful. Starbucks decided to drop the Starbucks name and the word "coffee" from its logo, giving it a more rounded appearance, which seems to appeal to collectivist consumers—found in China and other Asian countries.

In addition, there are other considerations in understanding the global market. Moving operations overseas to take advantage of lower labor costs has far-reaching implications for corporations. One example is the *maquiladoras*[4]—foreign-owned plants that use domestic labor—just across the U.S.-Mexican border. The U.S. companies that relocate their plants there benefit from lower labor costs and lack of environmental and other business regulations, while Mexican laborers benefit from the jobs. But there is a cost in terms of environmental hazards. Because Mexico has less stringent air and water pollution regulations than the United States, many of these *maquiladoras* have a negative environmental impact on the Mexican side of the border. Because the two nations are economically and environmentally interde pendent, they share the economic and environmental impact. Thus, these contexts present intercultural challenges for Mexicans and Americans alike.

To help bridge the cultural gap, many companies employ cross-cultural trainers, who assist people going abroad by giving them information about and strategies for dealing with cultural differences; such trainers report that Japanese and other business personnel often spend years in the United States studying English and learning about the country before they decide to build a factory or invest money there. By contrast, many U.S. companies provide little or no training before sending their workers overseas and expect business deals to be completed very quickly. They seem to have little regard for cultural idiosyncrasies, which can cause ill will and mistrust, enhance negative stereotypes, and result in lost business opportunities.

In the future, global economic development will create even more demand for intercultural communication. Economic exchanges will drive intercultural interactions. This development will create not only more jobs but also more consumers to purchase goods from around the world—and to travel in that world.

THE TECHNOLOGICAL IMPERATIVE

Communication technology is a constant. We are linked by technology to events in the most remote parts of the world and also to people that we may never meet face-to-face. In any given day you may text message or snapchat with friends about evening plans, post a Facebook message to a relative stationed overseas, participate in a discussion board for one of your courses, send an e-mail message to your professor and use Google Hangout for a virtual team project in an online course. It's possible not only to communicate with other people but also to develop complex relationships with them through such technology.

Technology and Human Communication

The extent of global connection and communication through social network sites is staggering. For example, Facebook was the first to surpass one billion monthly active users. These networks are often available in multiple languages and enable users to connect with friends or people across geographical, political, or economic borders. About two billion people now use social network sites like Facebook, Instagram, and Tumblr in the United States, VK in the United Kingdom, and QQ and WeChat in China. By some accounts, people spend more time on social networking sites (SNSs) like Facebook than any other online activity, and 80 percent of Facebook users are outside the United States and Canada. The effect of social media like Facebook and Twitter has far-reaching consequences, and it is important to understand that these technologies can have positive and negative impacts on intercultural encounters. For example, by using Twitter and Facebook, people were able to receive up-to-the-minute information and connect with friends and family in the immediate aftermath of the devastating Japanese tsunami in January 2011. Syrians, Egyptians, and Libyans were able to broadcast to the world—through text and videos—minute-by-minute reports of the progress and challenges of their fight for democracy against their repressive governments.

On the other hand, you may feel like you're too dependent on social media and suffer from FOMO (Fear of Missing Out)[5], checking your phone many times a day to see if you have messages or if there are new posts to Facebook that you have to see. An even worse impact of social media is the vicious trolls and nasty posts. For example, there was a multitude of vicious racist tweets posted in reaction to the crowning of the first Indian American as Miss America. These media videos and messages illustrate the far-reaching negative potential of communication technologies.

Some media experts worry that all the connectivity has not necessarily strengthened our relationships. Sometimes, in face-to-face encounters, we are not really present because we are checking our mobile phones for text messages or searching for information. One expert terms this the "absent presence." Another suggests that technology gives us control over our relationships and makes it easy for us to communicate when and how we wish, so that we often choose technologies, like texting or voice-mail messages, that actually distance us from each other.

That is said, more and more people around the world are using technology to communicate with each other. Consider these statistics:

- Mobile phone use in Africa has grown from 1 percent in 2000 to more than 54 percent today and people in South Africa and Nigeria have the same level of cellphone ownership as in America.
- The number of Internet users in Africa grew at seven times the global average, clocking more than 3,600 percent growth between 2000 and 2015, to 330 million users, according to data from Internet World Statistics (Internetstats. com).

What does this have to do with intercultural communication? Through high-tech communication, we come into contact with people who are very different from ourselves, often in ways we don't understand. The people we talk to on e-mail networks and blogs may speak languages different from our own, come from different countries, be of different ethnic backgrounds, and have had many different life experiences.

Technology has increased the frequency with which many people encounter multilingual situations; they must decide which language will be used. Contrast this situation with the everyday lives of people 100 years ago, in which they rarely communicated with people outside their own villages, much less people speaking different languages. Digital translation apps like Google Translate, Universal Translator, iTranslate can facilitate communication for travelers and business people and others in everyday intercultural encounters. Of course the use of some languages is privileged over others on the Internet. As experts note, if you want to do business online, it's more than likely going to be in English, the FIGS languages (French, Italian, German, Spanish), the CJK languages (Chinese, Japanese, Korean), and "the main languages of former colonial empires (Dutch, Russian, Portuguese)."

In addition to language and translation issues, online communication across cultures can present other challenges. For example, some online communication (e. g. , e-mail, text messages, tweets) filters out important nonverbal cues. When we are talking to individuals face-to-face we use nonverbal information to help us interpret what they are really saying—tone of voice, facial expressions, gestures, and so on. The absence of these cues in some online communication makes communication more difficult and can lead to misunderstandings, especially when communicating across cultures. One of our colleagues discovered in working in several virtual team projects that her colleagues in some countries (e. g. , India) tend to deliver part of their message with silence or nonverbal signs and prefer to communicate face-to-face. With this knowledge, she now uses Skype more to communicate with some team members rather than e-mail. One of our students, Lydia, described the challenges of online intercultural communication:

> In my last year of college, my roommate was from China and we became good friends. When she went back home in June, we decided to stay friends through Facebook and Skype. I find it much more difficult to communicate with her online because she doesn't always understand what I was writing and I couldn't repeat my sentences like I could if I were speaking to her, and the same applied to her. Skyping is definitely a lot easier, so we usually keep in touch this way.

Social media and other interactive media also give us the opportunity to stay in contact with people who are very similar to ourselves, with family members, friends, and others who share common interests. We can also turn to online groups and community for support. For example, international students can stay in touch with their local communities, keep up with what's going on at home, and receive emotional support during difficult time of cultural adaptation. Immigrants can stay in touch with friends and family at home or other immigrants from their country who are living all over the world. Similarly, discussion forums provide virtual communities of support for cultural minorities.

However, the social media can also provide a venue for like-minded people to promote prejudice and hatred. The number of websites that promote hatred against Americans, Muslims, Jews, gays, and people of non-European ancestry has increased exponentially to more than 30,000 and experts point out that young people are especially vulnerable to racist online flash games, jokes, and general hatefilled information on social media. One of the issues of interest to those who study intercultural communication is the "digital divide" that exists between those who have access to technologies like the Internet and those who do not.

Studies show that in the United States the people most likely to have access to and use the Internet are young or middle age, have a college degree or are students, and have a comfortable income. Race and ethnicity don't seem to play a role, if we compare similar levels of education and income. While the digital divide is shrinking, there are still some inequities, mostly related to income, urban-rural location, and physical ability. In addition, those Americans (mostly poor and some ethnic minorities) who have only a smartphone for online access at home have challenges. They are more likely than other users to encounter data-cap limits on smartphone service, frequently have to cancel or suspend service due to financial constraints, and face challenges when it comes to important tasks such as filling out job applications and writing (and reading) documents.

Even larger inequalities exist outside the United States. In many regions (Asia, Africa, and Middle East), only a fraction of the population has access to computers and the Internet, for example, Internet access in Africa is 29 percent compared to the worldwide average of about 50 percent.

These inequities have enormous implications for intercultural communication. In the global information society, information is an important commodity. Everybody needs its function. This ability is especially important in an increasingly "networked" society. It is easy to see how without these skills and knowledge one can feel marginalized and disconnected from the center of society.

THE DEMOGRAPHIC IMPERATIVE

Demographics refers to the general characteristics of a given population. As shown by the 2000 and 2010 U.S. Census data, the demographics of the United States is changing dramatically during your lifetime—the next 50 years. The workforce that you enter will differ significantly from the one that your parents entered. These changes come from two sources: changing demographics within the United States and changing immigration patterns.

Changing U.S. Demographics

According to the U.S. Population Reference Bureau, the nation's Hispanic and Asian populations are expected to triple by 2050, while non-Hispanic Whites are expected to grow more slowly to represent about one-half of the nation's population. People of Hispanic origin (who may be of any race) will increase from 36 million to 103 million. The Asian population is projected to triple, from 11 million to 33 million. The Black population is projected to grow from 36 million to 61 million in 2050, an increase of 71 percent. That change will increase Blacks' share of the nation's population from 13 percent in 2000 to 15 percent in 2050.

The population representing "all other races"—a category that includes American Indians, Alaska Natives, Hawaiian and other Pacific Islanders, as well as those who indicated two or more races on census forms—is also expected to triple between 2000 and 2050, growing from 7 million to about 22 million.

Another interesting projection involves the "multiracial" category, partly due to the increasing numbers of interracial couples. The 2000 Census was the first that allowed persons to categorize themselves as being of "two or more races"—2.4 percent of respondents did just that, and this number is projected to increase. The most recent statistics released from the 2010 Census shows that the projections for increasing diversity are right on target—reflecting dramatic changes in the ethnic and racial makeup of the United States. In fact, the nation is moving a step closer to a demographic milestone in which no group commands a majority, already true in 317 counties in four states (California, Hawaii, New Mexico, and Texas) and the District of Columbia with Nevada, Arizona, Florida, Georgia, and Maryland approaching this milestone. As you can see, the states with the most diverse populations tend to be in the southern and western regions of the United States. These statistics show rather dramatically that where you live determines to some extent how many opportunities you have to interact with people who are different from you ethnically or racially. Overall, the integration of new workers with the current ones will provide both opportunities and challenges for American businesses, as well as for the country as a whole.

Changing Immigration Patterns
The second source of demographic change is immigration. There are two contradictory faces to the story of immigration in the United States. The United States often is described as a nation of immigrants, but it is also a nation that established itself by subjugating the original inhabitants of the land and that prospered economically while forcibly importing millions of Africans to perform slave labor. It is important to recognize the many different experiences that people have had in the United States so that we can better understand what it means to be as a U.S. American. We cannot simply think of the American people as a nation of immigrants if we want to better understand contemporary U.S. society.

Current patterns of immigration are having a significant effect on the social landscape, as the foreign born population continues to rise as a percentage of the total population, up from almost 5 percent in 1970 to more than 12 percent in 2013. However, this is still lower than it was during the great migrations of the 1800s and 1900s when most Europeans came to the United States. According to the U.S. Census Bureau, the vast majority of today's immigrants now come from Latin America (52 percent) and Asia (25 percent). These immigrants also tend to settle in particular areas of the country. They are more likely to live in the western part of the United States and more likely to live in the central locations of metropolitan areas, adding to the diversity of these areas. These immigration changes, along with increasing domestic diversity clearly show that the United States is becoming more heterogeneous (diverse).

These demographic changes present many opportunities and challenges for students of intercultural communication and for society. Tensions among different racial and ethnic groups, as well as fear on the part of politically dominant groups, must be acknowledged. However, intercultural conflict is not necessarily a consequence of diversity. Intercultural encounters in certain types of conditions can lead to very positive outcomes, including reduced prejudice and positive intergroup relationships. Diverse college campuses, for example, can provide opportunities for the type of intercultural contact in which intercultural friendships can flourish—opportunities for extensive contact in a variety of formal and informal settings that promote communication and foster relationship development.

In fact, not surprisingly, the more diverse a campus is, the more likely students are to develop intercultural friendships—these friendships provide opportunities to expand our horizons linguistically, politically, and socially. We often profit from being exposed to different ways of doing things and incorporate these customs into our own lifestyles.

Historical Overview

To get a better sense of the sociocultural situation in the United States today, let's take a look at American history. As mentioned, the United States has always been a nation of immigrants. When Europeans began arriving on the shores of the New World, an estimated 8 to 10 million Native Americans were already living here. The outcome of the encounters between these groups—the colonizing Europeans and the native peoples—is well known. By 1940, the Native American population of the United States had been reduced to an estimated 250,000.

Today, there are about 2.5 million American Indians, from 542 recognized tribes, living in the United States.

African Americans are a special case in the history of U.S. immigration because they were brought to this country involuntarily. Some Europeans and Asians also arrived in the country as indentured or contract labor. However, by the middle of the seventeenth century this system of indenture was stopped because it was not economically viable for farmers and did not solve the problem of chronic labor shortage. Landowners needed captive workers who could neither escape servitude nor become competitors. The answer was slavery. Native Americans were not a good choice, given that they could always escape back to their own lands, but Africans were not. In fact, Europeans and Africans were already in the slave business, and so America became a prime market. The slave trade lasted about 350 years, during which 9 to 10 million Africans reached the Americas (the vast majority died in the brutal overseas passage). As James Baldwin has suggested, slavery is what makes U.S. history and current interracial relations different from those in Europe.

Historically, slavery presented a moral dilemma for many Whites, but today a common response is to ignore history. Many Whites say that because not all Whites owned slaves they should simply forget it and move on. For most African Americans, however, this is unacceptable. Rather, as Cornel West, a professor of Afro-American studies and the philosophy of religion at Harvard University, suggests, "we should begin by acknowledging the historical flaws in American society and recognizing the historical consequences of slavery." It is interesting to note that there are several Holocaust museums in the United States, but only recently has there been official national recognition of the horrors of slavery—with the Smithsonian National Museum of African American History and Culture which opened in Fall 2016. The second museum, Whitney Plantation on 2000 acres in Wallace Louisiana, was refurbished by real estate magnate John Cummings at his own expense of $8 million and is dedicated to telling the story of slavery. The site has the requisite 220-year-old genteel and beautifully furnished "big house" but also restored tiny slave cabins, a slave jail, blacksmith shop, and a number of memorials to the slaves who lived, worked, and died there.

Relationships between residents and immigrants—between old-timers and new-comers—often have been contentious. In the nineteenth century, Native Americans sometimes were caught in the middle of U.S. and European rivalries. During the War of 1812, for example, Indian allies of the British were severely punished by the United States when the war ended. In 1832, the U.S. Congress recognized Native Americans' right to self-government, but an 1871 congressional act prohibited treaties between the U.S. government and Indian tribes. In 1887, Congress passed the Dawes Severalty Act, terminating Native Americans' special relationship with the U.S. government and paving the way for the removal of Native Americans from their land.

As waves of immigrants continued to roll in from Europe, the more firmly established European—mainly English—immigrants tried to protect their way of life, language, and culture. James Banks has identified various conflicts throughout the nation's history, many of which were not uniquely American but were imported from Europe. In 1729, for example, an English mob prevented a group of Irish immigrants from landing in Boston. A few years later, another mob destroyed a new Scotch-Irish Presbyterian church in Worcester, Massachusetts. Subsequently, as immigrants from northern and western Europe came to dominate American culture, immigrants from southern, central, and eastern Europe were expected to assimilate into the so-called mainstream culture—to jump into the "melting pot" and come out "American."

In the late nineteenth and early twentieth centuries, an anti-immigrant, nativistic movement promoted violence against newer immigrants.

The anti-immigrant, nativistic sentiment was well supported at the government level as well. In 1924, the Johnson-Reed Act and the Oriental Exclusion Act established strict quotas on immigration and completely barred the immigration of Asians. According to Ronald Takaki, these 1924 laws "provided for immigration based on nationality quotas: the number of immigrants to be admitted annually was limited to 2 percent of the foreign-born individuals of each nationality residing in the United States in 1890." The underlying rationale was that economic and political opportunities should be reserved for Whites, native-born Americans or not. Thus, the dominance of Whites in the United States is not simply the result of more Europeans wanting to come here; the U.S. government designed our society in this way.

By the 1930s, immigrants from southern and eastern Europe were considered assimilable, or able to become members of White American society, and the concept of race assumed new meaning. All of the so-called White races were now considered one, so racial hostilities were directed toward members of non-White ethnic groups, such as Asian Americans, Native Americans, and Mexican Americans; this bias was particularly devastating for African Americans. In the growing but sometimes fragile economy of the first half of the twentieth century, only White workers were assured a place. White immigrants may have earned relatively low wages, but they were paid additional "psychological" wages in the form of better schools, increased access to public facilities, and more public deference.

Economic conditions make a big difference in attitudes toward foreign workers and immigration policies. Thus, during the Great Depression of the 1930s, Mexicans and Mexican Americans were forced to return to Mexico to free up jobs for White Americans. When prosperity returned in the 1940s, Mexicans were welcomed back as a source of cheap labor. In recent years, many businesses as well as the government favored a "guest worker program" with Mexico—which would allow Mexican workers to temporarily reside in the United States. In fact, this occurs all over the world. North African workers are alternately welcomed and rejected in France, depending on the condition of the French economy and the need for imported labor. The resulting discontent and marginalization of these immigrants were seen in the weeks of rioting in French cities in the fall of 2005 and 2007 and the riots that occurred in London in 2011. In France, it was primarily the children and grandchildren of North African immigrants; in London, many are children and grandchildren of Caribbean and African immigrants. The rioting in both England and France started with those from poor neighborhoods. The *Economist* suggests that in France "[a] much greater contributor to the malaise in the suburbs is the lack of jobs" and that in London, soaring property prices push the middle class into "ever-edgier" neighbor-hoods. Guest workers from Turkey have been subjected to similar uncertainties in Germany. Indian workers in Kenya, and many other workers toiling outside their native lands have suffered from the vagaries of fluctuating economies and inconsistent immigration policies.

The Current Situation

Ethnic and race relations in the United States are impacted by specific events and the economic climate. For example, Hispanic—Black relations were at a low in 2013 after George Zimmerman was acquitted in the killing of unarmed Black teenager Trayvon Martin, sparking a national debate over the nature of racism in the United States. The media described Zimmerman, whose father is a White American and whose mother is Peruvian, as both White and Hispanic. Similarly, relations between Hispanics and Whites were affected negatively over the contentious debates about immigration, and Whites and Blacks relations have suffered as a result of the many Black unarmed young men killed by White police. The racial divide is clear: 86 percent of Blacks say more needs to be done to achieve racial equality, compared to 53 percent of Whites; however a growing number of Americans, across all demographic groups, say that racism in society is a big problem—50 percent of Americans polled agreed in 2016, up from 33 percent in 2010.

Some of the conflict may be due to the economic disparity that exists among these different groups. To understand this disparity we need to look at issues of economic class. Most Americans are reluctant to admit that a class structure exists, let alone admit how difficult it is to move up in this structure. But the fact is that most people live their lives in the same economic class into which they were born. In addition, the U.S. cultural myth that anyone can move up in the class structure through hard work, known as the Horatio Alger myth, is not benign. Rather, it reinforces middle-class and upper-class beliefs in their own superiority and perpetuates a false hope among members of the working class that they can get ahead. And there are just enough success stories—for example, celebrity Oprah Winfrey, former President Bill Clinton, rapper Eminem, singer and songwriter Dolly Parton, Wendy's founder Dave Thomas—of impressive upward mobility to perpetuate the myth.

Studies have shown that U.S. Americans seriously underestimate the gap between the rich and not rich. The reality is strikingly grim. The top 20 percent of U.S. households own more than 84 percent of the wealth, and the bottom 40 percent combine for a mere 0.3 percent (that's right, not 3 percent, but 0.3 percent). Most of the recent growth after the recession is going to a tiny segment: 95 percent of the gains have gone to the richest 1 percent of people, whose share of overall income is once again close to its highest level in a century. The most unequal country in the rich world is thus becoming even more so. The Walton family, for example, has more wealth than 42 percent of American families combined, and the nation's official poverty rate in 2014 was 14.8 percent, which means there were 46.7 million people in poverty. The difference between CEO pay and unskilled worker is 354:1. Fifty years ago, it was 20:1. While many Americans acknowledge this gap between rich and poor, very few see it as a serious issue (one study reports only 5 percent). These two studies imply that the apathy about inequality may be due to rose-colored misperceptions.

A real consequence of this gap and the number of working poor is lowered economic growth in the nation and less equality of opportunity for the next generation. There are real material consequences. For example, the gap in test scores between rich and poor children is 30 to 40 percent wider than it was 25 years ago, suggesting that rich youngsters are benefiting more than ever from their economic and social advantages. Measures of social mobility between generations, already lower than in much of Europe, have stagnated.

This widening gap is partly due to the loss of stable industrial jobs as companies move to cheaper labor markets within the United States and abroad, and slow recovery from the recession with wages remaining low. Class and demographic issues also play a role, with racial and ethnic minorities typically hardest hit by economic down-turns. The impact of the downturn on household net worth of Whites, Black, and Hispanic families is dramatic. (Net worth is defined as what you have if you subtract your debt from what you own.) According to a recent Pew Research Center analysis of government data, the wealth of White households was 13 times the median wealth of Black households in 2013, compared with eight times the wealth in 2010.

The wealth of White households is now more than 10 times of Hispanic households, compared with nine times the wealth in 2010. Changing these differences will not be easy, but how will they influence our intercultural interaction?

Increasingly diverse groups mostly come in contact during the day in schools, businesses, and hospitals, but they bring different languages, histories, and economic backgrounds to these encounters. This presents a challenge for the society and for people as individuals to look beyond the Hollywood stereotypes, to be aware of this diversity, and to apply what we know about intercultural communication. Perhaps the first step is to realize that the melting pot metaphor—in which all immigrants enter and blend into American society—probably was never viable. That is, not all immigrants could be assimilated into the United States in the same way.

The legacy of the tensions over immigration remains today. With a stagnant economy, stalled wages, and fears about terrorist attacks, many U.S. Americans are not in favor of additional immigration; they see immigrants as additional competition for jobs. One area where this debate has taken place is over the immigration of highly skilled workers. These workers are typically given H-1B visas to work in the United States. Yet with a flagging economy and unfavorable immigration laws, highly skilled workers may not choose to remain in the United States. As Commerce Secretary Penny Pritzker said.

"These individuals are American families in waiting," "Many tire of waiting for green cards and leave the country to work for our competition ... we have to do more to retain and attract world-class talent to the United States."

What impact will changes in immigration make to the society? How will the loss of highly skilled workers impact the ability to recover economically and technologically? And how will these changes impact how people interact with others?

Fortunately, most individuals are able to negotiate day-to-day activities in schools, businesses, and other settings in spite of cultural differences. Diversity can even be a positive force. Demographic diversity in the United States has provided us with tremendous linguistic richness and culinary variety, has given us the resources to meet new social challenges, and has created domestic and international business opportunities.

THE SELF-AWARENESS IMPERATIVE

One of the most important reasons for studying intercultural communication is to gain an awareness of one's own cultural identity and background. This **self-awareness** is one of the least obvious reasons. Peter Adler, a noted social psychologist, observes that the study of intercultural communication begins as a journey into another culture and reality and ends as a journey into one's own culture.

Examples from the authors' own lives come to mind. Judith's earliest experiences in public school made her realize that not everyone wore "coverings" and "bonnets" and "cape dresses," the clothing worn by the females in her Amish/Mennonite family. She realized that her family was different from most of the others she came in contact with. Years later, when she was teaching high school in Algeria, a Muslim country, she realized something about her own religious identity as a Protestant. December 25 came and went, and she taught classes with no mention of Christmas. Judith had never thought about how special the celebration of Christmas was or how important the holiday was to her. She recognized on a personal level the uniqueness of this particular cultural practice.

When Tom, who is of Japanese descent, first started elementary school, he attended a White school in the segregated American South. By the time he reached the fourth grade, schools were integrated, and some African American students were intrigued by his very straight black hair. At that point, he recognized a connection between himself and the Black students, and he began to develop a kernel of self-awareness about his identity. Living in an increasingly diverse world, we can take the opportunity to learn more about our own cultural backgrounds and identities and about how we are similar to and different from the people we interact with. However, it is important to recognize intercultural learning is not always easy or comfortable. What you learn depends on your social and economic position in society. Self-awareness through intercultural contact for someone from a racial or minority group may mean learning to be wary and not surprised at subtle slights by members of the dominant majority—and reminders of their place in society. For example, an African American colleague has remarked that she notices some White cashiers avoid touching her hand when they return her change.

If you are White and middle class, intercultural learning may mean an enhanced awareness of your privilege. A White colleague tells of feeling uncomfortable staying in a Jamaican resort, being served by Blacks whose ancestors were brought there as slaves by European colonizers. On the one hand, it is a privilege that allows travelers like our colleague to experience new cultures and places. On the other hand, one might wonder, through this type of travel, people are reproducing those same historical postcolonial economic patterns.

Self-awareness, then, that comes through intercultural learning may involve an increased awareness of being caught up in political, economic, and historical systems not of our own making.

THE ETHICAL IMPERATIVE

Living in an intercultural world presents challenging ethical issues that can be addressed by the study of intercultural communication. **Ethics** may be thought as principles of conduct that help govern the behavior of individuals and groups. These principles often arise from communities views on what is good and bad behavior. Cultural values tell us what is "good" and what "ought" to be.

Ethical Judgments and Cultural Values

Ethical judgments focus more on the degrees of rightness and wrongness in human behavior than do cultural values.

Some judgments are stated very explicitly. For example, the Ten Commandments teach that it is wrong to steal, tell a lie, commit murder, and so on. Many Americans are taught the "Golden Rule"—do unto others as you would have them do unto you. Laws often reflect the cultural values of dominant groups. For instance, in the past, many states had miscegenation laws prohibiting interracial marriage. Contemporary debates about legalizing same-sex marriage reflect the role of cultural values in laws. Many other identifiable principles arise from our cultural experience that may be less explicit—for example, that people should be treated equally and that they should work hard.

Several issues come to mind in any discussion of ethics in intercultural communi- cation. For example, what happens when two ethical systems collide? While the desire to contribute to the development of a better society by doing the right thing can be an important motivation, it is not always easy to know what is "right" in more specific situations in intercultural communication. Ethical principles are often culture-bound, and intercultural conflicts arise from varying notions of what constitutes ethical behavior.

Another ethical dilemma involves standards of conducting business in multinational corporations. The U.S. Congress and the Securities and Exchange Commission consider it unethical for corporations to make payments to government officials of other countries to promote trade. Essentially, such payment smacks of bribery. However, in many countries, government officials are paid in this informal way instead of being supported by taxes. What is ethical behavior for personnel in multinational subsidiaries?

This book stresses the relativity of cultural behavior; no cultural pattern is inherently right or wrong. Is there any universality in ethics? Are any cultural behaviors always right or always wrong?

The answers depend on one's perspective. According to the universalist position, we need to identify those rules that apply across cultures. A universalist might try, for example, to identify acts and conditions that most societies think of as wrong, such as murder, treason, and theft. Someone who takes an extreme universalist position would insist that cultural differences are only superficial, that fundamental notions of right and wrong are universal. Some religions take universal positions—for example, that the Ten Commandments are a universal code of behavior. But Christian groups often disagree about the universality of the Bible. For example, are the teachings of the New Testament mainly guidelines for the Christians of Jesus's time, or can they be applied to Christians in the twenty-first century? These are difficult issues for many people searching for ethical guidelines.

By contrast, according to the relativist position, any cultural behavior can be judged only within the cultural context in which it occurs. This means that only a community can truly judge the ethics of its members. Intercultural scholar William S. Howell explains the relativist position:

> Ethical principles in action operate contingently. Circumstances and people exert powerful influences. The environment, the situation, the timing of an interaction, human relationships—all affect the way ethical standards are applied. Operationally, ethics are a function of context. All moral choices flow from the perceptions of the decision maker, and those perceptions are produced by unique experiences in one person's life, in the context in which the choices are made.

These are not easy issues, and philosophers and anthropologists have struggled to develop ethical guidelines that are universally applicable but that also reflect the tremendous cultural variability in the world.

Scholar David W. Kale has proposed a universal code of ethics for intercultural communicators. This code is based on a universal belief in the sanctity of the human spirit and the desirability of peace. While we may wish to assume that universal ethical principles exist, we must be careful not to assume that our ethical principles are shared by others. When we encounter other ethical principles in various situations, it is often difficult to know if we are imposing our ethical principles on others and whether we should. There are no easy answers to these ethical dilemmas.

Like David Kale, philosopher Kwame Appiah agrees that there are, and should be, values such as tolerance that are universal. He discusses how the misplaced belief of "my values are the only right ones" can lead to intolerance, cruelty, and even murder (e.g., bombings of abortion clinics or other buildings). He addresses the difficult question of how we can maintain universal values and still respect cultural distinctness. His answer is that we must all become cosmopolitans—citizens of the world-taking seriously the value of not just human life, but particular human life, never forgetting that each human being has responsibilities to every other.

The study of intercultural communication should not only provide insights into cultural patterns but also help us address these ethical issues involved in intercultural interaction. Appiah and other contemporary scholars stress the importance of dialogue and "conversations across differences," suggesting that as part of coordinating our lives with each other as world citizens, we critique existing norms together and arrive at more acceptable ethical standards. First, we should be able to judge what is ethical and unethical behavior given variations in cultural priorities. Second, we should be able to identify guidelines for ethical behavior in intercultural contexts where ethics clash.

Another ethical issue concerns the application of intercultural communication scholarship. Everett Kleinjans, an international educator, stresses that intercultural education differs from some other kinds of education: Although all education may be potentially transformative, learning as a result of intercultural contact is particularly so in that it deals with fundamental aspects of human behavior. Learning about intercultural communication sometimes calls into question the very core of our assumptive framework and challenges existing beliefs, values, and patterns of behavior.

Becoming an Ethical Student of Culture

Part of learning about intercultural communication is learning about cultural patterns and identities-your own and those of others. Four skills are important here: practicing self-reflexivity, learning about others, listening to the voices of others, and developing a sense of social justice.

Practicing Self-Reflexivity. Self-reflexivity refers to the process by which we "look in the mirror" to see ourselves. In studying intercultural communication, you must understand yourself and your position in society. When you learn about other cultures and cultural practices, you often learn much about yourself as well.

And the knowledge that you gain from experience is an important way to learn about intercultural communication. Intercultural experiences teach you much about how you react and interact in different cultural contexts and help you evaluate situations and deal with uncertainty. Self-reflection about your intercultural experiences will go a long way toward helping you learn about intercultural communication. When you consider ethical issues in intercultural communication, you need to recognize the strengths and limitations of your own intercultural experiences. Many immigrants have observed that they never felt so much like someone of their nationality until they left their homeland. As part of the process of self-reflexivity, when you gain more intercultural experiences, your views on ethics may change. For example, you may have thought that arranged marriages were misguided and unethical until you gained more experience with people in successful arranged marriages, which have very low divorce rates in comparison with traditional "romantic" marriages.

Many cultural attitudes and ideas are instilled in you and are difficult to unravel and identify. Discovering who you are is never a simple matter; rather, it is an ongoing process that can never fully capture the ever-emerging person. Not only do you grow older, but your intercultural experiences change who you are and who you think you are. When Judith compares her intercultural experiences in France and in Mexico, she noted that, while the two experiences were similar, her own reactions to these intercultural encounters differed markedly because she was younger and less settled into her identity when she went to France.

It is also important to reflect on your place in society. By knowing what social categories—groups defined by society—you fill and what the implications of those categories are, you will be in a better position to understand how to communicate. For example, your status as a male or female may influence how certain messages are interpreted as sexual harassment. Or your identification as a member of some groups may allow you to use certain words and humor, but using other words or telling some jokes may get you in trouble. Many Belgians, for example, are well aware that French sometimes tell *blagues belges*, or jokes about Belgians. Yet if the same joke is told by a Belgian, it has a different tenor. It is important to recognize which social categories you belong to, as well as which ones you are perceived by others as belonging to, as it influences how your message may be interpreted.

Learning about others. It is important to remember that the study of cultures is actually the study of other people. Never lose sight of the humanity of the topic of study. Try not to observe people as if they are zoo animals. Remember that you are studying real people who have real lives, and your conclusions about them may have very real consequences for them and for you.

When Tom was growing up, he was surprised to hear from an older woman that the first time she saw a foreign person was in the circus when she was a little girl. Judith remembers feeling uneasy watching White tourists at the Navajo Nation fair in Window Rock, Arizona, intrusively videotaping the Navajo dancers during their religious ceremonies. In each case, people who were different were viewed and treated as if their cultural practices were for the display and entertainment of others and there was no real attempt to understand them or their culture.

Cultural studies scholar Linda Alcoff discusses the ethical issue involved when students of culture try to describe cultural patterns of others. She acknowledges the difficulty of speaking "for" and "about" people from different cultures. Instead, she claims, students of culture should try to speak "with" and "to" people. Rather than merely describe other people from afar, it's better to listen to and engage them in a dialogue about their cultural realities.

Listening to the voices of others. We learn much from real-life experiences. Hearing about the experiences of people who are different from you can lead to different ways of viewing the world. Many differences-based on race, gender, sexual orientation, nationality, ethnicity, age, and so on-deeply affect the everyday lives of people. Listening carefully as people relate their experiences and their knowledge helps us learn about other cultures. What we mean by listening here involves more than face-to-face encounters with others. It may mean listening to the voices of others through websites or movies or blogs.

Communication scholars Starosta and Chen suggest that a focus on mutual listening, instead of talking, forms the core of successful intercultural understanding. They suggest that good intercultural listeners are receptive to "life stories" from a wide range of culturally different individuals, as a way of understanding and explaining the world around them. These listening skills are built on a foundation of openness, curiosity, and empathy.

Japanese scholar Ishii suggests that the very core of intercultural communication is listening. The effective intercultural communicator, sensitive to the other person, listens *carefully* before speaking. He or she hears the message from the other person, considers it, then reconsiders it, trying on different possible interpretations-trying to understand the speaker's possible intent. When the listener believes he or she has understood the point being made, he or she may respond, always in a nonthreatening manner. The point here is that we can only really understand another person when we have listened to him or her carefully.

Developing a sense of social justice. A final ethical issue involves the responsibility that comes with the acquisition of intercultural knowledge and insights. What constitutes ethical and unethical applications of intercultural knowledge? One questionable practice concerns people who study intercultural communication in order to proselytize others without their consent. For example, some religious organizations conduct Bible study sessions on college campuses for international students under the guise of English conversation lessons. Another questionable practice involves cross-cultural consultants who misrepresent or exaggerate their ability to deal with complex issues of prejudice and racism in brief, one-shot training sessions. Another way of looking at ethical responsibility suggests that intercultural learning is not just transformative for the individual, but should also benefit the larger society and other cultural groups in the increasingly interdependent world. The first step in working for social justice is acknowledging that oppression and inequities exist. As we have tried to point out, cultural differences are not just interesting and fascinating; they exist within a hierarchy where some are privileged and set the rules for others.

For example, how could you apply intercultural communication concepts in situations where gay and lesbian young people are the targets of bullying? Statistics show that these adolescents get bullied two to three times more than their heterosexual peers, and it often occurs through social media like Facebook and Twitter, where there is a large audience and relative anonymity. Why does this happen? What can be done to reduce harassment of this particular cultural group?

In the following chapters, you will learn about the causes and patterns of conflict between various cultural groups, the origins and expressions of prejudice and discrimination, as well as strategies for reducing conflict and discrimination. Consider the homeless—another cultural group rarely mentioned by cultural communication scholars—often the target of prejudice and violence. Perhaps increased knowledge about this group and ethical application of intercultural communication principles could lead to better understanding of these individuals and ultimately to less discrimination and prejudice. After working as an advocate for homeless people in Denver, one communication scholar, Professor Phil Tompkins, describes the link between communication skills and social justice. He defines social justice as the "process of communicating, inspiring, advocating, organizing, and working with others of similar and diverse organizational affiliations to help all people gain respect and participate fully in society in a way that benefits the community as well as the individual." This definition has three important components: (1) communication is central; (2) the outcome of social justice must be beneficial to society, not just the individuals involved; and (3) respect for and participation by all is important. We hope that as you read the following chapters, you will agree with us that learning about intercultural communication also involves ethical application of that knowledge.

As you learn about yourself and others as cultural beings, as you come to understand the larger economic, political, and historical contexts in which interaction occurs, is there an ethical obligation to continue learning? Can popular culture products, like films, play a part in motivating others to work for social justice? We believe that as members of an increasingly interdependent global community, intercultural communication students have a responsibility to educate themselves, not just about interesting cultural differences, but also about intercultural conflicts, the impacts of stereotyping and prejudice, and the larger systems that can oppress and deny basic human rights—and to apply this knowledge to the communities in which they live and interact.

SUMMARY

In this chapter, we identified six reasons for studying intercultural communication: the peace imperative, the economic imperative, the technological imperative, the demographic imperative, the self-awareness imperative, and the ethical imperative. Perhaps you can think of some other reasons. We stressed that the situations in which intercultural communication takes place are complex and challenging.

BUILDING INTERCULTURAL SKILLS

So what are the skills necessary to communicate effectively across cultures? It isn't easy to come up with specific suggestions that will always work in every situation. Communication is much too complex. However, we can identify several general skills that can be applied to the various aspects of intercultural communication covered in this book: (1) understanding cultural identity and history, (2) improving verbal and nonverbal communication, (3) understanding the role of popular culture in intercultural communication, and (4) building relationships and resolving conflicts.

Throughout the book, we'll focus on cultivating and improving the following communication skills:

1. Become more conscious of your communication. This may sound simple, but how often do you really think about your communication and whether it is working? Much of your communication, including intercultural communication, occurs at an unconscious level. A first step in improving your intercultural communication is to become aware of the messages you send and receive, both verbal and nonverbal, in both face-to-face and mediated contexts (Facebook, Twitter, text messaging). Do you communicate differently face-to-face or online? You cannot really work on improving your communication until you become aware of it on a conscious level.

2. Become more aware of others' communication. Understanding other people's communication requires the important intercultural skill of empathy—knowing where someone else is coming from, or "walking in his or her shoes." This is no easy task, especially in online

communication, but by doing things such as improving your observational skills and learning how to build better intercultural relations you can accomplish it.

3. Expand your own intercultural communication repertoire. This involves experimenting with different ways of looking at the world and of communicating, verbally and nonverbally, both face-to-face and online. Building this skill may require that you step outside your communication comfort zone and look at things in a different light. It may require that you question ideas and assumptions you've not thought about before. All this is part of expanding your communication options.

4. Become more flexible in your communication. Closely related to the previous skill—and perhaps the most important one—this involves avoiding what has been called "hardening of the categories."

5. Be an advocate for others. This is something that isn't often included in lists of communication skills. To improve intercultural communication among groups, however, everybody's voice must be heard. Improving relations among groups of people-whether based on ethnicity, race, gender, physical ability, or whatever difference—is not just about improving individual communication skills; it is also about forming coalitions with others.

It is important to remember that becoming a better intercultural communicator is not achieved quickly but rather is a lifelong process. In each of the following chapters, we invite you to take up the challenge of continuing to build these skills.

Notes

1. Adapted and abridged from *Experiencing Intercultural Communication: An Introduction*, 6th Edition, Judith N. Martin and Thomas K. Nakayama, McGraw-Hill Education, 2017.

2. Robert Muller: born in Belgium in 1923 and raised in the Alsace-Lorraine region in France. He created World Core Curriculum and is known throughout the world as the "father of global education." There are 29 Robert Muller schools around the world with more being established each year. The World Core Curriculum earned him the UNESCO Peace Education Prize in 1989. Based on this curriculum and his devotion to good causes, Dr. Muller has recently drawn up a "Framework for World Media Coverage" as a public service, as well as a "Framework for Planetary and Cosmic Consciousness" and a "Framework for the Arts and Culture." (http://www.robertmuller.org/)

3. "Proxy wars": A proxy war is defined to be a war fought between groups of smaller

countries that each represents the interests of other larger powers, and may have help and support from them. The United Nations does not wage war (or proxy war): its peacekeeping military actions are instead police actions.
4. *Maquiladoras*: A maquiladora is a mode of manufacturing in Mexico that is established by a foreign company, involving the export of the manufactured goods to the company's country of origin. The factories benefit from duty-free and tariff-free imports of raw materials, machinery, and equipment to be used in the manufacturing process. The manufactured goods are exported to other countries, mainly the United States and Canada.
5. FOMO (Fear of Missing Out): refers to the feeling or perception that others are having more fun, living better lives, or experiencing better things than you are. It involves a deep sense of envy and affects self-esteem. It is often exacerbated by social media sites like Instagram and Facebook.

Questions for Discussion

1. Describe and analyze your first intercultural encounter with someone of a different age, ethnicity, race, religion, and so on. What made it "intercultural"? How did you react to the encounter? What did you learn from the experience? Based on this experience, identify some characteristics that may be important for successful intercultural communication.
2. There are many reasons to study intercultural communication, including the six discussed in the selected reading. Can you identify other imperatives based on your perceptions?
3. The COVID-19 epidemic has impacted the whole world since the end of 2019. China's great spirit of combating the COVID-19 epidemic, features putting people's lives first, nationwide solidarity, sacrifice, respecting science, and a sense of mission for humanity. How could you relate such health challenge to the significance of studying intercultural communication?
4. There is a concern that the growing poverty and inequality resulting from globalization may escalate intercultural conflict. Can you elaborate your perspective?
5. "The U.S. companies that relocate their plants there benefit from lower labor costs and lack of environmental and other business regulations, while Mexican laborers benefit from the jobs." How do you apply the ethical imperative to the above quote?

Online Mini-Case Studies and Viewpoints-Sharing

Learning about Intercultural communication sometimes calls into question the core of our basic assumptions about ourselves, our culture, and our worldviews and challenges existing and preferred beliefs, values, and patterns of behavior. Liliana, a Colombian student, describes such a transformation:

"When I first came to the United States to study and live, I was surprised with all the diversity and different cultures I encountered. I realized I came from a country, society, school, and group of friends with little diversity. During all the years I lived in Colombia, I did not meet more than five people from other countries. Even at my school, there was little diversity—only two students of color among three thousand students. I realized that big difference when I was suddenly sharing a college classroom with students from all over the world, people of all colors and cultures. At the beginning, it was difficult getting used to it because of the wide diversity, but I like and enjoy it now and I wish my family and friends could experience and learn as much as I have."

Online Research

Exemplify the significance of studying intercultural communication by citing other cases from the commercials, diplomatic issues, international trades, etc.

Reading Two

Introductory Remarks

The beginning of intercultural communication was for the applied purposes rather than for the research studies nor the theoretical considerations, when the Foreign Service Institute (FSI) of the U.S. Department of State (DOS) targeted for the training of the American diplomats and development personnel prior to their dispatch abroad. In regard to the name of the field "Intercultural Communication," the credit is often given to American anthropologist Edward T. Hall, who used it for the first time in his book *The Silent Language* (1959), which is often called "the field's founding document." Hall was a staff member at the FSI between 1951 and 1955 before publishing the book. Since then, intercultural communication teaching and training gradually spread to the universities and other organizations. University courses were given and academic textbooks in Intercultural Communication started to appear in the USA in a larger scale in the 1970s.

    The selected reading offered four major arguments over Hall, Hall's work, and the emergence of field of intercultural communication: the significance of Hall's work, the origin and the historical context, the crucial decisions, and the ensuing contemporary literature. The four main elements of Hall's paradigm for the field are: first, systematic empirical study and the classification of nonverbal communication; Second, a diversion of the emphasis from earlier on macrolevel monocultural studies to the out-of-conscious level of information-exchange; Third, a non-judgmental view toward and an acceptance of cultural differences; Finally, the participatory training methods in intercultural communication.

Notes in the History of Intercultural Communication[1]

Wendy Leeds-Hurwitz[2]

Many articles discussing some aspect of intercultural communication begin with a paragraph in which the author reviews the history of the field and the major early publications. Typically, Edward Hall's book, *The Silent Language*, published in 1959, is listed as the first work in the field, and often specifically mentioned as the crucial starting point. The lack of attention to his motives and sources for the work is not surprising, since the young field still has little history written about it. But no book develops without a context, and no author invents a field without a reason. This study will look at the context in which Hall's work[3] was produced and will describe some of the events that led to the creation of the field of intercultural communication. Using this historical record, I argue that the parameters of the field were established in response to a particular set of problems. If we are to understand why we include some topics as appropriate and do not consider other types of work, we must understand the exigencies that generated the first study of intercultural communication.

Briefly, I will argue that intercultural communication emerged from occurrences at the Foreign Service Institute (FSI) of the U.S. Department of State (DOS) between 1946 and 1956. Because intercultural communication grew out of the need to apply abstract anthropological concepts to the practical world of foreign service diplomats, this early focus on training American diplomats led to the later, now standard use of intercultural communication training. Only recently has intercultural communication begun to discuss theoretical approaches; initially the concepts were accompanied only by examples, not by an elaboration of theory. In their first writings on the subject Hall and Hall and Whyte made no explicit attempt to create a new academic field with a novel research tradition. Establishing a new academic field was, rather, a secondary phase, based on Hall's early attempt to translate anthropological insights into cultural differences to an audience that wanted immediate and practical applications, not research studies.

My discussion offers four major arguments: first, that Hall's work was important to the development of the field of intercultural communication; second, that Hall's work originated in and was shaped by the specific context of the FSI; third, that this context resulted in a number of crucial decisions, which were continued by later researchers; and fourth, that these decisions illuminated some features of the contemporary literature. Assuming that the readers of this article will be most familiar with the contemporary literature, my effort will focus upon illuminating the historical context which set the stage for the current practices in the field.

The following specific connections between the work of Hall (and others) at the FSI and current intercultural communication research will be demonstrated:

1) Instead of the traditional anthropological focus on a single culture at a time, or at best, a comparison of two, Hall responded to the critique of his foreign service students by stressing interaction between members of different cultures. Hall is most explicit about this in a publication written jointly with William Foote Whyte:

> In the past, anthropologists have been primarily concerned with the internal pattern of a given culture. In giving attention to intercultural

problems, they have examined the impact of one culture upon another. Very little attention has been given to the actual communication process between representatives of different cultures.

This shift from viewing cultures one at a time to studying interactions between members of different cultures has been enormously influential on the study of intercultural communication and is what most completely defines the field today.

2) Hall narrowed the focus of study from culture as a general concept (macroanalysis) to smaller units within culture (microanalysis). This occurred in response to a particular problem: the students in the FSI classes had no interest in generalizations or specific examples that applied to countries other than the ones to which they were assigned; they wanted concrete, immediately useful details provided to them before they left the US, and they thought it appropriate that the anthropologists involved in their training should focus their energy on this level of culture. Hall, eventually agreeing that the complaints of his students were justified, began the move from a focus on the entire culture to specific small moments of interaction.

3) Hall enlarged the concept of culture to include the study of communication; he viewed much of his work as an extension of anthropological insight to a new topic, interactions between members of two or more different cultures. Those who study intercultural communication continue to use the concepts taken from anthropology in the 1940s and 1950s (culture, ethnocentrism, etc.), but this cross-fertilization moved primarily in one direction: now only a few anthropologists study proxemics, time, kinesics or paralanguage, or focus on interactions between members of different cultures. Although anthropology and intercultural communication were once closely allied, the two fields have grown apart as reflected in the shift from the qualitative methods of anthropology to the quantitative methods of communication generally used in intercultural communication today and in the recent surge of interest in applying traditional American communication theories to intercultural contexts. While intercultural communication sprang from anthropological insights, it has been on its own for some thirty years, and some shift in focus was predictable.

4) Implicit in Hall's work is the view that communication is patterned, learned, and analyzable, just as culture had been previously described. (Others later stated these insights more explicitly, but he implies them and should be given some credit for the ideas.) Researchers today make the same assumptions about communication. Without these assumptions, we could not have the abstract

theorizing about intercultural communication that now marks the field.

5) Hall decided that the majority of information potentially available about a culture was not really essential in situations of face-to-face interaction with members of that culture; only a small percentage of the total need be known. Thus he delineated several types of microcultural behavior as the focus of study; tone of voice, gestures, time, and spatial relationships. That intercultural research still pays extensive attention to these types of interaction over many other possibilities is a tribute to the influence of his work.

6) Several aspects of the training established by Hall are accepted as part of the repertoire of training procedures used today; a) Hall created teaching materials out of experiences abroad which students in the training sessions were willing to provide; b) Hall encouraged his students to meet with foreign nationals as part of the preparation for a trip abroad, as one way to increase their knowledge of other cultures; and c) Hall presented his insights as a beginning for his students, but assumed they would continue the learning process once they arrived at their destination.

7) Hall and his colleagues at FSI are responsible for the use of descriptive linguistics as the basic model for intercultural communication, a model which still implicitly serves as the basis for much current research. Explicit discussion of linguistic terminology is currently enjoying a renaissance through attention to what are now termed the "etic" and "emic" approaches to intercultural communication.

8) Hall expanded his audience beyond foreign diplomats to include all those involved in international business, today one of the largest markets for intercultural training. Intercultural communication continues to serve the function of training Americans to go abroad, although it has grown substantially beyond this initial mission to include such areas as the training of foreign students, recent immigrants, and teachers who work with students of different cultural backgrounds; it has established a university base now, and many practitioners engage in research, as well as teaching large numbers of undergraduate students the basics of an intercultural communication approach.

The innovations listed here were picked up by the fledgling field of communication, and they were crucial in the establishment of the area known as intercultural communication. They are today hallmarks of intercultural communication.

Background: The Foreign Service Institute

The story of intercultural communication began at the Foreign Service Institute. In the 1940s many persons recognized that American diplomats were not fully effective abroad, since they often did not speak the language and usually knew little of the host culture. After World War II Americans began to reevaluate their knowledge and understanding of other countries, both their languages and in terms of their cultural assumptions. Along with general concern about the ability of Americans to interact with foreign nationals, the training and knowledge of American diplomats were issues, since deficiencies in those areas having substantial repercussions. In 1946 Congress passed the Foreign Service Act, which reorganized the Foreign Service, and established a Foreign Service Institute to provide both initial training and in-service training on a regular basis throughout the careers of Foreign Service Officers and other staff members.

As one part of the preparation of the bill, in 1945 the American Foreign Service Journal sponsored a contest for ideas to improve the training program of the Foreign Service; Foreign Service personnel from around the world contributed essays. Those judged to be the best were published as a series of articles in the journal, and the comments were fascinating. Many themes recurred, among them the recommendation for better language training. Because American representatives abroad were often not well trained in foreign languages, many contributors argued that they would be more successful if they had fluency in at least one language other than English. Many authors also urged fuller education about the history, political structure, economics, and international relations with the United States, not only of the country to which the diplomat would be sent, but of the entire geographic region.

About the same time, a series of articles not submitted for the contest, but generally addressing the issue of change in the Foreign Service, was published. One of these specifically criticized the generally limited language fluency in the foreign service and highlighted the need for individuals who knew more than basic grammar and who could converse in a language other than English. In an unpublished history of the beginnings of FSI, Boswell pointed out that "Prior to 1946 the American Foreign Service placed less emphasis on language qualifications for entry than any other nation's foreign service". He attributed the deficiency to the poor language training available in American schools.

One factor which changed attitudes towards language training in the Foreign Service was the extensive language training program begun by the Army during World War II, which demonstrated the feasibility of language training on a largescale. Little excuse remained for Foreign Service diplomats to have inadequate language skills.

In 1939 Mortimer Graves, then the Executive Secretary of the American

Council of Learned Societies (ACLS), reasoned that linguists were capable of analyzing. Native American Indian languages (often funded through ACLS grants) should be able to analyze other, perhaps more politically useful, languages. Convinced that world-wide conflict was inevitable, he obtained funding from the Rockefeller Foundation to put a small group of linguists to work. Mary Haas, the first hired, was asked to analyze Thai from native speakers, to prepare basic teaching materials, and then to teach a group of students the language, combining the spoken words of native speakers with the written materials she had prepared.

When the United States formally entered World War II, Graves brought J Milton Cowan to Washington; together they organized the linguists to serve the war effort through what became known as the Intensive Language Program (ILP). Those who had been inducted served on the military side of the project, and those who had not participated as civilians through the ACLS. Henry Lee Smith, Jr., who was trained as a linguist, was in the Army Reserves at the time; he was recalled to active duty and put in charge of the military side.

The method, developed as the "linguistic method" of language training, became the "the Army method". Instead of the traditional focus on learning to read and write a language and on grammar as the key to a language, the method emphasized appropriate use of the spoken language, an innovative approach. Because the classroom teacher was a native speaker, students heard the idiomatic usages and pronunciations. These native speakers were under the close supervision of professional linguists, who worked with them on consistent organization of the materials. Ideally the material was organized as a series of natural speech situations: asking directions, going shopping, finding housing, etc. Through this division of labor, a small number of linguists supervised a large number of native speakers, and dozens of languages could be taught simultaneously with a minimum of full-time staff members.

Initially the Army program, formally one part of the larger Army Specialized Training Program (ASTP), was to serve 1,500 of the brightest and most qualified army recruits. However, believing that having a larger number of soldiers qualified to speak a variety of languages was desirable, officials increased the number of participants to 15,000. Not all of the techniques that had been established for 1,500 transferred easily to the larger group but, on the whole, the program was remarkably effective. The primary problem with ASTP was not in the training, but in the follow-through. For various reasons, soldiers trained to speak particular languages were assigned randomly and only rarely were able to use their linguistic training.

All of these efforts came together when the Foreign Service Institute was officially established. Because of the experience within an Army setting and due in part to the widespread agreement of a need for language training within the Foreign Service, FSI was immediately able to establish a language training program that had already been developed, tested, and proven effective. Frank Hopkins, the first Director of FSI, had studied linguistics and anthropology while at Harvard and had been impressed there with the work of Clyde Kluckhohn. "Hopkins was the linchpin in recruiting Haxie [Henry Lee] Smith and in the bringing of Social Science into FSI" (Hall, personal correspondence). Smith moved from the Army, where he had been serving as Director of the Language School, to a position as Director of Language Studies in the Division of Training Services for the Foreign Service in 1946; when the new Foreign Service Institute was formally established in 1947, he was made director of the School of Languages, one of the four schools established within FSI. Smith was later responsible for recruiting well-known linguist George L. Träger into the School of Languages, as well as Edward Kennard, an anthropologist who ran the School of Area Studies (Hall, personal correspondence). Bringing to FSI the knowledge of how to run a linguistically-based language training program, Smith adapted his experience to a new audience.

Smith maintained the model of native speakers in the classroom, combined with trained linguists available to prepare additional written materials where these were needed, although much of this work had already been prepared under ILP and ASTP auspices. The linguists could also work occasionally with the students. For the classes in descriptive linguistics, linguists such as Träger prepared the materials.

Träger summarized the basic approach quite well in this statement, described as the efforts of the entire group working together:

> Language has been indicated as being only one of the systematic arrangements of cultural items that societies possess. A culture consists of many such systems—language, social organization, religion, technology, law, etc. Each of these cultural systems other than language is dependent on language for its organization and existence, but otherwise constitutes an independent system whose patterning may be described. In theory, when one has arrived at the separate statements of each such cultural system, one can then proceed to a comparison with

the linguistic system. The full statement of the point-by-point and pattern-by-pattern relations between the language and any of the other cultural systems will contain all the "meanings" of the linguistic forms, and will constitute the metalinguistics of that culture.

Two important assumptions are apparent here: first, that the analysis of culture was dependent upon a prior linguistic model; and second, that linguistic meaning comes not from words alone but from a combination of the linguistic and what was then termed the "metalinguistic" levels. Both ideas are basic to Hall's 1959 book; both have influenced the contemporary field of intercultural communication.

The other members of the group to which Träger referred were: John M. Echols, Charles A. Ferguson, Carleton T. Hodge, Charles F. Hockett, Edward A. Kennard, Henry Hoenigswald, and John Kepke. Träger, Ferguson, and Hodge all had the advantage of having worked previously with Smith within the Army program. Edward Hall came into the group later than the others, in 1951, and frequently served a different administrative structure, although he was part of the FSI staff, and did participate in most of the orientation programs for Foreign Service personnel. In addition to learning how to speak a particular language, the students attended a seminar on general linguistics and another on discussing general principles for analyzing human societies. There Hall found his role, working to ensure that the students obtained general anthropological training to complement their specific language training. Shortly before Hall's arrival, Edward Kennard published an article describing the role of anthropology at the FSI, in which he mentioned developing the course, "Understanding Foreign Peoples," to combine anthropological insights with actual Foreign Service experiences.

Although a full member of the FSI staff with the rank of professor, Hall was under a different administrative branch of the Department of State, the Technical Cooperation Authority (TCA) also widely referred to as Point IV (Hall, personal correspondence). He worked closely with the linguists and anthropologists at FSI from 1951 to 1955 to provide the training TCA required, since no separate staff was available. A contemporary described TCA as "a stepchild in the organization [FSI]" for various reasons, a fact that did not facilitate its work. Hall pointed out that FSI acquired a reputation for having a large number of anthropologists. Later problems were attributed to the inappropriate numbers of anthropologists on staff, and two new directors were sent into the organization with orders to "get rid of the anthropologists". Hall wrote in detail about the administrative problems that academics in government faced: many of them could not use the proper procedures effectively, seeing them as unnecessary interference. Thus, they spent an inordinate amount of time trying to get their work done, and struggling to offer the training they were hired to provide. The basic four-week training course that Hall and the others offered to Point IV technicians was a modified version of the training given to foreign service personnel, including beginning instruction in the language of the country of assignment, orientation to the mission and its philosophy, limited study of the country and area, and a small amount of time devoted to anthropological and linguistic generalizations, including culture as a concept, change as a process, and common American assumptions.

Microcultural Analysis

The idea of culture, one of the central concepts taught in the anthropology seminars, was, and still is, one of the cornerstones of intercultural communication. Today, of course, the notion that each group of people has what can be described as a unique culture, consisting of traditional ways of doing things, traditional objects, oral traditions and belief systems, is taken for granted. In the 1940s and 1950s this was answer concept, requiring extensive discussion. Much to the astonishment of the anthropologists, many participants in the seminars viewed the concept itself as vague and viewed discussing it as a waste of time; instead, they wanted concrete information about how to interact with persons in the specific culture to which they were being sent. As Hall later wrote, "There seemed to be no 'practical' value attached to either what the anthropologist did or what he made of his discoveries". Faced with this reaction, Hall resolved to focus on what he termed micro cultural analysis: on tone of voice, gestures, time, and spatial relationships as aspects of communication. These smaller units of a culture, having obvious and immediate impaction interaction between members of different cultures, were very attractive to the foreign service personnel. Hall wrote: "Microcultural analysis, when used, seems to be much more acceptable and more readily handled by the layman". Thus, the focus of his training efforts gradually became all those parts of culture which are learned and used without conscious notice. By the time he published *The Silent Language*, this emphasis on aspects of interaction generally ignored by others was even more obvious: "If this book has a message it is that we must learn to understand the 'out-of-awareness' aspects of communication. We must never assume that we are fully aware of what we communicate to someone else".

Sometimes Hall termed these discussions "informal culture", which he contrasted with "formal culture", defined as traditional parts of knowledge, and "technical culture", the most explicit elements of knowledge, and those generally associated with particular sciences or technologies. In presenting this scheme, Hall emphasized that although lay persons assumed that informal culture has no rules or patterns governing it, the job of the anthropologist was to prove otherwise. At one time he explained informal culture through an extended description of the difference between what we assume schools are supposed to teach students, the formal and technical, and what they really teach, the informal. In the latter category he included: "all things are subservient to time; bureaucracies are real; what happens in the classroom is a game, and the teachers set the rule; and the teacher's primary mission is to keep order".

While discussing the complexity of the cultural systems governing interaction, Hall provides a clear statement of culture as a system of patterns which must be learned:

> the anthropologist knows that in spite of their apparent complexity, cultural systems are so organized that their content can be learned and controlled by all normal members of the group. Anything that can be learned has structure and can ultimately be analyzed and described. The anthropologist also knows that what he is looking for are patterned distinctions that transcend individual differences and are closely integrated into the social matrix in which they occur.

The extension from this view of culture to assuming that communication, as culture's counterpart, is equally patterned, learned, and analyzable is implicit in Hall's work, although others, writing later, made the point explicitly. These assumptions about culture and communication and the ways in which they are similar lie at the heart of much current research in intercultural communication; Hall's influence here is crucial. Hall viewed culture as communication, and others after him have had to come to terms with the ways in which the two ped.

For Hall, the practical implication of this theoretical extension of culture into communication was the feasibility of training those going overseas to attend deliberately to the more subtle aspects of interaction and to understand more fully the implications of their own behavior for others. Hall noted that the beginnings of his awareness of cultural impact on behavior occurred through observing his own interactions with others. While preparing the orientation materials for Americans going overseas, he was surrounded by people who represented many of the major languages and cultures of the world, some of whom would stop by his office to visit. "I would find myself impelled (as though pulled by hidden strings) to hold myself, sit, respond, and listen in quite different ways. I noted that when I was with Germans I would (without thinking) hold myself stiffly, while with Latin Americans I would be caught up and involved". It was exactly this sort of awareness of behavior that he then tried to foster in others. His instruction stressed understanding that others do not necessarily interpret our behavior as we do nor as we expect them to. Unlike typical anthropology students, the students in these classes were unwilling to arrive in a culture and simply observe interaction for several months before trying to draw conclusions as to what was occurring. In response, Hall gradually concluded that the majority of information potentially available about a culture was not really essential in situations of face-to-face interaction with members of that culture: only a small percentage of the total need be known, although that portion was critical.

One problem in implementing this insight was the dearth of information at the level of microcultural analysis. Hall had to create his own materials, primarily using details about experiences abroad which students in the training sessions were willing to provide. In addition, Hall was able to travel abroad to check the effectiveness of his program; he specifically listened to the problems Americans were having once they arrived at their destinations. These stories served as an additional resource for improving training.

In his earliest articles Hall already demonstrated what was to become a mark of his approach: providing a few generalizations, along with a large number of specific examples documenting interaction differences between members of different cultures. His students at FSI encouraged this approach, because they would tolerate only a few theoretical statements, although they paid attention to concrete details of real occurrences and were able to learn from them by drawing their own generalizations. This style also served him well with a broader audience, although scholars within intercultural communication, who hope for more extensive, less anecdotal, perhaps more traditionally academic studies, sometimes criticize it. As late as 1979 Robert L. Nwankwo suggested that most intercultural communication instructors "focus on the identification of communication barriers and on description and application rather than theory-building". This can be attributed largely to the origins of the field as a practical tool for training diplomats rather than as discipline based within a university setting, where the focus would have been on abstract theorizing. By 1983 this had changed with the publication of a volume specifically devoted to theories within intercultural communication.

Hall noted that the four weeks total training time for the general sessions as well as specific language training only permitted an orienting of students; he saw four months as ideal. A series of shortcuts designed to maximize the amount of learning possible despite a lack of available teaching time were used to make the endeavor feasible. For example, he mentioned the need to put Americans in touch with someone from the local culture with the task of discovering how many times they had to meet with someone in the country before they could begin official business. Through such assignments, Americans destined for the Middle East learned not to pursue business too quickly. Intercultural communication training still takes this approach of providing basic orientation to some problems that occur in intercultural interaction, leaving the balance of the learning to the student.

Proxemics, Time, Paralanguage, Kinesics

Major early statements on proxemics and nonverbal communication developed out of the training program at the Foreign Service Institute. In trying to adapt anthropological concepts for presentation to a new audience, Hall and the others established a whole new series of concepts: Hall's proxemics and related discussions of the use of time, occasionally called chronemics, Trager's paralanguage, and Birdwhistell's kinesics, were all initially begun by the group of linguists and anthropologists who were involved in the training courses presented through FSI. These areas are today standard parts of courses on intercultural communication and of most shorter training sessions, as well as standard parts of much research in other areas of communication.

Not until 1963 did Hall separate his work on cultural differences in use of space from the other aspects of microcultural analysis, and give it the name now popular, "proxemics". He reported having considered a series of other possible labels, including "topology", "chaology", the study of empty space, "oriology", the study of boundaries, and "choriology", the study of organized space. But he decided that proxemics was most descriptive. Since the widespread adoption of a new field of study is often delayed until a name has been chosen, this choice of a name was critical. Later, in 1972, he reunited the various aspects of nonverbal communication, saying "Proxemics represents one of several such out-of-awareness systems which fall within the general rubric Para communication". "Paracommunication", not a term generally used in the field then or now, but served as one of a series of ways of referring to the entire complex of what are today more generally termed nonverbal "channels" of communication. Other early terms included Trager's "metalinguistics", again not the term of choice today.

The materials Träger wrote while at FSI between 1948 and 1953 alluded to metalinguistics and the importance of extending the study of linguistics to more than words. Originally, all nonverbal communication was categorized under the rubric "metalinguistics", and all was viewed as being potentially of equal interest to linguists. Träger saw no reason for linguists to limit themselves to the study of language, arguing that nonverbal behaviors had an influence both on language choice and on how such choices were interpreted by participants in an interaction. Since virtually no one else was studying nonverbal communication at the time, there was little competition, and no one to complain if Träger and the others crossed the boundary between language and other aspects of culture and/or communication to "trespass" on territory covered in other disciplines. Although Trager's seminal article on paralanguage was not published until 1958, after research experience with The Natural History of an Interview team, among other influences, his position on the significance of that research was established while he was at FSI, as a direct result of the effort to put linguistic generalizations into a form which diplomats would be able to appreciate and put to immediate use.

Träger not only published general statements on the importance of metalinguistics as an extension of language study and the specific programmatic statement for research in paralanguage, but he was also the group member most directly involved in Hall's writings. In all of his early publications, Hall credited Träger as a collaborator. The draft for *The Silent Language* was actually published jointly, as *The Analysis of Culture*. This jointly authored text was issued only as a prepublication draft, by FSI in 1953, although at various times Hall commented that it was to be published shortly. Träger later decided it was not the best possible analysis, commenting in 1971: "No other edition ever published; no published criticism or discussion. GLT has completely replaced this scheme by another". His assessment reflected his effort to refine his work rather than substantive disagreements with the content of the work. In a parallel fashion, Hall also revised his understandings of intercultural communication as the years went by. He noted "My own description does not deviate in any significant degree from the joint version. However, I have come to feel that it was somewhat oversimplified and this I shall attempt to correct". In *The Silent Language* Hall sometimes uses the plural first person form and refers often to an idea or a problem as being a joint effort between himself and Träger. In later publications Trager's role has become significantly reduced, though still noticeable.

Since one of Hall's major statements about his work was published in *Current Anthropology* and accorded the CA treatment (being subjected to critique by peers, their comments published with the article), Träger had the opportunity to comment in print on the development of the work. After objecting to a rather minor linguistic point (Hockett's comment that language has the characteristic of duality, which he feels Hall has misunderstood and consequently misused), he added that he is able to "commend this article unreservedly". As this statement shows, and as Hall confirmed, any disagreements were minor (Hall, personal correspondence).

Although Ray L. Birdwhistell was at FSI only during the summer of 1952, his publication of Introduction to Kinesics through FSI established his reputation as the expert in that area of communication. In spite of his brief tenure, discussion at FSI during the time, particularly the need to focus attention on a microanalytic level, influenced his work. Like Träger he was later a part of The Natural History of an Interview team and developed his early insights in that context, adapting them to a new audience of psychiatrists. As with the study of proxemics, time, and paralanguage, kinesics obviously can be and now is fruitfully applied to almost any context of interaction. But all four originated with a particular context in mind, a context which shaped the way they developed.

My concern here is not to distinguish between the specific contributions of each member of the group at FSI, but rather to stress the importance of understanding that the influential work produced at FSI was partly due to the particular combination of talents drawn together at one time and place for a single purpose. As the person most immediately involved with Hall's work, Träger merited the title of co-author on the original major publication, but the presence of other scholars was equally significant since their ideas contributed to the whole. Although it is customary to attribute specific ideas to individual writers, sometimes an unusually fortuitous combination of individuals, brought together for the purposes of a specific research agenda, can encourage the development of new insights by all. Because he is the author of most of the early work on intercultural communication, giving Hall sole credit for the ideas is easy. However, the catalyst of the particular context, and informal discussions with particular individuals available, may well have been crucial to his thinking.

The Linguistic Model

Modelling paralanguage, kinesics, and proxemics after the analysis of language provided by descriptive linguistics was a deliberate attempt to make at least some aspects of culture as readily available to verbalization, and as readily taught, as language. Linguistics in the 1940s had acquired the reputation of being the most "scientific" of the social and behavioral sciences, and the FSI group wanted anthropology to be equally scientific. That two of the most influential descriptive linguists of the 1950s, Smith and Träger, were part of the group of peers Hall found at FSI was obviously a contributing factor. Not only did linguistics as a whole have the reputation of being scientific, but representatives were available daily and influenced Hall's ideas as they developed. Hall emphasized that the material he included in microcultural analysis was intended to be learned "in much the same way that language is learned", eventually making explicit the connection between linguistic analysis and cultural analysis: "Language is the most technical of the message systems. It is used as a model for the analysis of the others". In later writings he related this parallel more specifically to microculture analysis:

> A microcultural investigation and analysis properly conducted can provide material which can be compared in the same way that phonetic and phonemic material from different languages can be compared. The results of such studies are quite specific and can therefore be taught in much the same way that language can be taught.

Occasionally Hall had been explicit about why he saw the linguistic model as a particularly useful one, as when he specifically listed the strengths of linguistics: "it has distinguished between etic and emic events. ... and has been able to handle greater and greater complexity". He wished to utilize these strengths in intercultural communication. If anything, the linguistic model is even more important today to intercultural communication research, as the concepts of "etic" and "emic", in a slightly adapted form, are undergoing a strong resurgence ackey terms in the field.

For many of the same reasons that prompted Hall to utilize the model of descriptive linguistics in developing proxemics, Träger and Birdwhistell used descriptive linguistics as their model in developing paralanguage and kinesics. Trager's interest in paralanguage was an extension of his interest in language; he considered it obvious that paralanguage as a field of study would closely parallel formal linguistic analysis of language. Although the majority of his early work focused on a rather abstract level of analysis, developing the categories to be used in studying paralinguistic behavior, he subsequently published a description of paralinguistic behavior for a Native American language, Taos. Later authors described in detail the problems that divergent paralinguistic norms can cause when, members of different cultures attempt to interact, the application of the topic most directly relevant to the study of intercultural communication. Birdwhistell has been equally explicit about the deliberate use of descriptive linguistics as the model for kinesic analysis in his outlines of the historical development of kinesics, and about the influence of linguists such as Träger and Smith on his ideas. Hall was responsible for recommending to Kennard that Birdwhistell be brought into the FSI group; his intention was to permit him to work with the linguists there in refining his early model of kinesics (Hall, personal correspondence).

In addition to the ready and appropriate model linguistics provided for analysis of human symbolic behavior, Hall pointed out that the linguists at FSI were more successful in their efforts to teach language than the anthropologists were in their efforts to teach culture and added that this disparity led to direct comparisons of the methodologies of the two fields. "Träger and Smith thought that if language is a part of culture, and can be taught so that people speak with little or nonaccent, why would it not be possible to analyze the rest of culture in such a way so that people could learn by doing and thereby remove the accent from their behavior?" This provided yet another reason to use a linguistic model.

Culture and Communication

One goal of Hall's work was to extend the anthropological view of culture to include communication. At the time anthropologists paid attention to large cultural systems (e.g., economics or kinship) only and did not document directly interaction patterns in any detail. Statements relating culture and communication abound in his work; both *The Silent Language* and *The Hidden Dimension* have entire chapters devoted to the subject. In the early work, culture was seen as primary, communication as secondary, since it was only one aspect of culture. In the later work, Hall suggested "culture is basically a communicative process", thus reversing the order: communication was then viewed as primary. In light of this, it is important to note that *The Silent Language* was proposed as the first presentation of "the complete theory of culture as communication", not as the establishment of a new field to be called intercultural communication, not even as an outline of proxemics and/or the study of time as new foci for research.

Much of Hall's work is explicit about citing anthropological precedents, from the grandfather of American anthropology Franz Boas (who "laid the foundation of the view which I hold that communication constitutes the core of culture and indeed of life itself"), to the most significant of the early American linguists Edward Sapir, Leonard Bloomfield, and Benjamin Lee Whorf. Indeed, Whorf's essays were first gathered together and published by FSI during Hall's tenure there. Whorf's influence on Hall's work is obvious in *The Silent Language*, where he was called "one of the first to speak technically about the implications of differences which influence the way in which man experiences the universe". In *The Hidden Dimension*, Hall specifically says: "The thesis of this book and of *The Silent Language*, which preceded it, is that the principles laydown by Whorf and his fellow linguists in relation to language apply to the rest of human behavior as well—in fact to all culture".

The changing connections between intercultural communication and anthropology merit explicit comment. Culture as a concept had been and still is traditionally the domain of anthropology. Yet, for a variety of reasons, many of them political and bureaucratic in nature, anthropologists were no longer a part of FSI after the late 1950s. For other reasons relevant to disciplinary boundaries in American universities, anthropologists are not generally involved in intercultural communication as currently taught, whether as a full course or as a workshop.

Hall's first publication on intercultural communication, in 1955, was titled "The Anthropology of Manners", not "proxemics" or "the silent language", and not "intercultural communication". He suggested that:

> The role of the anthropologist in preparing people for service overseas is to open their eyes and sensitize them to the subtle qualities of behavior— tone of voice, gestures, space and time relationships—that so often build up feelings of frustration and hostility in other people with a different culture. Whether we are going to live in a particular foreign country or travel in many, we need a frame of reference that will enable us to observe and learn the significance of differences in manners. Progress is being made in this anthropological study, but it is also showing us how little is known about human behavior.

Hall's focus on establishing a "frame of reference" that would enable one to observe better and that would help us to discover the significant differences in manners (or, as more commonly described today, interaction styles), has remained important in the field. His emphasis on how much is still to be discovered, rather than what had already been learned, was an appropriate emphasis for a new field. His statement also illustrates how Hall clearly positioned his new field in relation to the discipline of anthropology, not communication. Only in looking back on the past thirty years of work do we know communication would provide an intellectual home to the new field rather than anthropology; in the 1950s there was no way to predict its future course. My suggestion is not that anthropology in some way abandoned intercultural communication, but that the expanding field of communication turned out to be an appropriate "foster home" for the new research into intercultural interaction, readily accepting the "infant" as a member of the its extended "family".

Anthropology originally addressed an academic audience, along with a smaller group in various government agencies. The original audience of intercultural communication was the reverse: primarily a sector of government (foreign service officers) with a small audience among academics. But this division changed over time. Intercultural communication today addresses a varied audience: Americans who travel for pleasure or business or school as well as foreign nationals coming to this country for any of the same reasons. Hall himself made this shift away from the original audience of diplomats. In at least one article, Hall drew explicit connections between his work with diplomats and what has become one of the largest groups interested in the results of intercultural communication research and training: international business. The rationale for this new, broader audience assumed that the same wide variety of factors that played a role in diplomatic interactions must play an equal role in business. Even in this early application, Hall saw the value of the case study approach; a major section of his article describes how a business deal "soured" due to cultural differences in timing, use of space, etc.. Comparable case studies still abound in intercultural communication training today as one of the best ways to provide participants concrete examples of problems caused by cultural differences in communication patterns.

Conclusion

FSI hired some of the best linguists and anthropologists of the day to train members of the Foreign Service. These academics had to adapt their knowledge for the new audience in a variety of ways; this adaptation led to new ideas about their work and to a burst of creativity in the late 1940s and early 1950s. The need to teach immediately practical aspects of their subject led to the study of small elements of culture, rather than the traditional topics anthropologists taught their college students. This shift, in turn, led to the creation of new fields of research, all centered on the role of nonverbal communication in social interaction: proxemics, time, kinesics, and paralanguage. Since the academics who had been assembled were not adept at nor interested in the political maneuvering necessary to survive in the federal bureaucracy, the group was disbanded in the mid-1950s.

But by that time their role in establishing what is now known as the field of intercultural communication had been completed and their influence assured.

Hall's writings have been instrumental in the development of intercultural communication as it is currently practiced; further, since Hall's approach was created in response to the context provided by the FSI, the field today owes much to the explicit requests of a small group of diplomats in the 1940s and 1950s for a way to apply general anthropological insights to specific problems of international discourse. Intercultural communication as a field obviously has changed in many ways over the past forty years, and no doubt will continue to change; understanding the roots of our own discipline and the reasons for some of the decisions that have come to be accepted as doctrine can only increase our ability to deliberately shape it to meet future needs.

Notes

1. From "Notes in the History of Intercultural Communication: The Foreign Service Institute and the Mandate for Intercultural Training." *Quarterly Journal of Speech*, 1990.
2. Wendy Leeds-Hurwitz: Wendy Leeds-Hurwitz is Director of the Center for Intercultural Dialogue, and Professor Emerita of Communication at the University of Wisconsin-Parkside. She is known for her research on intercultural communication, language and social interaction, semiotics, social construction theory, ethnography of communication, childhood socialization, and disciplinary history.
3. The use of case studies in this and other works by Hall can be viewed as part of a long tradition within anthropology of collecting both long and short "life histories" (details of autobiography from members of a culture under study as one way of learning what is normal and appropriate behavior). There is a related and comparable use of life histories within linguistics, where the focus was to gather extended examples of text for later analysis.

Questions for Discussion

1. What can you infer from the following quote? What are other essentials a student needs to fulfill the plan beyond the foreign language abilities?

    Many authors also urged fuller education about the history, political structure, economics, and international relations with the United States, not only of the country to which the diplomat would be sent, but of the entire geographic region.

2. At present, what are other professionals, in your opinion, necessary to promote Chinese culture to the whole world?

3. The author expressed her concerns about giving Edward T. Hall the sole credit for the significance of his work to the field. How do you think of other scholars' contributions? What can we learn from them?
4. After reading the historical context setting the stage for the field, what is/are your "aha" moment(s), if there is any?
5. In the past three years, people on the globe have been experiencing the pandemic. What are the possible new responsibilities for the intercultural communication scholars worldwide?

Online Mini-Case Studies and Viewpoints-Sharing

Americans sometimes have this belief that what we do here in the United States is the best and the only way to do things. We put these "cultural blinders" on and are oblivious to any other cultures and/or values. Although American tradition has been and can be a big influence on other markets and business sectors, we are failing to realize that the way we do business is not the basis for all businesses. Most of our international business ventures are failing and die to our stubbornness. In the past we felt that we could send someone to Mexico or Japan without any intercultural training and still show them how to do business. How wrong were we?

Today we realize it takes an understanding of others and their beliefs and values to truly gain respect and further our business and personal relationships. Businesses are taking the time and money to train their employees about the new culture that they will be submerged in. People in the past failed because we did not take into account that companies' attitudes and beliefs differed from ours. Good relations with other international businesses can produce a lifelong bond that can create great economic wealth for each country. The companies are not only training their employees for this culture shock but are training their families as well, because they know that without family support, this venture will surely fail. The United States has taken strides to correct their errors of the past and are continuing their efforts to produce intercultural employees, and I hope this trend continues.

Online Research

Find out the U.S. Peace Corps training programs and its volunteers' encounters when being dispatched overseas and share your findings.

Unit Two

Language and Culture

Reading One

Introductory Remarks

One of the recognized ways to understand the connection between language and culture is through language universals and language relativism. The former refers to linguistic characteristics which are salient of all cultures as an aspect of culture itself. The logical structure of such universals and their substantive content provide significant clues to their nature as well as their importance. While logical structure suggests the need for consistent characteristics throughout diversified languages, the substantive content of the universals includes such aspects as phonology, grammar, semantics, and symbols. Language universals indicate that beneath the surface all natural languages share certain features of similarity. In contrast, language relativism stresses the aspect of linguistic relativity, which was expounded by Sapir and his student Whorf in their hypothesis. The Sapir-Whorf hypothesis holds that every language is unique in its capacity to shape its culture and the individual thought-patterns of the culture, and that language has an even more persuasive influence than culture proper upon the language users in virtually every aspect including thinking-pattern, formulating notion of space, categorizing the material and spiritual worlds.

This selected reading begins with the study of the relationship between verbal linguistic codes and their implications in intercultural contexts. It then discusses the important aspects of the language-culture issue: language universals serving as a primary link between languages and cultures, whereas linguistic relativity theory dominant in answering many questions associated with language and culture. What is generally called Sapir-Whorf hypothesis (core of linguistic relativity), in Joshua Fishman's words, "does not concern itself too much about 'what was first, the language patterns or the cultural norms?' but was content to conclude that in the main they have grown up together, constantly influencing each other." Following that, the article elaborates on several assumptions underly generative grammar and some counter arguments to underly universality of language with examples. The selection ends with the language planning in Canada, leaving us with questions about language and culture to be explored through further readings.

Communicative Codes: Linguistic Aspects[1]

Michael H. Prosser

A code may be referred to as a system of laws or rules intended to augment or guide certain aspects of human interaction. Legal systems such as the Twelve Tables of the Romans, English Common Law, the United States Constitution, and International Law represent specific codes of justice. Religious rules in the Ten Commandments, the Torah, the Christian Bible, Roman Catholic or Episcopal Canon Law, and the Koran are codes for moral living. The language systems of the Indo-European family, with their similar patterns of grammar and syntax, provide a general code for the languages within that family. Each specific language in the family differs enough from the others that it is supplemented by its own specific code of rules.

Culture itself is a code which we learn and share with others. The socializing process in every culture for the young involves both written and unwritten codes of rules and laws. Likewise, within and between societies and cultures, communication proceeds by certain prescribed and inferred codes of behavior. Albert E. Scheflen argues that people are socially organized to perform and interpret repertoires of coded behavior. They have learned multichanneled, highly-patterned communicative behavior for multiple social roles and multiple occasions. The social organization for their interaction is not a simple alteration of speaker and listener, but involves kinship and other affiliational systems, dominance hierarchies, territorial arrangements, and other abstractable dimensions.

George Gerbner defines communication as "social interaction through symbols and message systems. The production and perception of message systems cultivating stable structures of generalized images—rather than any tactic calculated to result in 'desirable' (or any other response)—is at the heart of the communications transaction." David Berlo isolates the role of code as an aspect of the total communicative situation:

> A code can be defined as any group of symbols that can be structured in a way that is meaningful to some person ... Anything is a code which has a group of elements (a vocabulary) and a set of procedures for combining those elements meaningfully (a syntax). If we want to know whether a set of symbols is a code, we have to isolate its vocabulary, and check to see if there are systematic ways (structures) for combining

the elements.

In the same way, if we want to learn a code, to "break a code," we look for the elements that appear, and we look for consistent ways in which the elements are structured ... Whenever we encode a message, we must make certain decisions about the code we will select. Second, when we analyze communication behavior, messages, we need to include the source's decisions about the code in our analysis. It is for these reasons that we include codes as part of our analysis of structure.

Berlo emphasizes that in linking messages and codes, we must also be aware of the content of the message, which, like the code, has both elements and structure. We must also recognize the best ways to present our messages or how to select and arrange both our codes and message content. As message recipients we need to understand and accept messages. We must have the ability to interpret the codes as well as to perceive the intention of the messages. Berlo comments: "When we decode messages, we make inferences as to the source's purpose, his communication skills, his attitudes toward us, his knowledge, his status. We try to estimate what kind of person would have produced this kind of message. We often decide what the source's purpose was, what kind of 'personality' he or she has, what objects he or she values or believes in, what he or she thinks is worthless."

Verbal linguistic codes provide the link for cultural communication
Both the verbal linguistic and the nonverbal codes which we use in human communication are of considerable interest to the intercultural communicator and cross-cultural researcher. They add significantly to the ethnographic study of a community or mapping of a culture which Hymes recommends. As symbol-builders and manipulators, we can encode and decode a nearly limitless variety of verbal and nonverbal messages, depending upon our own capacities. Colin Cherry writes: "This great variety of roles which humans are able to adopt seems to be mediated by their phenomenal powers of a sign-usage, above all by those of language. It is their powers of language which set them apart from the creatures of a gulf, a gulf which Susanne Langer has seen as one whole day of nations, all tribes everywhere have language." Nonetheless, our capacity to use sign-systems such as language and conscious nonverbal codes serves both to unite and to divide us from each other. As Cherry stresses, the very fact that language forms a major part of our identity, of our view of ourselves and in relation to our friends, our

fellow citizens, and foreigners, helps to make us inseparable from our social groups. Thus, we accept certain groups and reject others. Cherry insists, however, that: "Man has endless uses of language, signs and ritual, significant of the fact that he is a member of a nation, or a class, or a tribe, or a race, of this or that group; but he has no common language, few signs, and virtually no universal ritual significant of the fact that he is a member of the human race."

By its nature, language is the key link between our ability to communicate and to pass on our cultural traditions to our children. Joseph H. Greenberg emphasizes that:

> Among all the aspects of the cultural inheritance, anthropologists are virtually unanimous in pointing to two, tools and speech, as the most fundamental, in that they provide the indispensable prerequisites for the remainder...
>
> The two basic human traits of toolmaking and speech are more similar to each other than might appear at first glance. They have in common indirectness of action on the environment: the natural environment, for tools, the social environment, in the case of speech...
>
> When we find, in the archeological record, specific types of such purposefully fashioned tools persisting over times in the form of a definite toolmaking tradition, we see a cultural trait that, we assume, could not have come into existence without language. From its transmission we infer the operation of a fundamental function of language: the communication of already acquired knowledge...

Speech is the basic coding procedure followed by language

In relating communication and codes, George A. Miller suggests: "Our analysis of communication begins with the most important encoding procedure of all human vocalization. Other ways of encoding information could be studied instead, but certainly speech is the first learned and most widely used. In many respects speech is the basic encoding procedure. Some linguists reserve the term 'language' exclusively for the code of vocal symbols; writing, gestures, Braille, etc., are also codes that can be used for communication but are not dignified by the title of languages." Most writers on language recognize that speech and language are not precisely the same. Language is seen as an abstract system which is realized through vocalized utterances. A person unable to speak may understand speech, but still has the innate ability to utilize language. Joseph DeVito observes: "Language is the potential vehicle whereas speech is the actual activity of communication. There is also an important distinction between speech and writing. Speech is clearly the primary form of communication; writing is a secondary and derived system—a system developed in imitation of the spoken language. Speech is not spoken writing, nor is writing simply written speech." The notion of speech as having among its partial origins the behavioral aspects of vocal behavior or oral gesture is widely held, as Miller observes: "To think of speech as audible movement and comparable to movements of the arms and legs is to think of speech as vocal behavior. Viewed in this way, speech is not essentially different from acts of other types. Its apparent uniqueness rests upon its importance to man, the talking animal. Speech accomplishes the same sort of result that other behaviors could, only more expeditiously."

A major concern for the study of speech is the patterning ability which allows us to make many different combinations of sounds. Without patterning its individual sounds, Miller suggests that there would be very few things such a language could talk about, as we can make and distinguish less than 100 different speech sounds. In the English language, there are about forty different sounds. We could produce fifty different sounds to discuss millions of different things, which is a feature of human speech sound combinations. Miller stresses that if "we use all the possible pairs of fifty sounds, we can make 25,000 different statements. If 25,000 statements are not enough, we can go on to use patterns of three or four or even a thousand sounds. There are many more patterns than there are individual sounds. The ability to use such patterns, however, is uniquely human." This patterning which occurs in English speech includes recognizable units called phonemes (the smallest meaningful elements of sound), words, and sentences. The patterning, often carefully prescribed by rules, becomes a grammar, which helps to structure the coding of a language. Miller suggests: "The grammar of any language has two main parts: (1) morphology deals with the structure of words, and (2) syntax deals with the combination of words in phrases and sentences. To define what a word is in any given language is to describe the morphology of that language. To define what a sentence is describes the syntax."

Language symbolizes and catalogs our perceived reality

As a code, language may be seen both as a component of communication and of culture. The noted sociolinguist Joseph Greenberg summarizes his view of language:

> Language is unique to man. No other species possesses a truly symbolic means of communication and no human society, however simple its material culture, lacks the basic human heritage of a well developed language. Language is the prerequisite for the accumulation and transmission of other cultural traits. Such fundamental aspects of human society as organized political life, legal systems, religion and science are inconceivable without that most basic and human of tools, a linguistic system of communication. Language is not only a necessary condition for culture, it is itself a part of culture. It, like other shared behavioral norms, is acquired by the individual as a member of a particular social group through a complex process of learning. Like other aspects of human culture, it characteristically varies from group to group and undergoes significant modification in the course of its transmission through time within the same society.

DeVito defines language as "a potentially self-reflective, structured system of symbols which catalog the objects, events, and relations in the world." He argues that symbols are arbitrary "stand-ins" for the actual things. For example the word "rain" is not the actual rain but serves as a symbol of rain. Signs, however, do bear real relationships to the things for which they stand. For example, "high fever" is a sign of sickness. Here there is a real, rather than arbitrary, relationship between the thing (sickness) and the sign (fever).

 DeVito notes that symbols are arbitrary according to certain rules, and many be made of any substance. He offers varied examples, such as pyramids, purple cloth for the royalty, black cloth for mourning, or vocal symbols as representative of speech. The symbols of language are words.

 DeVito contends that because language is potentially self-reflexive it is capable of being used on at least two different levels. It must permit symbolic reference to the real or object world, and it also must allow reference to itself or to talk about language. Language is language only if it can be used for language analysis that is, metalanguage.

 While it is possible for the "language" of bees to duplicate certain features of human language, it is a very limited duplication. Despite the work with certain members of the family of ape, researchers so far have not been able to develop any nonhuman being which can either systematically produce all of the human sounds in a meaningful way, or utilize the distinctively human features of language as the human can. David McNeil speaks of the centrality of the sentence to the development of language because virtually everything that occurs in language acquisition depends on prior knowledge of the basic aspects of sentence structure. He suggests that through the two-step alarm call produced by baboons, accepted at face value, they might be said to show sentence structure. However, "it is a structure sharply limited in use. If baboons have a language, it is a language with only one sentence. In contrast, sentences are obligatory in human language. Whatever favored sentence structure in the evolution of human language must have operated at an early point to have had such a wide scope."

Language universals serve as a primary link between language and cultures
Cultural universals are properties of all human cultures found in all groups, such as speech, material traits, art, knowledge, religion, society, organized social institutions, belief systems, property, government, and war in the abstract. While cultural universals represent only the minimum patterns of similarities in cultures across time and space, their study has led to crosscultural research to determine systematically what other more detailed universal statements can be made about human societies. In a similar way, a primary concern in linking language and culture is the concept of language universals. In an early attempt to distinguish the concept, Western linguists assumed that the Western descriptions of parts of speech were universally accepted, and that all sentences could properly be divided into subjects and predicates as bare minimums, without regard for the entirely different logical and thought-patterning prevalent among the other cultures and societies. Such statements have been unfounded crossculturally. As a simple example, while the English sentence does proceed in a subject-verb-object pattern (John ate a sandwich), the Japanese sentence proceeds instead in a subject-object-verb pattern. Such crosscutural differences obviously cause problems in intercultural communication.

Language universals are summary statements about all human speakers
A major contribution to the study of language universals has been their central place in the theoretical framework of the generative transformational school of linguistics, now the dominant trend in American language studies. Greenberg suggests: "Language universals are by their very nature summary statements about characteristics or tendencies shared by all human speakers. As such they constitute the most general laws of a science of linguistics." Further, he argues that since

language is both an aspect of individual behavior and human culture, its universals provide both the major point of contact with underlying psychological principles and the major source of implications for human culture in general. He stresses, however, that a major stumbling block for the proper development of a system of detailed language universals is first, the difficulty caused by making unwarranted assumptions based on the Greco-Roman grammatical and linguistic patterns and logic. A second important problem is the lack of a central source of data, or a crosscultural file for a large and representative sample of the world's 3,000 to 5,000 living languages.

Recognizing the principle of differences in studying culture, we become aware that the diversity of languages, even those within the same language families, is far greater than even most linguists have been willing to admit. As Clifford Geertz challenges the viability of the concept of cultural universals as being too simple, Greenberg argues that it is not enough to establish language universals by simply accepting statements that all languages have vowels; all languages have phonemes; and all language sound systems may be resolved into distinctive features. He believes that the concept of language universals must be expanded to include generalizations which hold true in more than a chance number of comparisons.

Language universals may be distinguished by logical structure and substantive content

Greenberg recommends viewing language universals as differentiated both in their *logical structure* and their *substantive content*. The *logical structures* of universals incorporate the ability to define universals as any statements which include all languages in their scope. Examples are characteristics possessed by all languages, the relationships between two characteristics in all languages, or the case of mutual implications between characteristics in all languages. The logical structure of universals also includes a certain characteristic which has a greater probability than some other characteristic. It includes "near universals" in some extreme cases. Additional considerations include the relation of several characteristics in terms of probability, and instances in which a certain measurement—for example, redundancy in information theory—may be applied to any language to demonstrate characteristic means and standard deviations from other languages.

Substantive classes of universals cut across the logical structure of languages, and include *phonological*, *grammatical*, *semantic*, and *symbolic* types. In the classification, Greenberg suggests that the first three involve either form without meaning or meaning without form. The last classification, which is concerned with sound symbolism, involves the connective between the two. For example, the near universality of nasals such as *m* and *n* is a phonological universal which is not concerned with semantic meaning of forms; and the semantic universal that all languages have some metaphorically transferred meaning is not concerned with the particular sounds of the forms as they occur. On the other hand, a statistical symbolic universal such as "there is a high probability that a word designating the female parent will have a nasal consonant" as in English "*mother*," French "*mère*," and the Latin "*mater*," involves both sound and meaning and is therefore of the symbolic type.

We are interested in the symbolic uses of social discourse in and between cultures. Thus, language universals relating to the ability for communicators to encode and decode messages symbolically through channels in time and space become more relevant and interesting to us than others. On a practical level, if we understand that we can begin to decode certain messages in various languages because language universals always or normally apply to certain aspects of these languages, our intercultural communication begins to become somewhat easier than if we had no methods at all for decoding. In the simplest way, if we are aware that the English word "me" has essentially the same basic form and meaning in dozens of languages, and if the paralinguistic pointing of a person points at himself or herself with approximately the same meaning, the initial step has been made in understanding a verbal and nonverbal cue offered in a different linguistic framework by a member of another culture. If a frantic vocal tension is added, some notion is provided to help decode a message of some urgency involving oneself. Naturally, a far more systematic probing into language universals is needed to assist in understanding the real or apparent connections even between very similar languages.

In a much more systematic and empirical way, the Cross-Cultural Universals of Affective Meaning Project which has been headed for the past several years by Charles E. Osgood at the University of Illinois is an example of an application of cultural and language universals theories in twenty-five cultures. It is designed to test the hypothesis that regardless of language or culture, human beings use the same qualifying and descriptive framework in allocating the affective meanings of concepts which involve values, stereotypes, attitudes, and feelings. Osgood and his colleagues, many of whom come from the cultures under consideration, maintain that hypothesis has proven valid, and that as the project continues it may be possible to isolate truly reliable cultural and linguistic universals.

Stability and change play a role in the understanding of language universals

Language universals can be stated by observing universally discoverable regularities of how languages remain the same. They can also be stated by emphasizing how languages change by various intracultural and intercultural influences over time and space.

The interrelationship of these approaches to language universals is important because one cannot be viewed systematically without understanding the other. The observer cannot develop universal rules for language without knowing how the language functions in a static position, relatively free of immediate change, and vice versa, especially in the context of the wide diversity of languages and language families. Such a study is of greater interest to the trained linguist than to us as regular intercultural communicators, but it is useful for us to know that there are universals which do powerfully affect and assist us as we try to communicate with persons from different language backgrounds.

Generative grammar argues that all natural languages have universally similar grammatical systems

In contrast to the Sapir-Whorf hypothesis that every language designates the culture and the cultural communicator's individual thought-patterning, David McNeil proposes that "the description of linguistic universals is included in the theory of universal grammar. As opposed to the grammar of a single language, the theory of a grammar is a description of the general form of human language ... The purpose is to state the universal conditions that the grammars describing individual languages must meet." Noam Chomsky, a chief proponent of the theory of generative or transformational grammar, states that two central problems are present in the descriptive study of a language: the primary concern is discover simple and "revealing" grammars for natural languages, and to arrive at a general theory of language structure crossculturally.

In many languages, there are certain cases of correct grammar and certain cases of incorrect grammar, for example, in English, "John ate a sandwich," and "Sandwich a ate John." In this case, Chomsky says that we can test the adequacy of the proposed linguistic theory by determining in each language whether or not clear cases are handled properly by the grammars in accordance with this theory. Chomsky calls the first step in the linguistic analysis of a language the provision of the limited system of representation for its sentences: "No matter how we ultimately decide to construct linguistic theory, we shall surely require that the grammar of any language must be finite. " It follows that only a countable set of grammars is made available by any linguistic theory; hence that many uncountable languages, in our general sense, are literally not describable in terms of the conception of linguistic structure. Chomsky asks: Are there interesting languages that are simply beyond the range of description of the proposed type? Can you construct reasonably simple grammars for all interesting languages? Are such grammars revealing in the sense that the syntactic structure that exhibit can support semantic analysis, can provide insight into the use and understanding of language?

Several basic assumptions underlie generative grammar
Joseph DeVito demonstrates that several basic assumptions underlie generative grammar in terms of the distinctions made between concepts and processes, that is, between *static* and *process descriptions*, between *competence* and *performance*, between *descriptive* and *prescriptive grammars*, and between *deep* and *surface structures*. In the distinctions between static and process descriptions, DeVito points out that earlier linguists attempted to describe language change as proceeded over time. More recently, especially in the twentieth century the emphasis developed so that they began describing the sound and structure of languages in a *static* or unchanging situation. Then, still later, the emphasis was placed on the description of the *process* of language with an emphasis on generative grammar and grammatical transformations, on processes or operations by which strings of elements are altered or changed by addition, deletion, substitution, or permutation. Chomsky provides an example of such a string with no general relation between the component parts and its grammaticalness: "colorless green ideas sleep furiously. " The string does have grammatical sense, even if it has no semantically correct meaning. Another example, this time of a string which has no grammatical correctness, is "furiously sleep ideas green colorless. " Both sentences can be improved syntactically or semantically by additions and deletions.

To delineate between *competence* and *performance*, DeVito utilizes the distinction offered by the generative grammarians which says that *competence*, similar to language, refers to the rules of grammar which the native speaker "knows," that is, can apply with a conscious understanding of them. *Performance*, similar to speech, is the actual vocal noise uttered and heard, and may have no relation to a conscious understanding of the rules behind it. DeVito asserts that the study of language is primarily concerned with *competence* and the generative grammarian will seek to discover the grammar which in turn generates grammatical sentences and offers no ungrammatical sentences. Such a grammar provides that while there are a limited number of linguistic elements and rules, there are an infinite number of possible sentences in any human language. Normal human adults can offer thousands and thousands of different sentences. This is an important factor for the intercultural communicator because once we know the basic rules and a substantial vocabulary in a second language, we become able to encode and decode a nearly limitless number of sentences or message components in that language as well as in our own. The generative or transformational grammar theory would lead us to believe that the same features can be duplicated over and over again to the extent that an individual's capacity for learning sets of rules and vocabularies is possible. This would seem a reasonable assumption, given the warning that the diversity of grammatical rules and vocabularies still makes it unusual for individuals to master more than several highly contrasting languages in terms of their structure and semantic range of meaning. This defines language (as opposed to language in general) as an infinite set of grammatical sentences, and defines grammar as the device for specifying or describing this infinite set of sentences. Chomsky has stimulated linguists to describe a universal grammar as a correlate of language universals.

Most contemporary linguists prefer *descriptive* grammar over *prescriptive* grammar because they wish to describe the competence of speakers rather than prescribe rules for instruction in proper language usage. Such linguists do not concern themselves with the nature and background of the specific user of the language nor with concepts such as "right" and "wrong" in language. They are less concerned about a speaker's use of "ain't" than whether it fits correctly in a sentence or a grammatical structural basis. Such language specialists would consider "black" English on this basis rather than on the basis that some of its usage and vocabulary seem incorrect to users of standard English. Chomsky distinguishes between deep and surface structure of a sentence universally by emphasizing that in addition to the surface or superficial structure of a sentence, there is also a deep structure and that sentences are understood on the basis of their deep rather than their surface structure. DeVito exemplifies a sentence whose surface structure is: "The criticisms of the student were negative," which has two confusing deep structures: "The student has given negative criticisms" and "Someone gives the student negative criticisms." DeVito suggests that another way in which the distinction between deep and surface structure becomes apparent is seen in sentences which are different on the surface but which have only one deep structure as in: "The boy hit the girl," and "The girl was hit by the boy."

These sentences are understood in essentially the same way, not because their surface structure reveals this similarity, but because their deep or underlying structure is the same. Interrogatives also form part of the deep structure and are generated semantically in any language, e. g. , "Did the boy hit the girl?" "Why did the boy hit the girl?" "The boy hit the girl, did he?" "How did the boy hit the girl?"

DeVito acknowledges that generative grammar is only one possible way of approaching language, but he argues: "It seems to me, however, that generative grammar is at present the only workable candidate for a theory of language simply because it is the only grammar which provides a convincing account of the speaker's linguistic competence... The influence of generative grammar on the study of psycholinguistics has far surpassed the influence exerted by any other approach." Comparing the argument between those who accept the linguistic relativity hypothesis of Sapir-Whorf, which makes each culture dependent upon its language, and the argument of Chomsky and others that generative grammars provide a sort of universal grammar, Condon and Yousef suggest: "If we expect to find great diversity in languages, it is only a matter of time until—as the transformational grammarians seemed to find—we discover how remarkably similar languages are at heart. That is, from the transformationalist point of view, the apparent differences in the ways languages code 'reality' are mostly superficial (if not exactly above the surface then at least not below the surface). If we go to a deeper structure on a level that ordinary speakers are not aware of, we can find remarkable consistency across languages."

A counterargument to the underlying universality of language

A major counter development in the Western world to the problems caused by the application of essentially a Greco-Roman grammatical tradition was structuralism. This emphasized linguistic structural differences rather than the uniformities of language. In structuralism, every language is perceived as an organized structural system which must be described in its own terms without the imposition of the observers' ethnocentrically derived categories. In this sense, the principle of differences was recognized as the basis for crosscultural linguistic research.

When we consider contemporary theories of language and culture which stress linguistic differences from culture to culture in contrast to the notion that language universals serve as a primary link between language and culture, the "linguistic relativity theory," associated primarily with Edward Sapir and Benjamin Lee Whorf and variously called the "Sapir-Whorf hypothesis" or "the Whorf hypothesis," is a dominant one. However, it is considered by many writers as out-of-date. It is not the sort of hypothesis that can be proven or disproven, and it is not even clear whether Sapir and Whorf meant what I considered as the focus of their theory today. Still, its staying power is the chief reason why it is of considerable interest to the student of intercultural and crosscultural communication. Sapir's statement of his hypothesis can be summarized as follows: "Language is a self-contained, creative, symbolic organization, which not only refers to experience largely acquired without its help but actually defines experience for us both by its structure and by our unconscious acceptance of the language's ability to influence all of our experience by shaping symbolic meanings for us." The argument is that meanings are not so much discovered in experience as imposed upon it, because of the tyrannical hold that linguistic form has upon our orientation of the world. Language is a guide to "social reality." According to this hypothesis, we are at the mercy of the particular language which has become the medium of expression for our society. Our reality is determined by our own language. No two languages are ever sufficiently similar to be considered as representing the same social reality. The world in which different societies live are distinct, not merely the same world with different labels attached. Sapir's student, Whorf, proposed essentially the same thesis several years later. Whorf argues that in the "constant ways of arranging data and its most ordinary every-day analysis of phenomena that we need to recognize the influence; ... [language] has no other activities, cultural and personal." He emphasizes both its structural and semantic aspects, including a self-contained system of meanings. It is of course easier to study language structure than its meaning, since meanings reside in the individual. It is still more difficult to link the structural aspects with its symbolic aspects.

In "A Systemization of the Whorfian Hypothesis," Joshua Fishman stresses that Whorf was not deeply concerned with "Which was first, the language patterns or the cultural norms?" but was content to conclude that "in the main they have grown up together, constantly influencing each other." Nevertheless, Fishman indicates that it was Whorf's feeling that if the two streams were separated from each other for the purpose of analysis, language is by far the more impervious, systematic, and rigid of the two, thus causing cultural innovations to have less influence on language than the other way around. Fishman suggests that Whorf apparently "considered language structure not only as interactingly reflective of 'cultural thought' but as directly formative of 'individual thought'." Fishman schematizes the Whorfian hypothesis at four levels; 1) languages differ "in the same ways" as the general cultures or surrounding environments of their speakers differ; 2) attempts at this level are made to codify some correspondence at the cultural level between language behaviors and nonlanguage behaviors; 3) the structure of language, for example, its grammar, shapes ideas in the particular culture; and 4) the actual prediction of individual and cultural behavior based on linguistic structure.

Fishman contends that while levels 1 and 3 could be seen as large group or collective phenomena, and levels 2 and 3 are concerned with individual interpersonal behavior, few studies have demonstrated the actual linkages between culture and language, which Sapir and Whorf seemed to feel possible. Fishman stresses that each level becomes progressively more debatable in terms of offering real proof. If the hypothesis were entirely valid, Fishman feels that its implications would be counterproductive to intercultural relations: "All of us in most walks of life and most of us in all walks of life are helplessly trapped by the language we speak; we cannot escape from it—and, even if we could flee, where would we turn but to some other language with its own blinders and its own vice-like embrace on what we think, what we perceive, and what we say? ... What hope can there be for mankind? What hope that one nation will ever fully communicate with the other?" In his critique of the linguistic relativity hypothesis, Fishman indicates that while evidence favoring it exists at each level, "It seems likely that linguistic relativity, though affecting some of our cognitive behavior, is nevertheless only a moderately powerful factor and a counteractable one at that."

To summarize, Fishman's critique of the Whorfian hypothesis seems reasonable. Obviously, language does have great power as a distinctive influence in culture and individual thought-patterning. Nevertheless, language may simply be one of many important influences on culture and thus on intercultural communication. Actually, though the individual language and culture are tightly linked, and therefore do cause important barriers for intercultural communication and for cultural spokespersons, the language problems may be less severe than other cultural barriers; for example, perceptions, attitudes, stereotypes, prejudices, beliefs, values, and thought-patterning itself. Additionally, the initial issues discussed earlier also may serve as even more formidable barriers for intercultural communication than the pervasive influence that language is likely to hold over culture and individual thinking. Based on my understanding of the inability to prove or disprove the linguistic relativity hypothesis, I believe that it is a less viable way of offering the primary link between language and culture than are the theories of language universals and generative grammar.

The notion of cultural pluralism vs. assimilation is relevant in an understanding of these two opposing theories. The Sapir-Whorf hypothesis, which stresses that language pervasively shapes each specific culture and the individual thought-patterns contained within the culture, may be seen as an expression of cultural pluralism. The generative grammar theory insists that all or most languages are governed by similar structural systems. While their surface structure may be vastly different, at the level below the surface, remarkable similarities appear. This theory attempts to assimilate a language into a common type at the "deep structure" level. The principle of similarities and differences also comes sharply into focus in considering these theories with the principle of similarities being favored by the generative grammar theory and the principle of differences begin favored by the Sapir-Whorf hypothesis. We must assume, then, that both theories do offer a degree of merit and that there are important cultural observations about linguistic and nonverbal coding which can be drawn from both theories. Taken together, without either theory being considered absolutely mutually exclusive, both do add to our understanding, especially of language as a chief component both of communication and culture, and of the problems and opportunities facing the intercultural communication and cultural spokesperson.

The focus of language contact is the bilingual or polylingual individual
Joseph Greenberg suggests that if the United States had the same linguistic diversity as Nigeria, more than 500 languages would be spoken within the American borders. He speculates that areas of high-linguistic diversity are those in which communication is poor and that the increase of communication which goes with greater economic productivity and more extensive political organization will lead typically to the spread of lingua franca, whether indigenous or imported. Such a condition results in widespread bilingualism and the ultimate disappearance of all except a single dominant language as the principal means of exchange between diverse peoples. In Africa, Greenberg indicates that tribal life and its extensive associations both with the living and their ancestors for formulating codes of social behavior is still a persistent mode of life, despite the increasing sense of national identity and urbanization. Since language is a social phenomenon whose fundamental role is to make possible "that accumulation of learned behavior which we call culture and which is the distinctively human mode of adjustment," the focus of language contact is the bilingual or polylingual individual. It is not the languages which are in contact so much as it is the individual in contact with his or her own culture and other cultural groupings.

Africa offers a prime example of the need for bilingualism and polylingualism
Though rural life in Africa tends to be defined in large measure by the first language, many Africans not only are forced to be bilingual but also polylingual, particularly in light of the linguistic diversity within tight geographical settings in Africa. Typical Africans may normally learn two or more African languages or dialects, often quite different in character and structure, simply to cope within the context of ethnic interaction. Their intercultural communication would be impossible without bilingualism and polylingualism. They are more likely to give allegiance to one language than the others, and may be required to think differently in each language. Additionally, the vast colonization of Africa, especially by France and Great Britain, has increasingly led to the imposition of a European lingua franca. Such a lingua franca can be used in urban African centers, in the schools, in political contacts with the government, in trade, in the ability to read printed materials, and in developing general literacy. In some parts of Africa, it remains predominantly French, while in still more parts it remains English.

Greenberg suggests that it is not enough simply to consider language from the utilitarian point of view, that is, as a chief means of communication but perhaps the most important single criterion of group identification, at least among groups sufficiently large to play a political role. He argues that if a common language did not have this important first "language" function, people who had learned a foreign lingua franca of wider usefulness than their native language would be likely to abandon their first language, or at least not insist that their children learn it. However, Greenberg states:

> In interviews I conducted in the Plateau Province of the Northern Region of Nigeria, a highly multilingual area in which Hausa is the undisputed lingua, practically all informants with children said that they taught them their tribal language as their first language, and Hausa somewhat later. In the words of one informant, "If we abandoned our own language, we would become Hausa just like the rest." Pagans said that their ancestors would be greatly angered by the abandonment of their language. Several illiterate informants ventured the opinion that the language itself had a positive aesthetic aspect. There was, however, no hostility to the learning of Hausa. In fact, my informants expressed a unanimous desire for their children to learn Hausa because it was the medium for

instruction in the lower grades and because ignorance of Hausa condemned a man to a restricted and economically marginal traditional agricultural existence.

Since most Africans speak tonal, nonstress native languages, they are likely to identify stress with high pitch and thus do not reduce unstressed vowels as native speakers of English would. Many Africans first encounter European languages through educated African speakers, causing them to use African renditions as a model. This helps to develop reasonably uniform "dialects" of English and French which may have a greater state of purity than in Great Britain and France. Even if such a European lingua franca is practically not one's first language, its purity is similar to that found among nonnative speakers of English in the Asian subcontinent. Such languages are relatively free of the linguistic inference often imposed by first languages in other situations and the rival allegiances which have developed toward various native languages. In any case, a European *lingua franca* such as English or French may serve more neutrally for interaction than either the first or second usual languages of potentially rival tribes. Thus, its power interculturally is markedly increased.

"Bilingual" is a euphemism for "linguistically handicapped"

Einar Haugen relates that as a bilingual from childhood he was unaware of the stigmata of bilingualism placed on him: "Without knowing it, I had been exposed to untold dangers of retardation, intellectual impoverishment, schizophrenia, anomie, and alienation, most of which I had apparently escaped, if only by a hair's breath. If my parents knew about these dangers, they firmly dismissed them and made me bilingual willy-nilly. They took the position that I would learn all the English I needed from my playmates and my teachers, and that only by learning and using Norwegian in the home could I maintain a fruitful contact with them and their friends and their culture." Sadly enough, Haugen believes, instead of properly defining bilingualism in terms of its positive relations to the learning of two languages, "for many people 'bilingual' is a euphemism for 'linguistically handicapped.' It is a nice way of referring to children whose parents have handicapped them in the race for success by teaching them their mother tongue, which happens not to be the dominant language in the country they now inhabit. The term has enjoyed a semantic development not unlike that of 'minority group'." In many countries and in many earlier societies bilingualism means to be educated. Haugen provides many more examples of countries in which bilingualism means to be uneducated, usually where a dependent and dominated social group has refused to submit to the imposition of the language of the culturally imperialistic and dominant group:

> The power relationship of victor over vanquished, of native over immigrant, of upper class over lower class; these have bred bilingualism as it is commonly understood. The fact that it is unilaterally imposed by a dominant group is a major source of the pejorative connotations where these exist. It is part of what keeps the underprivileged groups underprivileged, and it is taken up for general discussion only when it forms part of a syndrome of segregation. Our neighbor Canada offers a charming example of the ambiguities of the situation. The English speaking Canadians are heartily in favor of bilingualism, so long as it means that the French will learn English; the French, however, think of it as requiring that all the English learn French. But in the meanwhile the French are doing what they can to ensure that Quebec at least will remain all French—and no more bilingual than is absolutely necessary.

Both Haugen and Wallace Lambert note that many studies have been completed to demonstrate that bilingualism has a detrimental effect on intellectual functioning; very few indicate that there are favorable effects; and some indicate that bilingualism has no effect on intelligence. Lambert feels that the wide diversity of contradictory studies fails to establish any sort of generalized norm. He indicates that some recent studies have emphasized the importance for second-language learning of an individual's attitude toward the second-language community.

> Using a language involves persons, participation in a second culture...
> A bilingual person belongs to two different communities and possesses two personalities which may be in conflict if the two language communities are in social conflict. Changes in the bilingual's attitude toward a language community may account for the variation in his efficiency on intelligence tests... The fact that an individual becomes bilingual in a bicultural community may be attributable to a favorable disposition toward both the linguistic communities, whereas the monolingual may be retarded in his acquisition of a second language because of his unfavorable attitudes toward both the other culture and its language.

Lambert draws several conclusions from a study on the developmental aspects of second-language acquisition in Montreal between French and English native speakers who were either bilingual or were studying a second language. He feels that they may be generalizable in this one study from the hypotheses which were confirmed or not confirmed, based on the tested data. First, the acquisition of a second language entails a series of barriers to overcome, with the vocabulary barrier being easier to overcome as experience with the language progresses. However, the cultural barrier is more resistant, and to overcome this barrier, one must assimilate those aspects of a different culture which influence language behavior. Second, bilinguality needs to be tested at various stages of experience with a language, as individuals recently acquiring a second language might differ on the measures falling within a vocabulary cluster. The individuals who are more advanced in second-language acquisition might do equally well in terms of vocabulary, but might differ importantly with respect to measures falling within a cultural cluster. This would require testing from both clusters to assure success at various states of language acquisition. Third, one could speculate that when the adults acquire a second language, they develop in relatively the same way as small children when they learn their first language—that is, the task of amassing vocabulary is the first problem for both and can be done with relative ease. Incorporating the cultural aspects of the linguistic community seems to be at the more advanced state of development for both children and adults. Finally, the process of linguistic enculturation takes the most time both for the children learning their own first language and for adults learning a second language.

The true bilingual masters both languages at an early age and has facility with both as means of communication; O'Doherty states that there can be no question that genuine bilingualism is an intellectual advantage. Pseudobilinguals are the real problem, as they know a second language only superficially. Very often they fail to master either language. Genuine bilinguals may also be multicultured persons. In a parallel fashion, we might speculate that the same condition might exist between pseudocultural communicators and genuinely effective cultural communicators. The first know the second culture marginally, and may not even know their own culture well; the latter understand well both cultures and can function equally well in both.

Canada's decision to become bilingual and bicultural and the impact of language planning

The Canadian government's decision in 1969 to make Canada officially bilingual and bicultural has had profound effects on Canadian life. The October 1970 riots in Montreal essentially resulted from conflict which grew out of the implementation of the Bilingual and Bicultural Act[2]. In this case, the language planning which had been initiated earlier pointed to the social, political, and cultural need in Canada to recognize a factual situation and to help nurture an ecological linguistic balance already existing somewhat precariously between French and English-speaking Canada. The language planning was hastened by the acute fear that Quebec would secede from Canada, in part because of the language problem. The planning for a genuinely bilingual and bicultural country required not only the federal passage of extensive legislation, but also the involvement of social agencies, the media, labor, the schools and various other forms of Canadian cultural maximizes and elites.

The problems encountered simply at the business and labor level in such planning can be seen in microcosm in the decision of the jointly owned Stromberg Corporation and Miracle mart grocery chain. Since the company had considerable holdings both in Quebec and Ontario, and was based in Montreal with essentially an English-speaking management, frequent protests and boycotts and potential lawsuits were aimed at the chain in the early 1970s by the French-speaking population of Montreal and Quebec. The decision to become bilingual and bicultural from the top management down to store managers and clerks was not easily reached; nor was it simply a decision made in support of the country's official bilingualism and biculturalism. The company's economic base was the major consideration. Very real decisions had to be made about hiring and firing to achieve a linguistic balance at every level in the company. Decisions had to be made about whether the discussions themselves about the decisions had to be bilingual, about whether language classes in French and English must be offered by the company for those employees who were monolingual, about whether all printed messages for employees and customers would have to be offered in both French and English, and about whether all the merchandise must be labeled in French and English. Decisions were needed for whether all store employees would be required to respond to customers either in French or English, and whether all new employees should be required to pass written and spoken tests in both languages. The turmoil in the company, especially in top and middle management, was very real, but realistic long-term goals were set. Gradually a genuine ecological bilingual and bicultural balance is beginning to be reached in the company.

The company is starting to be known as a leader in the movement at the business and labor level for genuine adoption of bilingualism and biculturalism in Canada. Problems are continuing and much more time is needed to claim success for such a far-reaching organizational effort at intercultural communication. Even the most important goal to move toward a bilingual and bicultural status for the entire company was extremely courageous for the top management, especially since nearly all of them were monolingually English-speaking. Other companies based in Montreal with English-speaking managements simply made the decision to move out of Quebec or to maintain absolute linguistic stability, rather than change in the face of hostile reactions from the French population. Thus, we can see that key issues affecting intercultural communication are of very great practical importance in implementing a country's official decision to become bilingual and bicultural. The opportunities and problems for intercultural communicators and the cultural spokespersons in such a situation are very real and are not easily solved.

Notes

1. Adapted and abridged from *The Cultural Dialogue: An Introduction to Intercultural Communication*, 1989. Professor Prosser is one of the founders of American Association of Intercultural Communication Studies and initiator of the Speech Communication Association in the U.S.
2. In relation to the implementation of the Act, Pat Duffy Hutcheon has more to say.

Questions for Discussion

1. Do you think that language universals are by their very nature summary statements about the characteristics shared by all human speakers? Why or why not?
2. Point out loopholes in the viewpoints made by DeVito.
3. Share your understanding of Sapir-Whorf hypothesis with your fellow students and tell why its staying power is still strong.
4. Haugen believes that "bilingual" is a euphemism for "linguistically handicapped." Does it make sense?
5. Is it possible to make oneself a highly bilingual person without abandoning any aspect of his/her parental culture? If your answer is "Yeah", tell how you will work as a volunteer teacher in a Nairobi-based Confucius Institute, say, when you have an opportunity to Kenya?

Online Mini-Case Studies and Viewpoints-Sharing

Different Greeting Patterns

International students describe the different cultural and communication patterns they encounter in the United States. A graduate student from India noted the U.S. patterns of greeting. In her native culture people only say hello to those they know. Initially, she was surprised by the frequency with which Americans greet each other; she later became disillusioned: "I thought, they are really interested in how I am. They always go like ... I am fine and how about you? Then I realized that people are really not interested in the answer. It is just a way of acknowledging you."

Online Research

Find out at least five greeting patterns in different cultures and tell the possible causes of their differences.

Reading Two

Introductory Remarks

Language and culture are intertwined and interdependent. Studying a language without probing the culture in which it is nurtured equals studying an organism without considering the environment in which the being is living. Regarding the extended relationship among language, thought and action, Ward Beecher used a metaphor: Thought is the blossom; language the opening bud; action the fruit behind it. To state that language is important is to declare the obvious, yet, because we can all talk we often overlook the profound influence that languages have on human behavior. Language diversity is perhaps one of the most difficult and persistent problems that we find in intercultural communication.

This selection mainly concentrates on verbal language as well as relationships between verbal language and culture, and explains how their reciprocal relationships influence communication and understanding. Other important issues covered by this reading include the nature of language, components of language, and the use of argot in sub-cultural communities. The last section of the reading is about foreign language and translation, claiming that culturally-bound words and cultural orientations have no direct renditions.

Language and Culture: Sounds and Actions[1]

Larry A. Samovar and Richard E. Porter

The Nature of Language

As we have progressed through the various issues that affect intercultural communication, we have directed our attention to culturally influenced internal states that affect our behavior and perception. In fact, if we think about it for a moment, other than our physical self, everything that we are is internal. Most of this internal state is an electrochemical mélange residing within our brains. Here is the residence and locus of our beliefs, values, attitudes, world views, emotions, and myriad other aspects of our selves and personalities. In essence who and what we are is locked up inside of us.

If what we are is within us, how then do we share ourselves with others? As we pointed out earlier, we do not have a mechanism by which we can connect ourselves with others and have a direct electrochemical transfer that forms a physical communication link. This type of sharing is not yet possible. We can convey some aspects of ourselves nonverbally by touching, but to get to the deeper issues within us, we must resort to a method of symbolic substitution.

We already know that the purpose of communication is to be able to share ourselves with one another, and that intercultural communication is the special circumstance in which the sharing occurs between people of different cultures. This sharing happens through our use of language, which is our medium of exchange for sharing our internal states of being with one another.

In the simplest sense, a language is a set of symbols, with rules for combining the symbols, that a large community uses and understands. Verbal languages are the principal means by which we express our thoughts and feelings.

Verbal languages use word symbols that stand for or represent various concrete and abstract parts of our individual realities. Words, consequently, are abstractions of our realities; they are incapable of eliciting reactions that embody the totality of the objects or concepts they represent. Take, for instance, the word *dog*. What does that word represent? Dogs come in a variety of breeds and sizes. Are we talking about a small lap dog or perhaps a large guard dog? Are we representing a collie, a German shepherd, a poodle? Are we referring to a female or a male animal? Now notice the word that ended the last sentence, the word *animal*. This word is even more of an abstraction than the word *dog*. It could be referring to a dog, to a cow, to a horse, to a rat, or to a human being. Words are abstractions of the things they represent and are, therefore, always incomplete representations.

We may envision a verbal language as consisting of sounds, words, combinations of words, and communicative purposes. These dimensions of language are referred to as the phonemic, semantic, syntactic, and pragmatic.

The smallest unit of speech sound is called a phoneme. Hence the phonemic level of language is comprised of the sounds that are meaningful to a community of language users. Languages do not contain all of the same phonemes, nor do they make the same distinctions about the manner in which the sounds are produced. In the English language there are approximately forty-five phonemes, and we do not pay particular attention to minor differences in the way most of these sounds are produced. But in tonal languages such as Chinese, a minor difference in the way a phoneme is produced can be what distinguishes meaning.

The semantic level of language refers to the meanings that are attached to words. This level of language is critical to the process of translation, in which it is crucial to understand the meanings associated with words.

The syntactic level of language is the rules that govern the use of words. These rules specify what constitutes phrases, sentences, and larger sequences of words. They also specify such things as how a language expresses possession.

Finally, the pragmatic level of language contains the rules that govern language for the accomplishment of desired communicative goals. Here are specified the rules that determine whether a message will be persuasive, express anger or scorn, reveal feelings, or enforce social relationships.

If we include culture as a variable in the process of abstraction, the problems become all the more acute. When you are communicating with someone from your own culture, the abstraction process of using words to represent your experiences is much easier, because within a culture people share a number of similar experiences. But when the communication event involves people from different cultures, many experiences are different, and consequently the abstraction process is more troublesome. To illustrate, let us again use the word *dog*. Most of us think of an animal that is a companion and that possibly serves some useful purpose such as guarding our home. But to many Pacific Islanders and Southeast Asians, the word *dog* may represent a delicacy. Culture exerts a tremendous influence on this process of abstracting our realities into words.

Word symbols are governed by rules that tell us how to use them best to represent our experiences. These rules dictate both language structure in the form of grammar and syntax and how language is regulated through rules that govern turn-taking, feedback, and the like. Language, however, is much more than a mere set of word symbols governed by rules. It is far more complex than that because the language symbols are only abstractions of the real states of our being and, as such, are inadequate substitutes. But language symbols are all that we have, and we have learned to do relatively well using them. We are able to share symbolically our experiences with others and to achieve various levels of mutual understanding, at least among members of a particular language-using community.

The most common form of language that we use is the one with which we are more familiar: spoken language. Written language is merely a convenient way of recording spoken language by making marks on paper or some other suitable surface. If we recall our history, we remember that before paper was invented, language was recorded on clay tablets, papyrus, copper sheets, and many other surfaces that permitted humankind to record, share, and store knowledge for future use and for transmission to future generations.

For many of us, English is our primary language. It consists of symbols (words) and rules (grammar and syntax)—but so do Spanish, Swahili, Chinese,

German, and French. If we study another language, we soon discover that not only are the words different, but so are the rules. In English we live in a *house*. In Spanish, we live in a *casa*. In English, we show the possessive form by use of an apostrophe and say "Mary's house." In Spanish, the rules do not permit the use of an apostrophe to form a possessive, so in Spanish we learn to say "*lacasa de Maria*," or "*the house of Mary*," to form the possessive.

One of our most unusual characteristics as humans is our faculty and capacity to make sounds and marks serve as substitutes for things and feelings. That seemingly effortless process in which we all engage is at the very core of being human. Over millions of years we have evolved the anatomy necessary to produce and to receive sounds, and within a much shorter span of time have created a system whereby those sounds took on meaning by standing for things, feelings, or ideas. This evolution has led to the development of a four-part process that enables us to use sounds to our advantage: We have learned to receive, store, manipulate, and generate symbols. These four steps, working in combination, set humankind apart from other animals. The extent to which we use language is one of our most singular features.

The Importance of Language

It is through language that we reach out and make contact with our surrounding realities. And it is through language that we share with others our experiences of that reality. If we survey a normal day we will soon see that we use words for a variety of reasons. Even the first few minutes we are awake might find us using language for some of the following purposes.

"Good morning!" Here we use words as a way of becoming reunited with the world outside our skin, as a means of keeping in touch with other people.

"Let me tell you about the horrible dream I had last night... I was almost seduced by a strange creature in a flying saucer." In this case, we use words to share an experience. We even use words to get support from others so that we might feel better. This example also demonstrates how we employ words so that we can deal with the *past*, so that we can talk about something that has already happened.

"Please pass the salt and pepper." In this instance we use words so that we can exercise some control over the *present*. We each seek to affect our environment, to influence many of the daily situations in which we find ourselves. Words, and how we manipulate them, permit us to make those alterations through symbolic transactions with others. We use words to persuade, to exchange ideas to express views, to seek information, or to express feelings as we maintain contact with other people.

We also use words to form an image of the future. "Well, I guess I've got to go to work now. I've an important meeting with Jane today, but I dread seeing her, as I know she's going to be angry about the changes I'm going to make in her work schedule." Here we see how our word-using ability allows us to predict and to describe the future. Although our pictures of the future are not always accurate, at least language enables us to think about, talk about, and anticipate the future.

The ability to communicate with others depends not only upon our language faculty, but upon there being enough commonality of experience among people that the words they use basically mean the same things. The wider and more divergent the language communities from which people come, the more difficult mutual understanding becomes. Although both British and Americans speak English, they come from different language-using communities, and they may not always understand each other.

Language and Meaning

As children, most of us asked our parents, "What does that word mean?" Chances are we asked that question many times, and perhaps still ask it on occasion. This question reflects the way we view language. It suggests that we tend to look for meaning in the word itself. But we err if we think that words possess meaning. It is more accurate to say that people possess meaning and that words elicit the meanings in people. We can all have different meanings for the same word. Take the word *grass*, for instance. To one person it might mean something in front of the house that is green, has to be watered, and must be mowed once a week. To another person grass may mean something that is rolled in paper and smoked. There is no "real" meaning in this example, because all people, from their own personal backgrounds, decide what a word symbol means to them. People have similar meanings only to the extent that they have had or can anticipate similar experiences. Witness how various backgrounds and experiences can alter meanings. If our past experience is in baseball, a *rope* is a line drive. If our background lies in the rock music world, *monster* is not something ugly or evil, but rather a very successful record. And finally, it is likely that we and a physician respond differently to the word *cancer*.

A word, then, can elicit many meanings. Linguists have estimated that the five hundred most often-used words in the English language can produce over fourteen thousand meanings. This diversity of meanings suggests that words not only mean different things to different people, but also that words mean different things at different times and in different contexts. We simply have many more ideas, feelings, and things to represent than we have words to represent them. Tennyson said the same thing poetically when he wrote, "Words, like Nature, half reveal/And half conceal the Soul within."

Language and Culture

One of the most important theoretical formulations concerning language is the Sapir-Whorf hypothesis, which in essence states that language is a guide to social reality. This implies that language is not simply means of reporting experience but more importantly a way of defining experience. Sapir wrote in 1929:

> Human beings do not live in the objective world alone, nor alone in the world of social activity as ordinarily understood, but are very much at the mercy of the particular language which has become the medium of expression for their society ... The real world is to a large extent unconsciously built up on the language habits of the group. No two languages are ever sufficiently similar to be considered as representing the same social reality. The worlds in which different societies live are distinct worlds, not merely the same world with different labels attached.

From this position, we can see that language is distinctly a form of human cultural behavior. It is important that we realize the cultural dimension of language for several reasons. Language helps us understand not only one another but culture as well, for it is a reflection of its parent culture. If one is to use a language well, one must know the culture that uses the language. Each language presents us with a unique way of perceiving the world and interpreting experience. As Whorf has so frequently pointed out, the structure of our language influences the manner in which we understand our environment.

Our perceptions of the universe shift from tongue to tongue, and the forms of that shifting are worth considering. We shall look at but a few of literally thousands of examples that demonstrate the influence of culture on language.

In learning to use language, we have evolved elaborate, culturally diverse linguistic forms that assist in our efforts to represent our world symbolically. One such form is high and low context. High-context communication is that form in which most of the information to be conveyed is contained in the physical context or is internalized within the people who are communicating. Very little information is in the coded symbols that form the transmitted message. Many Asian and Middle Eastern nations prefer high-context communication. Low-context communication, on the other hand, contains almost all of the information to be shared in the explicit coded message. Low-context communication is the form found primarily in Western nations.

Cultural diversity in message context leads to differences in people's attitudes toward the function of verbal messages, and these differences in attitude can affect how communication is perceived. In low-context cultures, the primary function of language is to express thoughts, feelings, and ideas as clearly and logically as possible. Low-context cultures want to identify messages with specific speakers, so the speakers may be recognized for their ability to influence others. In high-context cultures, messages function to enhance social equality and to downplay the importance of individual speakers.

Language usage follows culturally determined patterns. These patterns not only influence the order in which people use words to form phrases; they also influence thinking patterns. The use of language to describe time, for instance, differs from culture. Western societies perceive time as something that can be kept, saved, lost, or wasted. Being on time is extremely important. In other societies, time takes on different values that are reflected in language. In the Vietnamese language, the verb system is such that only context can indicate time. The Sioux Indian language contains no words to represent the concepts of late or waiting. Some adherents of Zen Buddhism perceive time as an infinite pool in which acts cause waves or ripples that eventually subside. Time is a place with no past, no present, no future.

Language reflects the patterns of reasoning prevalent in a culture. The inductive and deductive reasoning patterns of the Western world, for instance, are very different from those of the Arabic world. The Arabic language tends to combine ideas through the use of conjunctions. The result is a lack of efficiency when speakers of Arabic use the English language because it is very difficult for English language speakers to locate the main idea in an Arab's message. Western forms of linear thinking thus cause difficulty for Arabic speakers using the English language. And conversely, those same patterns cause difficulty for someone who uses the thought patterns associated with the English language if that person is conversing in Arabic.

Nations tend to have their own national languages. Arensberg and Niehoff spell out the role of spoken language in distinguishing a culture:

Nothing more clearly distinguishes one culture from another than its language. We sometimes confuse writing systems with the spoken language of the people, otherwise we could say that the infallible sign of a separate culture is a separate language and the inevitable result of a separate language is a separate culture. For example, England, the United states, and Ireland all use English today as a literary written language, but they speak British, American, and the brogue (when not Gaelic). They are, in fact, three separate, though related, cultures. It is the spoken, not the written language that is basic.

That countries tend to have unique national languages is only partly true, however. For instance, both French and English are national languages in Quebec, Canada. English, French, and Spanish are national languages in over twenty countries. And more than a dozen countries share Arabic as a national language.

Because more than one nation uses a particular language, there will be some obvious cultural carryover between those countries; but in most cases the extension of a language has resulted from imperial conquest and the forcing of the language on the territory as its official language. Sharing the same official language, however, is no guarantee that nations share the same culture. In most instances where conquest has established English as the official language, most of the people in the country do not speak it. Such is the case in India and other former British colonies.

Besides in national languages, countries also differ in the language used within their boundaries. Although there are something like one hundred recognized official languages, at least three thousand languages are currently spoken in the world. In Zaire, for instance, there are over one hundred spoken tribal languages. Each tribal group's language not only identifies it but also separates it from other groups. India has several hundred spoken languages, with many of the same inherent problems.

Languages differ not only in the word symbols they use, the rules that govern them, and their phonemic structure, but also in how language serves adaptive functions. The Thai language contains many adaptations necessary for addressing members of the different levels in the hierarchical social system of Thailand. The Thai written language consists of forty-four consonants and thirty-two vowels. The sounds are combined with five different tones to produce a melodious language. Different classes use different pronouns, nouns, and verbs to represent rank and intimacy. There are at least forty-seven pronouns, including seventeen "I's" and nineteen "You's." Because it contains different forms for different classes, it is possible to distinguish four Thai languages: the royal one, the ecclesiastic one, the polite everyday type, and a slang.

The tonal dimension of the Thai language is typical of Asian languages. It produces a great deal of difficulty for someone who is not used to the tonal differences because the same sound pronounced with different intonations has distinctly different meanings. An American official visiting Vietnam discovered this while speaking to a Vietnamese audience. To show his respect to the Vietnamese, he wanted to say something in their language. He intended to make a patriotic declaration—"Vietnam for a thousand years!" But his tonal pronunciation was wrong, and the audience began to laugh when what the official actually said meant "The duck wants to lie down." A similar problem occurred when the Coca Cola Company introduced Coca Cola in China. The Chinese character selected to refer to Coca Cola translated into something akin to "Eat the wax tadpole."

Spanish is becoming by far the most widely spoken of the modern Romance languages. As a commercial and diplomatic language, it is quickly taking over the position long enjoyed by French. One important cultural group that speaks mostly Spanish is the eighty-five million Mexicans. Mexicans want to maintain the purity of their language, because they believe that Spanish without a mixture of English is a means of expressing their feelings of solidarity as well as their culture. The following examples show how the Spanish language expresses these feelings.

First of all, Mexicans cherish the art of conversation. They delight in verbal play, making wide use of double entendres, turns of phrases, and old quotations expressed at the right moment in an otherwise ordinary conversation. If there are opportunities to engage in talk, the Mexican is ready. Even among casual acquaintances, the Mexican seems anxious to lower his or her defenses and share in conversation. Once an emotional bond is established, he or she is open and generous willing to confide and be very hospitable.

The Spanish language tells us a great deal about the Mexican notion of the future through the structure of the future tense. To say "I will go to the store," a Mexican might say, "*Ire al la tienda.*" To the speaker of English, however, this means "I *may* go to the store." Spanish statements made about the future reveal its uncertainty by inferring probability.

The Spanish language reveals the strong male dominance of Mexican culture. The Spanish language is replete with gendered nouns and pronouns. A group of men, for instance, would be referred to as *ellos*, and a group of women as *ellas*, the *o* ending being masculine and the *a* ending being feminine. But if a group contains several men and one woman, the group is *ellos*—masculine gender. On the other hand, if a group contains several women and one man, the group is still *ellos*. A group of girls is called *niñas*, but a group of girls with a single boy is called *niños*.

The Spanish language also expresses formality. There are separate verb conjugations for formal and informal speech. Because Mexicans value formality, they use almost another language to carry on formal conversations. The pronouns meaning "you" differ between the formal and the informal or familiar forms of speech. In formal speech the pronoun *usted* is used, while in familiar speech the pronoun *tu* is appropriate.

Oriental languages provide another perspective on the relationship between language and culture. Asians use language cautiously, as they show in their high-context fondness for moderate or suppressed expression of negative and confrontational messages. They tend to be concerned more with the overall emotional quality of the interaction than with the meaning of particular words or sentences. Courtesy takes precedence over truth, and this is consistent with the cultural emphasis on the maintenance of social harmony as the primary function of speech. For certain Asian languages such as Chinese, Japanese, and Korean, the language structures themselves promote ambiguity. In the Japanese language, verbs come at the end of sentences, preventing one from understanding what is being said until the whole sentence has been uttered.

The Japanese language has borrowed from several other cultures. However, even though its writing system is derived from Chinese, grammatically Japanese is very unlike Chinese. It does share much with Korean, including an ancient use of vowel harmony. The Japanese language makes no sharp distinction between singular and plural. It does not distinguish masculine, neuter, and feminine nouns, and it has no articles.

The Japanese use language to communicate who belongs where and to support a carefully established hierarchy. This is perhaps the most significant difference between Japanese and Western communication. In Japan, the very structure of the language requires the speaker to focus primarily on human relationships, whereas Western languages focus on objects or referents and their logical relationships.

Not only do words that men and women use differ in Japanese, but a number of words take different forms for different situations and relationships between the speaker and the listener—or the person being talked about. There are many words for "you": *omae*, *kimi*, *ariata*, *kisama*, and *kisama*, and *anata-sama*. Certain words are used only between a husband and wife to express their delicate conjugal relationship. For example, a man uses the word *omae* (you) in two cases: when calling rudely to another man and when addressing his wife. Thus, *omae*, when the "You" is female, can be used only by a husband addressing his own wife. Only one man in the world, therefore, can call a woman *omae*—her husband.

Arabic gives us yet another perspective on the relationship between culture and language. First, the Arabic language helps to bond the Arab countries together linguistically. Anyone who speaks Arabic as a native is considered an Arab regardless of national origin.

Arabs attribute an exceptionally high value to rhetorical artistry, and this strongly influences communication patterns. Arabic is a language that can exercise an irresistible influence over the minds of its users. The language itself can be persuasive to the point that actual words sues to describe events are often more significant than the events themselves. Common rhetorical patterns include exaggeration, overassertion, and repetition. Sometimes words are used more for their own sake than for what they are understood to mean, and it is often difficult to obtain direct answers to questions. Someone may offer an answer such as *inshalla*, which means "God willing," because of the belief that God plays an integral role in all actions. No matter how badly someone wants something to happen, it will occur only if God wills it.

Although virtually every Saudi Arabian speaks Arabic, those who engage in international activities are usually fluent in English as well. As most intercultural communication between Saudis and Westerners is likely to utilize English, it is necessary to know about the transference of Arabic communication patterns into the English language. Arabs using English frequently transfer three facets of Arabic to their use of English: intonation patterns, a tendency toward overassertion and exaggeration, and the use of Arabic organizational logic. Native Arabic speakers tend to transfer certain preferred patterns of intonation when speaking English that may make it difficult for the English speaker to comprehend what the speaker is saying. This may be manifest by intonation and stress patterns transferring unwanted affective meanings because they sound aggressive or threatening to an English listener. The transfer of the flat Arabic intonation pattern to English declarative sentences can result in a monotonous voice pattern that native English speakers often feel demonstrates a lack of interest.

In social discourse, Arabs typically use an exaggerated speaking style. Where a North American can adequately express an idea in ten words, the Arabic speaker will typically use one hundred words. Boasting about the superiority of one's abilities, experiences, or friends is expected. Arabs ordinarily do not publicly admit to deficiencies in themselves. They will, however, spend hours elaborating upon the faults and failures of others who are not members of their clique.

The Greek language tends to express much of Greek culture in a variety of key sayings. In a sense these sayings are proverbs because they have the Greek morality attached to them and serve as a sort of generic form of expression that summarizes much meaning in a short phrase. For example, Greeks look harshly upon a lack of gratitude. A Greek who feels slighted might respond, "I taught him how to swim and he tried to drown me." When a Greek is at fault and has no excuse, he or she is liable to say, "I want to become a saint, but the demons won't let me." Greek men have a tendency toward arrogance and tend to boast often. If one succeeds in putting a halt to the bragging of another, he will say, "I cut out his cough." Greeks have a somewhat cavalier attitude toward the truth. This is expressed in proverbial sayings such as "Lies are the salt of life" and "Only from fools and children will you learn the truth."

Even the English language, with which we are most familiar, differs as we move among various cultures in which English predominates. In Great Britain, the language is interspersed with euphemisms that enable the speaker to avoid expressing strong feelings. For instance, when English persons wish to disagree with someone, they are liable to preface their comments with phrases such as "I may be wrong, but ... " or "There is just one thing in all that you have been saying that worries me a little... " Another example of this subtle form of speech is the frequent use of an expression of gratitude to preface a request, as in "I'd be awfully grateful if... " or "Thank you very much indeed... " This concern also appears in the difference between American and British word choice. Compare the following signs seen in the United States and in England. U.S. : No dogs allowed. Britain: We regret that in the interest of hygiene dogs are not allowed on these premises. U.S. : Video Controlled. Britain: Notice: In the interest of our regular customers these premises are now equipped with central security: closed circuit television. Or, U.S. : Pease Keep Hands Off Door. Britain: Obstructing the door causes delay and can be dangerous.

Differences between British and American language also appear in word meanings. Although some words are spelled and pronounced the same, they have different meanings. For instance, the words *boot*, *bonnet*, *lift*, and *biscuit* in British English translate properly into American English as car trunk, car hood, elevator, and cookie.

The relationship between language and culture by now should have begun to emerge. Both language acquisition and language meaning are directly related to our experience. These experiences are unique to each of us not only because of the differences we encountered as individuals while we were growing up and learning to use our language, but also because of what our culture has exposed us to. In short, each of us learns and language as we do because of both our individual and cultural backgrounds.

The Nature and Use of Argot
We indicated earlier, when discussing the Sapir-Whorf hypothesis, that language is a guide to dealing with and understanding social reality. From this notion comes the idea that cultures evolve different languages because their social realities are different, and their unique languages are best suited to describing and dealing with their specific social realities. This process works at all levels of culture but is most prevalent among nondominant co-cultures.

Co-cultures are groups of people that exist within a society but outside of the dominant culture. Their social realities, and values are generally quite different from those of the dominant culture. The process of language evolution in co-cultures, therefore, tends to mirror points or view and lifestyles quite different from those of the dominant culture; so we can examine co-cultures in terms of their language, values, and behavior. This method of analysis recognizes that experience and language work in combination.

A co-culture's use of language, the words its members select, and the meanings of those words offer us insight into the experiences of that co-culture. Because culture helps determine and shape our surroundings, it plays a crucial role in our deciding which experiences we learn to name. In many co-cultures, the name given to the experience clearly demonstrates how co-cultures perceive and interact with the dominant culture.

When we examine co-cultures, we find that their language frequently takes on added significance, a significance that lies in the need of co-cultures to have a language that permits them to share membership and to participate in their social and cultural communities. They need a means to identify themselves and their place in the universe, as well as to permit them to communicate with one another about their unique social realities. They do this by sharing modes and styles of verbal behavior. This form of language is known as argot, and we shall examine some of the forms of argot that various co-cultures use in the United States.

Argot is a more or less secret vocabulary peculiar to a particular group. In many respects, if a group cannot demonstrate an argot, it cannot be considered a co-culture. One major difference between an argot and a foreign language lies in the relationship between sounds and meanings. In a foreign language, the sounds are different but the referents are the same. In English the sound of the thing we sit at to eat dinner is *table*. In Spanish, it is *mesa*. In other words, the sounds are different, but the thing is the same. In argot, the sounds remain the same but the meanings change. Simple words may have multiple meanings unique to the social reality of the group. The word *pot*, for instance, may refer to the pot you smoke, to the pot that hangs over your belt, or to the pot in which you cook your dinner. The sound remains the same, but the meaning differs significantly. A second major difference between argot and dominant languages is the cultural reference. One can assume specific cultural identifications when referring to dominant languages such as English, Spanish, French, German, Chinese, Japanese, and Arabic. Here, the name of the language suggests the accompanying culture. But when we examine argot, we find that it does not refer to a specific dominant culture but to co-cultures such as black Americans, gays, prostitutes, prisoners, the hard-core poor, gangs, the drug-using community, and women.

Co-cultures in the United States that use argot are those that, by the norms of the eurocentric, monogamous, heterosexual, middle-to-upper-class dominant culture, exhibit some form of deviant behavior. This "deviant behavior" takes a variety of forms. Prisoners, for example, who have become deviants by breaking the law, have an argot. Hobos and vagabonds, not criminals by most standards, are also removed from the dominant culture, and hence they too have an argot. The important point is that argot is a language form limited to a particular co-culture whose members are outside the dominant culture. Oneway to gain insight into any co-culture, therefore, is to examine its use of language. "Argots are more than specialized forms of language, they reflect a way of life... They are keys to attitudes, to evaluation of man and society, to modes of thinking, to social organization and to technology."

Argot, then, is but one way in which language and behavior are linked together. And "because vocabulary is a part of language that is most immediately under the conscious manipulation and control of its users, it provides the most accessible place to begin exploration of shared and disparate experiences."

Functions of Argot

Argot serves several functions for the nondominant co-culture. First, argot assists countercultures in developing a means of self-defense by providing a code system that helps them survive in a hostile environment. Because many co-cultures function in a hostile environment, members of the co-culture use argot for communicating with each other in a manner that is difficult for outsiders to understand. The European Jews' use of Yiddish during harsh periods of discrimination is an obvious example of argot as a means of defense.

There are, however, even more subtle and contemporary instances. Prostitutes, because they are engaged in an illegal profession, also must use language for concealment. They must not only conceal the sexual acts themselves, but they must camouflage discussion of the acts to avoid arrest. Argot serves this purpose. The following might be a typical conversation between a prostitute and a pimp. "I have a steak if you're interested. I tried for some lobster but couldn't get it." Translated: *Steak* means a client who will pay fifty dollars to be with the prostitute. A seventy-five dollar client is often called *roast beef*, someone willing to pay one hundred and fifty dollars is a *lobster*, and a three-hundred-dollar client is labeled *champagne*.

In a similar manner, black Americans have evolved a distinctive language frequently referred to as Ebonics. This language contains a variety of terms denoting different ways of talking that depend on the context. Each way of talking is characterized by its own style and function. Through the study of Ebonics, we can gain insight into the black perspective and condition and develop an understanding of the values and attitudes that drive verbal behavior within the black community.

Rapping is an extremely fluent way of speaking. It is always lively and possesses a unique personal style, frequently taking the form of a narrative or story to describe some event in a particularly colorful manner. Rapping also may be used as a device to obtain something one desires or to create a favorable impression.

Rapping is not an interactive style of communication but rather a very functional activity. One does not rap with someone but *to* someone. Rapping may serve either an expressive or directive function. In the expressive form, a speaker attempts to project his or her personality onto the current social setting. In the directive form, the rap becomes persuasive and attempts to manipulate and control others. Rapping may be used to start a relationship by being impressive. It then may become persuasive if the initial impression-creating attempt is successful. A male, for instance, needs to throw an impressive rap when asking a woman for sex. His initial speaking seeks to demonstrate his verbal virtuosity and, if the woman appreciates this, he will transfer from expressive behavior to a directive behavior that becomes an appeal for sex.

Shucking and jiving both denote language behavior that blacks exhibit when confronted by the white establishment or authority figures. This language behavior evolved from the blacks' long history of mistreatment by the dominant white culture. Its roots are in fear, a respect for power, and a will to survive. Shucking has become an effective way for many blacks to stay out of trouble, to avoid arrest, or to get out of trouble when apprehended. Shucking and jiving work on the mind and emotions of the authority figure to get him or her to feel a certain way or to give up something that will be to the speaker's advantage. They include talk and gestures that are appropriate for putting someone on by creating a false impression.

Here is an example of shucking. A black gang member was coming downstairs from a club room with seven guns on him, when he encountered policemen who were going upstairs. If they stopped and searched him, they would arrest him. To avoid this, the black said something like, "Man, I gotta get away from up there. There's gonna be some trouble and I don't want no part of it." This shuck worked because it anticipated the policemen's questions about why the gang member was leaving the club and why he was in hurry. The shuck also gave the police a reason to get to the upstairs room fast.

Much of the colorfulness of the black language comes from the way in which blacks use words to describe their environment. Although the words usually come from the standard English language, their meanings are changed—sometimes even reversed—to reflect the perceptions and needs of the black community. A number of words and their meanings from the Ebonics vocabulary will demonstrate this. *Bad* takes on the opposite meaning and means the very best. *Candy* man refers to a drug pusher. *Charlie* is a term that refers to the white man. *Chickenhead* refers to a female with short-cropped hair; it also may refer to any unkempt or unattractive female. *Don't have papers on me* means that youdo not own me or that you are not married to me. *Feel draft* expresses a black's sense of racism in a white person. *Get down* means to engage in particular activity with enthusiasm. It especially refers to having a fight, having sex, dancing, or taking drugs. The word *haircut* takes on a unique meaning in that it refers to having been robbed or cheated. *High yella* denotes a particularly light-skinned African American, especially a female. *Hors d' oeuvres* doesnot refer to snacks with drinks but to capsules of the drug. *Lame* means socially inexperienced or unaware of what is happening. *Nairobi queen* refers to a particularly attractive dark-skinned female. The word *peckerwood* is used to indicate a white person. A Tom is any black person who attempts to emulate or to please the white man. Tom also refers both to someone who has sold out to whitey and to a black informer. *Woof* means to joke around or to put someone down playfully.

Argot also serves as a cultural storehouse for the hostility the users feel toward the dominant culture. It permits the expression of frustration and hatred without risk of reprisal from the dominant culture, as well as maintaining the identity and group solidarity of a co-culture or countercultures. A co-culture's use of a specialized linguistic code satisfies a number of significant and real needs.

A third major function of argot is to assert a co-culture's solidarity and cohesiveness through a uniform learned language code. Because a degree of secrecy is associated with the use of argot, a sense of identity and pride are associated with the realization that one is part of a group that developed its own private language; a bond forms among those members who understand the code. Homosexuals who know *AC-DC* (bisexual), *Bill* (a masculine homosexual), *Black Widow* (a person who takes love mates away from other gays), and *chicken* (a young male gay) are privy to an argot that is unique to a particular subculture.

The tramp and hobo are also set apart from the main culture, yet they can feel a type of in-group solidarity because they have learned that a *yap* is a newcomer, a *tool* is a pickpocket, a *paper* is a railroad ticket, to be *oiled* is to be intoxicated, and to *lace* is to punch.

Gangs have become prominent as co-cultures in the past several years because of the violence associated with their drug-dealing businesses. Like other co-cultures, gangs have a rich argot, as some examples will demonstrate. *Buster* refers to a gang member who does not stand up for his gang, who sells out his brothers. A *claim* is the area that gang members have stakes out as their turf. If persons are asked what they claim, they are being asked which gang they belong to or are associated with. A *claimer* is a person who pretends or wants to be a member of a gang but has not been accepted by the gang. *Crippin'* is a word that members of the Crip gang use and means survive an way you can. *Drive-bys* is a short term for drive-by shootings, which are surprise attacks from passenger cars. Gangs frequently use drive-by shootings to frighten rival gang members or to exact revenge from them. *Flashing signs* refers to using hand signals to communicate with other gang members. *Gang bangin'* means participating in any kind of gang activity ranging from hanging out, to dealing drugs, to being involved in drive-by shootings. A *homegirl* is a young woman who hangs out with gang members. *Jump in* is the initiation process whereby a claimer fights members of the gang to which he desires to belong. *Pancake* designates a person who has become a homosexual as a result of his experience in jail. And *strawberry* refers to a female who exchanges sexual favors for drugs.

A fourth function of argot is to help establish groups as real and viable social entities. During the 1960s, for example, when people began taking drugs as a way of life, they gathered at specific locations and immediately developed what became known as the "San Francisco drug language." As these individuals became more than a group of people simply taking drugs, they evolved a rather elaborate glossary of terms—terms that helped transform them from a collection of people into a subgroup. Some of their terms were *Bernice* for cocaine, *hay* for marijuana, *heat* for police, *pipe* for a large vein, *roach* for the butt of a marijuana cigarette, *octagon* for a square person, *lightning* for achieving a high, and *head* for a heavy drug user.

Women are another segment of our culture that uses language differently. Their language usage does not truly constitute an argot, but we include them here because of the need to understand how culture affects women in our society. Like any other group, women are susceptible to the conditioning applied by their culture. Because of their coexistence with the dominant male culture, they have learned linguistic ways of adapting to their cultural roles.

Women frequently use linguistic devices to avoid having to take a strong stand or to keep from being too direct or forceful. They may make an assertion that expresses their position, but then temper it with a tag line. "That was a good movie—*wasn't it?*" "This is a good dinner—*isn't it?*" To avoid directness or forcefulness, women also use more qualifiers than men do when speaking. Such phrases as "*Maybe* we should go … ," "*Perhaps* you are driving too fast … ," "I *guess* we can visit your mom first … ," and "I *sort of* don't want to do this" indicate this use of qualifiers.

In mixed conversation women talk less frequently than men, and they get the floor less often. When they do get the floor, they hold it for shorter amounts of time. Women interrupt less than men, and they have less control over the flow of the conversation. They tend to use language that is more precise than men's by including more adverbs, adjectives, and intensifiers. And finally, women use less profanity than men do.

Women have a tendency to ask more questions to keep a conversation going than men do. Again, this is part of their learned behavior and expected role. Questions such as "What did you do yesterday?" or "How was your drive over?" typify their use of language to keep a conversation going.

When examining the argot of various co-cultures, it is important to keep two things in mind. First, you will quickly discover that there is a great deal of overlap. This does not negate the notion that argot is a community's unique language. Instead it tells us that an individual may be a member of several co-cultures simultaneously. For instance, a person may be a hard-core poor, black, drug-using, gay prostitute who is in prison. This particular person then shares membership in the black, hard-core poor, gay, prostitute, drug-using, and prison co-cultures. Another person might be a convicted white, drug-using armed robber serving a prison term. This person is a member of the drug-using and prison co-cultures.

Second, we must remember that argots change. As the dominant culture becomes familiar with the specialized code being used, the co-culture will usually eliminate the word or phrase from its private glossary. Hence, many of the examples we cited in the last few pages may no longer be in use in the co-culture we are discussing. This need to alter words does not diminish the importance in studying argot. It is not a single word that is significant, but rather the idea that the words and phrases selected offer us valuable insight into the experiences of these groups, experiences to which may of us might not have access.

Foreign Languages and Translation
The translation of one language into another is far more complex than most people realize. Most people assume that text in one language can be accurately translated into another language, so long as the translator uses a good bilingual dictionary. Unfortunately, languages are not this simple, and direct translations in many cases are difficult if not impossible because (1) words have more than one meaning, (2) many words are culture-bound and have no direct translations, (3) cultural orientations can render a direct translation into nonsense, and (4) a culture may not have the experiential background to permit translation of experiences from other cultures. For instance, how does one translate Atlantic Ocean into the Hopi language?

A major problem in translation is that although messages may provide adequate interpretation of original text, there usually is no full equivalence through translation. Even what may appear to be synonymous messages may not be equivalent. There are several problems in the search for equivalence, including vocabulary, idiomatic, grammatical-syntactical, experiential-cultural, and conceptual equivalence. A brief glimpse of each should demonstrate some of the major difficulties in securing an adequate translation.

Vocabulary or lexical equivalence. Dictionary translations rarely reflect the language of the people. One of the goals of translation, of course, is to convey the meaning and style of the original. Problems can arise with the use of highly trained translators because their language style may not be representative of the original style. Translators also need to deal with the nuances of words and with words that have no equivalence in another language. For instance, there are really no good equivalent Tagalog language terms for *feminine* and *domestic*. On the other hand, the Tagalog words *hiya*, which relates to shyness, embarrassment, shame, and deference, and *pakikisama*, which relates to getting along with others and conformity, are difficult to translate into English.

Idiomatic equivalence. Idiomatic expressions are culture-bound; they do not translate well. Consider this example of an Italian idiom translated literally into English: "Giovanni sta menando il cane per l' aia. " Translated, this becomes "John is leading his dog around the threshing floor. " A better translation, with greater correspondence of meaning, would have been "John is beating around the bush. "

Grammatical-syntactical equivalence. Sometimes difficulties arise because there are no equivalent parts of speech in the language into which a message is being translated. For example, the Urdu language has no gerunds, and it is difficult to find an equivalent form for an English gerund.

Experiential-cultural equivalence. Translators must grapple not only with structural differences between languages but with cultural differences as well. The problem of transferring between cultures requires that the translator walk a fine line between the need for precision and the need for keeping the original author's approach or attitude. More importantly, the translator needs to consider shared experiences. *Peace* has various meanings for peoples of the world according to their conditions, time, and place; so does *war*. The meanings that we have for words are based on shared experiences. The ability of a word to convey or elicit meaning depends on culturally-informed perceptions by both source and receiver as message processors. When we lack cultural equivalents, we lack the words in our vocabulary to represent those experiences. For instance, when the vocabulary of a tribe in a mountainous jungle region has word for rivers and streams but not for oceans, how do you translate the notion of an ocean? Or what does a translator do when he or she is faced with the task of translating the Bible verse "Though you sins be as scarlet, they shall be as white as snow" into the language of a tribe that has never seen snow?

Conceptual equivalence. Another difficulty in translation lies in obtaining a concept match. Some concepts are culture-specific (**emic**) or culture-general (**etic**). By definition, it is impossible to translate perfectly an emic concept. So different, for instance, are the cultural experiences that many words cannot be translated directly from Spanish into English. Strong affection is expressed in English with the verb *to love*. In Spanish, there are two verbs, *te amo* and *te quiero*. *Te amo* refers to nurturant love, as between a parent and a child or between two adults. *Te quiero* translates literally into English as "I want you," which connotes an ownership aspect not present in the English expression *I love you*. Commonly used to express love between two adults, *te quiero* falls somewhere between the English statements *I love you* and *I like you*. Neither *te amo* nor *te quiero* has an exact English equivalent.

The Mexican Spanish language also has at least five terms indicating agreement in varying degree: *me compromento* (I promise or commit myself), *yo le asequro* (I assure you), *si, como no, lo haga* (maybe I might do it), *tal vez lo hago* (maybe I will do it), and *tal vez lo haga* (maybe I might do it). This agreement concept ranges from a durable agreement that everyone recognizes to agreement being unlikely. The problem, of course, is to understand the differences between *me compromeno* and *tal vez lo haga* in their cultural sense so that one can render a correct version in another language. If, for instance, we were rendering English translations of these Mexican Spanish terms, we could expect all sorts of misunderstandings and confusions to arise if we simply translated each of these phrases of agreement as "OK." About the only way in which an emic concept can be translated is to attempt to relate it to etic concepts by trying to tie it into the context in which the concept might be used.

Language translation is difficult, and it is easy to make mistakes. One of the better illustrations of a mistake is that of a missionary preaching in the West African Bantu language who instead of saying "The children of Israel crossed the Red Sea and followed Moses," mistakenly said "The children of Israel crossed the red mosquitoes and swallowed Moses." When translation is inept it can also have extreme consequences. Near the end of World War II, after Italy and Germany had surrendered, the Allies sent Japan an ultimatum to surrender. Japan's premier announced that his government would *mokusatsu* the surrender ultimatum. *Mokusatsu* was an unfortunate would-choice because it could mean both "to consider" and "to take notice." The premier, speaking in Japanese, apparently meant that the government would consider the surrender ultimatum. But the English-language translators in Japan's overseas broadcasting agency used the "to take notice" meaning of mokusatsu. Consequently, the would choice was heard that Japan had rejected the surrender ultimatum rather than that Japan was considering the ultimatum. The possible mistranslation led the United States to assume Japan was unwilling to surrender, and the atomic bombing of Hiroshima and Nagasaki followed. We realize that there has been much speculation on the reasons for the United States' use of the atomic bomb in the years since World War II, but it is quite possible that if the translators had selected the other meaning, the atomic bomb might not have been used in World War II. This example vividly illustrates the difficulties that can be found in foreign language translation and demonstrates the serious consequences that can follow inept translation of words with multiple meaning.

Language translations frequently produce misunderstanding or incomprehension because of cultural orientations reflected in the language. For instance, the Quechua language of Peru[2] uses orientations to past and future that are the opposite of those in the English language. Quechua visualizes the past as being in front of or ahead of one because it can be seen. It visualizes the future as being behind one because it cannot be seen. This is just the opposite of Americans, who speak of the past being behind them and the future being ahead of them. If this aspect of cultural orientation were not known or if it were ignored, it could lead to incomprehensible translations about time, the past, and the future. It might even imply that people must look behind them if they are to be able to see what normally lies ahead or them.

A good interpreter needs special, highly developed skills. He or she must be able to translate a message so that others understand it as though it had not been translated. This means that the interpreter must be skilled in understanding not only the words of the language being translated but the emotional aspects, thought processes, and communicative techniques of that culture as well.

The effective use of an interpreter requires the establishment of a three-way rapport. Rapport must exist between the speaker and the interpreter, between the speaker and the audience, and between the interpreter and the audience. This is an extremely difficult state to attain because of the complexity of translation in real time. Consider what an interpreter must be doing simultaneously. When the speaker says a phrase, the interpreter must listen to that phrase. While the speaker says the next phrase, the interpreter must not only be translating the first phrase, but must also be listening to the second phrase. Then while the speaker is saying the third phrase, the interpreter must remember the first phrase, be interpreting the second phrase, and listening to the third. This procedure goes on and on throughout the process of message delivery; and it requires that the interpreter be able to remember not only what the speaker has just said, but what he or she may have said several minutes ago, because the interpretation of the latest words spoken may reflect a reference to what the speaker said several minutes earlier.

In selecting an interpreter, there are several qualities or qualifications you should seek. First is compatibility. You need someone with whom you are comfortable. This means a translator that is neither domineering nor timid. Second is ethnic compatibility. You need a translator who is of the same tribe, religious group, or ethnic background as the people for whom he or she will be translating. Third, your translator should speak the same dialect as the people for whom he or she will be translating. And finally, the translator should have specialized experience in your field and its terminology.

Learning to help an interpreter can make speaking through an interpreter a much easier experience. You can do several things to make your interpreter's task easier. Before the meeting you should brief him or her on the tone, substance, and purpose of the presentation. You should review any technical terms that will be used. Ask the interpreter to brief you on any cultural differences in eye contact or other nonverbal behaviors that may be important in your presentation. Ask about local customs pertinent to your presentation, such as appropriate time of day for the presentation and how the audience regards time. Ask about unwritten rules of conversation. During the presentation, speak slowly enough for the interpreter to understand and to follow you. Speak in relatively short sentences and pause often, and look at the audience while you speak, not at the interpreter. Prepare yourself to give greetings and farewells in the foreign language. Do not use profanity, obscenities, slang, regional dialect, acronyms, high-tech shoptalk, or colloquialisms. At the end of your presentation, recap the major points and clear up any ambiguities.

Notes

1. Adapted and abridged from *Communication Between Cultures*, Belmont, CA: Wordsworth, Inc., 1991.
2. To know more about the official language of Tawantinsuyu, the Inca Empire, you may log on http://www.ullanta.com/quechua.

Questions for Discussion

1. "The limit of your language is the limit of your world." Comment on the statement with empirical evidence.
2. Does it make sense that people possess meanings and that words elicit the meanings in people?
3. Explain the culturally-bound difficulties that Chinese readers of English often

come across when they read English argumentative writings.
4. Why can't we achieve semantic equivalence in translation?
5. Read "La Dernière Classe" by Daudet and share each other's viewpoints on his remarks: *"To be fairly, the truth is — the most beautiful language is your mother tongue"*. And how do we love and protect our mother tongue?

Online Mini-Case Studies and Viewpoints-Sharing

Geronimo and its Controvercial Sense Across Cultures

On May 2, 2011, Osamna bin Laden was killed by U.S. military forces at his residence in Pakistan. In the course of the military action, the U.S. Defense Department chose the name "Geronimo" as the code word for Osama bin Laden or the operation itself. The use of Geronimo in this context created a controversy that highlights the ways the use of history can create conflict between cultural groups. Many Native Americans took great offense at the use of Geronimo's name. It's very important to think about how we use history for present needs, as heroes in one culture might be villains in another (and vice versa). Harlyn Geronimo, a great-grandson of Geronimo submitted a statement to the U.S. Senate Commission on Indian Affairs expressing his anger and confusion.

Online Research

Search the whole story online and elaborate on the complexity of meaning association across cultures.

Unit Three

Cultural Identity and Intercultural Communication

Reading One

Introductory Remarks

Americans tend to believe that dominant managerial values embrace much of what has been cherished in the USA, values such as achievement and success, hard work, pragmatism, optimism, Puritanism, rationality, competition, and individualism. This set of values, however, is not accorded equal importance in countries characteristic of collectivistic cultures and, therefore, does not bear universally shared features.

This selection probes the causalities of differences of management in individualistic cultures and in collectivistic cultures the Democratic of. The former emphasizes what you have achieved, as generally called "doing culture" while the latter places more importance on who you are, thus being labeled as "being culture." The different orientations—achievement vs. ascription—become largely the roots of internal consumption in multicultural companies and affect the managerial efficiency if not coped with properly. Against this, the author presents new dimensions (universalism vs. particularism, neutral vs. affective, individualism vs. communitarianism, achievement vs. ascription) and concludes with effective reconciliation strategies for successful management.

Intercultural Dilemma in Multicultural Setting: Doing vs. Being[1]

Fonds Trompenaars and Charles Hampern-Turner

All societies give certain groups of their members higher status than others, signaling that unusual attention should be focused upon such persons and their activities. While some societies accord status to people on the basis of their achievements, others ascribe it to them by virtue of age, class, gender, education, and so on. The first kind of status is called achieved status and the second ascribed status. While achieved status refers to doing, ascribed status refers to being.

When we look at other people we are partly influenced by their track record (top Eastern Division salesman for five consecutive years). We may also be influenced by their:

- age (a more experienced salesperson);
- gender (very masculine and aggressive);
- social connections (friends in the highest places);
- education (top scholar at the Ecole Polytechnique);
- profession (electronics is the future).

While there are ascriptions that are not logically connected with business effectiveness, such as masculine gender, white skin or noble birth, there are some ascriptions which do make good sense in predicting business performance: age and experience, education and professional qualifications. Education and professional qualifications, moreover, are related to an individual's earlier schooling and training and are therefore not unconnected with achievement. A culture may ascribe higher status to its better-educated employees in the belief that scholarly success will lead to corporate success. This is a generalized expectation and may show up as a "fast-track" or "management-trainee" programme that points a recruit to the top of the organization.

With the issue of status in mind, let us get back to the trials of Mr Johnson, who we may recall is struggling with a walk-out by Italian managers. Mr Gialli and Mr Pauli left the room furiously when their suggested modification to the pay-for-performance plan was called "a crazy idea" by Mr Bergman from the Netherlands. In order to save the situation Johnson has turned to shuttle diplomacy. Like a youthful Henry Kissinger (Johnson is only 35), he finds himself moving between the two parties to settle the dispute. He rapidly begins to feel less like Kissinger and more like Don Quixote[2].

> The Italian managers were far from assuaged. One even referred unpleasantly to "the American cult of youth; more boys who think they know everything." So when the Spanish HR manager, Mr Munoz, offered to mediate, Johnson readily agreed. It occurred to him that Spanish culture might be closer to Italian culture, apart from the fact that Munoz was some 20 years his senior, so could hardly be accused of inexperience.
>
> While hopeful that Munoz might succeed, Johnson was astonished to see him bring the Italians back into the conference room in minutes. Munoz was not, in Johnson's view, the most professional of HR

managers, but he was clearly expert at mending fences. It was at once apparent, however, that Munoz was now backing the Italians' call for modifications to the pay-for-performance plan. The problem as he saw it, and the Italians agreed, was that under the current plan winning salespeople were going to earn more than their bosses. Subordinates, they believed, should not be allowed to undermine their superiors in this way. Mr Munoz explained that back in Spain his sales force would probably simply refuse to embarrass a boss like this; or perhaps one or two, lacking in loyalty to the organization, might, in which case they would humiliate their boss into resignation. Furthermore, since the sales manager was largely responsible for the above-average performance of his team, was it not odd, to say the least, that the company would be rewarding everyone except the leader? The meeting broke for lunch, for which Johnson had little appetite.

As we can see, different societies confer status on individuals in different ways. Mr Munoz carried more clout with the Italians for the same reason that Johnson had less; they respected age and experience much more than the specific achievements that had made Johnson a fast-tracker in the company. Many Anglo-Saxons, including Mr Johnson, believe that ascribing status for reasons other than achievement is quite archaic and inappropriate to business. But is achievement orientation really a necessary feature of economic success?

Status-by-Achievement and Economic Development

Most of the literature on achievement orientation sees it as part of "modernisation", the key to economic and business success. The theory goes that once you start rewarding business achievement, the process is self-perpetuating. People work hard to assure themselves of the esteem of their culture and you get *The Achieving Society*, as David McClelland, the Harvard professor, defined his own culture in the late 1950s. Only nations setting out upon an empirical investigation of "what works best," and conferring status on those who apply it in business, can expect to conduct their economies successfully. This is the essence of Protestantism: the pursuit of justification through works which long ago gave achievers a religious sanction—and capitalism its moving spirit.

According to this view, societies which ascribe status are economically backward, because the reasons they have for conferring status do not facilitate commercial success. Catholic countries ascribing status to more passive ways of life, Hinduism associating practical achievements with delusion and Buddhism teaching detachment from earthly concerns are all forms of ascribed status which are thought to impede economic development. Ascription has been seen as a feature of countries either late to develop, or still underdeveloped. In fact ascribing status has been considered "dangerous for your economic health."

To measure the extent of achieving versus ascribing orientations in different cultures, we used the following statements, inviting participants to mark them on a five-point scale (1 = strongly agree, 5 = strongly disagree).

A The most important thing in life is to think and act in the ways that best suit the way you really are, even if you do not get things done.
B The respect a person gets is highly dependent on their family background.

The statistics shows the countries where only a minority disagree with "getting things done" are broadly speaking ascriptive cultures; very broadly speaking, because there are in fact less than ten societies—English-speaking and Scandinavian countries—where there is a majority in favour of getting things done even at the expense of personal freedom to live as you feel you should. The USA is clearly a culture in which status is mainly achieved, as shown by another research finding. 87% of Americans disagree that status depends mainly on family background. A number of societies which are ascriptive in the first research (the Czech Republic, for example) do in fact show majorities against the proposition that status is largely dependent on family; aspects of ascription vary greatly from country to country.

Both figures show that there is a correlation between Protestantism and achievement orientation, with Catholic, Buddhist and Hindu cultures scoring considerably more ascriptively. There is, incidentally, no correlation between support for achievement or ascription and the age, sex or education of respondents across our database as a whole, although there is for these factors in some societies.

A second glance at the scores shows that there are growing difficulties with the thesis that an achievement orientation is the key to economic success. In the first place, Protestant cultures are no longer growing faster than Catholic or Buddhist ones. Catholic Belgium, for example, has a slightly higher GDP per head than the more Protestant Netherlands. Catholic France and Italy have been growing faster than the UK or parts of Protestant Scandinavia. Japan, the Republic of Korea, Singapore are influenced by Buddhism and Confucianism. It is certainly not evident that Japan's habit of promoting by seniority has weighed its corporations down beneath piles of dead wood. In short, there is no evidence that either orientation belongs to a "higher" level of development, as modernization theorists used to claim.

What appears to be happening is that some very successful business cultures are ascribing status to persons, technologies or industries which they anticipate will be important to their future as an economy, with the result that these persons and sectors receive special encouragement. In other words, ascribing works with achieving by generating social and economic momentum towards visualized goals.

Ascription and Performance

Andrew, a British manager and trained geologist, had been working for a French oil company for 20 years and was still confused by one aspect of his colleagues' behaviour. He found that his fellow French geologists would simply not tolerate outside criticism of their profession. Initially he would get puzzled looks and frowns if he admitted he did not know the answer to some technical question in front of lay persons. Once when he said he would have to "look something up," his French colleagues were overtly annoyed with him. He was confused because in his view geologists are frequently asked questions for which they do not have answers right at hand, or for which there is no answer. But his French fellows would chide him for admitting this publicly. They believed he was letting his profession down.

This experience is supported by research undertaken at INSEAD business school in France by Andre Laurent. He found that French and Italian managers were much more emphatic about "knowing all the answers" than managers from many other cultures.

Notice, though, the effect that ascription has on performance. The French geologists are determined to live up to their ascribed status which, in turn, can lead to higher performance. Hence, it can be a self-fulfilling prophecy: through living up to the status ascribed to them, they "deserve" the status that was given to them before they actually earn it. In practice, then, achieving and ascribing status can be finely interwoven.

The European Union is a very good example of an ascribed self-fulfilling prophecy; its importance and power in the world was proclaimed before it had achieved anything.

The interweaving of ascribing and achieving orientations is a feature of the world's leading economies, Japan and Germany. Both cultures tend to confine achieving as individuals to the school days of their economic sectors. Thereafter, managers are supposed to co-operate. Achievement becomes less a task for individuals jostling each other for advantage than for whole groups, led by those who excelled earlier and individually.

We must bear these distinctions in mind when we examine the data presented earlier. Ascribing and achieving can be exclusive of each other, but are not necessarily so. Your achieving can drive your ascribing, as when you "land winners." Or ascribing can drive achieving, as when key industries are first targeted and then won by "national champions."

The belief that electronic equipment made by Olivetti, Bosch, Siemens or Alcatel is more important to the EC than enhanced expertise in distributing hamburgers or bottling colas is not entirely mistaken. You can ascribe greater importance to supposedly "key" industries on the basis of bad judgment or of good judgment. It is at least arguable than an economy needs to master electronics if it seeks to maintain competitiveness in manufacturing since machines are increasingly monitored, controlled and re-tooled electronically. You have a choice, then, of ascribing status to electronics before the achievements of manufacturing lapse, or afterwards. A culture that insists on waiting for dire results before changing course many handicap itself. Intelligent anticipation requires ascribing importance to certain projects, just as joint ventures, strategic alliances and partnerships require us to value a relationship before it proves successful.

Achievement- and Ascription-oriented Cultures' Negotiations

It can be extremely irritating to managers from achieving cultures when an ascriptive team of negotiators has some *eminence grise* hovering in the background to whom they have to submit any proposals or changes. It is not even clear what this person does. He (usually male) will not say what he wants, but simply expects deference not just from you but from his own team, which is forever watching him for faint signs of assent or dissent. It is, of course, equally upsetting for ascriptive cultures when the "achieving team" wheels on its aggressive young men and women who spout knowledge as if it were a kind of ammunition before which the team opposite is expected to surrender. It is rather like having to play a game with a toddler and a toy gun; there is a lot of noise coming from someone who is of no known authority or status.

Indeed, sending whiz-kids to deal with people 10-20 year their senior often insults the ascriptive culture. The reaction may be: "Do these people think they have reached our own level of experience in half the time? That a 30-year-old American is good enough to negotiate with a 50-year-old Greek or Italian?" Achievement cultures must understand that some ascriptive cultures, the Japanese especially, spend very heavily on training and in-house education to ensure that older people actually are wiser for the years they have spent in the corporation and for the sheer numbers of subordinates briefing them. It insults an ascriptive culture to do anything which prevents the self-fulfilling nature of its beliefs. Older people are held to be important so that they will be nourished and sustained by others' respect. A stranger is expected to facilitate this scheme, not challenge it.

Consider a Japanese-Dutch negotiating session. When Dutch experts in finance, marketing and human resources meet their Japanese opposite numbers, the Dutch approach is to try to clarify facts and determine who holds the decision-making power. To the Dutch, the Japanese will appear evasive and secretive, not revealing anything. For the Japanese, these are not "facts" so much as mutual understandings between their leaders and themselves, which the Dutch seem to be prying into. This may come across as disrespectful. Anyway, it is for the leader of the negotiating team to say what these relationships are if he or she chooses to.

At a conference on a Japanese-Dutch joint venture held in Rotterdam, a Japanese participant fell ill. A member of the Dutch delegation approached Mr Yoshi, another Japanese delegate with fluent English and outstanding technical knowledge, and asked if he would replace the sick man in a particular forum. Mr Yoshi demurred and the Dutchman was annoyed at the lack of a straight response. Several minutes later the leader of the Japanese delegation, Mr Kaminaki, announced that Mr Yoshi would replace the sick man because Mr Kaminaki was appointing him to the task. It was made very clear whose decision that had been.

The Translator's Role

In this and other negotiations it often becomes clear that the translator from an ascriptive culture behaves "unprofessionally" according to the standards of achieving cultures. According to British, German, North American, Scandinavian and Dutch values, the translator is an achiever like any other participant and the height of his or her achievement should be to give an accurate, unbiased account of what was said in one language to those speaking the other language. The translator is supposed to be neutral, a black box serving the interests of modern language comprehension, not the interests of either party who may seek to distort meanings for their own ends.

In other cultures, however, the translator is doing something else. A

Japanese translator, for example, will often take a minute or more to "translate" an English sentence 15 seconds long. And there is often extensive colloquy between the translator and the team he or she serves about what the opposite team just said. The translator on the Japanese side is an interpreter, not simply of language but of gesture, meaning and context. His role is to support his own team and possibly even to protect them from confrontational conduct by the western negotiators. He may protect superiors from rudeness and advise the team how to counter opposition tactics. The "translator" is very much on the ascribing team's side, and if the achievement-oriented team seeks flawless, if literal, translation they should bring their own. This may not actually improve relationships because Asian teams are quite used to speaking among themselves in the belief that foreigners do not understand. If you bring someone fluent in their tongue, they will have to withdraw in order to confer. Your "contribution" to mutual understanding may not be appreciated.

The Role of Titles
The use of and mention of titles with business cards and formal introductions can be complex. Both authors carry three kinds of cards to introduce themselves. In the Middle East and southern Europe formal titles received for formal education are diffused through several different contexts to elevate my status. In Britain, however, presenting myself as "doctor" may suggest a rather too academic bent for a business consultant. It may not be considered relevant for a consultant to have PhD, and if attention is drawn to it, the status claimed is not necessarily legitimate. Achievement in a university may even disqualify a person from likely achievement in a corporation.

We might expect a similar situation in the USA, another achievement-oriented, yet specific society. However, the "inflation" of qualifications in the USA makes it legitimate to draw attention to higher degrees from good universities, provided it is relevant to the task at hand. Typically the speciality is mentioned: MBA, Sociology and so on.

In diffuse cultures it is important to tie in your status with your organization. Indeed your achievement as an individual will be discounted compared with the status your organization ascribes to you. It is therefore important to say not just that you are chief, but what you are chief of: marketing, finance, human resources and so on. Many a deal has been lost because the representative was not seen to have high status back home. Ascriptive cultures must be assured that your organization has great respect for you and that you are at or near the top.

Relationship with Mother Company

In the value system of individualist, achievement-oriented cultures, the specific "word" of the representative pledges the company to any commitment made. The individual has delegated authority to use personal judgment. In ascriptive cultures, the individual, unless head of the organization, almost never has the personal discretion to commit the company without extensive consultations. An individual from an ascriptive culture may not really believe that the achieving representative has this authority either. Hence agreements are tentative and subject to back-home ratification. It is partly for this reason that your title and power "back home" is important to the ascriptive negotiator. How can you deliver your company if you are not high in its status hierarchy? If you send an impetuous, though clever youth, you cannot be very serious. It is important to send senior people if you are visiting an ascriptive culture, even if they are less knowledgeable about the product. It could also be important to ask for senior persons in the ascriptive culture to attend in person and meet their opposite numbers. The closer you get to the top, the more likely it is that promises made in negotiations will be kept.

Signs of Ascriptive Status Are Carefully Ordered

We are now beginning to see why pay-for-performance and bonuses to high achievers whatever their rank can be upsetting to ascriptive cultures. The superior is by definition responsible for increased performance, so that relative status is unaffected by higher group sales. If rewards are to be increased, this must be done proportionately to ascribed status, not given to the person closest to the sale. If the leader does something to reduce his own status, all his subordinates are downgraded as a consequence.

A British general manager upon arrival in Thailand refused to take his predecessor's car. The Thai finance manager asked the new GM what type of Mercedes he would like, then. The GM asked for a Suzuki or a Mini, anything that could be handled easily in the congested traffic in Bangkok.

Three weeks later the GM called the finance manager and asked about prospects for the delivery of his car. The Thai lost his reserve for a moment and exclaimed: "We can get you a new Mercedes by tomorrow, but Suzuki take much, much longer." The GM asked him to see what he could do to speed up the process. After four weeks the GM asked to see the purchase order for the car. The purchasing department replied that, because it would take so long to get a small car, they had decided to order a Mercedes.

The GM's patience had run out. At the first management meeting he brought the issue up and asked for an explanation. Somewhat shyly, the predominantly Thai management team explained they could hardly come to work on bicycles.

In this case the status of each member was interdependent. Had the British GM ordered an even more expensive car all the other managers might have moved up a notch. In ascriptive societies you "are" your status. It is as natural to you as your birth or formal education (rebirth) through which your innate powers were made manifest. Ascribed status simply "is" and requires no rational justification, although such justifications may exist. For example, a preference for males, for greater age or social connections is not usually justified or defended by the culture ascribing importance to older men from "good" families. That does not mean it is irrational or without competitive advantage; however, it simply means that justifications are not offered and not expected. It has always been so, and if this means a major effort to educate staff as they age, that is all the better, but it is not the basis for preferring older people in the first place.

Achievement-oriented organizations justify their hierarchies by claiming that senior persons have "achieved more" for the organization; their authority, justified by skill and knowledge, benefits the organization. Ascription-oriented organizations justify their hierarchies by "power-to-get-things-done." This may consist of power over people and be coercive, or power through people and be participative. There is high variation within ascriptive cultures and participative power has well-known advantages. Whatever form power takes, the ascription of status to person is intended to be exercised as power and that power is supposed to enhance the effectiveness of the organization. The sources of ascribed status may be multiple and trying to alter it by promotion-on-the-grounds-of-achievement can be hazardous.

An achievement-oriented Swedish manager was managing a project in Pakistan. A vacancy needed to be filled and after careful assessment the Swedish manager chose one of his two most promising Pakistani employees for promotion. Both candidates were highly educated, with PhDs in mechanical engineering, and in Pakistan both were known authorities in their field. Although both had excellent performance records, Mr Kahn was selected on the basis of some recent achievements.

Mr Saran, the candidate not chosen, was very upset by the turn of events. He went to his Swedish boss for an explanation. However, even an explanation based on the specific needs of the business did not calm him. How could this loss of face be allowed?

The Swedish manager tried to make the engineer understand that only one of the two could be promoted because there was only one vacancy. One of them was going to be hurt, even though they were both valued employees. He made no progress. The reason, as he eventually learned, was the fact that Mr Saran received his PhD two years before Mr Khan from the same American university. Saran was expected to have more status than his colleague because of this. His family would never understand. What was this western way of treating ascribed status so lightly? Should not more than just the achievements of the past months be considered?

It is important to see how different the logics of achievement and ascription are and not consider either as worthless. In achieving countries the actor is evaluated by how well he or she performed the allocated function. Relationships are functionally specific; I relate to you as, say, a sales manager. The justification of my role lies in the sales records. Another person in that role must be expected to be compared with me and I with that person. Success is universally defined as increased sales. My relationship to manufacturing, R&D, planning and so on is instrumental. I either sell what they have developed, manufactured and planned, or I do not. I am my functional role.

In ascribing cultures, status is attributed to those who "naturally" evoke admiration from others, that is, older people, males, highly qualified persons and/or persons skilled in a technology or project deemed to be of national importance. To show respect for status is to assist the person so distinguished to fulfill the expectations the society has of him or her. The status is generally independent of task of specific function. The individual is particular and not easily compared with others. His or her performance is partly determined by the loyalty and affection shown by subordinates and which they, in turn, display. He or she is the organization in the sense of personifying it and wielding its power.

Achievement-oriented corporations in western countries often send young, promising managers on challenging assignments to faraway countries without realizing that the local culture will not accept their youthfulness and/or gender however well they achieve. A young (aged 34) talented and female marketing manager had worked for an American company in both the USA and Britain. She was so successful in her second year there that she was named the most promising female manager in Britain. This vote of confidence influenced her decision to accept an offer to transfer as director of marketing to her company's operation in Ankara, Turkey. She knew she had always been able to win the support and trust of her subordinates and colleagues.

The first few weeks in Ankara were as usual in a new job, getting to know the local business, the staff and how to get things done. Luckily, she knew one of the marketing managers, Guz Akil, who had been her marketing assistant in London. They had worked very well together.

Working as hard as she could over the first few months, she found her authority gradually slipping away. The most experienced Turk, Hasan (aged 63), informally but consciously took over more and more of her authority, getting things done where her own efforts were frustrated, although his marketing knowledge was only a fraction of her own. She had to watch him exercise influence which most often led to unsatisfactory results. Through Guz she learned that head office complied with this arrangement, communicating more and more through Hasan, not her. She also heard that ten years earlier an American male manager the same age as her had been withdrawn for his inability to command local managers effectively. He was now working very effectively indeed for a competitor back in the USA.

When presenting this case in a workshop in San Francisco, pointing out the dangers of a universalist system for personnel planning, one female manager expressed concern. "You should not linger on this issue. You are advising us to discriminate on the basis of gender and age, or allow our overseas subsidiaries to do so. In this country you could get sued for that."

Indeed cultural preferences often have the force of law as well as custom. Refusal to send young women managers to Turkey because they are young and female is probably illegal, yet to send them is to confront them with difficulties which they may not have the capacity to surmount, through no fault of their own. The more they achieve, the more they seem to subvert the ascription process. A better tactic can be to make a young female an assistant or adviser to indigenous managers. She will make up for any deficits in knowledge they have, while using local seniority to get things done. Such a posting could be paid and evaluated in the same way as being chief in an achievement-oriented culture, perhaps with a bonus for culture-shock. You cannot replace Turkish with American cultural norms if you seek to be effective in Turkey. This will not be effective in the long run, and in the short run can be very expensive.

Towards Reconciliation

Despite far greater emphasis on ascription or achievement in certain cultures, they do in my view develop together. Those who "start" with ascribing usually ascribe not just status but future success or achievement and thereby help to bring it about.

Those who "start" with achievement usually start to ascribe importance and priority to the persons and projects which have been successful. Hence all societies ascribe and all achieve after a fashion. It is once again a question of where a cycle starts.

It was in 1985 that Belly Electronics (BE) started to manufacture in the Republic of Korea. The fast changing prices in consumer electronics had forced the San Francisco-based company to decentralize its production facilities. After some quite serious starting losses BE began to recover and late in 1989 it could report some promising profits. Early in 1991 margins came under pressure because of Thai and Vietnamese competition. BE decided to reengineer its business processes following its major competitors in the region.

For the first time BE flew in experienced US managers from the Bay area. Their approach was consistent and had made them managers of the year in BE for similar turnaround projects in California and Massachusetts. On the basis of a continuous improvement programme Korean managers were put under pressure to "get their act together." Something said by the first US manager is still remembered in Seoul: "Ladies and gentlemen, we are on a burning platform. Figures tell us there is not much time left. Competitors in the region are doing much better than us; in fact comparative research shows that in terms of quality our benchmark companies in California and Thailand are outperforming us by 35% on quality and 42% on quantity per worker. I therefore give you six months to get the numbers up and then to become a profit-generating company. Let us show that we are a worthwhile company in BE by achievements and not just promises."

After very disappointing results a second US manager was flown in, but his similar approach made no difference. Interviews with the key Korean players were not helpful. Loss after loss was defended by: "We are trying, but it is not easy in the Republic of Korea. Fierce competition explains a lot. But we need to stop turnover of personnel so we can trust each other more."

Jerome Don was asked to come to the rescue of the still loss. He was known for turning companies around with great skill in both South America and Asia. He started by telling Korean managers that his predecessors were quite right in their approach: "We are on a burning platform, but I ask you to help us to save this facility because it is so important to BE. I'll give you three years to get your act together and I'll help you whenever you need me."

Within six months BE-Korea was in profit. Quality went up and morale resulted in 60% lower staff turnover. Mr Don did not know exactly what happened, but he had done the same in South America and now in Asia.

Why would Jerome Don be successful in the Republic of Korea, while his predecessors had not been?

Achievement

- We need to reward what our people achieve based on skill, but ...
- Respect what people are so we can better take advantage of what they do
- We do not want to be hindered in our achievement by not challenging the status quo, so ...
- We want to avoid the instability that comes from only valuing most recent performance, so we must ...
- Respect who our people are based on their experience, although ...

Ascription

The initial actions by the American managers were counter-productive. In the great American tradition the turnaround managers started at the top (see the figure above) and focused on the reward which people could get for their achievements. The Koreans became even more nervous than they had been before the intervention, because basic trust seemed to be lacking. They were afraid to be judged on their past performance.

Jerome Don gave his Korean colleagues three years to get their act together.

By doing so he intuitively ascribed status to the Korean organization. This gave the Koreans the trust they needed because they were feeling that they were respected for who they were based on their years at BE. This made them work even harder. From ascribed status comes achievement.

Test Yourself

Consider the following problems:

There are different grounds for according status to employees, based on what people have succeeded in doing or on what qualities are attributed to them by the social system.

Consider the statements opposite:

1. Status should lie in the permanent attributes of employees, i. e. their education, seniority, age, position and the level of responsibility ascribed. Status should not change according to occasion or just because of recent successes. It reflects intrinsic worth, not the latest forays.
2. Status should lie in the permanent attributes of employees, i. e. their education, seniority, age, position and the level of responsibility ascribed. Such status tends to be self-fulfilling, with achievement and leadership resulting from what the corporation values in you and expects of you.
3. Status is a matter of what the employee has actually achieved, his or her track record. Yet over time this deserved reputation becomes a permanent attribute, allowing success to be renewed and enabling even more achievement to occur.
4. Achievement or success is the only legitimate source of status in business. The more recent the achievement, the better and more relevant it is to current challenges. Achievement gets its significance from the humble nature of the individual's birth and background, and from beating the odds.

Indicate with "1" the approach you believe would be favoured by your closest colleagues at work, and with "2" the approach which you believe would be their second choice.

If you have chosen 2 or 3 you have expressed a belief in reconciling achieved and ascribed status. Answer 2 affirms socially ascribed status which leads to achievement and success (the Korean case was based on a similar principle). Answer 3 affirms achieved status that is believed to lead to social ascription. In both cases the integrity lies in the self-fulfilling sense of self-worth. Answers 1 and 4 respectively reject achieved and ascribed status.

Practical tips for doing business in ascription-and achievement-oriented cultures

Recognising the differences

Achievement-oriented	Ascription-oriented
1. Use of titles only when relevant to the competence you bring to the task.	1. Extensive use of titles, especially when these clarify your status in the organization.
2. Respect for superior in hierarchy is based on how effectively his or her job is performed and how adequate their knowledge.	2. Respect for superior in hierarchy is seen as a measure of your commitment to the organization and its mission.
3. Most senior managers are of varying age and gender and have shown proficiency in specific jobs.	3. Most senior managers are male, middle-aged and qualified by their background.

Tips for doing business with

Achievement-oriented (for ascriptives)	Ascription-oriented (for achievers)
1. Make sure your negotiation team has enough data, technical advisers and knowledgeable people to convince the other company that the project, jointly pursued, will work.	1. Make sure your negotiation team has enough older, senior and formal position-holders to impress the other company that you consider this negotiation important.
2. Respect the knowledge and information of your counterparts even if you suspect they are short of influence back home.	2. Respect the status and influence of your counterparts, even if you suspect they are short of knowledge. Do **not** show them up.
3. Use the title that reflects how competent you are as an individual.	3. Use the title that reflects your degree of influence in your organization.
4. Do not underestimate the need of your counterparts to do better or do more than is expected.	4. Do not underestimate the need of your counterparts to make their ascriptions come true.

| When managing and being managed ||
Achievement-oriented	Ascription-oriented
1. Respect for a manager is based on knowledge and skills.	1. Respect for a manager is based on seniority.
2. MBO and pay-for-performance are affective tools.	2. MBO and pay-for-performance are less effective than direct rewards from the manager.
3. Decisions are challenged on technical and functional grounds.	3. Decisions are only challenged by people with higher authority.

Notes

1. Adapted and abridged from *Riding the Waves of Culture: Understanding Cultural Diversity in Business* (Second Edition), 1997. Fonds Trompenaars is the "new star of the world's management seminar circuit." In 1991 he was awarded the International Professional Practice Area Research Award by the ASTD. Charles Hampden-Turner is the leading management consultant with a DBA from Harvard and has authored 14 books, including *Maps of the Mind*.

2. Don Quixote is the hero of *Don Quixote*, an early 17th century novel. Quixote is a dreamer and a gentle buffoon, an aging gentleman who sets out from his village of La Mancha to perform acts of chivalry in the name of his grand love Dulcinea. He rides a decrepit horse, Rocinante, and is accompanied by his "squire," the peasant Sancho Panza. Quixote's imagination often gets the better of him; in once famous incident he tilts at windmills, imagining them to be giants. Throughout his many adventures Quixote often seems ridiculous, yet he maintains his staunchly hopeful attitude and belief in chivalry. The term quixotic now describes anyone who takes on an idealistic or foolish quest against great odds.

Questions for Discussion

1. Discuss how achievement orientation and ascription orientation affect the economic success. Which is more at work in Asian countries and why?
2. As a manager in a culturally diverse company, how can you reconcile the two forces?
3. How do you perceive people of ascriptive cultures in a multicultural company?
4. Discuss whether culture globalization will reduce the misunderstanding arising from the two differently oriented cultures in business.
5. Argue the position that cultural hegemony badly inhibits the fair exchange of

commodities and mutual learning among global businesses. Give examples where necessary to illustrate your point.

Online Mini-Case Studies and Viewpoints-Sharing

Interracial Marriage Calls for Cultural Reconciliation as Well

My aunt is full-blooded Mexican and her husband is full-blooded middle-Eastern. They have been married for about twelve years, and have three beautiful children. Despite many cultural differences, their relationship keeps going strong. One such difference is the language barrier. She only spoke Spanish, while he spoke Arabic and English. At the beginning of their relationship a friend translated for them in order to understand each other. A year later they got married and my aunt had to learn English to communicate with her husband and his family, while also trying to learn Arabic. Another difference was their religion. She is Catholic and he is Christian. Together, they have to cope with each other and educate their children. They have learned from each other's culture and are trying to take a little bit of both and combine it for their kids. (-Amilia's story)

Online Research

Read more about cultural reconciliation and pinpoint the possible challenges faced with by a multi-cultural company and an interracial marriage.

Reading Two

Introductory Remarks

Individualism and collectivism have been recognized as the most enduring pursuit for Westerners and Easterners respectively, thus bearing the irreplaceable features to distinguish the two communities of people in primary values. This discrepancy can be traced to ancient Greece and the Spring and Autumn and Warring-States Period of China, during which the concept of a self-determined individual "I" and the notion of other-concerned "we" emerged. Ever since then, they developed in their eventual social infrastructure and gradually enriched both in denotation and connotation, exerting enormous influence upon their people's identity construction and pattern of self-construal. Over time, more and more research gaps are detected, although myrads of researches and monographs were published to unearth the drastic differences between individualism and collectivism, between individualists and collectivists, between individualistic cultures and collectivisitc cultures from cognitive, affective, and behavioral and other perspectives.

    The article by Dr. Ting-Toomey was written to address the complex connection between identity and interpersonal relationship and their underlying variables. She maintains that for individualistic cultures, the "I" identity prevails over "we" identity, while for collectivistic cultures, "we" identity over "I" identity. Then quoting Giles' and Gudykunst's research findings as supporting evidence, she argues further that ethnic/cultural identity salience dimension has much to do with the forming of the collective identity of certain groups like a nation. In the following section, the author elaborates on the differences between individualistic cultures and collectivisitc cultures, pointing out that the former focuses on personal identity, views identity validation as an intensive affair, adopts the "equity norm", and accentuates verbal expressive communication while the latter emphasizes role identity that a person plays in the group, takes identity validation as a diffused activity, obeys "equality norm", and highlights nonverbal affiliative expressiveness. Compared with individualistic cultures whose members are the most susceptible to attacks to ego and get relational hurts, collectivist cultures often construct an interactive system in which "face" and the "face" identity seem to be the most vulnerable. In the end, Dr. Ting-Toomey concludes that the most fragile and sacred, the sense of self, takes different forms in individualistic and collectivistic cultures, and calls for much role-playing adrointness such as high sensitivity, security in ethnolinguistic identities and high other-orientation to achieve.

Identity and Interpersonal Bonding[1]

Stella Ting-Toomey

IDENTITY PERSPECTIVE

Cultural Variability Perspective

The cultural variability perspective is concerned primarily with how definable dimensions of a culture affect identity conceptions and relationship development. Dimensions of cultural variability influence the underlying social structures and norms of a situation, and the social norms, in turn, influence how one should or should not behave in a certain manner. The identity salience dimension, which is defined as the "degree to which an individual's relationships to particular others depended upon his or her being a given kind of person, playing a particular role, and having a particular identity", depends heavily on the cultural context in which the encounter takes place.

How one constructs and presents a "self" in a relationship is, to a large degree, situationally-dependent and culturally-dependent.

On a more specific level, when one examines the cultural variability dimensions that have been isolated by theorists in different disciplines, the one cross-cultural dimension that appears to have strong etic endorsement is individualism-collectivism. Individualism-collectivisim refers to the culturally grounded "cluster of attitudes, beliefs, and behaviors toward a wide variety of people". In an etic analysis[2] of the dimension in eight cultures (Chile, Costa Rica, France, Greece, India, Indonesia, the Netherlands, and three ethnic samples in the United States), Triandis et al. uncovered four stable etic factors: Individualism has two factors (separation from in-groups and self-reliance with hedonism) and collectivism has two factors (family integrity and interdependability with sociability).

Overall, members of the individualistic cultures (such as Australia and the United States) tend to place a high emphasis on the "I" identity over the "we" identity, the "I" assertion over the group assertion, and tend to maintain a considerable social distance between the "I" identity and in-group social influences. Conversely, members of the collectivistic cultures (such as China and Japan) tend to place a high premium on the "we" identity over the "I" identity, the group assertion over the individualistic assertion, and tend to be more susceptible to in-group influences than members in the individualistic cultures. Triandis[3] argued that there are two types of collectivism: "simple" collectivism and "contextual" collectivism. "Simple" collectivism allows members to choose how to behave when multiple in-groups are relevant, while "contextual" collectivism designates an in-group influence that is specific. In addition, while the boundary conditions between in-groups and out-groups are fairly diffused and loosely structured in individualistic cultures, the boundary conditions between in-groups and out-groups, and also between memberships in various in-groups (e.g., kin, coworkers, neighbors), are more sharply defined and tightly structured in collectivistic cultures.

In a recent study, for example, Triandis et al. found that individualism in the United States is reflected in (a) self-reliance with competition, (b) low concerns for in-groups and (c) distance from in-groups. In addition, a higher-order factor analysis suggests that subordination of in-group goals to personal goals may be the most important aspect of individualism in the United States. In comparison, samples from two collectivist cultures (Japan and Puerto Rico) indicate that which in-group is present, in what context, and what behavior (e.g., paying attention to the views of others, feelings similar to others, competing with others) are critical to role enactment and performance. Furthermore, the psychological dimension of idiocentrism-allocentrism (e.g., the personality dimension equivalent to individualism and collectivism, respectively) also asserts influence on individuals' behavior within cultures. Overall, allocentric individuals reported more social support and perceived a better quality of such support than idiocentric individuals, while idiocentric individuals reported being more lonely. Related research by Gudykunst and Nishida (1986) and Gudykunst, Yoon, and Nishida (1987) obtained results similar to Triandis et al's study (1986). For example, Gudykunst, Yoon, and Nishida found that members of collectivistic cultures (Japan and the Republic of Korea) perceive greater social penetration (personalization and synchronization) in their in-group relationships than do members of individualistic cultures (United States). Their data further revealed that perceived out-group relationships in collectivistic cultures are influenced by either "simple" collectivism or "contextual" collectivism. Overall, the Korean culture exhibits "simple" collectivistic patterns, while the Japanese exhibits "contextual" collectivistic patterns.

In cross-cultural interpersonal conflict literature, Chua and Gudykunst, Leung, and Ting-Toomey observed that members of individualistic cultures tend to use a direct conflict communication style and a solution-orientation style, and members of collectivistic cultures tend to use an indirect conflict communication style and a conflict-avoidance style. In addition, collectivists tend to use the equality norm (the equal distribution norm) with in-group members and use the equity norm (the deservingness norm) with out-group members more than individualists. Collectivists also display stronger preference for conflict mediation and bargaining procedure than individualists. Preferences for a direct conflict style, for the use of the equity norm[4], and for the direct settlement of disputes reflect the salience of the "I" identity in individualistic cultures; while preferences for an indirect conflict style, for the use of the equality norm, and for the use of mediation procedures reflect the salience of the "we" identity in the collectivistic cultures.

Ting-Toomey developed a theory of face-negotiation and cross-cultural conflict styles. Conflict is viewed as an identity-bound concept in which the "faces" or the "situated identities" of the conflict interactants are called into question. Based on the two dimensions of self-concern focus versus other-concern focus and positive-face need (inclusion need) versus negative-face need (autonomy need), twelve theoretical propositions were developed to account for the relationship between cultural variability and conflict style. The first four propositions, for example, were as follows:

(1) Members of individualistic cultures would tend to express a greater degree of self-face maintenance in a conflict situation than would members of collectivistic cultures.
(2) Members of collectivistic cultures would tend to express a greater degree of mutual-face or other-face maintenance than would members of individualistic cultures.
(3) Members of individualistic cultures would tend to use more autonomy-preserving strategies (negative face need) in managing conflict than would members of collectivistic cultures.
(4) Members of collectivistic cultures would tend to use more inclusion-seeking strategies (positive-face need) in managing conflict than would members of individualistic cultures.

Ethnolinguistic Identity Perspective

The ethnolinguistic identity perspective is concerned mainly with group membership influences on identity salience vis-a-vis the critical role of language. Giles and Johnson, for example, argue that language plays a critical role in shaping the ethnic/cultural identity salience dimension for individuals. Giles, Bourhis, and Taylor contend that perceived ethnolinguistic vitality influences the degree to which individuals will act as an ethnic/cultural group member in an intergroup encounter situation. Perceived high ethnolinguistic vitality means individuals perceive their own in-group language as assuming a high-status position and as receiving wide-based institutional support from the language community. Perceived low ethnolinguistic vitality means individuals perceive their own in-group language as assuming a low-status position and as receiving narrow-based institutional support from the government, education, industry, and the mass media.

In addition to the issue of ethnic/cultural identity salience dimension, Tajfel's and Turner's social identity theory argue for the critical role of social identity salience in the formation of an individual's self-concept. Tajfel states: "Social identity is that part of an individual's self-concept which derives from his or her knowledge of his or her membership in a social group (or groups) together with the value and emotional significance attached to that membership". Incorporating the main ideas in ethnolinguistic identity theory and social identity theory, Gudykunst identifies five factors that influence ethnolinguistic identity development: [(a) the strength of in-group identification; (b) the salience and overlaps of multiple group memberships; (c) the valence of intergroup comparisons; (d) the permeability of in-group/out-group boundaries; and (e) the perceived vitality of in-group language.] According to Gudykunst, the more secure and positive members of a group feel about their identity, the more positive the intergroup comparisons, the more tolerant and receptive they are toward members of other groups. He further theorizes that an increase in the strength of strangers' ethnolinguistic identities will produce an increase in their attributional confidence regarding the beliaviors of other groups' members. He contends that secure ethnolinguistic identity, positive expectations, perceived group similarity, shared intergroup networks, interpersonal salience, second-language competence, and personality factors affect the reduction of uncertainty and anxiety in intergroup encounter processes. Reducing uncertainty and anxiety, in turn, influences intergroup-interpersonal adaptation and effectiveness. Identity security, in short, brings about confidence in oneself to initiate the exploration of the world of a stranger, and the exploration, in turn, brings about greater knowledge and understanding of the stranger's background and normative culture.

Members who are secure in their ethnolinguistic identities will have an overall sense of positive self-concept. They will be likely to take risks in strangers' interaction. They will also be likely to explore and cultivate deeper levels of intergroup relationship with out-group members, and will be more receptive to move the relationship to different bonding stages such as close friendship, romantic relationship, or marital relationship than members with insecure ethnolinguistic identities. There exists, of course, an optimal level of the ethnolinguistic identification process. Members who are at the extreme far ends of the continuum of identification will have either extreme marginal identities or extreme ethnocentric identities. Secure ethnolinguistic identification in this writing means a healthy, optimal level of cultural role identities and social role identities that constitute the integral part of an individual's positive sense of "self".

INTERGROUP-INTERPERSONAL BONDING PROCESS

A Convergent Approach

Bochner in discussing the functions of human communication in interpersonal bonding, proposes five specific functions of relational communication: "(1) to foster favorable impressions; (2) to organize the relationship; (3) to construct and validate a conjoint world view; (4) to express feelings and thoughts; and (5) to protect vulnerabilities." As intercultural communication researchers, however, we cannot discuss the interpersonal bonding process adequately unless the dynamics of intergroup factors are taken into consideration. The factors of language, ethnolinguistic identity salience, preconceived expectations of out-group members, and the boundary conditions between in-group and out-group members are critical to the development of the evolving, long-term relationships of the intergroup-interpersonal dyad.

In order to examine the bonding ties between members of two ethnic or cultural communities, we have to make some basic assumptions. For example, the intergroup members have a common means (i. e., a common language) to communicate with one another. They are in close proximity with one another, they have the opportunities to communicate, and they have a sense of reciprocal awareness of the other's presence. The first intergroup bonding question asks: What are the conditions that promote the initiation of intergroup-interpersonal encounters?

The theories and research based on ethnolinguistic identity theory can provide initial observations to answer this question. Under the conditions that intergroup comparisons are positive, ethnolinguistic identities are strong, and group boundaries are permeable, members of culture X are more likely to venture out to initiate contact with members of culture Y, and vice versa. As Axiom 1 in Gudykunst's intergroup uncertainty reduction theory indicates: Strangers' positive ethnolinguistic identities are more likely to increase attributional confidence regarding out-group members' behavior and decrease initial anxiety they experience with out-group members' contact. The axiom, however, only holds when members of the out-group are perceived as "typical" and when ethnic status is activated. Nevertheless, while ethnolinguistic identities serve as a critical factor during the initial intergroup contact phase, it does not assume equal values and equal statuses during actual interactions in all cultures. In some cultures, personal identity salience outweighs the importance of role identity salience. In other cultures, cultural role and social role identities are of paramount importance to one's sense of "self" and personhood construction. Explaining these differences is where the cultural variability perspective can facilitate our understanding of the intergroup-interpersonal bonding process.

Applying the individualism-collectivism theoretical dimension, we can state the basic assumption that members of individualistic cultures will place a greater emphasis on the salience of personal identities over role identities, while members of collectivistic cultures will place a greater emphasis on the salience of role identities over personal identities during the intergroup encounter process. For example, members of individualistic cultures will emphasize personal identity factors such as personal ideals or achievements during initial attraction stages, while members of collectivistic cultures will emphasize role identity factors such as educational or occupational background during initial intergroup encounters. This basic assumption, in turn, influences how intergroup members attune to different aspects of the encounter—to foster favorable impressions, to validate a conjoint worldview, to organize the relationship, to express feelings and thoughts, and to protect relational vulnerabilities.

Fostering Impressions
Impression management is critical to the cultivation of intergroup-interpersonal ties. Both the cultural norms of the encounter situation and the identity negotiation process between the two individuals will have a profound influence on the further development of the relationship. If the intergroup encounter takes place in a hetero-geneous, individualistic culture, norms and rules will assert relatively less pressures on the dyad than if it does in a homogeneous, collectivistic culture like Japan. Beyond the contextual setting of the encounter, the identity negotiation process between the two individuals will be critical to the further evolution of the

relationship. While interpersonal attraction variables such as physical attraction, personality attraction, perceived attitudinal similarity, and close proximity may be necessary conditions for the intergroup-interpersonal bonding process to occur, identity negotiation and reciprocal support are the vital conditions that propel the intergroup relationship forward, moving toward an individualized relationship that is "close, deep, personal and intimate".

In attempting to foster a favorable impression, especially during actual initial encounters, the intergroup dyad has to grapple with two sets of problems: self-presentation versus other-validation. This section focuses on the self-presentation dimension, while the next section contains a discussion of the other-validation dimension.

In terms of self-presentation acts, there are four possible intergroup impression presentation options: (a) a member categorizes or identifies self as a typical cultural one, and behaves typically; (b) a member categorizes or identifies self as an atypical cultural one, and behaves atypically; (c) a member categorizes or identifies self as a "typical cultural one, but acts atypically; and (d) a member categorizes or identifies self as an atypical cultural one, but acts typically. All four options probably are influenced more by the dyadic partners perceptions and interpretations than by the member's projected sense of self in the encounter. The partner's knowledge of the culture, the degree of favorableness toward the out-group, the levels of expectations of the role enactment from out-group members, and the degree of tolerance of ambiguity will create either a positive or a negative climate for the initial intergroup contact. Past intergroup literature has indicated that positive feelings toward out-group members as a whole are more likely to be generated typical of his or her group rather than from interaction involving an out-group member who is perceived as atypical. We may want to qualify this finding, however, by adding on the variables of degree of favorable out-group attitude and the valence of typical/atypical out-group member's behavior. A favorable out-group attitude, in conjunction with desirable typical/atypical out-group member's behavior, will promote further intergroup-interpersonal relationship development, while the opposite attitude and behavior, will impede further relationship progress... .

The construction of personhood in individualistic cultures is based on intrinsic qualities and characteristics, while the one in collectivistic cultures is tied closely to the sociocultural webs of the system. As Shweder and Bourne summarized, in the individualistic cultures, "each person is conceived of as... a monadic replica of general humanity. A kind of sacred personalized self is developed and the individual qua individual is seen as inviolate, a supreme value in and of itself. The 'self' becomes an object of interest per se", whereas in collectivistic cultures, the "context-dependent, occasion-bound concept of the person" is expressed through "(a) no attempt to distinguish the individual from the status she or he occupies; (b) the view that obligations and rights are differentially apportioned by role, group, etc.; (c) a disinclination to ascribe intrinsic moral worth to persons merely because they are persons".

Validating the Other
Accurate coorientation and reciprocal, mutual support of identities occur in conjunction with fostering favorable impressions. Mutual validation and confirmation is vital to further relational growth and progress. Three issues (identity validation, the content of validation, and the means of validation) are of central concern in the intergroup-interpersonal validation process.

As mentioned in the previous section, identity presentation can come in different forms. Likewise, identity validation can take on different shapes. To validate someone's identities, we have to obtain the following identity information about other group members: (a) the extent to which he or she identifies with cultural role categories, social role categories, or personal identity categories; (b) the salience (important/unimportant) and the valence (positive/negative) in which he or she identifies with different role types; and (c) the consistency and frequency distributions in which he or she enacts each role category. Beyond obtaining the basic relational knowledge, the members have to possess a certain degree of attributional confidence in themselves to infer whether the obtained information is accurate or inaccurate.

Ethnolinguistic identity theory suggests some initial predictions. Members who are secure about their ethnolinguistic identities are more confident in their predictions of the out-group members' behavior, while members who are insecure about their ethnolinguistic identities are probably less confident in their predictions of out-group members' behavior. Members who are secure in their own identities possess a sense of awareness, knowledge, and acceptance of their own selves and behavior. Members who are self-aware are also likely to be alert and aware of their outer environment. Self-awareness leads to other-awareness, self-knowledge leads to other-knowledge, and self-acceptance leads to other-acceptance and tolerance. Members who have strong ethnolinguistic identities will be more ready to engage in an active information seeking process concerning strangers' behavior than members who have weak ethnolinguistic identities. Members who are secure in their identities are not afraid of losing their "selves" in the searching process, while those who are insecure in their identities will have a high apprehension level in losing their "selves" in interactions with dissimilar strangers.

Cross-cultural studies of uncertainty reduction indicate that the individualism-collectivism dimension influences uncertainty reduction content and modes of intergroup-interpersonal communication. Members of individualistic cultures tend to reduce uncertainty in the personal identity salience area, while members of collectivistic cultures tend to reduce uncertainty in the role identity salience area. Personal identity salience means a set of self-definitional personal identities that are derived from unique, idiosyncratic individual characteristics (e. g., active/passive, fast/slow). Role identity salience is conceptualized as a set of self-definitional role identities that are derived from cultural and/or social membership categories.

Applying the results of cross-cultural studies of uncertainty reduction to the intergroup-interpersonal validation process, the findings suggest that members of individualistic cultures are more likely to validate an out-group member's personal identity salience, while those of collectivistic cultures are likely to validate an out-group member's role identity salience. Furthermore, previous work reveals that members of individualistic cultures tend to use a direct verbal mode of communication to reduce relational uncertainty, while those of collectivistic cultures tend to use an indirect, nonverbal mode of communication. Individualistic cultures are low-context cultures and collectivistic cultures are high-context cultures (Hall, 1983). Low-context cultures emphasize direct verbal assertion, explicit meanings, and personal identity interactions, and high-context cultures value indirect verbal assertion, implicit meanings, and role identity interaction. In terms of intergroup modes of validation, members of low-context, individualistic cultures are likely to engage in a direct, explicit verbal mode of identity validation, while members of high-context, collectivistic cultures are likely to engage in an indirect, implicit nonverbal mode of identity validation.

Finally, social networks play a critical role in the intergroup-interpersonal identity validation process. According to Triandis et al., in collectivist cultures, "the in-group's influence on behavior is broad, profound, and diffuse; in the individualist cultures, it is narrow, superficial, and specific". In individualistic cultures, identity validation is a private and dyadic affair; while in the collectivistic cultures, identity validation is embedded within the approval of families and social networks. Identity validation is an intensive affair in individualistic cultures, while a diffused activity in collectivistic cultures... .

Organizing the Relationship

Organizing the relationship refers to how the intergroup couple establishes rules for the relationship, and the rules "constitute the definition of the relationship and form the organizational basis for controlling what actions will take place in the relationship, as well as how thoughts and feelings may be expressed". Different levels of rules concerning how a relationship should be conducted are reflective of basic cultural ideologies and themes surrounding the structure, content, and meanings of relationship. According to Bochner, there are four types of bonding rules: (a) common consent rules; (b) idiosyncratic rules; (c) explicit or implicit rules; and (d) metarules. Common consent rules are rules that are learned during primary socialization process via family interaction (i. e., are determined culturally); Idiosyncratic rules are rules that reflect the private beliefs concerning what is fair and just in the relationship by the involved parties; Explicit or implicit rules are prior agreement rules that are either publicly acknowledged or denied to a third party outside the relationship; Finally, metarules are rules about who, may set the rules, and also about against seeing or knowing about certain rules in the relationship.

Common consent rules are rules with high normative cultural forces. They constitute the cultural "scripts" of what it means to be a "good" friend, what it means to be a "dating" couple, or what it means to be a "harmonious" family. Argyle, in a series of studies testing 33 common rules in three cultures (Britain, Italy, and Japan), found that respect for privacy is a basic rule regulating all relationships across cultures. In addition, there are more rules about obedience, avoiding loss of face, maintaining harmonious relations in groups, and restraining emotional expression in the collectivistic cultures than in the individualistic ones.

The issue of privacy regulation is related directly to identity respect and the identity validation process. With respect to the influence of cultural variability on privacy negotiation[5], we can predict that members of individualistic cultures probably display a higher privacy need in interpersonal relationships than members of collec tivistic cultures. Members of individualistic cultures treasure autonomy and freedom in a relationship, while members of collectivistic cultures value mutual interdependence and restraint. While the dialectic of freedom and restraint is presented simultaneously in all intimate relationships, cultural variability will influence members' preference for one end of the dialectic over the other. In addition, members of individualistic cultures will be likely to articulate their need for privacy or privacy respect, while members of collectivistic cultures will be subdued about it. Privacy respect is a reflection of respect extended to the personhood of "I"; whereas privacy regulation, in the context of the collectivistic cultures, may mean dyadic privacy away from kinship network and social network influences, but may not necessarily mean the separation; autonomous privacy between the "you" and the "I".

Idiosyncratic rules are private beliefs concerning what constitutes "fairness" in a relationship. According to Leung and Iwawaki, collectivists typically follow the "equality norm" in reward allocation, while individualists typically follow the "equity norm" in reward distribution. The equality norm requires an equal allocation of a reward among the participants of their input to the obtaining of the reward, while the equity norm requires that reward distribution should be proportional to participants' input. In the initial intergroup-interpersonal interaction phase, members of individualistic cultures will probably practice the equity norm of self-deservingness, while members of collectivistic cultures will probably practice the equality norm for the sake of preserving relational harmony and solidarity. In addition, there are differences in the reciprocity norm in intergroup relationship development across cultures. The reciprocity norm in individualistic cultures means individualized responsibilities and exchange obligations, whereas in collectivistic cultures, it means role responsibilities and exchange obligations. To be attracted to a member of a collectivistic culture means to take on additional responsibilities and obligations toward the member's social networks. In terms of the explicit-implicit rules, while violation of relational rules in the public may be acknowledged explicitly in individualistic, low-context cultures, violation of relational rules will be noticed but may not be acknowledged explicitly in collectivistic, high-context cultures. To acknowledge relational rules' breakdowns in public will bring on enormous loss of face to members of the collectivistic cultures.

Expressing Thoughts and Feelings

According to Bochner, expressive communication refers to "messages that signify emotive and subjective experiences such as feelings, private sentiments, and personal qualities". Beyond normative rules of the culture, second-language competence is critical to expressive communication in intergroup encounters. The normative rules of individualistic, low-context cultures stress verbal expressive com munication, while the normative rules of collectivistic, high-context cultures emphasize nonverbal affiliative expressiveness. Second-language competence is critical for collectivists who are attracted to individualists, especially when the intergroup encounter takes place in individualistic, low-context cultures. On the other hand, nonverbal affiliative expressiveness is of paramount important for individualists who are attracted to collectivists, and, particularly when the intergroup encounter takes place in collectivistic, high-context cultures. As Gudykunst, Nishida, and Chua's study indicates, perceived second-language competence for the Japanese in the United States is correlated positively with the social penetration process of greater perceived personalization, greater perceived synchronization, and less perceived difficulty with U.S. members. The cultural context of expressive communication asserts strong influence over the critical role of second-language competence. While relational commitment will be expressed through verbal forms of communication in individualistic, low-context cultures, relational commitment will be expressed through subtle forms of nonverbal communication in collectivistic, high-context cultures.

The perceived ethnolinguistic identity dimension is also linked positively with second-language competence. The more secure and positive individuals feel about their identities, the greater the perceived competence in the out-group language, and also the more receptive they are of members of other groups. Members with secure ethnolinguistic identities tend to take more risks with cultivating second language competence and intergroup relationship competence. Successes in both areas probably act as a feedback loop to reinforce the security of the group members' identities.

Expressive communication or relational openness, however, does not follow a unidirectional trajectory in the development of intergroup-interpersonal relationships. As Bochner comments, "the dialectical qualities of interpersonal communication make it obvious that things are not always what they seem; yet interactants sometimes are pressured to act as if things are … . Talk may inhibit what it exhibits—expressiveness mandating protectiveness, revealing necessitating concealing, openness petitioning discretion, weakness used to dominate, freedom as a constraint"… .

Protecting Vulnerabilities

The sense of the "self", is the most vulnerable and the most sacred in any type of intimate relationships. In the individualistic cultures, the "I" identity is the most vulnerable to attack and to relational hurts. In the collectivistic cultures, the "face" identity is most sensitive to hurts and violations. To hurt someone's "I" identity in individualistic cultures means direct violation of the other person's sense of personal privacy, the betrayal of private information to a third person, or the bringing up of deeply personal taboo topics that hurt the other person's ego. To hurt someone's "face" identity in the collectivistic cultures means verbally assaulting the other person's face in front of a third party, separating the other person's connection with family and kinship network ties, or bringing up taboo topics that deal with in-groups' ineffectiveness or inadequacy.

Respecting and protecting relational vulnerabilities requires high role-taking ability. High rhetorically sensitive persons, high self-monitoring persons, or allocentric personality types probably possess a higher role-taking ability than low rhetorically sensitive persons, low self-monitoring persons, or idiocentric personality types. Members who are secure in their ethnolinguistic identities are also good role-takers because their sense of identity security will push them to take relational risks more easily than members with insecure ethnolinguistic identities. Members with ambivalent or insecure ethnolinguistic identities will have a harder time taking on the perspective of the other person because they have to spend time and energy struggling with their own identity problems and definitions. In addition, members of collectivistic cultures are probably better role-takers than members of individualistic cultures because members in collectivistic cultures have been socialized in cultural systems that emphasize a high other-orientation rather than a high I-orientation. Anticipating the other person's need, empathizing with the other's response, and learning the discretion and sensitivity of when to speak and when to remain silent are some of the fundamental training that collectivistsed early on in their family socialization process.

Finally, we also can predict that people with secure ethnolinguistic identities have few relational taboo topics, while people with insecure ethnolinguistic identities will have many relational taboo topics. If individuals do not feel secure about their ethnolinguistic identities, then conversations surrounding both the role identity salience dimension and the personal identity salience dimension will oftentimes become strained and awkward. Taboo topics and vulnerable feelings along these two dimensions will also accumulate.

Notes

1. Adapted and abridged from chapter with the same title in M. K. Asante & W. B. Gudykunst (Eds.), *Handbook of International and Intercultural Communication* (pp. 351-373). Newbury Park, CA: Sage, 1989.
2. Etic analysis, commonly used by cross-cultural researchers with the preference of social science approach, is aimed at searching for universal generalization from outside and with culture-general perspective. Relative to the etic analysis is emic

analysis, often the liking of the researchers of interpretive approach, which is often focused on understanding communication patterns from inside of a particular cultural community or context.
3. Harry Triandis, a professor Emeritus of Psychology at the University of Illinois at Urbana-Champaign, served as President of the International Association of Cross-cultural Psychology, and Chairman and Secretary General of the Society of Experimental Social Psychology. Harry C. Triandis is one of the key pioneers of the field of Cross-Cultural Psychology, which was established as a distinct discipline within psychology. His accomplishments in this international component of the field have included major theoretical and methodological innovations as well as educational and leadership contributions. His research interests have concerned the links between behavior and elements of subjective culture; and differences between individualistic and collectivist cultures. His work focused on the implications of these links for social behavior, personality, work behavior, intergroup relations, prejudice, attitude change, and cultural training; and applications to intercultural training for successful interaction in other cultures.
4. Equity norm, also called equity rules, means the fair and just distribution of resources to all the people which in a way represents partiality. Standing on the other end is equality norm, known as equality rules as well, which means the equal distribution of resources to everyone. The former is often viewed to work as a system of fairness and justice where people are given even-handed treatment. The needs and requirements of all members of this system are regarded and taken into account and given treatment accordingly, whereas the latter can be defined as treating every person in the same way without regarding their requirements and needs. Equality is practiced quite often in demographic societies. Its purpose is to give equal opportunities to everyone and avoid discrimination. Equality can be provided between rich and poor, men and women, people from different race and color, etc.
5. Privacy negotiation refers to the process in which interactants understand each other's extent to which their mutual understanding of privacy can be achieved, the limit to which their privacy is protected and the scope of their respective privacy is likely disclosed in their interaction. Usually, cross-cultural communication may get privacy involved as a more complex issue, thus calling for more adroitment for negotiation.

Questions for Discussion

1. Explain why people at the extreme far ends of the continuum of ethnolinguistic identification will have either extreme marginal identities or extreme ethnocentric identities.
2. Tell the differences between cross-cultural studies and transcultural studies and discuss how each of the research outcome can contribute to us in telling Chinese

stories abroad.
3. China has won its battle against poverty on schedule and achieved the poverty reduction goals because of the Chinese people's unremitting joint efforts under the firm Leadership of the CPC. Discuss how important a role that collectivism plays in winning the great war.
4. To acknowledge relational rules' breakdowns in public will bring on enormous "loss of face" to members of the collectivistic cultures. In what sense do you think the conclusion is probably a haste generalization?
5. In this article the author regards low-context, individualistic cultures as one category whereas high-context, collectivistic cultures as the opposite. Do you agree with her in making the classification? Why or why not?

Online Mini-Case Studies and Viewpoints-Sharing

How Can Undutiful Adult Children Make Trustworthy Businessmen?

Malcolm was picked up by Mr. Saud in person at the Bus Terminal. They had a lunch together in a local restaurant and enjoyed a wonderful time before their business talk kicked off. Mr. Saud inquired about the health of Malcolm's elderly parents. Without missing a beat Malcolm said that his father had been dead in a charity hospital since he was a teenager and his 80-year-old mother was doing fine, but that the last time he saw his mum at a hospice was half a year ago and she had a little trouble when walking alone because of her arthritis. From that point on Mr. Saud's demeanor changed abruptly from warm and hospitable to cool and aloof, and responded to his questions about the local market absent-mindedly. When asked how to start the business coop, Mr. Saud seemed to play dumb.

Online Research

Identify the possible cultures in which Malcolm and Mr. Saud were raised and find out reasons to justify Mr. Saud's sudden change in attitudes toward Malcolm. Then imagine if you were Mr. Saud, would you treat Malcolm the same way in that situation? Why or why not?

Unit Four

Verbal Communication

Reading One

Introductory Remarks

Verbal communication is the transferring of thoughts between individuals via spoken or written messages. It is a key component of communication, whose process involves encoding the sender's ideas into symbols, the presentation of words through a communication channel and the acceptance of the receiver. Verbal communication occurs when you are chatting with your friends, discussing an issue in a group, or making a public speech. It also takes place when you are composing an article, finishing a professor's assignment on campus or writing a report to your boss in a company. Skillful and effective verbal communication involves careful choice of language that takes into account logical and emotional effects, objective and subjective factors, and the needs of the message sender and receiver, especially when they come from different cultural backgrounds.

    The selection to follow explores the vital role of verbal codes in intercultural communication. It begins with a discussion of the characteristics and rule systems that create verbal codes. The nature of language and the five rule systems of phonology, morphology, semantics, syntactics and pragmatics are described. What follows is an analysis of the relationship among language, culture, thought, and intercultural communication. Both the stronger and softer versions of the Sapir-Whorf hypothesis of linguistic relativity are dealt with in great length with illustrations of supporting and opposing evidence. Then the significance of language variations in the identity of ethnic and cultural groups is described, and finally the interrelationship between verbal communication and intercultural competence is clarified and strengthened.

Verbal Intercultural Communication[1]

Myron W. Lustig[2] and Jolene Koester[3]

In this chapter we consider the effects of language systems on people's ability to communicate interculturally. In so doing we explore the accuracy of a statement by the world-famous linguistic philosopher Ludwig Wittgenstein[4], who asserted that "the limits of my language are the limits of my world."

The Power of Language in Intercultural Communication

Language—whether it is English, French, Swahili, Flemish, Hindi, or one of the world's other numerous languages—is a taken-for-granted aspect of people's lives. Language is learned unconsciously and without awareness. Children are capable of using their language competently before the age of formal schooling. Even during their school years, they learn the rules and words of the language and do not attend to how the language influences the way they think and perceive the world. It is usually only when people speak their language to those who do not understand it or when they struggle to become competent in another language that one recognizes language's central role in the ability to function; to accomplish tasks; and most important, to interact with others. It is only when the use of language no longer connects people to others or when individuals are denied the use of their language that they recognize its importance.

There is a set of circumstances involving communication with people from other cultural backgrounds in which awareness of language becomes paramount. Intercultural communication usually means interaction between people who speak different languages. Even when the individuals seem to be speaking the same language—a person from Spain interacting with someone from Venezuela, a French Canadian conversing with a French-speaking citizen of Belgium, or a British person visiting the United States—the differences in the specific dialects of the language and the different cultural practices that govern language use can mystify those involved and can realistically be portrayed as two people who speak different languages.

In this chapter we explore the nature of language and how verbal codes affect communication between people of different cultural backgrounds. We begin with a discussion of the characteristics and rule systems that create verbal codes. We then turn to a discussion of the all-important question of the relationship among language, culture, thought, and intercultural communication. As we consider this question, we explore the Sapir-Whorf hypothesis of linguistic relativity[5] and assess the scholarly evidence that has been amassed both in support of the hypothesis and opposed to it. We also consider the importance of language in the identity of ethnic and cultural groups. The chapter concludes with a consideration of verbal codes and intercultural competence.

Definition of Verbal Codes

Discussions about the uniqueness of human beings usually center around our capability to manipulate and understand symbols that allow interaction with others. In a discussion of the importance of language, Charles F. Hockett[6] noted that language allows people to understand messages about many different topics from literally thousands of different people. Language allows us to talk with others, to understand or disagree with them, to make plans, to remember the past, to imagine future events, and to describe and evaluate objects and experiences that exist in some other location. Hockett also pointed out that language is taught by individuals to others and thus is transmitted from generation to generation in much the same way that culture is. In other words, language is learned.

Popular references to language often include not only spoken and written language but also "body language." However, we prefer to study the latter under the more encompassing description of nonverbal codes in another chapter. In this chapter we concentrate on understanding the relationship of spoken and written language, or verbal codes, to intercultural communication competence.

The Features of Language

Verbal means "word." Therefore, a *verbal code is a set of rules about the use of words in the creation of spoken or written messages.* Words can obviously be either spoken or written. Verbal codes, then, include both oral (spoken) language and nonoral (written) language.

Children first learn the oral form of a language. Parents do not expect two-year-olds to read the words on the pages of books. Instead, as parents speak aloud to a child, they identify or name objects in order to teach the child the relationship between the language and the objects or ideas the language represents. In contrast, learning a second language as an adolescent or adult often proceeds more formally, with a combination of oral and nonoral approaches. Students in a foreign language class are usually required to buy a textbook that contains written forms of the language, which then guide students in understanding both the oral and the written use of the language.

The concept of a written language is familiar to all students enrolled in U.S. college and university classes, as they all require at least reasonable proficiency in the nonoral form of the English language. Fewer and fewer languages exist in only an oral form. When anthropologists and linguists discover a culture that has a unique oral language, they usually attempt to develop a written form of it in order to preserve it. Indeed, many Hmong[7] who immigrated to the United States from their hill tribes in Southeast Asia have had to learn not only the new language of English but also, in many instances, the basic fact that verbal codes can be expressed in written form. Imagine the enormous task it must be not only to learn a second language but also first to understand that language is written.

Rule Systems in Verbal Codes
Five different but interrelated sets of rules combine to create a verbal code, or language. These parts or components of language are called phonology, morphology, semantics, syntactics, and pragmatics.

Phonology. When you listen to someone who speaks a language other than your own, you will often hear different (some might even say "strange") sounds. The basic sound units of a language are called *phonemes*, and the rules for combining phonemes constitute the *phonology* of a language. Examples of phonemes in English include the sounds you make when speaking, such as [k], [t], or [a].

The phonological rules of a language tell speakers which sounds to use and how to order them. For instance, the word *cat* has three phonemes: a hard [k] sound, the short [a] vowel, and the [t] sound. These same three sounds, or phonemes, can be rearranged to form other combinations: *act*, *tack*, or even *tka*. Of course, as someone who speaks and writes English, your knowledge of the rules for creating appropriate combinations of phonemes undoubtedly suggests to you that *tka* is improper. Interestingly, you know that *tka* is incorrect even though you probably cannot describe the rules that make it so.

Languages have different numbers of phonemes. English, for example, depends on about 45 phonemes. The number of phonemes in other languages range from as few as 15 to as many as 85.

Mastery of another language requires practice in accurately reproducing its sounds. Sometimes it is difficult to hear the distinctions in the sounds made by those proficient in the language. Even when the differences can be heard, the mouths and tongues of those learning another language are sometimes unable to produce these sounds. In intercultural communication, imperfect rendering of the phonology of a language—in other words, not speaking the sounds as native speakers do—can make it difficult to be understood accurately. Accents of second-language speakers, which we discuss in more detail later in this chapter, can provoke negative reactions in native speakers.

Morphology. Phonemes combine to form *morphemes*, which are the smallest units of meaning in a language. The 45 English phonemes can be used to generate more than 50 million morphemes! For instance, the word *comfort*, whose meaning refers to a state of ease and contentment, contains one morpheme. But the word *comforted* contains two morphemes: *comfort* and *ed*. The latter is a suffix that means that the comforting action or activity happened in the past. Indeed, though all words contain at least one morpheme, some words (such as *uncomfortable*, which has three morphemes) can contain two or more. Note that morphemes refer only to meaning units. Though the word *comfort* contains smaller words such as *or* or *fort*, these other words are coincidental to the basic meaning of *comfort*.

Semantics. As we have just suggested, morphemes—either singly or in combination—are used to form words. The study of the meaning of words is called *semantics*. The most convenient and thorough source of information about the semantics of a language is the dictionary, which defines what a word means in a particular language. A more formal way of describing the study of semantics is to say that it is the study of the relationship between words and what they stand for or represent. You can see the semantics of a language in action when a baby is being taught to name the parts of the body. Someone skilled in the language points to and touches the baby's nose and simultaneously vocalizes the word *nose*. Essentially, the baby is being taught the vocabulary of a language. Competent communication in any language requires knowledge of the words needed to express ideas. You have probably experienced the frustration of trying to describe an event but not being able to think of words that accurately convey the intended meaning. Part of what we are trying to accomplish is to give you a vocabulary that can be used to understand and explain the nature of intercultural communication competence.

Communicating interculturally necessitates learning a new set of semantic rules. The baby that grows up where people speak Swahili does not learn to say *nose* when the protruding portion of the face is touched; instead, he or she is taught to say *pua*. For an English speaker to talk with a Swahili speaker about his or her nose, at least one of them must learn the word for nose in the other's language. When learning a second language, much time is devoted to learning the appropriate associations between the words and the specific objects, events, or feelings that the language system assigns to them. Even those whose intercultural communication occurs with people who speak the "same" language must learn at least some new vocabulary. The U.S. American visiting Great Britain will confront new meanings for words. *Boot* refers to the storage place in a car, or what the U.

S-English-speaking person would call the *trunk*. *Chips* to the British is *French fries to the* U.S. American. A Band-Aid in the United States is called a *plug* in Great Britain. As Winston Churchill[8] so wryly suggested, the two countries are indeed "divided by a common language."

The discussion of semantics is incomplete without noting one other important distinction: the difference between the denotative and connotative meanings of words. *Denotative meanings* are the public, objective, and legal meanings of a word. Denotative meanings are those found in the dictionary or law books. In contrast, *connotative meanings* are personal, emotionally charged, private, and specific to a particular person. Therefore, it is not possible to find the connotative meaning of a word in the dictionary.

As an illustration, consider a common classroom event known as a *test*. When used by a college professor to a group of undergraduate students, *test* is a relatively easy word to define denotatively. It is a formal examination that is used to assess one's degree of knowledge or skill. But the connotative meanings of *test* probably vary greatly from student to student; some react to the idea with panic, and others are indifferent and casual. Whereas denotative meanings tell us, in an abstract sense, what the words mean objectively, our interest in intercultural communication suggests that an understanding of the connotative meanings—the feelings and thoughts evoked in others as a result of the words used in the conversation—is critical to achieving intercultural competence.

As an example of the importance of connotative meanings, consider the experience reported by a Nigerian student who was attending a university in the United States. When working with a fellow male student who was African-American, the Nigerian called to him by saying, "Hey, boy, come over here." To the Nigerian student, the term *boy* connotes a friendly and familiar relationship, is a common form of address in Nigeria, and is often used to convey a perception of a strong interpersonal bond. To the African-American student, however, the term *boy* evokes images of racism, oppression, and an attempt to place him in an inferior social status. Fortunately, the two students were friends and were able to talk to each other to clarify how they each interpreted the Nigerian student's semantic choices; further misunderstandings were avoided. Often, however, such opportunities for clarification do not occur.

Syntactics. The fourth component of language is *syntactics*, which is the relationship of the words to one another. When children are first learning how to combine words into phrases, they are being introduced to the syntactics of their language. Each language stipulates the correct way to arrange the words. In

English it is not acceptable to create a sentence such as the following: "On by the book desk door is the the." It is incorrect to place the preposition *by* immediately following the preposition *on*. Instead, each preposition must have an object, which results in phrases such as "on the desk" and "by the door." Similarly, articles such as *the* in a sentence are not to be presented one right after the other. Instead, the article is placed near the noun, which produces a sentence that includes "the book," "the door," and "the desk." The syntactics of English grammar suggests that the words in the preceding nonsense sentence might be rearranged to form the grammatically correct sentence "The book is on the desk by the door." The order of the words helps establish the meaning of the utterance.

Each language has a set of rules that governs the sequence of the words. To learn another language requires you to learn those rules. The sentence "John has, to the store to buy some eggs, gone" is an incorrect example of English syntax but an accurate representation of German syntax.

Pragmatics. The final component of all verbal codes is *pragmatics*, which is the effect that language has on human perceptions and behaviors. The study of pragmatics focuses on how language is actually used. A pragmatic analysis of language goes beyond phonology, morphology, semantics, and syntactics. Instead, it considers how users of a particular language are able to understand the meanings of specific utterances in particular contexts. By learning the pragmatics of language use, you understand how to participate in a conversation and you know how to sequence the sentences you speak as part of a conversation. For example, when you are eating a meal with a group of people and somebody says, "Is there any salt?", you know that you should give the person the salt shaker rather than simply answer "yes."

To illustrate how the pragmatics of language use can affect intercultural communication, imagine yourself as a dinner guest in a Pakistani household. You have just eaten a delicious meal. You are relatively full but not so full that it would be impossible for you to eat more if it was considered socially appropriate to do so. Consider the following dialogue:

HOSTESS: I see that your plate is empty. Would you like some more curry?
YOU: No, thank you. It was delicious, but I'm quite full.
HOSTESS: Please, you must have some more to eat.
YOU: No, no, thank you. I've really had enough. It was just great, but I can't eat another bite.

HOSTESS: Are you sure that you won't have any more? You really seemed to enjoy the brinjals.

What is your next response? What is the socially appropriate answer? Is the hostess pressing you to have another helping because in her culture your reply is not interpreted as true negative response until you have given it at least three times? Or is it considered socially inappropriate for a dinner guest not to accept a second helping of food? Even if you knew Urdu, the language spoken in Pakistan, you would have to understand the pragmatics of language use in order to understand the language in use.

 The rules governing the pragmatics of a language are firmly embedded in the larger rules of the culture and are intimately associated with the cultural patterns. For example, cultures vary in the degree to which they encourage people to ask direct questions and to make direct statements to each other. Imagine a student from the United States who speaks some Japanese and who subsequently goes to Japan as an exchange student. The U.S. American's culturally learned tendency is to deal with problems directly, and he may therefore confront his Japanese roommate about the latter's habits in order to "clear the air" and establish an "open" relationship. Given the Japanese cultural preference for indirectness and face-saving behaviors, the U.S. American student's skill in Japanese does not extend to the pragmatics of language use. These differences in the pragmatic rule systems of language are also why it is very difficult to tell a joke—or even to understand a joke—in a second language. Humor requires a subtle knowledge of both the expected meanings of the words (semantics) and their intended effects (pragmatics).

Language, Thought, Culture, and Intercultural Communication

Every language has its own unique features and ways of allowing those who speak it to identify specific objects and experiences. These linguistic features, which distinguish each language from all others, affect how the speakers of the language perceive and experience the world. To understand the effects of language on intercultural communication, questions like the following must be explored:

- How do initial experiences with language shape or influence the way in which a person thinks?
- Do the categories of a language—its words, grammar, and usage—influence how people think and behave?

To make these questions more specific, consider the following question:

- Does a person who learns to speak and write Arabic, when growing up in Saudi Arabia, "see" and "experience" the world differently than does a person who grows up speaking and writing Tagalog[9] in the Philippines?

Although many scholars have advanced ideas and theories about the relationships among language, thought, culture, and intercultural communication, the names most often associated with these issues are Benjamin Lee Whorf and Edward Sapir. Their theory is called linguistic relativity.

The Sapir-Whorf Hypothesis of Linguistic Relativity

Until the early part of the twentieth century, language was generally assumed to be a neutral medium that did not influence the way people experienced the world. At that time, the answer to the preceding question would have been that regardless of whether people grew up learning and speaking Arabic or Tagalog, they would experience the world similarly. The varying qualities of language would not have been expected to affect those who spoke those languages. Language, from this point of view, was merely a vehicle by which ideas were presented rather than a shaper of the very substance of those ideas.

In 1921 the anthropologist Edward Sapir began to articulate an alternative view of language, which said that language influenced or even determined the ways in which people thought. Sapir's student, Benjamin Whorf, continued to present and develop Sapir's ideas into the 1950s. Together, their ideas became subsumed under several different labels, including the theory of linguistic determinism, the theory of linguistic relativity, the Sapir-Whorf hypothesis, and the Whorfian hypothesis. Typical of their statements is the following quotation from Sapir:

> Human beings do not live in the objective world alone, nor alone in the world of social activity as ordinarily understood, but are very much at the mercy of the particular language which has become the medium or expression for their society.
>
> It is quite an illusion to imagine that one adjusts to reality essentially without the use of language and that language is merely an

incidental means of solving specific problems of communication or reflection. The fact of the matter is that the "real world" is to a large extent unconsciously built up on the language habits of the group... We see and hear and otherwise experience very largely as we do because the language habits of our community predispose certain choices of interpretation.

Our discussion of the Sapir-Whorf hypothesis is not intended to provide a precise rendering as articulated by Sapir and Whorf, which is virtually impossible to do. During the three decades in which they formally presented their ideas to the scholarly community, their views shifted somewhat and their writings include "firmer" or more deterministic views of the relationship between language and thought and "softer" views that describe language as merely influencing or shaping thought.

In the "firm" or deterministic version of the hypothesis, language functions like a prison—once people learn a language, they are irrevocably affected by its particulars. Furthermore, it is never possible to translate effectively and successfully between languages, which makes competent intercultural communication an elusive goal.

The "softer" position is a less causal view of the nature of the language-thought relationship. In this version, language shapes how people think and experience their world, but this influence is not unceasing. Instead, it is possible for people from different initial language systems to learn words and categories sufficiently similar to their own so that communication can be accurate.

If substantial evidence had been found to support the strong version of the Sapir-Whorf hypothesis, it would represent a dismal prognosis for competent intercultural communication. Because so few people grow up bilingually, it would be impossible to transcend the boundaries of our linguistic experiences. Fortunately, the weight of the scholarly evidence, which we summarize in the following section, debunks the notion that people's first language traps them inescapably in a particular pattern of thinking. Instead, the evidence suggests that language plays a powerful role in *shaping* how people think and experience the world. Although the shaping properties of language are significant, linguistic equivalences can be established between people from different language systems.

Sapir and Whorf's major contribution to the study of intercultural communication is that they called attention to the integral relationship among thought, culture, and language. In the following section, we discuss some of the differences in the vocabulary of languages and consider the extent to which these differences can be used as evidence to support the two positions of the Sapir-Whorf hypothesis. As you consider the following ideas, examine the properties of the languages you know. Are there specialized vocabularies or grammatical characteristics that shape how you think and experience the world?

Variations in Vocabulary

The best-known example of vocabulary differences associated with the Sapir-Whorf hypothesis is the large number of words for snow in the Eskimo language (The language is variously called Inuktitut in Canada, Inupit in Alaska, and Kalaallisut in Greenland.). Depending on whom you ask, there are from 8 to 50 different words for snow in the Inuktitut language. For example, there are words that differentiate falling snow, or *gana*, and fully fallen snow, or *akilukak*. The English language has fewer words for snow and no terms for many of the distinctions made by Eskimos. The issue raised by the Sapir-Whorf hypothesis is whether the person who grows up speaking Inuktitut actually perceives snow differently than does someone who grew up in Southern California and may only know by second-hand descriptions. More important, could the Southern Californian who lives with the Inupit in Alaska learn to differentiate all of the variations of snow and to use appropriately the specific Eskimo words? The strong version of the Sapir-Whorf hypothesis suggests that linguistic differences are accompanied by perceptual differences, so that the English speaker looks at snow differently than does the Eskimo speaker.

There are numerous other examples of languages that have highly specialized vocabularies for particular features of the environment. For instance, on the South Sea islands, there are numerous words for coconut, which not only refer to the object of a coconut but also indicate how the coconut is being used or refer to a specific part of the coconut. Similarly, in classical Arabic over 6,000 words are used to refer to a camel.

Another variation in vocabulary concerns the terms a language uses to identify and divide places on the color spectrum. For example, the Kamayura Indians of Brazil have a single word that refers to the colors that English speakers would call blue and green. The best translation of the word the kamayuras use is "parakeet colored." The Dani of West New Guinea divide all colors into only two words, which are roughly equivalent in English to "dark" and "light." The important issue, however, is whether speakers of these languages are able to distinguish among the different colors when they see them or they can experience only the colors suggested by the words available for them to use. Do the Kamayura Indians actually see blue and green as the same color simply because they use the same word to identify both? Or does their language simply identify colors differently than does English?

Do you think you could learn to distinguish all of the variations of the object snow that are important to the Eskimos? Could you be taught to see all of the important characteristics of a camel or a coconut? Such questions are very important in accepting or rejecting the ideas presented in the firm and soft versions of the Sapir-Whorf hypothesis.

Researchers looking at the vocabulary variations in the color spectrum have generally found that although a language may restrict how a color can be labeled verbally, people can still see and differentiate among particular colors. In other words, the Kamayura Indians can, in fact, see both blue and green, even though they call both colors by the same linguistic referent. The deterministic version of the sapir-Whorf hypothesis, then, is not supported by the evidence on color perception and vocabulary.

What about all those variations for snow, camels, or coconuts? Are they evidence to support the strong version of the Sapir-Whorf hypothesis? A starting point for addressing this issue is to consider how English speakers use other words along with essentially the one word English has for "particles of water vapor that when frozen in the upper air fall to earth as soft, white, crystalline flakes." English speakers are able to describe verbally many variations of snow simply by adding modifiers to the root word. As readers who live in areas with a lot of snow can attest, they are quite familiar with *dry snow*, *heavy snow*, *slush*, or *dirty snow*. Skiers have a rich vocabulary to describe variations in snow on the slopes. It is possible, therefore, for a person who has facility in one language to approximate the categories of another language. The deterministic position of Sapir-Whorf, then, is difficult to support. Even Sapir and Whorf's own work can be used to argue against the deterministic interpretation of their position because in presenting all of the Eskiomo words for snow, Whorf provided their approximate English equivalences.

A better explanation for linguistic differences is that variations in the complexity and richness of a language's vocabulary reflect what is important to the people who speak that language. To an Eskimo, differentiating among varieties of snow is much more critical to survival and adaptation than it is to the Southern Californian, who may never see snow. Conversely, Southern Californians have numerous words to refer to four-wheeled motorized vehicles, which are very important objects in their environment. However, we are certain that differences in the words and concepts of a language do affect the ease with which a person can change from one language to another because there is a dynamic interrelationship among language, thought, and culture.

Linguistic Relativity and Intercultural Communication

The semantic and syntactic features of language are powerful shapers of the way people experience the physical and social world. Sapir and Whorf's assertions that language *determines* our reality have proven to be false. Language does not determine your ability to sense the physical world, nor does the language first learned create modes of thinking from which there is no escape. However, language shapes and influences our thoughts and behaviors. The vocabulary of a language reflects what you need to know to cope with the environment and the patterns of your culture. The semantics and syntactics of language gently nudge you to notice particular kinds of things in your world and to label them in particular ways. All of these components of language create habitual response patterns to the people, events, and messages that surround you. Your language intermingles with other aspects of your culture to reinforce the cultural patterns you are taught.

The influence of a particular language is something you can escape; it is possible to translate to or interact in a second language. But as the categories for coding or sorting the world are provided primarily by your language, you are predisposed to perceive the world in a particular way, and the reality you create is different from those who use other languages with other categories.

When the categories of languages are vastly different, people will have trouble communicating with one another. Differences in language affect what is relatively easy to say and what seems virtually impossible to say. As Wilma M. Roger has suggested, "Language and the cultural values, reactions, and expectations of speakers of that language are subtly melded."

We offer one final caution. For purposes of discussion we have artificially separated vocabulary and grammar, as if language is simply an adding together of these two elements. In use, language is instead a dynamic and interrelated system that has a powerful effect on people's thoughts and actions. The living, breathing qualities of language as spoken and used, with all the attendant feelings, emotions, and experiences, are difficult to convey adequately in an introductory discussion such as this one.

Language and Intercultural Communication

The earlier sections of this chapter may have given the impression that language is stable and used consistently by all who speak it. However, even in a country that has predominantly only one language, there are great variations in the way the language is spoken (accents) and there are wide deviations in how words are used and what they mean. Among U.S. Americans who speak English, it is quite common to hear many different accents. It is also quite common to hear words, phrases, and colloquial expressions that are common to only one region of the country. Think of the many voices associated with the speaking of English in the United States. Do you have an auditory image of the way someone sounds who grew up in New York City? How about someone who grew up in Georgia? Wisconsin? Oregon? The regional variations in the ways English is spoken reflect differences in accents and dialects.

Increasingly, U.S. Americans speak many first languages other than English. As is well-known, multiple language systems are represented in U.S. schools. Similarly, employers in businesses now must be conscious of the different languages of their workers. In addition, specialized linguistic structures develop for other functions within the context of a larger language. Because language differences are powerful factors that influence the relationships between ethnic and cultural groups who live next to and with each other in communities and countries, we will examine the variations among languages of groups of people who essentially share a common political union. We begin by considering the role of language in maintaining the identity of a cultural group and in the relationship between cultural groups who share a common social system. We then talk about nonstandard versions of a language, including accents, dialects, and argot, and we explore their effects on communication with others.

Language, Ethnic Group Identity, and Dominance

Each person commonly identifies with many different social groups. For example, you probably think of yourself as part of a certain age grouping, as male or female, as married or unmarried, and as a college student or someone who is simply interested in learning about intercultural communication. You may also think of yourself as African-American, German-American, Vietnamese-American, Latino, Navajo, or one of the many other cultural groups comprising the population of the Unites States. You may also identify with a culture from outside of the United States.

Henri Tajfel argues that humans categorize themselves and others into different groups to simplify their understanding of people. When you think of someone as part of a particular social group, you associate that person with the values that belong to the group. In this section we are particularly concerned with the ways in which language is used to identify people in a group, either by the people who are members of the group itself or by outsiders from other groups.

Some of the questions we are concerned with include the following: How important is language to the members of a culture? What is the role that language plays in the maintenance of a culture? Why do some language survive over time and others do not? What role does language play in the relationship of one culture to another?

The importance that cultures attribute to language has been well established. In fact, some would argue that the very heart of a culture is its language and that a culture dies if its language dies. However, it is difficult to determine the exact degree of importance that language has for someone who identifies with a particular group because there are so many factors that affect the strength of one's identification. For example, people are more likely to have a strong sense of ethnic and linguistic identity if their language is acknowledged in some way by members of other important cultural groups. In several U.S. states, for example, there have been legal battles to allow election ballots to be printed in languages other than English. Those advocating this option are actually fighting to gain official status and support for their language.

A language will remain vital and strong if groups of people who live near one another use the language regularly. The sheer number of people who identify with a particular language and their distribution within a particular country or region have a definite effect on the vigor of the language. For people who are rarely able to speak the language of their culture, the centrality of the language and the cultural or ethnic identity that goes along with it would certainly be diminished. Their inability to use the language results in lost opportunities to express their identification with the culture that it symbolizes.

The extent to which a culture maintains a powerful sense of identification with a particular language is called *perceived ethnolinguistic vitality*, which refers to "the individual's subjective perception of the status, demographic characteristics, and institutional support of the language community." Very high levels of perceived ethnolinguistic identity mean that members of a culture will be unwilling to assimilate their linguistic behavior with other cultures that surround them. Howard Giles, one of the foremost researchers in how languages are used in multilingual societies, concludes that there are likely to be intense pressures on cultural members to adopt the language of the larger social group and to discontinue the use of their own language when

1. the members of a culture lack a strong political, social, and economic status;

2. there are few members of the culture compared to the number of people in other groups in the community; and
3. institutional support to maintain their unique cultural heritage is weak.

When multiple languages are spoken within one political boundary, there are inevitably political and social consequences. In the United States, for example, English has maintained itself as the primary language over a long period of time. Immigrants to the United States had historically been required to learn English in order to participate in the wider political and commercial aspects of the society. Schools offered classes only in English, television and radio programs were almost exclusively in English, and the work of government and business also required English. However, in recent years there has been a change in this English-only pattern. Now in many areas of the country there are large numbers of people for whom English is not the primary language. As a consequence, teaching staffs are multilingual; government offices provide services to non-English speakers; and cable television has an extensive array of entertainment and news programming in Spanish, Chinese, Japanese, Arabic, and so on.

In some countries formal political agreements acknowledge the role of multiple languages in the government and educational system. Canada has two official languages: English and French. Switzerland uses three: French, German, and Italian. In Singapore, English, Mandarin, Malay, and Tamil are all official languages, and India has over a dozen.

When India was established in 1948, one of the major problems concerned a national language. Although Hindi was the language spoken by the largest number of people, the overwhelming majority of the people did not speak it. India's solution to this problem was to identify 16 national languages, thus formalizing in the constitution the right for government, schools, and commerce to operate in any of them. Even that solution has not quelled the fears of non-Hindi speakers that Hindi will predominate. In the mid-1950s there was political agitation to redraw the internal state boundaries based on the languages spoken in particular regions. Even now, major political upheavals periodically occur in India over language issues.

Because language is such a precious part of most people's identities, a great deal of emotion is attached to the political choices that are made about language preferences. However, what is most central to intercultural competence is the way in which one's linguistic identification influences the interaction that occurs between members of different cultural groups. In interpersonal communication, language is used to discern members of one's group from some other group. That is, language provides an obvious and highly accurate cue about whether people share one's cultural background. If others speak as you do, you are likely to assume that they are similar to you in other important ways.

People also make a positive or negative evaluation about the language that others use. Generally speaking, there is a pecking order among languages that is usually buttressed and supported by the prevailing political order. As Ellen Bouchard Ryan, Howard Giles, and Richard J. Sebastian suggest,

> In every society the differential power of particular social groups is reflected in language variation and in attitudes toward those variations. Typically, the dominant group promotes its patterns of language use as dialect or accents by minority group members reduce their opportunities for success in the society as a whole. Minority group members are often faced with difficult decisions regarding whether to gain social mobility by adopting the language patterns of the dominant group or to maintain their group identity by retaining their native speech style.

In the United States, there has been a clear preference for English over the multiple other languages that people speak, and those who speak English are evaluated according to their various accents and dialects. In the next section, we discuss the consequences of these evaluations and the effects of alternative forms of language use on intercultural communication competence.

Alternative Versions of a Language
No language is spoken precisely the same way by all who use it. The sounds made by a person from English when speaking English may be contrasted to the speech of English-speaking U.S. Americans. Even among those who share a similar language and reside in the same country, there are important variations in the way the language is spoken. These differences in language use include the way the words are pronounced, the meanings of particular words or phrases, and the patterns for arranging the words (grammar). Terms often associated with these alternative forms of a language include *dialect*, *accent*, *argot* (pronounced "are go"), and *jargon*.

Dialects and Accents
Dialects are versions of a language with distinctive vocabulary, grammar, and pronunciation that are spoken by particular groups of people or within particular regions. Dialects can play an important role in intercultural communication

because they often trigger a judgment and evaluation of a speaker. Dialects are measured against a "standard" spoken version of the language. The term *standard* does not describe inherent or naturally occurring characteristics but rather historical circumstances. For example, among many U.S. Americans, standard American English is often the preferred dialect and conveys power and dominance. But as John R. Edwards has suggested, "As a dialect, there is nothing intrinsic, either linguistically or esthetically, which gives Standard English special status." However, other dialects of English are frequently accorded less status and are often considered inappropriate or unacceptable in education, business, and government. Speakers of Black Standard English, for example, are sometimes unfairly assumed to be less reliable, less intelligent, and of lower status than those who speak Standard American English.

Accents, or distinguishable marks of pronunciation, are closely related to dialects. Research studies repeatedly demonstrate that speakers' accents are used as a cue to form impressions of them. Those of you who speak English with an accent or in a nonstandard version may have experienced the negative reactions of others, and you know the harmful effects such judgments can have on intercultural communication. Studies repeatedly find that accented speech and dialects provoke in listeners stereotyped reactions, so that the speakers are usually perceived as having less status, prestige, and overall competence. Interestingly, these negative perceptions and stereotyped responses sometimes occur even when the listeners themselves use a nonstandard dialect when they speak.

If you are a speaker of Standard American English, you speak English with an "acceptable" accent. Can you recall conversations with others whose dialect and accent did not match yours? In those conversations, did you make negative assessments of their character, intelligence, or goodwill? Such a response is fairly common. Negative judgments that are made of others simply on the basis of how they speak will obviously prove to be a formidable barrier to competence in intercultural communication. For example, an Iranian-American woman describes the frustration and anger experienced by her father, who is a physician, and her mother, who is a nurse, when they attempted to communicate with others by telephone. Though both of her parents had immigrated to the United States many years before, they spoke English with a heavy accent. These educated people were consistently responded to as if they lacked intelligence simply because of their accent. Out of sheer frustration they usually had their daughter, who spoke English with a U.S. accent, conduct whatever business needed to be accomplished on the telephone.

Jargon and Argot

Both jargon and argot are specialized forms of vocabulary. *Jargon* refers to a set of words or terms that are shared by those with a common profession or experience. For example, students at a particular college or university share a jargon related to general education requirements, registration techniques, add or drop procedures, activity fees, and the like. Members of a particular profession depend on a unique set of meanings for words that are understood only by members of that profession. The shorthand code used by law-enforcement officers, lawyers, those in the medical profession, and even by professors at colleges and universities are all instances of jargon.

Argot refers to a specialized language that is used by a large group within a culture to define the boundaries of their group from others who are in a more powerful position in the society. As you might expect, argot is an important feature in the study of intercultural communication. Unlike jargon, argot is typically used to keep those who are not part of the group from understanding what members say to one another. The specialized language is used to keep those from the outside, usually seen as hostile, at bay.

Verbal Codes and Intercultural Competence

The link between one's knowledge of other verbal codes and intercultural competence is obvious. To speak another language proficiently requires an enormous amount of effort, energy, and time. The opportunity, then, to study another language in your college curriculum is a choice we highly recommend to prepare you for the multicultural and multilingual world of the twenty-first century. Those world citizens with facility in a second or third language will be needed in every facet of society.

Many English speakers have a false sense of security because English is studied and spoken by so many people around the world. There is an arrogance in this position that should be obvious because it places all of the responsibility for learning another language on the non-English speaker. Furthermore, even if two people from different cultures are using the verbal code system of one of the interactants, significant influences on their communication arise from their initial language.

Despite our strong recommendation that you learn and be tolerant of other languages, it is virtually impossible for anyone to be proficient in all of the verbal codes that might be encountered in intercultural communication. The multicultural nature of the United States and the interdependence of world cultures means that multiple cultures and multiple languages will be a standard feature of people's lives. Simply admonishing you to learn all languages is not a feasible suggestion. However, there are important ways to improve competence in adjusting to differences in verbal codes when communicating interculturally.

First, the study of at least one other language is extraordinarily useful in understanding the role that differences in verbal codes can play in intercultural communication. Genuine fluency in a second language demonstrates experientially all of the ways in which language embodies another culture. It also reveals the ways in which languages vary and how the nuances of language use influence the meanings of symbols. The study of another language, even if you never become genuinely proficient in it, teaches much about the culture of those who use it and the categories of experience the language can create. Furthermore, such study demonstrates, better than words written on a page or spoken in a lecture, the difficulty in gaining proficiency in another language and may lead to an appreciation of those who are struggling to communicate in second or third languages.

Short of becoming proficient in another language, learning about its grammatical features can help you understand the messages of the other person. Study the connections between the features of a verbal code and the cultural patterns of those who use it. Even if you are going to communicate with people from another culture in your own first language, there is much that you can learn about the other person's language and the corresponding cultural patterns that can help you to behave appropriately and effectively.

Knowledge of another language is one component of the link between competence and verbal codes. Motivation, in the form of your emotional reactions and your intentions toward the culturally different others with whom you are communicating, becomes another critical component. Trying to get along in another language can be an exhilarating and very positive experience, but it can also be fatiguing and frustrating. The attempt to speak and understand a new verbal code requires energy and perseverance. Most second language learners, when immersed in its cultural setting, report a substantial toll on their energy.

Functioning in a culture that speaks a language different from your own can be equally tiring and exasperating. Making yourself understood, getting around, obtaining food, and making purchases can all require a great deal of effort. A recognition of the possibility of irritability and fatigue when functioning in an unfamiliar linguistic environment is an important prerequisite to intercultural competence. Without such knowledge, the communicator may well blame his or her personal feelings of discomfort on the cultures that are being experienced.

The other side of the motivation dimension concerns your reactions to those who are attempting to speak your language. In the United States, for example, those who speak English often lack sympathy for and patience with those who do not. If English is your first language, notice those learning it and provide whatever help you can. Respond patiently. If you do not understand, ask questions and clarify. Try making your verbal point in alternative ways by using different sets of words with approximately equivalent meanings. Speak slowly, but do not yell. Lack of skill in a new language is not caused by a hearing impairment. Be aware of the jargon in your speech and provide a definition of it. Above all, to the best of your ability, withhold judgments and negative evaluations; instead, show respect for the enormous difficulties associated with learning a new language.

An additional emotional factor to monitor in promoting intercultural competence is your reaction to the nonstandard versions of a language. The negative evaluations that nonstandard speech often triggers are a serious impediment to competence.

Competence in intercultural communication can be assisted by behaviors that indicate interest in the other person's verbal code. Even if you have never studied the language of those with whom you regularly interact, do attempt to learn and use appropriate words and phrases. Get a phrase book and a dictionary to learn standard comments or queries. Learn how to greet people and to acknowledge thanks. At the same time, recognize your own limitations and depend on a skilled interpreter when needed.

Intercultural competence requires knowledge, motivation, and actions that recognize the critical role verbal codes play in human interaction. Although learning another language is a very important goal, it is inevitably that you will also need to communicate with others with whom you do not share a common verbal code.

Notes

1. From *Intercultural Competence: Interpersonal Communication Across Cultures*, Myron W. Lustig and Jolene Loester, NY: Harper Collins, 1993.
2. Myron W. Lustig is a professor of communication at San Diego State University. He writes actively in the areas of intercultural and interpersonal communication. He likes talking with people, working with data, and eating Thai food.
3. Jolene Koester is provost and vice president for academic affairs as well as professor of communication studies at California State University, Sacramento. Despite her primarily administrative responsibilities, she is deeply committed to the importance of teaching and researching intercultural communication issues.
4. Ludwig Wittgenstein is an Austrian philosopher (1889 – 1951), whose two chief

works, *Tractatus Logico-Philosophicus* (1921) and *Philosophical Investigations* (published posthumously in 1953), have profoundly influenced the course of much recent British and US philosophy. The former dwells on the logical nature and limits of language, while the latter relates the meanings of sentences to their uses in particular contexts. Wittgenstein used to be a professor of philosophy at Cambridge University, England from 1929 to 1947.

5. Sapir-Whorf hypothesis of linguistic relativity: Edward Sapir (1884 – 1939) is an American anthropologist, poet and linguist whose most important work was on the relation between language and culture. He suggested that one's perception of the world is dominated by the language with which one articulates.

   Benjamin Lee Whorf (1897 – 1941) is also an American linguist and student of Sapir. He is best known for proposing the theory that a language's structure determines the thought processes of its speakers.

   Sapir-Whorf hypothesis is a theory of the relationship between language and thought, which asserts that language determines the way people perceive and organize their worlds.

6. Charles F. Hockett is considered as a star of Bloomfieldian linguistics. He was also well known for his *Manual of Phonology* and a textbook, *A Course in Modern Linguistics* (1955). He later became well known as an opponent to Chomsky's work, and published a monograph *Language, Mathematics, and Linguistics* with Mouton to show his own point of view on the application of mathematics. Eventually, in the later years of his life, he was tired of doing linguistics and became a composer of music. Hockett, a native of Ohio, spent his career at Cornell after receiving a Yale PhD, and died in Ithaca on November 3, 2000. He was a past president of the Linguistic Society of America.

7. Hmong are people from rural mountain areas in Laos. They are divided into clans or tribes that share the same paternal ancestry. Each clan has a leader who oversees all relations and a shaman (wise man/medicine man) who deals with spiritual and physical problems. Hmong education is oral, which leads many Americans to mislabel them as illiterate.

   The Hmong people have experienced an enormous cultural change in their move to the United States. No longer can they have the fresh variety of food available in their homeland. Because they were orally educated, a trip to the grocery store is quite difficult. The pictures on labels, for example, do not necessarily reflect the contents of the package and are often misleading.

8. Winston Churchill, also called Sir Winston Spencer Leonard (1874 – 1965), is one of the greatest modern British statesman, as a war leader of the architect of victory in WWII. During the Second World War, he was the lord of the admiralty from 1936 to 1940 and became one of the greatest-ever war leaders. His oratory maintained Britain's morale and he was one of the main shapers of Allied strategy. Churchill

was prime minister from 1940 to 1945 and then again from 1951 to 1955. He remained a nationally loved and revered figure for the rest of his life.
9. Tagalog: an official language of the Philippines（他加禄语）

Questions for Discussion

1. How do you comprehend the power of language in intercultural communication? Please use personal experience or anecdotes to illustrate your comprehension.
2. Can you briefly describe the features of language and explain how verbal codes affect communication between people of different cultural backgrounds?
3. How do you clarify the relationship among language, thought and culture? What stance do you take with regard to the Sapir-Whorf hypothesis? Please illustrate your viewpoints with examples.
4. How do you account for the impact of language variations on ethnic group identity and social or political dominance?
5. In which ways will your knowledge of verbal communication facilitate your future interactions with peoples from both the English-speaking countries and those countries associated with the "Belt and Road" Initiative?

Online Mini-Case Studies and Viewpoints-Sharing

A Letter of Complaint

Dear Mr. Lawson:

I wish to inform you that I was very unhappy during my last stay at your establishment for several reasons.

The lifts were not functioning properly, so I was forced to use the stairs. On the staircase, one of your charwomen refused to let me pass and insulted me. I was so distressed by this that I felt a bit ill so I went back to your main lobby only to find the hotel chemist's shop closed.

Thinking it best at this point to relax, I decided to have dinner at the hotel restaurant. However, even there the service was poor. I ordered an underdone undercut with French beans but received a nearly burnt joint with sautéed auberge.

When I returned to my room I attempted to make a trunk call home unsuccessfully. Finally, I called the front desk to ask them to knock me up in the morning and your clerk responded with a rude remark.

I have already shared my views on this with my booking clerk, but I felt that it would only be proper to share my views with you as well.

Sincerely,
Francine Faquhar

Online Research

Find out those terms of Mr. Farquhar, a British traveler, to Mr. Lawson, an American hotel manager, which may cause difficulty in understanding and check online for the meanings or those words and the reasons for the misunderstanding.

Reading Two

Introductory Remarks

To make progress in our study, gain achievements in our career, and succeed in our social lives, we have to pay sufficient attention to the relationships in face-to-face communication with people around us. How shall we greet different people on different occasions? What kind of styles shall we present in various relationships? How can we listen properly in our daily communication with others? What topics shall we talk about and how should we develop them appropriately in accordance with the contexts? The answers to these questions may greatly assist us in our daily face-to-face communication.

    The selection below is an extended and detailed discussion of the ways to express and create appropriate relationships in various face-to-face management communication contexts. After the introduction, the author shows that relationships are signaled by address terms, which differ according to the person and situation, and vary across cultures. Then the author discusses how stylistic features express different relationships. Formal styles convey authority but distance the speaker from the other people. Informal styles form and create closer relationships but convey relaxed authority and confidence. The author also deals with topics and the ways to develop them appropriately by controlling the topics tightly or loosely, arguing the point rationally and logically, reasoning with narration and using proverbs cautiously. Finally, the author suggests listening skills which may make communicators not only capable of encoding and sending appropriate messages but also able to decode and receive messages efficiently.

Relationships in Face-to-Face Communication[1]

Richard Mead

SECTION 1: INTRODUCTION

An Israeli engineer was invited to speak at a seminar in South Africa. All seats in the seminar hall had microphones controlled by a technician in a corner box. The speaker's microphone had yellow lights that flashed ten minutes before he or she was due to finish, and red lights four minutes before. Then at the precise moment the microphone was cut off, whether or not the speaker had finished. In practice, all speakers made a point of finishing in time.

    But in one session, the Israeli wished to continue in order to lead a group discussion of the issues. He was told that this was not possible; although the schedule showed a free hour following this session, the schedule had been set and could not be changed.

The Israeli felt frustrated by his failure to establish a less formal relationship with his audience. He explained:

> 'They're extremely disciplined and hierarchical. That wouldn't work in Israel, we would refuse to stop talking.'
> (What wouldn't work?)
> 'Having a guy in the corner cutting you off, a subordinate.'
> (But if the culture is so hierarchical, why do senior people allow a subordinate to cut them off?)
> 'Because he's not making the rules, he's only enforcing them. Everyone respects the discipline, and they're disciplined throughout society. This would never work in Israel. We're very democratic.'

This shows a problem in trying to communicate in one sort of relationship when social norms enforce a different sort of interaction. In this chapter, we deal with the problems of expressing management relationships across cultures. In a culture where management relationships are generally formal, trying to create less formal relationships may be counter-productive. Similarly, if you come from a formal management culture, you may need to adapt to a less formal mode when working in a normally informal culture.

We focus here on spoken communication at the micro level, and examine the expression of one-to-one relationships as a means of exerting influence. The speaker is more likely to be persuasive when he or she chooses a style that expresses the relationship with the other person appropriately.

SECTION 2: HOW ADDRESS TERMS SIGNAL THE RELATIONSHIP

More or less formal relationships are signaled by how people address each other. Here we deal with:

- address terms (e.g. first name, family name, title);
- pronoun systems (e.g. 'you', 'vous' or 'tu' in French).

Why are address terms and pronoun systems important? They reflect your relationship with the other person and help to create it. If you cease addressing your business acquaintance as Mr. Smith and start calling him John, you signal a closer relationship which implies a different level of trust. Across cultures this switch may be more or less welcomed for different reasons.

In Anglo cultures, all the alternatives below are (or in recent history, have been) appropriate in different relationships. Those at the top of the list tend to imply more formal relationships, and so in most situations are more formal, and those at the bottom imply closer relationships and so are less formal. However, use differs in different cultures and sub-cultures, and so a precise ordering is not possible.

> [without a name] Sir/Master/Madam (not in the US)/Ma'am/Miss/
> Missus/(in the UK, working-class connotations) Mister/Miz
> Mr. John Smith/Mrs. John Smith/Mrs. Ann Smith/Ms. Ann Smith/Miss
> Ann Smith/Messrs Smith (for plural of Mr; in written text only)
> Mr. Smith/Mrs. Smith/Ms. Smith/Miss Smith
> John Smith/Ann Smith
> Smith
> John /Ann
> Mr. John/Mrs. Ann/Ms. Ann/Mz. Ann
> man/woman/lady/boy (often derogatory in the US) girl/[plural forms]
> [nicknames] Jacko/Dimpy/etc.
> [terms of endearment] Love/Honey/etc.
> [family titles] Daddy/Mummy/etc.

Even in the individualist and narrow power distance Anglo cultures, the subordinate generally uses a more formal address term when speaking up to his superior than the superior uses down. For instance, at work the janitor addresses the manager as 'Mr Smith' and the manager responds with 'Charley'.

Address Terms Across Cultures
The cross-cultural manager cannot assume that his or her own address system is appropriate in the other culture. Some Anglo cultures pride themselves on their openness and equality in forming business relationships. The American or Australian manager may use first-name terms when meeting with a negotiating partner for the first time ('Just call me John'). But when the other culture does not share this trusting and optimistic view of human nature, approaching too

quickly has an effect opposite to that described. Instead of creating closeness it generates unease and suspicion.

An American manager working in his firm's British subsidiary asked to be transferred back home. When asked why, he explained that he found his British colleagues too 'reserved.' On his first day he had made clear that he expected to be called Chuck, but after six months they still insisted on referring to him by his family name or given name, Charles. The more he tried to break through their reserve the more they seemed to resent it and keep an emotional distance, and he could not be confident of his working relationships with them.

He had adopted a wrong strategy. His attempts to break down barriers too quickly had merely fortified them. If you are working in a cultural context more formal than your own, continue to use the formal term of address until it is clear that first names are now appropriate. Conversely, if you have come to a less formal culture, you can expect your colleagues to quickly adopt first name or nickname terms. If you resist this informality, you appear to be cold and untrusting.

Second, the cross-cultural manager cannot assume that the equivalent address term is appropriate in the other culture, even where power distances are equivalent. For instance, a Thai manager may have a title and full name of Khun Paron Kesboonchoo. ('Khun' is used with both men and women and so is equivalent to all of Mr., Mrs., Miss, Ms. Paron is a male name, and so here Khun can be translated as Mr.). But he is known generally as Khun Paron.

The Anglo manager, who expects to be called Mr Smith or John and never Mr John, may find this odd. But no Thai would refer to his colleague as Khun Kesboonchoo and only very close associates by his first name or nickname without the title Khun.

Third, the cross-cultural manager cannot assume that a form not used in his or her home management culture is meaningless in the other culture. Anglos do not normally use family titles in the workplace, but in India the family titles 'uncle' or 'aunty' may be used to denote a client relationship with a patron who is not a member of the immediate family. The young executive who announces that he is going to make a complaint to 'uncle,' who happens to be the CEO, is demonstrating both his status within a patronage network and his informal power in relation to third parties who do not belong to the network.

A young Indian may be brought up to use these terms for all friends of the parents. However, precise titles are used to denote family relationships. One Indian executive commented: 'When I first came to the United States, I was amazed how Americans call even their distant cousins uncle and aunt.'

Formality and Situation

How we address each other also depends on the situation. In different situations we use different terms to address the same person.

In the Anglo cultures, address terms can vary widely between the same two persons, in different situations. For instance, in the workplace the manager and janitor choose terms that signal their power difference. The manager addresses 'John' and the janitor replies to 'Mr. Brown'. But suppose that they belong to the same social club or worship at the same church; in that context, where they enjoy equal status, they are more likely to use a less formal differential: 'John' and 'David'. This reflects the fact that, in these cultures, status and power earned within the workplace does not apply outside (compared, for instance, with France).

A reasonably open Anglo company might accept a secretarial assistant greeting a boss by the first name and introducing the topic of conversation—perhaps even a non-work related topic. But in a culture where power differences are much greater, the junior might never start a casual conversation. The following is far more likely to occur in a Western office on a Monday morning:

> Assistant: 'Hi Jess, how was the golf?'
> Boss: 'Awful.'

But even in the West, would a secretarial assistant greet the CEO so casually? A new boss? The head of state? At what point would he or she substitute 'Good morning, Sir?' And how would the choice of greeting be affected by the presence of other people?

In the Anglo office, the manager and assistant of opposite sexes sometimes use pet names which are otherwise associated with an intimate relationship. But even when it occurs this use does not extend to outsiders. An American secretary writes to a syndicated agony column:

> 'Currently, I work in a professional office where clients, whom I call Mr., Mrs., Sir, Ma'am, or by their names, occasionally call me "Honey"—but only once. They are told, either by me or by my superior, that I will not tolerate such familiarity. They may be annoyed momentarily, but they never have to be told twice, and I usually get an

apology.

Pet names belong only between the closest friends and family, Please tell all those people who claim it's "just a habit," and have conned themselves into thinking it's cute or more informal, that it is nothing of the kind. It's extremely presumptuous and offensive, and they should not be surprised when someone is annoyed by it.'

The Anglo cultures are this flexible in their use of address terms because different areas of activity tend to be treated as distinct, and superiority in one area probably does not translate into another. In cultures where authority in the work place does apply in non-work activities, the address differential is more likely maintained.

The cross-cultural manager working in an Anglo culture learns to adjust to its address norms, but this does not mean that he wishes to continue them when back home.

Hiroki Kato explains that a Japanese businessman who has learned American ways may ask his American colleague to call him by his first name or nickname when in the United States. But it makes him acutely uncomfortable if you use the same form of address in Japan, particularly when he is surrounded by colleagues:

'The usual expectation of the Japanese is that everyone calls everyone else by their last name plus "-san", "-sensi", or by their title (e.g. Kacho, "section chief").

It made an interesting news item in Japan when then Prime Minister Nakasone reportedly mentioned that he dealt with President Reagan on a firstname basis and termed the two men's relationship as the "Ron-Yasu Relationship" (The Prime Minister's first name is Yasuhiro.). The fact remains, however, that no one, including his cabinet ministers, ever called him by his first name in Japan.'

In Japan, rules of status apply even to relationships between business partners. Buyers are assumed to have greater importance than sellers, and a seller says 'onsha' (your great company) whereas the buyer replies 'otaku' (your company).

Pronoun Systems

Modern English uses second person 'you' to denote both singular and plural, and it is neutral as regards the relationship between speaker and addressee. (A possible exception may be the Southern United States form 'you all' abbreviated to 'y' all', which can be used with either singular or plural audience and indicates the speaker's solidarity.)

In other languages, the selection of second person pronoun serves the same function as the address term. Where the language offers two alternatives, the plural form may be used to address one person. Whether you use singular or plural form is determined by the receiver's sex, age, superiority/ inferiority to yourself, and the closeness or distance of the relationship. In French, the singular form 'tu' is intimate, and when addressing even one person with whom you are not on intimate terms, use the polite form, plural 'vous'. Equivalents in Spanish are 'usted' and 'tu', and in German 'sie' and 'du'.

Many oriental languages have even more complex systems. Japanese has fourteen synonyms for 'you', and the appropriate choice depends on the other person's sex, age, occupation, and social and professional status.

SECTION 3: EXPRESSING THE RELATIONSHIP

The new British manager of a Brazilian subsidiary arranged a first meeting with his senior staff. He discussed aims, congratulated them on their work, and then said that he could already see the evidence of their determination to further improve productivity by the stack of reports on his desk. 'It seems you want me to take all the decisions around here. If this goes on I can see that I'm not going to see much of my family at weekends.' His audience laughed politely. The meeting broke up in a mood of good humor.

Two weeks later, the mood had changed. He complained bitterly that still too many minor decisions were coming to him. He had hoped by now to see some signs that routine problems were being resolved at lower levels. Why had nothing been done to prioritize decision-making processes?

The local managers were aghast. If this was what he had wanted why had he not made it clear? Of course the issue had been raised before, but in the form of a joke. Because it was accompanied by humor and a reference to his family needs, they had not taken it seriously. His style in making an important announcement had been inappropriate.

This section looks at the problem of style in spoken communication, and how it is expressed.

A formal style creates a sense of power and authority, but at the same time it marks the speaker as more committed to the topic than to the relationship, and creates emotional distance between him or her and the hearer. An informal and casual style down-plays authority and distances the speaker from the topic, but has the effect of making a closer relationship. The example above showed an important message misinterpreted because it came in the form of a joke.

Which style you use depends on
- who you are addressing;
- how you wish the other person to react;
- the cultural context—in this context, what style is most appropriate?

Style and Relationship

You create a closer relationship with the other person by using expressions of concern and admiration, a similarity in experience and needs, sympathy and understanding, and common views.

Assume that in a neutral situation in an Anglo culture, your boss asks about your weekend golf, then goes on to joke about his own poor performance. You interpret this choice of a non-task related topic and his self-disclosure and humor as an expression of personal interest and perhaps a willingness to create a closer relationship.

The subordinate does not expect to be called to his boss's office (which is a relatively formal and non-neutral situation) in order to talk only about golf, although this topic may serve to reduce the distance between them before moving on to the main topic.

The superior generally has greater freedom in deciding what topic is appropriate. In the office, a business-related topic conveys an impression of authority, reflects his or her power, and shows that the speaker has a clear objective in communicating. A change in the relationship towards a closer tie generally has to be initiated by the higher status person.

Style varies according to the situation. The manager adopts a more formal and distant style when addressing the same colleague in the board meeting than on the golf course, perhaps when communicating the same information. Whether or not other people are present may also affect style.

This means that if you wish to modify your relationship with a subordinate by changing the communicative style, make sure the style is appropriate to the situation.

Expressing Power by Direct and Indirect Requests

A powerful style reflects and helps assert wide power distances when the speaker is perceived to have the authority to enforce his or her will in this particular situation. A powerful style is direct, as in this example:

(a) Supervisor: 'Please complete this project by Friday.'
   Employee: 'Sure.'

In a flatter, more 'democratic' organization, the supervisor may feel it necessary to explain why the directive is justified, and a more indirect style is appropriate:

(b) Supervisor: 'Working on anything interesting now?'
   Employee: 'Not really.'
   Supervisor: 'Would you like to take on a project for me then?'
   Employee: 'Sure.'

In (a) the supervisor is much more committed to the project than in (b), and hence much more likely to lose face if the employee refuses the job. If the organization is hierarchical, the employee is far less likely to refuse it, and perhaps can do so only at risk to his job. In (b) the employee can refuse and the supervisor does not lose face. Now consider:

(c) Supervisor: 'Working on anything interesting now?'
   Employee: 'Yep, they sure keep us busy.'
   Supervisor: 'That's good, we like to keep you challenged.'

The direct style is as inappropriate in the democratic situation as the indirect style is in the hierarchical style. The imperative leaves the 'democratic' employee feeling bruised: 'Why can't he ask me politely?' The indirect form leaves the 'hierarchical' employee with the feeling that the supervisor is weak and indecisive: 'If he wants me to do a job, why can't he come out and say it?'

In an Anglo culture where organizations are flatter, giving a reason for a request seems more likely to win compliance. For example, when interrupting a colleague at the photocopier, the first request below stands a better chance of success: ①'Excuse me, I have five pages. May I use the machine because I'm in a rush?' ②'Excuse me, I have five pages. May I use the machine?'

The clauses 'Excuse me, I have five pages' and 'because I'm in a rush' frame the core request 'May I use the machine?'. In different situations and cultural contexts framing is more or less needed to signal politeness and avoid sounding peremptory.

In a wide power distance context, the relative statuses of the sender and receiver play the major part in determining whether a request is successful. This means that the superior may need to use little or no framing, and excessive framing sounds apologetic and cause him to appear weak or insincere. The subordinate uses more convincing frames, or risks being perceived as impertinent.

Expressing Distance and Closeness

The first in each pair of adjectives below expresses a more distant relationship but also carries greater credibility and effectiveness. The second in each pair expresses a more casual style and reflects a closer relationship:

(a) non-abbreviated/abbreviated style;
(b) self-monitored/casual style;
(c) elaborated/simple grammar.

These are dealt with below.

(a) Non-Abbreviated/Abbreviated Style

In a formal relationship, where sender and receiver are separated by power distances and/or a distant personal relationship, the speaker uses more complete forms, even when shared understanding of the context makes the full form redundant. Assume that the assistant is on his first day at work for a much older manager:

'cannot', 'rep' for 'reputation' all reflect informal contexts.

(b) Self-Monitored/Casual Style

The speaker conveys authority when he or she seems to be choosing the words with care. The speaker monitors the message and speaks clearly. Immediacy also conveys power, and is expressed by personal reference to what he or she wants done. Personal reference is more effective when it appears earlier rather than later in the message. Probability ('X will happen') is more powerful than possibility ('X may happen').

A casual style indicates a closer relationship with the receiver but may also signal less control over the content. Extreme forms may suggest the speaker's uncertainty and even powerlessness. These features typify a casual style and are generally not appropriate in formal situations:

   (a) slurring and running words into each other, and a lack of pausing;
   (b) overuse of intensifiers 'very', 'totally', etc. ;
   (c) empty modifiers—'kinda/kind of', 'sorta/sort of', etc. ;
   (d) empty adjectives—'cute', 'super'.

Anglos, in particular Americans, favor hyperbolic forms to give emphasis: 'I love those people', 'I hate it', 'I'm going to kill Bruce'. But these forms can lead to considerable confusion if used with Orientals not used to this style. Most Oriental cultures avoid these hyperbolic extremes in casual conversation and these forms may be taken literally.

(c) Elaborated/Simple Grammar

In English, hyper-correct grammar conveys authority within a formal context, but in an informal context it sounds inappropriate, and fails to exert the power that the speaker obviously wants. Hyper-correct forms include:

   (a) super-polite forms—'Would you be so kind as to close the window please?';
   (b) grammatical forms suited to written rather than spoken modes—'... to whom I wrote' as opposed to '... whom I wrote to', or even the strictly inaccurate '... who I wrote to';
   (c) elaborated verbal forms—'I would have gone if I had been able' as opposed to 'I would have gone if I could'.

The use of elaborated verbal forms offers the competent speaker a wide range of varieties in expression, and it typifies educated English. This style is sometimes difficult to handle. But although English modal forms ('can', 'might', etc.) tend to be more complex than in some Asian languages, for instance, where even future and past time markers are not always compulsory, they are considerably less complex than in Portuguese and Spanish. These languages have a far wider range of subjective expressions (expressing wishes, hopes, uncertainties, under different conditions), which are regularly used even in informal contexts.

Style and Culture
Stylistic differences are often associated with cultural groups, and groups tend to stereotype each in terms of their spoken style. Many Americans perceive British spoken style as over-formal, whereas the British may think American speech over-casual and think this reflects their behavior.

New Yorkers are perceived to be 'pushy' because they produce utterances which overlap with utterances produced by the other speaker and do not appear to wait to hear what is being said. For instance:

> George: 'John changed his schedule again and I thought that explains a lot about him.'
> Bill: 'What, that he works different from the others or thinks he's smarter or more important, or something?'
> George: 'It's not smarter or more important, it's different priorities.'

Bill interrupts George, and is interrupted in turn.

Overlapping shows that you are listening. But members of cultures educated to think that only one person should speak at a time find this difficult to handle. Tannen comments on data of interactions produced by speakers who overlapped their utterances and speakers who did not:

> ... when an overlap-avoiding speaker began to speak to show listenership, an overlap-avoiding speaker interpreted this as an interruption and stopped talking. The irony is that from the point of view of the culturally different speakers, each one thought the other created the interruption: the overlap-avoiding speaker thought the overlapper intended to interrupt, but the cooperative overlapper cannot understand why the speaker

interrupted himself by stopping.

Similarly, many Asians perceive Anglos to be aggressive because they ask too many questions in a machine-gun style. And Anglos think that the Indian's laughter when a potentially embarrassing subject is broached indicates lack of seriousness.

These stereotypes of style are particularly damaging because they are usually formed unconsciously and so are difficult to recognize and uproot. The cross-cultural manager needs to recognize when the speaker's stylistic choices reflect cultural priorities rather than decisions about the relationship.

In general, the cross-cultural manager should use the more formal or distant address form and style. Only switch to a less formal and less distant style with peers when the other person indicates that this is acceptable. Switching prematurely may be interpreted as presumptuous and 'pushy'.

SECTION 4: HOW THE TOPIC IS DEVELOPED

How you develop your point of view significantly reflects your perceptions of your relationship with the other person and modifies that relationship. We deal with topic development here in terms of:
- tight/loose development;
- argument/narrative.

Tight/Loose Development

How a speaker develops a topic is clearest in a monologue presentation. The presentation speaker creates a sense of authority and control by moving through the topic point by point, making clear that it has been planned and signposted at each stage ('That's all I have to say about X; I now want to move on to Y.') The speaker who slides between points and gives the impression of developing the ideas as he or she goes along conveys less authority, but may create a sense of informal closeness.

The same applies in face-to-face interaction. If an agenda is prepared for a meeting, this shows that it is expected to be more formal. When the chairperson uses the agenda items to impose structure on the interactions, he or she gives the meeting a sense of direction and formality, but at the expense of inhibiting unstructured brainstorming.

In an informal meeting, the development of ideas is looser and the style more casual. The direction is less obviously planned. The participants brainstorm with little concern for tight cohesion. They shift between different topics and make frequent side sequences, departing from the primary topic to a secondary topic, then back to the primary topic. For instance:

> Manager: 'Have Registration said anything about the income file yet?'
> Assistant: 'Yes, Jonah phoned after lunch. By the way, they need another programmer.'
> Manager: 'Again? I'll see who we've got.'
> Assistant: 'Yes, the new one has to relocate. Anyhow, they want some clarification on the resale figures ... '

In this example, the move out to the side sequence is marked by 'By the way... ', which suggests a lack of formal planning, and the move back by 'Anyhow ... '

Side sequences also occur in monologues. The presentation speaker uses them in order to introduce a relaxed mood and to 'soft-sell' an idea. But too many side-sequences risk confusing of frustrating the receiver who wants direction in the interaction.

In a cross-cultural context, the manager should be careful of shifting topics and using side sequences. When members of the other culture use the language only as a second language, non-linear topic development can be very confusing, even when topic shifts and side sequences are heavily marked.

Arguing the Point

Efficient planning, control, and decision making depends upon rational thinking directed to mapping out the future. Until recently it was generally accepted that this thinking process is best communicated by a rational, logical argument.

A logical argument makes a claim, that such-and-such is true or ought to be done. This claim is expressed by a 'therefore' statement. In order to justify this 'therefore,' the argument also presents a 'given' statement, which provides factual support, and a 'since' statement, which explains the relationship between the 'given' and the 'therefore.' Here are two examples.

GIVEN:	SINCE:	THEREFORE:
By innovating, our competitors have increased their market share.	This demonstrates the value of innovating.	We should also innovate.

The 'since' statement here justifies the relationship between 'given' and 'therefore' by emphasizing the general value of the 'given.'

GIVEN:	SINCE:	THEREFORE:
Advertising rates have increased by 10 percent.	Higher rates increase our sales costs.	We should increase prices.

The 'since' statement here shows the cause and effect relationship between the 'given' and 'therefore'.

This form of verbal logic can become complicated, using other types of 'sinces' including 'unless' statements, and replicated throughout the argument. Similar relationships between 'givens', 'sinces,' and 'therefores' are then created between sub-topics and topics.

A logical argument provides clear and persuasive justification for adopting a particular interpretation or policy. It reflects Western intellectual traditions of precise, scientific detachment, and appeals to an abstract sense of reason existing outside the relationship between the speaker and hearer. Thus it has the effect of establishing the distance between them. It is potentially divisive; the speaker is concerned with winning an argument, and this implies a possibility of conflict. However logical the argument presented, therefore, it is not persuasive when the hearer places a priority on a close relationship.

The Western cross-cultural manager cannot depend over-much on this form of logic when working in a culture where decision-making processes are based more on intuition and emotion as in Japan and the Republic Korea, and where members of the group are searching for consensus that unites them in a relationship rather than around an abstract idea, and so minimizes personal conflict.

Contrarily, the non-Western cross-cultural manager working in a Western scientific culture is liable to experience problems in adjusting away from his or her usual techniques of controlling and persuading. Appeals to emotion may not only fail, but create a resistance which damages relationships in the future.

Narration as a Form of Argument

A Canadian company was considering erecting a late-night entertainment center in a middle-class suburb. When plans were discussed in a board meeting, a fierce dispute broke out over whether much resistance could be expected from local residents. Figures produced by a marketing analyst could be interpreted ambiguously. Eventually an American board member described the history of the Chicago Clubs' move to introduce late play to the Wrigley Field ball-park and the unexpected opposition.

This use of narration rescued the argument from the logical *cul de sac* where it was stuck. The analogy did not fit precisely, as supporters of the scheme pointed out; but it threw the whole problem into a different light, the sense of nose-to-nose conflict lifted, and the board reached a decision.

Using narration as a means of argument includes using analogy and metaphor. It means reinterpreting basic human characteristics and appeals to a common sense of values and social coherence. It provides guidelines for action when insufficient data are available and logical argument is inadequate.

Narrative and analogous argument is a traditional form of reasoning, and the cross-cultural manager experiences it in societies where oral traditions are still strong. Analogous and non-logical reasoning is also a powerful tool in Western organizations, and new thinking on management communication indicates that its importance as a primary means of creating organizational coherence should be more widely recognized. Weick and Browning writes:

> The implied advice for managers who try to solve problems is that, when they try to be rational, they may overemphasize logic and forget that there are multiple logics and multiple rationalities and that stories incorporate much of what argument leaves out. If the manager can argue logically with facts and then cover the same points using stories that ring true and hold together, then he or she has understood the issue more thoroughly.

The cross-cultural manager similarly uses both analogous and logical arguments, balancing them to appeal most effectively to the other-culture receivers.

Proverbs

Among educated people in Anglo cultures, it is seldom considered sophisticated to use proverbs and maxims; no British business person says 'A stitch in time saves nine' in order to explain a renovation policy, for instance. In general, the cross-cultural manager working in an Anglo culture should avoid them. But in Oriental cultures, proverbs are quoted frequently. The Westerner can use those from his or her own culture (but be prepared to explain them), and better yet, show your empathy by citing proverbs from the host culture. For instance:

- from Burma, 'A man can practice virtue only when his stomach is full' —which seems to support Maslow's hierarchy of needs[2].
- from Thailand, 'Aim at a definite end' —the value of management by objectives.
- from Vietnam, 'Force binds for a time; education binds forever' — applicable to McGregor's theory X and theory Y[3].
- from the Philippines, 'The prompt man beats the industrious one.'

SECTION 5: LISTENING

This section deals with communication at the micro level of style. The features discussed operate very subtly to express power and solidarity relationships, and degrees of formality and informality. They reflect cultural perceptions about social status and responsibility.

A member of the other culture does not share your perceptions and so does not respond in the same way as do members of your culture to the stylistic features that you use. And he or she does not produce the same stylistic features with the same meanings in the same contexts. These differences create difficulties in cross-cultural communication. The cross-cultural manager needs to cultivate communication skills at a more sophisticated level than might be necessary when interacting within his or her own culture.

An effective communicator encodes and sends appropriate messages that are persuasive to the receiver. He or she *also* has to be efficient in decoding and receiving messages; if you cannot decode efficiently, you cannot give good feedback. In order to produce messages that the receiver can understand, the cross-cultural manager has to facilitate that person's listening; and in turn, to decode and understand messages coming back, he or she has to develop listening skills.

A good listener develops the following habits:
1. Adopt an inquiring attitude. The other person is telling you something he or she perceives to be of interest.
2. Evaluate the meaning of the words. Even when different cultures use the same first language, the same words have different meanings.
3. Evaluate the use of stylistic devices, including ambiguity.
4. Listen for what is *not* said; that is, for what the sender thinks is so

obvious as to be redundant or what is so new as to be outside his or her experience. This means processing the message in terms of the differences between your and the speaker's personal and cultural priorities.
5. Ask questions to check you understanding.
6. Give feedback based on the message and to check mutual understanding. If necessary, paraphrase the message in your feedback.
7. Do not jump to conclusions; listen for the whole message.
8. Give yourself time to think before replying. Make clear when you are adopting listening and speaking roles, and make the shift between roles clean-cut.

Remember that the other person has the same problems recognizing your cultural priorities and how they are expressed in the communication. Facilitate his or her listening so far as you can:

(a) Speak slowly and carefully when using your language. You cannot make a non-native speaker understand by shouting.

(b) So far as possible, avoid idioms, slang, metaphors, jargon.

(c) If necessary, explain complex words, but make clear that you are giving an explanation and not presenting an alternative message or adding a qualification.

(d) Use stylistic devices that are appropriate in the situational and cultural contexts (e.g. a declarative request rather than an imperative form); but keep them simple.

(e) Check that you are being understood as you go along.

(f) You may have to spell out the message and its purpose more clearly than you would with a member of your own culture, who could be expected to pick up the clues. So be prepared to explain not only WHAT you want done and WHAT you think important, but WHY you want it done and WHY it is important.

(g) Make clear those features in the context that demonstrate your purpose.

Bad listening was shown by the American manager of a British subsidiary. He had the habit of assessing the communications of his British subordinates on the basis of the first few words he heard and interrupting to answer within these terms. This meant that he often missed the important, new information that the speaker might have packaged at the end. His interruptions were perceived as aggressive and the faulty communication generated both resentment and expensive misunderstandings.

Listening is often assumed to be an automatic skill synonymous with hearing.

This is a false assumption. Developing effective listening skills is particularly important when you or the other receivers are using a second language.

At first, this communicative elaboration may not seem easy or natural. This is a small price to pay when measured against the costs in terms of human relations, management efficiency, and profits that may be incurred by a communications breakdown. As your relationship develops and each of you learns to recognize the other's personal and cultural priorities, you will know when to drop the elaboration.

Notes

1. From *International Management: Cross-Cultural Dimensions*, (2nd ed.), Richard Mead, Oxford: Blackwell Publishers, 1998.
2. Abraham Maslow (1908 – 1970) is an American psychologist. As a major figure in the humanistic school of psychology, he rejected behaviorism and psychoanalysis. He saw man as a creative being striving for self-actualization. His major books are *Motivation and Personality* (1954) and *Toward a Psychology of Being* (1960).

    Abraham Maslow is known for establishing the theory of a hierarchy of needs, writing that human beings are motivated by unsatisfied needs, and that certain lower needs need to be satisfied before higher needs can be satisfied. As long as we are motivated to satisfy these cravings, we are moving towards growth, toward self-actualization. Satisfying needs is healthy, and blocking gratification makes us sick or evil. The hierarchy of needs includes:

    1) Physiological needs

    Physiological needs are the very basic needs such as air, water, food, sleep, sex, etc. When these are not satisfied we may feel sickness, irritation, pain, discomfort, etc. These feelings motivate us to alleviate them as soon as possible to establish homeostasis. Once they are alleviated, we may think about other things.

    2) Safety needs

    Safety needs have to do with establishing stability and consistency in a chaotic world. These needs are mostly psychological in nature. We need the security of a home and family. Many in our society cry out for law and order because they do not feel safe enough to go for a walk in their neighborhood. In addition, safety needs sometimes motivate people to be religious. Religions comfort us with the promise of a safe secure place after we die and leave the insecurity of this world.

    3) Love needs

    Love and belongingness are next on the ladder. Humans have a desire to belong to groups: clubs, work groups, religious groups, family, gangs, etc. We need to feel loved (non-sexual) by others, to be accepted by others. Performers appreciate applause. We need to be needed.

4) Esteem needs

There are two types of esteem needs. First is self-esteem, which results from competence or mastery of a task. Second, there's the attention and recognition that comes from others. This is similar to the belongingness level, however, wanting admiration has to do with the need for power. People who have all of their lower needs satisfied, often drive very expensive cars because doing so raises their level of esteem.

5) Self-actualization

The need for self-actualization is "the desire to become more and more what one is, to become everything that one is capable of becoming." People who have everything can maximize their potential. They can seek knowledge, peace, esthetic experiences, self-fulfillment, etc. It is usually middle-class to upper-class students who take up environmental causes, join the Peace Corps, go off to a monastery, etc.

3. Douglas McGregor is an American social psychologist who proposed his famous X-Y theory in his 1960 book T*he Human Side Of Enterprise*. McGregor maintained that there are two fundamental approaches to managing people. Many managers tend towards Theory X, and generally get poor results. Enlightened managers use Theory Y, which produces better performance and results, and allows people to grow and develop. The two theories are as follows:

1) Theory X ('authoritarian management' style)

The average person dislikes work and will avoid it whenever he/she can. Therefore most people must be forced with the threat of punishment to work towards organizational objectives. The average person prefers to be directed; to avoid responsibility; is relatively not ambitious, and wants security above all else.

2) Theory Y ('participative management' style)

Effort in work is as natural as work and play. People will apply self-control and self-direction in the pursuit of organizational objectives, without external control or the threat of punishment. Commitment to objectives is a function of rewards associated with their achievement. People usually accept and often seek responsibility. The capacity to use a high degree of imagination, ingenuity and creativity in solving organizational problems is widely, not narrowly, distributed in the population. In industry the intellectual potential of the average person is only partly utilized.

Questions for Discussion

1. What is your comment on the changes of address terms in China? How would you introduce the appropriate Chinese ways of greeting to some foreigners who have newly arrived in China for study or work?
2. As discussed in the text, formal styles convey authority but distance the speaker

from the other people. Informal styles form and create closer relationships but familiarity makes contempt. How should one balance the two according to different contexts?
3. Describe both your successful and unsuccessful experiences in carrying out conversations or talks with foreigners. What are some of the helpful factors for developing the topic and what are some of the major obstacles?
4. As we are told in the text that we can use narration by way of analogy or metaphor as a means of argument to appeal to a common sense of values and social coherence and to provide guidelines for action when insufficient data are available and logical argument is inadequate. Can you illustrate this point?
5. For each of the following business situations, decide whether the local behavior is appropriate or inappropriate in terms of the Chinese and Anglo cultures, and supply reasons to back up your decision.
    1) On your first day, your boss (whom you have only met once before, at the airport on arrival) walks into your office unannounced, sits down, and asks how you and your family are settling in. You tell him everything is fine. You then suggest discussing your responsibilities. He looks surprised, says there is plenty of time for that, and leaves.
    2) At an office party, your immediate subordinate asks you detailed questions about how plans for a new project are progressing.
    3) Your boss calls you and your colleagues to a meeting where he explains his marketing strategy. This monologue is delivered in an authoritative and formal style. Twice you try to interrupt with comments. He looks pained and makes clear that you should keep quiet until he has finished.

Online Mini-Case Studies and Viewpoints-Sharing

Challenge of Intercultural E-mails

I met a girl from the Republic of Korea in my junior year of college, and we became good friends. When it came time for her to go back to her county we decided we would stay friends and become pen pals via e-mail. Nevertheless, I found it much more difficult to communicate with her via e-mail because she didn't always understand what I was writing and I couldn't repeat my sentence like I could if I were speaking to her, and the same applied to her. It definitely puts a strain on our relationship.

Online Research

Check online and find one successful and one unsuccessful cases of international friendship or romantic relationships. Then explore whether it is the culture factor or linguistic factor that accounts for either the success or failure.

Unit Five

Nonverbal Communication

Reading One

Introductory Remarks

Successful interaction in intercultural settings requires the understanding of not only verbal messages but also nonverbal messages. Nonverbal communication refers to all intentional and unintentional stimuli between communicating parties, other than spoken word. These nonverbal processes often account for as much as 70% of the communication. As the silent language of communication, nonverbal communication is culture-bound and ambiguous. Nonverbal code systems are less precise and systematized and less consciously used and interpreted than verbal code systems; however, they oftentimes exert greater effects on the results of our intercultural communication.

Nonverbal messages can be used to accent, complement, contradict, regulate, or substitute for the verbal message. The nonverbal code system can be roughly divided into four categories of kinesics, proxemics, paralanguage and chronemics. Kinesics, also called body language, refers to the body movements in communication including facial expressions, eye contact, hand gestures and touch. Proxemics refers to the study of how we use space in the communication process, which can mean anything from architecture and furniture to the distance between interactants in communication situations. Paralanguage comprises of all the sounds we produce with our voices that are not words, which includes laughter, tone and pace of voice and "empty" words such as "um," "uh" or "you know." Chronemics is the study of how we use time in communication, such as Edward T. Hall's time orientations (monochronic and polychronic) and our understanding of the present, past and future.

The following selection begins with the definition of nonverbal codes by pointing out their significance, characteristics and relationship with verbal codes. Second, the cultural universals and variations in nonverbal communication are discussed. It is the variations that are of particular interest in intercultural communication. Third, such nonverbal codes as body movements, space, touch, time and voice are described in detail to demonstrate their importance in understanding how members of a culture attempt to understand, organize, and interpret the behaviors of others. Finally, the interrelationship of the above nonverbal code systems with one another and with the verbal code system is explored.

Nonverbal Intercultural Communication[1]

Myron W. Lustig and Jolene Koester

Learning to communicate as a native member of a culture involves knowing far more than the culture's verbal code. Vocabulary and grammar, which are the words of a language combined with the rules to string those words together in meaningful units, are actually only a small portion of the message that people exchange when they communicate with one another.

As stated earlier, intercultural communication is a transactional process, which suggests that multiple types or streams of messages are simultaneously being sent and received throughout a conversation. In this chapter we would like to explain the types of messages that, taken together, constitute the nonverbal communication system.

DEFINITION OF NONVERBAL CODES

The importance of nonverbal codes in communication has been well established. Nonverbal communication is a multi-channeled process that is usually performed spontaneously, and it typically involves a subtle set of nonlinguistic behaviors that are often enacted outside of a person's conscious awareness. Nonverbal behaviors become part of the communication process when someone intentionally tries to convey a message or when someone attributes meaning to the nonverbal behavior of another, whether or not the person intended to communicate a particular meaning.

An important caution related to the distinction between verbal and nonverbal communication must be made as you learn about nonverbal code systems. Though we have provided, for explanatory convenience, separate chapters to describe the communication of verbal and nonverbal messages, it would be a mistake to assume that they are actually separate and independent communication systems. Rather, they are inseparably linked together to form the code systems through which the members of a culture convey their beliefs, values, thoughts, feelings, and intentions to one another. As Sheila Ramsey[2] has suggested,

> Verbal and nonverbal behaviors are inextricably intertwined; speaking of one without the other is, as Birdwhistell[3] says, like trying to study "noncardiac physiology." Whether in opposition or complementary to each other, both modes work to create the meaning of an interpersonal

event. According to culturally prescribed codes, we use eye movement and contact to manage conversations and to regulate interactions; we follow rigid rules governing intra- and inter-personal touch, our bodies synchronously join in the rhythm of others in a group, and gestures modulate our speech. We must internalize all of this in order to become and remain fully functioning and socially appropriate members of any culture.

Thus our distinction between verbal and nonverbal messages is a convenient, but perhaps misleading, way to sensitize you to the communication exchanges within and between cultures.

Characteristics of Nonverbal Codes

Unlike verbal communication systems, there are no dictionaries or formal sets of rules to provide a systematic list of the meanings of a culture's nonverbal code systems. The meanings of nonverbal messages are usually less precise than are those of verbal codes. It is difficult, for example, to define precisely the meaning of a raised eyebrow in a particular culture.

Nonverbal communication messages function as a "silent language" and impart their meanings in more subtle and covert ways. People process nonverbal messages, both the sending and receiving of them, with less awareness than they process verbal messages. Contributing to the silent character of nonverbal messages is the fact that most of them are continuous and natural, and they tend to blur into one another. For example, raising your hand to wave goodbye is a gesture made up of multiple muscular movements, yet it is interpreted as one continuous movement.

Skill in the use of nonverbal message systems has only recently begun to receive formal attention in the educational process, a reflection of the out-of-awareness character of nonverbal codes.

Relationship of Nonverbal to Verbal Communication

The relationship of nonverbal communication systems to the verbal message system can take a variety of forms. Nonverbal messages can be used to accent, complement, contradict, regulate, or substitute for the verbal message.

Nonverbal messages are often used to *accent* the verbal message by emphasizing a particular word phrase, in much the same way as italics add emphasis to written messages. For instance, the sentence "He did it" takes on somewhat different meanings, depending on whether the subject (*He* did it), the verb (He *did* it), or the object of the verb (He did *it*) is emphasized.

Nonverbal messages that function to clarify, elaborate, explain, reinforce, and repeat the meaning of verbal messages help to *complement* the verbal message. Many U.S. Americans shake their heads up and down while saying yes to reinforce the verbal affirmation. Similarly, a smile when talking to another helps to convey a generally pleasant tone and encourages a positive interpretation of the verbal message. Pointing forcefully at someone while saying "*He* did it!" helps to elaborate and underscore the verbal message.

Nonverbal messages can also *contradict* the verbal message. These contradictions could occur purposefully, as when you say yes while indicating no with a wink or a gesture; or they may be out of your conscious awareness, as when you say, "I'm not upset," while your facial expression and tone of voice indicate just the opposite. Contradictions between the verbal and nonverbal channels often indicate that something is amiss. Though the contradictory cues might sometimes indicate an attempt at deception, a less evaluative interpretation might simply be that the verbal message is not all that the person could convey. In intercultural communication, these apparent incongruities, when they occur, might serve as a cue that something is wrong.

When nonverbal messages help to maintain the back-and-forth sequencing of conversations, they function to *regulate* the interaction. Conversations are highly structured, with people typically taking turns at talking in a smooth and highly organized sequence. Speakers use nonverbal means to convey that they want the other person to talk or that they do not wish to be interrupted, just as listeners indicate when they wish to talk and when they prefer to continue listening. Looking behaviors, vocal inflections, gestures, and general cues of readiness or relaxation all help to signal one's conversational intentions.

Finally, nonverbal messages that are used in place of the verbal ones function as a *substitute* for the verbal channel. They are used when the verbal channel is blocked or when people choose not to use it. Head nods, hand gestures, facial displays, body movements, and various forms of physical contact are often used as a substitute for the verbal message.

The specific nonverbal messages used to accent, complement, contradict, regulate, or substitute for the verbal messages will vary, however, from culture to culture. In intercultural communication, difficulties in achieving competence in another verbal code are compounded by variations in the nonverbal codes that accompany the spoken word.

CULTURAL UNIVERSALS IN NONVERBAL COMMUNICATION

Charles Darwin[4] believed that certain emblems were universal. The shoulder shrug, for example, is used to convey such messages as "I can't do it," "I can't stop it from happening," "It wasn't my fault," "Be patient," and "I do not intend to resist." Michael Argyle[5] has listed a number of characteristics of nonverbal communication that are universal across all cultures: (1) the same body parts are used for nonverbal expressions; (2) nonverbal channels are used to convey similar information, emotions, values, norms, and self-disclosing messages; (3) nonverbal messages accompany verbal communication and are used in art and ritual; (4) the motives for using the nonverbal channel, such as when speech is impossible, are similar across cultures; and (5) nonverbal messages are used to coordinate and control a range of contexts and relationships that are similar across cultures.

Paul Ekman's[6] research on facial expressions demonstrates the universality of many nonverbal emotional displays. Ekman discovered that three separate sets of facial muscles that operate independently and can be manipulated to form a variety of emotional expressions. These muscle sets include the forehead and brow; the eyes, eyelids, and base of the nose; and the cheeks, mouth, chin, and the rest of the nose. The muscles in each of these facial regions are combined in a variety of unique patterns to display emotional states. For example, fear is indicated by a furrowed brow, raised eyebrows, wide-open eyes, creased or pinched base of the nose, taut cheeks, partially open mouth, and upturned upper lip. Ekman found that the interpretation of various emotional displays is consistent across cultures. Because of this consistency, there is probably a biological or genetic basis in all humans to interpret these behaviors in a particular way.

Another universal aspect of nonverbal communication is the need to be territorial. Robert Ardrey[7], an ethnologist, has concluded that territoriality is an innate, evolutionary characteristic that occurs in both animals and humans. Humans from all cultures mark and claim certain spaces as their own.

Although some aspects of nonverbal code systems are universal, it is also clear that cultures choose how to express emotions and territoriality in differing ways. It is these variations that are of particular interest in intercultural communication.

CULTURAL VATIATIONS IN NONVERBAL COMMUNICATION

Most forms of nonverbal communication can be interpreted only within the framework of the culture in which they occur. Cultures vary in their nonverbal behaviors in three ways. First, cultures differ in the specific *repertoire* of behaviors that are enacted. Movements, body positions, postures, vocal intonations, gestures, spatial requirements, and even dances and ritualized actions are specific to a particular culture.

Second, all cultures have *display rules* that govern when and under what circumstances various nonverbal expressions are required, preferred, permitted, or prohibited. Thus, children learn both how to communicate nonverbally and the appropriate display rules that govern their nonverbal expressions. Display rules indicate such things as how far apart people should stand while talking, whom to touch and where, the speed and timing of movements and gestures, when to look directly at others in a conversation and when to look away, whether loud talking and expansive gestures or quietness and controlled movements should be used, when to smile and when to frown, and the overall pacing of communication.

Differences in display rules can cause discomfort and misinterpretations. For instance, a Mexican-American female visited her relatives in Mexico. Upon her arrival, she reports,

> All of the relatives came to greet me and everyone shook my hand, hugged me, and kissed me on the cheek. I didn't find this very odd at first, because even though I had never seen some of these relatives, we were a family and being affectionate doesn't bother me. The difference occurred when I would go out with my cousins and their friends. When Maria would drop off Monica and me, they would kiss each other on the cheek. When a friend would come to the house, the greeting would always be a kiss on the cheek. It didn't matter if it was in public or private. It was as natural to them as shaking hands or hugging.

Display rules also indicate the intensity of the behavioral display that is acceptable. In showing grief or intense sadness, for instance, people from southern Mediterranean cultures may tend to exaggerate or amplify their displays, Euro-Americans may try to remain calm and somewhat neutral, the British may understate their emotional displays by showing only a little of their inner feelings, and the Japanese and Thai may attempt to mask their sorrow completely by covering it with smiling and laughter.

Third, cultures vary in the *interpretations* or meanings that are attributed to particular nonverbal behaviors. Three possible interpretations could be imposed on a given instance of nonverbal behavior: It is random, it is idiosyncratic, or it is shared. An interpretation that the behavior is random means that it has no particular meaning to anyone. An idiosyncratic interpretation suggests that the behaviors are unique to special individuals or relationships, and they therefore have particular meanings only to these specific people. For example, family members often recognize that certain unique behaviors of a person signify a specific emotional state. Thus, a family member who tugs on her ear may indicate, to other family members, that she is about to explode in anger. The third interpretation is that the behaviors have shared meaning and significance, as when a group of people jointly attribute the same meaning to a particular nonverbal act.

However, cultures differ in what they regard as random, idiosyncratic, and shared. Thus behaviors that are regarded as random in one culture may have shared significance in another. For example, John Condon[8] and Fathi Yousef describe an incident in which a British professor in Cairo inadvertently showed the soles of his shoes to his class while leaning back in his chair; the Egyptian students were supremely insulted. The professor's random behavior of leaning back and allowing the soles of his feet to be seen was a nonverbal behavior with the shared meaning of "insult" in Egyptian culture. Such differences in how cultures define *random* can lead to problems in intercultural communication; if one culture defines a particular behavior as random, that behavior will probably be ignored when someone from a different culture uses it to communicate something.

Even nonverbal behaviors that have shared significance in each of two cultures may mean something very different to their members. As Ray Birdwhistell suggests, "A smile in one society portrays friendliness, in another embarrassment, and in still another may contain a warning that unless tension is reduced, hostility and attack will follow." Aaron Wolfgang noted similar differences in interpretations when he compared Jamaican and Canadian reactions to such commonplace behaviors as clapping the hands for attention:

> In Barbados, a waiter in the dining room attempting to get the attention of some Canadian diners to show them to their table by clapping, shrugged his shoulders when they would not respond. In the English-Canadian culture clapping the hands would be considered inappropriate, or for that matter almost any expressive or gestural movement for

attention would be frowned upon.

Nonverbal repertoires, their corresponding display rules, and their preferred interpretations are not taught verbally. Rather, they are learned directly through observation and personal experience in a culture. Because they are frequently acquired outside of conscious awareness, they are rarely questioned or challenged by their users and are often noticed only when they are violated. In intercultural communication, therefore, misunderstandings often occur in the interpretations of nonverbal behaviors because different display rules create very different meanings about the appropriateness and effectiveness of particular interaction sequences. Consider, for instance, the following example:

> An American college student, while having a dinner party with a group of foreigners, learns that her favorite cousin has just died. She bites her lip, pulls herself up, and politely excuses herself from the group. The Italian student thinks, "How insincere; she doesn't even cry." The Russian student thinks, "How unfriendly; she didn't care enough to share her grief with her friends." The fellow American student thinks, "How brave; she wanted to bear her burden by herself."

As you can see, cultural variations in nonverbal communication alter the behaviors that are displayed, the meanings that are imposed on those behaviors, and therefore the interpretations of the messages.

NONVERBAL MESSAGES IN INTERCULTURAL COMMUNICATION

As you may recall from previous chapters, messages are transmitted between people over some sort of channel. Unlike written or spoken words, however, nonverbal communication is *multi-channeled*. Thus, several types of nonverbal messages can be generated by a single speaker at a given instant. When we "read" or observe the nonverbal behaviors of others, we might notice where they look, how they move, how they orient themselves in space and time, what they wear, and the characteristics of their voice. All of these nonverbal codes use particular channels or means of communicating messages, which are interpreted in a similar fashion by members of a given culture. We will discuss five types of nonverbal codes to demonstrate their importance in understanding how members of a culture attempt to understand, organize, and interpret the behaviors of others. Included is a discussion of body movements, space, touch, time, and voice.

Body Movements

The study of body movements, or body language, is known as *kinesics*. Kinesic behaviors include gestures, head movements, facial expressions, eye behaviors, and other physical displays that can be used to communicate. Of course, like all other forms of communication, no single type of behavior exists in isolation. Specific body movements can be understood only by taking the person's total behavior into account.

Paul Ekman and Wallace Friesen have suggested that there are five categories of kinesic behaviors: emblems, illustrators, affect displays, regulators, and adaptors. We will consider each of these types of kinesic behaviors in turn.

Emblems are nonverbal behaviors that have a direct verbal counterpart. Emblems that are familiar to most U.S. Americans are such gestures as the two-fingered peace symbol and arm waving to indicate hello or goodbye. Emblems are typically used as a substitute for the verbal channel, either by choice or when it is blocked for some reason. Underwater divers, for example, have a rich vocabulary of kinesic behaviors that are used to communicate with their fellow divers. Similarly a baseball coach uses kinesic signals to indicate a particular pitch or type of play, which is usually conveyed by an elaborate pattern of hand motions that involve touching the cap, chest, wrist, and other areas in a pattern known to the players.

Emblems, like all verbal languages, are symbols that have been arbitrarily selected by the members of a culture to convey their intended meanings. There is nothing peace-like in the peace symbol. Indeed, in other cultures the peace symbol has other meanings, some of which are quite derogatory. The meanings of emblems are learned within a culture and, like verbal codes, are used consciously by the culture's members when they wish to convey specific ideas to others. Because emblems have to be learned to be understood, they are culturally specific.

Emblems can be a rich source of misunderstanding in intercultural communication because the shared meanings for an emblem in one culture may be different in another. In Turkey, for instance, to say no nonverbally,

> Nod your head up and back, raising your eyebrows at the same time. Or just raise your eyebrows; that's "no."...
>
> By contrast, wagging your head from side to side doesn't mean "no" in Turkish; it means "I don't understand." So if a Turk asks you,

"Are you looking for the bus to Ankara?" and you shake your head, he'll assume you don't understand English, and will probably ask you the same question again, this time in German.

Illustrators are nonverbal behaviors that are directly tied to, or accompany, the verbal message. They are used to emphasize, explain, and support a word or phrase. They literally illustrate and provide a visual representation of the verbal message. In saying "The huge mountain," for example, you may simultaneously lift your arms and move them in a large half-circle. Similarly, you may point your index finger to emphasize an important idea or use hand motions to convey directions to a particular address. Unlike emblems, none of these gestures has meaning in itself. Rather, like all illustrators, it depends on and underscores the verbal message.

Illustrators are less arbitrary than emblems, which makes them more likely to be universally understood. But differences in both the rules for displaying illustrators and in the interpretations of them can be sources of intercultural misunderstanding. In Asian cultures, for example, calling for a person or a taxi while waving an index finger is very inappropriate, akin to calling a dog. Instead, the whole right hand is used, palm down, with the fingers together in a scooping motion toward one's body. Similarly, punching the fist into the open palm as a display of strength may be misinterpreted as an obscene gesture whose meaning is similar to a Westerner's use of the middle finger extended from a closed fist.

Affect displays are facial and body movements that show feelings and emotions. Expressions of happiness or surprise, for instance, are displayed by the face and convey the person's inner feelings. Though affect displays are shown primarily through the face, postures and other body displays can also convey an emotional state.

Many affect displays are universally recognized. The research of Paul Ekman, Wallace V. Friesen, and Phoebe Ellsworth indicates that regardless of culture, the primary emotional states include happiness, sadness, anger, fear, surprise, disgust, contempt, and interest. In addition to these *primary affect displays*, there are about 30 *affect blends*, which are combinations of the primary emotions.

Affect displays may be unconscious and unintentional, such as a startled look of surprise, a blush of embarrassment, or dilated pupils due to pleasure or interest. Or affect displays may be conscious and intentional, such as when we purposely smile and look at another person to convey warmth and affection.

Cultural norms often govern both what kind of and how much of affect displays are shown.

Regulators are nonverbal behaviors that help to synchronize the back-and-forth nature of conversations. This class of kinesic behaviors helps to control the flow and sequencing of communication and may include head nods, eye contact, postural shifts, back-channel signals (such as "Uhhuhm" or "Mmm-mmm"), and other turn-taking cues.

Regulators are used by speakers to indicate whether others should take a turn and by listeners to indicate whether they wish to speak or would prefer to continue listening. They also convey information about the preferred speed or pacing of conversations and the degree to which the other person is understood and believed.

Regardless of culture, taking turns is required in all conversations. Thus, for interpersonal communication to occur, talk sequences must be highly coordinated. Regulators are those subtle cues that allow people to maintain this high degree of coordination.

Regulators are culturally specific. For instance, high-context cultures are especially concerned with meanings that are conveyed by the eyes. In an interesting study comparing looking behaviors of African-Americans and Euro-Americans in a conversation, Marianne LaFrance and Clara Mayo found that there were many differences in the interpretations of turn-taking cues. Euro-Americans tend to look directly into the eyes of the other person when they are the listeners, whereas African-Americans look away. Unfortunately, to African-Americans such behaviors by Euro-Americans may be regarded as invasive or confrontational when interest and involvement are intended. Conversely, the behaviors of the African-Americans could be regarded by the Euro-Americans as a sign of indifference or inattention when respect is intended. LaFrance and Mayo also found that when African-American speakers pause while simultaneously looking directly at their Euro-American listeners, the listeners often interpret this as a signal to speak, only to find that the African-American person is also speaking."

Adaptors are personal body movements that occur as a reaction to an individual's physical or psychological state. Scratching an itch, fidgeting, tapping a pencil, and smoothing one's hair are all behaviors that fulfill some individualized need.

Adaptors are usually performed unintentionally, without conscious awareness. They seem to be more frequent under conditions of stress, impatience, enthusiasm, or nervousness, and they are often interpreted by others as a sign of discomfort, uneasiness, irritation, or other negative feelings.

Space

The use of space functions as an important communication system in all cultures. Cultures are organized in some spatial pattern, which can reveal the character of the people in that culture. Two important features of the way cultures use the space around them are the different needs for personal space and the messages that are used to indicate territoriality

Cultural differences in the use of personal space. Wherever you go, whatever you do, you are surrounded at all moments by a personal space "bubble." Edward Hall, who coined the term *proxemics* to refer to the study of how people differ in their use of personal space, has suggested that people interact within four spatial zones or distance ranges: intimate, personal, social, and public. These proxemic zones are characterized by differences in the ways that people relate to one another and in the behaviors that typify the communication that will probably occur in them.

Personal space distances are culturally specific. People from colder climates, for instance, typically use large physical distances when they communicate, whereas those from warm-weather climates prefer close distances. The personal space bubbles for northern Europeans are therefore large, and people expect others to keep their distance. The personal space bubbles for Europeans get smaller and smaller, however, as one travels south toward the Mediterranean. Indeed, the distance that is regarded as intimate in Germany, Scandinavia, and England overlaps with what is regarded as a normal conversational distance in France and the Mediterranean countries of Italy, Greece, and Spain. Consequently, southern Europeans are thought by their northern counterparts to get "too close for comfort," whereas the northern Europeans are regarded by their southern neighbors as "too distant and aloof."

The habitual use of the culturally proper spacing difference is accompanied by a predictable level and kind of sensory information. For example, if the standard cultural spacing distance in a personal conversation with an acquaintance is about 3 feet, people will become accustomed to the sights, sounds, and smells of others that are usually acquired at that distance. For someone who is accustomed to a larger spacing distance, at 3 feet the voices will sound too loud, it might be possible to smell the other person's breath, the other person will seem too close and perhaps out of the "normal" focal range, and the habitual ways of holding the body may no longer work. Then the culturally learned cues, which are so helpful within one's culture, can become a hindrance. One Euro-American student, for instance, in commenting on a party that was attended by many Italians and Spaniards, exclaimed, "They would stand close enough that I could almost feel the air coming from their mouths." Similar reactions to intercultural encounters is very common. As Edward and Mildred Hall have suggested,

> Since most people don't think about personal distance as something that is culturally patterned, foreign spatial cues are almost inevitably misinterpreted. This can lead to bad feelings, which are then projected onto the people from the other culture in a most personal way. When a foreigner appears aggressive and pushy, or remote and cold, it may mean only that her or his personal distance is different from yours.

Cultural differences in territoriality. Do you have a favorite chair or classroom seat that you think "belongs" to you? Or do you have a room, or perhaps just a portion of a room, that you consider to be off limits to others? The need to protect and defend a particular spatial area is known as *territoriality*, a set of behaviors that people display to show that they "own" or have the right to control the use of a particular geographic area.

People mark their territories in a variety of ways. It could be done formally by using actual barriers such as fences and signs that say "No Trespassing" or "Keep Off the Grass." Territories can also be marked informally by nonverbal markers such as clothing, books, and other personal items, which indicate that one intends to control or occupy a given area.

Cultural differences in territoriality can be exhibited in three ways. First, cultures can differ in the general degree of territoriality that its members tend to exhibit. Some cultures are far more territorial than others. For instance, as Hall and Hall point out in their comparison of Germans and French,

> People like the Germans are highly territorial; they barricade themselves behind heavy doors and soundproof walls to try to seal themselves from others in order to concentrate on their work. The French have a close personal distance and are not as territorial. They are tied to people and thrive on constant interaction and high-information flow to provide them the context they need.

Second, cultures can differ in the range of possible places or spaces about which they are territorial. A comparison of Euro-Americans with Germans, for example, reveals that both groups tend to be very highly territorial. They both have a strong tendency to establish areas that they consider to be their own. In Germany, however, this feeling of territoriality extends to "all possessions, including the automobile. If a German's car is touched, it is as though the individual himself has been touched."

Finally, cultures can differ in the typical reactions to invasions or contaminations of the territory that are exhibited. Members of some cultures prefer to react by withdrawing or avoiding confrontations whenever possible. Others respond by insulating themselves from the possibility of territorial invasion by using barriers or other boundary markers. Still others react forcefully and vigorously in an attempt to defend their "turf" and their honor.

Touch

Touch is probably the most basic component of human communication. It is experienced long before we are able to see and speak, and it is a fundamental part of the human experience.

The meanings of touch. Stanley Jones and A. Elaine Yarbrough have identified five meanings of touch that are important in understanding the nature of intercultural communication. Touch is often used to indicate *affect*, which is the expression of positive and negative feelings and emotions. Protection, reassurance, support, hatred, dislike, and disapproval are all messages conveyed through touch; hugging, stroking, kissing, slapping, hitting, and kicking are all ways in which these messages can be conveyed. Touch is also used as a sign of *playfulness*. Whether affectionately or aggressively, touch can be used to signal that the other's behavior should not be taken seriously. Touch is frequently used as a means to *control*. "Stay here," "move over," and similar messages are communicated through touch. Touching for control may also indicate social *dominance*. High-status individuals in most Western countries, for instance, are more likely to touch than be touched, whereas low-status individuals are likely to receive touching behaviors from their superiors. Touching for ritual purposes occurs mainly on occasions involving introductions or departures. Shaking hands, clasping shoulders, hugging, and kissing the cheeks or lips are all forms of greeting rituals. Touching is also used in *task-related* activities. These touches may be as casual as a brief contact of hands when passing something, or they may be as formal and prolonged as a physician taking a pulse at the wrist or neck.

Cultural differences in touch. Cultures differ in the overall amount of touching that they prefer. High-contact cultures such as those in the Middle East,

Latin America, and southern Europe touch each other in social conversations much more than do people from non-contact cultures such as Asia and northern Europe. These cultural differences can lead to difficulties in intercultural communication. Germans, Scandinavians, and Japanese, for example, may be perceived as cold and aloof by Brazilians and Italians, who in turn may be regarded as aggressive, pushy and overly familiar by the northern Europeans. As Edward and Mildred Hall have noted, "In northern Europe one does not touch others. Even the brushing of the overcoat sleeve used to elicit an apology." A comparable difference was observed by Dean Barnlund, who found that U.S. American students reported being touched twice as much as did Japanese students.

Cultures also differ in where people can be touched. In Thailand and Malaysia, for instance, the head should not be touched because it is considered to be sacred and the locus of a person's spiritual and intellectual powers. In the United States, the head is far more likely to be touched.

Cultures vary in their expectations about who touches whom. In Japan, for instance, there are deeply held feelings against the touch of a stranger. These expectations are culture-specific, and even cultures that live near one another can have very different norms. Among the Chinese, for instance, shaking hands among people of the opposite sex is perfectly acceptable; among many Malay it is not. Many Euro-Americans, react negatively to same-sex touching (particularly among men) but usually do not mind opposite-sex touching.

Finally, cultures differ in the settings or occasions in which touch is acceptable. Business meetings, street conversations, and household settings all evoke different norms for what is considered to be appropriate. Cultures make distinctions between those settings that they regard as public and those considered to be private. Although some cultures regard touching between men and women as perfectly acceptable in public conversations, others think that such activities should occur only in the privacy of the home; touch to them is a highly personal and sensitive activity that should not occur where others might see it.

Time

The study of how people use, structure, interpret, and understand the passage of time is called *chronemics*. We consider chronemics from two perspectives: time orientations and time systems.

Time orientations refer to the value or importance placed on the passage of time by the members of a culture. We indicated earlier that communication is a process, which means that people's behaviors must be understood as part of an ongoing stream of events that changes over a period of time. We suggested that individuals in a culture share a similar worldview about the nature of time. We also indicated that different cultures can have very different conceptions about the appropriate ways to comprehend how events and experiences should be understood. Specifically, some cultures are predominantly past-oriented, others are present-oriented, and still others prefer a future-oriented worldview. As we briefly review these cultural orientations about time, take note of the amazing degree of interrelationship—in this case the link between a culture's nonverbal code system and its cultural patterns—that characterize the various aspects of a culture.

Past-oriented cultures regard previous experiences and events as most important. These cultures place a primary emphasis on tradition and the wisdom passed down from the older generations. Consequently, they show a great deal of deference and respect for parents and other elders, who are the links to these past sources of knowledge. Events are circular, as important patterns perpetually reoccur in the present, and therefore tried-and-true methods for overcoming obstacles and dealing with problems can be applied to current difficulties. Many aspects of the British, Chinese, and Native American experiences, for instance, can be understood only by reference to their reverence for past traditions, family experiences, or tribal customs. An example of a past-oriented culture is the Samburu, a nomadic tribe from northern Kenya who revere their elders.

> The elders are an invaluable source of essential knowledge, and in an environment that by its very nature allows only a narrow margin for error, the oldest survivors must possess the most valuable knowledge of all. The elders know their environment intimately—every line and twist of it. The land, the water, the vegetation; trees, shrubs, herbs—nutritious, medicinal, poisonous. They know each cow and have a host of specific names for the distinctive shape and skin patterns of each animal in just the same way that Europeans distinguish within the general term flower, or tree.

Present-oriented cultures regard current experiences as most important. These cultures place a major emphasis on spontaneity and immediacy and on experiencing each moment as fully as possible. Consequently, people do not participate in particular events or experiences because of some potential future gain; rather, they participate because of the immediate pleasure that the activity provides. Present-oriented cultures typically believe that unseen and even unknown outside forces, such as fate or luck, control their lives. Cultures such as those in the Philippines and many Central and South American countries are usually present-oriented, and they have found ways to encourage a rich appreciation for the simple pleasures that arise in daily activities.

Future-oriented cultures believe that tomorrow—or some other moment in the future—is most important. Current activities are not accomplished and appreciated for their own sake but for the potential future benefits that might be obtained. For example, you go to school, study for your examinations, work hard, and delay or deny present rewards for the potential future gain that a rewarding career might provide. People from future-oriented cultures, which include many Euro-Americans, believe that their fate is at least partially in their own hands and that therefore they can control the consequences of their actions.

Time Systems are the implicit cultural rules that are used to arrange sets of experiences in some meaningful way. There are three types of time systems: technical, formal, and informal.

Technical time systems are the precise, scientific measurements of time that are calculated in units such as light years or atomic pulses. Technical time is not used by the typical member of a culture because it is most applicable to specialized settings like the research laboratory. Consequently, it is of little relevance to the common experiences that members of a culture share.

Formal time systems refer to the ways in which units of time are described and comprehended by the members of a culture. Time units can vary greatly from culture to culture. Among many Native American cultures, for instance, time is segmented by the phases of the moon, the changing seasons, the rising and falling of the tides, or the movements of the sun. Similarly when a Peruvian woman was asked for the distance to certain Inca ruins, she indicated their location by referring nonverbally to a position in the sky that represented the distance the sun would travel toward the horizon before the journey would be complete. Among Euro-Americans, the passage of time is segmented into seconds, minutes, hours, days, weeks, months, and years.

Time's passage may likewise be indicated by reference to significant events such as the birth of a royal son or an important victory in a battle. Time intervals for particular events or activities may also be based on significant external events such as the length of a day or the phases of the moon. Alternatively, time intervals may be more arbitrary, as in the length of a soccer game or the number of days in a week. These ways of representing the passage of time, however

193

arbitrary are the culture's formal time system. Sequences such as the months in the year are formally named and are explicitly taught to children and newcomers as an important part of the acculturation process.

The formal time system includes agreements among the members of a culture on such important issues as the extent to which time is regarded as valuable and tangible. Euro-Americans, of course, typically regard time as a valuable, tangible commodity that is used or consumed to a greater or lesser degree.

Informal time systems refer to the assumptions that cultures make about how time should be used or experienced. How long should you wait for someone who will be ready soon, in a minute, in a while, or shortly? When is the proper time to arrive for a 9:00 A. M. appointment or an 8:00 P. M. party? As a dinner guest, how long after your arrival would you expect the meal to be served? How long should you stay after the meal has been concluded? Cultures have unstated expectations about the timing and duration of events such as these. Although these expectations differ, depending on such factors as the occasion and the relative importance of those being met or visited, they are widely held and consistently imposed as the proper or appropriate way to conduct oneself as a competent member of the culture. In this regard, Edward Hall has reported,

> The time that it takes to reach an agreement or for someone to make up his mind operates within culturally defined limits. In the U.S. one has about four minutes in the business world to sell an idea. In Japan the well-known process of "nemawashi" —consensus building, without which nothing can happen—can take weeks or months. None of this four-minute sell.

Perhaps the most important aspect of the culture's informal time system is the degree to which it is monochronic or polychronic. A *monochronic* time system means that things should be done one at a time, and time is segmented into precise, small units. In a monochronic time system, time is viewed as a commodity; it is scheduled, managed, and arranged. Euro-Americans, like members of other monochronic cultures, are very time-driven. The ubiquitous calendar or scheduler that many Euro-Americans carry, which tells them when, where, and with whom to engage in activities, is an apt symbol of a monochronic culture. An event is regarded as separate and distinct from all others and should receive the exclusive focus of attention it deserves. These events also have limits or boundaries, so that there is an expected beginning and ending point that has been scheduled in advance. Thus Euro-Americans

> find it disconcerting to enter an office overseas with an appointment only to discover that other matters require the attention of the man we are to meet. Our ideal is to center the attention first on one thing and then move on to something else.

A *polychronic* time system means that several things are being done at the same time. In Spain and among many Spanish-speaking cultures in Central and South America, for instance, relationships are far more important than schedules. Appointments will be quickly broken, schedules readily set aside, and deadlines unmet without guilt or apology when friends or family members require attention. Those who use polychronic time systems often schedule multiple appointments simultaneously, so keeping "on schedule" is an impossibility that was never really a goal. Euro-Americans, of course, are upset when they are kept waiting for a scheduled appointment, particularly when they discover that they are the third of three appointments that have been scheduled for the same hour.

Cultural differences in perceptions and use of time. Cultures differ in their time orientations and in the time systems they use to give order to experiences. Cultures can collide and individual misunderstandings can occur between people who have different time orientations. For instance, someone from a present-oriented culture might view people from past-oriented cultures as too tied to tradition, whereas people from future-oriented cultures may be regarded as passionless slaves to efficiency and materialism. Alternatively, someone from a future-oriented culture might view those from present-oriented cultures as self-centered, hedonistic, inefficient, and foolish. This natural tendency to view one's own practices as superior to all others is a common source of problems in intercultural communication.

Cultures also differ in the formal and informal time systems used to describe and evaluate such events and experiences as how long an event should take, and even how long is regarded as "long." Misinterpretations often occur when individuals from monochronic and polychronic cultures attempt to interact. Each usually views the others' responses to time "commitments" as disrespectful and unfriendly.

Voice

Earlier in this chapter we stated that nonverbal messages are often used to accent or underscore the verbal message by adding emphasis to particular words or phrases. Indeed, the many qualities of the voice itself, in addition to the actual meaning of the words, form the *vocalic* nonverbal communication system. Vocalics also include many nonspeech sounds such as belching, laughing, and crying and vocal "filler" sounds like "*uh, er, um,* and *Uh-huh.*"

Vocal vs. verbal communication. Vocalic qualities include pitch (high to low), rate of talking (fast to slow), conversational rhythm (smooth to staccato), and volume (loud to soft). Because spoken (i.e., verbal) language always has some vocal elements, it is difficult to separate the meaning conveyed by the language from that conveyed by the vocalic components. However, if you can imagine that these words you are now reading are a transcript of a lecture the authors have given, you will be able to understand clearly the distinctions we are describing. Although our words—the language spoken—are here on the printed page, the vocalics are not. Are we speaking rapidly or slowly? How does our inflection change to emphasize a point or to signal a question? Are we yelling, whispering, drawling, or speaking with an accent? Does our voice indicate that we are tense, relaxed, strained, calm, bored, or excited? The answers to these types of questions are conveyed by the speaker's voice.

Cultural differences in vocal communication. There are vast cultural differences in vocalic behaviors. For example, unlike English, many Asian languages are tonal. The same Chinese words when said with a different vocalic tone or pitch can have vastly different meanings. *Ma*, for example, could mean "mother," "jute," "horse," or "scold," depending on the tone used in its expression.

The emotional meanings conveyed by the voice are usually taken for granted by native language users, but they can be the cause of considerable problems when they fail to conform to preconceived expectations. For instance, when a Saudi Arabian man is speaking in English, he will usually transfer his native intonation patterns without necessarily being aware that he has done so. In Arabic, the intonation pattern is such that many of the individual words in the sentence are stressed. Although a flat intonation pattern is used in declarative sentences, the intonation pattern for exclamatory sentences is much stronger and more emotional than that in English. The higher pitch of Arabic speakers also conveys a more emotional tone than that of English speakers. Consequently, differences in vocal characteristics may result in unwarranted negative impressions. The U.S. American may incorrectly perceive that the Saudi Arabian is excited or angry when in fact he is not. Questions by the Saudi that merely seek information may sound accusing.

The monotonous tone of declarative sentences may be perceived as demonstrating apathy or a lack of interest. Vocal stress and intonation differences may be perceived as aggressive or abrasive when only polite conversation is intended.

Conversely, the Saudi Arabian may incorrectly interpret certain behaviors of the U.S. American speaker as an expression of calmness and pleasantness when anger or annoyance is being conveyed. Similarly, a statement that seems to be a firm assertion to the U.S. American speaker may sound weak and doubtful to the Saudi Arabian.

Synchrony of Nonverbal Communication Codes

Cultures train their members to synchronize the various nonverbal behaviors to form a response pattern that typifies the expected behaviors in that culture. Subtle variations in the response patterns are clearly noticed, even when they differ by only a few thousandths of a second. William Condon, who describes himself as "a white, middle-class male," suggests that interactional synchrony is learned from birth onward and occurs within a fraction of a second. Condon compares the differences in the speech and gestures of African-Americans and Euro-Americans:

> If I say the word "because" both my hands may extend exactly together. In Black behavior, however, the right hand may begin to extend with the "be" portion slightly ahead of the left hand and the left hand will extend rapidly across the "cause" portion. This creates the syncopation, mentioned before, which can appear anywhere in the body. A person moves in the rhythm and timing of his or her culture, and this rhythm is in the whole body ... It may be that those having different cultural rhythms are unable to really "synch-in" fully with each other... I think that infants from the first moments of life and even in the womb are getting the rhythm and structure and style of sound, the rhythms of their culture, so that they imprint to them and the rhythms become part of their very being.

Behavioral synchrony in the use of nonverbal codes can be found in virtually all cultures. Not only must an individual's many behaviors be coordinated appropriately, they must also mesh properly with the words and movements of the other interactants. Coordination in Japanese bowing behaviors, for example, requires an adaptation to the status relationships of the participants; the inferior must begin the bow and the superior decides when the bow is complete. If the participants are of equal status, they must begin and end their bows simultaneously. This is not as easy as it seems, for as one Japanese man relates,

> Perfect synchrony is absolutely essential to bowing. Whenever an American tries to bow to me, I often feel extremely awkward and uncomfortable because I simply cannot synchronize bowing with him or her... bowing occurs in a flash of a second, before you have time to think. And both parties must know precisely when to start bowing, how deep, how long to stay in the bowed position, and when to bring their heads up.

Similar degrees of coordination and synchrony can be found in everyday activities. A sensitivity to these different nonverbal codes can help you to become more interculturally competent.

Nonverbal Communication and Intercultural Competence

The rules and norms that govern most nonverbal communication behaviors are both culturally specific and not in conscious awareness. That is, although members of a culture know and follow their culture's expectations, the norms may never have been articulated verbally. Sometimes, the only way to know that a cultural norm exists is to break it.

An important consequence of this out-of-awareness feature is that members of a culture use their norms to determine appropriate nonverbal behaviors and then make negative judgments about others' feelings, motives, and intentions when the norms are violated. Often the violations will be attributed, inaccurately, to aspects of personality attitudes, or intelligence rather than to a mismatch between learned nonverbal codes. But because the norms governing the behaviors are not coded verbally, inaccurate judgments are difficult to recognize and correct.

The following suggestions will help you use your knowledge of nonverbal communication to improve your intercultural competence. These suggestions are designed to help you notice, interpret, and use nonverbal communication behaviors to function more appropriately and more effectively in intercultural encounters.

Researchers have been known to take weeks or even months to analyze the delicate interaction rhythms involved in a single conversation. Of course, most people do not have the luxury of a month to analyze someone's comments before a response must be made. However, the knowledge that the patterns of behavior will probably be very complex will help to sensitize you to them and may encourage you to notice the many details.

No set of behaviors is universally correct, so the "right" behaviors can never be described in a catalog or list. Rather, the proper behaviors are those that are appropriate and effective in the context of the culture, setting, and occasion. What is right in one set of circumstances may be totally wrong in another. Although it is useful to gather culture-specific information about appropriate nonverbal behaviors, even this knowledge should be approached as relative because prescriptions of "right" behavior rarely can identify all of the situational characteristics that cultural natives "know."

By monitoring your emotional reactions to the differences in nonverbal behaviors, you can be alert to the interpretations you are making and, therefore, to the possibility of alternative meanings. Strong visceral responses to differences in smell, body movement, and personal spacing are quite common in intercultural communication. Knowledge that these might occur followed by care in the interpretation of meanings, is critical.

Skillful interpretation includes observation of general tendencies. Focus on what the members of the other culture prefer and the ways in which they typically behave. How, when, and with whom do they gesture, move, look, and touch? How are time and space used to define and maintain social relationships? It is much harder to pay attention to these general tendencies than you might think because in all likelihood you have not had much practice in consciously looking for patterns in the commonplace, taken-for-granted activities through which cultural effects are displayed. Nevertheless, it is possible, with practice, to improve your skills in observation.

Even after making observations, be tentative in your interpretations and generalizations. You could be wrong. You will be far more successful in making sense of the behaviors of others if you avoid the premature closure that comes with knowing for certain what something means. Think of your explanations as tentative working hypotheses rather than as unchanging facts.

Next, look for exceptions to your generalizations. These exceptions are very important because they help you to recognize that no specific individual, regardless of the thoroughness and accuracy with which you have come to understand a culture, will exactly fit the useful generalizations you have formed. The exceptions that you note can help you to limit the scope of your generalizations and to recognize the boundaries beyond which your judgments may simply not apply. Maybe your interpretations apply only to men or students or government officials or potential customers. Maybe your evaluations of the way that time and space are structured are applicable only to business settings or among those whose status is equal or with particular people like yourself. Though it is necessary to make useful generalizations to get along in another culture, it is equally necessary to recognize the limits of the generalizations that you have made.

Finally, practice to improve your ability in observing, evaluating, and behaving in appropriate and effective ways. Practice will increase your skill in first recognizing that there are specific patterns to another's behavior, then correctly interpreting their meanings and likely consequences, and finally selecting a response that is both appropriate and effective. Like all skills, your level of intercultural competence can improve with practice. Of course, the most appropriate form of practice is one that closely approximates the situations in which you will have to use the skills you are trying to acquire. This statement suggests that you should seek out and willingly engage in intercultural communication experiences. We wholeheartedly encourage you to do so.

SUMMARY

Although there is some evidence that certain nonverbal communication tendencies are common to all humans, cultures vary greatly in the repertoire of behaviors and circumstances in which nonverbal exchanges occur. A smile, a head nod, and eye contact may all have different meanings in different cultures.

This chapter has considered the important nonverbal code systems used to supplement, reinforce, or substitute for the verbal code systems. Nonverbal code systems are the silent language of communication. They are less precise and less consciously used and interpreted, but they can have powerful effects on perceptions of and interpretations about others. The nonverbal code systems relating to body movements, space, touch, time, voice, and other nonverbal code systems were each described. Finally, the interrelationship of these nonverbal code systems with one another and with the verbal code system was explored.

Notes

1. From *Intercultural Competence: Interpersonal Communication Across Cultures*, Myron W. Lustig and Jolene Koester, NY: Harper Collins, 1993.
2. Sheila Ramsey has a Ph. D. in communication as well as a background in theater and anthropology. She is known internationally for her work in the field of intercultural relations, international leadership development, team training and the facilitation of

individual and group creativity and innovation.

3. Ray L. Birdwhistell (1918 – 1994) was an American anthropologist who studied and became an expert in kinesics and nonverbal communication. He analyzed the way people interacted through watching films. Based on his research results, he wrote two books: *Introduction to Kinesics* published in 1952 and *Kinesics and Context*, which he's more known for, was published in 1970 by the University of Pennsylvania Press. His first book discusses his studies of body motion and gesture using nonverbal communication. His second book is about body motion and the use of nonverbal communication. Ray L. Birdwhistell was a very successful anthropologist and made many new observations when dealing with kinesics and nonverbal communication.

4. Charles Darwin (1809 – 1882) was a British naturalist famous for his theories of evolution and natural selection. Like several scientists before him, Darwin believed all the life on earth evolved over millions of years from a few common ancestors. From 1831 to 1836 Darwin served as naturalist aboard the H. M. S. Beagle on a British science expedition around the world. Darwin's theory of evolutionary selection holds that variation within species occurs randomly and that the survival or extinction of each organism is determined by that organism's ability to adapt to its environment. He set these theories forth in his book called, *On the Origin of Species by Means of Natural Selection, or the Preservation of Favoured Races in the Struggle for Life* (1859) or *The Origin of Species* for short.

5. Michael Argyle (1925 – 2002) was a pioneer in the study of Social Psychology in Britain. He has been engaged in research in various aspects of nonverbal communication and social skills. With a series of hypotheses and experiments to examine which nonverbal cues served which interactive social functions and how, Michael Argyle opened up a whole new field of inquiry. He wrote more than 25 books on a wide variety of topics such as cooperation, happiness, leisure, social interaction, social relationships, body language, gaze, mutual gaze and religious faith. Michael Argyle is the author of, to name just a few, *The Scientific Study of Social Behavior*, *Psychology and Social Problems*, and *Bodily Communication*.

6. Paul Ekman is a professor of psychology, in the Department of Psychiatry at the University of California Medical School, San Francisco. His interests have focused on two separate but related topics. He originally focused on "nonverbal" behavior, but by the middle 1960s focused more specifically on the expression and physiology of emotion. His second interest, dating from the same period of time is interpersonal deception.

7. Robert Ardrey (1908 – 1980) was an American anthropologist interested in human behavior, and also a Hollywood screenwriter. Ardrey was born on October 16, 1908 in Chicago, Illinois. He attended college at the University of Chicago, where he studied in the Natural and Social Science Department. Some of his books are *The*

Territorial Imperative, *The Social Contract*, *The Hunting Hypothesis*, *Social Contract*, and *Man and Aggression*.

8. John Condon is one of the pioneers of intercultural communication study. He has played important roles as writer, teacher and integrator. He is well known for his books on Mexican and Japanese cultures. He is currently Professor of Communication at the University of New Mexico. In the early 1970s Condon co-wrote one of the first textbooks with Fathi Yousef on intercultural communication titled *Introduction to Intercultural Communication*. Condon and Yousef's textbook and the first edition of *Intercultural Communication: A Reader* (Samovar and Porter, 1972) are seen as "the two major forces from the early 1970s in the integration of the study of intercultural communication in the 1980s."

Questions for Discussion

1. How do you understand the differences between verbal and nonverbal communication? How should nonverbal communication be "taught" in a foreign language classroom?
2. What are the cultural universals and variations in nonverbal communication? What is the significance of becoming aware of them for foreign language learners?
3. What are the five types of nonverbal codes people use to communicate messages? Which type bears the greatest significance to you in your life? Why and how?
4. What are the suggestions put forward in the text to help people apply their knowledge of nonverbal communication to improve their intercultural competence? What do you think of the suggestions? What new suggestions do you have?
5. Due to the cultural difference of self-enhancement in the West and self-effacement in the East, many international students from oriental countries tend to appear much more humble and modest than their over-confident and fully-assertive counterparts from the English-speaking countries. Do you think we Chinese people should still maintain our traditions of modesty in non-verbal intercultural communication? Why?

Online Mini-Case Studies and Viewpoints-Sharing

A Packed Lunch

An American family living in Japan for one year wanted their son (age 10) to attend a Japanese elementary school. When they so indicated to their landlord, the latter sent his English-speaking daughter to act as a go-between (chukaisha). The boy was duly enrolled and began school. He had to take a lunch (bento) every day, so he took a regular American meal of sandwich, chips, cookies, and drink. The teacher subsequently contacted the go-between to have her talk with the parents about the inappropriateness of the lunch and to request the parents provide a more Japanese-style bento.

Why was the school teacher perturbed by the child's American-style lunch?
A. The teacher feared that the Japanese children would become dissatisfied with their own lunches
B. It was felt the lunch was not sufficiently nutritious.
C. The typical Japanese bento has symbolic significance, and it was felt that the child was breaking with tradition.
D. Conformity in Japanese society is valued more than individuality.

Online Research

Search online for more information concerning food etiquette in both Japanese and American cultures and provide reasonable explanations for your choice among A, B, C, or D in the previous exercise.

Reading Two

Introductory Remarks

Since only about 30% of what is communicated in a conversation is verbal, the significance of nonverbal communication can never be overemphasized. Whether we are truly successful communicators or not depends a lot on our ability to use nonverbal skills appropriately. However, it is no easy job to apply and interpret the subtle and implicit nonverbal cues effectively. It is estimated that the human body can produce over 270, 000 discrete gestures, but there are neither set rules nor ready dictionaries for us to turn to for help. What we can do is "doing what comes naturally" as most of our knowledge about nonverbal communication stems from social, cultural and environmental factors.

The selection below consists of two main parts. The first part reinforces our awareness of nonverbal communication by some overlapping but somewhat detailed discussions of the definition of nonverbal communication and such nonverbal codes as facial expression, personal space, eye contact, use of time and conversational silence. Then, the authors broaden our knowledge of nonverbal communication by the introduction of semiotics including signs, cultural codes and myths. The second part discusses cultural space, which is an important aspect of nonverbal behavior. Finally, the authors explore the tenuous and dynamic postmodern cultural spaces in order to show how coexisting people of different cultural identities communicate.

Nonverbal Codes and Cultural Space[1]

Judith N. Martin and Thomas K. Nakayama

Nonverbal elements of cultural communication play an important role in understanding intercultural communication. Reading nonverbal communication within various cultural spaces can be a key to survival, depending upon the situation. Fletcher, a communication scholar, notes "Urban police officers are one group for whom taking 'everyday life' for granted by screening out the discomfiting or confusing elements can have tragic consequences for both cops and citizens."

You may never become a police officer, but you certainly will find yourself in many intercultural communication situations and cultural spaces. Your own nonverbal communication may create additional problems in some cases and, if the behaviors are inappropriate for the particular cultural space, may exacerbate existing tensions. In other cases, your use of nonverbals might reduce tension and confusion.

The first part of this chapter discusses the importance of understanding nonverbal aspects of intercultural communication. The second section explores cultural patterns of specific nonverbal communication codes (personal space, gestures, facial expressions, and so on) and how these nonverbal codes express power in intercultural contexts. The third section investigates the concept of cultural space and how cultural identity is shaped and negotiated by the cultural spaces (home, neighborhood, and so on) that people occupy.

As urban police officers know, there can never be a guidebook to "reading the streets." The nonverbals of the street change constantly. For the same reason, we believe it is useless to list nonverbals to memorize. Instead, it will be more beneficial for you to learn the framework of nonverbal communication and cultural spaces, so that you can unpack and learn the nonverbal systems of whatever cultural groups become relevant to your life. Understanding communication is a matter of understanding how to figure out systems of meaning, rather than discrete elements. Nonverbal intercultural communication is no exception.

Defining Nonverbal Communication

In this chapter we discuss two forms of communication beyond speech. The first includes facial expression, personal space, eye contact, use of time, and conversational silence (What is not said is often as important as what is spoken.).

A second aspect of nonverbal behavior includes the cultural spaces that we occupy and negotiate. Cultural spaces are the social and cultural contexts that form our identity—where we grow up and where we live (not necessarily the physical homes and neighborhoods, but the cultural meanings created in these places).

Comparing Verbal and Nonverbal Communication

Both verbal and nonverbal communication are symbolic, communicating meaning, and are patterned; that is, they are governed by rules that are contextually determined. Societies have different nonverbal languages, just as they have different spoken languages. However, some differences between nonverbal and verbal communication codes have important implications for intercultural interaction.

Let's look at some examples of these differences. The following incident occurred to Judith, one of the authors of this book, when she was new to Algeria, where she lived for a while. One day she stood at her balcony and waved to one of the young Algerian teachers, who was walking across the school yard. Two minutes later, the young teacher knocked on the door, looking expectantly at Judith, as if summoned. Because Judith knew that it was uncommon in Algeria for men to visit women they didn't know well, she was confused. Why had he come to her door? Was it because she was foreign? After a few awkward moments, he left. A few weeks later, Judith figured it out. In Algeria (as in many other places), the U.S. "wave" is the nonverbal signal for "come here." The young teacher had assumed that Judith had summoned him to her apartment. As this example illustrates, rules for nonverbal communication vary among cultures and contexts.

Let's consider another example. Two U.S. students attending school in France were hitchhiking to the university in Grenoble for the first day of classes. A French motorist picked them up and immediately started speaking English to them. They wondered how he knew they spoke English. Later, they took a train to Germany. The conductor walked into their compartment and berated them in English for putting their feet on the opposite seat. How had he known that they spoke English? As this example shows, nonverbal communication entails more than gestures. Even our appearance can communicate loudly (The students' very appearance probably was a sufficient clue to their national identity.). As this example also shows, nonverbal behavior operates at a subconscious level. We rarely think about the way we stand, the hand gestures we use, and so on. Occasionally, someone points out such behaviors, which brings them to a conscious level.

When misunderstandings arise, we are more likely to question our verbal communication than our nonverbal communication. We can search for a different way to explain verbally what we mean. We can look up words in a dictionary or ask someone to explain unfamiliar words. By contrast, it is more difficult to identify nonverbal miscommunications or misperceptions.

Learning nonverbal behavior. Whereas we learn rules and meanings for language behavior in grammar and spelling lessons, we learn nonverbal meanings and behaviors by more implicit socialization. No one explains, "When you talk with someone you like, lean forward, smile, and touch the person frequently, because that will communicate that you really care about him or her." In many contexts in the United States, these behaviors communicate immediacy and positive meanings. How is it interpreted if one does not display these behaviors?

Sometimes we learn strategies for nonverbal communication. Have you ever been told to shake hands firmly when you meet someone? You may have learned that a limp handshake indicates a weak person. Likewise, many young women learn to cross their legs at the ankles and keep their legs together when they sit. These strategies combine socialization and the teaching of nonverbal codes.

Researchers in the 1960s conducted microanalyses of nonverbal interactions in therapy sessions. They found that when things were going well, the therapist and patient mirrored each other's behavior, almost like a dance. When one person leaned back, so did the other. When one crossed his or her legs, so did the other. More recent research seems to support these early studies, showing that when people feel positively or warmly toward each other in conversations, they tend to mimic each other's nonverbal behavior.

Coordinating nonverbal and verbal behaviors. Nonverbal behaviors can reinforce, substitute for, or contradict verbal behaviors. When we shake our heads and say "no," we are reinforcing verbal behavior. When we point instead of saying "over there," our nonverbal behavior is substituting for our verbal communication. If we tell a friend, "I can't wait to see you," and then don't show up at the friend's house, the nonverbal behavior is contradicting the verbal behavior.

What would you think if someone told you that your outfit was wonderful but then rolled his or her eyes? The nonverbal behavior contradicts the verbal message. Which message would you believe, and why? Generally, people believe the nonverbal behavior. Because nonverbal communication operates at a more unconscious level, we tend to think that people have less control over their nonverbal behavior. Therefore, we often think of nonverbal behaviors as the "real" message.

What Nonverbal Behavior Communicates

Relational messages. Although language is effective and efficient at communicating explicit information and the content of messages, nonverbal communication often communicates the metamessage, or the relational aspect of messages: how we really feel about the person, and so on. Nonverbal behavior often forms the basis of our judgments about people we meet for the first time. In addition, we usually communicate how we feel about others nonverbally—by facial expression, eye contact, posture, and so on. Nonverbal communication plays a significant role in establishing the relations we have with others.

Status. Nonverbal behavior also communicates status and power. For example, a supervisor may be able to touch subordinates, but usually it is unacceptable for subordinates to touch a supervisor. Large expansive gestures are associated with status; conversely, holding the body in a tight, closed position communicates low status. In general, the more space a person controls in the office or home, the greater that person's status. Similarly, the presence of quantity of office windows communicates employees' relative power in an organization: the more power an employee has, the more windows in his or her office.

Deception. Nonverbal behavior also communicates deception. Early research studies concentrated on leakage in nonverbal communication. Researchers tried to identify which parts of the body people were least able to control and, therefore, which parts communicated "true" feelings. They believed that some nonverbal behaviors (avoiding eye contact, touching or rubbing the face, and so on) indicated lying.

Research shows that deception is communicated by fairly idiosyncratic behaviors and probably as much by verbal communication. Each individual may have his or her own unique way of communicating deception depending on personality, motivation, planning, and age. Only a few nonverbal behaviors (such as pupil dilation, blinking, and higher pitch) are consistently related to deception.

Most nonverbal communication about affect, status, and deception happens at an unconscious level. For this reason, it plays an important role in intercultural interactions. It is pervasive and unconscious. It communicates how we feel about each other and about cultural groups.

The Universality of Nonverbal Behavior

Most traditional research in intercultural communication focuses on identifying cross-cultural differences in nonverbal behavior. How do culture, ethnicity, and gender influence nonverbal communication patterns? How universal is most nonverbal communication? Traditional research seeks to answer these questions.

As we have observed in earlier chapters, it is neither beneficial nor accurate to try to reduce an individual to one element of his or her identity (gender, ethnicity, or nationality). Attempts to classify people in discrete categories tend to reduce their complexities and create enormous communication misunderstandings. However, we often classify people according to various categories to help us find universalities. For example, although we may know that not all Germans are alike, we may seek information that helps us communicate better with Germans. In this section, we explore the extent to which nonverbal communication codes are universally shared. We also look for possible cultural variations in these codes that may serve as tentative guidelines to help us communicate better with others.

Recent Research Findings

Research investigating the universality of nonverbal communication has focused on three areas:

1. The relationship of human behavior to that of primates (Particularly chimpanzees)
2. Nonverbal communication of sensory-deprived children who are blind or deaf
3. Cross-cultural studies on facial expression

Chimpanzees and humans share many nonverbal behaviors. Both, for example, exhibit the eyebrow flash—a slight raising of the eyebrow that communicates a recognition. This is one of the most primitive and universal animal behaviors. Humans do it when they see someone they know. Primates and humans also share some facial expressions. However, animal communication appears to be less complex, with fewer facial blends.

Researchers conducted studies that compared the facial expressions of children who were blind with those of sighted children and found many similarities. Even though the children who were blind couldn't see the facial expressions of others to mimic them, they still made the same expressions. This seems to suggest some innate, genetic basis for these behaviors. However, the blind children's facial expressions were less complex, with fewer facial blends, than sighted children's expressions. The face of a blind child might show a blank expression and then a smile, whereas the face of a sighted child might show subtle changes from a smile to a frown, for example. Or the sighted child's expression might combine a smile and a frown.

Many cross-cultural studies support the notion that facial expressions are universal, to some extent. Six basic emotions are communicated by facial expressions. They include happiness, sadness, disgust, fear, anger, and surprise. Expressions for these emotions are recognized by most cultural groups as having the same meaning.

These research findings may support universalities in nonverbal communication. However, some variations also exist. The evoking stimuli (that is, what causes the nonverbal behavior) may vary from one culture to another. Smiling, for example, is universal. But what prompts a person to smile may be culture-specific.

There are variations in the rules for the nonverbal behavior and in what contexts the nonverbal communication takes place. Whereas people kiss in most cultures, there is variation in who kisses whom and in what contexts. For example, when French friends greet, they often kiss on both cheeks but never on the mouth. Friends in the United States usually kiss on greeting only after long absence and then usually accompanied by a hug. The rules for kissing also vary along gender lines.

Finally it is important to look for larger cultural patterns to the nonverbal behavior, rather than trying to identify and memorize all of the cultural differences. Researcher David Matsumoto[2] suggests that, although cultural differences in nonverbal patterns are interesting, noting these differences is not sufficient. Studying every variation in every aspect of nonverbal behavior would be an overwhelming task. Instead, he suggests studying nonverbal communication patterns that vary with other cultural patterns, such as values.

For example, Matsumoto links cultural patterns in facial expressions with cultural values of power distance and individualism and collectivism. Hypothetically cultural groups that emphasize status differences most likely would express emotions that preserve these status differences. Matsumoto also suggests that within individualistic cultures the degree of difference in emotional display between in-groups and out-groups is greater than the degree of difference between the same groups in collectivist societies. If these theoretical relationships hold true, we could generalize about the nonverbal behavior of many different cultural groups.

Nonverbal Codes
Proxemics is the study of how people use personal space, or the "bubble" that is around us that marks the territory between ourselves and others. O. M. Watson, a proxemics specialist, investigated nonverbal communication between Arab and U.S. students after hearing many complaints from each group about the other. The Arab students complained that the U.S. students were distant and rude. The U.S. students characterized the Arab students as pushy, arrogant, and rude. His investigations showed that the two groups operated with different rules concerning personal space. Watson's research supported Edward Hall's observations about the cultural variations in how much distance individuals placed between themselves and others.

Hall made a distinction between *contact cultures* and *noncontact cultures*. He described contact cultures as those societies in which people stood closer together while talking, engaged in more direct eye contact, used face-to-face body orientations more often while talking, touched more frequently and spoke in louder voices. He suggested that societies in South America and Southern Europe are contact cultures, whereas those in Northern Europe, the United States, East Asia, and the Far East are noncontact cultures—in which people tend to stand farther apart when conversing, maintain less eye contact, and touch less often.

Of course, many other factors besides national culture determine how far we stand from someone. Gender, age, ethnicity, the context of the interaction, and the topic of discussion all influence the use of personal space. In fact, some studies show that national culture is perhaps the least important factor. For example, in Algeria, gender might be the overriding factor. Unmarried young women and men would rarely stand close together, touch each other, or maintain direct eye contact.

Eye contact is often included in proxemics because it regulates interpersonal distance. Direct eye contact shortens the distance between two people, whereas less eye contact increases the distance. Eye contact communicates meanings about respect and status and often regulates turn-taking.

Patterns of eye contact vary from culture to culture. In many societies, avoiding eye contact communicates respect and deference, although this may vary from context to context. For many U.S. Americans, maintaining eye contact communicates that one is paying attention, showing respect.

When they speak with others, most U.S. Americans look away from their listeners most of the time. They might look at their listeners every 10 to 15 seconds. When a speaker is finished taking a turn, he or she looks directly at the listener to signal completion. However, some cultural groups within the United States use even less eye contact while they speak. For example, some Native Americans tend to avert eye gaze during conversations.

Facial expression. As noted earlier in this chapter, there have been many investigations of the universality of facial expression. Psychologists Ekman and Friesen conducted extensive and systematic work in nonverbal communication. They first took pictures of U.S. Americans' facial expressions reflecting six emotions thought to be universal. They then showed these photographs to people in various cultural groups.

However, Ekman and Friesen's studies have been criticized for a few reasons. First, the studies don't tap into universality; people may be able to recognize and identify the six emotions because of exposure to media. Also, the researchers presented a limited number of responses (multiple choice answers) when they asked respondents to identify emotions expressed.

Later studies improved on this research. Researchers took many photographs, not always posed, of facial expressions of members from many different cultural groups; then they asked the subjects to identify the emotion expressed by the facial expression. Researchers then showed these photographs to many different individuals in many different countries, including some without exposure to media. The conclusion supports the notion of universality of facial expression. Some basic human emotions are expressed in a fairly finite number of facial expressions and these expressions can be recognized and identified universally.

Chronemics concerns concepts of time and the rules that govern its use. There are many cultural variations regarding how people understand and use time. Edward Hall distinguished between monochromic and polychronic time orientation. People who have a monochronic concept of time regard it as a commodity: Time can be gained, lost, spent, wasted, or saved. In this orientation, time is linear, with one event happening at a time. In general, monochronic cultures value highly punctuality, completing tasks, and keeping to schedules. Most university staff and faculty in the United States maintain a monochronic orientation to time. Classes, meetings, and office appointments start when scheduled. Faculty members see one student at a time, hold one meeting at a time, and keep appointments almost regardless of any relational emergency. Family problems are considered poor reasons for not fulfilling academic obligations—for both faculty and students.

In contrast, a polychronic orientation conceptualizes time as more holistic, perhaps more circular: Many events can happen at once. U.S. business people often complain that meetings in the Middle East do not start "on time," that people socialize during meetings, and that meetings may be canceled because of personal obligations. Often, tasks are accomplished *because* of personal relationships, not in spite of them.

Many international business negotiations and technical assistance projects fail because of differences in time orientation. International students and business personnel often complain that U.S. Americans seem too busy, too tied to their schedules; they complain that U.S. Americans do not care enough about relationships and about the personal aspects of living.

Silence. Cultural groups may vary in the relative emphasis placed on speaking and silence. Silence can be as meaningful as language. In most U.S. American contexts, silence is not highly valued. Particularly in developing relationships, silence communicates awkwardness and sometimes causes people to be uncomfortable. According to scholar William B. Gudykunst[3], the major reason for communicating verbally in initial interactions with people is to reduce uncertainty. In U.S. American contexts, people employ active uncertainty reduction strategies (such as asking questions). However, in many other cultural contexts, one reduces uncertainty by more passive strategies, by being silent, observing, perhaps asking a third party about someone's behavior.

In a classic study on the rules for silence among the Western Apache in Arizona, researcher Keith Basso[4] identified five contexts in which silence was appropriate: meeting strangers, courtship, seeing friends after a long absence, being with people who are grieving, and getting cussed out. Verbal reticence with strangers is directly related to the conviction that the establishment of social relationships is a serious matter that calls for caution, careful judgment and plenty of time.

In courting, individuals can go without speaking for a very long time. Similarly encounters between individuals who have been apart for a long time may call for silence. For example, parents and children may remain silent for a while after the children have returned from boarding schools. The time of silence is to see if the returnee has changed adversely.

The Western Apache also believe that silence is an appropriate response to an individual who becomes enraged and starts shouting insults and criticism. The silence acknowledges that the angry person is not really him or herself—that the person has temporarily taken leave of his or her senses, is not responsible, and therefore may be dangerous. In this instance, silence is a safe way to deal with the person.

Being with people who are sad or bereaved also calls for silence. Basso gives several reasons for this silence. First, talking is unnecessary because everyone knows how it feels to be sad. Secondly the Western Apache believe that intense grief, like intense rage, produces personality changes and personal instability.

Basso hypothesizes that the underlying commonality in these social situations is that participants perceive their relationships vis-à-vis one another to be ambiguous and/or unpredictable, and silence is an appropriate response to uncertainty and unpredictability. He also hypothesizes that this same contextual rule may apply to other cultural groups.

Communication scholar C. Braithwaite tried to find out if Basso's rule applied to other communities. He compiled ethnographic accounts from 13 speech communities in which silence seemed to play a similar role. His research included groups of Warm Springs Indians, Japanese Hawaiians, and 17th-century Quakers[5]. Braithwaite extended Basso's rule when he determined that in many communities silence was not just associated with uncertainty. Silence was also associated with social situations in which a known and unequal distribution of power existed among participants.

Cultural Variation or Stereotype?

As noted earlier, one of the problems with identifying cultural variations in nonverbal codes is that it is tempting to overgeneralize these variations and stereotype people. For example, we may think that *all* Amish[6] are silent in all contexts or that all Arabs stand close to one another in all contexts. Rather, cultural variations are tentative guidelines that we can use in intercultural interaction. They should serve as examples, to help us understand that there is a great deal of variation in nonverbal behavior. Even if we can't anticipate how someone's behavior may be different from our own, we can be flexible when we do encounter differences in how close a person stands, uses eye contact, or conceptualizes time.

Prejudice is often based on nonverbal aspects of behavior. That is, the negative prejudgment is triggered by physical appearances or physical behavior. The following excerpt from a news article underscores the importance of physical appearances in prejudice:

> In December, an Asian American male was hit with a glass bottle at his business in San Francisco by an inebriated European American male. The assailant's threats included "I'm not gonna leave, you f***ing gook or jap or whatever you are. I'm gonna smash your windows and smash you. Go back to wherever you came from."

As in many other instances of hate crimes, the victim's appearance is more significant than the victim's specific cultural heritage.

Semiotics

The study of semiotics, or semiology, offers a useful approach to understanding how many nonverbal codes and signs communicate meaning. The process of producing meaning is called semiosis. A particularly useful framework for understanding semiosis comes from literary critic Roland Barthes[7]. In his system, meaning is constructed through the interpretation of signs—combinations of *signifiers* and *signifieds*. Signifiers are the culturally constricted, arbitrary words or symbols we use to refer to something else, the signified. Think about this example: The word *man* is a signifier that refers to some signified, an adult male human being.

Obviously, *man* is a general signifier that does not refer to any particular man. The relationship between this signifier and the sign (the meaning) depends on how the signifier is used (for example, as in the sentence, "There is a man sitting in the first chair on the left") or on our general sense of what *man* means. The difference between the signifier *man* and the sign rests on the difference between the word *man* and the meaning of that word. At its most basic level, *man* means an adult human, but the semiotic process does not end there. *Man* carries many other layers of meaning. Roland Barthes calls these layers *myths*. The expression, "Man is the measure of all things," for example, is loaded with many levels of meaning, including the centering of male experience as the norm. *Man* may or may not refer to any particular adult male, but it provides a concept that you can use to construct particular meanings based on the way the sign *man* functions.

What do you have in mind when you think of the term *man*? How do you know when to use this signifier (and when not to use it) to communicate to others? Think of all of the adult males you know: How do they "fit" under this sign? In what ways does this sign reign over their behaviors, both verbal and nonverbal, to communicate particular ideas about them?

Intercultural communication is not concerned simply with the cultural differences in nonverbal systems, although that is certainly a central interest. Semiotics can be useful in unpacking the ways that the cultural codes regulate nonverbal communication systems. That is, semiotics allows us one way to "crack the codes" of another cultural framework. The goal is to establish entire systems of semiosis and the ways that those systems create meaning. We are not so much interested in the discrete, individual signifiers, but rather the ways that signifiers are combined and configured.

The use of these semiotic systems relies on many codes taken from a variety of places: economic institutions, history politics, religion, and so on. For example, when Nazi swastikas were spray-painted on Jewish graves in Lyon, France in 1992, the message they communicated relied on semiotic systems from the past. The history of the Nazi persecution of Jews during World War II is well known: the power behind the signifier, the swastika, comes from that historical knowledge and the codes of antisemitism that it invokes to communicate its message. Relations from the past influence the construction and maintenance of intercultural relations in the present.

Because we seek the larger semiotic systems, we need to be aware of the cultural contexts that regulate the semiotic frameworks. When we are in different cultural contexts, the semiotic systems transform the communication situations. Consider the following example, an observation by writer Edmundo Desnoes, who discusses the work of photographer Susan Meiselas on her trip to Nicaragua. Desnoes comments that Meiselas: "discovered one of the keys to understanding Latin America: a different context creates a different discourse. What she saw and what she shot in Nicaragua could not be plucked away and packaged in New York." That is, the photographs that Meiselas took could not communicate what she saw and experienced and wanted to communicate through the photos. The U.S. context would be regulated by a different semiotic system that would construct different signs and different meanings for the images.

It is wise to be sensitive to the many levels of cultural context that are regulated by different semiotic systems. In other words, it's a good idea to avoid framing cultural context as simply a "nation." Nation-states have other cultural contexts within their borders—for example, commercial and financial districts, residential areas, and bars, which are all regulated by their own semiotic systems. Consider, for example, the clothes that people might wear to a bar. Wearing the same clothes to a business setting would not communicate the same message. Yet, cultural contexts are not fixed and rigid. Rather, they are dynamic and fleeting.

Defining Cultural Space

The discourses that construct the meanings of cultural spaces are dynamic, ever-changing. In addition, the relations between those cultural spaces and our identities are negotiated in complex ways. Thus, because someone is from India does not mean that his or her identity and communication practices are reducible to the history of that cultural space.

What is the communicative (discursive) relationship between cultural spaces and intercultural communication? We define cultural space as the particular configuration of the communication (discourse) that constructs meanings of various places. This may seem like an unwieldy definition, but it underscores the complexity of cultural spaces.

A cultural space is not simply a particular location that has culturally constructed meanings. It can also be a metaphorical place from which we communicate. We can speak from a number of social locations, marked on the map of society that give added meaning to our communication. Sometimes we speak as parents, sometimes as children, sometimes as colleagues, siblings, customers, Nebraskans, and a myriad of other "places." All of these are cultural spaces.

Cultural Identity and Cultural Space

Home. Cultural spaces are important influences in the ways that we think about ourselves and others. One of the earliest cultural spaces we experience is our home. Although it is not always the case, home can be a place of safety and security. African American writer Bell Hooks remembers:

> When I was a young girl the journey across town to my grandmother's house was one of the most intriguing experiences... I remember this journey not just because of the stories I would hear. It was a movement away from the segregated blackness of our community into a poor white neighborhood [where] we would have to pass that terrifying whiteness—those white faces on porches staring down on us with hate... Oh! That feeling of safety, of arrival, of homecoming when we finally reached the edges of her yard.

Home, of course, is not the same as the physical location it occupies, nor the building (the house) on that location. Home is variously defined as specific addresses, cities, states, regions, even nations. Although we might have historical ties to a particular place, not everyone feels the same relationship between those places and their own identities.

The relationship between place and cultural identity varies. Writer Steven Saylor explains:

> Texas is a long way, on the map and otherwise, from San Francisco. "Steven," said my mother once, "you live in another country out there." She was right, and what I feel when I fly from California to Texas must be what an expatriate from any country feels returning to his childhood home ... Texas is home, but Texas is also a country whose citizenship I voluntarily renounced.

The discourses surrounding Texas are giving meaning to Texas no longer "fit" Saylor's sense of who he is or who he wants to be. We all negotiate various relationships to the cultural meanings attached to particular places or spaces we inhabit. Consider writer Harlan Greene's relationship to his hometown in South Carolina. Greene writes:

> Now that I no longer live there, I often think longingly of my hometown of Charleston. My heart beats faster and color rushes to my cheek whenever I hear someone mentioning her; I lean over and listen, for even bearing the name casts a spell. Mirages rise up, and I am as overcome and drenched in images as a runner just come from running. I see the steeples, the streets, the lush setting.

Despite his own attachment to Charleston, compared to Saylor's rejection of Texas, Greene does not believe that Charleston feels the same way toward him. He explains, "But I still think of Charleston; I return to her often and always will. I think of her warmly. I claim her now; even though I know she will never claim me."

The complex relationships we have between various places and our identities resist simplistic reduction. These three writers (Hooks, Saylor, and Greene) have negotiated different sentiments toward "home."

Neighborhood. One significant type of cultural space that emerged in U.S. cities in the latter part of the 19th century and the early 20th century was the ethnic or racial neighborhood. By law and custom, some cities developed segregated neighborhoods under different political pressures. Malcolm X[8], in his autobiography tells of the strict laws that governed where his family could live after their house burned down:

> My father prevailed on some friends to clothe and house us temporarily; then he moved us into another house on the outskirts of East Lansing. In those days Negroes weren't allowed after dark in East Lansing proper. There's where Michigan State University is located; I related all of this to an audience of students when I spoke there in January, 1963. I told them how East Lansing harassed us so much that we had to move again, this time two miles out of town, into the country.

The history of "White-only" areas pervades the history of the United States and the development of its cultural geography. Neighborhoods exemplify how power influences intercultural contact. Some cultural groups define who gets to live where and dictate the rules by which other groups must live. These rules were enforced through legal means and by harassment. For Bell Hooks and Malcolm X, the lines of segregation were clear and unmistakable.

In San Francisco, different racial politics constructed and isolated Chinatown.

The boundaries that demarcated the acceptable place for Chinese and Chinese Americans were clear and were carefully guarded through violence:

> The sense of being physically sealed within the boundaries of Chinatown was impressed on the few immigrants coming into the settlement by frequent stonings which occurred as they came up Washington or Clay Street from the piers. It was perpetuated by attacks of white toughs in the adjacent North Beach area and downtown around Union Square, who amused themselves by beating Chinese who came into these areas. "In those days, the boundaries were from Kearny to Powell, and from California to Broadway. If you ever passed them and went out there, the white kids would throw stones at you."

In contrast to Malcolm X's exclusion from East Lansing, Michigan, the Chinese of San Francisco were forced to live in a marked-off territory. Yet, we must be careful not to confuse the experience of Chinese in San Francisco with the experiences of all Chinese in the U.S. Nor should we assume that vast migrations of Chinese have led to the development of Chinatowns in other cities outside of China. The settlement of Chinese immigrants in the 13th Arrondissement of Paris, for example, reflects a completely different intersection between cultures. As two sociologists noted, "There is no American-style Chinatown" in Paris.

Within the context of different power relations and historical forces, settlement patterns of other cultural groups created various kinds of ethnic enclaves across the U.S. landscape. Many small towns across the Midwest were settled by particular European groups—Germans in Amana, Iowa; Dutch in Pella, Iowa; and so on. Cities, too, have their neighborhoods, based on settlement patterns. South Philadelphia is largely Italian American; South Boston is largely Irish American; Overtown in Miami is largely African American. Although it is no longer legal to mandate that people live in particular districts or neighborhoods based on their racial or ethnic backgrounds, the continued existence of such neighborhoods underscores their historical development and ongoing function. Economics, family ties, social needs, and education are some factors in the perpetuation of these cultural spaces.

The relationships between identity, power, and cultural space are quite complex. Power relations influence who (or what) gets to claim who (or what), and under what conditions. Some subcultures are accepted and promoted within a particular cultural space. Some are tolerated, but others may be unacceptable.

Identifying with various cultural spaces is a negotiated process that is difficult (sometimes impossible) to predict and control.

Regionalism. The rise of regional conflict, nationalism, ethnic revival, and religious conflict point to the continuing struggles over who gets to define whom. Such conflicts are not new, though. In fact, some cultural spaces (such as Jerusalem) have been ongoing sites of struggle for a very long time.

Although regions may not always be clearly marked on maps of the world, many people identify quite strongly with particular regions. Regionalism can take many different forms of expression, from symbolic expressions of identification to armed conflict. Within the United States, people may identify themselves or others as Southerners or Midwesterners. People from Montreal might identify more strongly with the province of Quebec than their country, Canada. Similarly some Corsicans might feel a need to negotiate their identity with France. Sometimes people fly regional flags, wear particular kinds of clothes, celebrate regional holidays, and participate in other cultural activities to communicate their regional identification.

National borders may appear simple, but they often conceal conflicting regional identities. To understand how intercultural communications may be affected by national borders, we must consider how history, power, identity, culture, and context come into play. Understanding these issues will enable you to approach the complex process of human communication.

Changing Cultural Space

In the following we'd like to focus on some of the driving needs of those who change cultural spaces.

Traveling. We often change cultural spaces when we travel. Traveling is frequently viewed as an unimportant leisure activity but it is more than that. In terms of intercultural communication, traveling changes cultural spaces in a way that often transforms the traveler. Changing cultural spaces means changing who you are and how you interact with others. Perhaps the old saying, "When in Rome, do as the Romans do," holds true today as we cross cultural spaces with more frequency than ever.

Do you alter your communication style when you encounter travelers who are not in their traditional cultural space? Do you assume that they should interact in the ways prescribed by your cultural space? These are some of the issues that travel raises.

Migration. People also change cultural spaces when they relocate. Moving, of course, involves a different kind of change in cultural spaces than traveling. In traveling, the change is fleeting, temporary and usually desirable. It is something that we seek out. People who migrate do not always seek out this change. For example, many people were forced from their homelands of Rwanda and Bosnia and settled elsewhere. Many immigrants leave their homelands and move so they can survive. They often find it difficult to adjust to the change, especially if the language and customs of the new cultural space are unfamiliar.

Even within the United States, people often find it difficult to adapt to new surroundings when they move. Tom, one of this book's authors, remembers that when Yankees[9] moved to the South they often were unfamiliar with the custom of banks closing early on Wednesday or with the traditional New Year's Day foods in the South. Ridiculing customs of their new cultural space simply led to further intercultural communication problems.

Postmodern Cultural Spaces

When one of the authors, Tom, spent a summer in New York City, a small group of his friends met with him at least once a week to have dinner at a restaurant. They followed a few rules: First, they went to a different restaurant each time; second, they spoke French exclusively (except when they spoke with waiters); and third, they were allowed to invite others who would follow the rules. The group fluctuated but included academics and business people, Europeans, and people from the United States who had traveled or lived abroad.

The group highlighted the dynamic nature of cultural space. Indeed, while group members ate, they not only spoke French, but they also used European table manners. They created a cultural space that was fluid in place and time. It was a moving space that was not quite French but not exactly New York, either. The group traveled throughout lower and mid-Manhattan, taking its cultural space with it. Unmarked by boundaries or ethnic ties, the cultural space the group created remained fluid—a postmodern cultural space.

The fluidity and fleeting nature of this cultural space stand in sharp contrast to the 18th-century notions of space, which promoted land ownership, surveys, borders, colonies, territories. No passport is needed to travel in the postmodern cultural space, because there is no border guarding. The dynamic nature of postmodern cultural spaces underscores its response to changing cultural needs. The space exists only as long as it is needed in its present form.

Postmodern cultural spaces are tenuous and dynamic. They are created within existing places, without following any particular guide: there is no marking off of territory, no sense of permanence or official recognition. The post-modern cultural space exists only while it is used.

The ideology of fixed spaces and categories is currently being challenged by postmodernist notions of space and location. Phoenix, for example, which became a city only in the past few decades, has no Chinatown, no Japantown, no Irish district, no Polish neighborhood, no Italian area. Instead, people of Polish descent, for example, might live anywhere in the metropolitan area, but might congregate for special occasions or for specific reasons. On Sundays, the Polish Catholic service draws many people from throughout Phoenix. When people want to buy Polish breads and pastries, they can go to the Polish bakery and also speak Polish there. Ethnic identity is only one of several identities that these people negotiate. When they desire recognition and interaction based on their Polish heritage, they may do so. When they seek other forms of identification, they may go to places where they can be Phoenix Suns fans, and so on. Ethnic identity is neither the sole factor nor necessarily the most important factor at all times in their lives.

The markers of ethnic life in Phoenix are the urban sites where people congregate when they desire ethnic cultural contact. At other times, they may frequent other locations in expressing other aspects of their identities. In this sense, the postmodern urban space is dynamic and allows people to participate in the communication of identity in new ways.

Summary

This chapter has examined both nonverbal communication principles and cultural spaces. Nonverbal communication compares to verbal communication and operates at a subconscious level. It is learned implicitly and can reinforce, substitute for or contradict verbal behaviors.

Nonverbal behaviors can communicate relational meaning, status, and deception. Nonverbal codes are influenced by culture, although many cultures share some nonverbal behaviors. Nonverbal codes include proxemics, eye contact, facial expressions, chronemics, and silence. Sometimes cultural differences in nonverbal behaviors can lead to stereotyping of other cultures.

Semiotics is one approach to studying nonverbal communication. Signs, cultural codes, and myths are discussed as they relate to semiotics.

Cultural space influences cultural identity. Cultural spaces relate to issues of power and intercultural communication. Homes, neighborhoods, regions, and nations are all examples of cultural spaces. Two ways of changing cultural spaces are travel and migration. Postmodern cultural spaces are tenuous and dynamic, accommodating people of different cultural identities who coexist.

Notes

1. From *Intercultural Communication in Contexts*, Judith N. Martin, and Thomas K. Nakayama, California: Mayfield Publishing Company, 1997.
2. David Matsumoto received his Bachelor of Arts from the University of Michigan (High Honors) and Master's and Ph. D. Degree in Psychology from the University of California at Berkeley. He is an elected Fellow of the Western Psychological Association. Dr. Matsumoto is also active in the Olympic sport of Judo. He served as the Executive Secretary and Director of the United States Judo Federation from 1988 to 1994. He is currently the Director of Development for the United States Judo Federation.
3. William B. Gudykunst is Professor of Speech Communication at the College of Communications, California State University, Fullerton. He has written and edited numerous works including the *Handbook of Intercultural and International Communication* and *Bridging Differences: Effective Intergroup Communication* as well as the best-selling introductory undergraduate texts *Building Bridges: Interpersonal Skills for a Changing World* (Houghton Mifflin) and *Communicating with Strangers: An Approach to Intercultural Communication* (McGraw-Hill). He is extremely well known in the discipline and is one of its most prolific writers/scholars in the areas of intercultural communication and human communication theory.
4. Keith Basso is an anthropologist who studies language and culture. He has done fieldwork in Australia and the American Southwest. Basso's fieldwork includes a long-term relationship with the Western Apache community of Cibecue which began in 1959 and is still there today. He received his B. A. from Harvard University in 1962 and his Ph. D. from Stanford University. Basso is currently a member of the Anthropology Department at the University of New Mexico. He has written and edited many books. Basso has also written numerous articles dealing with language and culture.
5. Quakers, also called Society of Friends, are believers of a church known for its pacifism, humanitarianism and emphasis on inner quiet. Founded in 17th-century England by George Fox, it was persecuted for its rejection of organized churches and of any dogmatic creed. Many Quakers emigrated to America, where in spite of early persecution they were prominent among the colonizers. In 1681, William Penn established his "Holy Experiment" in Pennsylvania, and from that point the church's main growth took place in America.
6. Amish are a conservative group of the Mennonite sect, which was founded by Jakob

Ammann in Switzerland in the 1690s. In the 18th century, members settled in what are now Ind. Ohio and Pa. and today they live in other states too in the USA. Literal interpretation of the Bible leads their farm communities to reject modern life (including electricity and cars). Amish wear old-style clothes, plow with horses and observe the Sabbath strictly.

7. Roland Barthes is a key figure in international intellectual life. He is one of the most important intellectual figures to have emerged in postwar France and his writings continue to have an influence on critical debates today. When he died in 1981, he left a body of major work but, as many of his friends and his admirers claimed, with still more important work to come. *Mythologies* is one of Barthes's most popular works because in it we see the intellectual as humourist, satirist, master stylist and debunker of the myths that surround us all in our daily lives.

8. Malcolm X is the adopted name of Malcolm Little (1925—1965). He is an American black nationalist leader.

9. Yankee is initially a disparaging term for Dutch free-booter, later it applied to English settlers by colonial Dutch in New York. Now it may be a colloquial term for a New Englander, any US northerner (used in the South), or any American (used outside the USA).

Questions for Discussion

1. What are the major similarities and differences between verbal and nonverbal communication? Can you provide some examples?
2. What is meant by metamessage? Why do the authors say that nonverbal communication plays an important role in establishing the relations we have with others?
3. What is your understanding of cultural stereotypes? How should people deal with them in intercultural communication?
4. What does semiotics mean to you? How can the study of semiotics help you understand the meanings communicated by nonverbal codes?
5. There is a proverb of "Speech is silver, and silence is gold" in English, while in Chinese, there is the Confucian caveat: "A clever tongue and fine appearance are rarely signs of benevolence" in the *Analects of Confucius*. How do you interpret the two and what suggestions would you offer to those Chinese who are planning to go abroad for further study, temporary jobs, or long-term settlement?

Online Mini-Case Studies and Viewpoints-Sharing

Obama's Lapels

In a television interview in fall 2007, presidential candidate Barack Obama was asked why he wasn't wearing an American flag lapel pin worn by many politicians. Some in the audience felt that wearing a flag pin is a sign of patriotism and shows visible support for the United States in a time of war—a prerequisite for being a viable candidate for the office of the president of the United States.

"The truth is that right after 9/11 I had a pin," Mr. Obama replied, "Shortly after 9/11, particularly because as we're talking about the Iraq war, that became a substitute for, I think, true patriotism, which is speaking out on issues that are of importance to our national security. I decided I won't wear that pin on my chest," he added. "Instead I'm going to try to tell the American people what I believe will make this country great and hopefully that will be a testimony to my patriotism... . My attitude is that I'm less concerned about what you're wearing on your lapel than what is in your heart. And you show your patriotism by how you treat your fellow Americans, especially those who served."

Online Research

Search online for more stories concerning Barack Obama's intercultural efforts adapting to the American culture and finally becoming the President of the United States.

Unit Six

Cultural Patterns and Perception

Reading One

Introductory Remarks

Cultural patterns are defined as shared beliefs, values, and norms. Because of cultural patterns, members of a culture behave almost similarly in similar situations. The present selection discusses three major conceptual taxonomies of the variations in cultural patterns.

The first taxonomy mainly developed by Edward Stewart gives a detailed explanation of the variations in beliefs, values, and norms, which are associated with cultural patterns. This taxonomy addresses the way a culture orients itself to activities, social relations, the self, and the world. The second taxonomy developed by Edward T. Hall places culture on a continuum from high context to low context. High context cultures prefer messages in which most of the meaning is implicit or implied. Low context cultures prefer messages in which the information is expressed explicitly. The third taxonomy developed by Geert Hofstede identifies four dimensions of cultural variation: power distance, uncertainty avoidance, individualism-collectivism, and masculinity-femininity. The first dimension assesses the degree to which the culture believes that institutional power should be distributed equally or unequally. The second describes the extent to which cultures prefer and can tolerate ambiguity and change. The third discusses the degree to which a culture relies on and has allegiance to the self or the group. The last indicates the degree to which a culture values assertiveness and the quality of life.

The three taxonomies provide us with alternative ways to understand and appreciate cultures more rationally and with the multiple frames of reference to comprehend intercultural communication.

Cultural Patterns and Communication: Taxonomies[1]

Myron W. Lustig and Jolene Koester

The present chapter focuses on specific conceptual taxonomies that are useful for understanding cultural differences. We have chosen three different but related taxonomies to describe variations in cultural patterns. The first, developed principally by Edward Stewart, was selected because it explains, with a great deal of detail, the variations in beliefs, values, and norms that are typically associated with cultural patterns. The second was developed by Edward Hall, who noted that cultures differ in the extent to which their primary message patterns are high context or low context. Finally, we describe the ideas of Geert Hofstede[2], who identifies four dimensions on which cultures vary. Hofstede's work is impressive principally because he provides a statistical profile of how and to what degree cultures actually differ from one another.

TAXONOMIES OF CULTURAL PATTERNS

As you read the descriptions of cultural patterns by Stewart, Hall, and Hofstede, we caution you to remember three points. First there is nothing sacred about these approaches and the internal categories they employ. Each approach takes the whole of cultural patterns (beliefs, values, and norms) and divides them in different ways. A rather crude comparison is the different ways in which people could slice pizza. It is possible to take a round pizza and slice it into pieces by cutting from the edges through the center, which would result in pie-shaped pieces. It would also be possible to take the same round pizza and, with multiple horizontal and vertical cuts, produce primarily rectangular or square pieces except for those slices on the edges, which would be rounded. Either way, it is the same pizza, though it is sliced or presented in different ways. Similarly, the Stewart, Hall, and Hofstede approaches simply slice up the domain of cultural patterns into pieces of different shapes and sizes.

Our second caution about the descriptions of cultural patterns is that the parts of each of the systems are interrelated. We begin the description of each system at an arbitrarily chosen point, but what we say at one point presupposes other parts of the system that have not yet been described. Cultural patterns are understandable not in isolation but as a unique whole.

Finally, we caution you that individual members of a culture may vary greatly from the pattern that is typical within that culture. Therefore, as you study these approaches to cultural patterns, we encourage you to make some judgments about how your own culture fits into the pattern. Then, as you place it within the pattern, also try to discern how you, as an individual, fit into the patterns described. Similarly, as you learn about other cultural patterns, please remember that a specific person may or may not be a typical representative of that culture.

Stewart's Cultural Patterns

Edward Stewart compared the preferred cultural patterns of the typical middle class Euro-Americans with those of other cultures. The taxonomy of cultural patterns in this section is adapted from Stewart's work, with modifications and refinements based on the work of John Condon and Fathi Yousef.

Members of a culture generally have a preferred set of responses to the world. Imagine that for each experience, there is a range of possible responses from which a culture selects its preferred response. In this section we will describe these alternative responses to events that members of a culture might select. In so doing, we will compare and contrast the cultural patterns of different cultural groups and suggest their implications on the process of interpersonal communication. Comparing the patterns of different cultures can sometimes be tricky because a characteristic of one culture, when compared to a second culture, may appear very different than it would when compared to a third culture. Stewart's work is particularly useful because it describes a broad range of cultural patterns against which a particular culture can be understood.

The four major elements of Stewart's taxonomy address the manner in which a culture orients itself to activities, social relations, the self and the world. As you read the descriptions in the sections that follow, try to recognize the preferred patterns of your culture. Also focus on your own beliefs, values, and norms, as they may differ in certain respects from your culture's predominant pattern.

Activity orientation defines how the people of a culture view human actions and the expression of self through activities. This orientation provides answers to questions like the following:

- Is it important to be engaged in activities in order to be a "good" member of one's culture?
- Can and should people change the circumstances of their lives?
- Is the desirable pace of life fast or slow?
- Is work very different from play?
- Which is more important, work or play?
- Is life a series of problems to be solved or simply a collection of events to be experienced?

To define their activity orientation, cultures usually choose a point on the being-becoming-doing continuum. "Being" is an activity orientation that values nonaction and an acceptance of the status quo. African-American and Greek cultures are usually regarded as "being" cultures. Another characterization of this orientation is a willingness to believe that all events are determined by fate and are therefore inevitable or fatalistic. Hindus[3] from India often espouse this view.

A "becoming" orientation sees humans as evolving and changing; people with this orientation, including Native Americans and most South Americans, are predisposed to think of ways to change themselves as a means to change the world.

"Doing" is the dominant characteristic of Euro-Americans, who rarely question the assumption that it is important to get things done. Thus, Euro-Americans ask, "What do you do?" when they first meet someone, and Monday morning conversations between co-workers often center on what each person "did" over the weekend. Similarly, young children are asked what they want to be when they grow up, and cultural heroes are those who do things. The "doing" culture is often the striving culture, in which people seek to change and control what is happening to them. The common adage "Where there's a will there's a way" captures the essence of this cultural pattern. When faced with adversity, for example, Euro-Americans encourage one another to fight on, to work hard, and not to give up.

A culture's activity orientation also suggests the pace of life. The fast, hectic pace of Euro-Americans, governed by clocks, appointments, and schedules, has become so commonly accepted that it is almost a cliché. The pace of life in cultures such as India, Kenya, Argentina, and among African-Americans is less hectic, more relaxed, and more comfortably paced. In African-Americanculture, for example, orientations to time are driven less by a need to "get things done" and conform to external demands than by a sense of participation in events that create their own rhythm. As Jack Daniel[4] and Geneva Smitherman[5] suggest about time in African-American culture,

> Being on time has to do with participating in the fulfillment of an activity that is vital to the sustenance of a basic rhythm, rather than with appearing on the scene at, say "twelve o'clock sharp." The key is not to be "on time" but "in time."

How a person measures her or his success is also related to the activity orientation. In cultures with a "doing" orientation, activity is evaluated by scrutinizing a tangible product or by evaluating some observable action directed at others. In other words, activity should have a purpose or a goal. In the "being" and "becoming" cultures, activity is not necessarily connected to external products or actions; the contemplative monk or the great thinker are examples of those who are most valued. Thus the process of striving toward the goal is sometimes far more important than accomplishing it.

In "doing" cultures, work is seen as a separate activity from play and an end in itself. In the "being" and "becoming" cultures, work is a means to an end, and there is no clear-cut separation between work and play. The social life for these individuals spills over into their work life. When members of a "being" culture work in the environment of a "doing" culture, there are often misinterpretations of behavior. A Latina employee described her conversation with a Euro-American co-worker when the latter expressed anger that she spent so much "work" time on the telephone with family and friends. For the Latina, it was important to keep in contact with her friends and family; for the Euro-American, only work was done at work, and one's social and personal relationships were totally separated from the working environment. In a "doing" culture, employees who spend too much time chatting with their fellow employees may be reprimanded by a supervisor. In the "being" and "becoming" cultures, those in charge fully expect their workers to mix working and socializing. Along with the activity orientation of "doing" comes a problem-solution orientation. The preferred way of dealing with a difficulty is to see it as a challenge to be met or a problem to be solved. The world is viewed as something that ought to be changed in order to solve problems rather than as something that ought to be accepted as it is, with whatever characteristics it has.

In every culture, these preferences for particular orientations to activities shape the interpersonal communication patterns that will occur. In "doing" cultures, interpersonal communication is characterized by concerns about what people do and how they solve problems. There are expectations that people should be involved in activities, that work comes before play, and that people should sacrifice in other parts of their lives in order to achieve their work responsibilities. In "being" cultures, interpersonal communication is characterized by being together rather than by accomplishing specific tasks, and there is generally greater balance between work and play.

Social relations orientation describes how the people in a culture organize themselves and relate to one another. This orientation provides answers to questions like the following:

· To what extent are some people in the culture considered better or superior

to others?
- Can social superiority be obtained through birth, age, good deeds, or material achievement and success?
- Are formal, ritualized interaction sequences expected?
- In what ways does the culture's language require one to make social distinctions?
- What responsibilities and obligations do people have to their extended families, their neighbors, their employers or employees, and others?

A social relations orientation can range from one that emphasizes differences and social hierarchy to one that strives for equality and the absence of hierarchy. Many Euro-Americans, for example, emphasize equality and evenness in their interpersonal relationships, even though certain groups have been treated in discriminatory and unequal ways. Nevertheless, equality as a value and belief is frequently expressed and is called on to justify one's actions. The phrase "We are all human, aren't we?" captures the essence of this cultural tenet. From within this cultural framework, distinctions based on age, gender, role, or occupation are discouraged. Conversely, cultures such as Korean emphasize status differences between individuals. Mexican-American culture, drawing on its cultural roots in traditional Mexican values, also celebrates status differences and formalizes different ways of communicating with people depending on who they are and what their social characteristics happen to be.

One way to notice differences in social relations orientations is in the degree of importance a culture places on formality. In cultures that emphasize formality, people address others by appropriate titles, and highly prescriptive rules govern the interaction. Conversely, in cultures that stress equality, people believe that human relationships develop best when those involved can be informal with one another. Students from other cultures who study in the United States are usually taken aback by the seeming informality that exists between teachers and students. Professors allow, even ask, students to call them by their first names, and students disagree and challenge their teachers in front of the class. The quickness with which interpersonal relationships in the United States move to a first-name basis is mystifying to those from cultures where the personal form of address is used only for selected, special individuals. Many U.S. Americans who share aspects of both Euro-American culture and another culture also express difficulty with this aspect of cultural behavior.

In cultures such as Japan, the Republic of Korea, and China, individuals identify with only a few distinct groups, and the ties binding people to these groups are so strong that group membership may endure for a lifetime. Examples of these relationships include nuclear and extended families, school friends, neighbors, work groups, and voluntary organizations. In contrast, Euro-Americans typically belong to many groups throughout their lifetimes, and although the groups may be very important for a period of time, they are easily discarded when they are no longer needed. That is, voluntary and informal groups are meant to be important for brief periods of time, often serving a transitory purpose. In addition, it is accepted and even expected that Euro-Americans will change jobs and companies quite often. "Best friends" may only be best friends for brief periods.

Another important way in which social relations orientations can vary is the way in which people define their social roles or their place in a culture. In some cultures, one's place is determined by the family and the position into which one is born. At the other extreme are cultures in which all people, regardless of family position, can achieve success and high status. Among African-Americans and Euro-Americans, for instance, there is a widespread belief that social and economic class should not predetermine a person's opportunities and choices. From the story of poor Abraham Lincoln, who went from a log cabin to the White House, to the heroine in the movie *Working Girl*, who went from an unsophisticated secretary to a polished financier, there is a common belief that people should not be restricted by their birth.

Cultural patterns can also prescribe the appropriate behaviors for men and women. In some cultures, very specific behaviors are expected; other cultures allow more ambiguity in the expected roles of women and men.

A culture's social relations orientation affects the style of interpersonal communication that is most preferred. Cultures may emphasize directness or confrontation, which is the typical Euro-American pattern, or it may emphasize indirectness, obliqueness, ambiguity, and the use of intermediaries.

The Euro-American preference for "Putting your cards on the table" and "Telling it like it is" presupposes a world in which it is desirable to be explicit, direct, and specific about personal reactions and ideas, even at the expense of social discomfort on the part of the person with whom one is interacting. For Euro-Americans, good interpersonal communication skills include stating directly one's personal need and reactions to the behaviors of others. Thus, if Euro-Americans hear that others have complained about them, they would probably wonder, "Why didn't they tell me directly if they have a problem with something that I have done?"

Contrast this approach to that of Asian cultures such as Japan, the Republic of Korea, Thailand, and China, where saving face and maintaining interpersonal harmony are so highly valued that it would be catastrophic to confront another person directly and verbally express one's anger. In the many Asian-American cultures in the United States, the same values are also usually preferred. Yet a Filipino-American man describes being very discouraged and upset when, on a visit to the Phillipines, he would ask people to accompany him and, although it seemed to him that they had agreed verbally, subsequently they did not appear. As he says of the experience, "They would never say no; rather they would say yes or I'll try." Unfortunately, he felt as if he had been "stood up" several times, until someone explained to him that Filipinos think it is rude to turn down an invitation directly.

The tendency to be verbally explicit in face-to-face interactions is related to a preference for direct interaction rather than interaction through intermediaries. Among Euro-Americans there is a belief that ideally people should depend only on themselves to accomplish what needs to be done. Therefore, the notion of using intermediaries to accomplish either personal or professional business goals is not widely accepted.

Although African-Americans prefer indirectness and ambiguity in conversations with fellow cultural members, they do not choose to use intermediaries in these conversations. In many cultures, however, the use of intermediaries is the preferred method of conducting business or passing on information. Marriages are arranged, business deals are made, homes are purchased, and other major negotiations are all conducted through third parties. These third parties soften and interpret the messages of both sides, thereby shielding the parties from direct, and therefore risky and potentially embarrassing, transactions with each other. Similarly, among many cultures from southern Africa, such as in Swaziland, there is a distinct preference for the use of intermediaries to deal with negotiations and conflict situations. Consider also the experience of the director of an English program in Tunisia, a culture that depends on intermediaries. One of the Tunisian teachers had been consistently late to his morning classes. Rather than calling the teacher in and directly explaining the problem, the director asked the teacher's friend about the teacher's health and happiness. The director indicated that the teacher's late arrival for class may have been a sign that something was wrong. The friend then simply indirectly conveyed the director's concern to the late teacher, who was late no more.

A culture's social relations orientation also affects the sense of social reciprocity, that is, the underlying sense of obligation and responsibility between people. Some cultures prefer independence and a minimum number of obligations and responsibilities; alternatively, other cultures accept obligations and encourage dependence. The nature of the dependence is often related to the types of status and the degree of formality that exists between the individuals. Cultures that depend on hierarchy and formality to guide their social interactions are also likely to have both a formal means for fulfilling social obligations and clearly defined norms for expressing them.

Self-orientation describes how people's identities are formed, whether the culture views the self as changeable, what motivates individual actions, and the kinds of people who are valued and respected. A culture's self-orientation provides answers to questions like the following:

- Do people believe they have their own unique identities that separate them from others?
- Does the self reside in the individual or in the groups to which the individual belongs?
- What responsibilities does the individual have to others?
- What motivates people to behave as they do?
- Is it possible to respect a person who is judged "bad" in one part of life but is successful in another part of life?

For most Euro-Americans, the emphasis on the individual self is so strong and so pervasive that it is almost impossible for them to comprehend a different point of view. Thus, many Euro-Americans believe that the self is located solely within the individual and the individual is definitely separate from others. From a very young age, children are encouraged to make their own decisions. Alternatively, cultures may define who people are only through their associations with others because individuals' self-definitions may not be separate from that of the larger group. Consequently, there is a heightened sense of interdependence, and what happens to the group (family, work group, or social group) happens to the person. For example, scholars like Mary Jane Collier[6] found that Mexican-Americans "place a great deal of emphasis on affiliation and relational solidarity." The sense of being bonded or connected to others is very important to members of this cultural group.

The significance to intercultural communication of a culture's preferences for defining the self is evident in the statement of a Latina student who is describing her friendship with a second-generation Italian-American woman, whose family has also maintained "traditional values."

> I think we are able to communicate so well because our cultural backgrounds are very similar. I have always been family-oriented and so has she. This not only allowed us to get along, but it allowed us to bring our families into our friendship. (For instance) A rule that the two of us had to live by up to this point has been that no matter how old we may get, as long as we are living at home we must ask our parents for permission to go out.

Related to self-orientation is the culture's view of whether people are changeable. Naturally, if a culture believes that people can change, it is likely to expect that human beings will strive to be "better," as the culture defines and describes what "better" means.

The source of motivation for human behavior is also part of a culture's self-orientation. Among Euro-Americans and African-Americans, individuals are motivated to achieve external success in the form of possessions, positions, and power. Self-orientation combines with the "doing" orientation to create a set of beliefs and values that place individuals in total control of their own fate. Individuals must set their own goals and identify the means necessary to achieve them. Consequently, failure is viewed as a lack of will power and a disinclination to give the fullest individual effort. In this cultural framework, individuals regard it as necessary to rely on themselves rather than on others.

Another distinguishing feature of the cultural definition of self is whether the culture emphasizes duties, rights, or some combination of the two. One culture that induces its members to act because it is their duty to do so is Japan. A contrasting culture is the Euro-American, in which the concept of duties to others is not a powerful motivator.

An additional part of self-orientation is the set of characteristics of those individuals who are valued and cherished. Cultures vary in their allegiance to the old or to the young, for example. Many cultures venerate their elders and view them as a source of wisdom and valuable life experience. Individuals in these cultures base decisions on the preferences and desires of their elders. Many Asian and Asian-American cultures illustrate this preference. The value on youth typifies the Euro-American culture, in which innovation and new ideas, rather than the wisdom of the past, are regarded as important. Euro-Americans venerate the upstart, the innovator, and the person who tries something new.

World orientation. Cultural patterns also tell people how to locate themselves in relation to the spiritual world, nature, and other living things. A world orientation provides answers to questions like the following:

- Are human beings intrinsically good or evil?
- Are humans different from other animals and plants?
- Are people in control of, subjugated by, or living in harmony with the forces of nature?
- Do spirits of the dead inhabit and affect the human world?
- How should time be valued and understood?

In the African and African-American worldview human beings live in an interactive state with the natural and spiritual world. Daniel and Smitherman describe a fundamental tenet of the traditional African worldview as that of "a dynamic, hierarchical unity between God, man, and nature with God serving as the head of the hierarchy." This relationship between the spiritual and material world, then, considers humans to be an integral part of nature. Thus, in the African and African-American world-view, "One becomes a 'living witness' when he aligns himself with the forces of nature and instead of being a proselytized 'true believer' strives to live in harmony with the universe." Native American groups, as well, clearly have a view of humans as living in harmony with nature. Latino culture places a great value on spirituality but views humans as being subjugated to nature and with little power to control circumstances that influence their lives.

Most Euro-Americans view humans as separate and distinct from nature and other forms of life. Because of the supremacy of the individual and the presumed uniqueness of each person, most Euro-Americans regard nature as something to be manipulated and controlled in order to make human life better. Excellent examples of this cultural belief can be found in news reports whenever a natural disaster occurs in the United States. For instance, when a large earthquake hit San Francisco in fall 1989 and 22 people were killed because a portion of a double-decker freeway collapsed, political leaders from California were outraged that they had not been told that the state's bridges could be unsafe. The assumption in these pronouncements was that the consequences of natural forces such as earthquakes could have been prevented simply by using better technology and by reinforcing the bridges to withstand the forces of nature.

This position is also associated with a belief that disease, poverty, and adversity can be overcome in order to achieve health and wealth. In this cultural framework the "natural" part of the human experience—illness, loss, even death—can be overcome, or at least postponed, by selecting the right courses of action and having the right kinds of attitudes.

The spiritual and physical worlds can be viewed as distinct or as one. Among Euro-Americans there is generally a clear understanding that the physical world, of which humans are a part, is separate from the spiritual world. If people believe in a spiritual world, it exists apart from the everyday places where people live, work, and play. Individuals who say they are psychic or who are mind-readers are viewed with suspicion and curiosity. Those who have seen ghosts are questioned to find a more "logical" and "rational" explanation. In other cultural frameworks, however, it is "logical" and "rational" for spirits to live in both animate and inanimate objects.

The final aspect of a culture's world orientation concerns how people conceptualize time. Some cultures choose to describe the past as most important, others emphasize the present, and still others emphasize the future. Native Americans and Latinos are present-oriented. Euro-Americans, of course, are future-oriented.

A culture's underlying patterns, according to Stewart, consist of orientations to activity, social relations, the self, and the world. The interdependence among these aspects of culture are obvious from the preceding discussion. Stewart's taxonomy provides a way to understand, rather than to judge, different cultural predispositions, and it demonstrates that there are different ways of defining what is the "real," "good," and "correct" way to behave.

Hall's High- and Low-Context Cultural Patterns

Edward T. Hall, a well-known writer about the relationship between culture and communication, organizes cultures by the amount of information implied by the setting or context itself, regardless of the specific words that are spoken. Hall argues that every human being is faced with so many perceptual stimuli—sights, sounds, smells, tastes, and bodily sensations—that it is impossible to pay attention to them all. Therefore, one of the functions of culture is to provide a screen between the person and all of those stimuli to indicate what perceptions to notice and how to interpret them. Hall's approach is compatible with the other approaches discussed in this chapter. Where it differs is the importance he places on the role of context.

According to Hall, cultures differ on a continuum that ranges from high to low context. High-context (HC) cultures prefer to use high-context messages, in which most of the meaning is either implied by the physical setting or is presumed to be part of the individual's internalized beliefs, values, and norms; very little is provided in the coded, explicit, transmitted part of the message. Examples of high-context cultures include Japanese, African-American, Mexican, and Latino cultures. Low-context (LC) cultures prefer to use low-context messages, which are just the opposite of high-context messages; the majority of the information in low-context messages is vested in the explicit code. Low-context cultures include German, Swedish, Euro-American, and English cultures.

A very simple example of high-context communication can be found in the interactions that take place in long-term relationship between two people, who are often able to interpret even the slightest gesture or the briefest comment. The message does not need to be stated explicitly because it is carried in the shared understandings about the relationship.

A simple example of low-context communication is now experienced by more and more people as they interact with computers. For computers to "understand" a message, every statement must be very precise. Many computers will not know how to understand instructions that do not have every space, period, letter, and number in precisely the right location. The message must be overt and very explicit.

Hall's description of high- and low-context cultures is based on the idea that some cultures have a preponderance of messages that are high-context, others have messages that are mostly low-context, and some cultures have mixtures of both. Hall also describes other characteristics of high- and low-context cultures, which reveal the beliefs, values, and norms of the cultural system. These characteristics include the use of covert or overt messages, the importance of in-groups and out-groups, and the culture's orientation to time.

Use of covert and overt messages. In a high-context culture such as Japan, meanings are internalized and there is a large emphasis on nonverbal codes. Hall describes messages in high-context cultures as almost preprogrammed, in which very little of the interpretation of the message is left to chance because people already know that in the context of the current situation the communicative behaviors will have a specific and particular message. In low-context cultures, people look for the meaning of others' behaviors in the messages that are plainly and explicitly coded. The details of the message are expressed precisely and specifically in the words that the people use as they try to communicate with others.

Another way to think about the difference between high- and low-context cultures is to imagine something with which you are very familiar, such as repairing a car, cooking, sewing, or playing a particular sport. When you talk about that activity with someone else who is also very familiar with it, you will probably be less explicit and instead use a more succinct set of verbal and nonverbal messages. You will talk in a verbal shorthand that does not require you to be specific and precise about every aspect of the ideas that you are expressing because the others know what you mean without their specific presentation. However, if you talk to someone who does not know very much about the activity, you will have to explain more, be more precise and specific, and provide more background information.

In a high-context culture, much more is taken for granted and assumed to be shared, and consequently the overwhelming preponderance of messages are coded in such a way that they do not need to be explicitly and verbally transmitted. Instead, the demands of the situation and the shared meanings among the interactants mean that the preferred interpretation of the messages is already known.

The difference between high-context and low-context cultural styles is illustrated in a dialogue between a Euro-American (low-context culture) and Malaysian (high-context culture); the Malaysian's message is revealed only by implication. Both people in the dialogue teach at a community college in the United States, and the Malaysian's objective in this conversation is to have the Euro-American drive him off campus for lunch because he does not have a car.

MALAYSIAN: Can I ask you a question?
EURO-AMERICAN: Yes, of course.
MALAYSIAN: Do you know what time it is?
EURO-AMERICAN: Yes, it's two o'clock.
MALAYSIAN: Might you have a little soup left in the pot?
EURO-AMERICAN: What? I don't understand.
MALAYSIAN: (*Becoming more explicit since the colleague is not getting the point*): I will be on campus teaching until nine o'clock tonight, a very long day for any person, let alone a hungry one!

> EURO-AMERICAN: (*Finally getting the point*) Would you like me to drive you to a restaurant off campus so you can have lunch?
>
> MALAYSIAN: What a very good idea you have!

Reactions in high-context cultures are likely to be reserved, whereas reactions in low-context cultures are frequently very explicit and readily observable. It is easy to understand why this is so. In high-context cultures, an important purpose in communicating is to promote and sustain harmony among the interactants. Unconstrained reactions could threaten the face or social esteem of the others. In low-context cultures, however, an important purpose in communicating is to convey exact meanings. Explicit messages help to achieve this goal. If messages need to be explicit, so will people's reactions. Even when the message is understood, one cannot assume that the meanings are clear in the absence of verbal messages coded specifically to provide feedback.

Importance of in-groups and out-groups. In high-context cultures, it is very easy to determine who is a member of the group and who is not. Because so much of the meaning of messages is embedded in the rules and rituals of situations, it is easy to tell who is acting according to those norms. As there are fixed and specific expectations for behaviors, deviations are easy to detect.

Another distinction concerns the emphasis placed on the individual in contrast to the group as a source of self-identity. In a high-context culture, the commitment between people is very strong and deep, and responsibility to others takes precedence over responsibility to oneself. Loyalties to families and the members of one's social and work groups are long-lasting and unchanging. This degree of loyalty differs from that found in a low-context culture, in which the bonds between people are very fragile, and the extent of involvement and commitment to long-term relationships is lower.

Orientation to time. The final distinguishable characteristic of high- and low-context cultures is their orientations to time. In the former, time is viewed as more open, less structured, more responsive to the immediate needs of people, and less subject to external goals and constraints. In low-context cultures, time is highly organized, in part because of the additional energy required to understand the messages of others. Low-context cultures are almost forced to pay more attention to time in order to complete the work of living with others.

Edward Hall's placement of cultures onto a continuum that is anchored by preferences for high-context messages and low context messages offers a way to understand other variations in cultural patterns. A high-context culture chooses to use covert and implicit messages that rely heavily on nonverbal code systems. In a high-context culture, the group is very important, as are traditional ways of doing things, and members of the in-group are easily recognized. Time is less structured and more responsive to people's needs. Low-context cultures are characterized by the opposite attributes: Messages are explicit and dependent on verbal codes, group memberships change rapidly, innovation is valued, and time is highly structured. There is a similarity between the Stewart and Hall taxonomies, yet each scholar highlights different aspects of the relationship between universal human issues and the specific choices that a particular culture makes.

Hofstede's Cultural Patterns

Geert Hofstede's impressive studies of cultural differences in work-related value orientations offer another approach to understanding the range of cultural differences. Hofstede's approach is based on the assertion that people carry "mental programs" that are developed during childhood and are reinforced by their culture. These mental programs contain the ideas of one's culture and are expressed through its dominant values. To identify the principal values of different cultures, Hofstede surveyed over 88,000 employees of a large multinational business organization that has branches in 66 countries. The following descriptions are based on the information obtained in 40 countries with sample sizes large enough to permit valid inferences.

Through theoretical reasoning and statistical analyses, Hofstede identified four dimensions along which dominant patterns of a culture can be ordered: power distance, uncertainty avoidance, individualism-collectivism, and masculinity-femininity. Recent evidence suggests that Hofstede's dimensions are applicable not only to work-related values but also to cultural values generally.

Power distance. One of the basic concerns in all cultures, and for which they must all find a solution, is the issue of human inequality. Contrary to the claim in the U.S. *Declaration of Independence* that "all men are created equal," all people in a culture do not have equal levels of status or social power. Depending on the culture, some people might be regarded as superior to others because of their wealth, age, gender, education, physical strength, birth order, personal achievements, family background, occupation, or a wide variety of other characteristics.

Cultures also differ in the extent to which they view such status inequalities as good or bad, right or wrong, just or unjust, and fair or unfair. That is, all cultures have particular value orientations about the appropriateness or importance of status differences and social hierarchies. Hofstede refers to these variations as the power distance dimension, which reflects the degree to which the culture believes that institutional and organizational power should be distributed unequally and the decisions of the power holders should be challenged or accepted.

Hofstede has created a power distance index (PDI) to assess a culture's relative location on the power distance dimension. At one extreme are such cultures as Austria, Denmark, Israel, and New Zealand. These cultures, which all have relatively low PDIs and prefer small power distances as a cultural value, believe in the importance of minimizing social or class inequalities, questioning or challenging authority figures, reducing hierarchical organizational structures, and using power only for legitimate purposes. Conversely, cultures in India, Mexico, the Philippines, and Venezuela all have relatively high PDIs and prefer large power distances. They believe in a social order in which each person has a rightful and protected place, the actions of authorities should not be challenged or questioned, hierarchy and inequality are appropriate and beneficial, and those with social status have a right to use their power for whatever purposes and in whatever ways they deem desirable.

Predictors of power distance. What can account for the differences in a culture's preferred level of power distance? Surprisingly, Hofstede suggests that three factors—climate, population size, and wealth—are strongly implicated.

Climate as measured by geographical latitude, is by far the best single predictor of a culture's power distance. Cultures that live in high-latitude climates that are far from the equator, and therefore have moderate to cold climates, tend to have low PDI scores. Cultures that live in low-latitude climates that are near the equator, and therefore have tropical or subtropical climates, tend to have high PDI scores. Hofstede speculates that the relationship between climate and power distance occurs because of the extent to which a culture's climate requires the culture to invent technological solutions to the weather problems that threaten its very survival. His reasoning is as follows:

In colder and more extreme climates, human survival requires more protection against the hardships of nature. Consequently, survival and population growth can occur only if the culture can develop solutions that counteract the extreme forces of nature. The need for solutions to its climatic problems predisposes the culture to seek less traditional and more innovative answers to its common problems, which leads in turn to a greater need for modernization, mass literacy, independent thinking, decentralization of political power, technological innovations, and a general questioning of authority. Conversely, survival in warmer climates is far less dependent on intervention with nature. The need for technological solutions to problems is low, more traditional approaches to obstacles are preferred, formal mass education is not required for survival, and independent thinking is not as necessary. People are therefore more likely to learn from their elders, and consequently there is less questioning of authority in general.

Population size is another predictor of power distance. Generally speaking, the larger the culture, the greater the power distance is likely to be. As the size of any social group increases, it must inevitably develop additional rules and formal procedures for coping with the increased complexities that arise. Additionally, large social groups will require more centralized concentrations of political power to function effectively. Consequently, for cultures with large populations to function effectively, they must adopt a political hierarch that is more distant, more impersonal, and less accessible than that needed by cultures with small populations. The need to concentrate political power in the hands of a few select people will help to create and reinforce a cultural norm that social hierarchy is desirable and that authorities should not be questioned or challenged.

Hofstede's third predictor of power distance is wealth. However, Hofstede suggests that it is the distribution of wealth, rather than the sheer amount of wealth, that best predicts power distance. His analyses reveal that the more unequally that wealth is distributed within a culture, the greater the culture's power distance. More evenly distributed wealth is related to cultures that value education, technology, and a decentralization of political power. As we suggested, these attributes lead to an increased tendency to question authority and to value a small power distance. Conversely, an unequal distribution of wealth is related to a centralized political system, a decreased tendency to question the actions of authorities, and a large power distance.

Uncertainty avoidance. A second concern of all cultures is related to the means they select to adapt to changes and cope with uncertainties. The future will always be, at least in some respects, unknown. This unpredictability and the resultant anxiety that inevitably occurs are basic in human experience.

Cultures differ in the extent to which they prefer and can tolerate ambiguity, and therefore in the means they select for coping with change. Thus, all cultures differ in their perceived need to be changeable and adaptable. Hofstede refers to these variations as the *uncertainty avoidance* dimension, which describes the extent to which the culture feels threatened by ambiguous, uncertain situations and tries to avoid them by establishing more structure.

Hofstede has created an uncertainty avoidance index (UAI) to assess a culture's relative location on the uncertainty avoidance dimension. At one extreme are cultures like Great Britain, Ireland, and Sweden. Such cultures, which all have relatively low UAIs and therefore have a high tolerance for uncertainty and ambiguity, believe in minimizing the number of rules and rituals that govern social conduct and human behavior, in accepting and encouraging dissent among cultural members, in tolerating people who behave in ways that are considered socially deviant, and in taking risks and trying new things. Conversely, Belgium, Greece, Japan, and Portugal all have relatively high UAIs and prefer to avoid uncertainty as a cultural value. These cultures desire or even demand consensus about societal goals, and they do not tolerate dissent or allow deviation in the behaviors of cultural members. These cultures, which usually have a strong inner urge to work hard, try to ensure certainty and security through an extensive set of rules and regulations.

Predictors of uncertainty avoidance. Unlike the power distance dimension, there are no straightforward explanations to account for the differences in a culture's preferred level of uncertainty avoidance. In general, high-UAI cultures tend to be those that are beginning to modernize and that therefore are characterized by a high rate of change. Historically, these cultures tend to have an extensive system of legislative rules and laws with which to resolve disputes, and they often embrace religions such as Catholicism, which stresses absolute certainties. Conversely, low-UAI cultures tend to be those that are advanced in their level of modernization and that are therefore more stable and predictable in their rate of change. These cultures are likely to have far fewer rules and laws that govern social conduct, instead preferring to resolve disputes by negotiation or conflict. They are also more likely to adopt religions such as Buddhism and Unitarianism, which emphasize relativity.

Individualism-collectivism. A third concern of all cultures is related to people's relationships to the larger social groups of which they are a part. People must live and interact together for the culture to survive. In so doing, they must develop a way of relating that strikes a balance between showing concern for oneself and concern for others.

Cultures differ in the extent to which individual autonomy is regarded favorably or unfavorably. Thus cultures vary in their tendency to encourage people to be unique and independent or conforming and interdependent. Hofstede refers to these variations as the *individualism-collectivism* dimension, which describes the degree to which a culture relies on and has allegiance to the self or the group.

Hofstede has created an individualism index (IDV) to assess a culture's relative location on the individualism-collectivism dimension. At one extreme are Australia, Belgium, the Netherlands, and the United States. Such cultures, which all have relatively high IDVs and therefore are highly individualistic, believe that people are supposed to take care of themselves only and, perhaps, their immediate families. In individualist cultures, the autonomy of the individual person is paramount. Key words used to invoke this cultural pattern include *independence*, *privacy*, *self*, and the all-important *I*. Decisions are based on what is good for the individual, not the group, because the person is the primary source of motivation. Similarly, a judgment about what is right or wrong can be made only from the point of view of each individual.

Such cultures as Pakistan, Peru, Thailand, and Venezuela all have relatively low IDVs and prefer a collectivist orientation as a cultural value. These cultures require an absolute loyalty to the group, though the relevant group might be as varied as the nuclear family, the organization for which one works. In collectivist cultures, decisions that juxtapose the benefits to the individual against the benefits to the group are always based on what is best for the group, and the groups to which a person belongs are the most important social units. In turn, the group is expected to look out for and take care of its individual members. Consequently, collectivist cultures believe in obligations to the group, dependence of the individual on organizations and institutions, a "we" consciousness, and an emphasis on belongingness. Hui-Ching Chang and C. Richard Holt, emphasize that the Chinese cultural pattern of relationships is built on an other-oriented perspective. Interpersonal bonding, from this point of view, is not due solely to "honest communication" but also has its basis in obligations and expectations that are already established and ongoing.

Predictors of individualism-collectivism. There is a strong relationship between a culture's location on the power distance dimension and its location on the individualism-collectivism dimension. High-PDI cultures tend to be collectivistic, whereas low-PDI cultures tend to be individualistic. Consequently, there are some similarities to the power distance dimension in predicting a culture's level of individualism-collectivism.

The best predictor of individualism-collectivism is economic development; wealthy cultures tend to be individualistic, whereas poor cultures tend to be collectivistic. Though it is impossible to determine if increased economic development leads to increased levels of individualism or vice versa, there is strong evidence to suggest that cultures become more individualistic as they become more economically advanced.

Another predictor is climate. Cultures in colder climates tend to be individualistic, whereas cultures in warmer climates tend to be collectivistic. As we suggested in the discussion of power distance, colder climates are likely to foster and support individual initiative and innovative solutions to problems, whereas warmer climates make individual achievements far less necessary.

Masculinity-femininity. The final issue that concerns all cultures, and for which they must all find solutions, pertains to the extent to which they prefer achievement and assertiveness or nurturance and social support. Hofstede refers to these variations as the masculinity-femininity dimension, though an alternative label is achievement-nurturance. This dimension indicates the degree to which a culture values such behaviors as assertiveness and the acquisition of wealth or caring for others and the quality of life.

Hofstede has created a masculinity index (MAS) to assess a culture's relative location on the masculinity-femininity dimension. At one extreme are such cultures as Austria, Italy, Japan, and Mexico. These cultures, which all have a relatively high MAS, believe in achievement and ambition, in judging people on the basis of their performance, and in the right to display the material goods that have been acquired. The people in high-MAS cultures also believe in ostentatious manliness, with very specific behaviors and products associated with appropriate male behavior.

Low-MAS cultures, such as Chile, Norway, Portugal, and Thailand, believe less in external achievements and shows of manliness and more in the importance of life choices that improve intrinsic aspects of the quality of life, such as service to others and sympathy for the unfortunate. People in feminine cultures are also likely to prefer equality between the sexes, less prescriptive role behaviors associated with each gender, and an acceptance of nurturing roles for both women and men.

Predictors of masculinity-femininity. The best predictor of masculinity-femininity is climate. Masculine cultures tend to live in warmer climates near the equator, and feminine cultures typically reside in colder climates away from the equator. As he suggested in the argument relating climate to power distance, Hofstede speculates that colder climates require a greater need for technology for the culture to survive, which in turn imposes a need for education and equality. Hofstede extends this argument to include equality between the sexes because cold-weather climates impose a need for both men and women to master a set of complex skills that make sexual inequality less functional and therefore less likely.

CULTURAL PATTERNS AND INTERCULTURAL COMPETENCE

The major lesson in this chapter is that cultures vary systematically in their choices about basic human problems. The taxonomies presented offer lenses by which cultural variations can be understood and appreciated rather than negatively evaluated or disregarded. The categories in these taxonomies can help you to describe the fundamental aspects of cultures. As frames of reference, they provide mechanisms to understand all intercultural communication events. In any intercultural encounter, people may be communicating from very different perceptions of what "reality" is, what is "good," and what is "correct" behavior. The competent intercultural communicator must recognize that cultural variations in addressing basic human issues such as social relations, emphasis on self or group, and preferences for verbal or nonverbal code usage will *always* be a factor in intercultural communication.

The taxonomies presented allow you to use culture-specific knowledge to improve intercultural competence. First, begin by seeking out information about the cultural patterns of those individuals with whom you engage in intercultural communication. To assist your understanding of the culture, select one of the taxonomies presented and seek information that allows you to create a profile of the culture's preferred choices. Libraries are a natural starting place for this kind of knowledge. So, too, are representatives of the culture. Engage them in conversation as you try to understand their culture. Most people welcome questions from a genuinely curious person. Be systematic in your search for information by using the categories thoroughly. Think about the interrelatedness of the various aspects of the culture's patterns.

Second, study the patterns of your own culture. Because your beliefs, values, and norms also are taken for granted, stepping outside of your cultural patterns by researching them is very useful. You might want to describe the preferences of your own culture by using one of the taxonomies.

The third step requires only one resource—a willingness to reflect on your personal preferences. Do your beliefs, values, and norms match those of the typical person in your culture? How do your choices coincide with and differ from the general cultural description?

Finally, mentally consider your own preferences by juxtaposing them with the description of the typical person from another culture. Note the similarities in beliefs, values, and norms. Note also the differences. Can you predict where misinterpretations may occur because of contrasting assumptions about what is important and good? For example, the Euro-American who shares the culture's preference for directness would inevitably encounter difficulties in communication with a typical member of the Japanese culture or a typical Chicano cultural member. Similarly, knowing that you value informality, and usually act accordingly, can help you to monitor your expressions when communicating with someone from a culture that prefers formality. The Euro-American's concept of time as linear often causes numerous problems in communication with people from other cultures. Interpretations of behavior as "late," "inattentive," or "disrespectful," rather than just "different," can produce alternative ways of viewing the ticking of the clock.

SUMMARY

This chapter discusses three important taxonomies that can be used to describe cultural variations. Edward Stewart focuses on the way cultures orient themselves to activities, social relations, the self, and the world. The activity orientation defines how people express themselves through activities and locate themselves on the being-becoming-doing continuum. The social relations orientation describes the preferred forms of interpersonal relationships within a culture. The self-orientation indicates the culture's conception of how people understand who they are in relation to others. The world orientation locates a culture in the physical and spiritual worlds.

Edward Hall placed cultures on a continuum from high-context to low-context. High-context cultures prefer messages in which most of the meaning is either implied by the physical setting or is presumed to be part of the individual's internalized beliefs, values, and norms; low-context cultures prefer messages in which the information is contained within the explicit code.

Geert Hofstede identified four dimensions along which dominant patterns of a culture can be ordered: power distance, uncertainty avoidance, individualism-collectivism, and masculinity-femininity. The power distance dimension assesses the degree to which the culture believes that institutional power should be distributed equally or unequally. The uncertainty avoidance dimension describes the extent to which cultures prefer and can tolerate ambiguity and change. The individualism-collectivism dimension describes the degree to which a culture relies on and has allegiance to the self or the group. The masculinity-femininity dimension indicates the degree to which a culture values assertiveness and the acquisition of wealth or caring for others and the quality of life.

The taxonomies presented in this chapter offer alternative lenses through which cultures can be understood and appreciated. Taken together, they provide multiple frames of reference that can be used to understand intercultural communication.

Notes

1. From *Intercultural Competence: Interpersonal Communication Across Cultures*, Myron W. Lustig and Jolene Koester, NY: Harper Collins, 1993.
2. Geert H. Hofstede was born on October 2, 1928 in Haarlem, the Netherlands, Geert H. Hofstede received his M. S. from the Delft Institute of Technology in 1953, his Ph. D. from Groningen University in 1967. Hofstede is most well known for his work on four dimensions of cultural variability, commonly referred to as "Hofstede's Dimensions." These include: Uncertainty Avoidance, Power Distance, Masculinity-Femininity, Individualism-Collectivism. These dimensions were arrived in his 1980 publication, "Culture's consequences: International differences in work-related values." The study took existing survey data (sample size of 116,000) collected from a multinational corporation. The result was a score in each of the dimensions for 40 different countries.
3. Hindu refers to a person, esp. of North India, whose religion is Hinduism, which is characterized by the beliefs in reincarnation, worship of several gods and the caste system.
4. Jack Daniel is Vice Provost for Undergraduate Studies and Dean of Students, and Professor of Communication at the University of Pittsburgh, USA. He earned all of his degrees—a B. S. in Psychology, a M. A. in Communication, and a Ph. D. in Communication—at the University of Pittsburgh. Dr. Daniel teaches in the area of African American communication, and his current research and writing interests include African American family communications.
5. Geneva Smitherman is a professor in the Department of Speech, Theater and Journalism at Wayne State University of the USA.
6. Mary Jane Collier got her Ph. D. degree at University of Southern California in 1982. She is Professor and Chair of the Department of Human Communication Studies, School of Communication, at the University of Denver. Her research interests focus on cultural identities and discourses across multiple contexts. Her work appears in such journals as: *Communication Monographs*, *International Journal of Intercultural Relations*, *Communication Quarterly*, and *Howard Journal of Communication*, and in various scholarly books and texts.

Questions for Discussion

1. Why do the authors say that the three major taxonomies of cultural patterns may

be used as lenses through which cultural variations can be understood and appreciated?
2. In what way can you make use of the three major taxonomies to improve your intercultural competence?
3. What are the beliefs, values, and norms that are taken for granted in your culture? What are the main features of your cultural pattern?
4. Can you be regarded as a typical person of your culture? Why? Why not?
5. All the three taxonomies of cultural patterns of Edward Stewart, Edward T. Hall, and Geert Hofstede originated from the Western world. In the process of globalization, should peoples from other cultures, adapt themselves to these existing cultural patterns or should they try to construct their own?

Online Mini-Case Studies and Viewpoints-Sharing

Cultural Differences: Easy or Difficult to Accept?

John Engle, a professor of Anglo-American literature and civilization, teaches a course, "French and North African Cultural Patterns," to American students studying in France. In a recent article, he describes how difficult it is for many Americans to accept the notion of cultural difference — a problem — that he attributes to their own cultural value of individualism. He says he starts his course with important distinctions between stereotypes and generalizations — pointing out that stereotypes are limiting and dangerous while generalizations can be useful, allowing for individual exceptions while permitting categorization, which is necessary for intelligent analysis. However, one of the students resist his way of thinking:

"You can't say that!", "For instance, the ritualized sit-down dinner or the five-week vacation might tell us something broadly significant about the French attitude toward the present moment. I know people back home who eat long meals. Everyone is different. You can't generalize like that."...

Online Research

Search online for more responses from other students in Professor Engle's course or similar cases involving Chinese students or Chinese culture.

Reading Two

Introductory Remarks

The Allegory of the Cave[3] by Plato is a metaphoric comparison between what we perceive and what we believe in reality. The thesis is that all we perceive are imperfect "reflections" of the ultimate Forms[4], which subsequently represent truth and reality. In his story, Plato establishes a cave in which prisoners are chained down and forced to look upon the front wall of the cave. To the back of them lie the puppeteers who are casting the shadows on the wall, which the prisoners are perceiving as reality. The allegory conveys the point that the prisoners would be fundamentally mistaken as to what is reality. Likewise, the terms of our language are not "names" of the physical objects that we can see. They are actually names of things that are not visible to us, things that we can only grasp with the mind.

Furthermore, Plato describes the vision of the real truth to be "aching" to the eyes of the prisoners. Once the prisoner climbs out of the cave and is fully immersed in the sun's rays, he would be filled with bewilderment, fear, and blindness to the objects he was now being told were real. When the prisoner looks up to the sky and looks into the Sun, and recognizes it as the cause of all that is around him, he may perceive the "Form of the Good." Upon returning to the Cave, the prisoner would be entering a world of darkness yet again, and would be faced with the other unreleased prisoners laughing at the released prisoner, and ridiculing him for taking the useless rise out of the cave in the first place.

The Allegory doesn't solely represent our own misconceptions of reality, but also Plato's vision of what a solid leader should be. The prisoner is expected to return to the cave and live amongst his former prisoners as someone who can see more and better than all the rest, someone who is now able to govern from truth and goodness. He is expected to care for his fellow citizens. The story as told by Socrates and Glaucon presents a unique look at the way in which reality plays such an important part in our own existence, and how one understands it can be used as a qualification for leadership and government. The stages of thought combined with the progress of human development represent our own path to complete awareness in which the most virtuous and distinguished will reach, and upon doing so shall lead the public.

The Allegory of the Cave

Plato[2]

Socrates: Next, I said, compare the effect of education and the lack of it on our nature to an experience like this: Imagine human beings living in an underground, cave-like dwelling, with an entrance a long way up, which is both open to the light and as wide as the cave itself[3]. They've been there since childhood, fixed in the same place, with their necks and legs fettered, able to see only in front of them, because their bonds prevent them from turning their heads around. Light is provided by a fire burning far above and behind them. Also behind them, but on higher ground, there's a path stretching between them and the fire. Imagine that along this path a low wall has been built, like the screen in front of puppeteers above which they show their puppets.

Glaucon: I'm imagining it.

Socrates: Then also imagine that there are people along the wall, carrying all kinds of artifacts that project above it—statues of people and other animals, made out of stone, wood, and every material. And, as you'd expect, some of the carriers are talking, and some are silent.

Glaucon: It's a strange image you're describing, and strange prisoners.

Socrates: They're like us. Do you suppose, first of all, that these prisoners see anything of themselves and one another besides the shadows that the fire casts on the wall in front of them?

Glaucon: How could they, if they have to keep their heads motionless throughout life?

Socrates: What about the things being carried along the wall? Isn't the same true of them?

Glaucon: Of course.

Socrates: And if they could talk to one another, don't you think they'd suppose that the names they used applied to the things they see passing before them?

Glaucon: They'd have to.

Socrates: And what if their prison also had an echo from the wall facing them? Don't you think they'd believe that the shadows passing in front of them were talking whenever one of the carriers passing along the wall was doing so?

Glaucon: I certainly do.

Socrates: Then the prisoners would in every way believe that the truth is nothing other than the shadows of those artifacts.

Glaucon: They must surely believe that.

Socrates: Consider, then, what being released from their bonds and cured of their ignorance would naturally be like. When one of them was freed and suddenly compelled to stand up, turn his head, walk, and look up toward the light, he'd be pained and dazzled and unable to see the things whose shadows he'd seen before[4]. What do you think he'd say, if we told him that what he'd seen before was inconsequential, but that now—because he is a bit closer to the things that are and is turned toward things that are more—he sees more correctly? Or, to put it another way, if we pointed to each of the things passing by, asked him what each of them is, and compelled him to answer, don't you think he'd be at a loss and that he'd believe that the things he saw earlier were truer than the ones he was now being shown?

Glaucon: Much truer.

Socrates: And if someone compelled him to look at the light itself, wouldn't his eyes hurt, and wouldn't he turn around and flee towards the things he's able to see, believing that they're really clearer than the ones he's being shown?

Glaucon: He would.

Socrates: And if someone dragged him away from there by force, up the rough, steep path, and didn't let him go until he dragged him into the sunlight, wouldn't he be pained and irritated at being treated that way? And when he came into the light, with the sun filling his eyes, wouldn't he be unable to see a single one of the things now said to be true?

Glaucon: He would be unable to see them, at least at first.

Socrates: I suppose, then, that he'd need time to get adjusted before he could see things in the world above. At first, he'd see shadows most easily, then images of men and other things in water, then the things themselves. Of these, he'd be able to study the things in the sky and the sky itself more easily at night, looking at the light of the stars and the moon, than during the day, looking at the sun and the light of the sun.

Glaucon: Of course.

Socrates: Finally, I suppose, he'd be able to see the sun, not images of it in water or some alien place, but the sun itself, in its own place, and be able to study it.

Glaucon: Necessarily so.

Socrates: And at this point he would infer and conclude that the sun provides the seasons and the years, governs everything in the visible world, and is in some way the cause of all the things that he used to see.

Glaucon: It's clear that would be his next step.

Socrates: What about when he reminds himself of his first dwelling place, his fellow prisoners, and what passed for wisdom there? Don't you think that he'd count himself happy for the change and pity the others?

Glaucon: Certainly.

Socrates: And if there had been any honors, praises, or prizes among them for the one who was sharpest at identifying the shadows as they passed by and who best remembered which usually came earlier, which later, and which simultaneously, and who could thus best divine the future, do you think that our man would desire these rewards or envy those among the prisoners who were honored and held power? Instead, wouldn't he feel, with Homer, that he'd much prefer to "work the earth as a serf to another, one without possessions," and go through any sufferings, rather than share their opinions and live as they do?

Glaucon: I suppose he would rather suffer anything than live like that.

Socrates: Consider this too. If this man went down into the cave again and sat down in his same seat, wouldn't his eyes—coming suddenly out of the sun like that—be filled with darkness?

Glaucon: They certainly would.

Socrates: And before his eyes had recovered—and the adjustment would not be quick—while his vision was still dim, if he had to compete again with the perpetual prisoners in recognizing the shadows, wouldn't he invite ridicule? Wouldn't it be said of him that he'd returned from his upward journey with his eyesight ruined and that it isn't worthwhile even to try to travel upward? And, as for anyone who tried to free them and lead them upward, if they could somehow get their hands on him, wouldn't they kill him?

Glaucon: They certainly would.

Socrates: This whole image, Glaucon, must be fitted together with what we said before. The visible realm should be likened to the prison dwelling, and the light of the fire inside it to the power of the sun. And if you interpret the upward journey and the study of things above as the upward journey of the soul to the intelligible realm, you'll grasp what I hope to convey, since that is what you wanted to hear about. Whether it's true or not, only the god knows. But this is how I see it: In the knowable realm, the form of the good is the last thing to be seen, and it is reached only with difficulty. Once one has seen it, however, one must conclude that it is the cause of all that is correct and beautiful in anything, that it produces both light and its source in the visible realm, and that in the intelligible realm it controls and provides truth and understanding, so that anyone who is to act sensibly in private or public must see it.

Glaucon: I have the same thoughts, at least as far as I'm able.

Socrates: Come, then, share with me this thought also: It isn't surprising that the ones who get to this point are unwilling to occupy themselves with human affairs and that their souls are always pressing upwards, eager to spend their time above, for, after all, this is surely what we'd expect, if indeed things fit the image I described before.

Glaucon: It is.

Socrates: What about what happens when someone turns from divine study to the evils of human life? Do you think it surprising, since his sight is still dim, and he hasn't yet become accustomed to the darkness around him, that he behaves awkwardly and appears completely ridiculous if he's compelled, either in the courts or elsewhere, to contend about the shadows of justice or the statues of which they are the shadows and to dispute about the way these things are understood by people who have never seen justice itself?

Glaucon: That's not surprising at all.

Socrates: No, it isn't. But anyone with any understanding would remember that the eyes may be confused in two ways and from two causes, namely, when they've come from the light into the darkness and when they've come from the darkness into the light. Realizing that the same applies to the soul, when someone sees a soul disturbed and unable to see something, he won't laugh mindlessly, but he'll take into consideration whether it has come from a brighter life and is dimmed through not yet having become accustomed to the dark or whether it has come from greater ignorance into greater light and is dazzled by the increased brilliance. Then he'll declare the first soul happy in its experience in life, and he'll pity the latter—but even if he chose to make fun of it, at least he'd be less ridiculous than if he laughed at a soul that has come from the light above.[5]

Glaucon: What you say is very reasonable.

Socrates: If that's true, then here's what we must think about these matters: Education isn't what some people declare to be, namely, putting knowledge into souls that lack it, like putting sight into blind eyes.

Glaucon: They do say that.

Socrates: But our present discussion, on the other hand, shows that the power to learn is present in everyone's soul and that the instrument with which each learns is like an eye that cannot be turned around from darkness to light without turning the whole body. This instrument cannot be turned around from that which is coming into being without turning the whole soul until it is able to study that which is and the brightest thing that is, namely, the one we call the good. Isn't that right?

Glaucon: Yes.

Socrates: Then education[6] is the craft concerned with doing this very thing, this turning around, and with how the soul can most easily and effectively be made to do it. It isn't the craft of putting sight into the soul. Education takes for granted that sight is there but that it isn't turned the right way or looking where it ought to look, and it tries to redirect it appropriately.

Glaucon: So it seems.

Notes

1. Retrieved from https://wmpeople.wm.edu/asset/index/cvance/Plato. *The Republic* is Plato's most ambitious dialogue, and one of the fullest expressions of both his political ideals, and his theories of ontology (the nature of existence) and epistemology (the nature of knowledge). The dialogue recounts a discussion among Socrates and some of his students (including Plato's brother, Glaucon) about the nature of justice. Socrates gets his students to agree that justice is best understood as a social good, and suggests they form a definition of justice by first imagining what kind of social structure would be necessary to produce it. The bulk of the dialogue is an exposition by Socrates of what justice in the state is, making it not only one of the first extended works of political philosophy, but also one of the earliest known works of utopian literature.

Plato's *The Allegory of the Cave* is a meditation on "the essence of truth" and its paradoxical relation to human comportment. Plato uses this allegory to gradually guide readers toward a personal realization of knowledge and philosophy as the key elements for freedom and enlightenment. This fable also contains exquisite reflections on concepts such as knowledge, education, perception, and politics. It is one of the most famous pieces of philosophical literature and a pillar of western philosophy. To this day, it remains the best known and most critically assessed of Plato's works.

Underlying Plato's image of the cave is his "theory of forms." The theory assumes the existence of a level of reality inhabited by ideal "forms" of all things and concepts. Thus a form exists for all objects (like chairs and ducks), and for all concepts (such as beauty and justice). The forms are eternal and changeless, but inhabit changeable matter, to produce the objects and examples of concepts that we perceive in the physical, temporal world. These are always in a state of "becoming"—that is, on the way to another state. The ever-changing temporal world can therefore only be the source of opinion. In the "Allegory," Plato likens our opinions about the temporal world to the prisoners' perception of shadows on the wall of a cave. True knowledge requires that one perceive the forms themselves, which is eternal and unchanging. Thus for Plato the realm of ideal forms is "real," while the constantly changing world of time and matter is illusory and unreal.

2. The son of a wealthy and noble family, Plato (427 BCE - 347 BCE) was preparing for a career in politics when the trial and eventual execution of Socrates (469 BCE - 399 BCE) changed the course of his life. He abandoned his political career and turned to philosophy, opening a school on the outskirts of Athens dedicated to the Socratic search for wisdom. Plato's school, then known as the Academy, was the first university in western history and operated from 387 BCE until 529 CE, when it was closed by Justinian. The writings of Plato are the primary source of knowledge about the ideas of his teacher, the Athenian philosopher Socrates. Plato's thirty dramatic dialogues all feature Socrates as the main character; it is, therefore, difficult to say where Socrates's philosophy begins and Plato's begins. For the sake of convenience, then, the ideas conveyed in Plato's dialogues are usually referred to as Platonic, while Socrates's method of instruction through dialectical question-and-answer is usually referred to as Socratic.

3. Living in this world is like living in an underground cave in which you can only see shadows and hear echoes. The idea of humanity being a dazed mass of confused people comes from Parmenides, and the idea that they live in a dim cave and must strive to get free comes from Empedocles (remember his two principles, love and strife).

4. The freed prisoner turns around 180° before he can start toward the truth. To get to the truth you must turn completely around, you must turn your back on the shadows in the cave, turn your back on what this world calls truth and reality. This separating oneself from mob-mind is probably Plato's version of Empedocles' strife principle, that we must separate ourselves from the herd and from Aphrodite's herd-

consciousness enchantment.
5. When the man goes back into the cave, he is ridiculed, and even threatened with violence. The people in the cave don't WANT to leave. People living in ignorance often resist truth, and don't want to be led to the truth. Sticking with what is familiar is just too COMFORTABLE for most to risk giving up. They may even respond with hate or violence if pushed toward truth. Plato knew this all too well. His own teacher, Socrates, was executed for trying to lead others to Truth.
6. The path to education is really about turning your attention toward the right things (i.e., justice, beauty, truth, and goodness). Plato repeatedly uses the imagery of turning around. Then, knowledge will come to you naturally (just as seeing the things instead of their shadows will come naturally in time to one whose eyes are turned toward them). The task of an educator is to get her students to turn their attention in the right direction (namely, toward Truth and Goodness), where she will realize that those things are the things that matter. The method by which one "turns" is philosophy.

Questions for Discussion

1. Plato's *The Allegory of the Cave* is a meditation on "the essence of truth" and its paradoxical relation to human comportment. Plato uses this allegory to gradually guide readers toward a personal realization of knowledge and philosophy as the key elements for freedom and enlightenment. Please retell the fable to each other and comment on the enlightenment you have obtained.
2. To Plato, getting educated is a painful process, which involves the uncomfortable realization of (1) your own ignorance and (2) the fact that many of your dearest, most closely-held beliefs and assumptions about the world were false. Do you agree with Plato's idea and how do you usually resolve the painful challenge of giving up what has been dear to you?
3. From the above allegory, we realize that the path to education is really about turning one's attention toward the right things such as justice, beauty, truth, and goodness. As a result, the task of an educator is to get his or her students to turn their attention in the right direction where they realize that those things they are absorbing are the things that matter. What are your thoughts? How would you make sure that what the teachers are teaching and what you are learning really matter?
4. What is Plato's theory of the form really about? To Plato there was another realm beyond the visible that was more real than the things themselves. Just as the above allegory illustrates the shadows are (1) dependent on, (2) caused by, and (3) inferior representations of the things themselves. Please share your thoughts with each other and support your thoughts with real-life evidence.

5. In *The Allegory of the Cave*, Plato describes the physical world as a "dark place" which is not a realm where humans can obtain knowledge of true reality. Instead, there is another realm beyond the heaven and the earth to obtain truth through "forms". Please make your argument or counter-argument basing on the dialectical materialism as proposed by Karl Marx.

Online Mini-Case Studies and Viewpoints-Sharing

The Cave

Some prisoners are chained inside of a cave, facing the back wall. Behind them is a fire, with people passing in front of it. The prisoners cannot turn their heads, and have always been chained this way. All they can see and hear are shadows passing back and forth and the echoes bouncing off the wall in front of them. One day, a prisoner is freed, and dragged outside of the cave. He is blinded by the light, and confused, and resists being led outside. But, eventually his eyes adjusts so that he is able to see the things around him, and even the sun itself. He comes to realize that the things he thought were real were merely shadows of real things, and that life outside of the cave is far better than his previous life in chains. He pities those still inside. He ventures back into the cave to share his discovery with the others—only to be ridiculed. The other prisoners violently resists his story, refuses to be freed and led outside, and even tries to kill him.

Online Research

Search online for more information about Socrates, Plato, and Aristotle, especially the main thoughts of the three great philosophers and their enduring impacts upon both the West and the East.

Unit Seven

Intercultural Communication—East and West

Reading One

Introductory Remarks

Individualism-collectivism, one of the most profound dimensions of cultural values, has long been discussed and investigated among historians, sociologists, psychologists, and philosophers. Max Weber (1930), the German sociologist and historian, contrasts collectivism and individualism through the lens of religion. Weber believes that Catholics were more collectivistic and inclined to have hierarchical, interdependent, group-oriented relationships compared to Protestants who were more individualistic and self-reliant. A collectivism-individualism model was proposed by the German sociologist Ferdinand Tönnies (1957) who describes *Gemeinschaft* (community) relationships as the characteristic of small, rural village communities, in which communalism is prioritized. This notion coincided with the American anthropologist Robert Redfield's (1941) contrast of folk society with urban society. The Dutch sociologist Geert Hofstede (1980) ushering in an era of cross-cultural research makes comparisons along the dimension of collectivism versus individualism. Hofstede conceptualizes collectivism and individualism as part of a single continuum, with each cultural construct representing an opposite pole.

Harry C. Triandis (2001), the author of the following passage, argues that compared to those in individualist cultures, people in collectivist cultures have the tendency to define themselves as members of groups, to prioritize in-group goals, to pay more attention to context than the content in making attributions and in communicating, to focus more on external than internal processes as determinants of social behavior, to define most relationships with in-group members as communal, to make more situational attributions, and tend to be self-effacing. As a member living in the collectivistic culture, what is your reflection on the cultural infusion into one's personality?

Individualism-Collectivism and Personality[1]

Harry C. Triandis[2]

The individualism-collectivism cultural syndrome appears to be the most significant cultural difference among cultures. Greenfield calls it the "deep structure" of cultural differences. While there are a myriad of cultural differences, this one seems to be important both historically and cross-culturally. Almost 100 publications per year now use this dimension in discussing cultural differences.

This article will review the findings concerning the relationship between this dimension of cultural differences and personality. It will begin with definitions of key terms and examine differences obtained when data are analyzed at the cultural (N = number of cultures) and the individual (N = number of participants) levels of analysis. A review of the consequences of individualism and collectivism will constitute the most important part of the paper. A discussion of needed future research will complete it.

Definitions

Culture. One way to think about culture is that "culture is to society what memory is to individuals". It includes what "has worked" in the experience of a society that was worth transmitting to future generations. *Language*, *time*, and *place* are important in determining the difference between one and another culture, since language is needed to transmit culture and it is desirable to have the same historical period and geography to do so efficiently. Sperber used the analogy of an epidemic. An idea (e.g., how to make a tool) that is useful is adopted by more and more people and becomes an element of culture.

Elements of culture are *shared* standard operating procedures, unstated assumptions, tools, norms, values, habits about sampling the environment, and the like. Since perception and cognition depend on the information that is sampled from the environment, the latter elements are of particular interest to psychologists. Cultures develop conventions about what to pay attention to and how much to weigh the elements that are sampled. For example, people in hierarchical cultures are more likely to sample clues about hierarchy than clues about aesthetics.

Triandis argued that people in individualist cultures, such as those of North and Western Europe and North America, sample, with high probability, elements of the personal self (e.g., "I am kind"). People from collectivist cultures, such as those of Asia, Africa and South America, tend to sample elements of the collective self (e.g., "my family thinks I am kind").

Personality. Funder defined personality as "an individual's characteristic pattern of thought, emotion, and behavior, together with the psychological mechanisms—hidden or not—behind those patterns". Characteristic sampling of the information in the environment, which corresponds to the sampling that occurs in different cultures, can be one of the bases of individual differences in personality.

Another way of discussing personality is that it is a configuration of cognitions, emotions, and habits which are activated when situations stimulate their expression. They generally determine the individual's unique adjustment to the world.

Collectivism. In collectivist cultures people are interdependent within their in-groups (family, tribe, nation, etc.), give priority to the goals of their in-groups, shape their behavior primarily on the basis of in-group norms, and behave in a communal way. People in collectivist cultures are especially concerned with relationships. For example, showed that collectivists in conflict situations are primarily concerned with maintaining their relationship with others, whereas individualists are primarily concerned with achieving justice. Thus, collectivists prefer methods of conflict resolution that do not destroy relationships (e.g., mediation), whereas individualists are willing to go to court to settle disputes.

Individualism. In individualist societies people are autonomous and independent from their in-groups; they give priority to their personal goals over the goals of their in-groups, they behave primarily on the basis of their attitudes rather than the norms of their in-groups, and exchange theory adequately predicts their social behavior.

Individualism and collectivism as ideal types. It should not be assumed that everybody in individualist cultures has all the characteristics of these cultures, and that every one in collectivist cultures has the characteristics of those cultures. Rather, people sample from both the individualist and collectivist cognitive structures, depending on the situation.

Measurement of individualism and collectivism. Measurement of these constructs has been very difficult, and while there are approximately 20 different methods, none has proven satisfactory. The reader is directed to Triandis and Gelfand for an overview of some of the measurement problems.

Vertical and horizontal varieties of collectivism and individualism. There are as many varieties of collectivism as there are collectivist cultures. For instance, Korean collectivism is not the same as the collectivism of the Israeli kibbutz. One dimension that is especially important is the horizontal-vertical aspect. Some cultures emphasize equality (e. g. , Australians, Swedes, kibbutzim), and others emphasize hierarchy (e. g. , India, highly competitive Americans who want to be "the best").

We can thus identify four types of cultures: Horizontal Individualist (HI), where people want to be unique and do "their own thing"; Vertical Individualist (VI), where people want to do their own thing and also to be "the best"; Horizontal Collectivism (HC), where people merge their selves with their in-groups; and Vertical Collectivism (VC), where people submit to the authorities of the in-group and are willing to sacrifice themselves for their in-group. Triandis argued that, in addition to the vertical-horizontal dimension, there are many other dimensions defining different varieties of individualism and collectivism.

The Cultural and Personality Levels of Analysis

When studying the relationship of culture and psychology, it is imperative to keep the level of analysis distinct, because results obtained when the number of cultures is the unit of analysis[3] (K cultures) are often different from results obtained when the number of participants (N = participants in one culture) are the units of analysis. For example, at the cultural level, factor analysis indicates that individualism and collectivism are opposite sides of a single dimension. *Family integrity* is the only aspect of collectivism that emerges. However, when data are analyzed within culture, with individuals as the units of analysis, there are usually several orthogonal factors reflecting individualism (e. g. , competition, emotional distance from in-groups, self-reliance, hedonism) and collectivism (e. g. , sociability, interdependence, family integrity).

Thus, it is useful to use a different terminology for findings at the cultural and individual levels of analysis. Triandis, Leung, Villareal, and Clack proposed the use of *allocentrism* and *idiocentrism*[4] to correspond at the personality level to individualism and collectivism. Smith and Bond, and many others, adopted this terminology. They used it consistently in their social psychology textbook. This allows us to discuss the behavior of idiocentrics in collectivist cultures and allocentrics in individualist cultures. The former find their culture stifling and try to escape it. The latter join groups, gangs, unions, and other collectives. There are more allocentrics than idiocentrics in collectivist and more idiocentrics than allocentrics in individualist cultures.

We can link the cultural and individual levels of analysis by noting that *customs* are aspects of culture and *habits* aspects of personality. Thus, we hypothesize a correspondence between customs, norms, and values on the one hand and habits and patterns of individual behavior on the other hand.

Theoretical Perspectives for the Study of Culture and Personality

A serviceable, though overly simple, theoretical framework is that ecology shapes culture, which includes child-rearing patterns, which influence personality. Ecology includes features of the geography, resources, and the history of a society. For example, societies where fish is available in the environment are more likely to use fish as food, and to have fish-based economies. Societies that have experienced failures throughout their history are likely to be less optimistic than societies that have experienced mostly successes, and so on.

Relatively isolated societies, such as those on islands, tend to be high in *tightness* (people provide sanctions for even minor deviations from norms). In such cultures people have clear ideas about what behaviors are appropriate; they agree among themselves that sanctions are needed when people do not follow the norms and since they are less influenced by neighboring cultures, they are less likely to accept other norms. Tight societies tend to include members who are highly interdependent, and tend to be densely populated, in the sense that surveillance is high. Tight cultures are high on collectivism.

In *loose* cultures there is tolerance of deviation. Such tolerance for deviation from norms is found in relatively heterogeneous societies (where several normative systems coexist), where people do not depend on each other much, and where population density (opportunity for surveillance) is low. The open frontier is related to looseness.

The more *complex* the culture, the more individualist it is likely to be. Cultures differ in complexity. The most contrast is found between hunters and gatherers on the one hand and service-information societies on the other hand. Gross national product per capita, although not sufficient, is one index of cultural complexity. Other indices include the percent of the population that is urban, the size of cities, personal computers per capita, and so forth. Obviously, in complex cultures (e.g., urban rather than rural environment), there are more choices and lifestyles. Thus, it is understandable that people in individualist cultures desire to have more choices and are motivated more when they have many choices than people in collectivist cultures.

In collectivist cultures, child rearing emphasizes conformity, obedience, security, and reliability; in individualist cultures, child rearing emphasizes independence, exploration, creativity, and self-reliance.

Thus, at least in principle, one should be able to trace links between ecology and personality. For example, in ecologies where one makes a living by acting self-reliantly, as is often the case among hunters, there is greater emphasis on self-reliance and less emphasis on conformity than in ecologies that require conformity for survival, as is more common in agricultural societies.

This theoretical framework is certainly not the only one. Church and Lonner edited a special issue of the *Journal of Cross-Cultural Psychology* that included papers that linked personality and culture from the perspective of cultural, indigenous, and evolutionary psychology. Church has provided an impressive model of culture and personality that integrates many of these approaches, especially the trait and cultural psychological approaches. Traits exist in all cultures but account for behavior less in collectivist than in individualist cultures. Situational determinants of behavior are important universally but are more so in collectivist than in individualist cultures. Cognitive consistency among psychological processes and between psychological processes and behavior occurs universally, but it is less important in collectivist than in individualist cultures.

The Importance of the Situation

Allocentrism and idiocentrism are best conceived as situation-specific dispositions. This is clear from studies that randomly assigned idiocentrics and allocentrics to situations that were individualist or collectivist. An interesting example is a study by Chatman and Barsade who randomly assigned participants who were either allocentric or idiocentric to simulated cultures that were collectivist or individualist. The allocentrics assigned to a collectivist culture were the most cooperative; all those assigned to the individualist culture (no matter whether they were idiocentric or allocentric) were low in cooperation; idiocentrics assigned to the collectivist situation were somewhat cooperative. Thus, it is clear that the situation is a powerful predictor of the level of cooperation, and cooperation is maximal when personality and situation jointly call for it.

Nevertheless, personality does include, as well, elements that are transituational. Allocentrics, even in individualistic cultures, will try to make relationships more intimate; idiocentrics, even in collectivist cultures, will be more likely to use individual goals to determine their behavior. In short, we see allocentrism and idiocentrism as having a transituational component, as well as a situation-specific component. Future research should examine the amount of variance that is determined by each of these components. At this writing it appears that the situational component accounts for more variance than the transituational one.

Correlates and Consequences of Allocentrism and Idiocentrism

Self-definitions. Allocentrics tend to define themselves with reference to social entities. Traditional samples who have acculturated to individualist cultures show this tendency less, especially when they are highly educated. For example, Altrocchi and Altrocchi found that the least acculturated Cook Islanders used about 57% social content in describing themselves, whereas Cook Islanders born in New Zealand used 20% and New Zealanders used 17% social content. Similarly Ma and Schoeneman (1997) reported 84% social content for Sumbaru Kenyans, 80% for Maasai Kenyans, but only 12% for American students, and 17% for Kenyan students. These results are quite consistent with those reported by Triandis, McCusker, and Hui who argued that the self-definitions of samples from collectivist cultures contain social content between 30% and 50% of the time, whereas those of samples from individualist cultures contain social content between zero and 20% of the time. The mode of the percent social content of the self-descriptions of 500 University of Illinois students was zero!

Internalization of norms. Allocentrics often have internalized the norms of their in-groups, so they enjoy doing what their in-groups expect them to do. Allocentrics receive much social support and are less likely to be lonely than idiocentrics.

Self-esteem. The self-esteem of allocentrics is more based on "getting along" than on "getting ahead" (Whatley, submitted, whereas vertical idiocentrics are especially interested in getting ahead and being the best.

Attributions. Idiocentrics tend to use traits in describing other people and focus on internal dispositions in making attributions. Compared to idiocentrics, allocentrics making attributions use the context, the situation, and group disposition, and tend to be more field dependent and to think more holistically. Norenzayan, Choi, and Nisbett make the case that dispositional attributions may be universal, but people in collectivist cultures make more situational attributions than those in individualist cultures. When collectivists make dispositional attributions, the traits they use are malleable, whereas when people in individualist cultures make such attributions they tend to use traits that are fixed. There is also evidence that idiocentrics think of the self as stable and the environment as changeable (e. g., if you do not like your job, you change jobs), whereas allocentrics think of the social environment as stable (duties, obligations) and the self as changeable (ready to fit into the environment).

Ethnocentrism. Allocentrics are often more ethnocentric than idiocentrics, have very positive attitudes about their in-groups, and report negative attitudes toward their out-groups. Triandis observed that collectivists see more of a difference between in-group and out-group than do individualists. Iyengar, Lepper, and Ross confirmed this. They presented a behavior by the "Self", a "Friend", and an "Enemy" and asked samples from the United States and Japan whether they "couldn't say" why they did this, because, in that behavioral domain, the behavior "depends on the situation". They found that the Japanese saw the self and the friend's behavior as dependent on the situation, whereas the enemy's behavior did not depend on the situation. However, Americans saw the behavior of both friend and enemy as not depending on the situation. In short, the largest distinction in individualist cultures is between self and others; the largest distinction in collectivist cultures is between in-group and out-groups.

Other personality correlates. Idiocentrics tend toward dominance, whereas allocentrics tend to be agreeable. The motive structure of collectivists reflects receptivity to others, adjustment to the needs of others, and restraint of own needs and desires. The basic motive structure of individualists reflects their internal needs, rights and capacities, including the ability to withstand social pressures.

Matsumoto, Weissman, Preston, Brown, and Kupperbusch developed and validated an inventory that measures these tendencies. Americans reported more positive disengaged emotions (superior, proud, top of the world), whereas Japanese reported more interpersonally engaged emotions (friendly feelings, feel close, respect). Also, Americans reported more positive than negative emotions, whereas Japanese reported more engaged than disengaged emotions (Kitayama, Markus, & Kurokawa, in press).

Grimm, Church, Katigbak, and Reyes examined the self-described personality traits, values, and moods of students in an individualist culture (U.S.) and a collectivist culture (Philippines). They predicted that the Filipino sample would rate themselves lower than the U.S. sample on individualist traits (independence, pleasure seeking, assertiveness, creativity, curiosity, competitiveness, self-assurance, efficiency, initiative, and directness) and higher on collectivist traits (attentiveness, respectfulness, humility, deference, obedience, dutifulness, reciprocity, self-sacrifice, security, traditionalism, conformity, and cooperativeness). The data were generally supportive of the differences on the individualist traits, but there were no statistically significant differences on the collectivist traits.

In studies by Dion and Dion, idiocentrism was related to less intimacy and poorer adjustment in romantic love relationships. Specifically, among idiocentrics, self-actualization, which is a prototypical individualist construct, was shown to be related to more gratification with love, yet less love for the partner, and less caring for the needs of the partner, suggesting that idiocentrism may be a factor in the high divorce rate of individualist countries.

Watson, Sherbak, and Morris found that allocentrism was correlated with social responsibility and negatively with normlessness; idiocentrism was correlated with self-esteem and normlessness. Singelis, Bond, Sharkey and Lai found that allocentrism is related to embarrassability and low self-esteem. Yamaguchi, Kuhlman, and Sugimori found that in the United States, Japan, and the Republic of Korea allocentrics show greater tendencies toward affiliation, higher sensitivity to the social rejection, and a lower need for uniqueness than idiocentrics. Lay and the colleagues found a relationship between allocentrism and depression. People who experienced a lot of hassles were more depressed. This relationship was stronger in the case of those who were low in allocentrism than those who were high in allocentrism.

People in collectivist cultures are rather shy when they have to enter new groups; people in individualist cultures are rather skilled in entering new groups and in dealing with others in superficial ways, such as at a cocktail party.

During communication, those from collectivist cultures pay a lot of attention to the context, that is, how is something said; people in individualist cultures pay most attention to content, that is, what was said. The specific language is very important in individualist cultures, and of secondary importance than the level of voice, body posture, eye contact, and accompanying gestures that are important in collectivist cultures.

When distributing resources to in-group members, people in collectivist cultures use mostly equality; people in individualist cultures use equity. When distributing resources to out-group members, people in most cultures use the equity principle.

Morality. Collectivist cultures differ from individualist cultures in the notions of morality that are emphasized. According to Rozin, Lowery, Imada, and Haidt, there are three moral codes: community, autonomy, and divinity. The first two codes are especially important in collectivist and individualist cultures, respectively, and they evoke different emotions. Violation of communal codes, including hierarchy, evokes contempt; violation of the autonomy code (e. g., individual rights) evokes anger; and violation of the divinity code (purity, sanctity) evokes disgust. Data from Japan and the United States support this theory linking morality and emotions.

Helping an in-group member is seen in duty-based terms by Indians, whereas Americans see it more as a matter of personal choice. In fact, Americans less frequently than Indians judged that they had a responsibility to help siblings or colleagues in cases involving low as contrasted to high liking. The judgments of Indians were not affected by liking. Morality among collectivists is more contextual; the supreme value is the welfare of the collective. Ma has provided a Chinese perspective on moral judgment that is different from the individualistic perspective of Kohlberg.

Lying is an acceptable behavior in collectivist cultures, if it saves face or helps the in-group. There are traditional ways of lying that are understood as "correct behavior." Trilling makes the point that when people have a strong sense that they themselves determine who they are, as is characteristic of individualists, they are more likely to seek sincerity and authenticity than when they feel swept up by traditions and obligations, as is more characteristic of collectivists. Triandis, Carnevale, Robert, Gelfand, Kessler, Probst, Radhakrishnan, Kashima, Dragonas, Chan, Chen, Kim, Kim, de Dreu, van Fliert, Iwao, Ohbuchi, and Schmitz found some evidence of greater tendencies toward deception among collectivist samples. However, in that study, vertical idiocentrics, who tend to be very competitive, were also high in deception, because they had to lie in order to win. Thus, everybody lied and only the horizontal idiocentrics were honest.

Many observers have emphasized the importance of face in collectivist cultures. A moral person behaves as his or her role is specified by in-group members and society. If the individual deviates from such ideal behavior, there is loss of face, not only for the individual, but also for the whole in-group. In many collectivist cultures, morality consists of doing what the in-group expects. When interacting with the out-group, it is "moral" to exploit and deceive. In other words, morality is not applicable to all but only to some members of one's social environment.

Relation to Big Five. Realo, Allik, and Vadi developed a measure of allocentrism in Estonia and tested its convergence with the Big Five. They found a negative correlation between Openness and allocentrism and positive correlations between Agreeableness and Conscientiousness and allocentrism. If indeed the Big-Five traits are substantially heritable, this suggests that future research may find some biological bases of allocentrism and idiocentrism, over and above the environmental bases emphasized in this paper.

Comparison of This Approach to Other Approaches

It should be clear that the major thrust of the approach described above is from the perspective of cross-cultural psychology. The individualism-collectivism syndrome is itself an etic construct that will take a myriad of culture-specific manifestations across cultures, though the emphasis on individual versus group processes will be found across all manifestations.

A discussion of comparisons between fruit provides a suitable metaphor. When we compare apples and oranges, we can use etic dimensions such as price or weight. Although these etic dimensions are important, they do not provide, by any stretch of the imagination, an adequate description of apples or oranges. In fact, it is the emic dimensions (such as apple/orange flavor) that provide the crucial information.

This observation suggests support for the ethnoscientific approach advocated by Marsella, Dubanoski, Hamada, and Morse. The ethnosemantic methods include (1) the elicitation of all personality terms in the particular language; (2) the organization by research participants of the terms into naturally occurring structures; (3) the derivation of the meanings (e. g. , spontaneous associations) of these structures; and (4) the linking of the terms to actual behaviors. For example, researchers might use the antecedent-consequent method (If one is Y [the name of the personality structure], then one "would" or "would not" do X) to determine the link between personality terms and behaviors in different cultures. These methods are emic and do not impose any Western assumptions when the data are gathered. Yet it is very likely that the emic structures obtained with these methods will have some resemblance to the etic structures obtained by Western methods. Finding such convergence allows us to compare personalities across cultures, using the etic dimensions, and also to describe personalities with culturally sensitive elements, using the emic dimensions.

When ethnoscientific methods for the study of personality are used, we are likely to obtain emic dimensions for the description of personality in each culture. It is likely that some of these emic dimensions will have some resemblance to the etic dimensions that we discussed as allocentrism and idiocentrism. However, the fit is not likely to be excellent. The traits that we use in the West cut the pie of experience in ways that implicitly assume that individuals are autonomous entities. That assumption is not likely to be used in collectivist cultures.

The ethnoscientific methods were developed mostly by anthropologists and are close to the methods advocated by indigenous and cultural psychologists. They complement the methods of crosscultural psychologists. Triandis argued that it is desirable to use all three approaches and look for convergence.

The evolutionary perspectives can also increase our understanding of the way events over a long period of time increased some trait. For example, it has been argued that humans evolved over 200, 000 years from the warm African climates to cold Northern climates, where they were required to exhibit much more self-control (a personality attribute). Thus, Africans tend to be more spontaneous and show less impulse control than people in the North because, in that environment for thousands of years, one did not need as much self-control as in harsher climates, where a mistake such as stepping out of an igloo in minus 40 degree weather wearing inadequate clothing, could be fatal.

Needed Future Research

Spiro provided an extensive critique of the work of Markus and Kitayama and others who contrast individualist and collectivist cultures. He thinks that their characterization of such cultures is "wildly overdrawn." He emphasizes that culturally normative conceptions are not necessarily manifested in the behavior of individuals. This suggests the need for research that will examine how the constructs are to be conceived. Is the probabilistic conception presented by Triandis desirable? How is that conception related to behaviors?

In this article, the constructs of individualism and collectivism have been defined tentatively, since we do not know at this time which elements of the definitions are essential, account for most of the variance, and are most clearly linked to the ecology. We indicated the child-rearing and personality consequences of these constructs. But we need many studies, with structural equation modeling, to determine whether the consequences are directly linked to the elements of the constructs or to third variables that covary with them. Variables such as affluence, cultural homogeneity, etc. may have direct or indirect links to the consequences.

This has been a serious problem with the work on these constructs so far. Similarly, we need studies that will unconfound the constructs from modernity, affluence, urban status, migration to a new culture, exposure to Hollywood-made TV, and so on.

A global culture is emerging, which is especially compatible with idiocentrism. However, as cultures interact, acculturation is likely to result in changes in some domains, such as job behaviors, and not in other domains, such as religious or family life. Thus, we need to study the constructs, taking the domain into account, and examining how acculturation results in different patterns of individualism and collectivism in each society.

Kagitcibasi distinguished *normative individualism*, with its emphasis on individual rights and avoidance of the oppression of the in-group, from *relational individualism*, with its emphasis on the distance between self and in-group. We do not have, as yet, specific measures of each of these aspects, or many variables, in addition to the vertical and horizontal dimensions, that may define different kinds of individualism and collectivism. Specifically, we need to examine differences between the relationship of self to close in-group, distant in-group (e. g., the state), neutral out-group (e. g., strangers) and hostile out-group (e. g., people with whom one has a zero-sum relationship), in private and public settings, that are characterized by differing levels of tightness.

Conclusions

Changes in the ecology result in changes in culture which result in changes in personality. We reviewed attributes of individualism and collectivism and corresponding attributes of idiocentrism and allocentrism. We found several correlates of individualism, such as greater emphasis on internal processes, more emphasis on consistency, and more self-enhancement. The correlates of collectivism included more focus on contexts, less concern for consistency, and less sel-fenhancement.

People in collectivist cultures see themselves as interdependent with their in-groups, which provide for them a stable social environment to which they must adjust. So their personality is flexible, and their personality traits are not so clear. People in individualist cultures see the self as stable and the social environment as changeable, so they tend to shape the social environment to fit their personalities. Since personality has both genetic and environmental bases, when, in the future, we trace the links between genes and personality, we may find clearer links in individualist than in collectivist cultures.

Notes

1. Adapted and abridged from Harry C. Triandis's "Individualism-Collectivism and Personality." *Journal of Personality*, vol. 69, no. 6, 2001, pp. 907 – 924.
2. Harry Charalambos Triandis (1926 – 2019) is acknowledged as the father of cross-cultural social psychology as well as a leader of industrial/organizational and attitude research, Triandis realized that cross-cultural research had to employ different methods if the results were to be valid, which required the involvement of scholars from the cultures being studied at every step in the process, including instrument

design, hypothesis specification and analyses, joint publication, and so on. He was a prolific author, publishing over 200 papers, book chapters, and books. His work has been translated into Chinese, Farsi, German, Japanese, Russian, and Spanish and spans 60 years (1955 – 2015).

3. Unit of analysis: The unit of analysis refers to the main parameter that you're investigating in your research project or study. Example of the different types of unit analysis that may be used in a project include: individual people, groups of people, objects such as photographs, newspapers and books, geographical unit based on parameters such as cities or counties, and social parameters such as births, deaths, divorces. The unit of analysis is named as such because the unit type is determined based on the actual data analysis that you perform in your project or study.

4. Allocentrism and idiocentrism: Allocentrism and idiocentrism are the individual equivalents of collectivism and individualism. Collectivism and individualism are intended to refer to cultural or societal descriptions of the interrelations among inhabitants of those cultures or societies. Thus, an individual can be allocentric or idiocentric in a collectivistic society, or an individual can be allocentric or idiocentric in an individualistic society. Much of the early work on this has been by Triandis and his associates (e. g. , Hui & Triandis, 1986; Hui, Triandis, & Yee, 1991; Triandis et al. , 1986; Triandis, Bontempo, Villareal, Asai, & Lucca, 1988; Triandis, Chan, Bhawuk, Iwao, & Sinha, 1995). These studies tended to focus on describing allocentrism and idiocentrism or on measuring these constructs. Later studies (e. g. , Caldwell-Harris & Ayçiçegi, 2006; Dutta-Bergman & Wells, 2002; Zhang, Norvilitis, & Ingersoll, 2007) tended to examine when individuals' tendencies mismatch their societal norms, such as an allocentric individual in an individualistic society or an idiocentric individual in a collectivistic society.

Questions for Discussion

1. What is/are your reflection(s) on the author's argumentations? Do you agree with him? In what way(s)? Or if you do not agree with him, how and why?
2. In American society, Asian-Americans, especially those from East Asian countries, are called "Model Minority" because of their stereotypical images of achieving higher socioeconomic status, silence, hard-working, well-educated, etc. What is your justification, upon the author's argumentations, for Asian-Americans' "model" tag or our traveling abroad being "obedient" in contrast to some foreigners' violations of China's rules, regulations, even laws during their traveling or living in China.
3. What's your opinion about the new generation in China? Are they somewhat idiocentric, allocentric, half-half, or not applicable to Chinese anymore? In what way?

4. In the section of "*Relation to Big Five*," the author suggested that "future research may find some biological bases of allocentrism and idiocentrism, over and above the environmental bases emphasized in this paper." In your viewpoint, does nature or nurture outweigh in an individual's development?
5. How do you evaluate the dichotomic categorization, such as "individualism vs. collectivism," "etic vs. emic," "loose vs. tight," comparing with the quartering classification in "horizontal/vertical-individualism/collectivism"

Online Mini-Case Studies and Viewpoints-Sharing

My roommate is from Poland, we are allies. We have similar traits in common. We also study the same major. Having the same course of study really helps us understand one another as it takes a certain type of personality to be successful. Understanding what it takes to be a good intercultural ally is indeed a learning process. There are many things that my Polish roommate does that I disagree with. But because he is from another culture, I learn to understand what makes him unique and different. I have shared many meals with his extended family and even had him translate-d a Polish television show. I have met and enjoyed being around his Polish friends.

Online Research

Beyond the differences in language, culture, and personality, try to identify other distinctive factors that may affect intercultural communication.

Reading Two

Introductory Remarks

"Face" as a metaphor for the projected self-image in a social relational network (Ting-Toomey, 1988) symbolizes one's social position achieved via the successful performance of one's social roles that are well recognized by other members in the society (Hu, 1944). Face is one's public identity, which is acquired, maintained, and lost through social interaction. The process is called "facework," defined as "a set of coordinated practices in which communicators build, maintain, protect, or threaten personal dignity, honor, and respect." (Domenici and Littlejohn 2006, p. 10). Ting-Toomey (1988) found that low-context/individualistic cultures emphasize "I" identity, self-face concern, negative-face need, and direct verbal and nonverbal expression; Whereas, high-context/collectivistic cultures emphasize "we" identity, other-face concern, positive-face need, and indirect verbal and nonverbal expression. In Chinese society, losing one's face is one of the worst ways to injure one's self-esteem, which in turn results in emotional uneasiness or serious conflict (Hwang, 1987). Thus, Chinese people tend to "earn face" by all means in the social situation (Chu, 1983), and to enhance the other's face (Chiao, 1981).

The following reading investigates the relationship between facework maintenance and intercultural conflict styles, in which the two dimensions of self-face concern and other-face concern, and negative face and positive face are used to develop a set of theoretical propositions that account for conflict communication style differences in individualistic, low-context cultures, and collectivistic, high-context cultures. Hopefully, it could help readers to have a more in-depth and comprehensive understanding of both interpersonal and intercultural communication conflicts.

Intercultural Conflict Styles: A Face-Negotiation Theory[1]

Stella Ting-Toomey[2]

Conflict is a pervasive phenomenon that penetrates all forms of social and personal relationships in all cultures. Partners in a conflict situation typically bargain over many facets of the conflict process. They bargain over their goal differences, they bargain over the process, and they bargain over their situated identities. Conflict, as a class of threatening situations, poses threats to the situated identities of the negotiators. It is a communication process that involves different styles of interchanges between two interdependent negotiators who perceive incompatible needs or goals and perceive each other's potential interference in achieving those goals. More specifically, conflict is viewed, in this chapter, as a problematic situation that demands active facework management from the two interdependent conflict parties.

"Facework" and conflict style," however, are two culturally grounded concepts. Culture provides the larger interpretive frame in which "face" and "conflict style" can be meaningfully expressed and maintained. The negotiators' predispositions toward the concept of "face," their face-need and face-concern levels, and their modes and styles of managing the conflict episode are, for the most part, influenced by the cultural premises from which they draw their values and norms. The cultural values and norms will influence and shape how members in a cultural system manage facework and, in turn, how they should appropriately handle and manage a conflict situation. While there has been a plethora of studies on interpersonal-organization conflict negotiation in the past 20 years, there is a paucity of studies addressing the critical role of culture and its effect on face-management and conflict negotiation style. Most conflict researchers have acknowledged the importance of studying conflict context, but the concept of "context" typically refers to the situational context rather than the cultural context. In addition, while most conflict studies have engaged in a critical examination of conflict styles in the U.S. culture, a theoretical explanation has not been fully articulated as to why individual members engage in certain conflict styles over others (for example, confrontational style over avoidance style, integrating style over obliging style).

Hence, the objective of this chapter is a general one: to explore the role of culture in both face-management and conflict style processes. Conflict is viewed as a face-negotiation process in which the "faces" or the situated identities of the conflict parties are being threatened and called into question. The relationships among culture, facework, and conflict style are analyzed in five sections: (1) the basic assumptions of the facework process will be introduced; (2) relevant cross-cultural conflict style studies will be reviewed; (3) the basic axioms of the conflict face-negotiation theory will be presented; (4) specific theoretical propositions that are derived from the conflict face-negotiation theory will be enumerated; and (5) the implications of the face-negotiation theory to the study of cross-cultural problematic situations will be discussed.

FACEWORK PROCESSES

Culture and Facework

According to the observations of cross-cultural researchers, "facework" is a ubiquitous concept that exists in all cultures. The concept of "face" has been defined variously as "something that is diffusedly located in the flow of events", "a psychological image that can be granted and lost and fought for and presented as a gift", and "the public self-image that every member of a society wants to claim for himself/herself". Face, in essence, is a projected image of one's self in a relational situation. It is an identity that is conjointly defined by the participants in a setting. However, the degree to which one wishes to project an "authentic self" in a situation and the degree to which one chooses to maintain a "social self" in a situation varies in accordance to the cultural orientations toward the conceptualization of selfhood. In other words, a different degree of selfhood is being projected into this public self-image known as "face." In individualistic cultures, such as those of Australia, Germany, and the United States, the consistency between maintaining a private self-image and a public self-image is of paramount importance. An individual's public self-presentation of "face" should correspond to an invariant "core self" within an individual to a certain degree. In collectivistic cultures, such as those of China, the Republic of Korea, and Japan, the "self" is a situationally and relationally based concept. In analyzing selfhood and otherness in Confucian thoughts in China, Tu pointed out that "a distinctive feature of Confucian ritualization is an ever-deepening and broadening awareness of the presence of the other in one's self-cultivation. This is perhaps the single most important reason why the Confucian idea of the self as a center of relationships is an open system".

The self, in the Chinese cultural context, is defined through an intersecting web of social and personal relationships. The self in most collectivistic cultures, in fact, is maintained and codified through the active negotiation of facework. Whereas in individualistic cultures, such as that found in the United States, however, the self is often defined as an intra psychic phenomenon. The public "face," then, should ideally correspond lo the internal states of the negotiators. Providing "face-support" to another person in a problematic situation means lending support and confirmation to his or her idealized sense of self, which in tum should be ideally consistent with his or her core "authentic self". As Bellah, Madsen, Sullivan, Swidler, & Tipton commented in analyzing individualism and commitment in North American life: "In the absence of any objectifiable criteria of right and wrong, good or evil, the self and its feelings become our only moral guidance ... . There each individual is entitled to his or her own 'bit of space' and is utterly free within its boundaries". From the collectivistic perspective of selfhood, the self is never free. It is bounded by mutual role obligations and duties and it is structured by a patterned process of give-and-take reciprocal facework negotiation. Facework, in this context, is focused on how to lend role-support to another's face and at the same time not to bring shame to one's own self-face. From the individualistic perspective of selfhood, the self is ideally a free entity—free to pursue its own personal wants, needs, and desires. Facework, in this context, is heavily emphasized on how one can preserve one's own autonomyi territory, and space, simultaneously respecting the other person's need for space and privacy.

Positive and Negative Face

Brown and Levinson developed an elaborate theory of politeness based on two underlying assumptions: (1) All competent adult members of a society have (and know each other to have) "face"—the public self-image that every member wants to claim for himself or herself. The "face" has two related components: (a) negative face-the basic claim to territories, person. al reserves, rights to nondistraction, and (b) positive face—the basic claim over this projected self-image to be appreciated and to be approved by others; and (2) all competent adult members of a society have certain rational capacities and modes to achieve these ends.

Negative facework means the negotiation process between two interdependent parties concerning the degree of threat or respect each gives to one another's sense of freedom and individual autonomy. Positive facework entails the degree of threat or respect each gives to one another's need for inclusion and approval. Negative facework (speech acts such as apology for imposition, prerequest ritual, compliance—resistance act, and command act) emphasizes the need for dissociation. Positive facework (speech acts such as self-disclosure, compliment, and promise) emphasizes the need for association. Both concepts (association and dissociation), in fact, have been extensively documented by cross-cultural researchers as psychological universals that cut across cultural boundaries. However, while one might expect that both negative facework and positive facework are present in all cultures, the value orientations of a culture will influence cultural members' attitudes toward pursuing one set of facework more actively than others in a face-negotiation situation. Facework then, is viewed as a symbolic front that members in all cultures strive to maintain and uphold; while the modes and styles of expressing and negotiating face-need would vary from one culture to the next.

Types of Strategies

In addition to the concepts of "negative face and upositive face," Brown and Levinson identified five levels of facework strategies that potentially threaten either the negative face or the positive face of the involved parties in a politeness situation. These face-threatening acts (FTA) are arranged in different hierarchical levels of direct to indirect verbal speech acts. Direct FTA are viewed as posing the highest threat to the negotiators' faces, and indirect FTA are viewed as posing the least threat, and hence the most polite verbal acts. Again, the correlations between the direct mode and the perceived threat level, and between the indirect mode and the politeness level would vary from one culture to the next. In cultures that foster a direct mode of interaction in everyday life (such as low-context cultures like those in Germany, Scandinavia, Switzerland, and the United States), a direct mode of behavior probably is perceived to be not so threatening as an ambiguous mode of interacting. In cultures that nurture an indirect mode of interacting (such as high-context cultures like those in China, Japan, the Republic of Korea, and Vietnam), a direct mode of communicating can be perceived as highly threatening and unsettling to one's own face. While Brown and Levinson focused mainly on the concept of "face-threat," the concept of "face-respect" has not been explicitly dealt with in their politeness theory[3].

More recently, Shimanoff reconceptualized Brown and Levinson's FTA typology and identified four types of affective strategies in terms of the degree they respect or threaten the face-needs of the negotiators in a problematic situation. These four suprastrategies concerning facework negotiation are: (1) face-honoring (FH) type, (2) face-compensating (FC) type, (3) face-neutral (FN) type, and (4) face-threatening (FT) type. While the first three types represent respect strategies for other's face, the last type is viewed as a negative face-confronting strategy. Overall, Shimanoff reported that in the marital context, marital partners tend to use more face-honoring, face-compensating, and face-neutral strategies than face-threatening strategies. Baxter, in studying politeness strategies between males and females, found that people tend to use more face-politeness strategies in close relationships than in distant relationships. Tracy, Craig, Smith, and Spisak, in testing discourse strategies in multiple "favor-asking" situations, discovered that favor-asking messages varied in the degree to which they acknowledged the hearer's desire to be liked and appreciated (positive-face need) and the hearer's desire for autonomy and freedom of action (negative-face need). In addition, favor-asking messages varied in the attention they gave to the speaker's own positive face need. Finally, Leichty and Applegate's research analyzing individual differences in face-saving strategies revealed that actors are not overly concerned with intimate face-wants on relatively small requests, but that they give considerable attention to the intimate face-wants when substantial autonomy threat is involved. Also, speaker power, request magnitude, and relational familiarity all influence the degree to which the autonomy desire of the person being persuaded is attended to. Craig, Tracy, and Spisak, and Leichty and Applegate recommended that a new theory of facework should make a clear distinction between strategies that threaten self-face and other-face, and also strategies that gear toward negative-face maintenance and positive-face maintenance.

A Model of Facework

The facework literature to date suggests that when two interdependent parties come together in a facework negotiation session, they negotiate over two implicit principles: (1) face-concern principle: self-face, other-face, or mutual-face, and (2) face-need principle: negative face (concern for autonomy), and positive face (concern for inclusion). Negative-face need can be viewed as the need for autonomy or dissociation, and positive-face need can be viewed as the need for inclusion or association. These two principles are expressed through the two-dimensional grid in Figure 1.

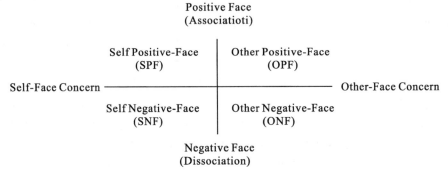

Figure 1　Two-dimensional grid of facework maintenance

Figure 1 consists of two conceptual dimensions: the self-concern and other-concern dimension and the positive-face and negative-face need dimension. The self-concern and other-concern dimension refers to the individual's orientation toward attention for self versus other. The positive-face and negative-face dimension refers to the individual's perceived need for association or dissociation. Self positive-face (SPF) maintenance means the use of certain communication strategies to defend and protect one's need for inclusion and association. Other positive-face (OPF) maintenance means the use of certain communication strategies to defend and support the other person's need for inclusion and association. Self negative-face (SNF) maintenance means the use of certain interaction strategies to give oneself freedom and space, and to protect self from other's infringement on one's autonomy. Finally, other negative-face (ONF) maintenance means the use of certain interaction strategies to signal respect for the other person's need for freedom, space, and dissociation. All four face types (SPF, OPF, SNF, and ONF) are subjected to differential treatments by the hearer in the negotiation process. The hearer can defend, respect, threaten, or confront the speaker's concern for self or other image, and the speaker's need for either positive face or negative face maintenance. While existing facework literature recognizes the functional importance of facework and the linguistic acts that accompany various face-needs and face-concerns, no study to date has explicated the critical role of culture in the facework negotiation process. In addition, there have been many interpersonal communication studies that used the concept of facework in compliance-gaining research, but no study has yet applied the face-negotiation concept in interpersonal conflict process. The rest of this chapter then will integrate the construct of facework with the conflict negotiation process.

To summarize, the basic assumptions of the facework negotiation process are: (1) members in all cultures negotiate over the concept of face; (2) the concept of face is especially problematic in uncertain situations (for example, request situation, complaint situation, embar-rassment situation, and conflict situation) when the situated identities of the interactants are called into question; (3) all face-negotiation entails multiple-goal orientations (self-concern and other-concern, negative-face and positive-face); (4) all negotiators express a concern for self-face protection or other-face support (or both) in problematic situations; (5) all negotiators express a need for dissociation (negative face) and/or a need for association (positive face) in problematic situations; (6) the self-other orientation dimension and the association-dissociation dimen-sion would be influenced by the relational variables (such as low-high familiarity level, low-high intimacy level), the situational variables (such as informal-formal level, public-private level) of the context, and the salience (such as topic magnitude, topic commitment) of the problematic issue; (7) the self-other dimension and the positive-face and negative-face need dimension would be influenced by the cultural interpretation and the cultural expectation levels of the context; and (8) while the four sets of suprastrategy—SPF, OPF, SNF, and ONF—are present in all negotiation settings in all cultures, certain sets of suprastrategy would be favorably preferred by members of a culture more often than others. The next two sections will develop along the lines of the last two assumptions in which the concept of facework is placed in the context of cross-cultural conflict situations.

CONFLICT STYLES

Interpersonal Conflict Styles

There have been many interpersonal and organizational communication studies that set out to test conflict communication styles in both relational and organizational settings. For example, Blake and Mouton used a two-dimensional framework: (a) the degree (low or high) of desire to meet personal needs or goals, and (b) the degree (low or high) of desire to maintain interpersonal needs. They analyzed the conflict process in terms of five styles: forcing, confronting, sharing, withdrawing, and smoothing. Putnam and Wilson concluded that these conflict styles can be clustered into three styles: (a) control style: acts that lead to direct confrontation, arguments, imposition of ideas on another person; (b) solution-oriented style: acts that aim to find solutions to the conflict and integrate the needs of both parties; and (c) nonconfrontational style: acts that entail indirectness, avoidance, and withdrawal. Ross and DeWine concurred with Putnam and Wilson's three-style approach, and came up with a forcing style, an issue style, and a smoothing style.

Rahim, Rahim and Bonoma, however, in developing a conflict typology based on the dimensions of concern for self and concern for others, still maintained the importance of a five-style approach. The first dimension explains the degree (low or high) to which a person attempts to satisfy his or her own concern or own face-need. The second dimension explains the degree (low or high) to which a person wants to satisfy the concern of others or, in other words, satisfy others' face-need. Their conflict styles include: (a) dominating (high self-concern, low other-concern), (b) obliging (low self-concern, high other-concern), (c) integrating (high self-concern, high other-concern), (d) avoiding (low self-concern, low other-concern), and (e) compromising (intermediate self-concern and other-concern). Finally, Brown, Yelsma, and Keller discussed the importance of an individual's predispositions to conflict process. They suggested that researchers should pay close attention to conflict predispositional factors, such as an individual's range of affective feelings, task energy level, concern for self-uniqueness, concern for control, respect for others, and concern for one's community.

Unfortunately, amidst the enthusiastic debate between three-style versus five-style approach to conflict, interpersonal and organizational conflict researchers typically have failed to provide cross-cultural evidence for both their theoretical and methodological claims over the various styles of conflict negotiation. We may summarize that overall, for the U.S. sample, conflict styles have been developed by various researchers along the lines of concern for self or concern for other, issue-oriented or relationship-oriented, and conflict-approach or conflict-avoidance attitude. In relating various conflict styles with face-management process, the concern for self is related to the concern for self-face protection; the concern for other is related to the concern for other-face support. Issue-oriented approach is reflective of the need for control, for choices, and for negative face of autonomy; relationship-oriented approach is reflective of the need for connection, for approval, and for positive face of association. Finally, conflict-approach attitude leads to the use of either direct confrontational strategies or solution-oriented strategies. Conflict-avoidance attitude leads to the use of either passive obliging strategies or withdrawal-exit strategies. The concern for self-face protection, the issue-oriented approach, and the conflict-approach attitude leads to a direct mode of handling conflict. Finally, the concern for other-face violation, the relationship-oriented approach, and the conflict-avoidance attitude leads to an indirect mode of managing conflict. In most conflict situations, members in all cultures typically face a set of dialectical choices: between protecting self-face and preserving other-face, and between defending self-face and con-fronting other-face. In addition, they have to search for the balance point between negotiating for self-concern and other-concern, and between association need and dissociation need.

Cross-Cultural Conflict Styles
It is only in the past five years that intercultural researchers have become actively engaged in cross-cultural conflict style research. For example, Tafoya used a barrier perspective to study the relationship between conflict style and culture. He found that two types of cultural barriers—personal psychological barriers and

interpersonal conflict style barriers—can detract from the functional conflict process. Wolfson and Norden, using the Coordinated Management of Meaning (CMM) Theorory[4], found that Chinese subjects tend to use more passive strategies in handling conflict, while North American subjects tend to use more active strategies in managing conflict. In addition, Chinese subjects felt that they had a limited range of choices in handling teacher-student conflicts, while North American subjects perceived a wider range of behavioral options.

Cushman and King, using a "national culture" approach, tried to explain conflict style differences in Japan, Yugoslavia, and the United States. They found that the Japanese culture values the importance of maintaining public face in the conflict process and would prefer the use of a collaborative style to resolve conflict. Yugoslavian culture values the equality norm in a conflict situation and would prefer a compromising style in handling conflict. Finally, the U.S. culture values the competitive norm in a conflict process, and would prefer a competitive style of conflict management. Nomura and llarnlund, also using a "national culture" approach, found that Japanese subjects tend to use more passive, accommodating strategies in the interpersonal criticism process, while American subjects tend to use more active, confrontational strategies. Kumagai and Straus, in examining Japanese and North American conflict style differences, presented similar findings to Nomura and Barnlund's study. Kagan, Knight, and Martinez-Romero, in testing for conflict style differences between Mexicans and Anglo-Americans, found that Mexican subjects tend to use more passive, avoidance conflict strategies, while Anglo-Americans tend to use more active, confrontational strategies. In testing for Black and White differences in conflict styles, Ting-Toomey found that Black subjects tend to use more controlling style strategies than do White subjects, and that White subjects tend to use more solution-oriented style strategies than do Black subjects. Ross and DeWine, in analyzing cross-cultural conflict styles in Denmark and the United States, discovered that North American subjects tend to prefer more issue-oriented strategies to manage conflict than do Danish subjects. As the cross-cultural conflict literature has indicated so far, conflict style is a cultural-relative construct. Research findings con-sistently point out that Whites in the U.S. culture tend to use two predominant styles of conflict: dominating (confrontation-oriented) style and integrating (solution-oriented) style. However, the reasoning behind the apparent conflict style differences in various cultures have not been satisfactorily addressed. Most cross-cultural conflict studies remain on a descriptive level of national culture differences, while the theoretical underpinnings of why cultural members choose certain conflict strategies over others remain thin and unpersuasive.

Moving beyond a "national culture" explanation, Nadler, Nadler, and Broome, in examining conflict situations across cultures, used a negotiation perspective to the study of conflict style and culture. They proposed that the three most critical components in understanding cross-cultural conflict are: perspectives toward conflict (orientations and criteria toward conflict), personal constructs (such as fairness, trust, and power), and message strategies (such as the use of threats, promises, use of time, and decision-making style). Finally, Ting-Toomey and Chua and Gudykunst used Hall's low-context culture (LCC) and high-context culture (HCC) framework to study the relationship between conflict style and culture. They found that low-context members tend to prefer a direct mode of conflict style (such as the use of confrontational strategies or solution-oriented strategies), while high-context members tend to prefer an indirect mode of conflict style (such as the use of smoothing strategies or avoidance strategies). Rather than treating culture as a static variable, the cultural variability dimensions (individualism-collectivism dimension, low-context/high-context dimension) were used in these studies to explain the conflict style differences in different cultures. With the various cross-cultural conflict studies in mind the following section will present the cultural variability dimensions in relationship to the conflict face-negotiation theory.

FACE-NEGOTIATION THEORY

Individualism-Collectivism
Numerous cross-cultural studies in the last five years have provided empirical evidence that the theoretical dimension of individualism-collectivism is the primary dimension that differentiates different clusters of cultures from an international perspective. Hofstede analyzed organiza-tional behaviors in 40 cultures identifying individualism-collectivism as one out of the four primary dimensions . that links organizational life with culture. Cross-cultural studies that have analyzed the relationship between interpersonal perception and culture also provide strong support for the critical role of the individualism-collectivism dimension in understanding communication style differences in different sets of cultures. Hui and Triandis, after surveying cross-cultural anthropologists and psychologists from all parts of the world, concluded that the dimension of individualism-collectivism can be used as a powerful theoretical construct to explain the degree of interactional differences and similarities between cultures.

In sum, the terms individualism and collectivism refer to "a cluster of attitudes, beliefs, and behaviors toward a wide variety of people". While individualistic cultures draw upon the "I" identity as the prime focus, collectivistic cultures draw upon the "we" identity. Individualistic cultures are concerned with the authenticity of self-presentation style. Collectivistic cultures are concerned with the adaptability of self-presentation image. Overall, individualistic cultures (such as that in Australia and the United States) emphasize individualistic goals over group goals, individualistic concerns over group concerns, and individual rights and needs over collective responsibilities and obligations. Collectivistic cultures (such as those in China and Japan), in contrast, value group goals over individual goals, group concerns over individual concerns, and collective needs over individual needs. While individualistic cultures are concerned with self-face maintenance, collectivistic cultures are concerned with both self-face and other-face maintenance. Individualistic cultures value autonomy, choices, and negative-face need, while collectivistic cultures value interdependence, reciprocal obligations, and positive-face need.

Low- and High-Context

In addition to the individualism-collectivism dimension, Hall's low-context culture and high-context culture (LCC-HCC) dimension serves as a good theoretical foundation to account for communication style differences across a range of cultures. While the individualism-collectivism dimension points to the underlying values of different clusters of cultures, the LCC-HCC dimension points to communication style differences across a set of cultures. Hall's LCC-HCC framework provides a conceptual grounding to understand groups of cultures from a communication perspective.

According to Hall and Ting-Toomey, LCC system (cultures such as those in Germany, Scandinavia, Switzerland, and the United States) and HCC system (cultures such as those in China, Japan, the Republic of Korea, and Vietnam) exist on a continuum of cultural communication differences. The LCC system (with the U.S. culture as the prime example) values individual value orientation, line logic, direct verbal interaction, and individualistic nonverbal style. The HCC system (with the Japanese culture as the prime example) values group value orientation, spiral logic, indirect verbal interaction, and contextual nonverbal style. Individualistic verbal and nonverbal communication style means intentions are displayed clearly and have direct correspondence with verbal and nonverbal patterns. Contextual verbal and nonverbal style means intentions and meanings are situated within the larger shared knowledge of the cultural context. While meanings in the LCC are overtly displayed through direct communication forms, meanings in the HCC are implicitly embedded at different levels of the sociocultural context.

Hence, in the LCC system, face-negotiation is an overt communication process. The face-giving and face-protection moves and counter-moves have to be overtly spelled out, and the arguments and the persuasions in a conflict situation would typically follow a linear logic pattern. Face-negotiation in the LCC system would be based on an immediate cost-reward-comparison model[5], whereas in the HCC system, face-negotiation is an accumulative, long-term process. Since members in the HCC system are interlocked in a group-value perspective, every face-support or face-violation act on another person will have larger social and group implications. The arguments and disagreements in a conflict situation would be ambiguously expressed and the face-giving and face-saving appeals would typically follow a spiral logic pattern. Face-negotiation in the HCC system would probably be based on a long-term, cost-reward-comparison model. In LCC systems, immediate reciprocity of face-giving and face-saving is important to the success of face-negotiation moves. In HCC systems, eventual reciprocity of face-honoring and face-compensating is important for the maintenance of both social and personal relationship developments.

The face-conflict axioms that are derived from both the individualism-collectivism dimension and the LCC-HCC dimension are posited as follows: (1) Both LCC and HCC systems have the concept of "face" a public image that an interactant claims for himself or herself; (2) LCC members project the "I" identity in facework negotiation, and HCC members project the "we" identity in facework negotiation; (3) the "I" identity facework maintenance makes facework negotiation a competitive process, and the "we" identity facework maintenance makes facework negotiation a collaborative process; (4) the "I" identity orientation means interactants will focus more on self-face perseverance and other-face threat strategies, the "we" identity orientation means interactants will focus more on mutual-face perseverance and other-face honoring strategies; (5) members in both LCC and HCC systems negotiate both face types, negative-face and positive-face, with LCC systems focusing more on negative-face maintenance process, and HCC system focusing more on positive-face maintenance processes; (6) members in both LCC and HCC systems use all four types of face-maintenance suprastrategy: SPF, OPF, SNF, and ONF, however, LCC members tend to use more SPF and SNF strategies while HCC members tend to use more OPF and ONF strategies in interpersonal problematic situations.

THEORETICAL PROPOSITIONS

Altogether 12 theoretical propositions are derived from the preceding discussion of facework negotiation and cross-cultural conflict styles. The first two propositions are presented as follows:

> Proposition 1: Members of individualistic, LC cultures tend to express a greater degree of self-face maintenance in a conflict situation than do members of collectivistic, HC cultures.
>
> Proposition 2: Members of collectivistic, HC cultures tend to express a greater degree of mutual-face or other-face maintenance than do members of individualistic, LC cultures.

Members of individualistic cultures tend to operate from the "I" identity system and members from the collectivistic cultures tend to operate from the "we" identity system. The "I" identity system influences one's perception and attention toward "self" as the most important entity of choices. In the LCC system, the concept of "face" is fused with a strong sense of "I" image in the negotiation process. The "we" identity system influences one's perception and orientation to seek outward for connection and approval. In the HCC system, the concept of "face" is always an other-directed concept. Without the approval or disapproval of other people surrounding the self, the concept of "face" does not exist. The third and fourth propositions are as follows:

> Proposition 3: Members of individualistic, LC cultures would tend to use more autonomy-preserving strategies (negative-face need) in managing conflict than would members of collectivistic, HC cultures.
>
> Proposition 4: Members of collectivistic, HC cultures would tend to use more approval-seeking strategies (positive-face need) in managing conflict than would members of individualistic, LC cultures.

While privacy and autonomy are the trademarks of individualistic LC cultures, interdependence and inclusion are the hallmarks of collectivistic HC cultures. Ina conflict uncertainty situation, face threat means, to members of LC cultures, threatening their need for autonomy and control over self and other. Face threat means, to the members of HC cultures, threatening their need for inclusion and approval by others. Face-violation acts, to the LCC members, would be communicative acts that violate their sense for independence and privacy. Face-violation acts, to the HCC members, would be communicative acts that violate their sense for interconnection and mutuality. Different cultural members, in a sense, would perceive different degrees of threat and different thematic variations of threat in a conflict situation. Propositions 5 and 6 are presented as follows:

> Proposition 5: Members of individualistic, LC cultures would tend to use more self positive-face (SPF) and self negative-face (SNF) suprastrategies than would members of collectivistic, HC cultures.
>
> Proposition 6: Members of collectivistic, HC cultures would tend to use more other positive-face (OPF) and other negative-face (ONF) suprastrategies than would members of individualistic, LC cultures.

Self positive-face and self negative-face strategies are defend-attack strategies that aim at protecting self-inclusion need and self-autonomy need while assaulting the face of the other conflict partner. Other positive-face and other negative-face strategies are pleasing and nonimposition strategies that aim, perhaps, at protecting one's self or face from the other's direct criticisms and rejections. Members in the LC cultures tend to use overt face-negotiation tactics, while members in the HC cultures tend to use functionally ambiguous face tactics. Overt face-negotiation tactics promote competition, ambiguous face-negotiation tactics aim at preserving group harmony. The seventh and eighth propositions are presented as follows:

> Proposition 7: Members of individualistic, LC cultures tend to use a greater degree of direct face-negotiation strategies than do members of collectivistic, HC cultures.
>
> Proposition 8: Members of collectivistic, HC cultures tend to use a greater degree of indirect face-negotiation strategies than do members of individualistic, LC cultures.

"Face" in LC cultures is a commodity that can be explicitly bargained and counter-bargained. "Face" in the HC cultures is a psychological-affective construct that ties closely with other concepts such as "honor," " shame," and "obligation." In the LC cultures, "face" exists only in the immediate time-space that involves the two conflict parties, unfortunately, "face" in the HC cultures involves the multiple faces of relatives, friends, and family members that are closely linked to the HCC interactants. "Face" is a relatively "free" concept in the LC cultures; "face" is an obligatory concept in the HCC system that reflects one's status hierarchy, role position, and power resource. The more one is in power, the more one knows how to bestow, maintain, honor, and destroy face. For LC cultures, the direct dealing with "face" in a conflict situation signifies an honest, up-front way of handling a problematic situation. For HC cultures, the indirect, subtle dealing with "face" in a conflict situation reflects good taste and tactfulness. The ninth and tenth propositions are proffered as follows:

> Proposition 9: Members of individualistic, LC cultures tend to use more dominating or controlling strategies to manage conflict than do members of collectivistic, HC cultures.
> Proposition 10: Members of collectivistic, HC cultures tend to use more obliging or smoothing strategies to manage conflict than do members of individualistic, LC cultures.

Dominating or controlling conflict strategies reflect the importance of self-face concern in individualistic, LC cultures. Obliging or smoothing conflict strategies reflect the other-face concern in collectivistic, HC cultures. In LC cultures, "control" of one's freedom, autonomy, and choices is of paramount importance to one's sense of ego. In HC cultures, "blending in" with other's wishes, desires;i and needs is of utmost importance in upholding one's own face and at the same time not embarrassing the other person's face. From the HCC perspective, dominating or confrontational conflict strategies are viewed as posing a direct threat to the other person's face without leaving room for further negotiations and maneuvers in the conflict process. From the LCC perspective, the obliging or the roundabout way of handling conflict in the HCC system poses a direct insult to the face of the negotiators in the LCC conflict situation. While the LCC members would view the indirect way of handling conflict as a cowardly act, the HCC members would view the direct way of handling conflict as lacking in good taste. On both the verbal and nonverbal levels, LCC members would tend to use more direct speech acts (such as direct demands and direct compliance-gaining strategies) and direct, personalized nonverbal style to deal with the face-negotiation process, while HCC members would tend to use more indirect speech acts (such as indirect requests and indirect compliance-gaining strategies) and indirect, contextualistic, nonverbal style to deal with the conflict-confrontation process. The eleventh and twelfth propositions are presented as follows:

Proposition 11: Members of individualistic, LC cultures would use a greater degree of solution-oriented conflict style than would members of collectivistic, HC cultures.

Proposition 12: Members of collectivistic, HC cultures would use a greater degree of avoidance-oriented conflict style than would members of individualistic, LC cultures.

While members in the LC cultures can separate the conflict issue from the person, members in the HC cultures typically view conflict as an integration between the issue and the problem in the person. While LCC members are able to analyze the logic of conflict from a task-oriented viewpoint, HCC members typically combine the instrumental dimension with the affective dimension. Hence, for LCC members, while they can manage conflict face-negotiation from an instrumental, solution oriented perspective, HCC members would typically take the conflict flight approach and try to avoid the conflict person at all costs. Table 1 presents the major characteristics of individualistic, LCC and collec-tivistic, HCC face-negotiation processes.

Table 1 A Summary of Low-Context and High-Context Face-Negotiation Processes

Key Constructs of "Face"	Individualistic, Low-Context Cultures	Collectivistic, High-Context Cultures
Identity	emphasis on "I" identity	emphasis on "we" identity
Concern	self-face concern	other-face concern
Need	autonomy, dissociation, negative-face need	inclusion, association, positive-face need
Suprastrategy	self positive-face and self negative-face	other positive-face and other negative-face
Mode	direct mode	indirect mode

Continued

Key Constructs of "Face"	Individualistic, Low-Context Cultures	Collectivistic, High-Context Cultures
Style	controlling style or confrontation style, and solution-oriented style	obliging style or avoidance style, and affective-oriented style
Strategy	distributive or competitive strategies	integrative or collaborative strategies
Speech act	direct speech acts	indirect speech acts
Nonverbal act	individualistic nonverbal acts, direct emotional expressions	contextualistic (role-oriented) nonverbal acts, indirect emotional expressions

IMPLICATIONS

Five implications can be drawn from the face-negotiation theory: (1) The theory can be applicable to any intercultural problematic situations that entail active facework negotiation process; (2) tile theory can be applied to situations that involve a high degree of threat (or uncertainty) to the face of the intercultural interactants; (3) the theory can be used in situations that demand a high degree of politeness between the intercultural interactants; (4) the theory can be used in conjunction with other speech act types (such as request act, compliment act, complaint act, and insult act); and (5) the theory can be used in relationship to other conceptional variables such as compliance-gaining, compliance-resistance, and communication competent behaviors.

The face-negotiation theory states basically that while all intercultural interactants come to a problematic situation with the need for facework management, their focus and orientation toward what aspects of the face need to be tend to vary from one culture to the next. In individualistic, low-context cultures, it is predicted that members would be more likely to turn to self positive-face management and self negative-face management strategies in resolving threat or uncertainty in a problematic situation. In collectivistic, high-context cultures, it is predicted that members would be more likely to use other positive-face strategies and other negative-face management strategies to satisfy the inclusion and approval need.

It is also predicted that because of the different concerns for either negative-face protection (concern for autonomy) or positive-face protection (concern for inclusion), these concerns will be translated to the actual choices of certain conflict styles over others. For LCC members, the concern for autonomy and freedom of actions would influence the LCC individuals to select controlling strategies to preserve distance between the two interactants, and to choose confrontational strategies to fend off opponents in their space-violation acts. For HCC members, the concern for inclusion and other-approval would influence the HCC individuals to select obliging strategies to seek approval for self-face from the other interactant, or to pick avoidance strategies to avoid the problematic issue altogether.

In continuing the theorizing process in interculturat. facework negotiation, future studies need to pay close attention to: (1) the basic taxonomies and metaphors that members use in different cultures that have direct or indirect bearing in the facework negotiation process; (2) the underlying logic and interpretation that cultural members have concerning the use of face-saving, face-violating, and face-honoring communication behaviors; (3) what classes of facework constitute face-threatening acts and what classes of facework constitute face-respecting acts; (4) the fundamental communication acts that are viewed as face-violation behaviors, face-honoring behaviors, and face-compensating behaviors; and (5) the face-negotiation patterns (such as symmetrical patterns or complementary patterns) that constitute optimal communication competence and performance in each culture.

The concept of "face" is viewed in this chapter as a symbolic resource that members in all cultures strive to maintain. However, while "face" is a transcultural concept that governs the active negotiation processes in all cultures, the nuances and subtleties that attach to different facets of facework management would vary from one culture to the next. The dimensions of individualism-collectivism and low-context and high-context have been used as a starting point to aid in the theorizing process of conflict face-negotiation. It is hoped that as more data emerge concerning the theory of face-negotiation, specific propositions concerning specific problematic situations in specific cultures can be systematically introduced and developed. This study provides the groundwork for more integrated efforts between researchers whose work is in language behavior, conflict styles, or interpersonal intercultural communication competence process, to collaborate with and to contribute to a common understanding of the face-negotiation process in all cultures.

Notes

1. Adapted and abridged from Stella Ting-Toomey, 'Intercultural Conflict Styles: A Face-Negotiation Theory' in Kim, Young Y., and William B. Gudykunst. *Theories*

  in Intercultural Communication. vol. 12. , New York: Sage Publications, 1988.
2. Stella Ting-Toomey: Professor of Human Communication Studies at California State University, Fullerton. Her teaching interests are in intercultural (IC) communication theory, IC communication training, and IC conflict management. Her research program focuses on testing the conflict face-negotiation theory and fine-tuning the cultural/ethnic identity negotiation model. She is the author and editor of numerous books. Dr. Ting-Toomey has lectured widely throughout the U.S., Asia, and Europe on the theme of managing intercultural conflict effectively. She has also conducted many training workshops for corporations, universities, and non-profit organizations in the area of intercultural competence practice.
3. Politeness Theory: A major framework that combines these differing politeness strategies has been developed by the two linguists Penelope Brown and Stephen Levinson. They distinguish between negative politeness strategies: strategies that are performed to avoid offense through deference and positive politeness strategies: strategies that are performed to avoid offense by emphasizing friendliness.
4. Coordinated Management of Meaning (CMM) Theory: The CMM theory lays down the process that helps us to socially communicate that makes us create meaning and also manage the social reality. This theory of CMM advocates on articulation of a process on developing prepositions on given situation by the people. The process happens in an order to present the appropriate action/reaction. And to help the people enriching them with communication patterns is seen important like following the set rules and apply them to resolve/conflict the situations that is entirely different from the views set. The theorists believe that the co-construct of social realities are shaped as they are created and human beings create an hierarchy to organize the meanings to it that is associated with assumptions. So the organizing of meaning will help the people to determine the output/the throw of the message sent.
5. Cost-reward-comparison model: It is derived from the arousal: cost-reward model proposed by Dovidio, Piliavin, Gaertner, Schroeder, and Clark (1991). The arousal: cost-reward model operates in accordance with an individual's cognitive decision-making process. This theory holds that the ultimate determinate of helping is subjective mental calculation. People will be most likely to help when the costs of helping are low, and the costs of not helping are high. Helping can be viewed as an economic behavior based upon the weighing of situational and intrinsic variables. For example, time required and diffusion of responsibility can be considered costs, moreover, if the time required is low (1 hour) and the individual is unable to diffuse responsibility, then it is likely that this individual will help. In summary, there exist variables which through a subjective weighing process will determine whether or not a person will help (Dovidio et al. , 1991; Schroeder et al. , 1995). The arousal: cost-reward model includes two categories concerned with the cost variables: the costs of helping and the costs of not helping.

Questions for Discussion

1. Conflict and opposition permeate human relationship development. In one of the most influential Chinese philosophical classic *Book of Changes*, "*Heaven and earth are opposites, but their action is concerted. Man and woman are opposites, but they strive for union. All beings stand in opposition to one another; what they do takes on order thereby. Great indeed is the effect of the time of opposition.*"
   How do you understand "conflict" in the view of traditional Chinese philosophical doctrine in *Book of Changes*?
2. Social Anxiety Disorder (SAD) is prevalent among young people in China now. The possible and potential triggers vary greatly. Do you think there is any correlation between SAD and facework?
3. Cyber-bullying is currently one of the most notorious social issues. People anonymously use mean-spirited language with ill-will under the shield of the screen. How can we relate the cyber-bullying behavior to the Face-Negotiation Theory?
4. Have you ever had any conflict with your parents or grandparents due to face maintenance? Is/Are there any difference(s) in your conflicts with the two older generations respectively beyond the cause of the generation gaps? Do you think it is strategic in your family culture or typical of Chinese culture in general?
5. Are there any similarities of and/or differences in international conflict between two countries (e.g., China vs. the U.S.) and interpersonal conflict between two individuals (e.g., you and your roommate/classmate/colleague)? Can you apply the cross-cultural conflict styles and the interpersonal conflict styles to justify your response?

Online Mini-Case Studies and Viewpoints-Sharing

At my work, I have leaned to be somewhat of a "chameleon" in adapting to different cultural styles of conflict. I supervise a number of workers, a mixture of collectivists and individualists-some from Mexico, Mexican Americans, and white U.S. Americans. I have learned to play to each person's cultural style, soften them up for my suggestions on how to solve the conflict. With the collectivists, like people from Mexico, it takes a little time for them to open up to me. I have to build a relationship before they start to resolve the conflict. Since I've figured this out, they have been more cooperative with me in dealing with conflict issues While. With the individualists, they come right out and tell me what's wrong, but I still play to their emotional style and make them feel comfortable, calm them down so that we can move on with the resolution process.

Online Research

Compare and contrast the scenarios of intercultural and intracultural conflicts and elucidate the strategies to deal with each.

Unit Eight

Intercultural Barriers

Reading One

Introductory Remarks

Decades of research reveals that intercultural communication barriers usually result from group differences in cognition, affect, and patterns of behavior. Therefore, effective intercultural communication requires that participants in an intergroup encounter pay due attention to cognitive, affective, and behavioral adaptations. Although intercultural communication scholars and educators have attached great importance to the research on intercultural communication, the relationship between intercultural communication barriers and intergroup attitudes remains relatively unexplored.

In this paper, Spencer-Rodgers and McGovern, two well-known professors of psychology from the University of California at Berkeley and the University of California at Santa Barbara, examined the psychological impact of intercultural communication barriers on intergroup attitudes by testing a model of global attitudes toward the culturally different. Finding that the existing literature has largely overlooked the role of intercultural communication in determining people's evaluative orientation toward ethnolinguistic out-groups, the authors investigated intercultural communication emotions as determinants of prejudice and researched on the causal factors that are widely recognized as central to intergroup judgments. They submit that prejudice toward certain ethnolinguistic out-groups may derive from adverse emotions related to linguistic and cultural barriers. This antecedent of out-group attitudes, labeled intercultural communication affect, should be especially relevant in international settings, as well as multicultural and linguistically diverse societies. To testify their hypotheses, the two researchers used a sample of 154 undergraduate and graduate students enrolled at two large West Coast universities in the United States. The participants were invited to participate in a study on social attitudes toward foreign students and complete a questionnaire survey. Regression analyses indicated that intercultural communication emotions were strongly and uniquely related to prejudice toward a culturally diverse out-group: foreign students. Consistent with the contact hypothesis, moderated regression analyses indicated that the structure of intergroup attitudes was modified by social contact with the international community.

Today, American colleges and universities host the world's largest foreign student population, and it is predicted that international enrollments will keep increasing. The present research indicates that promoting contact with foreign students can not only reduce negative stereotypes and potential conflicts but also enhance mutual benefits from the diversity of student body on campus. Actual or symbolic threats can be greatly attenuated by the dissemination of information about the economic, cultural, and intellectual contributions of foreign students to the university community, especially through university programs such as integrated residential facilities and recreational activities.

Attitudes toward the Culturally Different: The Role of Intercultural Communication Barriers, Affective Responses, Consensual Stereotypes, and Perceived Threat[1]

Julie Spencer-Rodgers and Timothy McGovern

1. Introduction

Effective intercultural communication is critical to the establishment and maintenance of favorable intergroup relations. Factors that have been identified as central to intercultural communication competence, such as cultural knowledge and awareness, communication skills, and tolerance for ambiguity, strongly impact the favorability of intergroup contacts. As an area of inquiry, intercultural communication has been studied extensively in fields such as cultural anthropology, sociolinguistics, sociology of language, and communication science. Within psychology, research on intercultural communication has contributed greatly to our understanding of ethnolinguistic identity, language attitudes, speech accommodation, and the significance of language in stereotyping. Intercultural communication scholars and educators have called for more research on intercultural communication within the discipline of psychology. Relatively unexplored within social psychology, for example, is the relationship between intercultural communication barriers and intergroup attitudes.

Intercultural communication barriers arise from group differences in cognition (e. g., fundamental epistemologies, values, norms, etc.), affect (e. g., types and levels of emotional expressivity), and patterns of behavior (e. g., language, customs, communication styles, etc.). Effective intercultural communication requires cognitive, affective, and behavioral (including linguistic) adaptations that can be arduous and troublesome to participants in an intergroup encounter. Several decades of research on intercultural communication points to the relative difficulty of achieving effective and satisfying communication between ethnolinguistic out-groups. Individuals must meet the challenges of language barriers, unfamiliar customs and practices, and cultural variations in verbal and nonverbal communication styles in order to achieve successful intercultural understanding. As a result, linguistic and cultural barriers often carry evaluative and affective consequences for interactants in an intercultural context.

Communication with the culturally different is frequently associated with adverse emotional responses. To illustrate, individuals may feel awkward and anxious when interacting with culturally different others, in part, because of communication obstacles. Members of a dominant ethnolinguistic group may experience feelings of impatience and frustration when communicating with non-native speakers of a language. Although accented speech is sometimes viewed as socially attractive, processing accented speech is cognitively and emotionally taxing, and non-native speakers of a language are rated less favorable than native speakers on a wide range of attributes, including competence and trust-worthiness. Intercultural encounters may also be confusing due to group differences in emotional expressivity and non-verbal communication styles, and cultural variations in values, norms, and customs may lead to cultural misunderstandings and instances of communication breakdown that are stressful and unpleasant. Ultimately, repeated communication failures and emotionally laden cultural misunderstandings can give rise to a negative evaluative orientation toward the culturally different.

2. Intercultural Communication and Prejudice

Since the Cognitive Revolution[2] in social psychology in the 1970s, research on intergroup attitudes has largely emphasized cognitive causal factors (e.g., stereotypes) to the neglect of affective determinants. Social psychologists are increasingly recognizing the significance of emotions in determining people's evaluative orientation toward out-groups. Seminal work on intergroup anxiety demonstrated that negative affect-generalized feelings of awkwardness, anxiety, and apprehension elicited during intergroup contact strongly influences people's attitudes and behaviors. Anxiety and apprehension directly associated with communication barriers has also been shown to predict inimical attitudes toward ethnolinguistic out-groups (e.g., non-native teaching assistants).

The psychological literature has also largely overlooked intercultural communication difficulties as a potential causal factor underlying prejudice and discrimination. Whereas social psychologists have extensively documented the impact of stereotypes on intergroup attitudes, intercultural communication scholars have investigated diverse variables that influence communication effectiveness. In addition to affecting communication quality, constructs such as anxiety/uncertainty, cultural competence, and communication apprehension impact the favorability of intergroup attitudes and relations. Some correlational and experimental evidence points to a connection between intercultural communication barriers and prejudice. Much of this research has examined American college students' judgments of international teaching assistants. Communication difficulties between US nationals and foreign student-instructors are a significant source of intergroup conflict and hostility.

In an attempt to integrate further intergroup emotion, intercultural communication, and prejudice research, the present article examined a special class of intergroup emotions related to intercultural communication experiences, and more specifically, intercultural communication difficulties. Rather than stemming from strongly held beliefs about the negative attributes of a group, we submit that prejudice toward certain ethnolinguistic out-groups may derive from adverse emotions related to linguistic and cultural barriers. This antecedent of out-group attitudes, labeled *intercultural communication affect*, should be especially relevant in international settings, as well as multicultural and linguistically diverse societies, such as the United States, where intercultural communication is "virtually unavoidable." To our knowledge, the present study is the first to examine the contribution of intercultural communication emotions, relative to factors such as stereotypic beliefs, in predicting prejudice toward the culturally different.

3. The Relative Contribution of Intercultural Communication Emotions

The psychological impact of intercultural communication barriers on prejudicial attitudes can be examined in relation to factors that are widely accepted by social psychologists as germane to intergroup judgments. Intergroup attitudes have been conceptualized as a global evaluation of an attitude object that is based on multiple sources of information. Accordingly, much empirical work has investigated the relative contribution of various factors—such as realistic group conflict, values, stereotypes, and affective responses—in determining attitudes toward a wide range of social groups. The Integrated Threat Theory (ITT) of Prejudice posits that there are four basic causal factors or classes of threat that lead social perceivers to be biased against out-groups: negative stereotypes (cognitive beliefs), intergroup anxiety (affective responses), realistic threats (economic and physical concerns), and symbolic/cultural threats (perceived cultural differences and norm violations). Because communication between ethnolinguistic out-groups may be experienced as a type of intergroup threat, intercultural communication affect was examined within the context of this model. The ITT model also provided a useful framework for examining the relative contribution of intercultural communication emotions in predicting intergroup hostility.

Although intercultural communication barriers operate in most, if not all, intergroup situations, this source of attitudes is highly prevalent in international contexts where linguistic and cultural dissimilarities between group members are pronounced. International educational exchange—the movement of students and scholars across national boundaries presents a unique opportunity for studying intercultural communication. Representing over 185 countries, and many more distinct cultures, foreign students vary tremendously with respect to national, racial/ethnic, and linguistic background. Furthermore, it is widely recognized that members of this group are vulnerable to social isolation, prejudice, and discrimination. Foreign students rank negative attitudes and a lack of cultural sensitivity among US nationals as the greatest perceived barriers to successful intergroup relations.

An additional goal of this study was to investigate attitudes toward the international student community. Although a vast literature exists concerning this group, more research is needed on the nature and structure of Americans' attitudes toward their foreign guests. There is ample evidence indicating that unfavorable relations with host nationals have serious consequences for the psychological well-being of international students. Because social contact has been identified as a significant moderator of intergroup attitudes and has been studied extensively in international settings, prejudicial attitudes were also examined among domestic students who had experienced differing levels of social contact with the international community.

4. The Structure of Attitudes toward Foreign Students

The ITT posits that there are four causal factors that give rise to prejudice: negative stereotypes, intergroup anxiety, realistic threats, and symbolic/cultural threats. Stereotypic beliefs are a well-established source of inimical attitudes toward the culturally different, especially where there has been minimal prior intergroup and interpersonal contact. The international student literature indicates that a narrow set of negative attributes is commonly ascribed to this group as a whole. To illustrate, a prevalent view exists of foreign students as outsiders who are culturally maladjusted, naive, and confused. They are seen as psychologically unbalanced individuals who suffer from a "foreign student syndrome," a controversial condition characterized by a disheveled appearance, a passive and withdrawn interpersonal style, and a multitude of psychosomatic ailments. Consistent with the ITT, individual stereotypic beliefs are associated with prejudice toward international students.

Emotions are another fundamental source of intergroup judgments. Host nationals may view foreign students, especially those from developing nations, as a low-status or inferior group and they may feel contempt or disdain for the group. Highly ethnocentric individuals may feel suspicious, defensive, and hostile toward the international community. Intergroup anxiety—the apprehension individuals feel when anticipating or experiencing social contact with an out-group—is a highly prevalent emotion in intercultural contexts. On the other hand, international students may also evoke a number of positive emotions among members of the receiver-nation. Some research suggests that domestic students feel curious, interested, and inspired by their foreign guests. Because both positive and negative emotions have been shown to predict intergroup evaluations, a measure of general (positive and negative) affective responses toward foreign students was included in the study.

Intergroup competition represents a third type of intergroup threat underlying prejudice. Realistic threats are related to group conflict, competition for scarce resources, or threats to the physical well-being of an in-group. Realistic threat is a causal factor underlying hostility toward immigrant groups and may be a determinant of prejudice toward foreign students. Although most internationals pay for their education with funds from family members and overseas agencies, a popular belief exists that US institutions finance the education of foreign students. Foreign students may be regarded as illegitimate competitors who are depriving domestic students of valuable educational and material resources (e.g., admission to competitive academic programs, housing services, financial aid, employment opportunities, etc.). As a result, US nationals may oppose institutional policies and programs designed to benefit international students and perceptions of realistic threat may contribute to intergroup hostility.

Threats associated with value-laden beliefs and perceived group differences in cultural norms constitute a fourth determinant of prejudice. Symbolic threat is experienced when an in-group believes that its sociocultural system is being obstructed, undermined, or violated by an out-group. Although international students may be regarded as valuable cultural and intellectual resources that enrich the university community, they also possess values, norms, and patterns of behavior that conflict with those of domestic students. Foreign students can express opinions that challenge or threaten the world view of domestic students and they may represent social, religious, and political systems that are unpopular in the receiver-nation. Where the values, beliefs, and cultural norms of ethnolinguistic groups are greatly dissimilar, symbolic threats should impact the favorability of intergroup judgments.

5. Hypotheses

We hypothesized that intercultural communication emotions would constitute a unique and potent source of attitudes toward ethnolinguistic out-groups. Based on the sizable correlation found between stereotypic beliefs and judgments of foreign students in previous research, consensual stereotypic beliefs were expected to be a significant, but relatively weaker, determinant of attitudes. Given that the intergroup anxiety literature indicates a consistent association between intergroup emotions and prejudice, we predicted that general affective responses would be moderately related to host attitudes. Realistic and symbolic threats are generally less salient sources of prejudice toward subordinate groups. Because foreign students are unlikely to challenge seriously the economic position and sociocultural system of American students, weak positive relations were expected between both realistic and symbolic threats and intergroup judgments.

The quantity and quality of social contact experienced with members of an out-group should moderate the structure of intergroup attitudes. Accordingly, intercultural communication emotions were expected to be more strongly related to prejudice among individuals who have had less direct experience with foreign students. Stereotypic beliefs and affective reactions were hypothesized to be more potent predictors of prejudice among individuals who have experienced minimal contact with the international community. In contrast, realistic and symbolic threats would be stronger predictors of prejudice at higher levels of social contact with international students. To test these hypotheses, the structure of attitudes toward foreign students was examined among low-contact and high-contact host nationals.

6. Summary of Hypotheses

1) Intercultural communication emotions would be uniquely and strongly related to attitudes toward foreign students. Stereotypes and general affect would be moderate predictors, and realistic and symbolic threats would be weak predictors, of prejudice.

2) Social contact would moderate (decrease) the association between intercultural communication emotions, stereotypes, general affect, and prejudice; and increase the association between realistic threats, symbolic threats, and prejudice.

7. Method

7.1 Participants and procedures

A diverse group of undergraduate and graduate students enrolled at two large West Coast universities participated in the study. Approximately 64% of the students were recruited through the psychology research participant pool. These individuals received partial course credit for their participation in a 1-hour testing session. In order to increase the diversity of the sample, additional participants were recruited through classroom presentations and advertisements posted in various academic departments. The latter individuals were paid $5 for their participation. Nineteen individuals who were not citizens or permanent residents of the United States and three individuals who did not indicate their racial/ethnic category membership were eliminated from the study, resulting in a usable sample of $N = 154$. The demographic characteristics of the sample were as follows: 83(54%) identified as European American, 34 (22%) identified as Asian American, 26 (17%) identified as Latino/Hispanic, and 11(7%) identified as African American. The percentage of participants who were born in the United States was as follows: European American (98%), Asian American(93%), Latino/Hispanic (86%), and African American (100%). The sample consisted of 86 (56%) women. Eighty-two percent of the participants were undergraduate students and 18% were graduate students. The students ranged in age from 17 to 42, with a mean age of 23.

The students were invited to participate in a study on "social attitudes." In order to reduce demand, the written and oral instructions informed the participants that the researchers were interested in people's attitudes toward a wide variety of social groups. They were further instructed that they would be responding to questions about the group "foreign students" in the current testing session. The term "foreign students" was defined as "college students from other countries who are studying in the United States." Because the label "international students" may evoke socially desirable responding, the potentially more negative, but commonly used designation "foreign students" was selected for this study. The participants were assured that their responses to the questionnaire would be kept strictly confidential and they returned their completed questionnaires to an anonymous drop-box at the end of the testing session. They were subsequently debriefed and thanked for their participation.

7.2 Measures
7.2.1 *Global attitudes*
Scholars posit that prejudice may derive from a variety of sources, such as cognitive beliefs, affective responses, and values. These factors have been shown to be differentially important in predicting attitudes toward different social groups (e.g., immigrants, homosexuals, the disabled, etc.). In order to assess global evaluations of foreign students, semantic differential items that are essentially "content-free" were selected. Content-free items allow participants to make judgments on the basis of information (e.g., cognitions, emotions, values, etc.) that is most relevant and important to them. The participants indicated their overall attitude toward foreign students on three semantic differential scales: favorable-unfavorable, positive-negative, and good-bad. The 11-point scales ranged from 0 (*extremely favorable*) to 100 (*extremely unfavorable*). Variations of this instrument have been shown to possess high test-retest reliability, to be strongly correlated with longer attitude scales, and they have been used to assess attitudes toward a wide variety of groups. Cronbach's alpha was 0.90. For purposes of comparison, the participants also rated the group "American college students" (defined as college students who are citizens and permanent residents of the United States) on the same three-item measure. Cronbach's alpha for American students was 0.93. Higher scores indicate a less favorable attitude toward the group.

7.2.2 *Intercultural communication emotions*
As a measure of intercultural communication affect, the participants responded to a seven-item scale developed for this study. The items were as follows: (a) "I find it unpleasant to listen to foreign students who speak with a strong accent," (b) "I rarely feel annoyed when talking to foreign students who have poor English skills" (reverse-scored), (c) "I sometimes feel frustrated when interacting with foreign students who do not understand American customs and ways of behaving," (d) "I am comfortable interacting with foreign students who have different ethnic customs and practices" (reverse-scored), (e) "I become impatient when listening to foreign students who speak English poorly," (f) "I find it agreeable to talk to foreign students who speak with a strong accent" (reverse-scored), and (g) "I sometimes feel uncomfortable when interacting with foreign students because of cultural barriers (i.e., cultural differences in ways of

communicating). " The nine-point response scale was anchored by 1 (*strongly disagree*) and 9 (*strongly agree*). Factor analysis (principal components analysis with varimax rotation) indicated that all of the items loaded on a single factor, which explained 51% of the variance. Cronbach's alpha was 0.76. Higher scores correspond to greater negative affect associated with intercultural communication barriers.

7.2.3 *Preliminary stereotypic attributes*

A preliminary stereotype scale was composed of 40 attributes that have been specifically ascribed to foreign students. Thirty of the descriptors were adapted from a free-response study on international student stereotypes. Based on a review of the international student literature, 10 additional traits (e.g., competitive, homesick, etc.) were included to test specific hypotheses regarding the content of the consensual stereotype. Participants were asked to rate the extent to which each of the 40 attributes was characteristic or typical of foreign students as a group. The nine-point response format ranged from 1 (*not at all characteristic*) to 9 (*extremely characteristic*). To assess the evaluative content of the attributes, the participants rated each of the 40 descriptors on a favorability scale, ranging from -4 (*extremely negative*) to $+4$ (*extremely positive*).

7.2.4 *Consensual stereotype measure*

The impact of stereotypes on intergroup attitudes is related to both the strength and the valence of the components of a stereotype. Because valenced attributes that are strongly associated with a group have greater predictive utility and validity, we created a composite (strength × evaluation) stereotype index. For each of the 40 attributes, the strength rating of the trait ($1-9$) was multiplied by the valence rating (-4 to $+4$). The mean (strength × evaluation) score for each of the 40 descriptors was then calculated and the distribution of means was analyzed. Attributes that were rated as fairly to extremely negative (or positive) and as moderately to extremely characteristic of foreign students were selected as stereotypic attributes for the group. Table 1 presents the initial pool of 21 traits and the mean (strength × valence) rating and standard deviation for each of the attributes.

To create a reliable consensual stereotype index, the 21 attribute ratings were factor analyzed (principal components analysis with varimax rotation). Attributes that loaded on the principal negative stereotype factor (eigenvalue >1.0; e.g., culturally maladjusted, socially awkward, etc.) and traits that loaded on the positive stereotype factor (eigenvalue >1.0; e.g., hardworking, determined, etc.) were included in the final consensual stereotype measure. Next, each participant's (strength × evaluation) rating was summed across the 13 stereotypic traits and divided by the number of attributes. To create a measure of negative stereotypic beliefs, the scale was reverse-scored. Coefficient alpha was 0.81. Higher scores on the consensual stereotype measure indicate that participants hold predominantly negative stereotypic beliefs about foreign students.

Table 1 The Consensual Foreign Student Stereotype among American Host Nationals

Positive attributes	Composite[a] (strength[b] × valence[c]) mean (SD)	Negative attributes	Composite[a] (strength[b] × valence[c]) mean (SD)
1. Multilingual	22.59 (10.01)	1. Culturally maladjusted[d]	−11.97 (8.41)
2. Intelligent[d]	21.86 (7.46)	2. Clannish	−9.93 (10.78)
3. Eager to learn[d]	19.72 (9.33)	3. Socially awkward[d]	−9.71 (9.69)
4. Friendly	19.18 (9.07)	4. Frightened	−8.69 (11.57)
5. Hardworking[d]	17.31 (8.30)	5. Sad/depressed[d]	−8.03 (7.09)
6. Determined[d]	14.74 (9.49)	6. Confused/lost[d]	−7.96 (9.22)
7. Talented[d]	13.29 (9.61)	7. Anxious[d]	−7.57 (8.45)
8. Open-minded	11.43 (10.35)	8. Lonely[d]	−6.45 (7.01)
9. Worldly	10.88 (9.74)	9. Speak English poorly[d]	−6.18 (7.86)
10. Brave/adventurous	8.91 (8.96)	10. Arrogant	−6.01 (9.17)
11. Studious[d]	6.63 (10.27)		

[a] Note: Composite = mean (strength rating × valence rating) across all participants.
[b] Strength scores range from 1 (*not at all characteristic*) to 9 (*extremely characteristic*).
[c] Valence scores range from −4 (*extremely negative*) to +4 (*extremely positice*).
[d] Attributes included in the final consensual stereotype scale.

7.2.5 *General affective responses*

To assess general affective reactions associated with foreign students, the participants indicated the extent or degree to which they felt various emotions in response to the group. The nine-point response scale was anchored by 1 (*not at all*) and 9 (*extremely*). The eight negative emotions included were: awkward, anxious, uneasy, self-conscious, defensive, suspicious, hostile, and superior. The eight positive emotions were: admiration, respectful, happy, comfortable, confident, interested, curious, and inspired. To assess the evaluative content of the affective responses, the participants rated each of the 16 emotions on a favorability scale that ranged from −4 (*extremely negative*) to +4 (*extremely positive*).

For each of the 16 emotions, the strength rating (1 − 9) was multiplied by the favorability rating (-4 to $+4$) to create a (strength × evaluation) index. Emotions that were rated as fairly to extremely negative (or positive) and that were moderately to strongly associated with the group were included in the initial pool of affective responses. Factor analysis of the affect scale (principal components analysis with varimax rotation) yielded two emotion categories: positive emotions (eigenvalue > 1.0; e.g., interested, inspired, curious, etc.) and intergroup anxiety (eigenvalue > 1.0; e.g., awkward, anxious, uneasy, etc.). Each participant's (strength × evaluation) rating was then summed across the 12 affective responses and divided by the number of emotions. To create a measure of negative general affect, the scale was reverse-scored. Cronbach's alpha was 0.79. Higher scores on the composite index indicate that participants primarily associate negative emotions with foreign students.

7.3 Realistic threats

Perceptions of realistic threat were assessed by six items including: (a) "Foreign students take jobs away from American students (e.g., on-campus employment, teaching/research assistantships)," (b) "Foreign students pay their fair share for the education and services that they receive at US universities" (reverse-scored), (c) "Foreign students take valuable educational resources away from American students (e.g., financial aid, university housing, etc.)," and (d) "American colleges and universities are paying too much to finance the education of foreign students." The items were rated on a nine-point scale with endpoints 1 (*strongly disagree*) and 9 (*strongly agree*). Factor analysis (*principal components analysis with varimax rotation*) indicated that all six items loaded on one factor, which explained 61% of the variance. Cronbach's alpha was 0.78. Higher scores correspond to greater perceived realistic threat.

7.3.1 *Symbolic/cultural threats*

As a measure of symbolic threat, the participants responded to six statements, which included: (a) "Some American colleges and universities are losing their 'American' character because of increasing foreign student enrollments," (b) "Foreign students contribute positively to the ethnic mix at American universities" (reverse-scored), and (c) "Cherished American norms and traditions are threatened somewhat by increasing foreign student enrollment on US campuses." The statements were rated on a nine-point scale with the continuum ranging from 1 (*strongly disagree*) to 9 (*strongly agree*). Factor analysis (principal components analysis with varimax rotation) indicated that all six items loaded on a single factor, which explained 53% of the variance. Cronbach's alpha was 0.72. Higher scores indicate greater perceived symbolic/cultural threat.

7.3.2 *Social contact*

To assess social contact with the international community, the participants responded to three items (a) "How often do you talk to and engage in informal conversations with foreign students?," (b) "How often do you study or do other class work with foreign students?," (c) "How often do you do things socially with foreign students? (This includes things like sharing meals, going to movies and parties, etc.)." The items were rated on a nine-point scale that ranged from 1 (*never*) to 9 (*all the time*). Factor analysis (principal components analysis with varimax rotation) indicated that the items loaded on one factor, which explained 79% of the variance. Cronbach's alpha was 0.93. Higher scores correspond to greater social contact with the group.

The order of presentation of each of the scales was counterbalanced across all participants, with the following exceptions (1) the strength ratings preceded the favorability ratings for both the stereo typic attribute and affective response measures, and (2) the measure of attitudes toward "American college students" was presented at the end of the questionnaire.

8. Results

A multivariate analysis of variance (MANOVA) was conducted on the principal study variables (global attitudes, intercultural communication emotions, consensual stereotypes, general affect, and realistic and symbolic threats), using gender, ethnicity, and educational level (undergraduate vs. graduate) as the factors. There were no main effects of gender. However, there was a significant (gender × educational level) interaction on global attitudes, $F(1, 139) = 5.54$, $P < 0.05$, and general affect, $F(1, 139) = 4.77$, $p < 0.05$. Male graduate students reported significantly greater prejudice ($M = 46.67$) and less positive affect ($M = 0.39$) toward foreign students than did female graduate students ($M = 29.11$ and -4.64, respectively). There were no other interactions involving gender. There was a main effect of ethnicity on the following measures: global attitudes, $F(3, 139) = 3.93$, $p < 0.01$, general affect, $F(3, 139) = 2.89$, $p < 0.05$, and symbolic threats, $F(3, 139) = 3.05$, $P < 0.05$. However, post-hoc multiple comparisons (using the Games Howell test statistic for unequal cell sizes) indicated that group-level differences in global attitudes and general affect were not statistically significant. European Americans ($M = 3.48$) perceived significantly greater symbolic/cultural threats than did Latinos ($M = 2.57$). There was a main effect of educational level on realistic threats, $F(1, 139) =$

5.57, $p < 0.05$. Graduate students perceived significantly greater realistic threat ($M = 5.12$) than did undergraduate students ($M = 3.97$). In addition, we examined the intercorrelations between age and the principal study variables. Older students perceived greater symbolic/cultural threat ($r = 0.17$, $p < 0.05$) and they tended to perceive greater realistic threat ($r = 0.13$, ns) than younger students. The subsequent regression analyses were conducted controlling for gender, ethnicity, age, and the educational level of the participants.

On average, the participants' overall attitude toward foreign students ($M = 31.17$, $SD = 22.34$) corresponds to a "somewhat" favorable (positive, good) evaluative orientation. This mean evaluative score is comparable to that obtained for minority and immigrant groups. Notably, judgments of international students were relatively unfavorable: the mean evaluative rating for the target group "foreign students" was significantly less favorable than that obtained for "American college students" ($M = 23.89$, $SD = 15.92$), with $t(153) = 6.94$, $p < 0.001$.

Table 1 presents the consensual stereotype of foreign students. Table 2 presents the means and standard deviations for the intercultural communication emotions, stereotype, general affect, and threat scales. The mean score for intercultural communication emotions ($M = 4.54$) indicates that many American college students felt frustrated, impatient, and uncomfortable when encountering communication obstacles with the international student community. On average, stereotypic beliefs about foreign students were somewhat positive ($M = -2.73$, scale reverse-scored), although there was substantial variability on this measure. Descriptive statistics for the general affect scale suggest that emotional responses toward foreign students were also generally positive ($M = -3.43$, scale reverse-scored), with considerable variability existing in participants' affective orientation toward the group. The mean scores for realistic threats ($M = 4.26$) and symbolic/cultural threats ($M = 3.18$) suggest that foreign students are generally viewed as contributing positively to the university community on US campuses, although international students are viewed as illegitimate competitors by some host nationals.

Simultaneous regression analyses were conducted to determine the predictive utility of each of the attitudinal determinants. In preparation to run the analysis, correlations among the predictor variables were calculated and are presented in Table 2. All of the predictors were positively intercorrelated, which is indicative of intra-attitudinal consistency. Several of the predictors (e.g., realistic threats and symbolic/cultural threats) were highly correlated; however, the percentage of shared variance did not exceed 18% for any intercorrelation. This pattern of intercorrelations suggests that the attitudinal determinants are related, but distinct, sources of prejudice toward foreign students. The zero-order correlations between the predictor variables and the criterion measure of global attitudes are presented in the last row of Table 2. The five attitudinal determinants were entered simultaneously as predictors in the regression analysis in order to determine the unique contribution of each variable to overall attitudes.

Table 2 Means, Standard Deviations, and Intercorrelations among Predictor Variables and Global Attitudes toward Foreign Students

$N = 154$	Mean (SD)	Intercorrelations				
		1	2	3	4	5
1. Intercultural communication emotions	4.54 (2.31)					
2. Consensual stereotypes	-2.73 (6.33)[a]	0.29***	—			
3. General affective responses	-3.43 (4.77)[a]	0.31***	0.37***	—		
4. Realistic threats	4.26 (1.96)	0.23**	0.26**	0.14	—	
5. Symbolic/cultural threats	3.18 (2.15)	0.34***	0.41***	0.25**	0.42***	—
6. Global attitudes	31.17 (22.34)	0.48***	0.39***	0.43***	0.16*	0.30***

[a]*Note*: The stereotype and affect indexes were reverse-scored, such that negative mean scores indicate overall positive stereotypic beliefs and emotional responses.

*$p < 0.05$, **$p < 0.01$, ***$p < 0.001$.

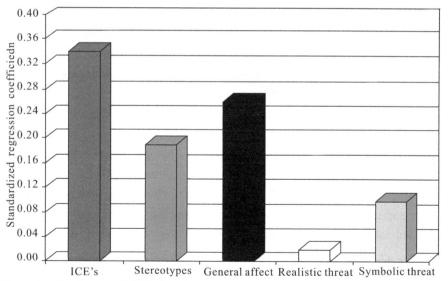

Figure 1 Predictors of Global Attitudes Toward Foreign Students Among American Host Nationals $N = 154$.

Note: ICEs = intercultural communication emotions (negative affect associated with perceived linguistic and cultural barriers)

The simultaneous regression analysis indicates that intercultural communication emotions ($B = 0.34$, $p < 0.001$) were strongly and uniquely related to attitudes toward foreign students. General affective responses ($B = 0.26$, $p < 0.001$) and consensual stereo typic beliefs ($B = 0.19$, $p < 0.01$) were unique, but less potent, predictors of prejudice. The standardized regression coefficient for symbolic/cultural threats was not significant ($B = 0.10$, ns). Particularly low was the association of intergroup attitudes with perceived realistic threats ($B = 0.02$, ns). The model including all five predictor variables accounted for 41% of the variance in global evaluations of foreign students.

The determinants of intergroup attitudes were also examined among individuals who had experienced differing levels of social contact with the target group. Moderated regression analyses, using social contact as the moderator variable, were conducted separately for each of the five predictor variables. Consistent with our hypotheses, consensual stereotypic beliefs (interaction $B = -0.09$, ns) and general affective responses (interaction $B = -0.10$, ns) tended to be less potent unique predictors of prejudice at higher levels of social contact with the international community. Contrary to prediction, social contact had no appreciable effect on the relation between intercultural communication emotions and intergroup judgments ($B = -0.01$, ns). That is, intercultural communication emotions were equally, and strongly, related to intergroup attitudes for both low-contact and high-contact host nationals. As hypothesized, realistic threats ($B = 0.11$, ns) and symbolic/cultural threats ($B = 0.14$, ns) tended to be more potent predictors of prejudice among individuals who had interacted more frequently with foreign students.

9. Discussion

In order to gain greater understanding of the psychological impact of intercultural communication barriers on attitudes toward the culturally different, we tested a model of global attitudes toward foreign students. Based on previous intergroup emotion and intercultural communication research; we hypothesized that prejudice toward ethnolinguistic out-groups may stem from intercultural communication emotions, or negative affect associated with perceived linguistic and cultural obstacles. This source of attitudes was examined within the context of the Integrated Threat Theory of Prejudice. The predictive utility of intercultural communication emotions was examined in relation to four causal factors or classes of threat that are widely acknowledged by social psychologists as relevant to intergroup judgments: stereo typic beliefs, affective responses, realistic threats, and symbolic/cultural threats.

Intercultural communication emotions were the strongest unique predictors of attitudes toward foreign students. This antecedent of prejudice may be particularly salient in international contexts, where language and cultural differences can greatly impair communication between ethnolinguistic out-groups. Many American college students reported feeling uncomfortable, impatient, and frustrated when encountering communication difficulties with the international student population on their campuses. Factors such as accented speech, cultural differences in non-verbal communication styles, and cultural variations in values, norms, and customs contribute to these communication problems. Intercultural interactants may also fear the negative consequences of communication failures and emotionally laden cultural misunderstandings, such as appearing foolish to others or experiencing rejection. In sum, negative affect elicited during communication with ethnolinguistic out-groups represents an additional type of intergroup threat associated with prejudice toward the culturally different. A large corpus of research on intergroup anxiety has established that individuals may experience generalized feelings of awkwardness, anxiety, and apprehension when experiencing or anticipating social contact with an out-group. The present research suggests that a broad range of adverse emotions, directly associated with communication between ethnolinguistic groups, can be a potent source of intergroup hostility.

Intercultural communication emotions may be especially germane to judgments of foreign students. The most derogatory attributes elicited in a free-response study on international student stereotypes were related to perceived English language deficits and intercultural communication obstacles. When foreign students perform in the capacity of student-instructor, they may be evaluated extremely negatively by American academic personnel, undergraduate students, and the general public. Both actual and assumed communication barriers are thought to underlie these strongly prejudicial evaluations. Brown found that perceptions of communication difficulties and foreign accentedness accounted for most of the variance in college students' ratings of international teaching assistants. In an experimental study, Rubin and Smith manipulated the level of accentedness of a foreign student-instructor and found that perceived—but not real—levels of accentedness predicted evaluations of the target. Our findings provide further evidence that intercultural communication difficulties underlie prejudice toward foreign students,

The structure of intergroup attitudes was expected to differ for host nationals who had experienced little or no social contact with the international community and individuals who had interacted more extensively with students from abroad. Frequent social interaction with foreign students should facilitate intercultural communication and understanding. With increased intercultural exposure, social perceivers become more accustomed to accented speech, more adept at communicating with non-native speakers of a language, and more sensitive and sympathetic toward cultural differences. Contrary to prediction, social contact did not moderate the relationship between intercultural communication emotions and global attitudes. That is, intercultural communication affect was strongly and uniquely related to prejudice for both low-contact and high-contact host nationals. It is noteworthy, however, that the social contact scale used in the present study primarily assessed quantitative, rather than qualitative, contact with the target group. High levels of social contact with members of an ethnolinguistic out-group may have the unfortunate effect of making intercultural communication difficulties more psychologically salient. These data are consistent with previous research indicating that frequent contact with members of an out-group does not necessarily translate into improved intergroup communication and relations. It is also notable that ethnic group membership did not affect the mean favorability of intercultural communication emotions and global attitudes. These findings parallel prior research indicating that individuals may be prejudiced toward culturally similar immigrant groups (e.g., Hispanic and Anglo American students may hold comparably unfavorable attitudes toward Mexican immigrants.).

A second purpose of the study was to examine the nature and structure of American college students' attitudes toward the international community. The structure of intergroup judgments has been found to vary according to the target group under investigation. That is, stereotypes, emotions, and other variables are differentially important as predictors of attitudes toward different out-groups. A major strength of the ITT model is that it permits comparison of causal factors that contribute to prejudice toward diverse groups. In addition to intercultural communication emotions, general affective responses and consensual stereotypic beliefs were significant and unique predictors of inimical attitudes toward foreign students. Symbolic/cultural threats were marginally related to intergroup judgments and realistic threats were not unique determinants of intergroup evaluations. These findings are consistent with ITT research indicating that realistic and symbolic threats are less salient sources of attitudes toward subordinate cultural groups.

10. Attitudes toward Foreign Students

This study is among the most comprehensive empirical investigations of foreign student stereotypes. The initial stereotype index was composed of 40 group-specific stereotypic attributes. As hypothesized by numerous cross-cultural scholars, many of the unfavorable attributes consensually ascribed to international students were related to perceived cultural and social adjustment problems. For example, foreign students were characterized as frightened, sad/depressed, and lonely. Moreover, these stereotypic beliefs were uniquely related to host attitudes. A theoretical explanation for why endorsement of the consensual stereotype was significantly related to host attitudes emphasizes the function of stereotypes as heuristic devices when social perceivers lack familiarity and experience with members of an out-group. Stereotypic beliefs, developed during brief encounters with foreign students, or through secondary sources such as classmates, family members, or the media, can subsequently guide evaluations and behaviors. On average, the participants in this study had experienced relatively little contact with the international community ($M = 3.89$). The moderated regression analyses lend further support to this theoretical explanation. Domestic students who had experienced less contact with the international student population were more likely to rely on stereotypic knowledge as a basis for intergroup judgments.

Although consensual stereotypes were a significant source of attitudes toward international students, the results of the simultaneous regression analysis suggest that emotional responses tend to be more uniquely related to evaluations of this group. Affective associates have been found to be potent predictors of inimical attitudes toward racial/ethnic minority and immigrant groups. A number of scholars have posited that intergroup attitudes are formed on the basis of emotionally significant, and hence, highly memorable and personally relevant encounters with representative members of an out-group. As a result, the quantity and quality of social contact experienced with members of an ethnolinguistic out-group should moderate the favorability and predictive utility of intergroup emotions. As expected, general affective responses tended to be more strongly related to attitudes among individuals who had experienced (minimal quantitative) contact with the target group. For high-contact host nationals, frequent interaction with members of an ethnolinguistic out-group may decrease feelings of intergroup anxiety and uncertainty, while increasing favorable emotions such as sympathy, respect, and admiration.

Overall, perceived symbolic/cultural threats made a marginal contribution to the prediction of prejudice. The relatively weak predictive utility of symbolic threats may be explained by several factors. As temporary sojourners and potential immigrants, foreign students are unlikely to obstruct, undermine, or violate the sociocultural system of American students. Rather, US nationals appear to value the cultural and intellectual contribution of the international student community. Foreign students add to the racial/ethnic diversity of the student body and they share their knowledge of different countries, social and political systems, and cultural customs and practices. Nonetheless, perceptions of cultural differences have been found to predict hostility toward international teaching assistants. Brown manipulated information about the demographic background of a foreign student-instructor and found that perceptions of cultural differences strongly contributed to evaluations of the target. Mean perceptions of symbolic threats were also higher among European American students (the dominant ethnolinguistic group) than Latino students, and symbolic/cultural threat was a stronger predictor of prejudice at higher levels of social contact. Frequent contact with an ethnolinguistic out-group may increase the psychological salience of cultural dissimilarities. Perceptions of cultural differences may also have an indirect, adverse effect on intergroup attitudes through increased perceptions of intercultural communication difficulties.

Realistic threats were not uniquely related to judgments of foreign students. Stephan et al. posited that realistic threats are a less salient source of attitudes toward minority groups. Given that foreign students are temporary sojourners and potential immigrants, international students are unlikely to pose a serious threat to the economic standing of domestic students. For many US colleges and universities, international students help maintain enrollments and they represent a substantial source of tuition revenue, teaching service, and intellectual capital. It is noteworthy, however, that mean perceptions of realistic threats were substantial. This finding may be explained, in part, by the sizable number of graduate students in the study sample. Perceptions of realistic threat were significantly higher among graduate than undergraduate students. Domestic graduate students compete directly with internationals for admission to competitive academic programs, teaching and research assistantships, certain fellowships, and post-graduate employment in competitive industries. Realistic threat was also a stronger predictor of attitudes at higher levels of social contact. Host nationals who interact more frequently with foreign students are more likely to compete with them for limited educational resources.

The correlational nature of the data limits the conclusions that can be drawn from this study. A significant association between ratings on a predictor variable (e.g., an affect or stereotype measure) and an attitude scale does not demonstrate that the predictor variable produced the attitude. Individuals may first retrieve a global evaluative orientation toward a target group and then construct a response to the predictor variable that is consistent with their overall attitude. Maio, Esses, and Bell provided some insight into these causal relations in an experimental study. The researchers manipulated information about the valence and relevance of stereotypic beliefs, values, and affective responses toward a fictitious immigrant group and found that the predictor variables influenced overall evaluations of the group. Furthermore, intercultural training programs designed to increase intercultural communication competence and to decrease anxiety/uncertainty, have been shown to improve attitudes toward ethnolinguistic out-groups. The causal relation between the quality of intercultural communication and prejudice may also be reciprocal.

Social desirability bias may account for the apparent discrepancy between foreign students' widely held perceptions of prejudice and discrimination in the United States and American college students' self-reported judgments of the group. Participants may have hesitated to report their negative beliefs, emotions, and attitudes toward foreign students. Alternatively, scholars maintain that intergroup attitudes in contemporary US society are no longer characterized by strong negative sentiments toward out-groups, but rather by the absence of positive characterizations of out-groups in comparison to in-groups. Indeed, judgments of "foreign students" in the present study did not compare favorably with those of "American college students".

Our findings help to explain why attitudes toward the international student community are relatively unfavorable. The combination of intercultural communication emotions, general affect, consensual stereotypes, and perceived threats accounted for a significant percentage of the variance in attitudes toward foreign students. Factors not included in the study, such as personality traits and past experiences and behaviors, have also been found to predict intergroup attitudes. Inclusion of these, and other variables, could significantly increase our ability to predict prejudice toward international students. The affective dimension of intercultural communication barriers may constitute a substantial source of hostility toward other ethnolinguistic groups, such as Latinos/Hispanics and Asian Americans. Replications with other cultural and linguistic groups would help to establish the generalizability of our findings.

11. Implications for International Student Exchange

In 1998, close to 500,000 international students were attending educational institutions in the United States. Presently, American colleges and universities host the world's largest foreign student population and international enrollments are increasing. Institutions of higher education are "internationalizing": they are creating specialized programs and services to attract the international student market and they are aggressively recruiting students from abroad. The large influx of international students and scholars to US educational institutions presents opportunities for intercultural contact, communication, and, potentially, conflict. International educational exchange enables foreign individuals and host nationals to acquire intercultural understanding and competence, factors that can enhance intergroup and international relations. Differences in language, cultural norms, and patterns of behavior, can also lead to serious communication and interaction problems between domestic and foreign students.

Educational administrators can take into account the various sources of prejudice toward foreign students when creating policies and programs designed to reduce inimical attitudes toward this group. In accordance with the Contact Hypothesis, the evaluative implication of negative stereotypes and general affect can be addressed by promoting contact with foreign students. Frequent contact alone, however, may not lead to favorable intercultural communication and relations. Increased social interaction with international students was associated with increased perceptions of threat. Realistic and symbolic threats could be attenuated by disseminating information about the economic, cultural, and intellectual contribution of foreign students to the university community. One strategy that could alter the evaluative implication of intercultural communication barriers would be to create structured opportunities for positive intergroup interaction. University programs such as integrated residential facilities and recreational programs are notable examples. Understanding the nature and structure of attitudes toward foreign student visitors and attempts to alter these attitudes are worthwhile endeavors. Unfavorable relations with host nationals strongly influence the personal and cultural adjustment of international students. Moreover, domestic students may develop enduring negative attitudes toward certain national and cultural groups as a result of their interactions with foreign student visitors.

More research is needed at the interface of intergroup emotion, intercultural communication, and prejudice research. Increasing intergroup conflict in the world today highlights the necessity of identifying the multiple sources of intergroup hostility. Communication difficulties and cultural barriers may evoke adverse emotions that, in turn, give rise to prejudicial attitudes and discriminatory behaviors. Intercultural communication affect was the strongest unique predictor of attitudes toward foreign students. Intercultural communication emotions may constitute a significant source of prejudice and discrimination toward other ethnolinguistic out-groups, such as racial/ethnic minority and immigrant groups. This antecedent of intergroup attitudes is especially relevant in international contexts and multicultural societies, and is likely to become increasingly important as international migration and globalization bring more ethnolinguistic groups into contact. This study also contributes to a growing body of evidence indicating that emotions are central determinants of intergroup attitudes. To comprehend and address prejudice toward the culturally different, scholars need to examine the broad range of intergroup emotions that influence prejudicial attitudes.

Notes

1. From *International Journal of Intercultural Relations*, Julie Spencer-Rodgers and Timothy McGovern, 26, 2002.
2. The cognitive revolution is the name for an intellectual movement in the 1950s that began what are known collectively as the cognitive sciences. It began in the modern context of greater interdisciplinary communication and research. The relevant areas of interchange were the combination of psychology, anthropology, and linguistics approaches developed within the fields of computer science and neuro-science, cognitive revolution in psychology was a response to behaviorism, which was the predominant school in experimental psychology at the time. This school proposed that psychology could only become an objective science were it based on observable behavior in test subjects. The cognitive approach was brought to prominence by Donald Broadbent's book *Perception and Communication* in 1958. The publication of the book *Cognitive Psychology* by Ulric Neisser in 1967 is also considered an important milestone. Other influential researchers included Noam Chomsky, Herbert Simon, Allen Newell. The cognitive revolution reached its height in the 1980s with publications by philosophers such as Daniel Dennett's *Artificial Intelligence*.

Questions for Discussion

1. When you recall your experience in communicating with us Chinese and foreigners, what are the similarities and differences between the two types of interaction as far as problems or difficulties are concerned?
2. What are the major intercultural communication barriers? Do you interact in the

same way with people from the so-called in-groups and out-groups?
3. Have you ever been abroad for travel or for study? If not, do you plan to go abroad to further your English study? What are the difficulties that you are probably going to encounter when you are studying or working in a foreign country?
4. Have you ever used a quantitative research method to deal with any intercultural topics? What do you think of the research findings of the present paper? How can the qualitative approach like the in-depth interview or focus group add validity to the present study?
5. What do you think are the effective and appropriate ways to deal with intercultural communication barriers in the present-day world? On various intercultural communication occasions, should the people from the host cultures make efforts adapting themselves to those from the guest cultures, or vice versa? Or do you still have other suggestions to make?

Online Mini-Case Studies and Viewpoints-Sharing

A U.S. Supreme Court Rule

In 1913, members of the Pueblo tribe challenged the degree of control that Congress exercised over tribal affairs. In its decision on United States vs. Sandoval, the Supreme Court ruled, "Always living in separate and isolated communities, adhering to primitive modes of life, largely influenced by superstition and fetishism, and chiefly governed according to crude customs inherited from their ancestors, [the Pueblos] are essentially a simple, uninformed and inferior people … . As a superior and civilized nation, [the U.S. government has both] the power and the duty of exercising a fostering care and protection over all dependent Indian communities within its borders."

Online Research

Search online for more information or cases concerning the U.S. mistreatment of the American Indian tribes and try to understand the nature of the intercultural communication barriers between the white people and the aboriginal Indian tribes.

Reading Two

Introductory Remarks

Problems and misunderstandings often occur when we are interacting with people from other cultures. It is, therefore, necessary that we identify and become alert to both the obvious and potential problems in our intercultural communication. Furthermore, we need to examine the reasons for both the overt and covert problems. Only when we become aware of the major reasons for the many types of problems can we hope to seek the means of improvement as an intercultural communicator.

The following selection explores some specific reasons for the problems and misunderstandings in intercultural communication. The author has identified six important causes for communication breakdowns across cultural boundaries. They are the assumption of similarity instead of difference, language problems, nonverbal misunderstanding, the presence of preconceptions and stereotypes, the tendency to evaluate and the high anxiety in intercultural encounters. Becoming aware of the six stumbling blocks is the first step toward understanding. More expertise from special training in our insight and the alteration of our conventional habits and thinking patterns will prepare us to become competent and effective intercultural communicators.

Stumbling Blocks in Intercultural Communication[1]

Laray M. Barna[2]

Why is it that contact with persons from other cultures so often is frustrating and fraught with misunderstanding? Good intentions, the use of what one considers to be a friendly approach, and even the possibility of mutual benefits don't seem to be sufficient—to many people's surprise. A worse scenario is when rejection occurs just because the group to which a person belongs is "different." It's appropriate at this time of major changes in the international scene to take a hard look at some of the reasons for this. New proximity and new types of relationships are presenting communication challenges that few people are ready to meet.

THE SIX STUMBLING BLOCKS

Assumption of Similarities

One answer to the question of why misunderstanding and/or rejection occurs is that many people naively assume there are sufficient similarities among peoples of the world to make communication easy. They expect that simply being human, having common requirements of food, shelter, security and so on, makes everyone alike. Unfortunately they overlook the fact that the forms of adaptation to these common biological and social needs and the values, beliefs, and attitudes surrounding them are vastly different from culture to culture. The biological commonalities are not much help when it comes to communication, where we need to exchange ideas and information, find ways to live and work together, or just make the kind of impression we want to make.

Another reason many people are lured into thinking that "people are people" is that it reduces the discomfort of dealing with difference. If someone acts or looks "strange" (different from them), it's then possible to evaluate this as "wrong" and treat everyone ethnocentrically.

The assumption of similarity does not often extend to the expectation of a common verbal language but it does interfere with caution in decoding nonverbal symbols, signs, and signals. No cross-cultural studies have proven the existence of a common nonverbal language except those in support of Darwin's theory that facial expressions are universal. Ekman found that "the particular visible pattern on the face, the combination of muscles contracted for anger, fear, surprise, sadness, disgust, happiness (and probably also for interest) is the same for all members of our species."

This seems helpful until it is realized that a person's cultural upbringing determines whether or not the emotion will be displayed or suppressed, as well as on which occasions and to what degree. The situations that bring about the emotional feeling also differ from culture to culture, for example the death of a loved one may be a cause for joy, sorrow, or some other emotion, depending upon the accepted cultural belief.

Since there seem to be no universals or "human nature" that can be used as a basis for automatic understanding, we must treat each encounter as an individual case, searching for whatever perceptions and communication means that are held in common and proceed from there. This is summarized by Vinh The Do[3] "If we realize that we are all culture bound and culturally modified, we will accept the fact that, being unlike, we do not really know what someone else 'is.' This is another way to view the 'people are people' idea. We now have to find a way to sort out the cultural modifiers in each separate encounter to find similarity."

Persons from the United States seem to hold this assumption of similarity more strongly than some other cultures. The Japanese, for example, have the reverse belief that they are distinctively different from the rest of the world. This notion brings intercultural communication problems of its own. Expecting no similarities they work hard to figure out the foreign stranger but do not expect foreigners to be able to understand them. This results in exclusionary attitudes and only passive efforts toward mutual understanding.

As Western trappings permeate more and more of the world the illusion of similarity increases. A look-alike facade deceives representatives from contrasting cultures when each wears Western dress, speaks English, and uses similar greeting rituals. It is like assuming that New York, Tokyo, and Tehran are all alike because each has the appearance of a modern city. But without being alert to possible underlying differences and the need to learn new rules for functioning, persons going from one city to the other will be in immediate trouble, even when taking on such simple roles as pedestrian or driver. Also, unless a foreigner expects subtle differences it will take a long time of noninsulated living in a new culture (not in an enclave of his or her own kind) before he or she can be jarred into a new perceptual and nonevaluative thinking.

The confidence that comes with the myth of similarity is much stronger than with the assumption of differences, the latter requiring tentative assumptions and behaviors and a willingness to accept the anxiety of "not knowing." Only with the assumption of differences, however, can reactions and interpretations be adjusted to fit "what's happening." Without it someone is likely to misread signs and symbols and judge the scene ethnocentrically.

The stumbling block of assumed similarity is a *troublem*, as one English learner expressed it, not only for the foreigner but for the people in the host country (United States or any other) with whom the international visitor comes into contact. The native inhabitants are likely to be lulled into the expectation that, since the foreign person is dressed appropriately and speaks some of the language, he or she will also have similar nonverbal codes, thoughts, and feelings. In the United States nodding, smiling, and affirmative comments from a foreigner will probably be confidently interpreted by straightforward, friendly Americans as meaning that they have informed, helped, and pleased the newcomer. It is likely, however, that the foreigner actually understood very little of the verbal and nonverbal content and was merely indicating polite interest or trying not to embarrass himself or herself or the host with verbalized questions. The conversation may even have confirmed a stereotype that Americans are insensitive and ethnocentric.

In instances like this, parties seldom compare impressions and correct misinterpretations. One place where opportunities for achieving insights does occur is in an intercultural communication classroom. Here, for example, U.S. students often complain that international student members of a discussion or project group seem uncooperative or uninterested. One person who had been thus judged offered the following explanation:

> I was surrounded by Americans with whom I couldn't follow their tempo of discussion half of the time. I have difficulty to listen and speak, but also with the way they handle the group. I felt uncomfortable because sometimes they believe their opinion strongly. I had been very serious about the whole subject but I was afraid I would say something wrong. I had the idea but not the words.

The classroom is also a good place to test whether one common nonverbal behavior, the smile, is actually the universal sign people assume it to be. The following enlightening comments came from international students newly arrived in the United States.

Japanese student: *On my way to and from school I have received a smile by non-acquaintance American girls several times. I have finally learned they have no interest for me; it means only a kind of greeting to a foreigner. If someone smiles at a stranger in Japan, especially a girl, she can assume he is either a sexual maniac or an impolite person.*

Korean student: *An American visited me in my country for one week. His inference was that people in Korea are not very friendly because they didn't smile or want to talk with foreign people. Most Korean people take time to get to be friendly with people. We never talk or smile at strangers.*

Arabic student: *When I walked around the campus my first day many people smiled at me. I was very embarrassed and rushed to the men's room to see if I had made a mistake with my clothes. But I could find nothing for them to smile at. Now I am used to all the smiles.*

Vietnamese student: *The reason why certain foreigners may think that Americans are superficial—and they are, some Americans even recognize this—is that they talk and smile too much. For people who come from placid cultures where nonverbal language is more used, and where a silence, a smile, a glance have their own meaning, it is true that Americans speak a lot. The superficiality of Americans can also be detected in their relations with others. Their friendships are, most of the time, so ephemeral compared to the friendships we have at home. Americans make friends very easily and leave their friends almost as quickly, while in my country it takes a long time to find out a possible friend and then she becomes your friend—with a very strong sense of the term.*

Statements from two U.S. students follow. The first comes from someone who has learned to look for differing perceptions and the second, unfortunately reflects the stumbling block of assumed similarity.

U.S. student: *I was waiting for my husband on a downtown corner when a man with a baby and two young children approached. Judging by small quirks of fashion he had not been in the U.S. long. I have a baby about the same age and in appreciation of his family and obvious involvement as a father I smiled at him. Immediately I realized I did the wrong thing as he stopped, looked me over from head to toe and said, "Are you waiting for me? You meet me later?" Apparently I had acted as a prostitute would in his country.*

U.S. student: *In general it seems to me that foreign people are not necessarily snobs but are very unfriendly. Some class members have told me that you shouldn't smile at others while passing them by on the street in their country. To me I can't stop smiling. It's just natural to be smiling and friendly. I can see now why so many foreign people stick together. They are impossible to get to know. It's like the Americans are big bad wolves. How do Americans break this barrier? I want friends from all over the world but how do you start to be friends without offending them or scaring them off—like sheep?*

The discussion thus far threatens the popular expectation that increased contact with representatives of diverse cultures through travel, student exchange programs, joint business ventures, and so on will automatically result in better understanding and friendship. Indeed, tests of that assumption have been disappointing. For example, research found that Vietnamese immigrants who speak English well and have the best jobs are suffering the most from psychosomatic complaints and mental problems and are less optimistic about the future than their counterparts who remain in ethnic enclaves without attempting to adjust to their new homeland. One explanation given is that these persons, unlike the less acculturated immigrants, "spend considerable time in the mainstream of society regularly facing the challenges and stresses of dealing with American attitudes."

After 24 years of listening to conversations between international and U.S. students and professors and seeing the frustrations of both groups as they try to understand each other, this author, for one, is inclined to agree with Charles Frankel who says, "Tensions exist within nations and between nations that never would have existed were these nations not in such intensive cultural communication with one another." Recent world events have proven this to be true.

From a communicative perspective it doesn't have to be that way. Just as more opportunities now exist for cross-cultural contact so does more information about how to meet this challenge. There are more orientation and training programs around the country, more courses in intercultural communication in educational institutions, and more published material. Until persons can squarely face the likelihood of meeting up with difference and misunderstanding, however, they will not be motivated to take advantage of these resources.

Many potential travelers who do try to prepare for out-of-country travel (for business conferences, government negotiations, study tours, or whatever) might gather information about the customs of the other country and a smattering of the language. Behaviors and attitudes of its people are sometimes researched, but necessarily from a secondhand source, such as a friend who has "been there." Experts realize that information gained in this fashion is general, seldom sufficient, and may or may not be applicable to the specific situation and area that the traveler visits. Also, knowing "what to expect" often blinds the observer to all but what confirms his or her image. Any contradictory evidence that does filter through the screens of preconception is likely to be treated as an exception and thus discounted.

A better approach is to begin by studying the history, political structure, art, literature, and language of the country if time permits. This provides a framework for on-site observations. Even more important is to develop an investigation, nonjudgmental attitude, and a high tolerance for ambiguity—all of which require lowered defenses. Margaret Mead suggests sensitizing persons to the kinds of things that need to be taken into account instead of developing behavior and attitude stereotypes. She reasons that there are individual differences in each encounter and that changes occur regularly in cultural patterns, making research information obsolete.

Stewart and Bennett also warn against providing lists of "do's and don'ts" for travelers for several reasons, mainly that behavior is ambiguous; the same action can have different meanings in different situations and no one can be armed with prescriptions for every contingency. Instead they encourage persons to understand the assumptions and values on which their own behavior rests. This can then be compared with what is found in the other culture, and a "third culture" can be adopted based on expanded cross-cultural understanding.

Language Differences

The remainder of this article will examine some of the variables of the intercultural communication process itself and point out danger zones therein. The first stumbling block has already been discussed at length, the hazard of assuming similarity instead of difference. A second danger will surprise no one: language difference. Vocabulary, syntax, idioms, slang, dialects, and so on, all cause difficulty but the person struggling with a different language is at least aware of being in trouble.

A worse language problem is the tenacity with which someone will cling to just one meaning of a word or phrase in the new language, regardless of connotation or context. The infinite variations possible, especially if inflection and tonal qualities are present, are so difficult to cope with that they are often waved aside. This complacency will stop a search for understanding. The nationwide misinterpretation of Krushchev's[4] statement "We'll bury you" is a classic example. Even "yes" and "no" cause trouble. When a non-native speaker first hears the English phrase, "Won't you have some tea?" he or she listens to the literal meaning of the sentence and answers, "No," meaning that he or she wants some. The U.S. hostess, on the other hand, ignores the double negative because of common usage, and the guest gets no tea. Also, in some cultures, it is polite to refuse the first or second offer of refreshment. Many foreign guests have gone hungry because they never got a third offer. This is another case of where "no" means "yes."

Nonverbal Misinterpretations

Learning the language, which most visitors to foreign countries consider their only barrier to understanding, is actually only the beginning. As Frankel says, "To enter into a culture is to be able to hear, in Lionel Trilling's phrase, its special 'hum and buzz of implication'." This suggests the third stumbling block, nonverbal misinterpretations. People from different cultures inhabit different sensory realities. They see, hear, feel, and smell only that which has some meaning or importance for them. They abstract whatever fits into their personal world of recognition and then interpret it through the frame of reference of their own culture. An example follows:

An Oregon girl in an intercultural communication class asked a young man from Saudi Arabia how he would nonverbally signal that he liked her. His response was to smooth back his hair, which to her was just a common nervous gesture signifying nothing. She repeated her question three times. He smoothed his hair three times. Then, realizing that she was not recognizing this movement as his reply to her question, automatically ducked his head and stuck out his tongue slightly in embarrassment. This behavior was noticed by the girl and she expressed astonishment that he would show liking for someone by sticking out his tongue.

The lack of comprehension of nonverbal signs and symbols that are easy to observe—such as gestures, postures, and other body movements—is a definite communication barrier. But it is possible to learn the meanings of these messages, usually in informal rather than formal ways. It is more difficult to note correctly the unspoken codes of the other culture that are less obvious such as the handling of time and spatial relationships and subtle signs of respect or formality.

Preconceptions and Stereotypes

The fourth stumbling block is the presence of preconceptions and stereotypes. If the label "inscrutable" has preceded the Japanese guest, his behaviors (including the constant and seemingly inappropriate smile) will probably be seen as such. The stereotype that Arabs are "inflammable" may cause U.S. students to keep their distance or even alert authorities when an animated and noisy group from the Middle East gathers. A professor who expects everyone from Indonesia, Mexico, and many other countries to "bargain" may unfairly interpret a hesitation or request from an international student as a move to manipulate preferential treatment.

Stereotypes help do what Ernest Becker[5] asserts the anxiety-prone human race must do—reduce the threat of the unknown by making the world predictable. Indeed, this is one of the basic functions of culture: to lay out a predictable world in which the individual is firmly oriented. Stereotypes are overgeneralized, secondhand beliefs that provide conceptual bases from which we "make sense" out of what goes on around us, whether or not they are accurate or fit the circumstance. In a foreign land their use increases our feeling of security and is psychologically necessary to the degree that we cannot tolerate ambiguity or the sense of helplessness resulting from inability to understand and deal with people and situations beyond our comprehension.

Stereotypes are stumbling blocks for communicators because they interfere with objective viewing of stimuli—the sensitive search for cues to guide the imagination toward the other person's reality. They are not easy to overcome in ourselves or to correct in others, even with the presentation of evidence.

Stereotypes persist because they are firmly established as myths or truisms by one's own national culture and because they sometimes rationalize prejudices. They are also sustained and fed by the tendency to perceive selectively only those pieces of new information that correspond to the image held. For example, the Asian or African visitor who is accustomed to privation and the values of self-denial and self-help cannot fail to experience American culture as materialistic and wasteful. The stereotype for the visitor becomes a reality.

Tendency to Evaluate
Another deterrent to understanding between persons of differing cultures or ethnic groups is the tendency to evaluate, to approve or disapprove, the statements and actions of the other person or group rather than to try to comprehend completely the thoughts and feelings expressed from the worldview of the other. Each person's culture or way of life always seems right, proper, and natural. This bias prevents the open-minded attention needed to look at the attitudes and behavior patterns from the other's point of view. A midday siesta changes from a "lazy habit" to a "pretty good idea" when someone listens long enough to realize the midday temperature in that country is over 115 °F.

The author, fresh from a conference in Tokyo where Japanese professors had emphasized the preference of the people of Japan for simple natural settings of rocks, moss, and water and of muted greens and misty ethereal landscapes, visited the Katsura Imperial Gardens in Kyoto. At the appointed time of the tour a young Japanese guide approached the group of 20 waiting U.S. Americans and remarked how fortunate it was that the day was cloudy. This brought hesitant smiles to the group who were less than pleased at the prospect of a shower. The guide's next statement was that the timing of the summer visit was particularly appropriate in that the azalea and rhododendron blossoms were gone and the trees had not yet turned to their brilliant fall colors. The group laughed loudly now convinced that the young man had a fine sense of humor. I winced at his bewildered expression, realizing that had I come before attending the conference I would have shared the group's inference that he could not be serious.

The communication cutoff caused by immediate evaluation is heightened when feelings and emotions are deeply involved, yet this is just the time when listening with understanding is most needed. As stated by Sherif and other scholars, "A person's commitment to his religion, politics, values of his family and his stand on the virtue of his way of life are ingredients in his self-picture—intimately felt and cherished." It takes both the awareness of the tendency to close our minds and the courage to risk changing our own perceptions and values to dare to comprehend why someone thinks and acts differently from us. Religious wars and negotiation deadlocks everywhere are examples of this.

On an interpersonal level there are innumerable illustrations of the tendency to evaluate, resulting in a breach in intercultural relationships. Two follow:

U.S. Student: *A Persian friend got offended because when we got in an argument with a third party, I didn't take his side. He says back home you are supposed to take a friend's or family's side even when they are wrong. When you get home then you can attack the "wrongdoer" but you are never supposed to go against a relative or a friend to a stranger. This I found strange because even if it is my mother and I think she is wrong, I say so.*

Korean student: *When I call on my American friend he said through the window, "I am sorry. I have no time because of my study." Then he shut the window. I couldn't understand through my cultural background. House owner should have welcome a visitor whether he likes or not and whether he is busy or not. Also the owner never speaks without opening his door.*

The admonition to resist the tendency to immediately evaluate does not intend to suggest that one should not develop one's own sense of right and wrong. The goal is to look and listen emphatically rather than through a thick screen of value judgments that would cause one to fail to achieve a fair and total understanding. Once comprehension is complete it can be determined whether or not there is a clash in values or ideology. If so, some form of adjustment or conflict resolution can be put into place.

High Anxiety

High anxiety or tension, also known as stress, is common in cross-cultural experiences due to the number of uncertainties present. The two words, "anxiety" and "tension," are linked because one cannot be mentally anxious without also being physically tense. Moderate tension and positive attitudes prepare one to meet challenges with energy. Too much anxiety or tension requires some form of relief which too often comes in the form of defenses, such as the skewing of perceptions, withdrawal, or hostility. That's why it is considered a serious stumbling block. As stated by Kim[6]:

> Stress, indeed, is considered to be inherent in intercultural encounters, disturbing the internal equilibrium of the individual system. Accordingly, to be interculturally competent means to be able to manage such stress,

regain internal balance, and carry out the communication process in such a way that contributes to successful interaction outcomes.

High anxiety or tension, unlike the other five stumbling blocks (assumption of similarity, language, nonverbal misinterpretations, preconceptions and stereotypes, and the practice of immediate evaluation), is not only distinct but often underlies and compounds the other stumbling blocks. The use of stereotypes and evaluations are defense mechanisms in themselves to alleviate the stress of the unknown or the intercultural encounter, as previously explained. If the person was tense or anxious to begin with, these would be used even more. Falling prey to the aura of similarity is also a protection from the stress of recognizing and accommodating to differences. Different language and nonverbal patterns are difficult to use or interpret under the best of conditions. The distraction of trying to reduce the feeling of anxiety (sometimes called "internal noise") makes mistakes even more likely. Jack Gibb remarks:

> Defense arousal prevents the listener from concentrating upon the message. Not only do defensive communicators send off multiple value, motive, and affect cues, but also defensive recipients distort what they receive. As a person becomes more and more defensive, he becomes less and less able to perceive accurately the motives, the values, and the emotions of the sender.

Anxious feelings usually permeate both parties in an intercultural dialogue. The host national is uncomfortable when talking with a foreigner because he or she cannot maintain the normal flow of verbal and nonverbal interaction. There are language and perception barriers, silences are too long or too short; proxemic and other norms may be violated. He or she is also threatened by the other's unknown knowledge, experience, and evaluation—the visitor's potential for scrutiny and rejection of the person and/or the country. The inevitable question "How do you like it here?" which the foreigner abhors, is a quest for reassurance, or at least a "feeler" that reduces the unknown. The reply is usually more polite than honest but this is seldom realized.

The foreign members of dyads are even more threatened. They feel strange and vulnerable, helpless to cope with messages that swamp them. Their own "normal" reactions are inappropriate. Their self-esteem is often intolerably undermined unless they employ such defenses as withdrawal into their own reference group or into themselves, screen out or misperceive stimuli, use rationalization or overcompensation, or become aggressive or hostile. None of these defenses leads to effective communication.

Culture shock. If a person remains in a foreign culture over time the stress of constantly being "on guard" to protect oneself against making "stupid mistakes" takes its toll and he or she will probably be affected by "culture fatigue," usually called culture shock. According to Barna:

> ... the innate physiological makeup of the human animal is such that discomfort of varying degrees occurs in the presence of alien stimuli. Without the normal props of one's own culture there is unpredictability, helplessness, a threat to self-esteem, and a general feeling of "walking on ice"—all of which are stress producing.

The result of several months of this sustained anxiety or tension (or excitation if the high activation is perceived positively) is that reserve energy supplies become depleted, the person's physical capacity is weakened, and a feeling of exhaustion, desperation, or depression may take over. He or she, consciously or unconsciously, would then use psychological defenses such as those described previously. If this temptation is resisted, the sojourner suffering from the strain of constant adjustment may find his or her body absorbing the stress in the form of stomach or backaches, insomnia, inability to concentrate, or other stress-related illnesses.

The following account by a sojourner to the United States illustrates the trauma of culture shock:

> Soon after arriving in the U.S. from Peru, I cried almost every day. I was so tense I heard without hearing, and this made me feel foolish. I also escaped into sleeping more than twelve hours at a time and dreamed of my life, family and friends in Lima. After three months of isolating myself in the house and speaking to none, I ventured out. I then began to have severe headaches. Finally I consulted a doctor, but she only gave me a lot of drugs to relieve the pain. Neither my doctor nor my teachers ever mentioned the two magic words that could have changed my life: culture shock! When I learned about this I began to see things from a new point of view and was better able to accept myself and my feelings.

I now realize most of the Americans I met in Lima before I came to the U.S. were also in one of the stages of culture shock. They demonstrated a somewhat hostile attitude toward Peru, which the Peruvians sensed and usually moved from an initially friendly attitude to a defensive, aggressive attitude or to avoidance. The Americans mostly stayed within the safe cultural familiarity of the embassy compound. Many seemed to feel that the difficulties they were experiencing in Peru were specially created by Peruvians to create discomfort for "gringos." In other words, they displaced their problem of adjustment and blamed everything on Peru.

Culture shock is a state of disease, and, like a disease, it has different effects, different degrees of severity and different time spans for different people. It is the least troublesome to those who learn to accept cultural diversity with interest instead of anxiety and manage normal stress reactions by practicing positive coping mechanisms, such as conscious physical relaxation.

Physiological reactions. Understanding the physiological component of the stumbling block of anxiety/tension helps in the search for ways to lessen its debilitating effects. It is hard to circumvent because, as human animals, our biological system is set so that anything that is perceived as being "not normal" automatically signals an alert. Depending on how serious the potential threat seems to be, extra adrenalin and noradrenalin pour into the system, muscles tighten; the heart rate, blood pressure, and breathing rate increase, the digestive process turns off, and other changes occur.

This "fight or flight" response was useful, actually a biological gift for survival or effective functioning, when the need was for vigorous action. However, if the "danger" is to one's social self, which is more often the case in today's world, too much anxiety or tension just gets in the way. This is particularly true in an intercultural setting where the need is for understanding, calm deliberation, and empathy in order to untangle misperceptions and enter into smooth relationships.

All is not "doom and gloom" however. As stated by Ursin, "The bodily response to changes in the environment and to threatening stimuli is simply activation." Researchers believe that individuals control their emotional response to that activation by their own cognitions. If a person expects something to be exciting rather than frightening, he is more likely to interpret the somatic changes that he feels in his body as excitement.

People also differ in their stress tolerance. Whatever the reasons, everyone knows people who "fall apart at the least thing" and others who seem unflappable in any crisis. If you are one of the former there are positive ways to handle the stress of intercultural situations, whether these be one-time encounters; frequent dialogues in multicultural settings like a school or workplace, vacation trips; or wherever. For starters, you can find opportunities to become familiar with many types of people so that differences become normal and interesting instead of threatening. And you can practice body awareness so that changes that signify a stress reaction can be identified and counteracted.

CONCLUSION

Being aware of the six stumbling blocks is certainly the first stop in avoiding them, but it isn't easy. For most people it takes insight, training, and sometimes an alteration of long-standing habits or thinking patterns before progress can be made. The increasing need for global understanding, however, gives all of us the responsibility for giving it our best effort.

We can study other languages and learn to expect differences in nonverbal forms and other cultural aspects. We can train ourselves to meet intercultural encounters with more attention to situational details. We can use an investigative approach rather than stereotypes and preconceptions. We can gradually expose ourselves to differences so that they become less threatening. We can even learn to lower our tension level when needed to avoid triggering defensive reactions.

The overall goal should be to achieve intercultural communication competence, which is defined by Kim as "the overall internal capability of an individual to manage key challenging features of intercultural communication: namely, cultural differences and unfamiliarity intergroup posture, and the accompanying experience of stress."

Roger Harrison adds a final thought:

> ... the communicator cannot stop at knowing that the people he is working with have different customs, goals, and thought patterns from his own. He must be able to feel his way into intimate contact with these alien values, attitudes, and feeling. He must be able to work with them and within them, neither losing his own values in the confrontation nor protecting himself behind a wall of intellectual detachment.

Notes

1. From *Intercultural Communication: A Reader*, 8th Ed., Larry A. Samovar and Richard E. Porter, Belmont: Wadsworth Publishing Company, 1997.
2. Laray M. Barna is an emeritus associate professor at Portland State University, Portland, Oregon, USA.
3. Vinh The Do is a multicultural specialist at Portland Public Schools, Portland, Oregon, USA.
4. Nikita Krushchev (1894—1971) was a Soviet politician, First Secretary of the Soviet Communist Party and prime minister. As a close associate of Stalin, he emerged victorious from the power struggle that followed Stalin's death. In 1956 he began a program of destalinization and of liberalization. His economic and foreign policies failed. Because of that he was ousted by Brezhnev and Kossygin.
5. Dr. Ernest Becker is a cultural anthropologist and interdisciplinary scientific thinker and writer. Because of his breadth of vision and avoidance of social science pigeonholes, Becker was an academic outcast in the last decade of his life. It was only with the award of the Pulitzer Prize in 1974 for his book, *Denial of Death* that his enormous contributions began to be recognized. The next book *Escape from Evil* (1975) developed the social and cultural implications of the concepts explored in the earlier book and is an equally important and brilliant companion volume. Many scholars in many fields are studying, teaching, researching and writing about the works of Ernest Becker.
6. Young Yun Kim was born and raised in Korea and now lives in Norman, Oklahoma. She is a professor of communication at the University of Oklahoma. Her research has been primarily aimed at explaining the role of communication in the cross-cultural adjustment process of immigrants, sojourners, and native-born ethnic minorities.

Questions for Discussion

1. Are there more similarities or differences among peoples of different cultures? Why do you think so?
2. What personal experiences do you have to illustrate the role of language differences in intercultural communication?
3. How can preconceptions and stereotypes act as stumbling blocks in our interactions with people from other cultures? What should we do to deal with the problem?
4. Do you have the tendency to evaluate other people's opinions and actions? How can you comprehend the thoughts and feelings of other people from their point of view?

5. Young Yun Kim was born and raised in Korea, but she is now teaching at the University of Oklahoma in the United States as a professor of communication studies. She is famous for her contributions of the "Association and Dissociation: A Contextual Theory of Interethnic Communication" and "Adapting to a New Culture: An Integrative Communication Theory". How much do you know about the two theories and how will you apply the theories to deal with the stumbling blocks in the intercultural interactions between the Chinese and peoples from other cultural backgrounds?

Online Mini-Case Studies and Viewpoints-Sharing

A Cultural Gulf of Time

The Hopi are separated from us by a tremendous cultural gulf. Time, for example, is not duration but many different things for them. It is not fixed or measurable as we think of it, nor is it a quantity. It is what happens when the corn matures or a sheep grows up-a characteristic sequence of events. It is the natural process that takes place while living substance acts out its life drama. Therefore, there is a different time for everything which can be altered by circumstances. One used to see Hopi houses that were in the process of being built for years and years. Apparently the Indians had no idea that a house could or should be built in a given length of time since they could not attribute to it its own inherent time system such as the corn and the sheep had. This way of looking at time cost the government untold thousands of dollars on construction projects because the Hopi could not conceive of there being a fixed time in which a dam or a road was supposed to be built. Attempts to get them to meet a schedule were interpreted as browbeating and only made things worse.

Online Research

Please search online the major types of blockades of intercultural communication. Based on your academic interests and future goals, narrow down the major types of intercultural communication obstacles in-between two specific national cultures while getting ready to explore the cultural roots for those major blockades or obstacles.

Unit Nine

Intercultural Communication in Business, Management and Negotiation

Reading One

Introductory Remarks

We are living in the world of negotiations. We negotiate, almost on a daily basis, with the other half of ourselves as well as with our spouses, children, colleagues, friends, landlords, customers, doctors and neighbors. In other words, the process of negotiation accompanies the process of our communication and relationship construction. Because of its non-replacement functions and wide permeation, negotiating becomes largely a process beyond our awareness most of the time. We don't have to think hard about how to go about it and it goes. As with so many aspects of our behavior, how we negotiate is shaped by our culture one way or the other. We encounter relatively few difficulties when negotiating with people who live in the same culture with us but must grapple with various obstacles when conducting negotiations in a different cultural context. The shared values, interests, goals, ethical principles, recognized practices, even familiar symbols no longer exist nor present themselves in the meaning that we take for granted in the home culture. Thus, the desired goals of negotiation become difficult for the negotiators to achieve.

This reading is selected to familiarize readers with the nature of cross-cultural negotiations, effective strategies for international negotiators and the significance attached to the venue of negotiations. The article addresses the differences between Western negotiators and their eastern counterparts in reaching agreements and concluding transactions. Over-reliance on cultural generalization leads to fruitless negotiations and the carry-over of host norms in cross-cultural business talks yields no better result. There is some obvious overlapping between this article and the following one in addressing the roles of interpreters and discussing strategies for business talks, but the two readings deal with the issues from different perspectives, which will help readers gain more insights.

Negotiating Across Cultures

Gary P. Ferraro[1]

The Nature of Cross-Cultural Negotiation

We frequently fail to define the act of negotiating because it is so central to our lives. Those who write about the process of negotiating, on the other hand, do define it—sometimes in excruciating detail—but fail to agree on a common definition. But, as Moran and Stripp remind us, the common theme running through all of the definitions is that two or more parties, who have both common and conflicting interests, interact with one another for the purpose of reaching a mutually beneficial agreement.

Effective negotiation does not involve bludgeoning the other side into submission. Rather, it involves the more subtle art of persuasion, whereby all parties feel as though they have benefited. There is no simple formula for success. Each situation must be assessed within its own unique set of circumstances. The successful negotiator must choose the appropriate strategy, protect the correct personal and organizational images, do the right type of homework, ask the most relevant questions, and offer and request the appropriate types of concession at the right time. Negotiating within one's own culture is sufficiently difficult, but the pitfalls increase geometrically when one enters the international/intercultural arena.

Being a skilled negotiator in any context entails being an intelligent, well-prepared, creative, flexible, and patient problem solver. International negotiators, however, face an additional set of problems, obstacles not ordinarily encountered by domestic negotiators. As we have tried to establish from the outset of this book, one very important obstacle to international negotiations is culture. Because culture involves everything that a people have, think, and do, it goes without saying that it will influence or color the negotiation process. The very fact that usually one party in a negotiation will travel to the country of the other party establishes a foreign negotiating setting for at least one party, and this "strangeness" can be a formidable barrier to communication, understanding, and agreement.

There are other barriers as well. For example, international negotiation entails working within the confines of two different, and sometimes conflicting, legal structures. Unless the negotiating parties are able to both understand and cope with the differing legal requirements, a joint international contract may be governed by two or more legal systems. Another barrier may be the extent to which government bureaucracies in other countries exert their influence on the negotiation process, a problem not always understood by Westerners whose governments are relatively unobtrusive in business negotiations.

And, finally, an additional obstacle that goes beyond cultural differences is the sometimes volatile, or at least unpredictable, geopolitical realities of the two countries of the negotiating parties. Sudden changes in governments, the enactment of new legislation, or even natural disasters can disrupt international business negotiations either temporarily or permanently. For example, the disintegration of the Soviet Union, Iraq's invasion of Kuwait, or an earthquake in Mexico could all have far-reaching implications for Western business persons who were in the process of negotiating business deals in those parts of the world.

While we recognize the importance to international negotiations of these non-cultural obstacles (different legal structures, interference by government bureaucracies, and geopolitical instability), our discussion of international business negotiation will focus on the cultural dimension.

It should be apparent by now that success in negotiating international business contracts requires a deep understanding of the culture of those on the other side of the table. The reason for this cultural awareness, however, is not for the purpose of bringing the other side to its knees—to make them do what we want them to do. Nor is it to accommodate them by giving up some of our own strongly adhered-to principles. Rather, an appreciation of the important cultural elements of the other side is essential if one is to get on with the business at hand so that all parties concerned can feel as though they are better off after the negotiations than before. Moreover, it is equally the responsibility of both sides in the negotiating process to understand the cultural realities of their negotiation partners. Intercultural communication, in other words, is a two-way street, with both sides sharing the burden and responsibility of cultural awareness.

Where to Negotiate

Earlier we defined negotiation as a process between people who share some common interests, people who stand to benefit from bringing the process to a successful conclusion. Both sides have a stake in the outcome, so it stands to reason that the place of negotiations could be on the home turf of either party or in a neutral environment. The selection of a site for the negotiations is of critical importance because there are a number of advantages of negotiating in your own backyard. In the world of international diplomatic negotiations, the question of where a summit meeting will occur is taken very seriously because it is assumed that the location will very likely affect the nature and the outcome of the negotiations. The business negotiator who travels abroad is confronted with an appreciable number of problems and challenges not faced by those who negotiate at home. Let us consider some of the difficulties encountered when negotiating abroad.

First, and perhaps most important, the negotiator abroad must adjust to an unfamiliar environment during the days, weeks, or even months of negotiations. This involves getting used to differences in language, foods, pace of life, and other aspects of culture. The negotiator who is well prepared will make a relatively smooth and quick adjustment, yet not without moments of discomfort, awkwardness, and general psychological disorientation. Time and effort must be spent learning about the new environment, such as how to make a telephone call, where to find a fax machine, or simply how to locate the restroom. For those who are less well prepared, the adjustment process may be so difficult that there is little energy left for the important work of negotiating.

Second, the business negotiator cannot avoid the deleterious effects of jet lag. Even for those international travelers who heed all of the conventional wisdom concerning minimizing jet lag (avoid alcohol and eat certain foods), an intercontinental flight will nevertheless take its toll on one's physical condition. Thus, the traveling negotiator is likely not to be as rested or alert as his or her counterpart who doesn't have to cope with jet lag.

Third, the negotiator has little or no control over the setting in which the discussions take place. The size of the conference room, the seating arrangements, and the scheduling of times for both negotiating and socializing are decisions made by the host negotiating team. The side that controls these various details of the process can use them to their own advantage.

Fourth, the negotiator working in a foreign country is further hampered by being physically separated from his or her business organization and its various support personnel. Frequently, before negotiators can agree to certain conditions of a contract, they must obtain additional information from the manufacturing, shipping, or financial department of their home office. Those negotiating at home have a marked advantage over the traveling negotiator because it is always easier to get a question answered by a colleague down the hall than by relying on transcontinental telephones or fax messages.

Finally, negotiators working on foreign soil are under pressure to conclude the negotiations as soon as possible, a type of pressure not experienced by those negotiating at home. The longer negotiations drag on, the longer the negotiator will be away from the other operations of the office that need attention, the longer his or her family and social life will be disrupted, and the more it will cost the firm in terms of travel-related expenses. Given these very real pressures, negotiators working abroad are more likely to make certain concessions than they might if they were negotiating at home.

It would appear that negotiating abroad has a number of distinct disadvantages as compared to negotiating at home, including the hassle of an unfamiliar cultural setting, uncertain lines of communication with the home office, lack of control over the negotiating setting, and considerable expenditure of both time and travel funds. There is little doubt that, given the choice, most Western business people would opt to conduct their negotiations at home. Yet, more often than not, Westerners are attempting to sell their products and ideas abroad. And if the potential international customers are to learn about the products or services, it is essential that the Westerners go to them. Moreover, in many parts of the world, particularly in developing areas, potential customers from both the private and public sectors have very limited resources for traveling. Thus, in many cases, if Westerners desire to remain competitive in the international marketplace, they will have no other choice than to do their negotiating on foreign soil.

Effective Strategies for International Negotiators
In keeping with the conceptual nature of this chapter, we do not attempt to list all of the do's and don'ts of negotiating in all of the cultures of the world. Such an approach—given the vast number of features found in each culture would be well beyond the scope of the present book and certainly beyond any single individual's capacity to comprehend. Whereas some works have taken a country-by-country approach to international negotiating, here we will focus on certain general principles of cross-cultural negotiating that can be applied to most, if not all, international situations. This chapter will not provide a cookbook-style guide for avoiding negotiating faux pas in ail of the major cultures of the world, but it will draw upon some of the most positive experiences of successful intercultural negotiator.

Concentrate on Long-term Relationships, Not Short-term Contracts
If there is one central theme running through the literature on international business negotiations it is that the single most important consideration is building

relationships over the long run rather than focusing on a single contract. At times U.S. business persons have been criticized for their short-term view of doing business. Some feel that they should not waste time; they should get in there and get the contract signed and get on other business. If the other side fails to meet their contractual obligations, the lawyers can sue. Frequently this approach carries with it the implicit analogy of a sports contest. Negotiating across cultures is like a football game, the purpose of which is to outmaneuver, outmanipulate, outsmart, and generally overpower the other side, which is seen as the opponent. And the wider the margin of victory, the better. But conventional wisdom, coupled with the experience of successful negotiators, strongly suggests that international business negotiating is not about winning big, humiliating the opposition, making a killing, and gaining all of the advantages. Rather, successful international business negotiating is conducted in a cooperative climate in which the needs of both sides are met and in which both sides can emerge as winners.

To be certain, there exists considerable variation throughout the world in terms of why people enter into business negotiation in the first place. In some societies, business people may enter into negotiations for the sake of obtaining the signed contract; other societies, however, view the regulations as primarily aimed at creating a long-standing relationship and only secondarily for the purpose of signing a short-term contract. As Salacuse reminds us, for many Americans a signed contract represents closing a deal, whereas to a Japanese, signing a contract is seen as opening a relationship. With those cultures that tend to emphasize the relationship over the contract, it is likely that there will be no contract unless a relationship of trust and mutual respect has been established. And even though relationship building may not conform to the typical American's time frame, the inescapable truth is that, because relationships are so important in the international arena, negotiations are unlikely to succeed without them.

Building relationships requires that negotiators take the time to get to know one another. Frequently this involves activities like eating, drinking, visiting national monuments, playing golf—that strike the typical North American as being outside the realm of business and consequently a waste of time. But this type of ritual socializing is vital because it represents an honest effort to understand, as fully as possible, the needs, goals, values, interests, and opinions of the negotiators on the other side. It is not necessary for the two sides to have similar needs, goals, and values in order to have a good relationship, for it is possible to disagree in a number of areas and shall have a good working relationship. However, both parties need to be willing to identify their shared interests while at the same time work at reconciling their conflicting interests in a spirit of cooperation and mutual respect. And this two-fold task, which is never easy to accomplish, has the very best chance of succeeding if a relationship built on trust and mutual respect has been established between the negotiating parties.

Focus on the Interests behind the Positions

After the parties in a negotiation have developed a relationship, the discussion of positions can begin. This stage of negotiating involves both sides setting forth what they want to achieve from the negotiations. From a seller's perspective, it may involve selling a certain number of sewing machines at X dollars per unit. From the perspective of the purchaser, it may involve receiving a certain number of sewing machines within 11-month's time at X minus $30 per unit. Once the positions have been clearly stated, the effective international negotiator will then look behind those positions for the underlying needs of the other party. The stated position is usually one way of satisfying needs. But often the position of one side is in direct opposition to the position of the other side. If the negotiators focus just on the positions, it is unlikely that they will resolve or reconcile their differences. But by looking beyond the position to the basic needs that gave rise to those positions in the first place, it is likely that creative solutions can be found that will satisfy both parties.

The need to distinguish between a position and the needs underlying the position has been effectively illustrated by Foster. The representative of a U.S. telecommunications firm had been negotiating with the communications representative from a Chinese enterprise. After months of relationship building and discussing terms, the finalization of the agreement appeared to be in sight. But at the eleventh hour the Chinese representative raised an additional condition that took the American by surprise. The Chinese representative argued that since they were about to embark on a long term business relationship between friends, the U.S. firm should give its Chinese friends a special reduced price that it would not give to other customers. The problem with this request was that the U.S. firm had a strict policy of uniform pricing for all countries with which it did business.

If we look at this situation solely in terms of the positions of the two parties, it would appear to be an impasse. For anything to be resolved, one party would have to get what it wanted while the other would have to abandon its position. But, by understanding the basic needs behind the positions, both sides have more room to maneuver so that a win-win situation can result. Let us consider the needs behind the positions. The Chinese position was based on two essential needs: to get a lower price, thus saving money, and to receive a special favor as a sign of the American's friendship and commitment to the relationship. The position of the U.S. firm was based on its need to adhere to the principle of uniform pricing. By looking at the situation from the perspective of underlying needs rather than positions, it now became possible to suggest some alternative solutions. In fact, the U.S. negotiator offered another proposal: to sell the Chinese some new additional equipment at a very favorable price in exchange for sticking with the original pricing agreement. Such an arrangement met all of the needs of both parties. The Chinese were saving money on the new equipment and they were receiving a special favor of friendship from the U.S. firm. At the same time, the U.S. company did not have to violate its own policy of uniform pricing. In this example, a win-win solution was possible because the negotiators were able to concentrate on the needs behind the positions rather than on the positions themselves. Once the negotiators were willing to look beyond a prepackaged, non-negotiable, unilateral position for having their own needs met, they were able to set out to explore new and creative ways of satisfying each other's needs.

Avoid Overreliance on Cultural Generalizations
The central theme of this unit has been that success in any aspect of international business is directly related to one's knowledge of the cultural environment in which one is operating. Simply put, the more knowledge a person has of the culture of his or her international business partners, the less likely he or she will be to misinterpret what is being said or done, and the more likely one's business objectives will be met. Communication patterns—both linguistic and nonverbal—need to be mastered as well as the myriad of the culture-specific details that can get in the way of effective intercultural business communication. But just as it would be imprudent to place too little emphasis on cultural information, it is equally inadvisable to be overly dependent on such knowledge.

As was pointed out, cultural "facts" are generalizations based on a sample of human behavior, and as such can only point out tendencies at the negotiating table. Not all Middle Easterners engage in verbal overkill, and not all Japanese are reluctant to give a direct answer. If we tend to interpret cultural generalizations too rigidly, we run the risk of turning the generalizations into cultural stereotypes. We may chuckle when we hear heaven defined as the place where the police are British, the cooks French, the mechanics German, the lovers Italian, and it's all organized by the Swiss; and, conversely, hell is defined as the place where the cooks are British, the mechanics French, the lovers Swiss, the police German, and it's all organized by Italians. Such cultural stereotypes can be offensive to those being lumped together uncritically, but they can be particularly harmful in the process of international business negotiations because they can be wrong. Sometimes negotiators on the other side of the table do not act the way the generalization would predict.

To be certain, people's negotiating behavior is influenced by their culture, but there may be some other factors at work as well. How a person behaves also may be conditioned by such variables as education, biology, or experience. To illustrate, a Mexican business negotiator who has an MBA from the Wharton School may not object to discussing business at lunch, as most other Mexicans might. We should not automatically assume that all Mexicans will act in a stereotypical way. Owing to this particular Mexican's education and experience, he has learned how to behave within the U.S. frame of reference. It is, therefore, important that we move beyond cultural stereotyping and get to know the negotiators on the other side not only as members of a particular cultural group, but also as individuals with their own unique set of personality traits and experiences.

Be Sensitive to Timing

Timing may not be everything, but in international negotiations it certainly can make a difference between success and failure. As pointed out, different cultures have different rhythms and different concepts of time. In cultures like our own, with tight schedules and a precise reckoning of time, it is anticipated that business will be conducted without wasting time. But in many parts of the world it is not realistic to expect to arrive one day and consummate a deal the next before jetting off to another client in another country. The more likely scenario involves spending what may seem like inordinately long periods on insignificant details, frustrating delays, and unanticipated postponements. Bringing the U.S. notion of time into an international negotiation will invariably result in either frustration or the eventual alienation of those with whom one is negotiating.

As a general rule, international negotiations, for a number of reasons, take longer than domestic negotiations. We should keep in mind that McDonald's engaged in negotiations for nearly a decade before it began selling hamburgers in Moscow. In another situation, a high-level salesperson for a U.S. modular office furniture company spent months negotiating a deal in Saudi Arabia. He made frequent courtesy calls, engaged in long discussions on a large number of topics other than office furniture, and drank enough coffee to float a small ship. But the months of patience paid off. His personal commission (not his company's profit) was in excess of $2 million dollars! The lesson here is clear. An international negotiator must first understand the local rhythm of time, and if it is slower than at home, exercise the good sense to be patient.

Another important dimension of time that must be understood is that some times of the year are better than others for negotiating internationally. All cultures have certain times of the year when people are preoccupied with social or religious concerns or when everything having to do with business simply shuts down. Before negotiating abroad, one should become familiar with the national calendar. To illustrate, one should not plan to do any global deal making with the Chinese on October 1, their national day; or with the Japanese during "Golden Week[2]," when most people take a vacation. Any attempt to conduct negotiations on these holidays, traditional vacation times, or hours of religious observance will generally meet with as much success as a non-American might have trying to conduct business negotiations in the United States during the week between Christmas and New Year's.

Still another consideration of time has to do with the different time zones between one's home office and the country in which the negotiations are taking place. Owing to these different hour zones, an American negotiating in Manila cannot fax the home office in New York and expect an answer within minutes, as might be expected if the negotiations were taking place in Boston. If at 4:00 P.M. (Manila time) a question is raised in the negotiations that requires clearance or clarification from the home office, it is not likely that an answer will be received until the next day because in New York it is 3:00 in the morning. Thus, attempting to operate between two distant time zones can be frustrating for most Americans because it tends to slow down the pace of the negotiations.

Remain Flexible
Whenever entering an international negotiating situation, the Western negotiator, despite the best preparation, will always have an imperfect command of how things work. In such an environment some of the best-laid plans frequently go unexecuted: schedules change unexpectedly; government bureaucrats become more recalcitrant than predicted; people don't follow through with what they promise. When things don't go as expected, it is important to be able to readjust quickly and efficiently. To be flexible does not mean to be weak; rather, it means being capable of responding to changing situations. Flexibility, in other words, means avoiding the all too common malady known as "hardening of the

categories."

The need for remaining open and flexible has been well illustrated by Foster, who tells of a U.S. businessman trying to sell data processing equipment to a high-level government official in India. After preparing himself thoroughly, the American was escorted into the official's office for their initial meeting. But much to the American's surprise, seated on a nearby sofa was another gentleman who was never introduced. For the entire meeting the host government official acted as if the third man were not there. The American became increasingly uncomfortable with the presence of this mystery man who was sitting in on the negotiations, particularly as they discussed specific details. After a while the American began having paranoid delusions. Who was this man listening in on these private discussions? He even imagined that the man might be one of his competitors. The American negotiator became so uncomfortable with this situation that he lost his capacity to concentrate on the negotiations and eventually lost the potential contract. Here was a perfect example of a negotiator who was unsuccessful because he could not adjust to an unfamiliar situation. In India, as in some other parts of the world as well, it is not unusual for a third party to be present at negotiations. They may be friends, relatives, or advisors of the host negotiator invited to listen in to provide advice—and perhaps a different perspective. Unaware of this customary practice in India, this U.S. negotiator began to imagine the worst until it had irreparably destroyed his capacity to focus on the negotiations at hand.

We can see how flexibility is important in order to most effectively adapt to unfamiliar cultural situations that are bound to emerge when negotiating internationally. But remaining flexible has another advantage as well. Flexibility creates an environment in which creative solutions to negotiating problems can emerge. We have said earlier that negotiations should be a win-win situation, whereby both sides can communicate their basic needs and interests, rather than just their positions, and then proceed to brainstorm on how best to meet the needs of both sides. A win-win type of negotiation is most likely to occur when both sides remain flexible and open to exploring nontraditional solutions.

Prepare Carefully

It is hard to imagine any undertaking—be it in business, government, education, or athletics—where advanced preparation would not be an asset. Nowhere is this more true than in the arena of international negotiating where the variables are so complex. There is a straight forward and direct relationship between the amount of preparation and the chances for success when engaging in global deal making. Those who take the rather cavalier attitude of "Let's go over and see what the Japanese have to say" are bound to be disappointed. Rather, what is needed is a substantial amount of advanced preparation, starting, of course, with as full an understanding as possible of the local cultural realities. But in addition, the would-be negotiator needs to seek answers to important questions concerning his or her own objectives, the bottom line position, the types of information needed as the negotiations progress, an agenda, and the accessibility of support services, to mention a few. These and many other questions need to be answered prior to getting on the plane. Failure to prepare adequately will have at least two negative consequences. First, it will communicate to the other side that you don't consider the negotiations sufficiently important to have done your homework. And second, ill-prepared negotiators frequently are forced into making certain concessions that they may later regret.

We often hear the old adage "knowledge is power." Although most North Americans would agree, we are a society that tends to downplay, at least in principle, status distinctions based on power. Our democratic philosophy, coupled with our insistence on universal education, encourages people from all parts of the society to get as much education (and information) as possible. Even the recent computer revolution in the United States now puts vast quantities of information into virtually anyone's hands. Consequently, Americans usually do not equate high status or power with the possession of information. In some other cultures, however, there is a very close association between knowledge and power. Unless Americans negotiating in such cultures have as much information as possible, they are likely to be seen as weak and, by implication, ineffectual negotiators.

A basic part of preparing for negotiations is self-knowledge. How well do you understand yourself, the assumptions of your own culture, and your own goals and objectives for this particular negotiation? If you are part of a negotiating team, a number of questions must be answered: Who are the team members? How have they been selected? Is there general consensus on what the team hopes to accomplish? Is there a proper balance between functional skills, cross-cultural experience, and negotiating expertise? Has a rational division of labor been agreed upon in terms of such tasks as note taking serving as a spokesperson, or making local arrangements? Has there been sufficient time for team building, including discussions of strategies and counter strategies?

A particularly important area of preparation has to do with getting to know the negotiator on the other side of the table. At the outset, it must be determined if the organization is the appropriate one to be negotiating with in the first place. Once that has been decided, it is important to know whether their negotiators have the authority and responsibility to make decisions. Having this information prior to the negotiations can eliminate the possibility of long delays stemming from the last-minute disclosure that the negotiators on the other side really cannot make final contractual decisions. But once involved in the negotiating process, it is important, as a general rule, to get to know the other team's negotiators as people rather than simply as members of a particular culture.

Learn to Listen, Not Just Speak
The style of oral discourse in the United States is essentially a very assertive one. Imbued with a high sense of competition, most North Americans want to make certain that their views and positions are presented as clearly and as powerfully as possible. As a consequence, they tend to concentrate far more on sending messages than on receiving them. Many Westerners treat a discussion as a debate, the objective of which is to win by convincing the other party of the superiority of their position. Operating under such an assumption, many North Americans are concentrating more on their own response than what the other party is actually saying. They seem to have a stronger desire to be heard than to hear. Although public speaking courses are quite common in our high schools and colleges, courses on how to listen are virtually nonexistent. Because effective listening is a vital component of the negotiating process, Westerners in general, and North Americans in particular, are at a marked disadvantage when they appear at the negotiating table.

If, as we have tried to suggest throughout this chapter, the best negotiator is the well-informed negotiator, then active listening is absolutely essential for understanding the other side's positions and interests. The understanding that comes from your active listening can have a positive persuasive effect on your negotiating partners in at least two important ways. First, the knowledge gleaned through listening can convince your negotiating partners that you are knowledgeable and, thus, worthy of entering into a long-term relationship. And second, the very fact that you made the effort to really hear what they were saying will, in almost every case, enhance the rapport and trust between the two parties.

Developing good listening skills may be easier said than done. Nevertheless, there are some general guidelines that, if followed, can help us receive oral messages more effectively.

1. Be aware of the phenomenon that psychologists call cognitive dissonance,

the tendency to discount, or simply not hear, any message that is inconsistent with what we already believe or want to believe. In other words, if the message does not conform to our preconceived way of thinking, we subconsciously tend to dismiss its importance. It is important to give yourself permission to actively hear all messages—those that you agree with and those that you don't. It is not necessary that you agree with everything that is being said, but it is important to hear the message so that you will then be in a position to seek creative ways of resolving whatever differences may exist.

2. Listen to the whole message before offering a response. Focus on understanding rather than interrupting the message so that you can give a rebuttal/response. Because no one likes to be cut off before he or she is finished speaking, it is vital for the effective negotiator to practice allowing other people to finish their ideas and sentences.

3. Concentrate on the message rather than the style of the presentation. It is easy to get distracted from what is being said by focusing instead on how it is presented. No matter how inarticulate, disorganized, or inept the speaker might be, try to look beyond those stylistic features and concentrate on the content of the message.

4. Learn to ask open-ended questions which are designed to allow the speaker to elaborate on a particular point.

5. Be conscious of staying in the present. All people bring into a negotiation session a wide variety of baggage from the past. It is tempting to start thinking about yesterday's racquet-ball game with a friend, this morning's intense conversation with your boss, or the argument you had with your spouse at breakfast, but to do so will distract you from actively hearing what is being said.

6. Consider the possibility of having a friend or close associate serve as an official listener whose job it is to listen to the other side with another set of ears. Such a person can provide a valuable new perspective on what is being said and can also serve as a check on your own perceptions.

7. In almost all situations, taking notes will help you become a more effective listener. Provided you don't attempt to record every word, selective note-taking can help to highlight what is being said. Not only will note-taking help to document the messages, but when the speaker notices that you are taking notes, he or she will, in all likelihood, make a special effort to be clear and accurate.

The Use of Interpreters

Throughout this article we have stressed the importance of knowing as much as possible about the language and culture of the people with whom one is doing business. To speak the language of your business partner gives you an enormous advantage, in that it enhances rapport and allows you to understand more fully the thought patterns of your business partners. However, when deciding on which language to use in the negotiation, you should not be guided by the principle that a little knowledge is better than none at all. In other words, unless you are extremely well versed in a foreign language, you should not try to negotiate in that language directly, but rather rely on the services of a competent interpreter. But even if the negotiator has a relatively good command of the language, it may be helpful to work through an interpreter because it allows you more time to formulate your response. On the other hand, use of an interpreter has certain disadvantages, such as increasing the number of people involved, increasing the costs of the negotiations, and serving as a barrier to the two sides really getting to know one another.

When considering the use of a linguistic intermediary in cross-cultural negotiations, it is important to make the distinction between a translator and an interpreter. Although both roles are aimed at turning the words of one language into the words of another language, the translator usually works with documents, whereas the interpreter works with the spoken word in a face-to-face situation. Translators have the luxury of using dictionaries and generally are not under any great time constraints. Interpreters, on the other hand, must listen to what is being said and then instantaneously translate those words into the other language. Interpreting is a demanding job, for it requires constant translating, evaluating, and weighing the meaning of specific words within the specific social context. A good interpreter not only will need to be aware of the usual meaning of the words in the two languages but must also consider the intent of the words and theme hangs of the nonverbal gestures as well. Because of these special demands, language interpretation is more exhausting and consequently, less accurate than language translation.

When selecting an interpreter, it is important for that person to be both intimately knowledgeable of the two languages and have a technical expertise in the area being negotiated. For example, while a U.S. ' university professor of Spanish literature may have an excellent command of the language, he or she may not be particularly effective at translating scientific terms or highly technical data on weaving equipment. It is this type of shortcoming that could lead an interpreter to translate the term "hydraulic ram" into the term "wet sheep."

Because the use of an interpreter involves placing an additional person between the two primary regulators, one should take a number of precautions to ensure that the interpreter clarifies communication rather than obscures it. First, the regulator and the interpreter should allow sufficient time before the negotiations begin to get to know one another. Only when the interpreter understands your goals and expectations can he or she represent your interests to the other side and be on the lookout for the type of information that you need. Second, help the interpreter by speaking slowly and in discreet sentences. By pausing moveably between sentences, you are actually providing a little more hour for the interpreter to do his or her job. Third, because interpreting is an exhausting job that requires intense concentration, interpreters should be given breaks periodically to recharge their intellectual batteries. Fourth, plan your words carefully so as to avoid ambiguities, slang, or other forms that do not translate well. And finally, it is imperative that interpreters be treated with respect and acknowledged as the highly qualified professionals that they are. The purposeful development of cordial relations with your interpreter can only help to facilitate the process of communication at the negotiating table.

The Global Negotiator
We have examined, in a very general way, some of the problems and challenges of negotiating abroad. This chapter is not intended to be a cookbook for the would-be international negotiator. Rather, it is offered as a set of general guidelines for those who find themselves negotiating across cultures. We should bear in mind that there are never any two negotiating situations that are exactly alike. But most of the strategies suggested here are applicable to whatever type of cross-cultural negotiating session one can imagine. We have suggested that international negotiators should: (a) concentrate on building long-term relationships rather than short-term contracts, (b) focus on the interests that lay behind the positions, (c) avoid over dependence on cultural generalizations, (d) develop a sensitivity to timing, (e) remain flexible, (f) prepare carefully ahead of time, (g) learn to listen effectively, and (h) know when to use interpreters.

A major theme running through the contemporary literature is that because negotiating across cultures involves mutual interdependence between the parties, it must be conducted in an atmosphere of mutual trust and cooperation. Quite apart from your position on the issues that are being negotiated, it is important to maintain a high degree of personal respect for those on the other side of the table. Even though it is very likely that the negotiators on the other side of the table view the world very differently than you do, they should always be approached with respect and with a willingness to learn. You should not try to reform the other culture at the negotiating table in hopes that they will eventually be more like yourself, for the simple reason that it will not work. On the other hand, you should not go overboard in the other direction by "going native." Most people tend to be suspicious of anyone imitating their gestures or behaviors. The soundest advice is to learn to understand and respect cultural differences while retaining one's own. This spirit of mutual respect and cooperation has been cogently expressed by Salacuse:

> At times the two sides at the negotiating table are like two persons in a canoe who must combine their skills and strength if they are to make headway against powerful currents, through dangerous rapids, around hidden rocks, and over rough portages. Alone they can make no progress and will probably lose control. Unless they cooperate, they risk wrecking or overturning the canoe on the obstacles in the river. Similarly, unless global deal makers find ways of working together, their negotiations will founder on the many barriers encountered in putting together an international business transaction.

Notes

1. Adapted and abridged from *The Cultural Dimensions of International Business* (Second Edition), Gary P. Ferraro, 1994.
2. Many Japanese seldom take the vacations they should enjoy, but with the coming of "Golden Week", a series of holidays following one after another (usually from April 27th to May 6th), they pour out of the country by tens of thousands. The most popular place they go to is Hawaii, but Bangkok, Manila, and Hong Kong are also favored. The typical Japanese abroad, as it is reported, travel for about a week and spend, on average, $2,800 on airline tickets, hotels and gifts for friends and relatives. It may seem high, but it's cheap for the Japanese, who would have to spend a lot more if they spend a week touring their own country.

Questions for Discussion

1. How do you understand the statement made by Salacuse "At times the two sides at the negotiating table are like two persons in a canoe who must combine their skills and strength if they are to make headway against powerful current?"
2. Refer to the example given in the part of "Focus on the Interests behind the Positions" and predict the likely response from the American counterpart.
3. Why is it important to listen, not just speak? Should it be highly recommended to Chinese negotiators? Why?
4. Interpreters for international negotiators merely serve as oral translators or more than that? Give your reasons.
5. Why should we avoid meeting our Irish business partners on March 17th and try not to do any business with an Israeli merchant at Rosh Hashana?

Online Mini-Case Studies and Viewpoints-Sharing

An American Executive in London

An American executive went to London to manage the company's British office. Although the initial few weeks were relatively uneventful, it bothered the executive that visitors were never sent directly to his office. A visitor had to first speak with the receptionist, then the secretary, and then the office manager. Finally the office manager escorted the visitor to see the American executive. The American executive became annoyed with this practice, which he considered a total waste of time. When he finally spoke with his British employees and urged them to be less formal and to send visitors directly to him, the employees were chagrined.

After a number of delicate conversations, the American executive began to understand the greater stress on formality and hierarchy in England. He slowly learned to ignore his feelings of impatience when the British used their proper channels for greeting guests. As a result, visitors continued to see the receptionist, secretary, and office manager before being sent in to meet the American executive.

Online Research

Explore online the different impact of power distance upon office work in different cultures and share your opinions about the case above.

Why did the American executive fail in the tug of war when coping with the British office rules? Do you have any good suggestions for him? If "yes", justify the workability of your suggestions.

Reading Two

Introductory Remarks

As globalization continues in depth and width, the economies of the world are becoming more interdependent and interconnected with virtually no regional limit in the business arena. For companies to develop in today's economically integrated environment, they must expand overseas to seek market for their products and partners for cost-effective opportunities. Like it or not, they are actually engaged in business with people whose culture is more often than not different from their own. The differences, if handled inappropriately to become the causes of dilemmas, may erode the common ground of a well-planned program and lead to a premature full stop. In consequence, the parties involved would blame each other for problems that arise, letting slip away the dilemmas that are likely to stumble them once again in another cooperation with people of another culture.

This selection discusses how transcultural competence can be achieved by being aware of cultural differences, respecting them and ultimately reconciling the dilemmas. To present it clearly, this article analyses the steps which people need to take to understand cultural differences. This is done through a case study which elicits the various problems that occur when professional people from different cultures meet. Then it argues forcefully why the idea should be dispelled that there is only one way to manage "locked horns" of culture and states in detail what are the alternative perspectives and how managers from different cultures can synergize their forces, reconcile the differences and establish empathy when scrutinizing their counterparts with perceptions other than their own.

Reconciling Cultural Dilemmas[1]

Fons Trompenaars and Charles Hampden-Turner

AWARENESS OF CULTURAL DIFFERENCES

An American CEO had exchanged customary, polite greetings with his Japanese opposite number, a ritual which the American felt had gone on far too long. They had at last come to the root of the problem and the Japanese president was being evasive, ducking all the straight questions and repeating that "with goodwill and sincerity" all such questions could be satisfactorily answered.

As part of the initial greeting ceremony the parties had exchanged *meishi* (business cards) and the American CEO, conscious of Japanese custom, had laid the cards on the table in front of him in the same pattern as the seating arrangement for the Japanese delegation. In this way he could call everyone by name, having a convenient reminder in front of him.

As the meeting grew more stressful and his impatience with evasive answers grew, he picked up one of the cards, absent-mindedly rolled it into a cylinder, unrolled it again and crossly cleaned his nails. Suddenly he felt the horrified eyes of the entire Japanese delegation on him! There was a long pause and then the Japanese president stood up and withdrew from the room. "We would like to call an intermission," the Japanese interpreter said. The American looked at the battered *meishi* in his hand. It was the one the Japanese president had given him.

This example aptly demonstrates the devastating effects which insufficient awareness of cultural differences may have. If the CEO had merely been following a long list of tips, or dos and don't, it is somehow unlikely that "don't abuse the *meishi*" would have been on the list. After all, there are thousands of possible mistakes.

But a systematic understanding of cultural differences would have enabled the CEO to have foreseen this pitfall and others. Had he remembered that the Japanese rarely answer directly, like to build a relationship before coming to the point, give their presidents very general duties, many of them ceremonial, so that they do not know the details, and regard *meishi* as symbolising the status of the person referred to, as well as the quality of the relationship being created, then he would never have dreamed of mangling someone's *meishi* while that person was watching!

Cultural awareness, then, is understanding states of mind, your own and those of the people you meet. You can never be fully informed, since there is an infinite range of potential errors, but our seven dimensions of culture provide us with a frame of reference for analysing ways in which people attribute meaning to the world around them.

One of the goals of cross-cultural training must therefore be to alert people to the fact that they are constantly involved in a process of assigning meaning to the actions and objects they observe. For cross-cultural training to be successful, it must not be limited to delivering more or less detailed information about other countries and cultures. If it is, even the most sophisticated model of cross-cultural differences will only enhance the particular stereotypes that the participants have about another culture. So if we are approached by participants after a training course with comments like, "Thank you, Dr Trompenaars, I already knew that I had difficulties working with the French. They are strange beings and you have proved it empirically. The information you just gave me proves that I am right," we know that something has gone wrong.

Increasingly, professionals in cross-cultural management, who seek to develop transcultural competence, sense the need to go beyond the defence of their own model. It is legitimate to have a mental model. We are all creatures of our culture. The problem is to learn to go beyond our own model, without being afraid that our long-held certainties will collapse. The need to win over others to our point of view, to prove the inferiority of their way of thinking, reveals our own in securities and doubts about the strength of our identity. Genuine self-awareness accepts that we follow a particular mental cultural program and that members of other cultures have different programs. We may find out more about ourselves by exploring those differences.

The seven dimensions all indicate ways in which another culture may start from seemingly "opposite" premises. But this does not invalidate our own frameworks. It is simply a different approach from which we can learn. Milton Bennett[2], a cross-cultural researcher, has found that people encountering foreign cultures may isolate themselves and separate their norms and values from those of the foreign culture. But this only impedes self-awareness. Both sameness and difference tell us who we are: "I am like A, but not like B."

RESPECTING CULTURAL DIFFERENCES

An initial step towards developing respect for cultural differences is to look for situations in our own life in which we would behave like a person from another culture. This is what helped a member of the purchasing department of a big European oil company who was negotiating an order with a Korean supplier. At the first meeting, the Korean partner offered a silver pen to the European manager. The latter, however, politely refused the present for fear of being bribed (even though he knew about the Korean custom of giving presents). Much to our manager's surprise, the second meeting began with the offer of a stereo system. Again the manager refused, his fear of being bribed probably heightened.

When he gazed at a piece of Korean vase on the third meeting, he finally realized what was going on. His refusal had not been taken to mean: "Let's get on with business right away", but rather: "If you want to get into business with me, you had better come up with something bigger." How embarrassing his refusal must have been for the Korean partner became clear to him when he remembered a similar situation in his own life. On one of his first dates with his wife, he had bought her a small present. But from the expression on her face, he could easily tell that it was not quite what she had expected. Remembering this made him accept the fact that the Korean partner was simply trying to establish a relationship and had no intention of bribing him. To avoid similar misunderstandings in future encounters with Korean partners, the manager decided to try to communicate that he, too, was interested in good relationships but that he felt no need to exchange expensive presents. (One alternative he might have come up with could have been to offer presents that were of little material value, but nevertheless signaled appreciation and interest.)

This story illustrates how we can learn to appreciate and respect behaviours and values different from our own. Thinking about situations in your own life might help you understand that behaviours that seemingly differ are often different only in terms of the type of situation in which you observe them, not in terms of their function. This will prevent you from prematurely valuing a behaviour as negative and, more importantly, help you understand what the other person is actually trying to do. In understanding the other's intentions, and in possibly signaling that you do understand those intentions, you take the first step towards developing a shared meaning with your partner.

Generally speaking, what is strong in another culture will also be present in some form in our own culture. We speak of "guilt cultures" and "shame cultures", for example: those which try to make us feel guilty for breaking rules, and those which demand public apologies and subject the miscreant to the hostile stares of their group, e.g. "loss of face". This is a significant difference between West and East: but who has never wished the ground would open up because of an excruciatingly embarrassing lapse?

Respect is most effectively developed once we realize that most cultural differences are in ourselves, even if we have not yet recognized them. For example, we often think that the Japanese are mysterious, even unreliable. You never know what they are feeling or thinking and they always say "yes", even when they are negative about something. But don't we have situations in which the same happens to us? If your own child has given a rather nervous and halting performance in her first solo in a school concert but must go on again after the interval, you might well say "Wonderful, darling" to give her confidence, even though you don't actually believe her performance was good.

Or suppose a minority employee who has been subject to discrimination in your company comes to see you in despair. You are worried that he might injure himself, sue the company or attack his supervisor. It is likely that you would work on re-establishing your relationship with this employee, gaining his confidence, before suggesting that he might consider alternative forms of behaviour. You would obviously be tactful and indirect in making these suggestions. You would be behaving in a "Japanese" manner, because the circumstances warrant it. But perhaps circumstances in Japan make the sense of self so vulnerable that one usually tip-toes around another person's sensibilities. If we assume that most Japanese have a frail sense of self, their behaviour makes very good senses. We would be wise to do the same when in Japan.

Consider another case encountered by a German engineer in South Africa. We all work for money and most of us have a sense of pride and duty in our work, but the money-duty continuum may be radically different in different cultures. The engineer gave his maid a Christmas bonus and she promptly disappeared for two months, since as she saw it she had no need to work. He was appalled. Of course we don't know her motives: she may have felt no obligation to an employer she disliked, but a sense of duty to an employer she did like. Or perhaps being a maid is only something she did in desperate circumstances. The engineer's wife concluded that she was "lazy", but such a judgment came from her own frame of reference.

To sum up, both awareness and respect are necessary steps towards developing transcultural competence. But even their combined power may not always suffice. In workshops, people often ask questions such as: "Why should only we respect and adapt to the other culture? Why don't they respect and adapt to ours?" We will come back to this question when we discuss reconciliation.

Another, perhaps more interesting problem is that of mutual empathy, a term employed by Milton Bennett. What happens when one person attempts to shift to another culture's perspective when at the same time the other person is trying to do the same thing?

Motorola University recently prepared carefully for a presentation in China. After considerable thought, the presenters entitled it "Relationships do not retire". The gist of the presentation was that Motorola had come to China in order to stay and help the economy to create wealth. Relationships with Chinese suppliers, subcontractors and employees would constitute a permanent commitment to building Chinese economic infrastructure and earning hard currency through exports.

The Chinese audience listened politely to this presentation but was quiet when invited to ask questions. Finally one manager put up his hand and said: "Can you tell us about pay for performance?"

What was happening here is very common. Even as we move towards the other person's perspective, they have started to move towards ours, and we pass each other invisibly like ships in the night. Remember that those Chinese who come to a presentation by a western company may already be pro-western and see western views as potentially liberating. This dynamic is especially strong when a country is small and poor. When a drug salesperson from a US company meets with the minister of health from Costa Rica, the former's salary may be ten times the latter's. This kind of encounter only hardens our prejudices: "See, they all want to be like us."

But foreign cultures have an integrity which only some of its members will abandon. In the Vietnam War the USA found that the genuine nationalists among the Vietnamese were very much tougher than their own opportunist allies. People who abandon their culture become weakened and corrupt. We need foreigners to be themselves if partnerships are to work. It is this very difference which makes relationships valuable.

This is why we need to reconcile differences, be ourselves but yet see and understand how the other's perspectives can help our own.

RECONCILING CULTURAL DIFFERENCES

Once we are aware of our own mental models and cultural predispositions, and can respect and understand that those of another culture are legitimately different, then it becomes possible to reconcile differences. Why do this? Because we are in the business of creating wealth and value, not just for ourselves, but for those who live in different cultural worlds. We need to share the values of buying, selling, of joint venturing, of working in partnership.

Take two companies, one in the Netherlands and one in Belgium. The first was innovation oriented. The second relied on its strong traditional reputation and the prestige ascribed to it by Belgian culture. The status of the two companies was derived from achievement and ascription respectively. They could have quarrelled endlessly about their comparative "worth", but they did not. Rather they jointly strove to establish a reputation for both innovation and quality which they then achieved.

There are ten steps which are useful in achieving reconciliation:
1 The theory of complementarity
2 Using humour
3 Mapping out a cultural space
4 From nouns to present participles and processes
5 Language and meta-language
6 Frames and contexts

7   Sequencing
8   Waving/cycling
9   Synergising and virtuous circling
10 The double helix

The Theory of Complementarity

The Danish scientist Niels Bohr proposed a theory of complementarity. The ultimate nature of matter is manifested both as specific particles and as diffuse waves. Nature reveals itself to us as a response to our measuring instruments. There is no one form "out there", but forms which depend on how we perceive them and how we measure them.

Throughout this book all our seven dimensions have represented continua with two extremes. Universalism and particularism are not separate but different, on a continuum between rules and exceptions. Things are more or less similar to the rule, or more or less dissimilar and hence exceptional. You could not even define rules without also knowing what exceptions were. The terms are therefore complementary.

It is the same for all seven dimensions. The individual is more or less separate from the group. "Being by yourself" requires a group if the difference is to register. There can be no specific part without a concept of the diffuse whole. Directing yourself from inside outwards is necessarily in contrast to being directed from the outside inwards. To say that we seek to integrate our values and that all cultures look for integrity and reconciliation is a recognition that values are holistic to begin with.

Using Humour

We become aware of dilemmas through humour, which signals an unexpected clash between two different perspectives.

Values taken to extremes often suggest that the opposite value is really present, rather than the proclaimed one: "The more he talked of his honour, the faster we counted our spoons." "Why does the ascent of the preacher's rhetoric in TV evangelism so often accompany the descent of his trousers?" the *New York Times* recently asked.

Corporations who announce that they "trust their people" may end up breaking into their offices at night and rifling their desks, because they cannot be seen distrusting them publicly but are secretly concerned about a spate of thefts. For the "lowdown" on what really happens in the corporation, look at the cartoons stuck on the walls of employees' offices. They are often incisive satires of the official line and reveal what the dilemmas really are.

Mapping Out a Cultural Space

Another effective process for exploring dilemmas is to turn their "two horns" into axes to create a cultural space. We can map some or all of the seven dimensions on this cultural space. The map is constructed through either interviews or questionnaires. Issues mapped recently include:

A) Given the pluralism of local initiatives in Europe, is it possible to exercise any strategic leadership from US headquarters which is applicable to all the units concerned? (Universalism-particularism dilemma)

B) Given the obvious desirability of getting our best products on to the market according to the value of their achievements, is it possible to attain this while giving the autonomous R&D for high potential products the space they need to mature? (Achievement-ascription dilemma)

C) Given the need for a quick response to very swiftly changing markets in the US, is it possible to keep ourselves committed to a long-term vision developed at our centre in the Republic of Korea? (Short-term-long-term dilemma)

Respondents drew attention to the first three dilemmas in words paraphrased below:

A) Universalism-particularism dilemma
- The markets in Europe could be served much better if our American HQ could only understand the particular needs we have over here.
- If the Europeans could only understand what it takes to become a truly global company.
- We know here in the US very well what different markets need, but we need to co-educate them in order not to fall into the trap of having very happy clients but no margins for us. Economies of scale force us to limit our offerings.

B) Achievement-ascription dilemma
- If we in R&D could get some more time to work out our very promising products without continuously being pushed by marketing, our products would be much better in the long run.
- You can't be innovative unless you are given some time to work things out Customers need to leave you alone for a while.
- R&D people tend to deliver too late products which the market frequently doesn't need. In marketing we should be more responsible

and give R&D strict guidelines and deadlines.
- In our company we should have more trust in what we are developing. It is good stuff. Let's go for it wholeheartedly.

C) *The short-term and long-term dilemma*
- The Americans hinder our long-term achievements because of their drive for quarterly results. Our vision is often jeopardized by a quest for the quick buck!
- It seems like in the Far East and in Europe there are no shareholders. The ease with which they accept quarterly losses would be unacceptable in the US.

Most of these remarks clearly show basic dilemmas that are inherent in cross-cultural debates. In intercultural encounters people frequently complain of excessive rivalry and an inability to harmonise the efforts of different units, representing different cultures.

Dilemma A can be mapped between the pluralism of local initiatives on the horizontal axis and the universal truth of HQ on the vertical axis (Figure 1).

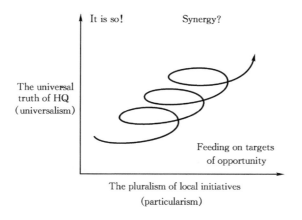

Figure 1 Dilemma A

Dilemma B is between identification with customers' viewpoints on the horizontal axis, because it is the customer who buys the achievements of the product. On the other hand, R&D wants to be committed to the product by ascribing status to it, which allows its development without being hindered by clients' needs too early or too frequently (Figure 2).

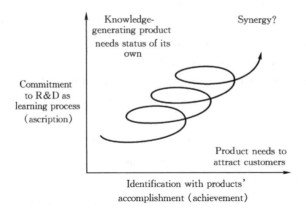

Figure 2 Dilemma B

Dilemma C is between short- and long-termism. On the one axis the market demands a quick response and US shareholders look for good returns every quarter. On the other axis we find the long-term needs to be framed by a vision which allows the short-term to have meaning (Figure 3).

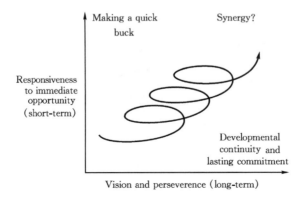

Figure 3 Dilemma C

The dilemma must be mapped before reconciling it, so that we and clients have a clear definition of what has to be reconciled. The remaining steps in the process show how genuine reconciliation can be attained.

From Nouns to Present Participles and Processes

A noun could be defined as "a person, place or thing". But a value is none of these and we get into difficulty when we use nouns like universalism or particularism, loyalty or dissent to describe the horns of a dilemma. We have done so in this book because it is the convention of the social sciences to make phenomena look and sound physical, but it is still misleading. So, as a step on the road to reconciliation, we shall turn all nouns into present participles, ending in -*ing*, which transforms them into processes. Thus:

Universalising – Particularising
Individualising – Communing
Specifying/analysing – Diffusing/Synthesising
Communicating neutrality – Communicating emotion
Achieving – Ascribing (status)
Directing oneself from inside – Going with the flow of the environment
Sequencing time – Synchronising time

Not all nouns can be made into present participles, but if we know what we want—to get rid of the "hard edges" and render the value as a process requiring the participation of people—then suitable words can be found. Since processes mingle in a way that things do not, we are now much closer to understanding that all seven dimensions are really continua, with a preponderance of one process at one end (*yin*) and a preponderance of the other process at the other end (*yang*). We have also softened the adversary structure of clashing nouns or "isms". This is what De Bono[3] calls "water logic".

Language and Meta-Language

Since we are stuck with the structure of language, it is as well to consider how language achieves reconciliation. It does so by using a ladder of abstraction and putting one value (or horn of the dilemma) above the other, that is, by using both an object language and a meta-language and allowing them to dovetail.

Consider this famous quotation from Scott Fitzgerald:

The test of a first rate intelligence is to hold two ideas in your mind at the same time and still retain the capacity to function. You must, for example, be able to see that things are hopeless, yet be determined to make them otherwise.

This might appear at first glance to be a contradiction, but it is not. Contradictions cancel each other out: they are meaningless. What the author has done here is to dovetail the two statements at different levels of language.

Meta-level   "*be determined to make them otherwise*"

Object level   *"sees that things are hopeless"*

The object level is about things being hopeless. The meta-level is about the determination of the person who sees. The two statements are not contradictory because they do not apply to the same "things". The second is about the person seeing, not about the things seen.

This applies equally to our seven dimensions. We could say: "The test of a first-rate manager is to hold two ideas in your mind at the same time and still retain the capacity to function."

You must, for example, be able to see that a particular customer request is outside the universal rules your company has set up, yet be determined to qualify the existing rule or create a new rule based on this case.

Meta-level   *Determined to qualify rule or create new one*
Object level   *Particular request breaks existing rule*

We could do the same for any of the seven dimensions. Take a small business unit which has enjoyed extraordinary success:

Meta-level   *Ascribe importance to this strategy company-wide*
Object level   *Admire and reward this form of achieving*

Top management has encouraged achievement in a particular unit and has ascribed universal importance to the strategy employed, so that other business units can benefit by emulating the particular achievement. Here both particularising and universalising, and achieving and ascribing have been reconciled.

Frames and Contexts

In the previous example of language levels, you could say that the metalevel frames the object level:

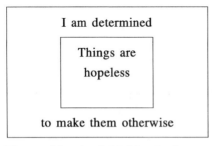
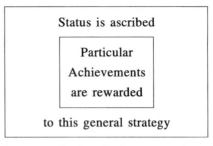

The usefulness of thinking in frame and contexts is that the latter contain and constrain the "picture" or the "text" within them. There is always a danger of people's value extremes "running away". "To see that things are hopeless" can lead to despair, unless framed by "a determination to make them otherwise". We might have concluded from the outstanding achievement of the business unit that

Unit Nine Intercultural Communication in Business, Management and Negotiation

top management should simply keep out of their way, but that would have prevented the organisation learning from a local success.

The important thing to grasp is that text and context are reversible, as are the picture and the frame. We could focus on a very intelligent person and say: or we could say:

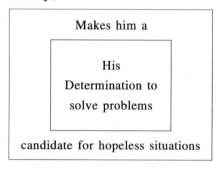
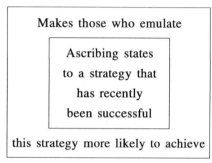

Sequencing

Values appear to clash and conflict when we assume that both must be expressed simultaneously. It isn't possible to be right and wrong, to universalise and particularise, to be steered from inside and from outside at the same time. One obviously precludes the other.

But it is possible to go wrong and then correct, to particularise and then generalise, to observe outer trends and dynamics and then direct yourself at your objective. So a major element in reconciling values is to sequence processes over time.

Indeed one of the frames and contexts comments on what your present action is leading to: or:

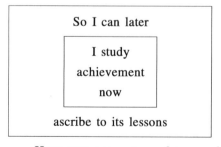
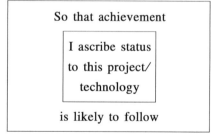

Have you every stopped to wonder what happens to our values if, instead of assuming they are things (i. e. colliding billiard balls), we assume that they are wave-forms? Common sense assumes values to be like coins, jewels or rocks. We could take the view that they are like water waves, electro-magnetic waves, sound waves, light waves etc. This makes a great deal of difference.

Consider the cycle of sleeping and waking, which looks like Figure 4.

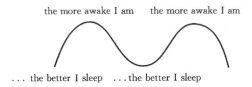

Figure 4 Sleeping and waking

Or consider music on various frequencies (Figure 5).

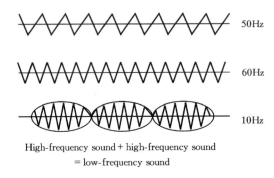

High-frequency sound + high-frequency sound
= low-frequency sound

Figure 5 High- and low-frequency sound

If we have two different frequencies, 50 Hz and 60 Hz, these combine to form a beat frequency of only 10 Hz, because a low-frequency wave has been created by harmonising the two waves. The high-frequency sound is now "within" the low-frequency beat. If values are like sound waves, no wonder their harmony (what south-east Asians call wa) can be more beautiful still.

If the wave-form is a legitimate expression of values and if the values alternate like sleeping and waking, relaxing and exciting, erring and correcting, then we can draw the wave-form between the axes as in Figure 6.

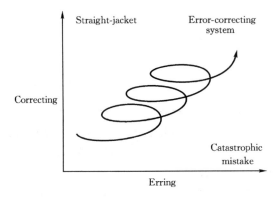

Figure 6 Process of continuing improvement

Here we first err, then correct, then err again, then correct again and so on. The entire process is called an error correcting system. We avoid both catastrophic mistakes (perhaps by using simulation) and the straight-jacket of never making a mistake. Arguably if we want to learn fast, many small errors which are corrected might be the best way. "Error", of course, is relative. If we call the bottom 35% of our performance "errors", we will go on improving. If we call only 5% "errors" we may come to ignore them or hush them up.

The notion of learning by error correction is so important that we include this idea in all our dilemmas, especially the seven dimensions. Suppose that we were to create a wave-form between universalising and particularising. It might look like Figure 7.

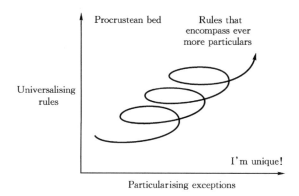

Figure 7 Generating new rules and reforming current ones

This is a diagram of how particular exceptions are encountered and noted before encompassing them within changed or reformed rules. No scientific law can ignore mounting anomalies. No legal statute can survive massive opposition. No corporate procedures can fail to account for a growing number of exceptions. In all such crises the old rules must be reformed or new ones created. The point is that rules must be open to refutation if we are to improve them. Nor can we properly appreciate what is unique and outstanding unless we know what the common standards are.

We have retained the idea of error correction by rendering our waveform as a cycle. This assumes that we will periodically get things wrong and have to make a second "try" or circuit before improving on both axes.

Synergising and Virtuous Circling

An important test of optimal reconciliation which includes both ends of the values continuum, in even greater harmony, is the criterion of synergy. The word comes from the Greek sunergos, meaning "to work with". When two values work with one another they are mutually facilitating and enhancing. Thus ascribing importance to a major project with France Telecom makes it more likely that your working group will be inspired to achieve that project. That your company has recently been seen to be achieving the project makes it far more likely that senior management will ascribe great importance to it in next year's strategy deliberation. The virtuous circle looks like Figure 8.

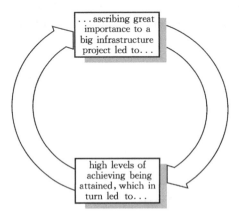

Figure 8　A virtuous circle between ascribing and achieving

Synergy is also present in nature. Steel alloys for jet engines are immensely stronger than the strength of all their components combined. The molecular chain in the alloy is simply a stronger structure.

The Double Helix

Finally we come to our model of models: DNA, the double helix molecular structure (Figure 9). Let us make it clear that we are using this as a metaphor, not trying to borrow the mantle of biological science. But then most, if not all, of the social sciences are based on metaphors. Since cultures are alive we have consciously borrowed from the life sciences.

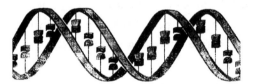

Figure 9　The double helix of reconciliation

The double helix model helps to summarise the steps to reconciliation. The ladder of protein synthesis has four rungs. We have a ladder of values synthesis with seven rungs. The twisted ladder is full of **complementarities**. When the "pairs" come together unexpectedly it can be **funny**. We can use the uprights on each side of the ladder as cultural space for **mapping**. The twisted elements of the ladder constitute a growth **process**. Each twist of the spiral speaks the **language** of growth and contains coded instructions. Each turn of the helix is framed and **contextualised** by the helix within and around it, containing and constraining. The process is **sequential**. It constitutes waves and cycles, with synthesis producing growth and **synergy**.

In short, the double helix helps summarise all nine processes by which values are reconciled.

Notes

1. Adapted from *Riding the Waves of Culture*, Fons Trompenaars and Charles Hampden-Turner, 1997.
2. Milton Bennett is well known for his Developmental Model of Intercultural Sensitivity and the Intercultural Development Inventory, which are used internationally to guide intercultural training design and to assess intercultural competence. He has received the highest awards for excellence from the Society for Intercultural Education, Training and Research (SIETAR) and from NAFSA: Association of International Educators. Earlier in his life, he was a Westinghouse Talent Search winner for his work in science. For 15 years, Dr. Bennett was a faculty member at Portland State University, where he created a graduate program in intercultural communication.
3. De Bono has written extensively about the process of lateral thinking—the generation of novel solutions to problems. The point of lateral thinking is that many problems require a different perspective to solve successfully. De Bono identifies four critical factors associated with lateral thinking: (1) recognize dominant ideas that polarize perception of a problem, (2) searching for different ways of looking at things, (3) relaxation of rigid control of thinking, and (4) use of chance to encourage other ideas. This last factor has to do with the fact that lateral thinking involves low-probability ideas which are unlikely to occur in the normal course of events.

Questions for Discussion

1. Review the 7D-Model in *Riding the Waves of Culture* and compare it with Hofstede's 5 Cultural Dimensions.
2. If a particular customer request is outside the universal rules your company has

set up, you are determined to create a new rule based on this case instead of qualifying the existing rule. Foretell the consequences that may follow.
3. Discuss the feasibility of solution 1.1 to Dilemma A and evaluate its practicality using at least two examples you are familiar with.
4. How do you understand the model of double helix of reconciliation? Why can double helix help summarize all nine processes by which values are reconciled?
5. What cultural issues would the management of a Chinese Abuja-based company probably have to address when he/she leads the culturally-diverse project team to work in Nigeria?

Online Mini-Case Studies and Viewpoints-Sharing

Bangkok with a Husband and Children

When a major oil company transferred a geologist to Bangkok, her husband, a diplomat, arranged a transfer to the same city. In describing their global lifestyle, the geologist explained that the availability of household help—including a driver, a nanny for their two small children, and a housekeeper—made it much easier for her to balance her three extremely time-consuming roles—as mother, wife, and geologist—in a way that would be financially impossible for her to achieve in the United States. "Even though everyone thought it would be completely impossible, the expatriate assignment has made my life easier, not more difficult. Time is my scarcest resource, and the household help available in Thailand gives me the time I need to be a good mother, a good wife, and a good manager."

Online Research

Research the value differences between American career women and their Asian counterparts regarding families and children and tell if there is a converging tendency as globalization continues.

Unit Ten

Cultural Adaptation and Intercultural Competence

Reading One

Introductory Remarks

When individuals leave their home culture and enter an unfamiliar culture, they may encounter certain mental, emotional and physical discomfort. How long its impact lasts before the normality returns mainly depends on how adaptable the individuals are when situated in the new environment of the host culture. The process to survive the new culture and overcome the disturbance is synonymous with the process of adaptation. This process is essentially a communication process in which strangers learn, understand and acquire communication patterns of the new culture. Just as individuals learn their own cultural communication patterns through interaction with significant people around them, strangers acquire the culturally-recognized communication norms of the host culture and build up relationships with the new cultural environment by various means of communication.

    This selection begins with the discussion about the strangers adapting to the new culture. The author maintains that in the communication system the strangers gradually undergo an adaptive transformation coupled with the dynamic interplay of acculturation and deculturation. Following that elucidation, the article proposes stress-adaptation-growth dynamics and elaborates on the internal dynamics of strangers cross-cultural experience in a "draw-back-to-leap" pattern similar to the movement of a wheel, a non-linear cycle in the process. In the final part, the author condenses the theoretical principles of the process and outcome of cross-cultural adaptation into 10 axioms which, undoubtedly, serve as guidelines for cross-cultural communicators to cope with various disturbances in their adaptation to the new culture.

Cross-Cultural Adaptation: Axioms[1]

Young Yun Kim[2]

Strangers Adapting

Intercultural encounters provide such situations of deviation from the familiar, assumed, and taken-for-granted, as individuals are faced with things that do not follow their unconscious cultural program. They now need to learn and acquire a new system of communication patterns acceptable in the host society. As strangers in the new land, they are subject to a greater or lesser necessity to conform to the communication patterns of the host society. Permanent immigrants or long-term settlers generally have a greater need to conform than temporary sojourners, yet no one is completely free from having to understand, and manage, the various communication patterns sanctioned and operating in the host culture.

Acculturation and Deculturation

This process of learning and acquiring the elements of the host culture is called *acculturation*. Specifically, acculturation of strangers involves the cultural patterns established in the host society at large and regarded by the majority of people as the 'standard' for that society. In many ethnically diverse societies, the standard cultural patterns refer mainly to those of the dominant culture. In the United States, for example, the standard cultural patterns refer mainly to those of the anglo-white Americans. Although acquiring minority cultural patterns is a part of the overall adaptation process of newcomers, the most compelling pressure to conform comes from the dominant elements of the host society.

In this process, strangers are re-enculturated, only this time into the host society. This second-time enculturation does not occur so smoothly as their childhood enculturation, because of the distinct cultural identity and communication patterns internalised in their childhood. As acculturation occurs in the strangers, *unlearning* (or undoing) of at least some of the old cultural patterns occurs (at least in the sense that new responses are adopted in situations that previously would have evoked old ones). The cost of acquiring something new is inevitably the 'losing' of something old in much the same way as 'being someone requires the forfeiture of being someone else.'

This cultural discontinuity in strangers' internal cultural identity and attributes has been recognised by a number of investigators as *desocialisation or* deculturation. These two phenomena are not necessarily observable in a direct one-on-one basis. Acquiring knowledge and skill in the host language may not necessarily result in the unlearning of the corresponding amount of knowledge and skill in the original language, as has been indicated in studies of bilingual children. As we consider the make-up of strangers after a given time in the host milieu, however, we will note that their internal attributes are no longer the same as they once were before being exposed to the host culture.

In this dynamic interplay of acculturation and deculturation, strangers gradually undergo an adaptive transformation in their communication system. Ultimately the new cultural patterns replace many of the old patterns and the overall transformation of strangers becomes noticeable, particularly to others.

Stress-adaptation-growth Dynamics
As discussed previously, human systems are characteristically homeostatic attempting to hold constant a variety of variables in our internal structure so as to achieve an ordered whole. When individuals receive messages that disrupt their existing internal order, they experience disequilibrium. In this state of disequilibrium, stress confronts the individual. As such, strangers inevitably experience acute stress as they go through the experiences of acculturation and deculturation. They lack 'intersubjective understanding' of the social world inhabited by the members of the host society. As Parrillo observed:

> For the natives, then, every social situation is the coming together not only of roles and identities, but also of shared realities—the intersubjective structure of consciousness. What is taken for granted by the native is problematic for the stranger. In a familiar world, people live through the day by responding to daily routine without questioning or reflection. To strangers, however, every situation is new and is therefore experienced as a crisis.

As long as there are discrepancies between the demands of the host environment and the capacities of the strangers' internal communication to meet those demands, the strangers must adjust and readjust themselves to better function in the host society. Everyone requires on-going validation of his or her 'place' in a given environment, and the inability to meet this basic human need can lead to symptoms of mental, emotional, and physical disturbance. The shifting of the self-world relationship brings about a heightened level of consciousness through an increased awareness of the split between inner, subjective experiences and external, objective circumstances.

When experiencing internal stress or disequilibrium, strangers 'instinctively' react to maintain or restore their inner balance and stability. Through various psychological maneuvers, they temporarily escape from the necessity of having to deal with stressful conditions. Often the 'problem-solving' approach is not used by strangers when they are under high stress, but, instead, more primitive, rigid, and less adequate attempts are made to protect feelings or master the situation. Consequently, strangers may become more aggressive or hostile toward the new country, attacking its values, customs, food, climate, and so on. As coping mechanisms, they may yearn for home, become dependent on others, be excessively concerned with unimportant details, rationalize their inabilities, or simply avoid problematic situations by ignoring them.

Unfortunately, these defensive reactions do not facilitate learning about a new environment. Although defensive reactions to stressful situations may temporarily reduce inner tension and anxiety, strangers cannot avoid the necessity to 'face' and cope with the host environment if they are to perform satisfactorily in it. Although internal protective reactions are frequently necessary for strangers, such reactions are generally temporary. Sooner or later, the strangers must stop protective reactions that merely postpone dealing with the impending problems of adaptation. As long as they remain in the host society, and as long as the equality of their performance in the host society depends on how well they can communicate with host nationals, they eventually must acquire the information that will improve their functional relationship with the host environment.

To acquire the necessary communication competence of the host society means going through many stressful emotional 'lows.' Strangers must weather internal conflicts—conflicts between their original cultural patterns and the host cultural patterns—through active communication participation in the host society. In this process, *stress* is inevitably present: it is 'part-and-parcel of the stress-adaptation cycle.' The psychological movements of individuals' internal systems into new dimensions of perception and experience often produce forms of temporary personality disintegration, or even 'breakdown' in some extreme cases. *Stress, in the present context, can be viewed as the internal resistance of the human organism against its own cultural evolution.*

As strangers face the demands of the host environment and cope with the accompanying stress, parts of their internal organisation undergo small changes. The interior organisation of strangers is in flux as they continue to communicate with and adapt to the host environment. The periods of 'crisis' will be temporary as the strangers work out new ways of handling problems through sources of strength in themselves and in their social environment. A crisis, once managed by the strangers, presents an opportunity to strengthen their coping abilities and potential for adaptive changes. Stress, then, is responsible not only for suffering, frustration, and anxiety, but also for providing the impetus for adaptive personal transformation and growth—the learning and creative responses to manage new cultural circumstances.

Stress, adaptation, and growth, together, define the internal dynamics of strangers' cross-cultural experiences in a 'draw-back-to-leap' pattern similar to the movement of a wheel. Each stressful experience is responded to by strangers with a 'draw back,' which then activates their adaptive energy to help them reorganise themselves and 'leap forward.' This stress-adaptation-growth cycle involves communication activities that shift between out-looking, information-seeking behavior and tension-reducing, defensive retreat, and the resultant capacity to see a situation 'with new eyes.' The break-up of the old internal conditions usually results not in chaos or breakdown, but in the creation of a whole new internal structure that is better adapted to the host environment.

The adaptation process, thus, is not a smooth, linear process, but a transformation of individuals through the successive interplay of *degeneration and regeneration*. The stress, adaptation, and resultant internal growth essentially characterise the strangers' conscious and unconscious movement forward and upward in the direction of greater success in meeting the demands of the host environment. The resolution of stressful difficulties promises the qualitative transformation of strangers toward a greater internal capacity to cope with varied environmental conditions. The increased internal capacity, in turn, facilitates the subsequent handling of stress and adaptation, learning and unlearning, acculturation and deculturation, crisis and resolution.

At this point, recall from the previous chapter that many studies of the 'culture shock' phenomenon have focused on these initial-phase stress reactions of strangers. These studies have typically viewed culture shock as a negative, problematic, and undesirable phenomenon to be avoided. Viewed in the present systems terms, however, *culture shock is a manifestation of a generic process that occurs whenever the capabilities of a living system are not sufficiently adequate to the demands of an unfamiliar cultural environment.* It is a necessary precondition to adaptive change, as individuals strive to regain their inner balance by adapting to the demands and opportunities of their new life circumstance.

In this view, the present theory conceptualises cross-cultural adaptation as a process of dynamic stress-adaptation-growth interplay. This conceptualisation shows the unity of stress and change in the adaptation process: neither occurs without the other and each occurs because of the other. To the extent that stress is said to be responsible for suffering, frustration, and anxiety, it also must be credited as an impetus for learning, growth and creativity for the individual. Temporary disintegration is thus viewed as the very basis for a subsequent increase in the awareness of life conditions and ways to deal with them.

Empirical research has provided some supportive indication, although indirect and rudimentary, that the stress of meeting with new cultural elements lays the groundwork for subsequent adaptation. For example, Eaton & Lasry reported that the stress level of more upwardly mobile immigrants was greater than those who were less upwardly mobile. Among Japanese-Americans and Mexican-American women, the better adapted immigrants had a somewhat greater frequency of stress-related symptoms (such as anxiety and need for psychotherapy) than the less adapted group. Additionally, Ruben & Kealey suggested that the Canadians in Kenya who would ultimately be the most effective in adapting to the new culture underwent the most intense culture shock during the transition period. Other acculturation studies of immigrants and foreign students in the United States have shown that, once the initial phase has been successfully managed, individuals demonstrate an increased cognitive complexity, a positive orientation toward the host environment and toward themselves, and behavioral capacities to communicate with the natives.

The stress-adaptation-growth dynamics of strangers' cross-cultural experiences speak of profound human pliability, resilience and potential for growth. Except for a small portion of strangers who are unable, or unwilling, to cope with the stress of cross-cultural adaptation, most strangers in foreign cultures have demonstrated an impressive capacity to manage their cross-cultural encounters successfully and without damaging their overall psychological health. This observation can be extended to individuals under even more extreme life conditions, such as those in concentration camps and prisons who have shown repeatedly that humans are capable of coping with severely stressful situations by adaptively transforming themselves.

It must be pointed out that not all individuals are equally successful in making transitions toward adaptation. Certain individuals, although in the minority, may strongly resist such change, thereby increasing the stress level and making the stress-adaptation-growth cycle intensely difficult. Some may not be able to cope with intense stress experiences due to lack of psychological resilience. Others may find themselves in situations that present too severe a challenge to manage. *Most individuals in most circumstances*, however, undergo the stress-adaptation-change cycle and achieve at least a minimum functional effectiveness in the host environment.

Strangers Communicating

As strangers accumulate adaptive experiences, they cultivate the capability to code and decode verbal and non-verbal messages so that the messages will be recognised, accepted, and responded to. Through prolonged and varied communication experiences, strangers gradually acquire the coping mechanisms that help discern and deal with the dynamics of the host environment. Once acquired, communication capabilities function as an instrumental, interpretive, and expressive means of coming to terms with the host environment, and of feeling more at ease and less stressed.

Indeed, communication is at the heart of cross-cultural adaptation—as it is in the enculturation process of native-born children. The cross-cultural adaptation process is essentially a process of achieving the communication capacities necessary for strangers to be functional in the host society. In the continuous process of message encoding and decoding, up-to-date information about the self, the host environment, and the relationship of the self to the host environment leads to the acquisition of appropriate techniques, and eventually increases the individual's mastery of life. Through effective communication, strangers are able to gradually increase their control over the environment and over life itself—just as the capacity of a balloon expands with the increased amount of incoming air.

Conversely, the development of adaptive communication capacity occurs through countless acts of communication. Communication activities of strangers serve to develop their internal communication capacities: one learns to communicate by communicating. Furthermore, the acquired host communication competence has a direct bearing on the overall cross-cultural adaptation of strangers, serving as their primary means of utilizing the resources of the host environment. It also functions as a set of adaptive tools assisting strangers to further participate in the communication processes of the host society, and to attempt to meet their personal and social needs. Through communication, they adapt to and relate to the new environment, and acquire membership and a sense of belonging in the various social groups of the host society on which they depend.

Dimensions of Communication

In understanding the complex process of communication between strangers and the host cultural environment, Ruben's parameter of human communication provides a useful and comprehensive framework. In this parameter, each person's communication activity is conceptualised in two closely interrelated, inseparable communication processes—*personal* (or intrapersonal) and *social*.

Personal communication refers to the 'private symbolization' activities of individuals—all the internal mental activities that occur in individuals that dispose and prepare them to act and react in certain ways in actual social situations. Geyer refers to this process as 'off-line functions,' that is, 'internal information exchange within the system' of individuals when

(1) no inputs are received from the environment,

(2) no outputs are given to the environment, or

(3) there are 'outputs' but the system directs these back into itself as 'inputs'—as when a conclusion of a thinking process is not transmitted to anybody else but is used as an element in a further line of thought.

Personal communication is linked to social communication when two or more individuals interact with one another, knowingly or not. Social communication is the process underlying 'intersubjectivisation,' a phenomenon that occurs as a consequence of 'public symbolization.' According to Geyer, these externalized communication processes of individuals are referred to as 'on-line functions' of human systems. The actual interface of individuals with their environment occurs through their on-line input-output transactions of messages.

Social communication activities occur in many different contexts—from communication in the macro-level society via newspapers, television and movies, to communication within the micro-level environment such as family, neighborhood, museum, workplace, bank, classroom, and friends. Social communication occurs when strangers make simple, passing observations of people on the street, when they listen to a newly released record album, or when they engage in serious dialogue with close friends. These and numerous other aspects of social communication activities can be grouped into two dimensions: (1) interpersonal communication and (2) mass communication.

Interpersonal communication of strangers refers to their social engagements through people in their immediate micro-level environment. Much of their adaptive learning takes place in the context of interpersonal communication. *Mass communication*, on the other hand, includes all other social processes that occur within larger, societal contexts. Through mass media communication experiences (such as radio, television, magazines, newspaper, movies, museums) and other forms of indirect communication (such as lectures, posters, and computerised networks), individuals participate in 'para-social' activities substituting for, or in conjunction with, direct person-to-person encounters. Mass communication, thus, is a more generalized, public form of communication by which individuals interact with their larger societal environment without involvement in any relationships with specific persons.

Along this line of systems thinking, the present theory focuses on host communication competence in examining personal (or 'off-line') communication processes of strangers. To understand social (or 'on-line') communication processes, we will examine the strangers' participation in the host society in general (host social communication) and in their ethnic community (ethnic social communication). Each of these two communication processes is explained below in relation to cross-cultural adaptation.

Personal Communication: Host Communication Competence

The successful adaptation of strangers is realized only when their internal communication systems sufficiently overlap with those of the natives. This internal capacity enables strangers to organise themselves in and with their sociocultural milieu, developing ways of seeing, hearing, understanding, and responding to the environment appropriately. As they become more competent in the host communication system, they are better able to discern the similarities and differences between their original home culture and the host culture and are able to act accordingly.

For the natives, such internal communication capacity has been acquired from so early in life and has been so completely internalised into their personal communication system that, by and large, it operates automatically and unconsciously. For immigrants or sojourners, however, the interpretive frames need to be learned and internalised (acculturation) and, at the same time, some of their original cultural communication patterns must be unlearned (deculturation). Through trial and error, with frequently accompanying stress and despair, they are able to gradually transform their personal communication patterns and achieve an increasing level of host communication competence. Until the strangers have acquired a sufficient level of host communication competence, they are handicapped in their ability to appropriately and effectively receive and transmit messages and retain information, and to perform operations in such a way that they may contribute to furthering their physical, psychological and social fulfillment in the host society.

In a way, strangers become more 'mature' members of the host society through acquiring host communication competence. They become less reliant on others for protection and correction of their behaviors in managing their daily activities, and feel a greater sense of belonging to the host society. Strangers' host communication competence, thus, faciliates the process of achieving the ultimate goal and outcome of cross-cultural adaptation—increased functional fitness and decreased cross-cultural stress. As Ruesch & Bateson stated. 'the ability to communicate successfully becomes synonymous with being mentally healthy.'

Host communication competence as presently conceptualised, then, is a *continuum*, on which different strangers can be plotted and analysed. At the lowest end of this continuum is a hypothetical 'zero competence,' that is, a complete inability to communicate in a new cultural environment. At the highest end, we can theoretically place those individuals whose capability to communicate is at the highest possible attainment.

Host Social Communication

Strangers actually participate in the reality of the host environment through social communication. Through such participation, they become actively 'engaged' in the host society and develop a functional relationship with it, and are given the opportunity to learn and enhance their host communication competence.

The critical importance of host social communication as a cross-cultural adaptation medium has been shown in numerous empirical studies, although findings are still scattered across several human science disciplines. Typically, the group-level anthropological studies of cultural contacts and change have taken communication as a 'given' condition that facilitates the adaptation flow between two or more contacting cultures, and thus, little scientific attention has been placed on the communication process itself. In sociological studies, strangers' communication behaviors have been included as part of the indexes of 'social integration' or as a factor that is positively associated with the 'majority-minority' relations among ethnic groups within societies.

Like interpersonal communication activities, mass communication activities (particularly the use of mass media) have been observed to promote adaptation of strangers. Gordon stated, for example, that the mass media (along with public schools) exert 'overwhelming acculturation powers' over immigrants' children.

Shibutani & Kwiln also supported this view indicating that:

> The extent to which members of a minority group become acculturated to the way of life of the dominant group depends upon the extent of their participation in the communication channels of their rulers.

The underlying assumption is that access to, exposure to, and use of the mass media of the dominant group influences ethnics and migrants in their processes of learning about and taking part in the dominant society.

Recently, a few communication researchers have begun to pay closer attention to the communication patterns of immigrants. Nagata, for example, made a first conceptualisation of the immigrant adaptation process based on various communication variables (such as interpersonal communication relations, mass media behavior, and perceptual and attitudinal orientations). In this study of Chicago area Japanese-Americans, Nagalta observed a progressive increase in such communication variables. Ryu's study ' suggested the positive role of mass media in the adaptation of Korean immigrants in the United States. Other studies of sojourners' and immigrants have repeatedly shown that individuals who are more active in interpersonal communication with members of the host society are better adjusted psychologically as well as financially.

Strangers themselves are also keenly aware of the vital role that communication plays in their overall functioning in the host society. The majority of the Indochinese refugees in the United States, for example, expressed a strong need for communication training and general cultural orientation. A similar view was expressed by the social and educational service agencies and organizations serving refugee resettlement and adaptation. The agencies considered cultural and communication barriers one of the most serious problems impairing their service delivery to refugee clients.

Indeed, the critical importance of the host communication activities of strangers cannot be over-emphasized. Adaptive transformation occurs in and through such communication activities, which, in turn, facilitate learning of all other aspects of the host culture including its economic, social, political and aesthetic dimensions.

Ethnic Social Communication

Along with host interpersonal and mass communication activities, strangers in many societies today have access to individuals of the same national or ethnic origin. Whether we speak of British compounds in India, American military posts in West Germany, Puerto Rican barrios in New York City, Chinatown in Tokyo, or a Japanese student association in a Canadian university, there are ethnic communities that provide strangers with opportunities to interact with fellow countrymen [women]. In large cities in countries like Australia, Canada, England, Germany, and the United States, where there has been a large influx of immigrants, many immigrant groups have organized some form of 'mutual aid' or 'self-help' ethnic community group. Such ethnic organizations render assistance to those who need material, informational, emotional, and other forms of social support. In many larger immigrant groups, ethnic media (including newspapers, radio stations, and television programs) perform various informational, educational, and entertainment services to their members.

These ethnic support systems serve adaptation-facilitating functions for new immigrants and sojourners during the initial phase of their adaptation process. Because many strangers initially lack host communication competence and other resources to be self-reliant in the new environment, they tend to rely on ethnic sources of support, compensating for the lack of support from host nationals. In the long run, however, heavy reliance on ethnic sources for their social activities would contribute to the sustenance of ethnic identity, and deter the development of strangers' host communication competence. Because of the relatively 'easy' communication experiences in dealing with ethnic individuals and media, strangers are likely to delay or avoid confronting the stressful experiences of host social communication that are essential for adaptation. The relatively stress-free ethnic communication activities offer temporary relief and refuge, but in doing so discourage the long-term development of host communication competence and participation in the host social processes.

Strangers, therefore, cannot remain rigidly ethnic and also become highly adapted to the host culture. The longer strangers avoid or only minimally interact with the host communication environment, the longer it will take for them to acquire host communication competence. To the extent that strangers participate in ethnic communication channels, they are likely to maintain perspectives different from the normative patterns of the host culture and will experience difficulty in understanding and relating to the host environment.

In sum, the personal and social communication processes are functionally interrelated by a reciprocal causal relationship. Strangers' host communication competence promotes their social engagements with the host environment. Their participation in host social communication processes, in turn, facilitates their host communication competence. This reciprocal and mutually defining relationship between host communication competence and social communication activities is analogous to computer operations in which the former is comparable to the capabilities of a software program and the latter to the actual application of the software for a specific purpose. Added to this interaction of host communication competence and participation in host social communication activities are ethnic social communication activities. Initially, ethnic social communication serves the adaptive process by compensating for the lack of host communication competence and host social communication activities. In time, ethnic social communication is likely to inhibit strangers' development of host communication competence and social participation.

Host Environment and Predisposition

The personal and social (interpersonal, mass) communication processes of strangers cannot be fully understood in isolation from the host environment or without understanding their individualised backgrounds. By adding these dimensions to the present discussion of communication and adaptation, we can address issues concerning the observed differences among individual strangers in their adaptation patterns.

Host Environment: Receptivity and Conformity Pressure

Host environment refers to the social milieu that strangers encounter through interpersonal and mass communication activities. Through interpersonal communication activities, strangers interact with a small part of the host society such as their work place, neighborhood, and community. Strangers share a direct functional relationship with this micro-environment. Through mass communication activities, strangers are exposed to the 'macro'-environment of the host society, its political, social, religious, economic, and other events and activities.

To understand and explain the cross-cultural adaptation process, both the micro- and macro-environment need to be examined. Specifically, the present theory is concerned with the extent to which the environment is receptive toward strangers and the extent to which it exerts pressure on strangers to conform to the host cultural patterns. Environmental receptivity refers to the opportunities offered to strangers to participate in on-going social activities. Other terms such as 'interaction potential' or 'acquaintance potential' have been used for environmental receptivity in relation to strangers' interpersonal communication activities. For instance, United States military personnel who live in a remote military camp have limited access to local people in their daily activities. On the other hand, Peace Corps volunteers who live primarily with natives in local residences have greater access to the host social processes.

The 'conformity pressure' of the host environment refers to the extent to which the environment challenges strangers to adopt the normative patterns of the host culture and its communication system. Although very few systematic studies have examined the role of environmental pressure in cross-cultural adaptation, societies and sub-societies clearly show different levels of tolerance (or rigidity) for strangers and their different cultural attributes. Generally, heterogeneous and 'free' societies such as the United States tend to exert less conformity pressure on strangers than homogeneous and 'rigid' societies such as the Soviet Union.

The above two environmental factors—receptivity and conformity pressure—help define the relative level of encouragement and challenge that a given environment offers to strangers. A society offering an optimal influence on strangers' adaptation would be one in which receptivity and conformity pressure are in an optimal balance.

Predisposition: Adaptive Potential

An additional dimension in explaining strangers' communication-adaptation is the nature of their experiential backgrounds prior to migrating to the host society. Strangers' predispositional factors precede the actual adaptation process, and set the tone for subsequent stranger—host communication encounters. The present analysis focuses on three predispositional factors that have direct bearing on strangers' communication-adaptation processes:

(1) cultural and racial background,
(2) personality attributes, and
(3) preparedness for change.

These predispositional factors collectively characterise the strangers' over-all *adaptive potential*.

Clearly, strangers from a culture similar to the host culture would begin their adaptation process with a greater advantage, compared to those who must bridge a more substantial cultural gap. A similar advantage is found among strangers whose racial/physical make-up closely resembles that of the natives. These cultural and racial similarities equip strangers with a greater potential for successful adaptation in the host environment. Strangers themselves also contribute to their own adaptive potential with differential personality attributes. Those who are more open-minded and receptive toward the host culture and who are stronger and more resilient under stressful circumstances are likely to be better able to manage the uncertainties and challenges of the host environment. In addition, strangers' adaptive potential is influenced by the degree of their preparedness for change. Those who are better educated and better informed about the host culture (through training and other forms of learning) begin their adaptation process with a greater adaptive potential.

Cross-Cultural Adaptation Outcomes

In time, changes take place within strangers as a cumulative result of prolonged communication and adaptation experiences with the host environment. Such adaptive changes in strangers have been examined innumerous aspects—from tastes for different foods, dress habits, and leisure activities, to religious practices, social values, and attitudes toward host culture and home culture. In the present theory, three interrelated aspects—functional fitness, psychological health, and intercultural identity—are examined as the most direct and critical changes that are likely to be observed in strangers.

Functional Fitness

Strangers conduct continuous 'experiments' in the host society. They try and fail, they try and fail less disastrously, they try another alternative and partially succeed. Learning some of the host culture and unlearning some of the original culture gradually brings about an internal transformation in strangers. In time, we see them deviate from the accepted patterns of their original culture and acquire the new patterns of the host culture. A natural outcome of this stress-adaptation-growth process is an increased functional fitness, that is, a greater congruence and compatibility between the strangers' internal conditions and the conditions of the host environment. This notion of person-environment fit implies an interactive system perspective that, unlike assessments based solely in terms of individual traits, regards human behavior as a function of both the person and the environment. Functional fitness, further, requires some 'compromise' in the internal structure of a person in the face of pressure from the host environment.

As such, the increased functional fitness of strangers promotes their life chances in the host society. Successfully adapted strangers have the desired level of appropriate and effective ways of communicating with the host environment. As they achieve an increasing level of fitness in the host culture, they are better able to meet their basic survival needs and social necessities (e. g. , friendship, occupation, and status), as well as philosophical drives (e. g. , creativity. actualisation and fulfilment). The increased functional fitness further enhances the potential effectiveness of the strangers' performance and control in the host environment.

Psychological Health
An increase in functional fitness will, in turn, reduce the stranger's overall cross-cultural stress, as well as defensive reactions to stress such as withdrawal, denial and hostility. As strangers achieve a greater functional fitness in the host environment with increased communication competence, their experience of internal stress due to cross-cultural challenges will decrease.

Issues of mental health (or illness) have been a subject of great interest among researchers, as well as practitioners. Culture shock studies have been mainly concerned with this psychological-health aspect of sojourn experiences, as was reviewed previously. Immigrant studies have also been conducted in psychology and psychiatry examining the issues of mental illnesses. In the present theoretical framework, the psychological health (or illness) of strangers is viewed as a direct outcome of their communication-adaptation experiences and as directly related to the level of functional fitness achieved in the host environment.

Intercultural Identity
Another related aspect of the cross-cultural adaptation outcome is the development of an intercultural identity. Strangers are capable of adapting to the host environment and of growing and developing through the process. The psychological movements of strangers into new dimensions of perception and experience produce 'boundary-ambiguity syndromes,' in which the original cultural identity begins to lose its definiteness and rigidity and the emergent identity shows an increasing 'interculturalness.'

From the present system's perspective, intercultural identity, like cultural identity, refers to the complex process of interpretive activity inside a stranger and the resultant *self-conception* in relation to a cultural group. As strangers undergo adaptive transformation, their internal attributes and self-identification change from being cultural to being increasingly intercultural, and their emotional adherence to the cultural of their childhood weakens, while accommodating the host culture into their self-conception. In other words, a stranger's cultural identity becomes increasingly flexible—no longer rigidly bound by membership to the original culture, or to the host culture—and begins to take on a more fluid intercultural identity.

Such an intercultural identity is likely to have the cognitive, affective, and behavioral flexibility to adapt to the situation and to creatively manage or avoid conflicts that could result from inappropriate switching between cultures. As pointed out earlier, the cross-cultural adaptation experiences of strangers contribute to the expansion of their internal capacity beyond the cultural parameters of the original culture. Through the dynamic and continuous process of stress-adaptation-transformation, strangers' internal conditions gradually transform toward becoming increasingly intercultural.

So far in this chapter, the process and outcomes of cross-cultural adaptation has been theoretically based on the General Systems perspective, focusing on strangers' communication experiences. The adaptation process has been described as a communication process in which strangers learn and acquire dominant communication patterns of the host society. Just as native-born individuals acquire their cultural communication patterns through interaction with their significant others, strangers acquire the cultural communication patterns of the host society and develop relationships with the new social environment through communication. Influencing this communication-adaptation process are the adaptive predisposition of strangers and the characteristics of the host environment. Three aspects of strangers' adaptive change—increased functional fitness, psychological health, and intercultural identity—have been identified as direct consequences of prolonged communication-adaptation experiences in the host society. These theoretical principles of the process and outcome of cross-cultural adaptation can be summarised into the axioms shown below.

Axioms

Axiom 1: Cross-cultural adaptation occurs in and through communication.

Axiom 2: Cross-cultural adaptation necessitates at least a minimum level of acculturation of the host culture and a minimum level of deculturation of the childhood culture.

Axiom 3: Individuals continually undergo the internal dynamics of stress-adaptation-growth *vis-a-vis* the host environment, maintaining their overall integrity.

Axiom 4: Host communication competence and host social (interpersonal, mass) communication interactively and collectively facilitate cross-cultural adaptation.

Axiom 5: Ethnic social (interpersonal, mass) communication indirectly facilitates the initial short-term cross-cultural adaptation, compensating for the lack of host communication competence and host social (interpersonal, mass) communication.

Axiom 6: Ethnic (interpersonal, mass) communication indirectly deters the subsequent cross-cultural adaptation by discouraging the long-term development of host communication competence and host social (interpersonal, mass) communication.

Axiom 7: Receptivity and conformity pressure of the host environment facilitates the development of host communication competence and host social (interpersonal, mass) communication.

Axiom 8: Adaptive predisposition facilitates the development of host communication competence and host social (interpersonal, mass) communication.

Axiom 9: Achieved outcomes of cross-cultural adaptation experiences at a given time include increased functional fitness, psychological health, and intercultural identity.

Axiom 10: The increased functional fitness, psychological health, and intercultural identity, in turn, facilitate subsequent development of host communication competence and host social (interpersonal, mass) communication.

Notes

1. Adapted and abridged from *Communication and Cross-Cultural Adaptation: An Integrative Theory*, Young Yun Kim, 1991.
2. Young Yun Kim is a professor of Communication at the University of Oklahoma. Her research activities mainly address two issues: (a) the role of communication in the cross-cultural adaptation process of immigrants; (b) the nature of behavior-context interface in interethnic and interracial communication.

Questions for Discussion

1. Overseas Chinese are generally respected and appreciated in the recipient cultures for their hard-working and peace-loving traits. Find out other characteristics they possess, say, in countries such as Malaysia, France, Britain, Australia and America.
2. According to stress-adaptation-growth dynamics, do you think the more stress people have in the host culture, the easier adaptation process there will be for them to go through?
3. Besides one's own culture, what other factors do you think influence a person's adaptation to the host culture?

4. To what extent do the personal communication and the social communication interact with each other?
5. As active intercultural communicators, how do we cultivate people's multi-cultural communication competence?

Online Mini-Case Studies and Viewpoints-Sharing

John Yelled Madly Before His Students

John is a Canadian exchange teacher with an M. S. in computer programming. Last semester he came to XYZ Machinery Building College to teach English. He won his students over and became popular with his colleagues soon. At the weekends by the end of the semester, he was asked to have some video taken while he was teaching in the sound lab so that the school's virtual campus could show some footage of vivid cultural exchange activities in it. John arrived in the lab as scheduled and his students got there even earlier but the school master and the video-shooting team were still out of sight. John and his class had to wait. Ten minutes had passed but no soul turned up. John looked a little bit impatient, so he sat back in a leather chair, rocking back and forth. Suddenly, the chair tore apart noisily, bounding John to the floor, which made all the students burst into laughing. Obviously, John got annoyed, yelling some dirty words, and picked the shattered object and threw it into a corner yards away under the window. At that very moment, the school head, the video-man and the beautiful anchor invited from a local TV station appeared at the door. All was in a terrible mess on the floor. John strode away from the lab, face thoroughly crimson, leaving the leaders and their distinguished guests and stunned students there in confusion. The planned video shooting was undone at all.

Online Research

Search online the possible causes of the conflict from the cultural perspective and tell how you would deal with the incident if you worked as a cultural mediator for the two sides and justify your resolution.

Reading Two

Introductory Remarks

If we concur with William Shakespeare that the world is a stage with actors and actresses, we must admit that these actors and actresses come from different cultures and they need to coordinate their scripts and actions in order to achieve their goals. It is, therefore, imperative for more significance to be attached to intercultural communication skills because the world has become more multi-cultural than ever before.

This article states first that intercultural communication is a complex and challenging activity. Intercultural competence, although attainable in varying degrees, will elude many people in at least some intercultural interactions. However, the discovery of something new would bring people joy and excitement when they interact with others from different cultures. Following that, the article addresses the basics of intercultural competence which include the display of respect, orientation of knowledge, empathy, and tolerance for ambiguity. The rest of the article discusses such factors as assimilation, integration, seclusion, and marginalization or hostility, which determine the outcome of communication.

The Potential for Intercultural Competence[1]

William B. Gudykunst[2]

Basic Tools for Improving Intercultural Competence

In the preceding chapters we have described how various aspects of culture affect interpersonal communication. We have suggested some ways for you to increase your intercultural competence by using your knowledge, motivation, and skills to deal appropriately and effectively with adherences in cultural patterns, verbal codes, nonverbal codes, and the developmental differences in interpersonal relationships. We now offer two additional tools to overcome some of the obstacles described in the previous chapter. These tools will help you improve your code usage and will facilitate the development of intercultural relationships.

The Basics of Intercultural Competence

The Behavioral Assessment Scale for Intercultural Competence (BASIC), which was developed by Jolene Koester and Margaret Olebe, is based on work done originally by Brent Ruben and his colleagues. A very simple idea provides the key to understanding how to use these BASIC skills:

Display of respect	The ability to show respect and positive regard for another person
Orientation to knowledge	The terms people use to explain themselves and the world around them
Empathy	The capacity to behave as though one understand the world as others do
Interaction management	Skill in regulating conversations
Task role behavior	Behaviors that involve the initiation of ideas related to group problem-solving activities
Relational role behavior	Behaviors associated with interpersonal harmony and mediation
Tolerance for ambiguity	The ability to react to new and ambiguous situations with little visible discomfort
Interaction posture	The ability to respond to others in descriptive, non-evaluative and nonjudgmental ways

What you actually do, rather than your internalized attitudes or your projections of what you might do, is what others use to determine if you are interculturally competent. The BASIC skills are a tool for examining the communication behaviors of people—yourself included—and in so doing provide a guide to the very basics of intercultural competence.

Eight categories of communication behavior are described in the BASIC instrument, each of which contributes to the achievement of intercultural competence (see the above Table). As each of the categories is described, mentally assess your own ability to communicate. Do you display the behaviors necessary to achieve intercultural competence? From what you now know about intercultural communication, what kinds of changes might make your behavior more appropriate and effective?

Before we describe each of the BASIC skills, we would like to emphasize that the BASIC descriptions of behaviors are culture-general. That is, in most cultures the types of behaviors that are described are used by their members to make judgments of competence. But within each culture there may be, and in all likelihood will be, different ways of exhibiting these behaviors.

Display of Respect   Although the need to display respect for others is a culture-general concept, within every culture there are specific ways to show respect and there are specific expectations about those to whom respect should be shown. What stands for respect in one culture, then, will not necessarily be so regarded in another culture.

Respect is shown through both verbal and nonverbal symbols. Language that can be interpreted as expressing concern, interest, and an understanding of others will often convey respect, as will formality in one's language, including the use of titles, the absence of jargon, and an increased attention to politeness rituals. Nonverbal displays of respect include showing attentiveness through the position of the body, facial expressions, and the use of eye contact in prescribed ways. A tone of voice that conveys interest in the other person is another vehicle by which respect is shown. The action of displaying respect increases the likelihood of a judgment of competence.

Orientation to Knowledge   Orientation to knowledge refers to the terms people use to explain themselves and the world around them. A competent orientation to knowledge occurs when people's actions demonstrate that all experiences and interpretations are individual and personal rather than universally shared by others.

Many actions exhibit people's orientation to knowledge, including the specific words that they use. Among Euro-Americans, for instance, declarative statements that express personal attitudes or opinions as facts and an absence of qualifiers or modifiers show an ineffective orientation to knowledge:

- "New Yorkers must be crazy to live in that city."
- "Parisians are rude and unfriendly."
- "The custom of arranged marriages is barbaric."
- "Every person wants to succeed—it's human nature."

In contrast, a competent intercultural communicator acknowledges a personal orientation to knowledge, as illustrated in the following examples:

- "I find New York a very difficult place to visit and would not want to live there."
- "Many of the people I interacted with when visiting Paris were not friendly or courteous to me."
- "I would not want my parents to arrange my marriage for me."
- "I want to succeed at what I do and I think most people do."

At least some of the time, all people have an orientation to knowledge that is not conducive to intercultural competence. In learning a culture, people develop beliefs about the "rightness" of a particular way of seeing events, behaviors, and people. It is actually very natural to think, and then to behave, as if your personal knowledge and experiences are universal. Intercultural competence, however, requires an ability to move beyond the perspective of your cultural framework.

Empathy Those individuals who are able to communicate an awareness of another person's thoughts, feelings, and experiences are regarded as more competent in intercultural interactions. Alternatively, those who lack empathy, and who therefore indicate little or no awareness of even the most obvious feelings and thoughts of others, will not be perceived as competent. Empathetic behaviors include verbal statements that identify the experiences of others and nonverbal codes that are complementary to the moods and thoughts of others.

It is necessary to make an important distinction here. Empathy does not mean "putting yourself in the shoes of another." It is both physically and psychologically impossible to do so. However, it is possible for people to be sufficiently interested and aware of others that they appear to be putting themselves in others' shoes. The skill we are describing here is the capacity to behave as if one understands the world as others do. Of course, empathy is not just responding to the tears and smiles of others, which may, in fact, mean something very different than your cultural interpretations would suggest. Although empathy does involve responding to the emotional context of another person's experiences, tears and smiles are often poor indicators of emotional states.

Interaction Management Some individuals are skilled at starting and ending interactions among participants and at taking turns and maintaining a discussion. These management skills are important because through them all participants in an interaction are able, as appropriate, to speak and contribute. In contrast, dominating a conversation or being non-responsive to the interaction is detrimental to competence. Continuing to engage people in conversation long after they have begun to display signs of disinterest and boredom, or ending conversations abruptly may also pose problems.

Interaction management skills require knowing how to indicate turn-taking both verbally and nonverbally.

Task Role Behavior Because intercultural communication often takes place where individuals are focused on work-related purposes, appropriate task-related role behaviors are very important. Task role behaviors are those that contribute to the group's problem-solving activities, for example, initiating new ideas, requesting further information or facts, seeking clarification of group tasks, evaluating the suggestions of others, and keeping a group on task. The difficulty in this important category is the display of culturally appropriate behaviors. The key is to recognize the strong link to a culture's underlying patterns and to be willing to acknowledge that tasks are accomplished by cultures in multiple ways. Task behaviors are so intimately entwined with cultural expectations about activity and work that it is often difficult to respond appropriately to task expectations that differ from one's own. What one culture defines as a social activity, another may define as a task. For example, socializing at a restaurant or a bar may be seen as a necessary prelude to the conduct of a business negotiation. Sometimes that socializing is expected to occur over many hours or days, which surprises and dismays many Euro-Americans, who believe that "doing business" is something separate from socializing.

Relational Role Behavior Relational role behaviors concern efforts to build or maintain personal relationships with group members. These behaviors may include verbal and nonverbal messages that demonstrate support for others and that help to solidify feelings of participation. Examples of competent relational role behaviors include harmonizing and mediating conflicts between group members, encouraging participation from others, general displays of interest, and a willingness to compromise one's position for the sake of others.

Tolerance for Ambiguity Tolerance for ambiguity concerns a person's responses to new, uncertain, and unpredictable intercultural encounters. Some people react to new situations with greater comfort than others. Some are extremely nervous, highly frustrated, or even hostile toward the new situations and those who may be present in them. Those who do not tolerate ambiguity well may respond to new and unpredictable situations with hostility, anger, shouting, sarcasm, withdrawal, or abruptness.

Others view new situations as a challenge; they seem to do well whenever the unexpected or unpredictable occurs, and they quickly adapt to the demands of changing environments. Competent intercultural communicators are able to cope with the nervousness and frustrations that accompany new or, unclear situations, and they are able to adapt quickly to changing demands.

Interaction Posture Interaction posture refers to the ability to respond to others in a way that is descriptive, non-evaluative, and non judgmental. Although the specific verbal and nonverbal messages that express judgments and evaluations can vary from culture to culture, the importance of selecting messages that do not convey evaluative judgments does not vary. Statements based on clear judgments of rights and wrongs indicate a closed or predetermined framework of attitudes, beliefs, and values, and they are used by the evaluative, and less competent, intercultural communicator. Non-evaluative and nonjudgmental actions are characterized by verbal and nonverbal messages based on descriptions rather than on interpretations or evaluations.

Description, Interpretation, and Evaluation

We have approached the study of intercultural competence by looking at the elements of culture that affect interpersonal communication. There is, however, a tool that allows people to control the meanings they attribute to the verbal and nonverbal symbols used by others. The tool is based on the differences in how people think about, and then verbally speak about, the people with whom they interact and the events in which they participate.

The interaction tool is called description, interpretation, and evaluation. It starts with the assumption that, when most people process the information around them, they use shorthand versions of thinking. Because people are taught what symbols mean, they are not very aware of the information they use to form their interpretations. In other words, when people see, hear, and in other ways receive information from the world around them, they generally form evaluations of it without being aware of the specific sensory information they have perceived. For example, students and teachers alike often comment about the sterile, institutional character of many of the classrooms at universities. Rarely do these conversations detail the specific perceptual information on which that interpretation is based. Rarely does someone say, for instance, "This room is about 20 by 40 feet in size, the walls are painted a cream color, there is no artwork on the walls, it is lit by eight fluorescent bulbs, and the floors are cream-colored tiles with multiple pieces of dirt." Yet when students and professors say that their classroom is "sterile, institutional-looking, and unattractive," most people who have spent a great deal of time in such rooms have a fairly accurate image of the classroom. Similarly if a friend is walking toward you, you might say, "Hi! What's wrong? You look really tired and upset." That kind of comment is considered normal, but if you said instead, "Hi! Your shoulders are drooping, you're not standing up straight, and you are walking much slower than usual," it would be considered strange. In both examples, the statements considered to be normal are really interpretations and evaluations of sensory information the individual has processed.

The skill we are introducing trains you to distinguish among statements of description, interpretation, and evaluation. These statements can be made about all characteristics, events, persons, or objects. A statement of description details the specific perceptual cues and information a person has received, without judgments or interpretations—in other words, without being distorted by opinion. A statement of interpretation provides a conjecture or hypothesis about what the perceptual information might mean. A statement of evaluation indicates an emotional or affective judgment about the information.

Often, the interpretations people make of perceptual information are very closely linked to their personal evaluation of that information. Any description can have many different interpretations; but because most people think in a mental shorthand, they are generally aware of only the interpretation that immediately comes to mind, which they use to explain the event. For example, teachers occasionally have students who arrive late to class. A statement of description about a particular student engaging in this behavior might be as follows:

- Kathryn arrived ten minutes after the start of the class.
- Kathryn also arrived late each of the previous times the class has met.

Statements of interpretation, which are designed to explain Kathryn's behavior, might include some of the following:

- Kathryn doesn't care very much about this particular class.
- Kathryn is always late for everything.
- Kathryn has a job on the other side of campus and is scheduled to work until ten minutes before this class. The person who should relieve her has been late, thus not allowing Kathryn to leave to be on time for class.
- Kathryn is new on campus this semester and is misinformed about the starting time for the class.

For each interpretation, the evaluation can vary. If the interpretation is Kathryn doesn't care very much about this class, different professors will have differing evaluations:

- I am really offended by that attitude.
- I like a student who chooses to be enthusiastic about only classes she really likes.

The interpretation a person selects to explain something like Kathryn's behavior influences the evaluation that is made of that behavior. In people's everyday interactions, the distinctions among description, interpretation, and evaluation are rarely made. Consequently, people deal with their interpretations and evaluations as if they were actually what they saw, heard, and experienced.

The purpose of making descriptive statements when you are communicating interculturally is that they allow you to identify the sensory information that forms the basis of your interpretations and evaluations. Descriptive statements also allow you to consider alternative hypotheses or interpretations. Interpretations, although highly personal, are very much affected by underlying cultural patterns. Sometimes when you engage in intercultural communication with specific persons or groups of people for an extended period of time, you will be able to test the various interpretations of behavior that you are considering. By testing the alternative interpretations, it is also possible to forestall the evaluations that can negatively affect your interactions. Consider the following situation, and notice how differences among description, interpretation, and evaluation affect the intercultural competence of John:

> John Richardson has been sent by his U.S.-based insurance company to discuss, and possibly to sell, his company's products to an Argentinian company that has expressed great interest in them. His secretary has set up four appointments with key company officials. John arrives promptly at his first appointment, identifies himself to the receptionist, and is asked to be seated. Some 30 minutes later he is ushered into the offices of the company official, who has one of his employees in the office with whom he is discussing another issue. John is brought into the office of his second appointment within a shorter period of time, but the conversation is constantly disrupted by telephone calls and drop-in visits from others. At the end of the day, John is very discouraged; he calls the home office and says, "This is a waste of time; these guys aren't interested in our products at all! I was left cooling my heels in their waiting rooms. They couldn't even give me their attention when I got in to see them. There were constant interruptions. I really tried to control myself, but I've had it. I'm getting on a plane and coming back tomorrow."

John would be better off if he approached this culturally puzzling behavior by separating his descriptions, interpretations, and evaluations. By doing so, he might choose very different actions for himself. Descriptive statements might be these:

- My appointments started anywhere from 15 to 30 minutes later than the time I scheduled them.
- The people with whom I had appointments also talked to other company employees when I was in their offices.
- The people with whom I had appointments accepted telephone calls when I

was in their offices.

Interpretations of this sensory information might include the following:

- Company officials were not interested in talking with me or in buying my company's products.
- Company officials had rescheduled my appointments for a different time, but they neglected to tell my secretary about the change.
- In Argentina, attitudes toward time are very different than they are in the United States; although appointments are scheduled for particular times, no one expects that people will be available at precisely that time.
- In Argentina it is an accepted norm of interaction between people who have appointments with each other to allow others to come into the room, either in person or by telephone, to ask their questions or to make their comments.

These interpretations suggest very different evaluations of John's experiences. His frustration with the lack of punctuality and the lack of exclusive focus on him and his ideas may still be a problem even if he selects the correct cultural interpretation, which is that in Argentina time is structured and valued very differently than it is in the United States. But by considering other interpretations, John's evaluations and his actions will be more functional, as he might say the following:

- I don't like waiting around and not meeting according to the schedule I had set, but maybe I can still make this important sale.
- Some of the people here are sure interesting and I am enjoying meeting so many more people than just the four with whom I had scheduled appointments.

The tool of description, interpretation, and evaluation increases your choices for understanding, responding positively, and behaving appropriately with people from different cultures. The simplicity of the tool makes it available in any set of circumstances and may allow the intercultural communicator to suspend judgment long enough to understand the symbols used by the culture involved.

Outcomes of Intercultural Contact

Both fictional and non-fictional accounts of intercultural contacts are replete with references to individual and cultural changes as a consequence. References are made to people who "go native" or who retain their own cultural identity by using only their original language and living in cultural ghettos. During the height of the British Empire in India, for example, many British officials and their families tried to re-create the British lifestyle in India, in a climate not conducive to tuxedos and fancy dresses, with layers and layers of slips and decorative fabrics. References are also made to those who seem to adjust or adapt to life in the new culture. Alternatively, the culture itself might change because of the influences of people from other cultures. The French, for example, have raised concerns about the effects of the English language on their own language and culture. Traditional societies have sometimes expressed this distress about the Westernization or urbanization of their cultures. We now turn to these two broad outcomes of intercultural communication: outcomes for people and outcomes for cultures.

Outcomes for People

It is generally accepted that intercultural communication creates stress for most individuals. In intercultural communication, the certainty of one's own cultural framework is gone, and there is a great deal of uncertainty about what other code systems mean. Individuals who have engaged in intercultural contacts for extended periods of time will respond to the stress in different ways.

Most will find themselves incorporating at least some behaviors from the new culture into their own repertoire. Some take on the characteristics, the norms, and even the values and beliefs of another culture willingly and easily others resist the new culture and retain their old ways, sometimes choosing to spend time in enclaves populated only by others like themselves. Still others simply find the problems of adapting to a new culture intolerably, and they leave if they can.

People's reactions may also change over time. That is, the initial reactions of acceptance or rejection often shift as increased intercultural contacts produce different kinds of outcomes. Such changes in the way people react to intercultural contacts are called acculturation.

The Acculturation Process Words such as *acculturation*, *assimilation*, *adjustment*, *adaptation*, and even coping are used to describe how individuals respond to their experiences in other cultures. Many of these terms refer to how people from one culture react to prolonged contact with those from another. Over the years, different emotional overtones have been attached to these terms. To some people, for instance, *assimilation* is a negative outcome to others it is positive. Some consider adjustment to be "good," whereas for others it is "bad."

We offer an approach that allows you, the reader, to make your own value judgment about what constitutes the right kind of outcome. We believe that a competent adjustment to another culture will vary greatly from situation to situation and from personal value to personal value. We will use the broader term of acculturation to characterize these adjustments because it subsumes various forms of cultural or individual adaptations.

Definition of Acculturation Acculturation, "culture change that results from continuous, firsthand contact between two distinct cultural groups," occurs both for individuals and for groups. When it occurs for individuals, it is called psychological acculturation, or the process by which individuals change their psychological characteristics, change the surrounding context, or change the amount of contact in order to achieve a better fit outcome with other features of the system in which they carry out their life.

Note that this definition suggests that when individuals acculturate they learn how to "fit" themselves into the situation. Again remember that different individuals and different groups will make the fit in different ways.

The process of acculturation includes changes that are physical, biological, and social. Physical changes occur because people are confronted with new physical stimuli—they eat different food, drink different water, live in different climates, and reside in different/kinds of housing. When people are exposed to a new culture, they may undergo actual physical changes, or biological changes. People deal with new viruses and bacteria; new foods cause new reactions and perhaps even new allergies. Prolonged contact between groups results in intermarriage, and the children of these marriages are born with a mixture of the genetic features of the people involved. Social relationships change with the introduction of new people. Outgroups may become bonded with the in-groups, for example, in opposition to the new out-group members. Changes also cause individuals to define themselves in new and different ways.

Forms of Acculturation Answers to two important questions shape the response of individuals and groups to prolonged intercultural contact, thus producing different acculturation outcomes. The first issue is whether it is considered important to maintain one's cultural identity and to display its characteristics. The second question centers on whether people believe it is important to maintain relationships with the out-groups. Assimilation occurs when it is deemed relatively unimportant to maintain one's original cultural identity but it is important to establish and maintain relationships with other cultures. The metaphor of the United States as a melting pot, which envisions many cultures giving up their individual characteristics to build the new homogenized cultural identity of the United States, illustrates the choice described in what is known as assimilation. Assimilation means taking on the new culture's beliefs, values, and norms.

When an individual or group retains its original cultural identity but also seeks to maintain harmonious relationships with other cultures, integration occurs. Countries like Switzerland, Belgium, and Canada, with their multilingual and multicultural populations, are good examples. Integration produces distinguishable cultural groups that work cooperatively to ensure that the society and the individuals continue to function well. Both integration and assimilation promote harmony and they result in an appropriate fit of individuals and groups to the larger culture.

When individuals or groups do not want to maintain positive relationships with members of other groups, the outcomes are starkly different. If, a culture does not want positive relationships with another culture and if it also wishes terrain its cultural characteristics, separation may result. If the separation occurs because the more politically and economically powerful culture does not want the intercultural contact, the result of the forced separation is called segregation. The history of the United States can provide numerous examples of segregation in its treatment of African-Americans. If, however, a non-dominant group chooses not to participate in the society in order to retain its own way of life, the separation is called *seclusion*. The Amish are a good example of this choice.

When individuals or groups neither retain their cultural heritage nor maintain positive contacts with the other groups, marginalization occurs. This form of acculturation is characterized by confusion and alienation. The choices of marginalization and separation are reactions against other cultures. The fit these outcomes achieve in the acculturation process is based on battling against, rather than working with, the other cultures in the environment. Many Euro-American women, whose actions arc based on the values of freedom and equality may find it difficult to respond positively to the Saudi Arabian cultural practices that require women to wear veils in public and to use male drivers or chaperones. The ethical dilemma that intercultural communicators face is the decision about how far to go in adapting their behaviors to another culture. Should people engage in behaviors that they regard as personally wrong or difficult? At what point do people lose their own sense of self, their cultural identities, and their moral integrity? One of the challenges and delights of intercultural communication is in discovering the boundaries and touchstones of one's own moral perspective while simultaneously learning to display respect for other ways of dealing with human problems.

Another perspective from which to explore the ethical issues embedded in the adage is that of the "Romans." A common point of view, often expressed by U.S. Americans about those who have recently immigrated to the United States or who still retain many of the underlying patterns of their own culture, is that since these people now live in the United States, they should adapt to its cultural ways. The same comments are often made about students from other countries who come to the United States to study.

We ask you to consider the experiences of those people who immigrate to or study in another country. Perhaps you are such a person. Or perhaps your parents or grandparents did so. Not all immigrants or students have so freely chosen the country where they now reside. Large numbers of people migrate from one country to another because of political, military and economic upheavals in their own country, which makes living and learning there nearly impossible. For many, the choice to leave is juxtaposed against a choice to die, to starve, or to be politically censored. We also ask you to consider how difficult it must be for people to give up their culture. Remember how fundamental one's cultural framework is, how it provides the logic for one's behavior and view of the world. How easy would it be for you if you were forced into new modes of behavior? Assimilation into another culture is not without its difficulties.

Are Cultural Values Relative or Universal?
A second ethical issue confronting the intercultural communicator is whether it is ever acceptable to judge the people of a culture when their behaviors are based on a radically different set of beliefs, values, and norms. Are there any values that transcend the boundaries of cultural differences? Are there any universally right or wrong values?

A culturally relativistic point of view suggests that every culture has its own set of values and that, judgments can be made only within the context of the particular culture. Most people do not completely subscribe to this view, partly because it would lead to individuals who lack any firm beliefs and values on which to build a sense of self-identity.

David Kale argues that there are two values that transcend all cultures. First, the human spirit, requires that all people must struggle to improve their world and to maintain their own sense of dignity, always within the context of their own particular culture. Thus Kale suggests that the "guiding principle of any universal code of intercultural communication, therefore, should be to protect the worth and dignity of the human spirit." The second universal value is a world at peace. Thus, all ethical codes must recognize the importance of working toward a world in which people can live at peace with themselves and with one another.

Ethical intercultural communicators continually struggle with the dilemmas presented by differences in cultural values. The tensions inherent in seeking to be tolerant of differences while simultaneously holding firm to one's own critical cultural values must always be reconciled. Kale's suggestions for ethical building blocks in responding to cultural differences in values are excellent starting points for the internal "dialogue that all competent intercultural communicators must" conduct.

Do the Ends Justify the Means?
The final ethical dilemma we wish to raise concerns this question: Should all intercultural contacts be encouraged? Are the outcomes of intercultural contacts positive? Are all circumstances appropriate for intercultural contact? In short, do the ends justify the means?

We have been shamelessly enthusiastic about the potential benefits and delights of intercultural interaction. Nevertheless, certain outcomes may not necessarily be justified by the means used to obtain them. Tourism, for example, can sometimes create an ethical dilemma. Although it often provides economic benefits for those living in the tourist destination and allows people from one culture to learn about another it can also produce serious negative consequences. In some popular tourist destinations, for instance, the tourists actually outnumber the native population, and tourists may consume natural resources at a greater rate than they can be naturally replaced.

Some of the following questions must be confronted:
- Is it ethical to go to another country for whatever reason, if you are naive and unprepared for cultural contact?
- Should intercultural contacts be encouraged for those who speak no language but their own?
- Should those who are prejudiced seek out intercultural contacts?
- Is it ethical to send missionaries to other countries?
- Is it acceptable to provide medical assistance to help a culture resist a disease, when in providing the assistance the very infrastructure and nature of the indigenous culture may be destroyed?
- Is it justifiable for the sojourner from one culture to encourage a person from another culture to disregard his or her own cultural values?

There are no simple answers to any of these questions, but the competent intercultural communicator must confront the ethical dilemmas posed within them.

Ethic—Your Choices

We have offered few specific answers to these ethical dilemmas because every person must provide his or her own response. In the context of your own experiences and your own intercultural interactions, therefore, you must resolve the ethical dilemmas that will inevitably occur in your life. Kale provides four principles to guide you as you develop your own personal code of ethics. Ethical communicators should:

- Address people of other cultures with the same respect that they would like to receive themselves
- Try to describe the world as they perceive it as accurately as possible.
- Encourage people of other culture to express themselves in their unique natures.
- Strive for identification with people of other cultures.

In brief, two tools can be used to improve intercultural competence. The first is provided in the culture-general concepts of the Behavioral Assessment Scale for Intercultural Competence (BASIC). Such concepts include the ability to display respect, a recognition that knowledge is personal rather than universal, an empathic sense about the experiences of others that results in behaviors appropriate to those experiences, the ability to manage interactions with others, skills in enacting appropriate task and relational role behaviors, the capacity to tolerate uncertainty without anxiety, and a non-evaluative posture toward the beliefs and actions of others. Within each culture there will be culturally specific ways of behaving that are used to demonstrate these culturally general competencies.

The second tool is to distinguish among the techniques of description, interpretation, and evaluation. This tool encourages communicators to describe the sensory information received and then to construct alternative interpretations about their perceptions by making correspondingly different evaluations.

When one cultural group lives near other cultural groups, various forms of acculturation occur. The desire to maintain both an identification with the culture of origin and positive relationships with other cultures influence the type of acculturation that is experienced. Intercultural transformation occurs when people are able to move beyond the limits of their own cultural experiences to incorporate the perspectives of other cultures into their own interpersonal interactions.

Ethical issues in the development of intercultural competence concern questions about whose responsibility it is to adjust to a different culture, issues about right and wrong, and the degree to which all intercultural contacts should be encouraged.

Notes

1. Adapted and abridged from *Assessment of Intercultural Communication*, 1996.
2. Wiliam B. Gudykunst is a professor of speech communication at California State University, Fullerton. Among his works *Bridging Differences* and *Communication in Personal Relationships Across Cultures* are highly recommended readers.

Questions for Discussion

1. Tell the differences among assimilation, integration, seclusion and marginalization using the representative people you are familiar with.
2. We, Chinese, the peace-loving people of the human community constantly suggest that dialogues of various forms and at levels be conducted to address intercultural disagreements, political confrontations, and even religious conflicts. In what sense do you think dialogues should be the first choice for nations and organizations to ease tension and regain peace?
3. What do you think about the ethical issues in the development of ICC?
4. As empathy can never be realized, why should we encourage ourselves to perceive the world the way others do?
5. Talk about the culturally-bound obstacles the Chinese often encounter when interacting with people from other countries.

Online Mini-Case Studies and Viewpoints-Sharing

The Teaching Secretary's Message to Dr. Hounslow

Miss Chuang, the secretary of the School of Physics, XYZ Electronics Engineering College, was notified by the president's office of the College that the lecture hall in the administrative building would be used for an important conference on inter-collegiate logistics the coming Friday. The participants would be from 30 higher learning institutions in the Province. Chuang knew it clearly that the decision by the school's immediate superior department cannot be changed easily, so she composed an email of explanation and sent it to the British visiting scholar Robert Hounslow (Phd. in Human Geography) at once. The email reads like this:

Dear Dr. Robert,

   Your Friday afternoon's lecture has been postponed till 2:00 p.m. next Monday. The venue remains unchanged.

   Please be punctual and I will be waiting for you at the hall gate then.

   Give my best regards to your wife and your kids and wish you a happy weekend.

Xiao Chuang, the secretary of teaching affairs

Online Research

Share on the Moments your specific comments and correct any pragmatic errors and cultural blunders.

Unit Eleven

Theories of Intercultural Communication

Reading One

Introductory Remarks

There are two major approaches to theorizing about intercultural communication: the subjectivist and the objectivist. To the subjectivists, there is no real world external to individuals as the reality is socially reconstructed. Thus, they try to understand individual communicators' perspectives and view communication as a function of free will. Objectivists, in contrast, see a real world external to individuals and expect to study the reality in a scientific way. Looking for regularities in human behavior, they see communication as determined by situations and environments. Gudykunst et al. argue that extreme objectivist or subjectivist perspectives are not defensible. They argue that both approaches are necessary to understand intercultural communication, and that the ideal is eventually to integrate the two perspectives.

In this article, Gudykunst et al. present a very comprehensive overview of both the subjectivistic and objectivistic theories in intercultural communication, with the intention to put the theories in context. By understanding the variability in the approaches used to construct theories, readers will be in a good position to understand and question the choices the theorists make. The authors have divided the relevant theories into seven categories that are not necessarily mutually exclusive: (1) theories that integrate culture with communication processes, (2) theories explaining cultural variability in communication, (3) intergroup/intercultural theories focusing on effective outcomes, (4) intergroup/intercultural theories focusing on accommodation or adaptation, (5) intergroup or intercultural theories focusing on identity management or negotiation, (6) intergroup/intercultural theories focusing on communication networks, and (7) intercultural theories focusing on acculturation or adjustment. Although both subjectivistic and objectivistic theories are included, the majority of the theories that have been developed are objectivistic.

At the end of the article, the authors hope that there will be more subjectivistic theorizing about intercultural communication and there is the need for integrating subjectivistic and objectivistic theories. Furthermore, the authors also note the lack of theories from outside the United States and call for indigenous theories developed by scholars outside the United States.

Theorizing about Intercultural Communication: An Introduction[1]

William B. Gudykunst, Carmen M. Lee, Tsukasa Nishida, Naoto Ogawa

Theorizing about intercultural communication has made tremendous progress in the last 20 years. When two of the authors (Gudykunst and Nishida) completed their doctorates, there were no theories of intercultural communication[2]. Initial attempts to theorize about interpersonal communication between people from different cultures were included in the first thematic volume of the *International and Intercultural Communication Annual* published by Sage. By the time the second volume of the *Annual* on theory was published, theorizing had increased in sophistication and there were theories supported by lines of research. There was another leap in the quality of theorizing when the most recent volume of the Annual on theory was published.

There are several approaches to incorporating culture into communication theories. First, culture can be integrated with the communication process in theories of communication (e. g. , Applegate & Sypher, 1983, 1988, integrate culture into constructivist theory; Cronen, Chen, & Pearce, 1988, integrate culture into coordinated management of meaning theory; cultural communication, Philipsen, Coutu, and Covarrubias, 1992). In other words, culture is linked to communication within the theory. Second, theories can be designed to describe or explain how communication varies across cultures[3]. Third, theories can be generated to describe or explain communication between people from different cultures. By far, the most theorizing exists in the third category.

Many of the theorists who attempt to describe or explain communication between members of different cultures focus on intergroup communication generally rather than intercultural communication specifically. Theorists using an intergroup approach tend to assume that culture is one of the many group memberships influencing communication. These theorists also tend to assume that the processes occurring in intercultural, interethnic, and intergenerational communication, among others, are similar. We divide the intergroup and intercultural theories into five categories that are not mutually exclusive: theories focusing on effective outcomes, theories focusing on accommodation and adaptation, theories focusing on identity management, theories focusing on communication networks, and theories focusing on adjustment and adaptation to new cultural environments.

Whatever the approach that is used to develop theories, the theories are based upon a set of metatheoretical assumptions. Gudykunst and Nishida use Burrell and Morgan's distinction between objectivist and subjectivist approaches to theory (see Table 1) to compare theories in intercultural communication. Objectivists, for example, see a "real world" external to individuals, look for regularities in behavior, and see communication as "determined" by situations and environments. Subjectivists, in contrast, contend that there is no "real world" external to individuals, try to understand individual communicators' perspectives, and view communication as a function of "free will." Gudykunst and Nishida contend that extreme objectivist or subjectivist perspectives are not defensible. They argue that both approaches are necessary to understand intercultural communication, and that the ideal is eventually to integrate the two perspectives.

Table 1   Assumptions About Theory

Subjective Approach (Human Action/Interaction)	Objectivist Approach (Causal Process)
ONTOLOGY	
Nominalism: There is no "real" world external to individual; "names," "concepts," and "labels" are artificial and are used to construct reality.	Realism: There is a "real" world external to individual; things exist, even if they are not perceived and labeled.
EPISTEMOLOGY	
Antipositivism: Communication can be understood only from the perspective of the individuals communicating; no search for underlying regulations.	Positivism: Attempts to explain and predict patterns of communication by looking for regularities and/or causal relationships.
HUMAN NATURE	
Voluntarism: Communicators are completely "autonomous" and have "free will."	Determinism: Communication is "determined" by the situation, environment in which it occurs or by individuals' traits.
METHODOLOGY	
Ideographic: To understand communication, "firsthand" knowledge must be obtained; analysis of subjective accounts.	Nomothetic: Research should be based on systematic protocols and "scientific" rigor.

The goals of theories in the objectivist and subjectivist perspectives tend to be different. Objectivists, for example, argue that theories should explain and predict the phenomena under study. Subjectivists, however, argue that theories should describe the phenomena under study. Both types of theorists might agree that theories should be heuristic; that is, they should generate future research. When evaluating theories, we must grant the theorists' assumptions and examine the theories for logical consistency and heuristic value. Theories rarely are designed to describe or explain the same thing. Unless they are, they are not directly comparable.

It is important to understand the metatheoretical assumptions that theorists make. The theoretical propositions in theories should be logically consistent with the metatheoretical assumptions on which the theories are based. The methods used to test theories also should be consistent with the metatheoretical assumptions. We can question a theory's metatheoretical assumptions, but when we evaluate the theory we must grant the assumptions and not impose other metatheoretical assumptions in our critiques.

In evaluating theories, we also need to look at logical consistency. Are the metatheoretical assumptions and the theoretical statements logically consistent? Are the theoretical statements logically consistent with each other? We also must pay attention to scope and boundary conditions that theorists specify when we evaluate their theories. Do theorists, for example, limit their theories to certain types of situations (e.g., initial interactions between strangers)?

If theorists limit their theories to initial interactions, then data in romantic relationships that are inconsistent with the theory do *not* call the theory into question. Theories should not be criticized because they do not explain something beyond the scope theorists specify for their theories. Theorists may limit complete theories to specific conditions or limit certain theoretical claims to only specific conditions. If a theorist claims that a statement holds only for people who feel secure in their identities, then data from respondents who do not feel secure do not test the theoretical claim.

Our purpose in this paper is to overview the theories in intercultural communication. Our goal is to put the theories in context. By understanding the variability in the approaches used to construct theories, readers will be in a good position to understand and question the choices the theorists make. We divide the theories into seven categories that are not necessarily mutually exclusive: (1) theories that integrate culture with communication processes, (2) theories explaining cultural variability in communication, (3) intergroup/intercultural theories focusing on effective outcomes, (4) intergroup/intercultural theories focusing on accommodation or adaptation, (5) intergroup/intercultural theories focusing on identity management or negotiation, (6) intergroup/intercultural theories focusing on communication networks, and (7) intercultural theories focusing on acculturation or adjustment. Both objectivistic and subjectivistic theories are included. The majority of the theories that have been developed, however, are objectivistic. Very few of the theorists attempt to integrate objectivistic and subjectivistic assumptions[4].

Theories in Which Culture and Communication are Integrated

Several theorists have integrated culture with communication processes. We briefly overview the three major approaches: (1) constructivist theory, (2) coordinated management of meaning, and (3) cultural communication.

Constructivist Theory

Applegate and Sypher integrate culture with constructivist theory. They make several assumptions, including that "theory should be interpretive," "dense and detailed accounts of everyday interaction ... are needed," "the focus of study should be the relationship between culture and communication," "value judgments should be made," and "theory and training should be linked closely".

Applegate and Sypher point out that communication occurs when individuals have "a mutually recognized interaction to share, exchange messages" in constructivist theory. This process is goal driven and individuals do what they think will help them accomplish their goals. Applegate and Sypher view complex message behavior (a function of the number of goals and situational factors incorporated in messages) as leading to "person-centered" communication (which involves the degree to which individuals adapt to their interactional partners). Individuals' constructs generate "communication and goal-relevant beliefs" that influence their definition of the situation and guide their "strategic behavior".

Applegate and Sypher believe that "culture defines the logic of communication" and that different cultures emphasize different goals and ways to achieve these goals. They go on to argue that "cultural communication theories specify how to place and organize events within larger contexts of meaning and elaboration". Hong et al. argue that construct activation is a major factor influencing cultural differences in social perception (they also review evidence for a dynamic constructivism approach). Applegate and Sypher conclude that intercultural communication training "should focus on developing flexible and integrative strategic means for accomplishing goals".

Coordinated Management of Meaning

Cronen et al. examine the role of culture in the coordinated management of meaning (CMM). They isolate three goals of CMM: (1) "CMM seeks to understand who we are, what it means to live a life, and how that is related to particular instances of communication", (2) "CMM seeks to render cultures comparable while acknowledging their incommensurability", and (3) "CMM seeks to generate an illuminating critique of cultural practices, including the researcher's own".

Cronen et al. isolate several propositions regarding CMM. To illustrate, they argue that "all communication is both idiosyncratic and social", "human communication is inherently imperfect", "moral orders emerge as aspects of communication", and "diversity is essential to elaboration and transformation through communication".

Cronen et al. propose three corollaries involving culture: "cultures are patterns of coevolving structures and actions", "cultures are polyphonic", and "research activity is part of social practice". They believe that it is necessary to describe the cultural context if we are going to understand communication within cultures and/or across cultures. It also is necessary to understand the individuals' interpretations of their communication.

CMM tends to be viewed as a "rules" theory that is based in U.S. pragmatism. CMM is used to analyze rules that are used as social episodes. The description of the episodes generates "a critical focus" on the situation being described.

Cultural Communication

Philipsen lays out the groundwork of cultural communication. Philipsen argues that:

> The function of communication in cultural communication is to maintain a healthy balance between the forces of individualism and community, to provide a sense of shared identity which nonetheless preserves individual dignity, freedom, and creativity. This function is performed through maintaining equilibrium between the two sub-processes of cultural communication, (1) the creation, and (2) the affirmation, of shared identity.

Cultural communication, therefore, involves the negotiation of cultural codes through communal conversations. Communal conversations are communicative processes through which individuals negotiate how they will "conduct their lives together".

Philipsen proposes speech code theory: a theory of "culturally distinctive codes of communication conduct". Speech code theory posits that communal conversations imply distinctive codes of communication. He suggests that "a speech code refers to a historically enacted, socially constructed system of terms, meanings, premises, and rules pertaining to communicative conduct".

Philipsen isolates two principles of cultural communication. Principle One states that "every communal conversation bears traces of culturally distinctive means and meanings of communicative conduct". Philipsen believes that the notion that members of groups engage in communal conversations is a universal of human life, but that each communal conversation has culture-specific aspects. The second principle of cultural communication is that "communication is a heuristic and performative resource for performing the cultural function in the lives of individuals and communities". The communal function involves "how individuals are to live as members of a community". Communication is "heuristic" because it is through communication that babies and newcomers to the community learn the specific means and meanings in the community. Communication is "performative" because it allows individuals to participate in the communal conversation.

Theories of Cultural Variability in Communication

A few theorists have attempted to explain cross-cultural differences in communication using cultural-level and/or individual-level dimensions. These theories include: face-negotiation theory, conversational constraints theory, and expectancy violations theory. EVT, however, is not a formal theory of cross-cultural communication. Rather, the focus is on cross-cultural variability of a theory designed in the United States. Each of these theories draws on Hofstede's dimensions of cultural variability. We, therefore, provide a brief introduction to these dimensions here.

Hofstede's Dimensions of Cultural Variability

Hofstede isolates four dimensions of cultural variability: individualism-collectivism, low-high uncertainty avoidance, low-high power distance, and masculinity-femininity. Both ends of each dimension exist in all cultures, but one end tends to predominate in a culture. Individual members of cultures learn the predominate tendencies in their cultures to various degrees. It, therefore, is necessary to take both cultural- and individual-level factors into consideration when explaining similarities and differences in communication across cultures.

Individuals' goals are emphasized more than groups' goals in individualistic cultures. Groups' goals, in contrast, take precedence over individuals' goals in collectivistic cultures. In individualistic cultures, "people are supposed to look after themselves and their immediate family only," and in collectivistic cultures, "people belong to in-groups or collectivities which are supposed to look after them in exchange for loyalty".

Triandis argues that the relative importance of in-groups is the major factor that differentiates individualistic and collectivistic cultures. Ingroups are groups that are important to their members and groups for which individuals will make sacrifices. Members of individualistic cultures have many specific in-groups that might influence their behavior in any particular social situation. Since there are many in-groups, specific in-groups exert relatively little influence on individuals' behavior. Members of collectivistic cultures have only a few general in-groups that influence their behavior across situations.

Cultural individualism-collectivism influences communication in a culture through the cultural norms and rules associated with the major cultural tendency (e.g., the U.S. tends to have individualistic norms/rules, Asian cultures tend to have collectivistic norms/rules). Cultural individualism-collectivism also indirectly influences communication through the characteristics individuals learn when they are socialized. There are at least three characteristics of individuals that mediate the influence of cultural individualism-collectivism on communication: their personalities, their individual values, and their self construals.

Individualism-collectivism provides an explanatory framework for understanding cultural similarities and differences in self-in-group behavior. Hall's differentiation between low- and high-context communication can be used to explain cultural differences in communication. High-context communication occurs when "most of the information is either in the physical context or internalized in the person, while very little is in the coded, explicit, transmitted part of the message". Low-context communication, in contrast, occurs when "the mass of information is vested in the explicit code". Low- and high-context communication are used in all cultures. One form, however, tends to predominate. Members of individualistic cultures tend to use low-context communication and communicate in a direct fashion. Members of collectivistic cultures, in contrast, tend to use high-context messages when maintaining in-group harmony is important and communicate in an indirect fashion.

High uncertainty avoidance cultures tend to have clear norms and rules to guide behavior for virtually all situations. Norms and rules in low uncertainty avoidance cultures are not as clear-cut and rigid as those in high uncertainty avoidance cultures. In high uncertainty avoidance cultures, aggressive behavior is acceptable, but individuals prefer to contain aggression by avoiding conflict and competition. There also is a strong desire for consensus in high uncertainty avoidance cultures, and deviant behavior is not acceptable. Tolerance for ambiguity and uncertainty orientation are two individual-level factors that mediate the influence of cultural uncertainty avoidance on communication.

Power distance is "the extent to which the less powerful members of institutions and organizations accept that power is distributed unequally". Members of high power distance cultures accept as part of society (e. g. , superiors consider their subordinates to be different from themselves and vice versa). Members of high power distance cultures see power as a basic factor in society, and stress coercive or referent power. Members of low distance cultures, in contrast, believe power should be used only when it is legitimate and prefer expert or legitimate power. Egalitarianism and social dominance orientation are two individual-level factors that mediate the influence of cultural power distance on communication.

The major differentiation between masculine and feminine cultures is how gender-roles are distributed in a culture.

> *Masculinity* pertains to societies in which social gender roles are clearly distinct (i. e. , men are supposed to be assertive, tough, and focused on material success whereas women are supposed to be more modest, concerned with the quality of life); *femininity* pertains to societies in which social gender roles overlap (i. e. , both men and women are supposed to be modest, tender, and concerned with the quality of life).

Members of cultures high in masculinity value performance, ambition, things, power, and assertiveness. Members of cultures high in femininity value quality of life, service, caring for others, and being nurturing. Psychological sex-roles are individual-level factors that mediate the influence of cultural masculinity-femininity on communication.

Face-Negotiation Theory

Cultural norms and values influence and shape how members of cultures manage face and how they manage conflict situations. Originally a theory focusing on conflict, face-negotiation theory (FNT) has been expanded to integrate cultural-level dimensions and individual-level attributes to explain face concerns, conflict styles, and facework behaviors.

Ting-Toomey argues that conflict is a face-negotiation process whereby individuals engaged in conflict have their situated identities or "faces" threatened or questioned. Face is "a claimed sense of favorable social self-worth that a person wants others to have of her or him". Although mentioned only briefly in the 1988 version of the theory, the concept of face is an integral part of the most recent version of the theory.

Ting-Toomey and Kurogi argue that members of collectivistic cultures use other-oriented face-saving strategies more than members of individualistic cultures. Conversely, members of individualistic cultures use more self-oriented face-saving strategies more than members of collectivistic cultures. Members of low power distance cultures defend and assert their personal rights more than members of high power distance cultures. Members of high power distance cultures, in contrast, perform their ascribed duties responsibly more than members of low power distance cultures. Members of low power distance cultures tend to minimize the respect-deference distance via information-based interactions more than members of high power distance cultures. Members of high power distance cultures are concerned with vertical facework interactions more than members of low power distance cultures.

Ting-Toomey and Kurogi contend that members of collectivistic cultures use relational, process-oriented conflict strategies more than members of individualistic cultures. Members of individualistic cultures, in contrast, tend to use more substantive, outcome-oriented conflict strategies than members of collectivistic cultures. High-status members of high power distance cultures tend to use verbally indirect facework strategies more than low-status members of high power distance cultures. High-status members of low power distance cultures tend to use verbally direct strategies more than high-status members of high power distance cultures.

Ting-Toomey and Kurogi also link individual-level mediators of the dimensions of cultural variability to face behaviors and conflict styles. Emphasizing self-face leads to using dominating/competing conflict styles and substantive conflict resolution modes. Emphasizing other-face leads to using avoiding/obliging conflict styles and relational conflict resolution modes. Independent self construal types tend to use dominating/competing conflict styles and substantive conflict resolution modes. Interdependent self construal types tend to use avoiding/obliging conflict styles and relational conflict resolution modes. Biconstrual types (high on both self construals) use substantive and relational conflict resolution modes, and ambivalent types (low on both self construals) tend not to use either.

Conversational Constraints Theory

Conversations are goal-directed and require coordination between communicators in CCT isolates two types of conversational constraints: social-relational and task-oriented. Social-relational constraints emphasize concern for others that focuses on avoiding hurting hearers' feelings and minimizing imposition on hearers. The task-oriented constraint emphasizes a concern for clarity (e.g., the degree to which the intentions of messages are communicated explicitly).

Kim explains cross-cultural differences in the selection of communicative strategies. Members of collectivistic cultures view face-supporting behavior (e.g., avoiding hurting the hearers' feelings, minimizing imposition, and avoiding negative evaluation by the hearer) as more important than members of individualistic cultures when pursuing goals. Members of individualistic cultures, in contrast, view clarity as more important than members of collectivistic cultures when pursuing goals.

Kim argues that individuals who activate interdependent self construals view not hurting hearers' feelings and minimizing impositions on hearers in the pursuit of their goals as more important than individuals who activate independent self construals. Individuals who activate independent self construals view clarity as more important in pursuing goals than individuals who activate interdependent self construals. Individuals who activate both self construals are concerned with relational and clarity constraints. Kim also argues that the more individuals need approval, the more important they view being concerned with hearers' feelings and minimizing impositions on hearers. The more individuals need to be dominant, the more importance they place on clarity. The more masculine individuals' psychological sex-roles, the more importance they place on clarity. The more feminine individuals' psychological sex-roles, the more importance they place on not hurting hearers' feelings and hearers.

Expectancy Violation Theory

Every culture has guidelines for human conduct that provide expectations for how others will behave. Expectancy violation theory (EVT) frames interpersonal communication within the context of expectations held by individuals and how individuals respond to violations of those expectations. Expectancies are based on social norms and rules as well as individual-specific patterns of typical behavior. Individual deviation in expected behavior causes arousal or alertness in others. Whether or not deviant behavior is interpreted as positive or negative depends on communicators' valences. Communicators valances refer to characteristics of individuals (e. g. , how attractive and familiar they are perceived to be). Burgoon argues that "communicator's positive or negative characteristics are posited to moderate how violations are interpreted and evaluated".

Burgoon contends that the "contents" of each culture's expectancies vary along Hofstede's dimensions of cultural variability. Specifically, members of collectivistic cultures expect greater verbal indirectness, politeness, and non-immediacy than members of individualistic cultures. Uncertainty avoidance is linked to expectancies to the extent that communication behavior is regulated by rules. Low uncertainty cultures have fewer rules and norms regulating behavior than high uncertainty avoidance cultures. Members of high uncertainty avoidance cultures tend to be more intolerant of deviant behavior than members of low uncertainty avoidance cultures. Power distance influences how violations of high status and low status are interpreted. A violation (e. g. , nonverbal proxemic violation) by a high-status person in a high power distance culture, for example, would be perceived as a violation of ascribed role behavior, and such an action would inevitably produce stress and anxiety, a negative outcome.

Theories Focusing on Effective Outcomes

One goal of theorizing is to explain specific outcomes. One outcome that intercultural theorists have used in developing theories is effective communication and effective group decisions. Four theories fit in this category: (1) cultural convergence theory, (2) anxiety/uncertainty management theory, (3) effective group decision making theory, (4) integrated theory of interethnic communication.

Cultural Convergence Theory

Cultural convergence theory is based upon Kincaid's convergence model of communication. Kincaid defines communication as "a process in which two or more individuals or groups share information in order to reach a mutual understanding of each other and the world in which they live". He argues that mutual understanding can be approached, but never perfectly achieved. "By means of several iterations of information exchange, two or more individuals may converge towards a more mutual understanding of each other's meaning".

Barnett and Kincaid use the convergence model of communication to develop a mathematical theory of the effects of communication on cultural differences. They argue that "the laws of thermodynamics predict that all participants in a closed system will converge over time on the mean collective pattern of thought if communication is allowed to continue indefinitely". Information that is introduced from outside the system can delay convergence or reverse it (i. e., lead to divergence). They present a mathematical model that predicts the convergence of the collective cognitive states of members of two cultures whose members are interacting. Kincaid's convergence model applies to individual-level communication, and Barnett and Kincaid's mathematical theory applies to group-level (e. g., culture) phenomena.

Kincaid presents the theory in verbal form. Kincaid summarizes the theory in two theorems and three hypotheses. Theorem 1, for example, states that, "In a relatively closed social system in which communication among members is unrestricted, the system as a whole will tend to *converge* over time toward a state of greater cultural *uniformity*". The system will tend to diverge toward diversity when communication is restricted (theorem 2). The hypotheses apply the theorems to the case of immigrant groups and native/host cultures.

Anxiety/Uncertainty Management Theory

Gudykunst extended Berger and Calabrese's uncertainty reduction theory (URT) to intergroup encounters as the first step in developing anxiety/uncertainty management (AUM) theory. Gudykunst and Hammer used uncertainty (e. g., the inability to predict or explain others' attitudes, behavior, feelings) and anxiety (e. g., feelings of being uneasy, tense, worried, or apprehensive) to explain intercultural adjustment (see adjustment section below).

Gudykunst proffered a general theory using uncertainty and anxiety reduction to explain effective interpersonal and intergroup communication (i. e., minimize misunderstandings; this theory was not referred to as AUM). Intercultural communication is one type of intergroup communication in AUM theory. Gudykunst used Simmel's notion of "the stranger" (e. g., individuals who are present in a situation, but are not members of the in-group) as a central organizing concept. Gudykunst applied the axioms of the 1988 version of the theory to diplomacy, a special case of intergroup communication.

Gudykunst expanded the theory using a competency framework (Note: the label AUM was first used in this version). Gudykunst specified the metatheoretical assumptions of the theory in this version. The assumptions underlying the theory avoid the extreme objectivist or subjectivist positions (e.g., he assumes that individuals' communication is influenced by their cultures and group memberships, but they also can choose how they communicate when they are mindful). This suggests that under some conditions objectivist assumptions hold and other conditions subjectivist assumptions hold. Further, Gudykunst expanded the number of axioms in the theory to make the theory easier to understand and easier to apply. This version of the theory also incorporates minimum and maximum thresholds for uncertainty and anxiety. Finally, Gudykunst integrated Langer's notion of mindfulness as a moderating process between AUM and effective communication in this version.

Following Lieberson, Gudykunst argues that there are "basic" and "superficial" causes of effective communication. He contends that anxiety and uncertainty management (including mindfulness) are the basic causes of effective communication, and the effect of other "superficial" variables (e.g., ability to empathize, attraction to strangers) on effective communication is mediated through anxiety and uncertainty management. The extent to which individuals are mindful of their behavior moderates the influence of their anxiety and uncertainty management on their communication effectiveness. Gudykunst suggests that dialectical processes are involved in AUM (e.g., the uncertainty dialectic involves novelty and predictability), but these processes have not been elaborated.

Effective Group Decision Making Theory

Oetzel proposes a theory of effective decision making in intercultural groups. Oetze integrates Hirokawa and Rost's vigilant interaction theory (VIT) and Ting-Toomey's cross-cultural theory of face negotiation and conflict management.

Hirokawar and Rost assume that the way members of groups talk about things (e.g., problems) associated with group decisions influences how they think about things associated with the decisions they must make. How group members think about things associated with the decision they make influences the quality of their decisions. A group's final decision is a result of "a series of interrelated subdecisions". Oetzel suggests that VIT may be limited to monocultural groups in the United States because different outcomes are emphasized in individualistic and collectivistic cultures. He, therefore, defines decision effectiveness in terms of quality appropriateness.

Oetzel's theory contains 14 propositions. The initial set of propositions focuses on homogeneous (e. g. , monocultural) and heterogeneous (e. g. , intercultural) groups. He contends that when members of homogeneous groups activate independent self construals, they emphasize task outcomes; when they activate interdependent self construals, they emphasize relational outcomes. Members of homogeneous groups who activate independent construals are less likely to reach consensus and will have more conflict and manage it less cooperatively than members of homogeneous groups who activate interdependent self construals. Member contributions tend to be more equal in homogeneous groups and members are more committed to the group than members in heterogeneous groups.

Oetzel contends that when most members activate independent self construals, they tend to use dominating conflict strategies. When most members activate interdependent self construals, in contrast, they tend to use avoiding, compromising, or obliging conflict strategies. Groups that use cooperative styles to manage conflict make more effective decisions than groups that use competing or avoiding styles. Groups in which members activate personal identities make better decisions than groups in which members activate social identities.

Oetzel's theory suggests that the more equal members' contributions and the more group members are committed to the group and its decision, the more effective the decisions. Consensus decisions are more effective than majority or compromise decisions. Finally, Oetzel believes that the "fundamental requisites" of VIT apply to intercultural groups: Groups that understand the problem, establish "good" criteria, develop many alternatives, and examine the positive/ negative consequences of the alternatives make more effective decisions than those that do not.

Integrated Theory of Interethnic Communication

Kim lays the groundwork for the integrated theory of interethnic communication. She uses general systems theory (open systems) as an organizing framework. Her organizing scheme consists of a set of four circles; a circle with behavior in the center surrounded by three circles representing contexts (from center to outer circles): (1) behavior (encoding/decoding), (2) communicator, (3) situation, and (4) environment.

Kim organizes various aspects of encoding and decoding using an associative—

disassociative behavior continuum. She argues that "behaviors that are closer to the associative end of this continuum facilitate the communication process by increasing the likelihood of mutual understanding, cooperation... behaviors at the disassociative end tend to contribute to misunderstanding, competition". To illustrate, associative decoding behaviors include processes like particularization, decategorization, personalization, and mindfulness. Disassociative decoding behaviors include processes like categorization, stereotyping, communicative distance, and making the ultimate attribution error. Associative encoding behaviors include processes like convergence, person-centered messages, and personalized communication. Disassociative encoding behaviors include processes like divergence, prejudiced talk, and the use of ethnophaulisms.

Kim examines the communicator in terms of "relatively stable psychological attributes". She includes such factors as cognitive structures (e.g., cognitive complexity, category width), identity strength (e.g., ethnic identity, ethnolinguistic identity, in-group loyalty), group biases (e.g., in-group favoritism, ethnocentrism), and related concepts (e.g., intercultural identity, moral inclusion).

Kim views the situation as defined by the physical setting. She isolates interethnic heterogeneity, interethnic salience, and interaction goals (e.g., goals) as critical factors of the situation. The environment includes national and international forces that influence interethnic communication such as institutional equity/inequity (e.g., history of subjugation, ethnic stratification), ethnic group strength (e.g., ethnolinguistic vitality), and interethnic contact (e.g., interaction potential of environment).

Kim argues that the organizing model provides a framework for integrating research in a variety of disciplines. It also serves as "a framework for pragmatic action... For instance, we can infer from the model that, by changing certain existing conditions in the environment, we can help facilitate associative communicative behaviors".

Theories Focusing on Accommodation or Adaptation

Another goal on which theorists focus is how communicators accommodate or adapt to each other. There are three theories that fit this category: (1) communication accommodation theory, (2) intercultural adaptation theory, and (3) co-cultural theory.

Communication Accommodation Theory

Communication accommodation theory (CAT) originated in Giles' work on accent mobility. CAT began as speech accommodation theory (SAT). SAT proposed that speakers use linguistic strategies to gain approval or to show distinctiveness in their interactions with others. The main strategies communicators use based on these motivations are speech convergence or divergence. These are "linguistic moves" to decrease or increase communicative distances, respectively.

Giles et al. expanded SAT in terms of the range of phenomena covered and relabeled it CAT. Coupland et al. adapted CAT to intergenerational communication and incorporated additional modifications to the theory (e. g., conceptualizing speaker strategies as based on an "addressee focus" and incorporating addressees' attributions about speakers' behavior). Gallois et al. adapted Coupland et al. 's model to intercultural communication. This modification integrated predictions from ethnolinguistic identity theory (EIT), and emphasized the influence of situations on intercultural communication. Gallois et al. updated the 1988 version of the theory incorporating research that had been conducted and cross-cultural variability in accommodative processes.

CAT begins with the "sociohistorical context" of the interaction. This includes the relations between the groups having contact and the social norms regarding contact (intercultural contact is one type of intergroup contact in CAT). This component also includes cultural variability.

The second component of CAT is the communicators' "accommodative orientation"; their tendencies to perceive encounters with out-group members in interpersonal terms, intergroup terms, or a combination of the two. There are three aspects to accommodative orientations: (1) "intrapersonal factors" (e. g., social and personal identities), (2) "intergroup factors" (e. g., factors that reflect communicators' orientations to out-groups, such as perceived in-group vitality), and "initial orientations" (e. g., perceived potential for conflict; long-term accommodative motivation toward out-groups).

The perceived relations between groups influence communicators' tendencies to perceive encounters as interpersonal or intergroup. Similarly, members of dominant groups who have insecure social identities and perceive threats from out-groups tend to perceive convergence by members of subordinate groups negatively. Also, individuals who are dependent on their groups and feel solidarity with them tend to see encounters in intergroup terms and tend to emphasize linguistic markers of their groups.

The third component in CAT is the "immediate situation." There are five aspects to the immediate situation: (1) "sociopsychological states" (e. g., communicators' interpersonal or intergroup orientation in the situation), (2) "goals and addressee focus" (e. g., motivations in the encounter, conversational needs, relational needs), (3) "sociolinguistic strategies" (e. g., approximation, discourse management), (4) "behavior and tactics" (e. g., language, accent, topic), and (5) "labeling and attributions." The five aspects of the immediate situation are interrelated.

The final component of CAT is "evaluation and future intentions." The propositions here focus on communicators' perceptions of their interlocutors' behavior in the interaction. Convergent behavior that is perceived to be based on "benevolent intent," for example, tends to be evaluated positively. When interlocutors who are perceived to be typical group members are evaluated positively, individuals are motivated to communicate with the interlocutors and other members of their groups in the future.

Intercultural Adaptation Theory

Ellingsworth assumes that all communication involves some degree of cultural variability. He, therefore, argues that explaining intercultural communication needs to start from interpersonal communication and cultural factors need to be incorporated. Ellingsworth's theory is designed to explain how communicators adapt to each other in "purpose-related encounters." He isolates eight "laws" (i. e., "ongoing relationships by which units affect one another,"). Examples of Ellingsworth's laws are "Adaptation of communication style affects invocation of culture-based belief differences" and "The burden of adaptive behavior is affected by the extent to which setting favors one or the other participant".

Ellingsworth argues that functionally adapting communication and equity in adaptation facilitate task completion. Nonfunctional adaptive communication leads to invocation of cultural differences and slowing task completion. When communicators have to cooperate there is equity in adapting communication. Using persuasive strategies leads to adapting communication. When the situation favors one communicator or one communicator has more power, the other communicator has the burden to adapt. The more adaptive behavior in which communicators engage, the more their cultural beliefs will change. Ellingsworth updated the theory by expanding discussion of the laws and propositions in the theory. The theory, however, remains essentially the same.

Co-Cultural Theory

Orbe uses a phenomenological approach to develop co-cultural theory. Co-cultural theory is based in muted group theory (e. g., social hierarchies in society privilege some groups over others) and standpoint theory (e. g., specific positions in society provide subjective ways that individuals look at the world). Co-cultures include, but are not limited to, nonwhites, women, people with disabilities, homosexuals, and those in the lower social classes.

Orbe points out that "in its most general form, co-cultural communication refers to interactions among underrepresented and dominant group members". The focus of co-cultural theory is providing a framework "by which co-cultural group members negotiate attempts by others to render their voices muted within dominant societal structures". Two premises guide co-cultural theory: (1) co-cultural group members are marginalized in the dominant societal structures, and (2) co-cultural group members use certain communication styles to achieve success when confronting the "oppressive dominant structures."

Orbe argues that co-cultural group members generally have one of three goals for their interactions with dominant group members: (1) assimilation (e. g., become part of the mainstream culture), (2) accommodation (e. g., try to get the dominant group members to accept co-cultural group members), and (3) separation (e. g., rejecting the possibility of common bonds with dominant group members). Other factors that influence co-cultural group members' communication are "field of experience" (e. g., past experiences), "abilities" (e. g., individuals' abilities to enact different practices), the "situational context" (e. g., where are they communicating with dominant group members?), "perceived costs and rewards" (e. g., the pros and cons of certain practices), and the "communication approach" (i. e., being aggressive, assertive or nonassertive).

Orbe isolates practices co-cultural group members use in their interaction with dominant group members. The practices used are a function of the co-cultural group members' goals and communication approaches. The combination of these yield nine communication orientations in which different practices tend to be used: (1) nonassertive separation involves practices of "avoiding" and "maintaining interpersonal barriers"; (2) nonassertive accommodation involves practices of "increasing visibility" and "dispelling stereotypes"; (3) nonassertive assimilation involves practices of "emphasizing commonalities," "developing positive face," "censoring self," and "averting controversy"; (4) assertive separation involves practices of "communicating oneself," "intragroup networking," "exemplifying strengths," and "embracing stereotypes"; (5) assertive accommodation involves practices of "communicating self," "intragroup networking," "utilizing liaisons," and "educating others"; (6) assertive assimilation involves practices of "extensive preparation," "overcompensating," "manipulating stereotypes," and "bargaining"; (7) aggressive separation involves practices of "attacking" and "sabotaging others"; (8) aggressive accommodation involves practices of "confronting" and "gaining advantage"; and (9) aggressive assimilation involves practices of "dissociating," "mirroring," "strategic distancing," and "ridiculing self."

Theories Focusing on Identity Negotiation or Management

Another goal that theorists use as a focus of their work is negotiating identities in intercultural interactions. These theories address adaptation of identities, not specific communication behaviors (as in the preceding section). Four theories focus on identity: (1) cultural identity theory, (2) identity management theory, (3) identity negotiation theory, and (4) Hecht's communication theory of identity.

Cultural Identity Theory

Collier and Thomas present an "interpretive" theory of how cultural identities are managed in intercultural interactions. Their theory is stated in six assumptions, five axioms, and one theorem. The assumptions are: (1) individuals "negotiate multiple identities in discourse"; (2) intercultural communication occurs "by the discursive assumption and avowal of differing cultural identities"; (3) intercultural communication competence involves managing meanings coherently, and engaging in rule-following (i. e. , appropriate) and outcomes that are positive (i. e. , effective); (4) intercultural communication competence involves negotiating "mutual meanings, rules, and positive outcomes"; (5) intercultural communication competence involves validating cultural identities (i. e. , "identification with and perceived acceptance into a group that has shared systems of symbols and meanings as well as norms/rules for conduct,"); and (6) cultural identities vary as a function of scope (e. g. , how general identities are), salience (e. g. , how important identities are), and intensity (e. g. , how strongly identities are communicated to others).

Given the six assumptions, Collier and Thomas develop five axioms. The first axiom states that "the more that norms and meanings differ in discourse, the more intercultural the contact". The second axiom suggests that the more individuals have intercultural communication competence, the better they are able to develop and maintain intercultural relationships. The third axiom is similar to the first and states that "the more that cultural identities differ in the discourse, the more intercultural the contact".

The fourth axiom in Collier and Thomas' theory suggests that the more one person's ascribed cultural identity for the other person matches the other person's avowed cultural identity, the more the intercultural competence. The final axiom states that "linguistic references to cultural identity systematically covary with sociocontextual factors such as participants, type of episode, and topic". The theorem claims that the more cultural identities are avowed, the more important they are relative to other identities.

Identity Management Theory

Cupach and Imahori's identity management theory (IMT) is based in interpersonal communication competence. IMT is based on Goffman's work on self-presentation and facework.

Cupach and Imahori view identity as providing "an interpretive frame for experience". Identities provide expectations for behavior and motivate individuals' behavior. Individuals have multiple identities, but Cupach and Imahori view cultural and relational identities (e. g. , identities within specific relationships) as central to identity management. Following Collier and Thomas, Cupach and Imahori view identities as varying as a function of scope (e. g. , number of individuals who share identity), salience (e. g. , importance of identity), and intensity (e. g. , strength with which identity is communicated to others). Intercultural communication occurs when interlocutors have different cultural identities and intracultural communication occurs when interlocutors share cultural identities.

Cupach and Imahori argue that aspects of individuals' identities are revealed through the presentation of face (e. g. , situated identities individuals claim). They contend "the maintenance of face is a natural and inevitable *condition* of human interaction". In IMT, "interpersonal communication competence should include the ability of an individual to successfully negotiate mutually acceptable identities in interaction". The ability to maintain face in interactions is one indicator of individuals' interpersonal communication competence. Cupach and Imahori believe this extends to intercultural communication competence as well.

Cupach and Imahori argue that since individuals often do not know much about others' cultures, they manage face in intercultural encounters using stereotypes. Stereotyping, however, is face-threatening because it is based on externally imposed identities. The result is a dialectic tension regarding three aspects of face: (1) fellowship face versus autonomy face, (2) competence face versus autonomy face, and (3) autonomy face versus fellowship or competence face. Intercultural communication competence involves successfully managing face, which involves managing these three dialectical tensions.

Cupach and Imahori contend that competence in developing intercultural relationships goes through three phases. The first phase involves "trial-and-error" processes of finding identities on which communicators share some similarities. The second phase involves enmeshment of the identities of the participants into "a mutually acceptable and convergent relational identity, in spite of the fact that their cultural identities are still divergent". The third phase involves renegotiating identities. "Competent intercultural interlocutors use their narrowly defined but emerging relational identity from the second phase as the basis for renegotiating their separate cultural identities". Cupach and Imahori argue that the three phases are "cyclical" and individuals in intercultural relationships may go through the three phases for each aspect of their identities that are relevant to their relationships.

Identity Negotiation Theory

Ting-Toomey argues that intercultural communication competence is "the effective identity negotiation process between two interactants in a novel communication episode". She makes several assumptions in constructing identity negotiation theory (INT): cultural variability influences the sense of self, self-identification involves security and vulnerability, identity boundary regulation motivates behavior, identity boundary regulation involves a tension between inclusion and differentiation, managing the inclusion differentiation dialectic influences the coherent sense of self, and a coherent sense of self influences individuals' communication resourcefulness (i. e. , "the knowledge and ability to apply cognitive, affective, and behavioral resources appropriately, effectively, and creatively in diverse interaction situations").

Ting-Toomey argues that the more secure individuals' self-identifications are, the more they are open to interacting with members of other cultures. The more vulnerable individuals feel, the more anxiety they experience in these interactions. Individuals' vulnerability is affected by their need for security. The more individuals need inclusion, the more they value in-group and relational boundaries. The more individuals need differentiation, the more distance they place between the self and others.

Individuals' resourcefulness in negotiating identities is affected by effectively managing the security-vulnerability and inclusion-differentiation dialectics. The more secure individuals' self-identifications, the greater their identity coherence and global self-esteem. The greater individuals' self-esteem and the greater their membership collective esteem, the more resourceful they are when interacting with strangers.

Individuals' motivation to communicate with strangers influences the degree to which they seek out communication resources. The greater individuals' cognitive, affective, and behavioral resourcefulness, the more effective they are in identity negotiation. The more diverse individuals' communication resources are, the more effective they are in interactive identity confirmation, coordination, and attunement. Finally, the more diverse individuals' communication resources, the more flexible they are in "co-creating interactive goals" and "developing mutual identity meanings and comprehensibility".

Communication Theory of Identity

Hecht lays the foundation for the theory. He argues that there are "polarities or contradictions in all social life ... elements of these polarities are present in all interactions". Hecht argues that identity is a "communicative process" and must be studied in the context of exchanged messages. He starts from several assumptions:

(1) Identities have individual, social, and communal properties;
(2) Identities are both enduring and changing;
(3) Identities are affective, cognitive, behavioral, and spiritual;
(4) Identities have both content and relationship levels of interpretation;
(5) Identities involve both subjective and ascribed meanings;
(6) Identities are codes that are expressed in conversations and define membership in communities;
(7) Identities have semantic properties that are expressed in core symbols, meaning, and labels;
(8) Identities prescribe modes of appropriate and effective communication.

Hecht contends that these assumptions are consistent with dialectical theory.

Hecht argues that there are four identity frames: personal, enacted, relational, and communal. Frames "are means of interpreting reality that provide a perspective for understanding the social world". Identity as a personal frame involves the characteristics of individuals. He makes three assumptions about the personal frame (1) "Identities are hierarchically ordered meanings," (2) "Identities are meanings ascribed to the self by others," and (3) "Identities are a source of expectation and motivation".

Hecht argues that identities are enacted in interactions with others. He contends that "not all messages are about identity, but identity is part of all messages". There are three assumptions about identity enactment: "Identities are emergent," "Identities are enacted in social behavior and symbols," and "Identities are hierarchically order[ed] social roles".

Hecht sees identities as emerging in relationships with others and part of the relationships because they are "jointly negotiated." He isolates three relationship frame assumptions: "Identities emerge in relationship to other people," "Identities are enacted in relationships," and "Relationships develop identities as social entities".

Hecht also views identities in a communal frame; "something held by a group of people which, in turn, bonds the group together". He isolates one proposition: "Identities emerge out of groups and networks".

Theories Focusing on Communication Networks

Network theories are based on the assumption that individuals' behavior is influenced by relationships between individuals rather than the characteristics of the individuals. "In network theory, the main focus is on positions and social relationships, rather than beliefs or internalized norms. Also, the focus is on series of interconnecting relationships, rather than static, bounded groups". These theories focus on explaining linkages between people from different cultures. Three theories focus on networks: (1) out-group communication competence theory, (2) intracultural versus intercultural networks theory, and (3) networks and acculturation theory.

Outgroup Communication Competence Theory

Kim uses a personal network approach to explain out-group communication competence. Personal networks emphasize the links between individuals. She argues that "one of the most important aspects of a personal network is ego's conscious and unconscious reliance on the network members for perceiving and interpreting various attributes and actions of others (and of self)".

Kim assumes that having out-group members in individuals' personal networks and the nature of these out-group ties influence their out-group communication competence. Theorem 1 states that "a higher level of heterogeneity of a personal network is associated with a higher level of ego's overall out-group communication competence". This theorem suggests that having out-group members in individuals' personal networks facilitates out-group communication competence.

Theorem 2 in Kim's theory proposes that "a higher level of centrality of out-group members in a personal network is associated with a higher level of the ego's out-group communication competence". This theorem suggests that having out-group members in central positions in individuals' personal networks facilitates out-group communication competence.

Theorem 3 contends that "a higher level of an ego's tie strength with out-group members is associated with a higher level of his/her ego's out-group communication competence". This theorem suggests that the more frequent the contact and the closer the ties individuals have with out-group members, the more their out-group communication competence.

Intracultural Versus Intercultural Networks Theory

Yum's theory is designed to explain the differences in individuals' intracultural and intercultural networks. She begins with the assumption that there is more variance in behavior between cultures than within cultures. There are six theorems in Yum's theory.

Yum's first theorem posits that intercultural networks tend to be radial (e. g., individuals are linked to others who are not linked to each other) and intracultural networks tend to be interlocking (e. g., individuals are linked to others who are linked to each other). Theorem 2 predicts that intracultural networks are more dense (e. g., the ratio of actual direct links to number of possible links) than intercultural networks.

Yum's third theorem proposes that intracultural networks are more multiplex (e. g., multiple messages flow through linkages) than intercultural networks. Theorem 4 states that intercultural network ties are more likely to be weak ties than strong ties". Strong ties involve frequent and close contact (e. g., friendships). Links between acquaintances and people with whom individuals have intermittent role relationships (e. g., hair dressers) tend to be weak ties.

Theorem 5 in Yum's theory states that "the roles of liaison and bridge will be more prevalent and more important for network connectedness in intercultural networks than in intracultural networks". Liaisons are individuals who link cliques

(e. g. , a group of connected individuals) but are not members of any of the cliques. Bridges are individuals who link cliques and are members of one of the cliques. Both are "intermediaries" and can form indirect linkages between members of different groups.

Yum's final theorem suggests that "transivity will play a much smaller role in creating intercultural networks than intracultural networks". Transivity occurs when "my friend's friends are my friends". Since intercultural networks tend to be uniplex and involve weak ties, they do facilitate forming networks with friends of out-group members in the network.

Networks and Acculturation Theory

Smith's theory links social networks to immigrant acculturation. The theory consists of seven assumptions about the nature of networks, and seven propositions. The first proposition suggests that immigrants tend to be linked to those individuals who define their identities (e. g. , other immigrants from their cultures or host nationals). The second proposition claims that the way immigrants experience their social networks is influenced by their native cultures.

Smith's third proposition suggests that the more host nationals are in immigrants' social networks, the more likely immigrants are to acculturate. The fourth proposition claims that as immigrants become integrated into host communities, their social networks change. Proposition 5 contends that factors like where immigrants live and their social class influence their abilities to form intercultural networks and acculturate.

Smith's sixth proposition states that dense networks (e. g. , links connected to each other) decrease immigrants' abilities to obtain the resources needed for acculturation. The final proposition contends that "intercultural networks will be less dense, with more radial ties in cultures reflecting a contextual-based relationship norm than those found in cultures reflecting a person-based relationship norm".

Theories Focusing on Acculturation and Adjustment

The acculturation of immigrants and the adjustment of sojourners have been of interest to scholars for over 50 years. Only in recent years, however, have formal theories focusing on communication been proposed. Five theories are examined in this section: (1) communication acculturation theory, (2) interactive acculturation model, (3) anxiety/uncertainty management theory of adjustment, (4) communication in assimilation, deviance, and alienation states theory, and (5) a schema theory of adaptation. The first two focus on the acculturation of immigrants and the other three focus on the adjustment of sojourners.

Communication Acculturation Theory

Kim has been developing her theory of communication and acculturation for over 20 years. The first version of the theory appeared in a causal model of Korean immigrants' acculturation to Chicago. She has refined the theory several times using an open-system perspective. One of the major changes incorporated into the theory is adding the "stress, adaptation, and growth dynamics" that immigrants go through, and focusing on immigrants becoming "intercultural." In addition, the current version of the theory attempts to portray "cross-cultural adaptation as a collaborative effort, in which a stranger and the receiving environment are engaged in a joint effort".

The current version of Kim's theory contains assumptions based on open-systems theory, axioms, and theorems. The axioms are "law like" statements about relationships between units in the theory. Theorems are derived from the axioms. The first five axioms are broad principles of cross-cultural adaptation: acculturation and deculturation are part of the cross-cultural adaptation process, the stress-adaptation-growth dynamic underlies the adaptation process, intercultural transformations are a function of the stress-adaptation-growth dynamic, the severity of the stress-adaptation-growth dynamic decreases as strangers go through intercultural transformations, and functional fitness and psychological health result from intercultural transformations. The final five axioms deal with the reciprocal relationship between intercultural transformations and host communication competence, host communication activities, ethnic communication activities, environmental conditions, and strangers' predispositions.

The first three theorems posit relationships between host communication competence and host communication activities (+), ethnic communication activities (−), and intercultural transformations (+). Host interpersonal and mass communication activities are related to ethnic communication activities (−), and intercultural transformations (+). Ethnic interpersonal and mass communication activities are related negatively to intercultural transformations.

The next three theorems relate host receptivity and conformity pressure to host communication competence (+), host communication activities (+), and ethnic communication activities (−). Ethnic group strength is related to host communication competence (−), host communication activities (−), and ethnic communication activities (+). Ethnic proximity is related to host communication competence (+), host communication activities (+), and ethnic communication activities (−).

Strangers' preparedness for change is related to host communication competence (+), host communication activities (+), and ethnic communication activities (+). Strangers' adaptive personalities are related to host communication competence (+), host communication activities (+), and ethnic communication activities (−).

Interactive Acculturation Model

Bourhis et al. 's interactive acculturation model (IAM) suggests that relational outcomes between host nationals and immigrant groups are a function of the "acculturation orientations of both the host majority and immigrant groups as influenced by state integration policies". They begin by adapting Berry's model of immigrant acculturation.

Berry's model is based on immigrants' responses to two issues: (1) do they want to maintain their native cultural identities, and (2) do they want to maintain good relations with members of the host culture. If the answer is "yes" on both issues, they use an "integration" orientation with respect to the host culture. If they answer "yes" to having relations with hosts and "no" to maintaining their cultural identities, immigrants have an "assimilation" orientation toward the host culture. If immigrants answer "yes" to maintaining their native cultural identities and "no" to having good relations with hosts, they have a "separation" orientation toward the host culture. If they answer "no" to both issues, they have a marginal orientation toward the host culture. Bourhis et al. divide the marginal orientation into "anomie" (e. g., cultural alienation) and "individualism" (e. g., they define themselves and hosts as individuals rather than as members of groups).

Bourhis et al. develop a similar model for hosts' acculturation orientation. The model is based on responses on two questions: "(1) Do you find it acceptable that immigrants maintain their cultural heritage? (2) Do you accept that immigrants adapt to the culture of your host culture?" If hosts answer "yes" to both questions, they have an "integration" orientation toward immigrants. If they answer "no" to question 1 and "yes" to question 2, they have an "assimilation" orientation. If hosts answer "yes" to question 1 and "no" to question 2, the "segregation" orientation. If hosts answer "no" to both questions, they have an "exclusion" or "individualism" orientation.

Bourhis et al. combine the two models to form the IAM. They use the IAM to predict whether there are "consensual," "problematic," or "conflictual" relational outcomes between hosts and immigrants. To illustrate, "the most consensual relational outcomes are predicted in three cells of the model, namely when both host community members and immigrant group members share either the integration, assimilation, or individualism acculturation orientations".

Anxiety/Uncertainty Management Theory of Adjustment
Defining strangers is a figure-ground phenomenon. The effective communication version of ADM theory is written from the perspective of individuals communicating with strangers (e.g., others approaching individuals' in-groups). The adjustment version of the theory is written from the perspective of strangers (e.g., sojourners) entering new cultures and interacting with host nationals.

The original version of ADM theory was a theory of adjustment. Gudykunst includes axioms comparable to the 1995 version of the effective communication version, plus two additional axioms focusing specifically on adjustment (i.e., pluralistic tendencies in host culture decreases and permanence of stay increases strangers' anxiety).

When strangers enter a new culture they have uncertainty about host nationals' attitudes, feelings, beliefs, values, and behaviors. Strangers need to be able to predict which of several alternative behavior patterns hosts will employ. When strangers communicate with hosts, they also experience anxiety. Anxiety is the tension, feelings of being uneasy, tension, or apprehension strangers have about what will happen when they communicate with hosts. The anxiety strangers experience when they communicate with hosts is based on negative expectations.

To adjust to other cultures, strangers do not want to try to reduce their anxiety and uncertainty totally. At the same time, strangers cannot communicate effectively with hosts if their uncertainty and anxiety are too high. If uncertainty is too high, strangers cannot accurately interpret hosts' messages or make accurate predictions about hosts' behaviors. When anxiety is too high, strangers communicate on automatic pilot and interpret hosts' behaviors using their own cultural frames of reference. Also, when anxiety is too high, the way strangers process information is very simple, thereby limiting their ability to predict hosts' behaviors. When uncertainty is too low, strangers become overconfident that they understand hosts' behaviors and do not question whether their predictions are accurate. When anxiety is too low, strangers are not motivated to communicate with hosts.

If strangers' anxiety is high, they must mindfully manage their anxiety to communicate effectively and adjust to the host cultures. Managing anxiety requires that strangers become mindful (e. g. , create new categories, be open to new information, be aware of alternative perspectives). When strangers have managed their anxiety, they need to try to develop accurate predictions and explanations for hosts' behaviors. When strangers communicate on automatic pilot, they predict and interpret hosts' behaviors using their own frames of reference. When strangers are mindful, in contrast, they are open to new information and aware of alternative perspectives (e. g. , hosts' perspectives) and they, therefore, can make accurate predictions.

Lieberson argues that it is necessary to isolate "basic" and "superficial" causes of the phenomenon being explained. In ADM theory, managing uncertainty and anxiety are the basic causes of strangers' intercultural adjustment. The amount of uncertainty and anxiety strangers experience in their interactions with hosts is a function of many superficial causes (e. g. , self-concepts, motivation, reactions to hosts, social categorization, situational processes, connections with hosts). Research supports the theoretical argument that the superficial causes of adjustment (e. g. , ability to adapt behavior) are linked to adjustment through uncertainty and anxiety.

Assimilation, Deviance, and Alienation

McGuire and McDermott argue that assimilation and adaptation are not permanent outcomes of the adaptation process, rather they are temporary outcomes of the communication process. The reason is that everyone, no matter how well integrated into their cultures, deviates from social norms and rules at some point. They contend that "individuals (or groups) have achieved the assimilation state when their perceptions are receiving positive reinforcement from others' communications …. the group accomplishes an assimilation state when an individual conforms to expected norms".

McGuire and McDermott contend that the hosts' response to immigrants' deviation from cultural norms is neglectful communication. Neglectful communication involves negative messages or the absence of messages. When immigrants are not deviant or engage in assimilative communication (e. g. , interact with hosts, increase fluency in host languages), host nationals respond with assimilative communication (e. g. , praise immigrants' behavior, being available to interact with immigrants).

When immigrants are in a deviance state they experience tension with their new cultures. Host nationals tend to respond with neglectful communication (e.g., low level of communication, negative feedback). One possible response to host nationals' neglectful communication is for immigrants to become alienated from the host cultures. Alienation involves feelings of "normlessness and social isolation". Immigrants, therefore, may feel that they cannot accomplish their goals and are being excluded from the host cultures. This does not, however, necessarily "involve hostility, aggression or conflict".

The way host nationals respond to immigrants when immigrants feel alienated influences whether immigrants stay in an alienated state. If host nationals respond in a way to strengthen alienation (e.g., refusing to interact with immigrants, being obscene, ridiculing immigrants), immigrants are likely to withdraw from host cultures, be hostile toward the host cultures, or refuse to use the host languages.

McGuire and McDermott argue that the way host nationals and immigrants respond to neglectful communication is similar. They conclude that "changes in the amount or kind of deviance or amount or kind of neglectful communication will push an individual toward or into either the alienation or the assimilation state ... . Alienation or assimilation, therefore, of a group or an individual is an outcome of the relationship between deviant behavior and neglectful communication".

A Schema Theory of Adaptation

Nishida uses schema theory to develop a theory of sojourner adaptation to new cultural environments. She defines schemas as "generalized collections of knowledge of past experiences which are organized into related knowledge groups and are used to guide our behaviors in familiar situations". Nishida contends that sojourners' failures to understand host nationals' behavior is due to sojourners' lack of schemas used in the host culture.

When sojourners do not have the schemas used in the host culture, they tend to focus on "data-driven processing which requires effort and attention". Data-driven processing is affected by sojourners' self-schemas. In other words, sojourners pay attention to information that is important to them (as opposed to what is important to host nationals). Nishida argues that sojourners "actively try to reorganize their native-culture schemas or to generate new schemas in order to adapt to the host culture environment".

Conclusion

As indicated earlier, theorizing about intercultural communication has improved tremendously in recent years. There are, however, still several issues that need to be addressed in future theorizing on intercultural communication.

First, the vast majority of the theories proposed to date are objectivistic in nature. Only a few of the theorists included here claim to have developed subjectivistic theories. Some objectivistic theories include subjectivistic components (e. g., mindfulness in AUM), but the general trend is for the two types of theorizing not to be integrated. Clearly, there is a need for more subjectivistic theorizing and for integrating subjectivistic and objectivistic theories.

Second, the vast majority of the theorists were born in the United States. Researchers born in other cultures, however, have developed several of the theories discussed. There may be theories of intercultural communication published in languages other than English of which we are not aware. The lack of theories from outside the United States may be a function of the role of theory in scholarship in different cultures (e. g., developing theories is not emphasized in many cultures). There is, nevertheless, a need for indigenous theories developed by scholars outside the United States.

Before theories of intercultural communication can be developed by theorists from outside the United States, indigenous theories of communication must be developed. There is extensive work on indigenous Asian concepts related to communication; for example, *amae* (roughly dependence); *awase* (roughly reciprocal adjustment to the other person); *chi/ki* (roughly energy flow); face; indirectness; *ishin-denshin* (roughly communicating without talk); *sasshi* (roughly guessing what others mean); and *sunao* (roughly being upright and obedient).

There also are beginning attempts to develop indigenous conceptualizations of topics like Japanese communication competence, and to develop indigenous models of communication (e. g., *enryo-sasshi*, *enryo* is roughly reserve), as well as discussions of how Asian philosophy influences communication and how Asian conceptualizations of self construals lead to different patterns of communication than Western conceptualizations of self construals. To date, however, none of this work approaches what might be called an indigenous theory of communication.

Dissanyake called for indigenous Asian approaches to the study of communication. Similarly, Chan argues that indigenous theories are needed to guide indigenous research. Miike suggests assumptions for an Asian-centric approach to theorizing about communication in English. It is important to recognize that indigenous theorizing cannot take place when authors write in English. Indigenous theories must be constructed in the theorists' native languages; they cannot be constructed in English. Once constructed in the native language, we hope indigenous theories are "translated" into English so that theorists in the United States can incorporate them in their theories of communication in general and intercultural communication in particular.

Third, the issue of power is not incorporated in very many of the theories constructed to date. Clearly, power plays a role in many, but not all, intercultural and intergroup encounters. Reid and Ng, for example, describe the relationships among language, power, and intergroup relations. Power needs to be incorporated in theories of intercultural communication. Berger examines power in interpersonal communication, and his analysis provides one starting point for looking at power in intercultural communication.

Fourth, many of the theories proposed to date are compatible with each other. Many of the theories proposed have different scopes and boundary conditions. This allows for the possibility of integration. Gallois et al., for example, indicate that CAT can incorporate other theoretical positions but do not present specifics (e. g., one possibility is co-cultural theory, which is not inconsistent with CAT). Similarly, Cupach and Imahori's theory appears to be theoretically compatible with Collier and Thomas' theory. Gudykunst suggests that dialectical theory can be integrated with AUM. We believe that integrating theories, especially objectivistic and subjectivistic theories, will increase our ability to understand intercultural communication.

Finally, there is little or no published research supporting some of the theories presented in this article. Given the state of theorizing in intercultural communication, conducting atheoretical research is unwarranted. Research designed to test theories is needed to advance the state of our understanding of intercultural communication, not more atheoretical research.

Notes

1. From *Theorizing about Intercultural Communication*, William B. Gudykunst (Ed), Thousand Oaks, CA: Sage Publications, Inc. 2005.
2. Hall (1976) had been published and this could be considered a cross-cultural theory of communication, but not an intercultural theory.
3. These approaches to integrating culture with communication theory are not necessarily incompatible. It is possible, for example, to integrate cultural communication and cross-cultural variability in communication. The integration tends not to occur because the theorists have different objectives.
4. The authors have not included theoretical discussions that are not developed into full

theories [e. g. , Martin & Nakayama's (1999) discussion of dialectical processes]. They also have not included rhetorical approaches to intercultural communication (e. g. , Gonzalez & Tanno, 2000).

Questions for Discussion

1. What is the importance of theories for intercultural communication study? How do the authors categorize the theories about intercultural communication? How many theories have been mentioned in this overview?
2. What are the epistemological and ontological backgrounds for subjectivistic and objectivistic research approaches? Why do we find much more objectivistic theories than subjectivistic ones? Why do the authors call for an integration of the two?
3. Which theory or theories about intercultural communication are you most interested in? Please share your knowledge of your favorite theory or theories and your experience in applying any of the theories discussed in the article.
4. What is the significance of using theories as framework in research? How do you comment on atheoretical research?
5. Scholars like Yoshitaka Miike and Chen Guoming call for the construction of indigenous Asian or Chinese intercultural communication theories. Do you agree with their suggestions? Based on your experience of applying indigenous Chinese communication or intercultural communication theories in your research projects, please either share your own experience or make some comments or suggestions in this regard.

Online Mini-Case Studies and Viewpoints-Sharing

Groupthink

Individuals make mistakes, and so do groups. Groupthink is a dysfunctional decision-making process that happens when group members are so focused on making a unanimous decision that they fail to fully analyze a problem. As such, groupthink was designed to explain and predict how bad decisions are made by groups. At its core, the notion of groupthink represents a failure of the group to demonstrate critical thinking. When groups "go along to get along," the end result of the decision-making process is likely to be less effective than if group members question the information at hand, being careful to look at the problem from a variety of perspectives. In 1982, Janis articulated three antecedent conditions to groupthink. According to Janis, these preexisting conditions make it more likely that groupthink will occur. Note that the existence of the antecedent conditions does not guarantee that groupthink will occur. Instead, these are what Janis calls "necessary but not sufficient" conditions. The antecedent conditions are high cohesion, structural flaws, and situational characteristics.

Online Research

To understand the three antecedent conditions of "high cohesion, structural flaws, and situational characteristics" of the groupthink theory, please search online for more information. Then analyze some real-life cases both at home and abroad.

Reading Two

Introductory Remarks

In 1980, Hofstede studied over 100,000 employees in over 40 countries and regions. The research results indicate that there are four cultural dimensions, i. e., individualism-collectivism (I-C), masculinity-femininity (M-F), power distance (PD) and uncertainty avoidance (UA) that are rooted in the basic problems with which all societies cope that classify the different ways cultural members respond to varying situations. To improve Hofstede's cultural dimensions, Hofstede and Bond together with other scholars expanded their Hofstede's studies and found that the Asian cultures had a greater long-term orientation (LTO) than Western cultures.

With the intention to update Hofstede's (1980) cultural dimensions, the author of the present paper tested Hofstede's country and region and VSM 94 instruments to see if differences exist and where future research should be headed given such results. The present paper is adapted from the author's doctoral dissertation research at Kent State University in 2000. Using a sample of 649 participants representing six countries and regions, the author in this study intends to examine specified relationships between Hofstede's cultural dimensions and consequential facework behaviors by using all of Hofstede's cultural dimensions: I-C, M-F, PD, UA and LTO in the context of strategy choice responses of culture members to a face-threatening situation.

The Research results show no significant difference between the samples used in this study on the basis of the demographic characteristics of age and education. However, there are substantive differences between Hofstede's (1980, 2001) original country and region classifications and results calculated from the VSM 94.

Measuring Culture:
The Utility of Verifying Hofstede's Cultural Dimensions[1]

Rebecca S. Merkin

Studying intercultural communication is essential at this time given the increasingly global nature of today's communication interactions. Furthermore, contexts such as international business, political, and even military alliances have mandated better understanding between members of different cultures. Intercultural understanding has also become vital because wide spread population migration (mainly resulting from better transportation and communication accessibility) has caused an increase of immigrants settling in the USA. In short, we need to understand each other in order to get along.

Hofstede's Cultural Dimensions

One major researcher who increased cultural understanding is Hofstede[2]. Hofstede studied over 100,000 employees in over 40 countries and regions. According to his study, there are four cultural dimensions rooted in the basic problems with which all societies cope that classify the different ways culture members respond to varying situations: individualism-collectivism (I-C), masculinity-femininity (M-F), power distance (PD) and uncertainty avoidance (UA).

Individualism stands for a society in which everyone is expected to look after him/herself and her/his immediate family only. *Collectivism* stands for a society in which people from birth onwards are integrated into cohesive in-groups which continue to protect them throughout their lifetime in exchange for unquestioning loyalty.

The *MF* dimension refers to the dominant sex-role patterns in societies. Just as male communication is oriented towards status and power, masculine cultures emphasize competition and strength. According to Hofstede, the gap between the values of women and men is very large in masculine cultures (e. g., Japan) and small in feminine cultures (e. g., Sweden).

PD is "the extent to which the less powerful members of institutions and organizations within a country and region expect and accept that power is distributed unequally". Hofstede's *UA* refers to the extent to which people are made nervous by situations they consider to be unstructured or unpredictable and the extent to which they try to avoid such situations by adopting strict codes of behavior.

The above cultural dimensions are used as a benchmark for distinguishing cultural differences and their effects in cross-cultural studies. After Hofstede concluded his study, however, some researchers found that his results did not completely represent the range of cultural characteristics that Asian culture members possess. According to the Chinese Culture Connection, Hofstede's notion of uncertainty avoidance was considered to have a predominantly Western European bias in that it left out various Confucian-based notions widely held by Eastern cultural members. These researchers together with Hofstede and Bond studied Asian participants previously not tested with regard to their cultural characteristics. Their results substantiated that *a fifth* dimension of cultural variation exists.

This dimension, Confucian dynamism, refers to characteristics reflecting a long-term orientation (LTO). LTO refers to virtues oriented towards future rewards, such as the promotion of cooperation and harmony for the good of all men. The Asian cultures studied by Hofstede and Bond had a greater long-term orientation than the more Western cultures tested by Hofstede.

Hofstede's original study reported on data collected between the late 1960s and early 1970s and Hofstede and Bond reported on data collected a few years later. Then Hofstede reassessed his results and included data from 10 supplementary countries and regions in three areas. Hofstede further revised and expanded his work adding the Long Term Orientation dimension and additional work on organizational culture. Hofstede's book, however, is a new edition, *not* a new study. Thus, Hofstede's country and region classifications are still founded on his original data.

Despite this, Hofstede's original cultural categorizations are still widely used to operationalize how countries and regions rank in a particular cultural dimension for analyses of phenomena pertaining to different cultures. While evidence exists supporting Hofstede's overall cultural dimensions, his ranking of over 50 countries and regions has not been individually tested to see whether or not it needs to be updated. Many factors could have caused cultural values to have drifted in the past twenty years.

For a case in point, Triandis listed a number of factors (such as affluence, urbanization, education level, and opportunities to travel abroad) likely to make a collectivist culture more individualist. Although Hofstede classified the USA as individualistic and Japan as collectivistic, Takano and Osaka analyzed the results of 15 studies comparing Japan with the USA on I-C and found that 14 of these studies failed to show Japan to be more collectivistic than the U.S. Additionally, despite the fact that Hofstede and Bond originally indicated that Hong Kong has a high LTO score, evidence exists indicating that Hong Kong scores *moderately* on LTO. Such exemplifications of discrepancies between Hofstede's classifications; and more recent findings signify a need to reevaluate Hofstede's country and region classifications.

Facework

Facework researchers tend to look at particularly face-threatening contexts (e.g., requests, conflict, embarrassment) in order to study the facework strategies people use to manage such situations. According to facework negotiation theory and subsequent research, people in all cultures try to preserve and negotiate face (using face work) in all communication situations.

Individuals have predominant facework strategy choices. While cultural factors have an indirect effect on facework strategy choices when mediated by individual-level factors, cultural factors also have a *direct* effect on facework strategy choices. It is in the context of facework strategies that the cultural-dimension measures were tested.

Research has shown Hofstede's dimensions to have significant implications for facework strategy behavior regardless of the context. Other inquiries are warranted, however, given the dearth of information regarding all of the actual effects of Hofstede's cultural dimensions. As a result, to gain a clearer view of cultural effects, Merkin tested culture by country and region, as designated by Hofstede's study and by calculated VSM 94 results to see if discrepancies between the two might help explain results better. A more complete description of Hofstede's VSM 94 follows.

Hofstede's Value Survey Module (VSM 94)

Besides operationalizing cultural dimensions by country and region in order to measure his cultural dimensions from actual population data, Hofstede developed his VSM 94 to quantify each of the five cultural dimensions: I-C, M-F, PD, UA and LTD. Hofstede's VSM 94 is made up of five 4-item questionnaire segments used to compare culturally determined values between people from different countries and regions. Each four-question set allows for the calculation of an index score. Because VSM 94 index scores can be calculated as a measure of any of Hofstede's five cultural dimensions, this questionnaire can actually test any chosen culture on any of these dimensions.

In order for researchers to examine whether cultures actually rank the way Hofstede originally ranked countries and regions on his cultural dimensions, it is proposed that researchers conduct cross-cultural research using the country and region classifications of Hofstede as a starting point together with his VSM 94 measure for substantiation.

A study that utilizes this process will follow. The results of research conducted on cross-cultural facework strategies using both Hofstede's country and region classifications and the VSM 94 will be reported. Findings will also be reported so that future researchers can move forward to update and fill in the gaps in Hofstede's original data.

Background to the Study

The purpose of this study was to update Hofstede's cultural dimensions by testing his country and region and his VSM 94 instruments to see if differences exist and where future research should be headed given such results. This study was part of an overall study testing specified relationships between Hofstede's cultural dimensions and consequential facework behaviors. This test was conducted with *all* of Hofstede's cultural dimensions: I-C, M-F, PD, UA and LTO in the context of strategy choice responses of culture members to a face-threatening situation. The process of facework (the behaviors people use to negotiate their face) is what individuals do to try to reestablish themselves after experiencing a face-threatening situation. Such conceptions that make up the self are influenced by culture.

According to Hofstede, culture is reflected in individuals' *mental programming*. This study takes into account *mental programming* on the collective level. The collective level of mental programming is common to people belonging to a particular category. Triandis described the collective level as the level of *subjective* human culture (in the mind) as opposed to more *objective* human artifacts.

To understand the process of facework on the collective level, one must first begin with a culture member's self. One's subjective self reflects cultural influences such as I-C and M-F. During face negotiation, one's face is an expression of one's self. Once one's face is presented, the negotiation of that presentation ensues. When a person's face is threatened—for example, when a person makes a request or is enmeshed in conflict—facework is the necessary action taken to restore one's desired identity.

Thus, Hofstede's country and region classifications were used to measure how culture influences face negotiation processes during a face-threatening situation. In this context, the following research question was investigated to see how Hofstede's country and region classifications corresponded to VSM 94 rankings from six countries and regions:

RQ1: Are Hofstede's cultural rankings classified the same or differently from more recently calculated VSM 94 results?

Hypotheses of the Study

In order to demonstrate whether differences exist between Hofstede's cultural rankings and calculated VSM 94 results, hypotheses based on Hofstede's theory that were used in Merkin's investigation are presented to exhibit how their results can help determine which measure of cultural dimensions is more accurate. H1-H3 test Hofstede's different cultural dimensions based on VSM results. A test of LTO VSM results versus his country and region classifications can be found in another source.

Hofstede stated that feminine culture members were more likely to value cooperation and consensus than their masculine counterparts. To test this claim while controlling for collectivism, the following hypothesis was posed:

> H1: Members of feminine collective cultures will use more feminine leveling (i. e., harmonious and cooperative) strategies than members of masculine collective cultures.

Hofstede found high-PD to be correlated with collectivism. Thus, testing high-PD represents tests of both cultural dimensions. Thus, the following hypothesis is posed:

> H2: High-PD-culture members are more likely to engage in face-saving indirect communication than their low-PD counterparts.

Finally, Hofstede described high-UA culture members as more likely to engage in ritualistic interactions to reduce uncertainty than their low-UA counterparts. Thus, the following hypothesis is posed:

> H3: Members of high-UA cultures are more likely to respond to interactions ritualistically than members of low-UA cultures.

Method

This test, based on Hofstede's theory of national and regional cultures, was carried out to confirm that the cultures measured actually possess the characteristics originally described by Hofstede. This was accomplished by comparing Hofstede's original scores against results that used the data that had been collected for this study and had been calculated according to Hofstede's VSM 94.

Participants

Participants to this study came from six countries: Chile, China, Israel, Japan, Sweden, and the U.S. The Asian participants were 98 students from Tezukama College in Nara, Japan, 92 students from Hong Kong, China [who came primarily from Hong Kong Baptist University ($n = 60$) and secondarily from the Chinese University of Hong Kong ($n = 32$)]. The 81 Israelis student participants came from three locations: Haifa University, Bar Ban University, and Tel Aviv University; and 70 Chilean students came primarily from two universities: the University of Chile and Universidad Diego Portales. The 92 Swedish student participants primarily came from three places: the University of Lund, the University of Hogskolan Trollhattan-Uddevalla, and the Royal Institute of Technology in Stockholm. The 241 U.S. students came from a large Midwestern university. A total of 649 participants took part in this study; 216 were males, and 443 were females.

Instrumentation

Hofstede specified that the best way to operationalize culture would be to use matching samples. If subjects are matched on as many characteristics as possible (e.g., age, education, sex), such factors could not act as competing effects with the calculation of cultural effects. Therefore, for the most part, participants in this study were matched. They were all college students between the ages of 18 and 23, with 13 to 15 years of education, and broken up into similar ratios between men and women, with women dominating the samples. According to Hofstede, the minimum number of respondents per country and region that would be useful in comparisons is 20; and the ideal number is at least 50. The samples used for this study all had over 70 participants.

Instruments used to measure the specific variables reported on in the examples that follow will be listed in the order of their presentation. Culture was measured using Hofstede's VSM 94 and country and region classifications. The VSM 94 is a 22-item questionnaire used to compare culturally determined values among people from two or more countries and regions. The 22 questions allow for the calculation of four index scores on the basis of four questions per dimension of national and regional cultures: I-C, M-F, UA, PD and LTO. The remaining six questions provide demographic data.

Cocroft's construction of response items for indirect and harmony strategies were used because Cocroft and Cocroft & Ting-Toomey were able to successfully utilize these response items with Japanese and U.S. respondents. An example of an indirect questionnaire item is *I would express my regrets indirectly*. The indirect reliability scores for each sample were as follows: 0.78 for the USA, 0.72 for Japan, 0.75 for Chile, 0.81 for China, 0.79 for Israel, and 0.76 for Sweden. An example from the harmonious strategy measure is *I would try to smile and express positive emotions only.* The harmonious reliability scores for each sample were as follows: 0.70 for the USA, 0.69 for Japan, 0.50 for Chile, 0.68 for China, 0.79 for Israel, and 0.68 for Sweden.

Cooperation was measured using the cooperation subscale of the Cooperative/Competitive Strategy Scale (CCSS) that measures the motivation to use cooperative strategies to achieve success. This scale measured items such as *Joint effort is the best way to achieve success.* This 8-item independent cooperation subscale was scored by adding all responses within the subscales and computing the aggregate average for this subscale. The reliability scores for each sample were as follows: 0.74 for the USA, 0.72 for Japan, 0.75 for Chile, 0.70 for China, 0.63 for Israel, and 0.73 for Sweden.

Merkin constructed a scale to measure behavioral ritualism (see Appendix A). Face validity for this scale was established by a group of four experts who viewed the scale. This scale's reliability was mostly acceptable in all six countries and regions tested. The reliability scores for each sample were as follows: 0.72 for the USA, 0.72 for Japan, 0.62 for Chile, 0.75 for China, 0.58 for Israel, and 0.69 for Sweden. In Japan and Chile, reported reliability results reflect the use of translated versions of the Intercultural Ritualism Scale. Using U.S. data, Merkin found a test-retest reliability of 0.81 as well as evidence of construct validity for this scale.

Procedure

Professors in their classes in their home countries and regions requested students to respond to questions by indicating on a 5-point Likert scale the extent to which they would agree or disagree with each statement. U.S. respondents and respondents from China, Israel, and Sweden received questionnaires in English because they were bilingual. Japanese respondents received surveys in Japanese; and Chilean respondents received questionnaires in Spanish. Both of the translated questionnaires were back-translated to assure that they were translated correctly. When the students finished, their professor collected their questionnaires.

Results

Results showed no significant difference between the samples used in this study on the basis of the demographic characteristics of age and education. Substantive differences do exist, however, between Hofstede's original country and region classifications and results calculated from the VSM 94. Table 1 presents the scores and ranks for the six cultures studied.

Table 1 Cultural Dimension Scores and Ranks for 6 Countries and Regions in CCa and VSMb

Country/Region	Power Distance		Uncertainty Avoidance		Individualism Collectivism		Masculinity Feminity		Long Term Orientation	
	CC	VSM	CC	VSM	CC	VSM	CC	VSM	CC	VSM
Chile	(3)28	63(2)	(1)93	86(2)	(2) 97	23(6)	(2)33	28(5)	(1)62	(NA)
China	(1)33	68(3)	(2)90	29(5)	(5) 70	25(5)	(5)14	57(3)	(3)47	96(1)
Israel	(5)22	13(6)	(6)61	81 (3)	(4) 92	54(3)	(4)15	47(4)	(5)30	(NA)
Japan	(4)24	54(3)	(4)73	92(1)	(6) 66	46(4)	(6) 7	95(1)	(2)60	80(2)
Sweden	(2)29	31 (5)	(5)67	29(5)	(1)119	71 (2)	(1)35	05(6)	(5)30	33(3)
USA	(6)20	40(4)	(3)77	46(4)	(3) 95	91(1)	(3)27	62(2)	(4)35	29(4)

Note. Ranks are in parentheses. I = Highest and 6 = Lowest. CC[a] = Culture's Consequences (Hofstede, 1980). VSM[b] 94 = Value Survey Module (Hofstede, 1994).

Hypotheses 1 to 3 corresponding to cases one to three respectively were tested using Hofstede's country and region classifications. Results of Hypothesis 1 demonstrated that members of feminine collective (Chilean) and masculine collective (Japanese) cultures significantly differed in their use of harmonious ($F[1,36] = 9.18$, $p < .001$, $h^2 = .10$) and cooperative strategies ($F[1,36] = 6.87$, $p < .001$, $h^2 = .08$). Contrary to expectations, members of feminine collective cultures were less likely to use harmonious strategies (Chile: $M = 2.31$; Japan: $M = 2.66$) and cooperative strategies (Chile: $M = 2.00$; Japan: $M = 2.19$) than their masculine collective counterparts. Thus, Merkin (2000) found discrepancies between the VSM 94 and Hofstede's (1980) cultural dimension scores vis-à-vis a collective masculine culture (i.e., Japanese), indicating that their culture members would be more likely to use harmonious and cooperative strategies (both culturally feminine behavior) than a collective-feminine culture (i.e., Chile) after experiencing a face-threatening event.

Hypothesis 2 results indicated that members of high-PD and low-PD cultures significantly differed in their use of indirect communication ($F[1,36] = 4.34$, $p < .006$, $h^2 = .08$). Contrary to expectations, indirect facework strategy used by high-PD culture members after a face-threatening situation was inconsistent (see Table 2).

Merkin's findings from hypothesis 2 are another example of discrepant results between Hofstede and his VSM 94 results. After significant differences were found between the effect of high and low PDs on indirect communication strategies, significant mean differences were closer to VSM 94 results than to Hostede's country and region rankings (see Table 2 below).

Table 2 Indirect Power Distance Means, VSM and Hofstede's Rankings

Rank	Indirect	Means	VSM 94 Ranking	Hofstede's 1980 Rank
1	Sweden	3.82	USA	China
2	China	3.45	Sweden	Chile
3	USA	3.41	China	Japan
4	Israel	3.27	Japan	USA
5	Chile	3.08	Israel	Sweden
6	Japan	2.72	Chile	Israel

Note: 1 = Highest and 6 = Lowest

According to Hypothesis 3, members of high-UA cultures significantly differed from low-UA culture members in their use of ritualistic communication ($F[1,36] = 17.77$, $p < .001$, $h^2 = .27$). Contrary to expectations, high-UA versus low-UA-culture members' use of ritualistic facework strategies after a face-threatening situation was inconsistent. The means were as follows: Chile (high UA) $M = 3.79$; USA (moderate UA) $M = 3.51$; China (low UA) $M = 3.40$; Sweden (low UA) $M = 3.39$; Japan (high UA) $M = 3.17$; Israel (high UA) $M = 3.17$).

According to Hofstede the following countries and regions rank from highest to lowest in UA: Japan, Chile, Israel, the USA, China, and Sweden. According to the VSM, however, the following countries and regions are highest to lowest in UA: Chile, China, USA., Japan, Sweden, and Israel (see Table 1). The corresponding means for ritualism are as follows: Chile ($M = 3.79$); China ($M = 3.40$); USA. ($M = 3.51$); Japan ($M = 3.17$); Sweden ($M = 3.39$); and Israel ($M = 3.13$). These means appear to correspond more to the VSM classifications of UA in that people from high-UA cultures used more ritualistic facework strategies than people from lower UA cultures, as Hofstede originally declared.

Discussion

Utility of VSM 94

The purpose of this study was to illustrate how to update Hofstede's country and region rankings using his VSM 94 instrument. This demonstration was carried out using examples taken from a 6-nation and region study testing specified relationships between Hofstede's cultural dimensions and consequential facework strategies.

Testing the same sample cultures by country and region and by the VSM 94 showed differences between calculated scores and Hofstede's country and region scores (see Table 1), in some cases large differences. This finding is very troubling because, although Merkin's (2000) study depended on Hofstede's (1980) designated country and region scores, it is not possible to be sure that such countries and regions actually possess the characteristics they are considered to have in all cases. Results requiring further thought can best be analyzed when viewing the calculated results in a rank order (Hofstede, personal communication, July 25, 2000; Hoppe, 1998). This is because calculated VSM 94 results are sample-dependent and, therefore, not necessarily on the same scale as Hofstede's original study.

Strengths and Limitations

This study's external validity was limited because the researcher employed the self-report method. While self-reports have the advantage of finding out cognitive intentions, they have the disadvantage of not representing an active relationship. Ideally, self-report studies should have triangulated results as well.

Another limitation in carrying out this study was that professors in the native countries and regions administered the questionnaires; thus, the researcher did not personally control the administration of the questionnaires. It cannot, therefore, be known if the samples used in this study could have affected results. It could be that the respondents who filled out the questionnaires had hidden characteristics that biased their responses. Strong attempts were made in this study to assure the most representative controlled sample possible. On the other hand, because they filled out questionnaires in their native country and region, a source of error was controlled.

Differences between what a person reported and what a person might actually do could not be controlled, although a social desirability check had been undertaken to rule out social desirability effects. The half-hour questionnaire used in this study was somewhat long to administer, and the entire data collection process from start to finish took approximately one year.

Despite the stated limitations, strong attempts were made in this study to assure the most representative controlled sample possible. To assure that respondents were truly representative of their culture, culture members filled out questionnaires in their native country and region. Finally, the participants were also quite similar to each other, which controlled for other possible predictors causing their responses. The samples used in this study were matched by gender, age, and education, thus eliminating competing explanations for the differences in this study. Without a random sample, however, it is not known if the results obtained are truly representative of the populations they are said to represent.

Importance of VSM 94 Rankings

Merkin's study highlights inconsistent results that could be explained by large discrepancies between Hofstede's country and region classifications and actual calculated scores on Hofstede's VSM 94 calculations. For example, there were two substantive differences between VSM 94 calculations and Hofstede's country and region classifications regarding Japan and China. Both discrepancies occur in the two cultural dimensions, I-C and M-F. Although both Japan and China are classified as collective and masculine according to Hofstede's categorizations, calculated VSM 94 scores showed these countries and regions to be individualistic and feminine (see Table 1). Sampling errors could occur, but this is a double instance of such an occurrence. It appears, therefore, that China and Japan's populations have changed their values of late.

The discrepant results are telling because based on Hofstede's cultural theory, the effects using Hofstede's designated countries and regions were opposite to the direction hypothesized. The VSM 94 results, on the other hand, classified Japan as feminine and Chile as masculine, which more accurately explains these findings. Therefore, VSM 94 calculations appear to measure Hofstede's theory more accurately than his country and region classifications.

The final case offered exemplified how using the VSM 94 could explain curious results obtained by employing Hofstede's country and region classifications. Uncertainty avoidance is the extent to which people feel threatened by ambiguous situations and create beliefs and institutions to avoid ambiguity. Part of the way members of high-UA cultures avoid ambiguity is through the construction of rules and sanctions to enforce such rules. Thus, Merkin originally hypothesized that members of high-UA cultures would be more likely to use ritualistic facework strategies after experiencing a face-threatening situation than members of low-UA cultures. Using the VSM-94 ranks supported this theoretical prediction; on the other hand, using Hofstede's country and region classifications produced conclusions in the opposite direction. Thus, while operationalizing culture by country and region could work in some cases, VSM94 scores could usefully explain instances when the country and region classifications do not hold up.

Suggested Future Studies

Given the convenience sample used for this study, follow up studies using different samples would be in order. In particular, future studies using a random sample need to be carried out with different populations to see if the results obtained in this study are corroborated. A complementary method of analysis, for example, behavioral observation could also be used in future studies to confirm conclusions arrived at in this investigation.

Future studies should also test known relationships as previously exemplified. Even if results of hypotheses are not absolutely known relationships; nonetheless, researchers have to choose a starting point to update Hofstede's findings. The Merkin tests highlight some further issues that intercultural researchers need to address.

Further methodological questions to be asked are how should a researcher measure cultural dimensions and which method is most valid? Although Hofstede's original cultural categorizations are still widely used to operationalize how countries and regions rank in a particular cultural dimension for analyses of phenomena pertaining to different cultures such analyses should be viewed with caution. Researchers should keep in mind that country and region categorizations might need to be updated when interpreting results.

While the construct validity and convergent validity have been established for the VSM 94, a final note should be made regarding the reliability of the VSM 94. This instrument measures culture on the cultural level as opposed to the individual level. Studies using the VSM 94 on the individual level have not always found the instrument's reliability to hold up. Investigations using the VSM 94, as with any intercultural study, need to match respondents on demographic categories as much as possible to assure valid results to cultural studies.

Future intercultural studies should attempt to simultaneously validate and/or reevaluate Hofstede's country and region classifications. Such attempts could act to verify that researchers are measuring what they think they are measuring. Finally, if researchers systematically update Hofstede's cultural dimensions while performing other intercultural research, they could again be confident using Hofstede's country and region classifications as a benchmark for studying cultural dimensions.

APPENDIX A

Intercultural Ritualism Scale

How often do the following statements below apply? Please indicate the extent to which the following occur in your culture. Write the answer that represents your response.

NEVER	RARELY	SOMETIMES	OFTEN	ALWAYS
1	2	3	4	5

1. In my culture, we have formal routines that we follow with business associates.
2. In my culture, we value formal introductions and leave-taking.
3. People from my culture develop routinized communication patterns with their close associates.
4. In my culture, there are particular communication routines that people use when communicating with strangers.
5. In my culture, we distinguish between different relationships by the way we say "hello" or "good-bye."
6. In most of the families of my culture, there are unspoken rules that we follow during family occasions.

Scoring: Items should be summed and averaged.

Notes

1. From *Taking Stock in Intercultural Communication: Where to Now?*, William J. Starosta and Guo-Ming Chen (Eds.), Washington, DC: National Communication Association, 2005.
2. Geert Hendrik Hofstede was born on Oct. 2, 1928. He is an influential Dutch writer on the interactions between nation, culture and organization. As an author, he has published several books including *Culture's Consequences* (2nd, fully revised edition, 2001) and *Cultures and Organizations, Software of the Mind* (2nd, revised edition, 2005), with his son Gert Jan Hofstede. Hofstede has demonstrated that there are national and regional cultural groupings that affect the behavior of societies and organizations, and that are very persistent across time.

Questions for Discussion

1. Who is Geert Hofstede? How did he obtain his cultural dimensions and what made him add the fifth dimension?

2. How do you understand Hofstede's five cultural dimensions? Can you elaborate on his fifth cultural dimension of long-term orientation? Are there any other Asian cultural dimensions that need further exploration? What are they and how can you prove that they are equally important?
3. Why does the author of this paper want to test Hofstede's cultural dimensions? How has he achieved his purpose? Can you say a few words about the reliability and validity of the present research?
4. With the dramatic changes in the process of globalization, Hofstede's cultural dimensions have grown from four (collectivism vs. individualism, power distance index, uncertainty avoidance index, and femininity vs. masculinity) to six (the original four plus short-term vs. long-term orientation, and restraint vs. indulgence). Even so, what are some of your critical comments on the feasibility and applicability of Hofstede's cultural dimensions theory to the on-going context of present-day China?
5. In his paper entitled "A Critique of Hofstede's Fifth National Culture Dimension," which appeared in *International Journal of Cross Cultural Management*, 3(3), 347 – 368, Tony Fang critiqued Hofstede's fifth national cultural dimension by using indigenous knowledge of Chinese culture and philosophy and found that there is a philosophical flaw inherent in this new' dimension. If possible, get access to Fang's paper to clarify the "philosophical flaw" and share your critique of Fang's critique.

Online Mini-Case Studies and Viewpoints-Sharing

Criteria for Evaluating Theory

Although theories serve as lenses in our academic research, some students still have difficulties selecting, evaluating, and applying theories in their research projects. Below is a table containing the necessary criteria for you to evaluate a theory:

Area of evaluation	What to look for
Accuracy	Has research supported that the theory works the way it says it does?
Practicality	Have real-world applications been found for the theory?
Succinctness	Has the theory been formulated with the appropriate number (fewest possible) of concepts or steps?
Consistency	Does the theory demonstrate coherence within its own premises and with other theories?
Acuity	To what extent does the theory make clear an otherwise complex experience?

Online Research

Search online for a proper theory to be applied in a research project of yours, and check the applicability of the theory with the five evaluation criteria.

Unit Twelve

Scholarship on Chinese Communication

Reading One

Introductory Remarks

Believing that the Western culture and the Chinese culture can benefit from each other, Jia Wenshan examines how Chinese communication scholarship may be considered an expansion of the communication and culture paradigm in the following comprehensive and thorough study. His developed argument is solid support for the viewpoint that Chinese communication research has now grown to a mature state. The author argues that Western scholars need to stand back a bit and allow Chinese scholars to develop their Eastern perspective on conceptions of communication and their characteristics in Chinese society and not approach Chinese notions of communication through the lens of their orientalism. Meanwhile, he also asks for more mainstream scholars in the Western world to take notice of the research in Chinese communication so that an intercultural dialogue can take place, which will advance a mutual understanding of communication in the East and the West.

Specifically, the author makes a metatheoretical critique of the cultural studies of Chinese communication in this paper. First, he analyzes the significance of the growth of Chinese communication scholarship in the American circle of communication studies. Then, he critiques orientalism in the cultural studies of Chinese communication. Finally, he discusses how the cultural studies of Chinese communication can be further developed in the early 21st century.

With the intention to promote a "mutual engagement" between Chinese communication research and Western communication research and to facilitate a mutual reconstruction of the two cultures, the author emphasizes that Chinese communication research should continue making creative uses of the good aspects of Western communication scholarship. The analysis of the Western biases is meant to make the Chinese communication research more productive and more useful to East-West intercultural communication.

Chinese Communication Scholarship as an Expansion of the Communication and Culture Paradigm[1]

Jia Wenshan

Introduction

Although the Chinese culture and the Western culture have known each other's presence for the past century, little mutual penetration has occurred at the every day level with many entrenched stereotypes and biases toward each other. While this is true in everyday and international interactions between the East and the West, it is also true in academic studies of communication practices. Instead of a mutual informing and mutual learning between the two cultures, research in Chinese communication[2], like many other fields, has been significantly informed and guided by the Western theories with the deeply entrenched modern Western biases, or what Edward Said[3] terms "orientalism." As a matter of fact, while the Western culture has much to benefit the Chinese culture, Chinese culture also has a lot to offer to the Western culture. Failure to do so for the Western culture would carry with it "great risk" and would "lead us to miss a singular opportunity to discover something momentous about ourselves" or the Western culture itself and about each other.

In this paper, I make a metatheoretical critique of the cultural studies of Chinese communication. First, I analyze the significance of the growth of Chinese communication scholarship in the American circle of communication studies. Then, I critique orientalism in the cultural studies of Chinese communication. Finally, I discuss how the cultural studies of Chinese communication can be further developed in the early 21st century. The goal of this study is to promote a "mutual engagement" between Chinese communication research and Western communication research and to facilitate a mutual reconstruction of the two cultures called for by Hall and Ames.

Since I am critiquing Chinese communication research with a central concentration on identifying and analyzing the Western biases in the body of literature, I am not suggesting that Western communication scholarship has little to contribute to Chinese communication research. As a matter of fact, the so-called Chinese communication research would not have been possible without the creative uses of the good aspects of Western communication scholarship. However, by analyzing the Western biases, Chinese communication research can be more productive and more useful to East-West intercultural communication.

Significance

In this part, I first provide a short history of the cultural studies of Chinese communication research in the United States, plus a short review of Chinese communication research reviews in the West. Then, I discuss its significance in the West and in China, respectively. Within the West, I discuss the impact of the growth of cultural studies of Chinese communication upon Western communication research. I also discuss its impact upon and its implications for Sinology and China Studies as significant parts of area studies in the West. Within China, I discuss its significance to China's traditional scholarship. Finally, I attempt to answer why cultural studies of Chinese communication have made these achievements.

A Short History: Research and Reflection

I define Chinese communication research here as micro- and text-based or data-based cultural studies of Chinese formal use of speech, such as rhetoric, and speech in Chinese social interaction, such as interpersonal communication. The term "cultural studies" I use here is loosely defined as an aggregate of studies that either explicitly or implicitly use a certain cultural concept, model, theory, or philosophy in analyzing Chinese rhetoric or interpersonal communication.

The cultural studies of Chinese communication in the West can be said to have formally begun in the United States in 1971. It was pioneered by Robert T. Oliver with his landmark book, *Communication and Culture in Ancient India and China*, published in 1971. Although some scholars of communication wrote and published about Chinese communication much earlier than Oliver or at about the same time as Oliver, their primary concentrations were Chinese Communism-related communication, mass communication, and development communication.

Overseas Chinese students and scholars of speech communication and other non-Chinese scholars of communication with a strong research interest in cultural studies of Chinese speech communication resumed and significantly expanded the research program in the early 1980s. *Communication Theory: Eastern and Western Perspectives*, *Communication Theory: The Asian Perspectives*, and J. O. Yum's article "The impact of Confucianism on Interpersonal Relationships and Communication Patterns in East Asia" embody some of the very significant research results in this decade. With the graduation of more speech communication Ph. D. s committed to research, cultural studies of Chinese speech communication have been further expanded, diversified and deepened in the 1990s. So far, there have been more than half a dozen books solely on Chinese speech communication from cultural perspectives published in English.

In addition, there have been hundreds of essays on Chinese communication published in a large variety of communication journals and communication-friendly journals or presented at all kinds of communication and communication-related conferences and forums in the United States and abroad. What is particularly noticeable is that several important conferences on Chinese speech communication research have been hosted in the 1990s. In 1995, a conference on communication and culture was held in Harbin. Peking University in Beijing, represented by Gong Wenxiang, and Kent State University, represented by D. Ray Heisey, hosted a conference on Chinese speech communication in Beijing in 1996. The School of Communication in Hong Kong Baptist University hosted a conference on Chinese communication in 1997. In 1998, Shixin University in Taiwan hosted a conference on Chinese communication. Unlike Lau's finding that there was no active research and major work in Chinese communication studies between 1931 and 1987, I conclude that there was an opening up of the field of Chinese speech communication research in the 1970s, a substantial growth in the 1980s, and an explosive development that moved toward maturity in the 1990s.

Although Chinese communication studies has a history of about 40 years, Chinese speech communication has been around about 30 years. Coupled with this was a repeated, albeit disconnected, series of reflections upon Chinese communication research. During these years, several scholarly studies have summarized and/or critiqued this growing research program. While Oliver was a pioneer in the cultural studies of Chinese speech communication, he was also the first in cautioning against using Western theories of rhetoric to study Chinese rhetoric: "Any attempt to discover in Asia prototypes of the Western rhetorical canons... would resemble trying to measure the salinity of water with a ruler". He argued that Chinese rhetoric should be studied in light of the Chinese cultural perspective that constitutes, in Oliver's mind, the Chinese religions and philosophies. Although Oliver's focus does not include interpersonal relationships and communication patterns in the Chinese context, his emphasis on understanding Chinese elite communication in light of the native perspective among the drowning waves of scientific approaches on communication regardless of cultural contexts in the West was really far-sighted in the then field of speech communication studies.

Unfortunately, Oliver's warning went largely unheeded in the field for a long time, until Godwin C. Chu repeated the warning for Chinese mass communication research in 1988. Though Chu was trained in mass communication, his research covered Chinese speech communication as well. Through his life-long study of Chinese communication and an overview of studies of Chinese communication, he found (he did not seem to have read Oliver's work and thus had fallen into the pitfalls himself, which Oliver had cautioned against) that there is a need to search a native Chinese perspective, which is not individual-based and which bedevils experimental studies. Lau's study is a mere citation analysis of studies of Chinese communication between 1931 and 1987. He not only missed a lot of key studies, such as Robert Oliver's, but also had a very broad, loose, and fuzzy definition of communication. Even studies of journalism were included as part of his data. However, very few studies of Chinese speech communication were reviewed in his study. Therefore, Lau's study cannot be said to be a metatheoretical analysis of Chinese communication from a cultural perspective at all.

My goal is to identify who was cited most and which journals in which disciplines cited which scholars more than others. Stowell's study is a mere summary of fewer than 20 largely unpublished cultural studies of Chinese communication that were available to her as a scholar who has a newfound interest in knowing about Chinese communication. The studies summarized are very limited, leaving out many key works. Stowell neither makes any critique nor any metatheoretical analysis of the works summarized. Although Oliver's warning in the 1970s and Chu's warning in the 1980s against Western cultural biases seem to have been heeded more and more in the 1980s and 1990s, Oliver and Chu's classics have been largely excluded out of the mainstream speech communication curricula in the West. The modern and postmodern Western theories of communication and methodologies have been the mainstay of the curricula. As a result, a majority of graduate students of speech communication who have a strong interest in and a deep commitment to Chinese speech communication studies have not been exposed to research literature on Chinese speech communication in their graduate classes. While such young scholars are beginning to take a cultural approach to the study of Chinese speech communication, many of them are adopting concepts and theories of communication and culture largely generated out of the Western cultural and communication traditions, thus doing a disservice to our understanding of Chinese speech communication in many instances. The present study is more than a general warning like Oliver's or Chu's. It is a metatheoretical analysis of achievements, weaknesses, and future directions of cultural studies of Chinese communication in light of a cultural perspective that is built upon Oliver, Chu, and Cheng, deeply grounded in the Chinese ontology, epistemology, and axiology and informed by ethnography in the views of Clifford Geertz.

Its Impact on the West and the East

When we try to summarize almost two decades of Chinese speech communication scholarship whose research results are primarily written in English, we find that Chinese communication research has made the following contributions:

First, it has been a growing force joining the postmodern transformation of the modern Western scientific paradigm of communication research. This occurs in three aspects. As research on Chinese communication has largely been defined by the cultural perspective (although different studies have divergent definitions of culture), it has been a counter-narrative to the waning modern scientific (quantitative) approach to communication studies dominant in the West, especially in the United States. It orchestrates with, joins in, and contributes to the emerging inter/cultural perspective and the qualitative approach to communication studies. It consists of a potential heuristic to the budding social approaches such as social constructionism and ethnography of communication to communication studies in the West. Most Chinese communication studies are done with the qualitative methods from natives' perspectives.

They are exemplified alphabetically by Hui-qing Chang and R. Holt's research on Chinese interpersonal relations, such as *guanxi*, *yuan*, and *renqing* and *mianzi*; Guo-Ming Chen's research on Chinese conflict; Chung-Ying Cheng's work on Chinese philosophy of communication; Wenshan Jia's research on Chinese concepts of face from a discourse analysis perspective and a historical perspective and Chinese civic discourse; Randy Kluver's work on contemporary Chinese political rhetoric of Chinese economic reform; and Casey Lum's ethnographic work on contemporary Chinese popular culture—Karaoke in overseas Chinese communities. Also, M. M. Garrett's work on classic Chinese rhetoric, specifically on the Chinese pathos and the Chinese concept of pure talk or *qingtan*; Xing (Lucy) Lu's work on ancient Chinese rhetoric; Ringo Ma's work on Chinese mediation and his research on the Chinese rule for "yes" and "no"; Xiao-shui Xiao's research on modern Chinese intellectual rhetoric, and so on. Such studies more or less consciously attempt to overcome the Western biases and carve out a Chinese perspective with varying degrees of success.

These studies share the following unique characteristics. First of all, they are grounded in the Chinese cultural contexts, instead of being acontextual like a lot of other quantitative studies of communication. Furthermore, many of these studies identify unique meanings and functions of uniquely Chinese communication terms and concepts that are nonexistent in Western communication terminologies, and unsubstitutable or incompatible with any terms or concepts in Western communication studies. All this in and of itself questions many of the truth claims about many of the philosophical, conceptual, theoretical, and methodological frameworks constructed both quantitatively and qualitatively from both the modern tradition and postmodern tradition in the West. Finally, the cultural uniqueness of Chinese communication described by these studies can help reveal minute but prevalent and hardly visible but perplexing sources of difficulty in communication between Chinese and Americans. Many of these studies have been used to help reflect upon, challenge, expand, and transform the discipline of intercultural communication.

Second, Chinese speech communication scholarship has helped enrich and expand Sinology and China studies, part of area studies in the West. Jessica Stowell, a professor of communication with an interest in Chinese communication, having found little literature on Chinese communication in the East-West Center—a premiere center of research in Sinology—and Peking University, had "a breakthrough" the last two years when she met and learned from a group of young, dedicated Chinese communication scholars at the Speech Communication Association. They are researching and writing as never before and provided much of the information for her paper, entitled "The Changing Face of Chinese Communication: A Synthesis of Interpersonal Concepts". I am sure that there are many like Stowell who have had similar experiences when they tried to find literature on Chinese communication in area studies centers, such as the East-West Center in Hawaii and the Fairbank Center at Harvard. Specifically, Chinese speech communication scholarship has moved beyond the cold war model of communication studies on China.

Studies representing the cold war model of Chinese communication are characterized by ideological, utilitarian, and strategic concerns for political and economic benefits. Such a model allowed a close look at the communication strategies, styles, and skills of the Chinese political elites in very strategic contexts such as diplomatic and trade negotiations between China and the West and China's domestic political campaigns. It disallowed more nuanced natives' points of view of average Chinese communication practices in everyday life in light of culturally sensitizing perspectives such as the pragmatic one that communication-oriented scholars of East-West intercultural philosophy David Hall and Roger Ames have used. Such nuanced native points of view have been a dominant trend in Chinese speech communication research in the past two decades. Contrary to the cold war elitist model, which aims for conquest, this cultural communication model allows for deep curiosity and appreciation for and detailed ongoing understanding of Chinese people and Chinese culture in real workings. It also furthers a realistic and constructive approach to intercultural conflicts—to making cultural amends and interculturally mutual empowerment rather than a cultural conquest.

Third, it has opened up a fresh disciplinary perspective little known in Chinese history. Although Chinese culture has an inherent communication perspective, it had never been systematically and explicitly studied from a social scientific perspective. Dominance in traditional Chinese scholarship has been largely humanistic scholarship that consists of philosophy/philology, literature, and history, which are usually treated as a unified academic discipline. This humanistic approach, maintained by Chinese scholars such as Tu Wei-ming, tends to be regulative, normative, and top-down. Thus, it seems to be rigid and restrictive in thinking, in theoretical perspectives and methodology, failing to make sense of many dimensions of Chinese culture.[4] Chinese speech communication scholarship is generating a fresh alternative or a complement to traditional Chinese humanistic and elitist approaches, for it tends to be descriptive, elaborative, and bottom-up, thus allowing more update description, more diversity, and tentativeness in thinking, interpretation, and critique of the status of Chinese communication practices in flux of change. It is also micro detail-oriented. The state of the art and the actual functioning/malfunctioning and transformation of the Chinese culture and society are much better understood in light of such communication studies.

Put together, the studies of Chinese communication have systematically redescribed, reinterpreted, and reanalyzed Chinese culture from a much more detailed and pragmatic approach, paving the way for a mature launch of communication-centered academic programs in Chinese higher education. Seeing the unique value of communication in constructing a peaceful world, Peking University, the national flagship university in China, has formally established a Department of International and Intercultural Communication in its School of International Studies. This is unusual compared to many of the Western universities that rarely have a department or a program of intercultural communication in their schools of international relations. The goal of academic programs of international relations in the West seems to train personnel good at maximizing national interests, national security, and selling Western cultural values to other countries, contrary to the goal of intercultural communication, which is to promote intercultural understanding, peaceful coexistence, and mutual learning. This perhaps suggests that Peking University's definition of the goal of international relations is much larger than the definition of international relations in the West. Peking University's definition of the goal of international relations explicitly embraces the goal of intercultural communication in the discipline of communication in the West. This indicates a growing impact of communication studies, specifically (inter) cultural communication studies and, more specifically, Chinese cultural and intercultural communication studies on Chinese higher education and Chinese diplomacy. With Peking University taking such an initiative, I am sure many other Chinese universities will follow suit.

Reasons for the Growth

The achievements in Chinese speech communication studies have been possible because of several factors, both internal and external. Internally, it is due to the diligence of scholars and students of Chinese speech communication studies and their establishment of a special research interest group—the Association of Chinese Communication Studies (ACCS), affiliated with NCA (formally SCA)[5]. The scholars reviewed above have all been active members of this organization. This organization was established in 1991 with only a few members, largely Chinese or Chinese Americans. Now, it consists of many members from China and many non-Chinese as well. There are also several external factors conducive to the achievements.

First of all, it is due to the diversity model of higher education adopted by the United States since the 1970s, which allows for the acceptance and training of a growing number of Chinese students of communication who later became professors in departments of communication largely within American institutions of higher education. This diversity model also encourages scholarly inquiries into other cultures. Furthermore, it is due to the transformation of the cold war into the post-cold war with the collapse of the Soviet Union. This signals a need for an understanding about cultures other than the one held during the cold war. Still further, it is due to postmodernism, which promotes the growth of indigenous cultures and which values the role of these cultures in critiquing and transforming the crisis-stricken modern Western culture in order to enhance the viability and sustainability of human species.

Finally, China's open-door policy allowed for more intercultural interaction and educational exchanges with the United States and other Western countries. This has made it possible for a growing number of Chinese students of communication to study in the U.S. and to travel back and forth between U.S. and China to do research in Chinese speech communication.

Orientalism

Enlightened by the concept of orientalism of Edward Said in 1979, which identifies a historically created and contemporarily functioning discourse of systematic Western biases on other non-Western cultures such as the Middle East, guided by Clifford Geertz's "emic" approach in understanding cultures, and inspired by Robert Oliver's call for assessing rhetorical theories in Asia "in their own terms — to go with them wherever they may take us", Godwin Chu's call for constructing an operationalizable Asian perspective to communication studies in general and Guo Shu Yang's call for a nativization (*bentuhua*) of social sciences in the Chinese cultural context or sinicization, I am going to identify the patterns of orientalism in Chinese speech communication research. Drawing upon the contemporary literature on Chinese philosophy written by Chinese philosophers such as Chung-Ying Cheng, Tu Wei-Ming, Donald Munro, Herbert Fingarette, and David L. Hall and Roger T. Ames, I will argue epistemologically, ontologically, and axiologically why much of the scholarship on Chinese communication is deeply inconsistent with the nature of Chinese philosophy, but deeply modern Western in nature or orientalist.

Patterns of Orientalism

For the small number of scholars who have been committed to Chinese communication research, the achievements in the past two decades can be said to be remarkable. However, for the fact that Chinese culture has been one of the largest, most sustainable and endurable cultural systems in the world, the amount of Chinese communication scholarship is far from enough. Perhaps it is no exaggeration when Ge Gao and Stella Ting-Toomey conclude: "There has been, however, little theorizing or research on communication in Chinese culture". A major reason for this, I think, is that scholars of communication interested in Chinese communication apply communication theories and concepts generated by Western scholars in the Western contexts to their studies of Chinese communication without any concern for cultural biases, for they tend to regard these theories and concepts as universal and generalizable to all cultures and see no need to theorize about Chinese communication itself. This is what Said calls "a system of reproduction" that "makes it inevitable that the Oriental scholar will use his American training to feel superior to his own people because he is able to 'manage' the Orientalist system; in his relations with his superiors, the European or American Orientalists, he will remain only a 'native informant' ".

Such an orientalist trend has been occasionally heeded against in mass communication research in the Asian context by some insightful scholars of communication, but not in Asian or Chinese speech communication research. In 1988, there was an attempt to reexamine modern Western media-oriented communication theories in light of Asian cultures and traditions and a call by Asian scholars of primarily media-oriented communication, led by Wimal Dissanayake and Godwin Chu, to be critical of uncritical application of Western communication theories and models in Asia-based mass communication research and a call to develop an Asian perspective of communication theory. However, this call seems to be rarely heeded by mass communication scholars with an Asian concentration and virtually unheard by scholars of Chinese speech communication. Recently, Akira Miyahara criticizes the orientalist practices—the "absence of Japanese culture-specific theory and research" in Japanese interpersonal communication research and calls for searching for Japanese culture-specific theory and research in Japanese interpersonal communication competence, which should be conceptually, theoretically, and methodologically consistent with Japanese epistemology and ontology. Likewise, Chinese speech communication research in the past decades seems to be plagued with problems of orientalization similar in nature to the ones Wimal Dissanayake's book describes in mass communication in Asian contexts in the previous decades and the ones in Japanese interpersonal communication research Miyahara criticizes. A critique of Western biases plaguing Chinese speech communication is comparatively late, thus becoming highly urgent and warranted.

Unreflective, uncritical, and uncreative applications of Western communication theories, concepts, and methodologies to the inquiries of Chinese communication have significantly distorted Chinese communication and culture. As a result, it expands or reproduces orientalism in Chinese communication in the West and fails to educate people in the West about exactly how Chinese communicate and why Chinese communicate in given ways and fail to help Westerners better understand the hows and whys about their communication in light of Chinese communication. Specifically, much of the Orientalist scholarship of Chinese communication carries the following modern Western biases into their research: Dichotomous thinking, linear thinking, individualism, analyticalism, absence of the Chinese cosmic, historical, moral, and ethical views, and ignorance of essential concepts of Chinese culture and communication.

Dichotomous Thinking. Dichotomous thinking is explicit in the application of the modern Western individualism versus collectivism framework and the self versus other framework, which are characteristic of the modern Western world view, but find themselves alien in the Confucian-dominated Chinese culture, which emphasizes appropriate, thoughtful, and reflective communication as the very process of self-cultivation and self-transformation. The individualism-collectivism framework used to understand Chinese communication in contrast to the modem Western culture without contexts produces stereotypes that Chinese use an indirect, "positive and affective style" of communication, value interdependence, and social harmony with all Chinese and all other kinds of people they interact with. As a matter of fact, these Chinese communication characteristics are only true with the in-group, or the people they regard as their own, such as members of their own family, group, their own superiors, and people with whom they are in a significant relationship. I would prefer a framework called "situational particularism." Yes, it is true that Chinese live in a web of relations, but this web is very insulated and walled. Beyond the web is a world the Chinese tend to perceive to be generally hostile, harsh, and cold, and thus they act accordingly. I would prefer a framework termed "situational particularism," which best describes Chinese communication. Although Gao and Ting-Toomey's study aims to develop an emic view of Chinese communication, the self-other conceptual divide, obviously influenced by the modern Western dichotomous view, excludes an indigenous Chinese conceptual framework which consists of 1 a core concept of Chinese communication—*li* (rules of propriety)— "the foundations of all human virtues" in the Confucian view; 2 gentlemanhood/sagehood; and 3 harmony. *Li* are instrumental to personal transformation into gentelmanhood or sagehood—the Confucianist ideal personhood, and instrumental to the creation and maintenance of social harmony and cosmic harmony. As a result, their self-other framework fails to penetrate the very depth of Chinese communication.

Linear Thinking. Some studies also apply the transmission model of communication, a typical modem Western model. However, typical of the Chinese culture is the transformative or constructionist model of communication as a means and process of "person making" or "ultimate self-transformation" grounded in the Chinese cultural context. In the Chinese worldview, human nature is malleable, plastic, and perfectible primarily through proper communication. However, in the modem West, communication is primarily concerned with effectiveness of passing objective information separable from the human agent as a sender to the human agent as a receiver. In other words, Chinese communication is conceptualized as a morality-centered activity to improve members' social behavior, whereas the Western scientific model of communication is primarily conceptualized as a scientific instrument to transmit knowledge to other people for the mere sake of knowledge. Communication in this Western sense is largely detached from moral reasoning or the purpose of bettering people's social behavior.

Individualism. Social exchange theory, compliance gaining strategies, Brown and Levinson's theory of politeness, self-disclosure, and, most recently, the use of Western concepts of communication satisfaction and communication competence used in the studies of Chinese communication are all individual-based. They generally do not fit with Chinese communication, which are primarily interpersonally and communally based. The building block of the Chinese culture is at least a pair or a triad instead of individualism, which is not regarded morally legitimate in Chinese culture. Underlying social exchange is a modem Western economic or commercial metaphor for communication that is a process of negotiating and meeting mutual needs, like two traders cutting a deal.

However, Chinese communication is hardly a rational instrument with which each rational and rugged individual tries to meet his or her own needs. It is but a holistic process of relationalism and rationalism in which two or more members try to meet their mutual needs by making the taken-for-granted assumption that the other understands my needs and voluntarily takes care of my needs without my own expression of them. An individual using compliance-gaining strategies is one whose only goal is to meet his own needs regardless of the negative consequences his strategies may bring to the other party. The name of the theory itself indicates the one-sidedness of communication that only includes the profiteer — the compliance-gaining strategist in the theory. To take advantage of the other as an explicit goal would be regarded as immoral in the Chinese context. Self-disclosure as a conceptual framework blinds itself to a unique Chinese interpersonal communication pattern called "heart-to-heart talk" (*tanxin*). In this kind of talk, each one's words are able to touch the heart of the other by talking about exactly what the other party thinks or feels about himself or herself and the interpersonal situation. Politeness is but a tactic of impression management that does not allow any self-sacrifice. Politeness is always coupled with assertiveness. The concept of politeness used to interpret Chinese communication is too superficial to capture the essence of humility and humbleness that are mostly coupled with self-sacrifice or self-effacement, a pervasive ritual in Chinese communication. Communication satisfaction and communication competence used in the studies of Chinese communication are conceptualized in light of the individual. Researchers need to reconceptualize satisfaction and competence from a systemic and contextual perspective in order to understand the Chinese view of communication satisfaction and the Chinese view of communication competence in specific cultural contexts.

Analyticalism. This primarily refers to sole reliance on statistical measurement and analysis in the studies of Chinese communication. Contemporary English is already quite an analytical language. But, Chinese communication is a relatively introspective, reflective, holistic, dialectic, ritualistic, particularistic, and transformative process. If studies of Chinese communication are written in English without any creative effort for appropriate linguistic expressions, they hardly resist this analytical bias. When experimental methods are applied, this analytical bias is even more evident. This bias consists of the following:

1. Chinese concepts of communication are usually substituted with the Western concepts of communication; for example, the modern Western concept of value, which is nonexistent in Chinese culture in lieu of the Chinese concept of ethics and the modern Western intrapsychic concept of attitude, which is nonexistent in Chinese culture in lieu of the Chinese concept of *li* are used as the conceptual framework in the studies of Chinese communication and culture; the concept of value indicates that values are regarded as abstract near-Truth, which is generalizable to all situations and highly stable in all times, whereas the concept of ethics is a relatively particularistic set of rules for social action in a given time and place, which are not regarded as Truth as much as a set of right public performances;

2. Culture and communication are thought to be made up of structural variables and bounded values; this neopositivist view of communication and culture pervasive in the modern West is incompatible with the relatively holistic and dialectic Chinese view of culture and communication as a moral and ethical process of self-cultivation;

3. Since experimental methods used in the above studies only take observable verbal behavior into consideration, much of the nonverbals that constitute Chinese embodied ritualistic communication is excluded;

4. Statistical measurements attempt to come up with mathematically accurate truth claims about a specific dimension of Chinese communication across all situations; however, Chinese communication is defined more by ethical and moral standards than truth standards.

To conclude, applying experimental methods in the studies of Chinese communication without any creative translation is very likely to implicitly assume without researchers' awareness that Chinese subjects think, act, and feel like an ideal modern Western man and are likely to paint a static picture of Chinese communication and culture.

Absence of cosmic, historical, and moral perspectives. As I have already suggested above, due to the mechanistic use of modern Western conceptual and analytical frameworks and the employment of quantitative methods in the studies of Chinese communication reviewed above, the studies, with an explicit goal of understanding Chinese communication and culture, have blinded themselves to the Chinese cosmic view, which includes the historical view and moral view, deeply embedded in and formative of Chinese communication and culture.

Indigenous Chinese concepts ignored. Although some indigenous Chinese concepts of communication, such as face, *guanxi*, and *renqing* have been elaborated, many other concepts of the similar kind remain undefined from a communication perspective. These include *ren* (cohumanity), *yi* (cultivated sense of morality), *li* (rites of propriety), *zhi* (moral knowing), *de* (intelligent virtue), *xiao* (piety), *ren* (tolerance), *qian* (humility), and so on. A communication perspective on such concepts may discover Chinese culture as a unique culture of communication, quite different from Western views of communication and quite different from interpretations of Chinese culture generated out of modern Western Sinology.

Pervasive apathy toward Chinese communication. Although there are a few far-sighted Western scholars of communication, such as Michael Prosser, D. Ray Heisey, William Starosta, and others, who have demonstrated a serious commitment to Chinese communication research and research support in the manner of publishing books and articles on Chinese communication, a majority of the "mainstream" scholars regrettably believe in their theories of communication without bothering to delve into Chinese communication. This attitude not only reflects on their research, but also on their exclusion of studies of Chinese communication in their curricula and in their nonattendance to panels specifically addressing Chinese communication.

For instance, the Association of Chinese Communication Studies (ACCS), as a special research interest group, is perhaps sometimes forced to be an enclave within the international field of communication studies. There seems to be a Great Wall around it, blocking its avenues to communicate with other lines of communication scholars. Membership and leadership are primarily dominated by scholars and students of the Chinese ethnic/national origins, with relatively few scholars of communication from other ethnic/national origins. Like many other similar divisions and special interest groups in NCA, it lacks an institutionalized scholarly dialogue and debates with other interest groups in NCA, particularly at the annual conventions. I do not know of a single panel that addresses a given communication topic from the Chinese cultural perspective and another cultural perspective, such as the European American cultural perspective, African cultural perspective, or the Latin American cultural perspective, in the past five NCA (SCA) annual conventions in which I participated. This apathy of the "mainstream" scholars has helped popularize and perpetuate the above patterns of orientalism in Chinese communication scholarship in the field of communication, although scholars of Chinese communication should also have gone extra miles to break this Great Wall.

Psychologists of Chinese psychology, such as Yang and Wen (1982), learned a lesson from unreflectively applying modern Western psychological theories to the Chinese context and started an indigenization movement in research in Chinese social psychology in the early 1980s. Ten years ago, Asian scholars of mass communication called for a reexamination of Western biases in the study of Asian communication and attempted to establish Asian perspectives of communication. However, it does not seem to have acted as a warning to research on speech communication in the Chinese context in the past decade. At the dawn of the 21st century, with the uncovering of patterns of orientalism, I am making a similar call to scholars of Chinese speech communication and "mainstream" scholars of speech communication: It is high time that we should have avoided the detour; it is high time "mainstream" scholars of speech communication grasped the "singular opportunity to discover something momentous" about yourselves and about your theories by looking into the magic Chinese mirror of Chinese communication and culture.

Chinese Communication in the 21st Century

Given the fact that Chinese communication research has made big strides but is constrained with patterns of orientalism, naturally questions about the future of Chinese communication come to mind. In this section, I first address the question: How can patterns of orientalism in Chinese communication research be broken in future Chinese communication research? Then, I answer the question: Given the emergent trend of and prospect for communication education in China in the 21st century, how can patterns of orientalism be not perpetuated and how can occidentalism be minimized? Finally, what is the prospect of Chinese communication in the 21st century?

Breaking Patterns of Orientalism in the West
This can be done in three steps. First, one must metatheoretically ground his/her study in Chinese philosophy in contrast to the modern Western philosophy. Although I have implicitly addressed this question above, I will address it more explicitly here. Given the fact that Chinese communication is directly and deeply shaped by Chinese philosophy—its cosmology, ontology, epistemology, and axiology—Chinese communication research must be conceptually consistent with Chinese philosophy and Chinese culture. This is very important because "Eastern philosophy almost always has had a direct rhetorical concern", and by extension a direct concern for communication in general. Based on Hall and Ames and De Bary's argument for the centrality of communication in Confucianism and Chung Ying Cheng's argument for communication as a unique perspective to Sinology, with communication's central role in cultural transformation, I even venture to say that to a significant extent, Chinese philosophy is a unique philosophy of communication and Chinese culture is a unique culture of communication. This is because in the Chinese context, philosophy, culture, and communication are not as conceptually distinct as in the modem West.

They conceptually intertwine and share a blurred rather than a distinct and uncrossable boundary. To be able to break the orientalist patterns, a researcher needs to be well trained in Chinese philosophy and culture in comparison to the modern Western analytical philosophy "which may be only accidentally and occasionally concerned with rhetoric", including communication in general, due to its sole interest in abstract truth as irrelevant to or even alienating and annihilating human life in the name of progress. This behooves communication education at both graduate and undergraduate levels in both the West and the East to bear explicitly upon Eastern and Western philosophies, which have been barely touched upon in the Western history of communication education.

Second, he or she must be able to translate the unique essence of indigenous Chinese concepts of culture and communication into English and to interpret the nuances of the concepts in light of a culturally sensitive framework made up of the least value-laden Western terms. Usually, if certain Chinese concepts are found to be unique in meaning, the seemingly similar concepts in English are not to be used to substitute the Chinese ones. Rather, they are sound translated to indicate their unique repertoires of meanings. For example, the Chinese concepts of face should be translated as they are pronounced in *Chinese* —*lianmian*, *mianzi*, and so on— instead of letting these indigenous terms be substituted by face or facework as

Goffman and Brown and Levinson did. Given the fact that the Chinese concepts of mind and heart are conceptually inseparable, unlike the Western ones, which are conceptually distinct from each other, the Chinese term "*xin*" should be creatively and meaningfully translated into something like "mind-heart" (if not literally sound translated) to capture the essence of the term. He or she must also be able to develop research methodologies on the basis of the indigenous cultural and philosophical resources instead of solely relying on the research methods that are solely developed out of the Western cultural context. For instance, since Chinese value *renqing*, *mianzi*, and *guanxi*, a researcher should create a strong sense of obligation on the part of his/her informants instead of highlighting one's rights as a researcher and his/her informants' rights based on the protocols of the human subjects review developed in the West. Instead of paying the informants (which may be perceived to be demeaning or a *lianmian* threat), the researcher is advised to send a relatively recyclable gift to the informants as an effort to establish a long-term relationship. Instead of relying on a Western type of rapport that may be perceived to be superficial, the researcher is advised to act as a new relative of Chinese informants.

Finally, he or she must be able to develop a very intimate knowledge of possible cultural biases of the modern Western concepts and theories and be acutely aware of such negative theoretical and practical impacts of such biases in his/her Chinese communication studies on intercultural communication between China and the West. For example, the Western concept of "value" refers to eternal, relatively immutable abstract truths, which Westerners and all other people are supposed to hold true and hold as guides for behavior during all times in all places. Value is conceptually separate from action and behavior. However, as soon as the concept "value" is used to study Chinese communication and culture, it falsely assumes that Chinese culture shares the concept of value with the modern West. By extension, it falsely implies that Chinese have a dichotomous view of value versus behavior and Chinese believe abstract truths as modem Western men; Chinese culture has the same close-ended definition of culture as the modern West; Chinese try to convert other people as much as modern Western man does.

In fact, Chinese culture did not develop an indigenous concept of value. "*Jiazhi*," which is an invention in modern Chinese, is but a creative translation from English. Evidently, researchers who employ the concept of value in their studies of Chinese communication and culture with the goal of promoting intercultural understandings might have found themselves having done something opposite — having distorted the Chinese culture and communication system and having perpetuated Orientalism. He or she must also be able to translate creatively distinct Western concepts, theories, and methodologies into the Chinese contexts so that there will be substantial relevancy to and insights into the subject under inquiry. For example, the Western concept of value, when appropriated to describe or analyze certain sallent subsystems of Chinese culture, can be creatively translated as "quasi-value," "open-ended value," "relative value," or "pragmatic value" and so on to alleviate Orientalism.

Avoiding Patterns of Orientalism and Occidentalism in China

Communication will be most likely incorporated into related majors such as English, business, journalism, tourism, and Chinese or as a formal discipline of academic study in Chinese universities in the 21st century due to the following forces: the influence of communication departments in universities in China, the overseas Chinese scholars who are originally from China, communication scholars who are of non-Chinese ethnic origins in the U.S. and other countries interested in promoting communication education in China. Peking University, for example, has already established the Department of International and Intercultural Communication in the School of International Studies, perhaps the first department of communication with an emphasis on speech communication and intercultural communication in China.

Communication scholars who are participating in such a bright trend of communication education in China should be especially vigilant about and critical of Orientalist patterns in the Chinese communication scholarship published in the West, which they are appropriating. Instead of treating Western communication scholarship and Chinese communication scholarship in the West as received knowledge applicable to China, they should treat them as heuristic tools at most and try to advance them in the Chinese contexts. They should also watch for and be critical of their own Sinocentric biases in their understanding of modern Western communication that I term as "Chinese Occidentalism." They should establish communication programs that keep both Eastern and Western perspectives (of course many other cultural perspectives, too) without one subordinate and the other dominant.

The Prospect for Chinese Communication Research in the 21st Century

Chinese communication research can be understood to join the third wave of Confucianism articulated by Tu Wei-ming in 1979 and promoted by Hall and Ames in 1987. This third wave is the Confucian-dominated Chinese philosophy/

culture's impact on the evolution of the Western philosophy/culture after its first wave—the birth of the Confucian culture around 200 B. C. and the second wave—Confucianism's expanding impact upon Korea, Japan, and Southeast Asia about 10 centuries ago. Extending and echoing Tu's theory of the third wave Confucianism to the study of Chinese communication, Randy Kluver predicts: "[The] twenty-first century would be the century of Chinese communication research. It would be the century when the entire field of communication is to be revolutionized by Chinese communication studies". Although Kluver does not elaborate his statement, he resonates with my own vision based on my studies of communication theory from a dual East-West cultural perspective. I think that this revolution will occur in the 21st century and will occur in several ways:

First, the 21st century will witness de-westernization and indigenization of Chinese communication research. This will happen in several aspects. First of all, indigenous Chinese communication or interpersonal concepts, such as *mianzi* (face), *renqing* (humanness), and *guanxi* (connections), will be further interpreted and theorized in their own terms. This means that these Chinese interpersonal communication concepts will less likely be interpreted in light of the highly culture-laden Western communication concepts and theoretical frameworks. Many elements of modern Western theories of communication will need to be reformulated and many of these theories will be found to be incomplete in the Chinese context as well as in the Western context by "the introduction of a well-grounded conceptualization of Chinese communication theory and practice". This also means that more Chinese communication research results will be published in Chinese. This will be made possible by the confluence of reflective thinking and self-critique growing within the postmodern paradigm of communication research in the West, the growing self-discovery of its own cultural resources for communication research and possible broad-scale institutionalization of communication research and education in cultural China and other Far East areas such as Japan, Korea, and Singapore, which have received the historical impact of Chinese culture.

Second, this also will be the century when the Eastern culture and the Western culture inform, complement, and transform each other through two independent, equally powerful, mutually interactive systems of communication. For example, the pluralist model of communication studies in the West can be a very useful heuristic for the management of diversity against the backdrop of the deeply-engrained Sinocentrism in cultural China, whereas elements of the Chinese cultural practices such as *renqing* (humanness), *guanxi* (connections), and *mianzi* (face) have a transformative potential for interpersonal relations in the contemporary West, which are excessively dependent on laws, technologies, capital, and other impersonal forces. The fully established Chinese communication research will make its own unique contribution in communication theory development and in promoting intercultural communication between the East and the West.

Third, in terms of communication philosophizing and theorizing in general, the two cultures can be mutually complementary if understood and used well. Ronald Gordon seems to be the one of the first scholars in communication who has conducted a very provocative theoretical study of communication as social transformation by drawing upon the relevant cultural resources from both the West, such as Merleau-Ponty, Sapir Whorf, and Kenneth Burke, and from Chinese Taoism. This type of theoretical scholarship in communication that draws upon more than one cultural resource should be a new direction for research in the 21st century. The reason is clear. Our cultures do not remain as distinct as they used to be in this era of globalization. Thus, while research on culturally distinctive cultural patterns of communication is still possible, building communication theories by creatively drawing upon and synthesizing useful aspects of many cultural and philosophical traditions not only seems to be possible, but also seems to be more and more necessary and practical in this age of unprecedented degree of racial and cultural intermixing.

Conclusion

Orientalism is perhaps the biggest obstacle to a breakthrough in Chinese communication research. Given the fact that the history of Chinese communication, which consists of rhetoric, group communication, and interpersonal communication, have been very long, rich, and unique. Chinese communication research should have been much more developed without Orientalist influence. Unfortunately, Western communication scholarship has been treated as knowledge and has been dominating the Chinese communication research agenda and communication curricula in the Western universities. Perpetuating Orientalism in Chinese communication research will prevent both Chinese and Westerners from better understanding each other. Communication scholars should never forget that there are relevant resources in each cultural tradition that may shed new light on the received knowledge about communication in both the Chinese and Western societies.

It is our responsibility as scholars of communication at the turn of the century to unearth, translate, synthesize, and advance both the Chinese scholarship and the Western scholarship on communication most creatively. It is our responsibility to critique, improve, and enrich or transform the received knowledge in the West in light of the Chinese communication scholarship, and vice versa. It is our responsibility to incorporate such an improved and enriched scholarship into our curricula in both cultures so as to help train our younger generation to become competent communicators and qualified communication professionals who are able to meet the unprecedented demands and challenges of the 21st century. It is out of a deep sense of responsibility that I am doing a critical overview of and painting a prospect for Chinese communication research at the dawn of the new century. I hope that this will help contribute to the construction of communication theories applicable to diverse cultures in this increasingly globalized and simultaneously diversified world.

Notes

1. From *Chinese Perspectives in Rhetoric and Communication*, D. Ray Heisey (Ed.), Stamford, Connecticut: Ablex Publishing Corporation.
2. The term "Chinese communication" here primarily refers to Chinese speech communication published in English. It does not include Chinese mass communication.
3. Edward Wadie Saïd (Nov. 1, 1935—2003), Palestinian American, a political activist and an outspoken advocate for a Palestinian state. He was University Professor of English and Comparative Literature at Columbia University, and was regarded as a founding figure in Postcolonial theory. Saïd is best known for "describing and critiquing Orientalism", which he perceived as a constellation of false assumptions underlying Western world attitudes toward the Middle East.
4. For example, Godwin C. Chu in 1988 has made a similar argument that understanding philosophical traditions, such as Confucianism, Taoism, and Buddhism, does not equate an independent understanding of the Chinese culture in light of communication. This perhaps explains why Tu Weiming's Confucianist project in 1979, the third-wave Confucianism, has largely been ineffective. He seems to have made the mistake of equating the Confucianist teachings with the culture of the Chinese people. Thus, Jia Wenshan thinks that a contextually grounded communication perspective to Chinese studies will help salvage Tu's third-wave Confucianism.
5. NCA is the oldest and largest national organization in the United States to promote communications studies scholarship and education. Founded in 1914 as the National Association of Academic Teachers of Public Speaking, the society incorporated in 1950 as the Speech Association of America. The organization changed its name to Speech Communication Association, in 1970. It adopted its present name in 1997. NCA is a non-profit organization of approximately 7,700 educators, practitioners,

and students who work and reside in every state and more than 20 countries. The purpose of the association is to promote study, criticism, research, teaching, and application of the artistic, humanistic, and scientific principles of communication. As a scholarly society, NCA works to enhance the research, teaching, and service produced by its members on topics of both intellectual and social significance.

Questions for Discussion

1. What does the concept of "Chinese communication" mean to you? Can you name some major scholars on Chinese communication both within and outside China? Chen Guoming, a well-known communication scholar in the University of Rhode Island in the United States posits that the discipline of Chinese communication needs to be established with Chinese characteristics. How do you comment on Chen's viewpoint?
2. Who is Edward Saïd? How do you understand his critique of Orientalism? What is the significance and impact of his critique?
3. What are some of the achievements in Chinese communication research? Can you list some major factors for the achievements and predict the future trends of development?
4. What are the patterns of Orientalism and how can you break such patterns in your own intercultural communication study and research?
5. Scholars like Ji Xianlin, Cai Canrong, and Zhang Weiwei claim that the 21st century is the century of China. By the same token, some communication scholars predict that the 21st century is the century of Chinese communication studies. How do you understand the "taking China as the method" phenomenon?

Online Mini-Case Studies and Viewpoints-Sharing

Amanda's First Business in Mexico

Here is the story of Amanda, an entrepreneur who went to Mexico with a dream of expanding her business overseas. She expressed to me how challenging and frustrating it was to get things done on time and to get feedback from her local team. She said she would ask her Mexican staff to do certain tasks and they would always agree only to disappoint her by not meeting her expectations and deadlines.

When I asked Amanda about her interactions with staff outside of work, she said that she refused to mix work with pleasure. She normally grabbed lunch alone and ate it at her desk so that she could continue working. After listening to Amanda, it was clear to me that she had no idea how different her American cultural behaviors were from the Mexico and how it was deterring her from launching a successful business in Mexican.

After 18 months, Amanda called it quits and returned to San Francisco.

I stayed in touch with Amanda and asked her if she would do anything differently. She paused for a while. Then I proceeded to ask her if she would dive into the ocean without learning how to swim? She said, "Of course not. But what does swimming have to do with my Mexican business?" I told her that it was my analogy for why she would go to Mexico without first understanding the Mexican language and culture, prior to launching her business there.

Online Research

Search online for similar cases, either successful or unsuccessful, and try to offer solutions from an intercultural communication perspective as the author did in the above case.

Reading Two

Introductory Remarks

In this paper, the author looks into the interrelationships of the communication strategies and game intentions in-between China and the US in the arena of the present-day world, with the purpose of constructing a water and game theory for intercultural communication. Through the theoretical lenses of cultural gaming and Chen's paradigmatic assumptions of Eastern and Western cultures and via a thematic analysis of the Chinese traditional cultural classics, from the Chinese Text Project, three featured themes of water including the best and the softest, carrying boats and capsizing boats, and the most violent and the strongest have emerged in correspondence to the positive zero sum, zero sum and negative zero sum game intentions. Thus, a water and game theory for intercultural communication has been constructed, which is applicable to managing various intercultural communication barriers or conflicts.

This theory differs from the major existent ones in three aspects. First, the decisions to choose the communication strategies in correspondence to the conventional or unconventional game intentions are within a continuum with all possible choices included. This breaks through the simple two-element relationships between variables and reflects the intricate player relationships changeable at any time and game intentions sometimes explicit, sometimes half-hidden, and some other times totally hidden. Second, the theory is representative of the Chinese cultural characteristics of water, capable of handling the multiple possibilities of game intentions. Finally, the theory can be applied to manage ICC barriers, especially strategic misunderstanding or distrust between individuals from China and the West, between Chinese enterprises and their counterparts in other countries, and between China and other countries on various ICC occasions.

To seek the cultural roots for the application of the above theory, one can adopt Pang[1]'s Three-Layer Culture Structure. In his article, "Culture Structure and Contemporary China," Pang posited that the structure of culture comprises layers, with an outer layer of the material culture, an inner mixed layer of the partially material and partially spiritual cultures and the spiritual culture at the core. The material layer of culture refers to all the human-processed objects created to meet the needs of human life, especially those articles essential for the sustenance and perpetuation of human life. The mixed layer refers to the mechanic principles, social management, educational systems, and political organizations, and the spiritual culture means the cultural psychological state, which is composed of values, perceptions, aesthetic tastes, thinking patterns, moral sentiment, aesthetic taste, religious feelings, and national character, etc. Related to each other, the three layers of culture form a system or constitute an organism, which stipulates its own development and choice to absorb, transform or exclude the elements of different cultures. Definitely, different cultural models can be adopted when the above theory is applied in various cultural contexts.

Construction of a Water and Game Theory for Intercultural Communication[2]

Tian Dexin

In today's globalized world, connections in-between countries in all social aspects have been becoming tighter than ever before. Although there are different voices and even anti-globalization movements regarding the trend of globalization, interactions among peoples from various cultural backgrounds and different parts of the world are the norm of our times instead of vice versa. Nevertheless, intercultural communication (ICC) barriers, especially those closely related to the value systems bring about misunderstandings or strategic misunderstandings interpersonally due to the mismatch between the cognitive and cultural environments of the communicators. In bilateral relations, strategic distrust occurs due to the fundamental differences in their political traditions, value systems and cultures; insufficient understanding and appreciation of each other's policy-making processes; and growing fear of power competitions. Such ICC challenges are beyond practical pieces of advice because they call for theoretical solutions based on the abstraction of rich cultural resources.

Fortunately, Chinese scholars have been working on the construction of native communication theories and they have made apparent achievements. However, the existing researches have rarely been conducted from the perspectives of cross-cultural gaming and ICC. The present paper aims to fill this gap by looking into the Chinese communication strategies in correspondence to cross-cultural games. On this basis, a native water and game theory for managing ICC barriers is constructed. In a sense, this study traces the thematic resonances of the water image in the Chinese conventional culture so as to explore the Chinese communication strategies in the face of regular and irregular game intentions. On the one hand, 'The highest excellence is like that of water' has been a household saying for centuries in China. On the other hand, metaphors drawing on the image of water convey a significant Chinese philosophical proposition and political doctrine, which functions as the primary source of understanding modern Chinese ideas. To achieve the purposes of this study, three research questions (RQ) are raised:

RQ1: What are the Chinese cultural and philosophical roots for the construction of the water and game theory for intercultural communication in this study?

RQ2: What is the situation of the native ICC theory construction among Chinese scholars like and what are their strengths and weaknesses?

RQ3: How is the water and game theory constructed and how is it applicable to intercultural communication?

LITERATURE REVIEW

To provide the contextualization for the present study, the review of literature herein includes three aspects: first, paradigm shifts from Euro-centrism to Asia-centrism and to contemporary Chinese discourse; second, the concepts, elements, functions and principles of an ICC theory; and third, the achievements and shortcomings of the existing native ICC theories in China.

Paradigm Shifts from Euro-centrism to Asia-centricity and to Chinese Discourse

First, a paradigm refers to 'a summation of the value and technology that are acknowledged and believed among a certain community'. For centuries, it is the developed Western countries that have established and maintained control of the global discourse system. Today, it is more or less the same though there are rising powers fighting for more rights of speech and non-Euro-American scholars advocating de-Euro-centrism. Asante[3] first proposed the concept of 'Afro-centricity' in 1980, advocating the correction of Euro-centrism in the field of ICC, and the adoption of Africa's own cultural basis to construct African centricity.

To follow up, Miike[4] put forward the concept of Asia-centricity in 2003. In his opinion, Asian communication must take Asian culture as the theoretical source. When describing, analyzing and understanding the preconditions and behaviors of Asian communication, Asian culture itself should be placed at the center of exploration, and the following six points should be reflected as far as possible: (1) taking Asians as the subject and agent; (2) focusing on collective and human interests of Asia and Asian's benefits; (3) focusing on the cultural concepts and values of Asian people when understanding their thoughts and behaviors; (4) based on the historical experience of Asia; (5) processing data with an orientation to the Asian context; and (6) criticizing and correcting Asian ethics for the dislocation of Asia and Asians. Thus, the above two scholars have established the first non-western theoretical systems of ICC and laid paved the way for further academic researches along this line.

Regarding Asante's 'Afro-centricity' and Miike's 'Asia-centricity' as paradigmatic shifts from 'Euro-centrism', we agree with their emphasis on understanding the thoughts and behaviors of a people by focusing on their cultural concepts and values. Meanwhile, we hold the idea that any communication theory based on ethnic groups can be biased. Upon further reflections of the cultural games between China and the West, we are fully aware that the contradiction between the Chinese and Western cultures is still very prominent and quite sharp, and the cross-cultural games between the two sides will continue for a long time. However, it is possible and feasible for the two sides to enter a complementary and interactive process of communication and understanding through mutual contacts and dialogues. Du seconded in 2007, all ethnic groups and civilizations should exchange ideas on an equal footing, enhance mutual understanding and reach cross-cultural consensus, so as to create a series of rules for peaceful coexistence, exchanges and mutual learning and form a world civilization. Based on these stimulating ideas, this paper proposes the construction of a water and game theory for ICC.

As for how to construct a native ICC theory based on the Chinese culture, Professor Yu Yelu replied that 'the art of communication has been deeply rooted in the Chinese culture and the blood of the Chinese people, and only systematic and scientific explorations and integrations are needed'. Xu stressed in 2006 that, if they are to make their own contributions, Chinese communication scholars ought to start studying the communication reality in China. Shi has advocated for years, multicultural co-equality should be sought in the construction of contemporary Chinese discourse system to avoid falling into the trap of an eye for an eye vicious cycle or becoming the victim of the myth of cultural incompatibility. Chen also suggested in 2009, 'the intellectual inquiry can be transformed from opposition to fellowship and bring the continuity into the pursuit of humanness on the basis of comprehensive harmony'. To this end, Chinese scholars should begin from the specific historical and cultural contexts of China, effectively combine the cultural wisdom of the East and the West, create an open mechanism of new ICC theories in China, and establish a contemporary Chinese discourse research system with Chinese characteristics.

The Concepts, Elements, Functions, and Principles of an ICC Theory
Every theory is an attempt to explain and illustrate a certain experience or phenomenon. Just as the macro communication theory is a systematic conclusion of the nature of the communication process, a concrete ICC theory is 'the

systematic, abstract and rational explanation and conclusion of the intercultural communication behavior and value' according to Dai in 2011. Wiseman and Horn noted in 1995 each ICC theory includes four elements: (1) research problems, which refer to abstract research problems generated in social practices rather than concrete problems in daily lives; (2) fundamental assumptions, which refer to the attempts to answer the academic questions based on the foundations of research; (3) concepts and variables, in which a concept means the inner feature refined from numerous and shifting phenomena or facts by researchers while a variable refers to the external basic feature that reflects the phenomena or facts, including their status, speed and scale etc. ; and (4) propositions related to concepts and variables, which refer to the statements of relevant concepts and variables usually in the form of axioms, hypotheses and empirical generations.

In addition, Wiseman and Horn remarked in 1995 that a theory has three functions: (1) providing explanations, which means that a theory helps people understand things with systematic knowledge; (2) providing predictions, which means that a theory provides people with enlightenment and verifiable predictions of the ongoing work; (3) the power given by the explanation and prediction of a theory will help people obtain the measures of controlling the progress of a certain event or phenomenon. Therefore, 'theory construction should be viewed as the central issue of intercultural communication study'.

Dai further noted in 2011 that, in spite of various evaluation criteria of theories, at least four principles could be applied in the evaluation process of the quality of ICC theories, namely: (1) logicality, which means a self-justification in logical aspects; (2) explanatory and predictive power, which means a compelling explanation to why and how a certain thing happens, as well as predicting the result and trend of it; (3) enlightening, which serves as an enlightenment for people to do new research and explore more; and (4) simplicity, which means hitting the mark with clear words while explicating the reasons logically, or to put it another way, which is easy to understand and convenient to operate. Accordingly, the water and game theory to be constructed in this study comprises the elements, display the functions and observe the principles of an ICC theory.

The Achievements and Shortcomings of the Existing Native ICC Theories in China

After making a close investigation into China's National Knowledge Infrastructure (CNKI), one of China's biggest online databases, we have found three major categories of native ICC theories: theories based on extracting the condensed essence of China's traditional culture; and theories based on visualizing the metaphoric functions of the Chinese traditional culture; and theories based on the integration of both Eastern and Western communication principles. Limited to space, here are just three examples respectively representing the three categories.

Embryo of an ICC Theory: Ten Concepts of Chinese Communication. Example 1 was contributed by Shao and Yao in 2016. As well-known scholars of cultural studies, the two authors have profound knowledge of traditional Chinese culture. After a patient and careful analysis of Chinese cultural texts, they have extracted and sorted out ten pairs of precious traditional Chinese cultural ideas: '阴-阳' [yīn yáng, yin vs. yang]、'和-合' [hé hé, harmony vs. integration]、'交-通' [jiāo tōng, communication vs. understanding]、'感-应' [gǎn yìng, proper perception vs. ethical response]、'中-正' [zhōng zhèng, centrality vs. uprightness]、'时-位' [shí wèi, temporal contingencies vs. spatial contingencies]、'名-实' [míng shí, name vs. reality]、'言-行' [yán xíng, words vs. deeds]、'心-受' [xīn shòu, heart vs. reception]、'易-简' [yì jiǎn, easy vs. simple].

Being intertwined and inseparable, the first pair of 'yin' and 'yang' keep flowing, transforming, and complementing each other while forming the opposite of each other. In the process, harmony and integration are achieved, and the Chinese learn to adopt the intuitive and dialectical ways of thinking instead being rigid in all situations. As for the second pair, the Chinese culture seeks 'harmony' while putting differences aside and emphasizes 'integration' while maintaining the distinct features of each component. Thus, this pair contributes to the ultimate goals of the Chinese people's interpersonal interactions and diplomatic relations. Regarding the third pair, 'communication' is meant for 'understanding', so a meaningful understanding of each other results from a two-way interaction with necessary feedback. In the fourth pair, individuals are regarded as parts of the whole universe, who can *perceive* the state and demand of the whole while interacting with one another, thus able to *respond* with appropriate behaviors.

With regard to the fifth pair, 'centrality' means showing unbiased attitudes and 'uprightness' proper positions. The implementation of the fifth pair depends on the sixth pair of 'temporal contingencies' and 'spatial contingencies,' with the former referring to the time factors and the latter such space factors as the social background and communication environment. The seventh pair of 'name' and 'reality' are philosophical concepts since ancient China. The former means the form or name of objects while the latter means the content or real objects themselves. However, the relationships between the two concepts have been debated without a definite result. Similarly, the eighth pair of 'words' and 'deeds' are also controversial concepts, with some regarding the two as separate terms, others giving priority to the latter, and still others emphasizing that the two are inseparable. In the ninth pair, 'heart' is oftentimes used to refer to communication itself such as having a heart-to heart talk or taking one's heart. 'Reception' means understanding or getting the message. In fact, the subjectivity of the receiver has been emphasized so much that teachers in various fields tend to ask their students to engage themselves in self-realization. As for the final pair, 'easy' vs. 'simple', the Chinese are accustomed to the emphasis on using easy language or simple terms in social interactions. For instance, Lao Zi claimed that Tao is such a complicated concept that no human languages can convey the essence of its meaning. In the end, he simply used 'yin' and 'yang' and the metaphor of the water image to make it clear.

Shao and Yao are sensitive enough to realize that, with thousands of years in its history, the Chinese traditional culture contains some abstract, systematic and theoretical pairs of thoughts. Although they are invisible, the pairs of thoughts permeate the minds of the Chinese and flow in their blood, guiding and regulating the Chinese people's words and behaviors.

Prototype of an ICC Theory: 'Wind-grass Theory'. According to Xie and Chen's introduction in 2015, the 'wind-grass theory' in Example 2 was originated from Professor Huang Xingmin's speech at an academic conference of Xiamen University. Its main connotation includes: (1) paying attention to the popular decency in the process of natural dissemination like wind; (2) focusing on the audience's subjectivity in terms of laying down like grass; (3) emphasizing the dissemination effect in terms of rising up as wind. The theory is based on what Confucius stressed in *The Analects*:

> The relation between superiors and inferiors is like that between the wind and the grass. The essence of a gentleman is that of wind; the essence of small people is that of grass. The grass must bend, when the wind blows across it. And when a wind passes over the grass, it cannot choose but bend.

Likewise, the 'wind-grass theory' clarifies the interrelationship between the administrators and their subjects by emphasizing the fact that the ordinary people follow the example of their superiors. That means the behavior of a politician or a gentleman is like that of the wind while the conduct of the ruled people is like that of the grass. The latter complies with the moral demeanor of the former. If the former is good, the people will be good; if the former is observant, so is the latter. To be specific, 'natural dissemination like wind' is to popularize the rulers' political ethics and codes of conduct to the public in a natural and subtle way. 'Laying down like grass' and 'rising up as wind' indicate that, in the traditional Chinese context, the ordinary people will go with the stream or wind and compromise with favorable governance and rise up and even fight back with the violent and cruel ruling forces.

It should be noted here that readers familiar with liberal democracy in the West may find it hard to appreciate the dialectical interrelationship between leaders and the people in the Chinese culture. The wind-grass theory may leave them the impressions that the leaders blow and the people bend, and the latter have no ready way to pressurize the former just as the grass cannot tell the wind how to blow. However, in this metaphor, grass does have life, and its actions of laying down and rising up vividly reveal the essence of the Chinese proverb 'A just cause gains great support whereas an unjust one gains little'. In our case, we can just replace the word 'cause' with 'leaders'. In the long history of China, many a violent and cruel government was overthrown by the peasants' uprisings.

Confucian Ethics and the Spirit of the World Order: The Chinese Way of Tolerance. In Example 3, Gu Mingdong[5] found in 2016 that in the face of various crises in the world today, the Western value system alone, which is based on liberalism, seems increasingly inadequate and even at a loss of what to do effectively. Thus, it is necessary to deal with global issues from an integrated perspective based on the common ethics of all nations in the world. In Gu's opinion, the 'way of tolerance' advocated by Confucius in China more than 2,000 years ago can be a key to solving the ethical conflicts and crises between peoples and nations. Although the Western culture also contains similar concepts of 'tolerance' such as 'love your neighbor as yourself', its 'tolerance' has the mandatory ethics, which is difficult to put into practice. On the contrary, 'tolerance' in the Confucian culture is a kind of moral consciousness. Based on the Confucian doctrine of forgiveness combined with the reality of today's world, Gu reconstructed a new Confucian doctrine of tolerance in the form of a pyramid. The ethical base of the pyramid is the Golden Rule: 'Do not do to others what you do not want yourself'. Hence upward is the Silver Rule: 'Recommend to others what you want yourself', the Platinum Rule: 'Help others realize what is good in what they desire', the Iron Rule: 'Repay kindness with kindness and repay injury with justice', and the Jade Rule: 'A civilized person seeks harmony but not conformity. If another person does not follow you, try to win him over by your exemplary cultivated virtues'. The five rules are structured into a pyramid of practical ethics as can be seen below:

Figure 1　A Pyramid of Practical Ethics

As a renowned scholar familiar with the philosophical underpinnings and cultural values of both the East and West, Gu has created reconstructed the Confucian ethics and offered practical solutions to human ethical conflicts and world crises. In the process, both the liberal and democratic conception and the Confucian concepts of the individual have been taken into consideration. With the pyramid structure, Gu presents a 'visual representation of the interrelations of the rules showing an internal logic based on an order of importance and an inverse order of practical applicability … grounded on a model of moral virtues and a humanistic model'.

Obviously, each of the three examples above has its own characteristics and merits. The first example is a preliminary attempt to creatively transform Chinese traditional communication thoughts into native ICC theories. Although the ten pairs of traditional Chinese cultural concepts that represent the dialectical unity of thoughts cannot be regarded as communication theories either independently or as a whole, each pair of concepts is crucial to the further development of the 'contemporary Chinese discourse system'. The communication concept of Example 2 was originated from the social phenomenon of the political management in ancient China, where officials and the ordinary people interacted with one another. Although the 'wind-grass theory' is still 'far from being a theory with a systematic framework' according to Xie and Chen in 2015, it is a great breakthrough in the localization of communication theories by Chinese scholars. Based on the exploring, refining and theorizing of the source of ancient Chinese classical culture, the 'wind-grass theory' has left an indelible imprint on the contemporary Chinese discourse system, especially the construction history of Chinese ICC theories. Example 3, the theoretical pyramid of rebuilt Confucian ethics of tolerance and *tao* [way] has potential universal value. By overcoming the abstractness and poor operationality of Kantian ethics, the theory makes up for the deficiency of liberal ethics. As the spiritual core of the new world order, it can be of certain reference value to meet the moral needs of the new era of globalization.

Nonetheless, as Zhu critiqued in 2007, due to the lack of operationality and falsifiability, it does not help much to explore and sort out traditional Chinese cultural communication speeches and ancient sayings. Without the necessary reliability and validity statistics usually expected in research reports, speculative research findings have little guiding significance for empirical researchers. Even for qualitative researchers, the ten pairs of traditional Chinese cultural concepts in Example 1 are not exclusive of other similar concepts. Both the "wind-grass theory" and "pyramid ethics theory of tolerance" can still be further improved in terms of the accurate descriptions of the different situations and the actual operation procedures of corresponding countermeasures.

THEORETICAL FRAMEWORKS

To seek theoretical guidance, this study observes the principles of the cultural game theory and the paradigmatic assumptions of Eastern and Western cultures.

The Cultural Game Theory
Scholars believed that a game is an activity of how people choose and how this choice achieves equilibrium. It can also be regarded as an act of how to make the

best decisions for maximum benefits. A game theory is 'a study on the rational behaviors of rational participants and their realization of participation equilibrium when the behaviors of multiple participants interact with each other in the case of risk uncertainty' according to Wang in 2005. Liu noted in 2018 that a game theory is a theory concerning two parties or multiple parties which pursue the best interests of their respective parties on the basis of fully understanding the information of all parties in the contexts of competition, cooperation, and conflicts. As a formal discipline, it is the American mathematicians Von Neumann and Oskar Morgenstern that firstly extended a game from a two-player game to a multiple player game, and applied the systematic game theory into the economic field. Thus, the game theory came into being. Later on, with further contributions worth Nobel Prizes by John Forbes Nash, Jr., John Harsanyi, Reinhard Seltern, James Morris, James A. Mirrlees and William Vickrey from Britain and the United States, the game theory has become all the more popular and extensively applied in such disciplines as politics, economics, management, military affairs as well as cultural studies.

Liu found in 2018 that the game theory has four basic elements: (1) no less than two participants; (2) participants striving for maximum benefits; (3) game strategies; and (4) game information. Depending on whether they are subject to binding restrictions, games are divided into cooperative games and non-cooperative games. From the perspective of strategy selection, games are further divided into static games and dynamic games. From the perspective of information mastery, there are also complete information games and incomplete information games. Generally speaking, there are three results in a game: (1) the negative sum game, which means that the participants in the game are ultimately less rewarded than what have been paid, and both parties suffer from losses; (2) the zero-sum game, which means that one participant benefits while the other loses, and the sum of the benefits and losses obtained between the participants is zero; and (3) the positive sum game, meaning that the participants can all benefit and play a win-win game. The above elements and outcomes apply to games in various fields, and of course in cultural games as well.

A cultural game refers to the 'symbiosis between communication and collision, dialogue and confrontation that emerges in cultural exchanges' according to Wang in 2005. Gong and Zhao applied the game theory in 2015 in the field of Chinese and Western cultural security. According to the main cultural differences between China and the West, they found that the games between the Chinese and Western countries has three characteristics: (1) the personification of the sovereign states, that is, the game participants are personified sovereign states; (2) the incompleteness of the game information, which means that the games can start before the players possess complete understanding of each other's characteristics, strategy space. or expected benefits; (3) the non-cooperative nature of the game mode; that is, in most cases the game participating countries find it inconvenient to cooperate and can only make decisions based on their own interests. Of course, the above accounts about the game characteristics have profound cultural roots. In the construction of the water and game theory, the present study takes both the characteristics of the cultural game theory and its cultural roots seriously.

The Paradigmatic Assumptions of Eastern and Western Cultures

Scholars found that the Chinese traditional culture is based on Confucianism, Buddhism and Taoism, and the Chinese culture presents a harmonious, natural, and inductive cultural view with an emphasis on the unity between human beings and the natural world or 'heaven.' Outwardly, it longs for the peaceful harmony between people and nature. Inwardly, it pursues self-improvement through 'cultivating the persons, regulating the families, governing the states, and maintaining the whole kingdom tranquil and happy'. Therefore, when the Chinese people interact with others, they often show a kind of behavior that is forbearing, flexible, and leisurely. The main purpose of using language is to 'establish morality' so as to establish and maintain a harmonious social relationship. In brief, the Chinese culture emphasizes the overall thinking of dialectics, integrating people with words, words with actions, and doing things with morality to carry out a comprehensive and profound understanding.

In contrast, the Western culture inherits the characteristics of individualism and adventurous spirit in ancient Greece. First, Westerners advocate individualism and pragmatism. While pursuing equality, freedom, science, and reason, they tend to impose their own preferences on other nations and cultures, and assume that language is a tool for personal goals. Second, the West, influenced by Descartes' dualism, tries to find a simple and mechanical causal relationship between the two polarized items. Finally, Western scholars, influenced by Derrida's postmodernism and Saussure's structuralism, believe that the observable language form is the carrier of meaning, and thus pay greater attention to language forms and content while paying less attention to the roles of language users and the context.

After looking into the cultural roots and communication preferences between the East and the West, we further empower this study with Chen Guoming's[6] contribution of the paradigmatic assumptions of Eastern and Western cultures in 2009. According to Chen, a paradigm refers to the worldview or philosophical assumptions of a group of people, with the functions of guiding the people to believe, think, and behave in certain ways. A paradigm consists of four elements: ontology, axiology, epistemology, and methodology. Chen summarized the paradigmatic assumptions of Eastern and Western cultures in the table below.

Table 1 The Paradigmatic Assumptions of Eastern and Western Cultures

Ontology		Axiology	
East	West	East	West
Holistic	Atomistic	Harmonious	Confrontational
submerged collectivistic	discrete individualistic	indirect subtle adaptative consensual agreeable	direct expressive dialectical divisive sermonic

Epistemology		Methodology	
East	West	East	West
Interconnected	Reductionistic	Intuitive	Logical
reciprocity we hierarchical associative ascribed	independent I equal free will achieved	subjective non-linear ambiguous ritual accommodative	objective linear analytical justificatory manipulative

As can be seen from the table, ontologically the Eastern cultures tend to hold a holistic view of human communication whereas the Western cultures hold an atomistic view, with the former emphasizing the collectivistic orientation in social interactions and the latter individualistic orientation. Axiologically, people in the East treat harmony as the guidepost and ultimate goal of human communication, thus adopting indirect, subtle, adaptive, consensual and agreeable styles in everyday social interactions. In contrast, people in the West consider confrontation the best way to resolve a problem or overcoming one's rivals in social interactions by using direct, expressive, dialectical, divisive, and sermonic styles of communication. Epistemologically, the Eastern cultures stress the interconnectedness in-between the knower and the known and reciprocal, we-sense, hierarchical, associative, and ascribed human communication. However, Western cultures emphasize the reductionistic way of knowing and independent, I-sense, equal, free-will, and achieved processes of human communication. Finally, in methodology, people in the East trust their intuitive thinking and tend to adopt a more subjective, non-linear, ambiguous, ritual, and accommodative pattern of communication. Nevertheless, people in the West trust logical reasoning and are likely to employ the objective, linear, analytical, justificatory, and manipulative patterns of communication. It is Chen's idea that the cultural differences in the paradigmatic assumptions between the East and the West 'create a discrepancy of insurmountable gap' which requires 'a culture specific or emic approach to the understanding of a cultural group'.

Because of the fundamental differences between Chinese and Western cultural values, their thinking patterns and behavioral norms are quite different. In the cultural games between China and the West, it is unwise and impractical to try to impose one party's cultural values onto the other party based on racial or cultural superiority. We believe that the best way to maximize the benefits of both sides is to 'absorb each other's advanced culture to make up for the shortcomings of one's own culture' according to Chu in 2011. As Du also voiced in 2007 that all ethnic groups and civilizations should exchange ideas on an equal footing, enhance mutual understanding and reach a cross-cultural consensus, so as to create a series of rules for peaceful coexistence, exchanges and mutual learning and ultimately form a world civilization.

RESEARCH METHODS

This study adopted the online field observation for data collection. According to the purposes of this study, the present paper selected its primary data from the Chinese Text Project on the website of https://ctext. org, with a total number of 675 paragraphs regarding 'water'. After deleting 165 paragraphs which are irrelevant or do not make sense, 510 paragraphs were selected for analysis. The reasons for selecting this website are threefold: first, the website has been designed, edited, and maintained by Dr. Donald Sturgeon, a professor of computer science at Durham University in the UK. Second, although the texts on the website are predominantly pre-Qin (221 BCE—206 BCE) and Han (206 BCE—220 CE), they also include selections through the other dynasties in the history of China in an organized and searchable format. Finally, the website presents the texts in both Chinese and English, thus keeping the quality of English versions acceptable to English native speakers.

For the analysis of the 510 paragraphs, thematic analysis was adopted, which is "a method for identifying, analyzing, and reporting themes within qualitative data" (Braun & Clark, 2006, p. 79). Themes are 'units derived from patterns such as conversation topics, vocabulary, recurring activities, meanings, feelings, or folk sayings and proverbs' according to Taylor and Bogdan in 1989. Following Owen's three criteria for the generation of a theme in 1984, the author and two of his graduate students independently coded the selected paragraphs, analyzed them comparatively at the message level from the perspective of the message authors rather than from the viewpoints of the message inter-coders. By categorizing the selected paragraphs based on the nature of the messages, we further divided them into sub-categories according to the featured themes. Finally, guided by the theoretical framework and through constant comparison and contrast between us as coders, we made every endeavor to build a valid argument for the themes. The featured themes are as follows.

RESEARCH FINDINGS AND DISCUSSION

Under the guidance of the cultural game theory and paradigmatic assumptions of Eastern and Western cultures and via the research methods of online field observation and thematic analysis for data collection and analysis, this study has achieved the following three main findings. Below is a report of the findings with necessary comments and explanations.

The Best and the Softest

As a material condition for the survival and development of human beings, water has not only nurtured and forged the Chinese nation, but also become an important source for the traditional cultural concepts of Confucianism, Buddhism and Taoism. In the eighth chapter of *Dao De Jing*, Daoist Lao Zi said: 'The highest excellence is like [that of] water, benefiting all things and occupying the low place which all men dislike. Hence [its way] is near to [that of] the Dao'. Moreover, the "highest excellence" of water is also compared to the kindest and the best character of a noble person. Therefore, the highest tenderness of water is called 'highest virtue.' As the operating law of the universe and the highest idea, Dao is invisible and difficult to describe in language. Lao Zi believed that the form, mode of operation and function of water were closest to the Dao he discussed.

In *The Analects*, Confucius said: 'The wise find pleasure in water; the virtuous find pleasure in hills'. Because water possesses such virtuous features as benevolence, wisdom, and chastity. Water is not contesting with other things, but the place that people hate is where it stays for a long time. Although water is the weakest thing in the world, it can penetrate the hardest. No matter how filthy a place is, sufficient water can finally cleanse it. Water bears the burden of humiliation, contains all things, and eventually becomes an indisputable king. Meanwhile, Buddhism advocates 'observing Buddha with water, cultivating the mind with water.' Buddhists believe that water is the embodiment of Buddhist wisdom. 'Although the utensils are square and round, the water in it stays clear by clearing the dirt. It spares no efforts reaching everywhere. Thus, it is all over the place and unpredictable'. In addition, a Buddhist saying goes: the sea does not allow dead bodies. This means that water seems to be indiscriminate, but in fact it does not allow dirt and what is left is the purest. All this makes the Buddhists realize and appreciate the connotations of water: 'Pureness', 'emptiness' and 'brightness'.

To learn from the best and the softest nature of water from the perspective of ICC is to adopt the highest moral standards and the willingness to bring benefits to all while giving priority to human beings by seeking harmony and integration. In order to formulate a series of ICC rules for peaceful coexistence, exchange and mutual learning, and construct a universal civilization of the world, the Chinese tend to embrace the attitudes of extensive consultation, joint contribution, win-win cooperation and openness and inclusiveness.

Carrying Boats and Capsizing Boats

It is recorded in *Xunzi: Aigong*, '... the king, is like a boat, and the people, water. Water can carry the boat, and it can also overturn the boat. If you think about danger in this way, you will not be in danger'. By talking about water which can carry and overturn boats, it is meant that rulers and ordinary people function interdependently. The rulers are expected to keep the country in good order and peaceful for further development and possible survival of the people. Meanwhile, the ordinary people can make the boat sail smoothly and also overturn it. Such experience of governing a country and lessons of subjugation are based on the relationship between the government and the people, which were repeatedly alluded to in the Tang Dynasty by Wei Zheng, the Prime Minister, to Li Shimin, the second emperor in the Tang Dynasty. It is fair to say that, thanks to the prime minister's timely advice by alluding to the water metaphor, the emperor who had felt increasingly self-important, was successfully pulled back once and again from abusing his power and endangering the interrelationship between him and his subjects.

Thus, it is of paramount significance for a ruler to understand and remember that water can carry boats and overturn them. Reflecting upon the changes of the past dynasties in China which violated the moral of the water metaphor, quite a number of them simply experienced 'overwhelming prosperity' followed by 'abrupt collapses'. Actually, the water metaphor of 'carrying or overturning the boats' embodies the idea of dialectical unity in the popular statement of 'those who win the hearts of the people gain the world while those who lose the hearts of the people lose the world'. This dialectical view in the spiritual attributes of water is also reflected in such pairs of ideas as the clear and turbid, rigid and soft, dynamic and static, and beneficial and harmful. The point here is that among the four pairs of opposites, without the former in each pair, the latter can become so blurred that it draws insufficient or even no attention. It also indicates that the opposites can transform into one another under certain circumstances.

To learn from the nature of water capable of carrying boats and capsizing boats from the vantage of ICC, it is necessary to first understand the interdependence between communicators and audiences, and behave flexibly according to the specific environment and different objects. At the same time, effective ICC communicators should be good at distinguishing the dialectical relationships such as the clear and turbid, rigid and soft, dynamic and static, beneficial and harmful in the real society. Finally, in accordance with the communication laws, ICC communicators should creatively apply such strategies as using the soft to fight against the rigid and taking advantage of the benefits of both the rigid and the soft under various contexts.

The Most Violent and the Strongest
Zhang (2012) found that the relationship between human beings and water has gone through four stages: 'awe', 'development', 'plunder' and 'symbiosis' in the process of human history. It can also be described as a spiral rising process of 'harmony—imbalance—harmony'. From a cultural point of view, there is extreme human centralism based on 'man is the spirit of all things' and 'man is better than heaven'. There is also natural centralism, treating the earth as the 'mother'. In addition, there is the Chinese cultural value of seeking harmony between human beings and nature, based on the unity of heaven and mankind. As Marx and Engels put it: 'Human plans that are not based on the great laws of nature will only bring disaster'. In fact, before the 1940s, China had disasters and famines almost every year in more than 3000 years. No wonder the Chinese people have drawn so much experience from their fights against floods and in their

construction of water conservancy projects.

To learn from the most violent and strongest character of water for better ICC is definitely not to learn how to bring disasters to other human beings and the earth, but to learn that the softest water contains extremely fierce and great impacts. The same is true of the power of discourse in human communication. Anytime when we are endowed with the rights of speech, we need to apply the rights with great caution, especially when we are dealing with serious and important issues on various ICC occasions involving individuals, communities, ethnic groups, and nations. Otherwise, the gentle water may act as a runaway wild horse, become a flood and beast, ravage the world, and bring harm to the lives and property of human beings.

The Construction of the Water and Game Theory

As Gong and Zhao emphasized in 2015, the game participants discussed in this paper are the personified sovereign states of China and its counterparts in the West. In addition to the incomplete game information and the non-cooperative game characteristics, the countries participating in the games, the focus of the games and the intensity of the games are changing all the time according to the changes in the current global situation, the focus of the respective country's national interests, and most importantly, the differences in the paradigmatic assumptions between Eastern and Western cultures. Therefore, the present Chinese water and game theory for ICC is about making flexible and creative choices of communication strategies between the range of the 'best and the softest' through 'carrying boats and capsizing boats' and 'the most violent and the strongest.'

The choices are made in response to the positive zero sum, zero sum and negative zero sum game intentions in the case of cooperative or non-cooperative, static or dynamic, or conventional or unconventional situations. The ultimate goals are: the best possible publicity effects and optimal game outcomes.

On the one hand, this theory uses water as a metaphor to indicate a range of communication strategies between the most desirable and most undesirable choices for ICC. Along the vertical axis on the left side of Figure 1, the nodes from 'the best and the softest' through 'carrying boats and capsizing boats to 'the most violent and the strongest' communication strategies are marked from the bottom to the top. First, the most desirable and most undesirable are two dynamic concepts in relation to each other, rather than two absolute static concepts. Depending on the rival player's conventional or unconventional intentions, the final decision regarding the communication strategies shifts between the most acceptable and the most unacceptable. Second, between the most desirable and the most undesirable strategies, there are countless choices along the continuum. The continuum here refers to the 'integration of the points, and the solid line as a continuum is exactly the same as the real integration. That is, each point on the line corresponds to each real number, and the division of the line is like the division of real numbers' according to Zhang in 2011. Finally, the midpoint on the vertical axis ('carrying boats and capsizing boats') is a reference for discussion. The choices above this point tend to move towards the 'most undesirable' while those below this point tend to move towards the 'most desirable.' Therefore, this mid point or node itself does not participate in the representation of the hypothetical relationships between the vertical axis and the parallel axis.

On the other hand, this theory uses gaming as an analogy, which indicates that there are three options: i. e. , the positive zero sum (Win-win or both sides win.), zero sum (One side wins, and the other side loses.) and negative zero sum (Double losses or both sides lose.) in the range from the most favorable to the most unfavorable outcomes along the horizontal axis at the bottom of Figure 1. In general, each player wants to achieve the ideal result of either a win-win or a win-lose situation. However, it cannot be ruled out that in some special or unconventional situations, the player may purposely aim at the zero sum or even negative zero sum outcome. Facing such extreme cases, Gu's Jade Rule of Confucian tolerance may be taken. The rule is 'A civilized person seeks harmony but not conformity. If another person does not follow you, try to win him over by your exemplary cultivated virtues'. When conditioned tolerance still does not work, zero-tolerance of tit-for-tat measures will be adopted. Thus, the decisions to choose the best possible communication strategy must be flexibly and creatively made within the most desirable and most undesirable range to deal with the gamers' explicit, semi-hidden or hidden agendas.

Based on the above, we propose our basic assumptions. For the convenience of description, we divide the two sides of players into the host and the rival. In fact, the host is also a rival in the eye of the rival. In other words, the host and the rival take turns to make their communication strategies and convey their game intentions. Below are our six assumptions:

(1) If the rival player shows an obvious positive zero sum intention, and the host player makes decisions likely to move towards the best and the softest communication strategy, then the game is likely to end with a win-win outcome.

(2) If the rival player shows an obvious positive zero sum intention, but the host player makes decisions likely to move towards the most violent and strongest

communication strategy, then the game is likely to end with a winning rival and losing host.

(3) If the rival player shows a clear zero sum intention, and the host player makes decisions likely to move towards the best and the softest communication strategy, then the game is likely to end with a winning host and losing rival.

(4) If the rival player shows a clear zero sum intention, but the host player makes decisions likely to move towards the most violent and the strongest communication strategy, then the game is likely to end with a winning rival and losing host.

(5) If the rival player shows an obvious negative zero sum intention, but the host player makes decisions likely to move towards the best and the softest communication strategy, then the game is likely to end with a winning host and losing rival.

(6) If the rival player shows an obvious negative zero sum intention, and the host player chooses the path that tends to move towards the most violent and strongest communication strategy, then the game is likely to end with a lose-lose outcome.

The above native water and game theory for ICC can be illustrated as follows:

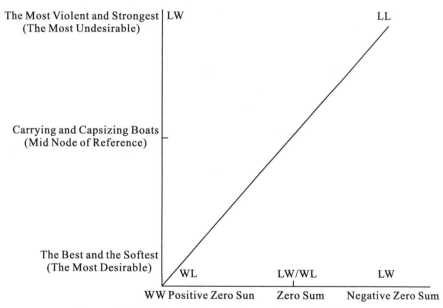

Figure 2　A Native Water and Game theory ICC Theory

In Figure 2, WW refers to win-win, LL refers to lose-lose, WL refers to the host-player win and rival player lose, and LW refers to the host-player lose and rival player win. Upon reflections of the previous literature, this theory contains the three functions and four elements of an ICC theory as Wiseman and Horn emphasized in 1995. It also meets the four criteria which Dai proposed in 2011 to measure the quality of a theory. Of course, the reliability, credibility and practical value of the present theory needs to be further tested by actual case analyses.

The Applicability of the Water and Game Theory to ICC

First and foremost, ICC occurs when an interaction happens between peoples from different cultures. In the case of the present study, we discuss cross-cultural games between China and Western countries. The verbal and nonverbal communication in the course of the games between the personified sovereign states and their representatives are intercultural in nature.

Second, considering China as a rising power and the impacts on its diplomatic relations, the intentions of the cross-cultural game participants include all the possibilities of the positive zero sum, zero sum and negative zero sum in cooperative or non-cooperative, static or dynamic, and conventional or unconventional situations. In response to the uncertainties in the game intentions, the level of difficulty in the choice of communication strategies increases dramatically. Seeking solutions to addressing the tension between the cross-cultural intentions and communication strategies has thus created an ICC need calling for a theoretical resolution.

Finally, the compatibility between choosing the communication strategies based on the functions of the water image in the Chinese culture and handling the cross-cultural game intentions lies in the fact that the intentions are from cross-cultural games and communication strategies stem from cultural sources as well. Although the relationships between the game players become complicated and unpredictable, the decisions to choose the relevant communication strategies as countermeasures are accessible and available within the overall structure of the theory.

CONCLUSION

The purposes of the present paper were to look into the interrelationships between Chinese and Western game intentions and communication strategies and, on this basis, construct a native water and game theory for managing ICC barriers. Through the theoretical lenses of cultural gaming and Chen's paradigmatic assumptions of Eastern and Western cultures and via the research methods of online field observation and thematic analysis, three featured themes of water including the best and the softest, carrying boats and capsizing boats, and the most violent and strongest have emerged from the Chinese cultural classics. In correspondence to the positive zero sum, zero sum and negative zero sum game outcomes or intentions, a native water game theory for ICC with six basic assumptions has been constructed. In brief, this theory is meant for applying the most desirable communication strategies to obtain the best possible game outcomes or in changeable and tricky game situations.

This theory differs from the above three sample theories in three aspects. First, the decisions to choose the communication strategies in correspondence to the conventional or unconventional game intentions are within a continuum with all possible choices included. This breaks through the simple two-element relationships between variables and reflects the intricate player relationships changeable at any time and game intentions sometimes explicit, sometimes half-hidden, and some other times totally hidden. Second, the theory is representative of the Chinese cultural characteristics of water, capable of handling the multiple possibilities of game intentions. Finally, the theory can be applied to manage ICC barriers, especially strategic misunderstanding or distrust between individuals from China and the West, between Chinese enterprises and their counterparts in other countries, and between China and other countries on various ICC occasions.

There are at least three limitations with the present paper. First, the primary data just comes from the Chinese Text Project on the website of https://ctext.org. Second, the paper has mainly examined the Chinese cultural texts. Finally, the six assumptions of the proposed theory still need to be verified. Thus, suggestions for future research are twofold: On the one hand, an expansion of the data sources should be made to include not only more Chinese cultural texts but Western ones as well. On the other hand, a balanced, comparative study can be more fruitful.

Notes

1. Pang Pu (庞朴) was originally named Shenglu. As a famous contemporary Chinese historian, cultural historian, philosophical historian, and Fang Yizhi research expert, Pang was born in Huaiyin County, Jiangsu Province in October, 1928. He graduated from the Philosophy Department of Renmin University of China in 1954. He used to be a lecturer at Shandong University, editor in chief of historical studies, a researcher at the Chinese Academy of Social Sciences, the international editorial board of UNESCO's history of human scientific and cultural development, the director of the international bamboo and silk research center, a lifelong professor at Shandong University, vice chairman of the board of trustees and director of the

academic committee of the Academy of Confucianism. He is committed to the study of the history of Chinese philosophy, ideology, culture and unearthed bamboo and silk.

  Throughout the 1980s, Pang Pu has made dozens of speeches and written articles on the issues of culturology, cultural history, cultural tradition and modernization, explaining his various ideological understandings of culture, thus promoting the progress of the upsurge of cultural research. Pang Pu's series of important points can be summarized into three: first, a definition, what is culture? Culture is humanization. The second is that culture has two attributes: nationality and timeliness. Third, culture has three levels: material, spiritual and institutional. Pang Pu's exposition of the definition, two attributes and three-tier structure of culture has attracted great attention in the academic circles and has become an important theoretical guide to explore Chinese culture.

2. From Tian Dexin, Construction of a Water and Game Theory for Intercultural Communication, *The International Communication Gazette*, 2021, 83(7), 662-684.

3. Molefi Kete Asante is Professor and Chair, Department of Africology and African American Studies at Temple University in Philadelphia. He also serves as the International Organizer for Afrocentricity International and is President of the Molefi Kete Asante Institute for Afrocentric Studies. Asante is a Guest Professor, Zhejiang University, Hangzhou, China and Professor Extraordinarius at the University of South Africa.

  Asante, often called the most prolific African American scholar, has published 85 books, among the most recent are *Radical Insurgencies*, *The History of Africa*, 3rd Edition; *The African American People: A Global History*; *Erasing Racism: The Survival of the American Nation*; *Revolutionary Pedagogy*; *African American History: A Journey of Liberation*; *African Pyramids of Knowledge*; *Facing South to Africa*, and, the memoir, *As I Run Toward Africa*. Asante has published more than 500 articles and is considered one of the most quoted living African authors as well as one of the most distinguished thinkers in the African world. He has been recognized as one of the 10 most widely cited African scholars. Asante has been recognized as one of the most influential leaders in education.

4. Dr. Yoshitaka Miike joined the UH Hilo faculty in 2004. He holds one of the first M. A. s in Communication Studies from Dokkyo University (Japan) and earned, with distinction, his Ph. D. in Intercultural Communication from the University of New Mexico (USA). He was named as Fellow at the Molefi Kete Asante Institute for Afrocentric Studies in Philadelphia and was elected to serve as Vice-Chair Elect (2011—2012), Vice-Chair (2012—2013), Chair (2013—2014), Immediate Past Chair (2014—2015), and Past Chair (2015—2016) of the International and Intercultural Communication Division (IICD) of the National Communication

Association (NCA) in Washington, D. C.

Dr. Miike is best known for his pioneering work on the paradigmatic and pragmatic idea of Asiacentricity. He co-edited *The Global Intercultural Communication Reader* (1st and 2nd Editions, Routledge, USA) and guest-edited four journal special issues/section on Asian communication theory. His numerous essays have been published in such outlets as *Asiacentric Theories of Communication* (Zhejiang University Press, China), *Communication Monographs* (NCA/Routledge, USA), *Encyclopedia of Identity* (Sage, USA), *Essays in Honor of an Intellectual Warrior, Molefi Kete Asante* (Editions Menaibuc, France).

5. Gu Mingdong (顾明栋) is currently Professor of Chinese and Comparative Literature at the University of Texas at Dallas. He is the author of four monographs in English: (1) *Fusion of Critical Horizons in Chinese and Western Language, Poetics, Aesthetics* (Palgrave Macmillan, 2021); (2) *Sinologism: An Alternative to Orientalism and Post-colonialism* (Routledge, 2013); (3) *Chinese Theories of Reading and Writing* (SUNY Press 2005), (4) *Chinese Theories of Fiction* (SUNY Press 2006), and 1 book in Chinese: (5) *Anxiety of Originality* (Nanjing University Press, 2009); editor of three English books: *Translating China for Western Readers* (SUNY Press, 2014), *Why Traditional Chinese Philosophy Still Matters* (Routledge 2018), and *Routledge Handbook of Modern Chinese Literature* (2019); and a co-editor of three volumes: *Nobel Prize Winners on Literary Creation* (Peking University Press, 1987), *Collected Essays on the Critical Inquiry of Sinologism, and and Sinologism* (China Social Science Press, 2017), and *New Sinology: Discussions and Debates on China-West Studies* (Special Issue for Contemporary Chinese Thought 2018).

6. Chen Guoming (陈国明) is Professor of Communication Studies at the University of Rhode Island. He was the recipient of the 1987 outstanding dissertation award presented by the NCA International and Intercultural Communication Division. Chen is the founding president of the Association for Chinese Communication Studies. He served as Chair of the ECA Intercultural Communication Interest Group and at-large member of the SCA Legislative Council, and currently he is the President of the International Association for Intercultural Communication Studies. He is also the co-editor of Intercultural Communication Studies, China Media Research, and International and Intercultural Communication Annual, and serves on the editorial board of different professional journals.

Chen's primary research interests are in intercultural/organizational/global communication. In addition to receiving various awards and honors, Chen has published over 150 papers, book chapters, and essays in *Communication Yearbook, Journal of Cross-Cultural Psychology, China Media Research, Human Communication, Communication Research Reports, Intercultural Communication Studies, The Howard Journal of Communications, Journal of Psychology*, etc. Chen has (co) authored and (co) edited 35 books and journal special issues, including *Foundations of Intercultural Communication*, *Communication and Global Society*, *A Study of Intercultural Communication Competence*, *Dialogue Among Diversities*, *Study of Chinese Communication Behaviors*, *Chinese Conflict Management and Resolution*, *Introduction to Intercultural Communication*, *Theories and Principles of Chinese Communication*, *Asian Perspective of Culture and communication*, *Communication Research Methods*, *Communication Theories*, and others. Chen continues to be active in teaching, scholarship and in professional, university, and community services.

Questions for Discussion

1. In the process of paradigm shifts, Asante and Miike contributed "Afro-centricity" and "Asia-centricity" respectively, how do you comment on the paradigm shifts and how do you like the two scholars' achievements?
2. Three major categories of native ICC theories have been introduced, namely: (1) theories based on extracting the condensed essence of China's traditional culture; (2) theories based on visualizing the metaphoric functions of the Chinese traditional culture; and (3) theories based on the integration of both Eastern and Western communication principles. How do you like the categorization and what comments do you intend to make on the selected indigenous Chinese communication theories?
3. In 2009, Dr. Chen Guoming made his contribution of the paradigmatic assumptions of Eastern and Western cultures, comprising four elements: ontology, axiology, epistemology, and methodology as can be seen in Table 1. What critical thoughts do you have on Dr. Chen's contribution?
4. In brief, the water and game theory for ICC in the reading is about making flexible and creative choices of communication strategies between the range of the 'best and the softest' through 'carrying boats and capsizing boats' and 'the most violent and the strongest'. The choices are made in response to the positive zero sum, zero sum, and negative zero sum game intentions in the case of cooperative or non-cooperative, static or dynamic, or conventional or unconventional situations. The ultimate goals are the best possible publicity effects and optimal game outcomes. How do you like the construction of the theory? What values do you see in the application of it?
5. To seek the cultural roots for the application of the said theory, it is suggested that one can adopt Pang's Three-Layer Culture Structure at the material, spiritual and institutional levels. How do you like the suggestion? What other cultural models can you suggest in different cultural contexts?

Online Mini-Case Studies and Viewpoints-Sharing

Misunderstood Humor in an Online Course

When humor is misunderstood, it often takes complicated explanations to clarify, as one communication professor discovered:

One of the classmates in my online course made a remark, meant to be slightly sarcastic and humorous, about one of the group projects he was involved in for our course. However, the remark was perceived by some of the international members of his group to be in poor taste. Some thought it very rude and insulting. Others just found it childish. It took almost half the semester to figure out what had gone wrong, why the remark was misunderstood and how to get things back on a good footing. I can't imagine it would have taken even half that long if the interactions had been face-to-face instead of on the Internet.

Online Research

Search online and find out if more and more online courses are being offered nowadays and if online teaching will become a normal phenomenon instead of an exception in the future. Based on your experience, please compare and contrast traditional classroom teaching with online teaching, while taking their respective impacts upon effective and appropriate intercultural communication into consideration.

Glossary

Acculturation The process of cultural change that results from ongoing contact between two or more culturally different groups.

Adaptors Mostly unconscious nonverbal actions that satisfy physiological or psychological needs, such as searching an itch.

Adjustment The principle of verbal interaction that claims that effective communication depends on the extent to which communicators share the same system of signals.

Affect display Also called affective display, refers to an interactant's externally displayed affect. The affect can be displayed by facial, vocal, and gestural means.

Affective resources The emotional responses and ways of managing our emotions that help us communicate effectively with others. Some affective resources include the abilities to tolerate ambiguity, manage anxiety, manage anger, and forgiving others.

Affinity seeking The process by which individuals attempt to get others to like and feel positive toward them.

Affirmation The communication of support and approval.

Age identity The identification with the cultural conventions of how we should act, look, and behave according to our age.

Allness The illogical assumption that all can be known or said about a given person, issue, object, or event.

Alter-adaptors Body movements you make in response to your current interactions, for example, crossing your arms over your chest when someone unpleasant approaches or moving closer to someone you like.

Anthropology The science of man in his physical, social, and cultural variation.

Anxiety A diffuse state of being uneasy or worried about what may happen.

Argot The cant and jargon of a particular class, generally an underworld or a criminal class, which is difficult and sometimes impossible for outsiders to understand.

Assertiveness A willingness to stand up for your rights but with respect for the rights of others.

Assimilation The degree to which an individual takes on the behaviours and language habits and practices the basic rules and norms of the host culture while relinquishing ties with the native culture.

Attitudes An individual's dispositions or mental sets. As a component of intercultural communication competence, attitudes include tolerance for ambiguity, empathy, and non-judgmentalness.

Attraction theory The theory that people develop relationships on the basis of attractiveness, proximity, and similarity.

Avowal The process by which an individual portrays himself or herself.

Barriers to intercultural communication Those physical or psychological factors that prevent or hinder effective communication, such as ignoring differences between yourself and the culturally different, ignoring differences among the culturally different, ignoring differences in meaning, violating cultural rules and customs, and evaluating differences negatively.

Behavioral synchrony The similarity in the behavior, usually nonverbal (such as postural stance or facial expressions) of two persons, generally, taken as an indicator of liking.

Boundary markers Markers that set boundaries around or divide one person's territory from another's, such as a fence.

Bureaucracy A form of organization based on strict rules and competences attached to positions.

Channel The vehicle or medium through which signals are sent such as the vocal-auditory channel.

Cherishing behaviors Small behaviors you enjoy receiving from others, especially from your relational partner like a kiss before leaving for work.

Chronemics The perception and use of time.

Civil inattention Polite ignoring of others (after a brief sign of awareness) so as not to invade their privacy.

Code switching A technical term in communication that refers to the phenomenon of changing languages, dialects, or even accents.

Code A set of symbols used to translate a message from one form to another.

Cognitive complexity The use of a large number of constructs to understand other people's behavior. Cognitive simplicity, in contrast, involves the use of a small number of constructs to understand other people's behavior.

Collectivism The opposite of individualism; together, they form one of the dimensions of national cultures. Collectivism stands for a society in which people from birth onwards are integrated into strong, cohesive in-groups, which throughout people's lifetime continue to protect them in exchange for unquestioning loyalty.

Collectivist culture A culture in which the group's goals rather than the individual's are given greater importance and in which, for instance, benevolence, tradition, and conformity are given special emphasis. Opposed to individualist culture.

Color communication The use of color to communicate different meanings; each culture seems to define the meanings colors communicate somewhat differently.

Communication apprehension Fear or anxiety associated with either real or anticipated communication with another person or group of persons.

Communication Basically means a dynamic, systemic process in which meanings are created, negotiated and reflected in human interaction with symbols.

Communicology The study of communication, particularly the subsection concerned with human communication.

Competence "Language competence" is a speaker's ability to use the language; it is a knowledge of the elements and rules of the language. "Communication competence" generally refers to both the knowledge of communication and also to the ability to engage in communication effectively.

Complementary relationship A relationship in which the behavior of one person serves as the stimulus for the complementary behavior of the other; in complementary relationships, behavioral differences are maximized.

Compliance-gaining strategies Behaviors designed to gain the agreement of others, to persuade others to do as you wish.

Compliance-resisting strategies Behaviors directed at resisting the persuasive attempts of others.

Confirmation A communication pattern that acknowledges another person's presence and indicates an acceptance of this person, this person's definition of self, and the relationship as defined or viewed by this other person. Opposed to rejection and disconfirmation.

Conflict The interference between two or more interdependent individuals or groups of people who perceive incompatible goals, values, or expectations in attaining those ends.

Confrontation Direct resistance, often to the dominant forces.

Confucian dynamism A dimension of national cultures found through research among student samples using the Chinese Value Survey. See Long-term vs. Short-term orientation by Hofstede and Bond.

Congruence A condition in which both verbal and nonverbal behaviors reinforce each other.

Contact cultures Cultural groups in which people tend to stand close together and touch frequently when they interact—for example, cultural groups in South

America, the Middle East, and southern Europe.

Context The physical, psychological, social, cultural, and temporal environment in which communication takes place.

Conversational management The management of the way in which messages are exchanged in conversation.

Conversational maxims Principles that are followed in conversation to ensure that the goal of the conversation is achieved.

Conversational turns The process of passing the speaker and listener roles during conversation.

Conversation Two-person communication usually following five stages: opening, feedforward, business, feedback, and closing.

Correlation A term from mathematical statistics express the degree of common variation of two sets of numbers. The coefficient of correlation can vary from a maximum of 1.00 (perfect agreement) via the value 0 (no relationship) to a minimum of −1.0 (perfect disagreement).

Co-cultural group Non-dominant cultural groups that exist in a national culture, such as African American or Chinese American.

Critical approach A meta-theoretical approach that includes many assumptions of the interpretive approach but that focuses more on macro-contexts, such as the political and social structures that influence communication.

Critical thinking The process of logically evaluating reasons and evidence and reaching a judgment on the basis of this analysis.

Cross-cultural training Training people to become familiar with other cultural norms and to improve their interactions with people of different domestic and international background.

Cultural adaptation A process by which individuals learn the rules and customs of new cultural contexts.

Cultural assimilation The process by which a person's culture is given up and he or she takes on the values and beliefs of another culture as when, for example, an immigrant gives up his or her native culture to become a member of this new adopted culture.

Cultural display Signs that communicate one's cultural identification, like clothing or religious jewelry.

Cultural identity The social identity associated with being a member of our culture.

Cultural imperialism Domination through the spread of cultural products.

Cultural inversion The process of regarding certain forms of behavior as inappropriate for a minority-group member because they are seen as characteristic of the dominant culture.

Cultural rules Rules that are specific to a given culture.

Cultural shock A relatively short-term feeling of disorientation and discomfort due to the lack of familiar cues in the environment.

Cultural space Where people grow up and live in terms of culture.

Cultural texts Cultural artifacts (magazines, TV programs, movies, and so on) that convey cultural norms, values, and beliefs.

Culture assimilator A programmed learning tool for developing intercultural communication skills.

Culture brokers Individuals who act as bridges between cultures, facilitating intercultural interaction.

Culture industry Industries that produce and sell popular culture as commodities.

Culture shock A state of distress following the transfer of a person to an unfamiliar cultural environment. It may be accompanied by physical symptons.

Culture time The meanings given to the ways time is treated in a particular culture.

Culture An accumuated pattern of values, beliefs, worldviews and behaviors shared mostly by an identifiable group of people with a common history and verbal and non-verbal symbols of system.

Deception Leading others to false conclusions.

Deceptive communication Message distortion resulting from deliberate falsification or omission of information by a communicator with the intent of stimulating in another, or others, a belief that the communicator himself or herself does not believe.

Decoder Something that takes a message in one form and translates it into another form from which meaning can be formulated. In human communication, the decoder is the auditory mechanism; in electronic communication, the decoder is, for example, the telephone earpiece. Decoding is the process of extracting a message from a code, for example, translating speech sounds into nerve impulses.

Delphi method A small-group technique in which a group of experts is established but there's no interaction among them; instead they communicate by repeatedly responding to questionnaires.

Determinism, principle of The principle of verbal interaction that holds that all verbalizations are to some extent purposeful, that there is a reason for every verbalization.

Dialect A language variety associated with a particular region or social group.

Dialectical approach An approach to intercultural communication that integrates three approaches—functionalist (or social science), interpretive, and critical—in understanding culture and communication. It recognizes and accepts that the three approaches are interconnected and sometimes contradictory.

Diaspora A massive migration often caused by war, famine, or persecution that results in the dispersal of a unified group.

Dimensional model A set of dimensions used in combination in order to describe a phenomenon.

Dimension An aspect of a phenomenon that can be measured, usually expressed by a number. See 6 Dimensions of Cultures by Hofstede: individualism versus collectivism, power distance (from small to large), femininity versus masculinity, uncertainty avoidance (from weak to strong), long-/ short-term orientation, and restraint vesus indulgent.

Disclaimer Statement that asks the listener to receive what you say without its reflecting negatively on you.

Disconfirmation The process by which one ignores or denies the right of the individual even to define himself or herself.

Discourse The ways in which language is actually used by particular communities of people, in particular contexts, for particular purposes.

Distance zones The areas, defined by physical space, within which people interact, according to Edward Hall's theory of proxemics. The four distance zones for individuals are intimate, personal, social, and public.

Downward communication Communication sent from the higher levels of the hierarchy to the lower levels, for example, messages sent by managers to workers, or from deans to faculty members.

Dyadic communication Two-person communication.

Dyadic consciousness An awareness on the part of the participants that an interpersonal relationship or paring exists between them; distinguished from situations in which two individuals are together but do not see themselves as a unit or twosome.

Dyadic effect The tendency for the behaviors of one person to stimulate similar behaviors in the other interactant; often used to refer to the tendency of one person's self-disclosures to prompt the other to also self-disclose.

Egocentric bias The tendency to see our own behavior as normal, and compare other people's behavior to our own.

Elaborate style Mode of speaking that emphasizes rich, expressive language.

Primarily hand gestures that have a direct verbal translation; can be used to repeat or to substitute for verbal communication.

Emic A term stemming from phonemic. The emic way of inquiry focuses on understanding communication patterns from inside a particular cultural community or context. Opposed to etic.

Empathy The feeling of another person's feeling; the capacity to feel or perceive something as does another person.

Enclaves (1) The territories that are surrounded by another country's territory; (2) cultural territory groups that live within a larger cultural group's territory.

Encoder Something that takes a message in one form and translates it into another form. In human communication, the encoder is the speaking mechanism; in electronic communication, the encoder is, for example, the telephone mouthpiece. Encoding is the process of putting a message into speech sounds.

Enculturation The process by which culture is transmitted from one generation to another.

Equilibrium theory A theory of proxiemics holding that intimacy and physical closeness are positively related; as a relationship becomes more intimate, the individuals will maintain shorter distances between themselves.

Equity theory A theory claiming that the two people in a relationship experience relational satisfaction when there is an equal distribution of rewards and costs between them.

Ethics The branch of philosophy that deals with the rightness or wrongness of actions; the study of moral values; in communication, the morality of message behavior.

Ethnic identity The degree to which a person identifies, associates, and empathizes with his or her ethnic group. Often, this is accomplished and recognized via language use.

Ethnocentric attributional bias The tendency to make internal attributions for the positive behavior of the in-group while making external attributions for its negative behavior.

Ethnocentrism The tendency to place one's own group (cultural, ethnic or religious) in a position of centrality and worth, and to create negative attitudes and behaviors toward other groups.

Ethnography A discipline that examines the patterned interactions and significant symbols of specific cultural groups to identify the cultural norms.

Etic A term stemming from phonetic. The etic inquiry searches for universal generalizations across cultures from a distance. Opposed to emic.

Expectancy violations theory A theory of proxemics holding that people have a certain expectancy for certain relationships. When that is violated (a person stands too close to you, or a romantic partner maintains abnormally large distances from you), the relationship comes into clearer focus and you wonder why this "normal distance" is being violated.

Experiential limitation The limit on an individual's ability to communicate, as set by the nature and extent of that individual's experiences.

Extended family A family group including relatives in the second and third degree (or beyond), like grandparents, uncles, aunts, and cousins.

Eye contact A nonverbal code, eye gaze, that communicates meanings about respect and status and often regulates turn-taking during interactions.

Face In collectivist societies, a quality attributed to someone who meets the essential requirements related to his or her social position.

Facework Communication strategies employed to "save" one's own "face", someone else's "face", or public image.

Facial feedback hypothesis The hypothesis or theory that your facial expressions can produce physiological and emotional effects.

Facial management techniques Techniques used to mask certain emotions and to emphasize others, for example, intensifying your expression of happiness to make a friend feel good about a promotion.

Factor analysis A technique from mathematical statistics designed to assist minimum number of undelying common factors. Fact-inference confusion A misevaluation in which one makes an inference, regards it as a fact, and acts upon it as if it were a fact.

Feedback Information that is given back to the source. Feedback may come from the source's own messages or from the receiver(s) in the form of applause, yawning, puzzled looks, questions, letters to the editor of a newspaper, increased or decreased subscriptions to a magazine.

Feedforward Information that is sent prior to the regular messages, telling the listener something about what is to follow; messages that are prefatory to more central messages.

Feminine culture A culture in which both men and women are encouraged to be modest, oriented to maintaining the quality of life, and tender. Feminine cultures emphasize the quality of life and so socialize their people to be modest and to emphasize close interpersonal relationships. Opposed to masculine culture.

Femininity   The opposite of masculinity; together, they form one of the dimensions of national cultures. Femininity stands for a society in which social gender roles overlap: both men and women are supposed to be modest, tender, and concerned with quality of life.

Field studies   Formal investigations conducted by researchers in the target culture. The purpose of field studies is to gain insiders' insights.

Functionalist approach   A study of intercultural communication, also called the social science approach, based on the assumptions that (1) there is a describable, external reality; (2) human beings are predictable; (3) culture is a variable that can be measured. This approach aims to identify and explain cultural variations in communication and to predict future communication.

Fundamentalism   The belief that there is one Truth and that one's own group is in possession of this Truth which is usually defined in great detail.

Fundamentalism   The belief that there is only one Truth and that one own group is in possession of this Truth which is usually defined in great detail.

Gender   A socially constructed and learned creation usually associated with one's sex, masculinity and femininity. People are born into sex group, but learn to become masculine or feminine. The meaning of gender stems from the particular culture's value system.

Gestalt   An integrated whole which should be studied as such and loses its meaning when divided into parts; from a German word meaning 'form'.

Global nomads   People who grow up in many different cultural contexts because their parents relocated.

Global village   A term coined by Marshall McLuhan in the 1960s that refers to a world in which communication technology unite people in remote parts of the world.

Gossip   Oral or written communication about someone not present, some third party, usually about matters that are private to this third party.

Grapevine messages   Messages that do not follow any formal organizational structures; office-related gossip.

Guanxi   A Chinese term for relational network.

Halo effect   The tendency to generalize a person's virtue or expertise from one area to other areas.

Haptics   Nonverbal communication through physical contact or touch.

Heroes   Persons, alive or dead, real or imaginary, assumed to possess characteristics highly prized in a culture, and which thus serve as models for behavior.

Heterogeneity   Consisting of different or dissimilar elements.

High context Cultural orientation where meanings are gleaned from the physical, social and psychological contact.

High-context culture A culture in which much of the information in communication messages is left implied; it's "understood," it's considered to be in the context or in the person rather than explicitly coded in the verbal messages. Collectivtic cultures are generally high contexts. Opposed to low-context cultures.

Home field advantage The increased power that comes from being in your own territory.

Horizontal collectivism Cultural orientation where the self is seen as a member of an in-group whose members are similar to each other.

Horizontalindividualism Cultural orientation where the self is seen as a member of an in-group whose members are similar to each other.

Hyphenated Americans U.S. Americans who identify not only with being U.S. citizens but also as members of ethnic groups.

Identity The concept of who we are. Characteristics of identity may be understood differently depending on the perspectives that people take—for example, social psychological, communication, or critical perspectives.

Illustrators Primarily hand and arm movements that function to accent or complement speech.

Implicit personality theory A theory of personality, complete with rules about what characteristics go with what other characteristics, that you maintain and through which you perceive others.

Incompatibility A state of incongruity in goals, values, or expectations between two or more individuals.

Individualist culture A culture in which the individual's rather than the group's goals and preferences are given greater importance.

Individualism The opposite of collectivism; together, they from one of the dimensions of national cultures.

Informal time terms Terms that are approximate rather than exact, for example, "soon," "early," and "in a while."

Ingroup A cohesive group which offers protection in exchange for loyalty and provides its members with a sense of identity.

Instrumental style Sender-focused manner of speaking that is goal and outcome oriented. Instrumental speakers use communication to achieve some goal or purpose.

Integration A type of cultural adaptation in which individuals maintain both their original culture and their daily interactions with other groups.

Integration Mode of acculturation in which the individual develops a kind of bicultural orientation that successfully blends and synthesizes cultural dimensions from both groups while maintaining an identity in each group.

Intentionality During communication, the volutary and conscious encoding and decoding of messages.

Intercultural communication Communication that takes place between persons of different cultures or persons who have different cultural beliefs, values, or ways of behaving.

Intercultural competence The ability to behave effectively and appropriately in interacting across cultures.

Interpellation The communication process by which one is pulled into the social forces that place people into specific identity.

Interpersonal communication Communication between two persons or among a small group of persons and distinguished from public or mass communication.

Interpretive approach An approach to intercultural communication that aims to understand and describe human behavior within specific cultural groups based on the assumptions that (1) human experience is subjective; (2) human behavior is creative rather than determined or easily predicted; (3) culture is created and maintained through communication.

Intercultural competence The ability to adapt one's verbal and nonverbal messages to the appropriate cultural context.

Interview A question and answer form of communication.

Intimate distance The closest distance in proxemics, ranging from touching to 18 inches.

Intrapersonal communication Communication with oneself.

In-group talk Talk about a subject or in a vocabulary that some group members understand and others do not; has the effect of excluding those who don't understand.

Irreversibility A principle of communication holding that communication cannot be reversed; once something has been communicated, it cannot be uncommunicated.

I-messages Messages in which the speaker accepts responsibility for personal thoughts and behaviors; messages in which the speaker's point of view is stated explicitly. Opposed to you-messages.

Jargon The technical language of any specialized group, often a professional class, which is unintelligible to individuals not belonging to the group; shop

Glossary

talk.

Johari window A diagram of the four selves (open, blind, hidden, and unknown).

Kinesics General category of body motion, including emblems, illustrators, affect display, and adaptors.

Knowledge As an individual component of intercultural communication competence, the quality of knowing about oneself (that is, one's strengths and weaknesses), others, and various aspects of communication.

Lateral communication Communication between equals—manager to manager, worker to worker.

Leave-taking cues Verbal and nonverbal signals that indicate a desire to terminate a conversation.

Linguistic relativity hypothesis The theory that the language you speak influences your perceptions of the world and your behaviors and that therefore people speaking widely differing languages will perceive and behave differently as a result of the language differences.

Long-term orientation The opposite of short-term orientation; together they form a dimension of national cultures originally labeled "Confucian dynamism." Long-term orientation stands for the fostering of virtues oriented towards future rewards, in particular perseverance and thrift.

Low context Cultural orientation where meanings are encoded in the verbal code.

Low-context culture A culture in which most of the information in communication is explicitly slated in the verbal message, rather than left implied or assumed to be "understood." Low-context cultures are usually individualistic cultures. Opposed to High-context culture.

Marginalization A type of cultural adaptation in which an individual expresses little interest in maintaining cultural ties with either the dominant culture or the migrant culture.

Masculine culture A culture in which men are viewed as assertive, oriented to material success, and strong; women on the other hand are viewed modest, focused on life, and tender. Masculine cultures emphasizes success and so socialize their people to be assertive, ambitious, and competitive. Opposed to feminine culture.

Messages Signals or combinations of signals that serve as stimuli for a receiver.

Metacommunication A message that makes reference to another message: for example, the statements "Did I make myself clear?" or "That's a lie." are metamessages because they refer to other messages.

Microculture An identifiable group of people coexisting within some dominant cultural context.

Model minorities A stereotype that characterizes Asian Americans as a good, successful minority.

Monochronic time system Cultural temporal orientation that stresses the compartmentaliztion and segmenting of measurable units of time.

Monochronic A view of time in which things are done sequentially; one thing is scheduled at a time. Opposed to polychronic.

Monologue A form of communication in which one person speaks and the other listens; there's no real interaction among participants. Opposed to dialogue.

Multiphrenia The splitting of the individual psychologically into multiple selves.

Muted groups Microcultures whose members are forced to express themselves (for example, speak, write) within the dominant mode of expression.

Nativistic Extremely patriotic to the point of being anti-immigrant.

Negative feedback Feedback that serves a corrective function by informing the source that his or her message is not being received in the way intended. Looks of boredom, shouts of disagreement, letters critical of newspaper policy, and teachers' instructions on how better to approach a problem would be examples of negative feedback and would serve to redirect the speaker's behavior.

Nonverbal communication Communication without words; communication by means of space, gestures, facial expressions, touching, vocal variation, and silence, for example.

Nonverbal dominance Nonverbal behavior that allows one person to achieve psychological dominance over another.

Nuclear family A family group including only relatives in the first degree (parents and children).

Obliging style During conflict, asserting the other-face need while also attending to the need of the other-face.

Olfactics The perception and use of smell, scent, and odor.

Olfactory communication Communication by smell.

Openness A quality of interpersonal effectiveness encompassing (1) a willingness to interact openly with others, to self-disclose as appropriate; (2) a willingness to react honestly to incoming stimuli; and (3) a willingness to own one's feelings and thoughts.

Organizational culture An organized pattern of values, beliefs, behaviors, and communication channels held by the members of an organization.

Outgroup   A group whose attributes are dissimilar from an in-group and who opposes the realization of in-group goals.

Paradigms   A framework that servers as the worldview of researchers. Different paradigms assume different interpretation of reality, human behavior, culture, and communication.

Paralanguage   Characteristics of the voice, such as pitch, rhythm, intensity, volume and rate.

Particularism   A way of thinking prevailing in collectivist societies, in which the standards for the way a person should be treated depend on the group to which this person belongs.

Passive listening   Listening that is attentive and supportive but occurs without talking and without directing the speaker in any nonverbal way; also used negatively to refer to inattentive and uninvolved listening.

Perception checking   The process of verifying your understanding of some message, situation, or feeling.

Perception   The mental interpretation of external stimuli via sensation.

Perceptual Context   The attitudes, emotions, and motivations of the persons engaged in communication and hw they affect information processing.

Personal distance   The second-closest distance in proxemics, ranging from 18 inches to 4 feet.

Personal rejection   An unproductive conflict strategy in which you withhold love and affection and seek to win the argument by getting the other person to break down under this withdrawal.

Phatic communication   Communication that is primarily social; communication designed to open the channels of communication rather than to communicate something about the external world; "Hello" and "How are you?" in everyday interaction are examples.

Polarization   A form of fallacious reasoning by which only two extremes are considered; also referred to as "black-or-white" and "either-or" thinking or two-valued orientation.

Polychronic   A view of time in which several things may be scheduled or engaged in at the same time. Opposed to monochronic time orientation.

Polychronictime system   Cultural temporal orientation that stresses the involvement of people and completion of tasks as opposed to strict adherence to schedules.

Positive feedback   Feedback that supports or reinforces the continuation of behavior along the same lines in which it is already proceeding—for example, applause during a speech encourages the speaker to continue speaking this way.

Power distance The extent to which the less powerful members of institutions and organizations within a country expect and accept that power is distributed unequally. One of the dimesnions of national cultures (from small to large)

Power plays Consistent patterns of behavior in which one person tries to control the behavior of another.

Pragmatics In interpersonal communication, an approach that focuses on communication behaviors and effects and on communication effectiveness.

Prejudice An attitude (usually negative) toward a cultural group based on little or no evidence.

Primary affect displays The communication of the six primary emotions: happiness, surprise, fear, anger, sadness, and disgust/contempt.

Privacy The degree to which an individual can control the visual, auditory and olfactiv interaction with others.

Projection A psychological process whereby you attribute characteristics or feelings of your own to others; often used to refer to the process whereby you attribute your faults to others.

Protection theory A theory of proxemics holding that people establish a body-buffer zone to protect themselves from unwanted closeness, touching, or attack.

Proxemics The perception and use of space, including territoriality and personal space.

Proxemics The study of the communicative function of space; the study of how people unconsciously structure their space—the distance between people in their interactions, the organization of space in homes and offices, and even the design of cities.

Proximity As a principle of perception, the tendency to perceive people or events that are physically close as belonging together or representing some unit; physical closeness—one of the qualities influencing interpersonal attraction.

Psychological time The importance you place on past, present, and future time.

Public distance The farthest distance in proxemics, ranging from 12 feet to more than 25 feet.

Pupil dilation The extent to which the pupil of the eye is expanded; generally large pupils indicate positive reactions.

Qualitative methods Research methods that attempt to capture people's own meanings for their everyday behavior in specific contexts. These methods use participant observation and field studies.

Quality maxim A principle of conversation that holds that speakers cooperate by saying what they think is true and by not saying what they think is false.

Quantitative methods Research methods that employ numerical indicators to capture and ascertain the relationships among variables. These methods use survey and observation.

Quantity maxim A principle of conversation that holds that speakers cooperate by being only as informative as necessary to communicate their intended meanings.

Reconciliation strategies Behaviors designed to repair a broken relationship.

Reentry shock The effects associated with the tensions and anxiety of returning to one's native culture after an extended stay in a foreign culture.

Reference group A group to which a person may or may not belong, but identifies in some way with the values and goals of the group.

Regulators Nonverbal act that manage and govern communication between people, such as stance, distance, and eye contact.

Relationship dialectics theory A theory that describes relationships along a series of opposites representing competing desires or motivations, such as the desire for autonomy and the desire to belong to someone, for novelty and predictability, and for closeness and openness.

Relativism A willingness to consider other persons' or groups' theories and values as equally reasonable as one's own.

Rhetorical approach A research method, dating back to ancient Greece, in which scholars try to interpret the meanings or persuasion used in texts or oral discourses in the contexts in which they occur.

Rituals Collective activities, technically superfluous in reaching desired ends, but which within a culture are considered as socially essential: they are therefore carried out for their own sake.

Role One's relative hierarchical position or rank in a group. A role is a prescribed set of behaviors that is expected in order to fulfill the role. Roles prescribe with whom, about what, and how to interact with others.

Schemata Ways of organizing perceptions; mental templates or structures that help you to organize the millions of items of information you come into contact with every day as well as those you already have in memory; general ideas about people, for yourself, or social roles.

Self-adaptors Movements that usually satisfy a physical need, especially to make you more comfortable, like scratching your head to relieve an itch, moistening your lips because they feel dry, or pushing your hair out of your eyes.

Self-disclosure Revealing information about oneself.

Self-serving bias　A bias that operates in the self-attribution process and leads you to take credit for the positive consequences and to deny responsibility for the negative consequences of your behaviors.

Separation　A type of cultural adaptation in which an individual retains his or her original cultural while interacting minimally with other groups. Separation may be voluntary, or it may be initiated and enforced by the dominate society, in which case it becomes segregation.

Short-term orientation　The opposite of long-term orientation; together, they form a dimension of national cultures originally labelled 'Confucian dynamism'. Short-term orientation stands for the fostering of virtues related to the past and present, in particular respect for tradition, preservation of face, and fulfilling social obligations.

Situational features　The extent to which the environmental context, previous contact, status differential, and third-party intervention affect one's competence during intercultural communication.

Social comparison processes　The processes by which you compare yourself with others and then assess and evaluate yourself on the basis of the comparison; one of the sources of self-concept.

Social penetration theory　A theory concerned with relationship development from the superficial to the intimate levels (depth) and from few to many areas of interpersonal interaction (breadth).

Social stratification　A culture's organization of roles into a hierarchical vertical status structure.

Socialization　The acquisition of the values and practices belonging to a culture, by participating in that culture.

Sojourners　People who move into new cultural contexts for a limited period of time and for a specific purpose, such as for study or business.

State apprehension　Communication apprehension for specific types of communication situations like public speaking or interview situations.

Stereotypes　A subset of categorizing and involving the attribution of characteristics of a group to an individual based on the individual's membership in that group. Stereotypes are categories with an attitude.

Stimuli　Any external or internal changes that impinge on or arouse an organism.

Stimulus-response models of communication　Models of communication that assumes that the process of communication is linear, beginning with a stimulus that then leads to a response.

Subcultures　Groups within a culture whose members share many of the values of the culture but also have some values that differ from those of the larger culture.

Succinct style symbol Manner of very concise speaking often accompanied by silence. An arbitraily selected and learned stimulus representing something else.

Sympathy The imaginative placing of ourselves in another person's position.

Taboo Forbidden; culturally censored.

Taboo language It is language that is frowned upon by "polite society." Topics and specific words may be considered taboo-death, sex, certain forms of illness and various words denoting sexual activities and excretory functions.

Tactile communication Communication by touch; communication received by the skin.

Temporal communication The messages that your time orientation and treatment of time communicates.

Tolerance for ambiguity The ability to deal successfully with situations, even when a great deal of information needed to interact effectively is unknown.

Trait apprehension Communication apprehension generally; a fear of communication situations regardless of their specific form.

Uncertainty avoidance The extent to which the members of a culture feel threatened by uncertain of unknown situations. On of the dimensions of national cultures (from weak to strong)

Uncertainty reduction theory Applied to interpersonal relationships, the theory holds that as relationships develop, uncertainty is reduced; relationship development is seen as a process of reducing uncertainty about one another.

Uncertainty The amount of unpredictability during communication.

Universal of interpersonal communication A feature of communication common to all interpersonal communication acts.

Universalism A way of thinking prevailing in individualist societies, in which the standards for the way a person should be treated are the same for everybody.

Upward communication Communication sent from the lower levels of the hierarchy to the upper levels—worker to manager, faculty to dean.

U-curve theory A theory of cultural adaptation positing that migrants go through fairly predictable phases—excitement (anticipation, shock) disorientation, adaptation—in adapting to a new cultural situation.

Validation Testing the conclusions from one piece of research against data from independent other sources.

Values Criteria for selecting and justifying behavior. Values have a cognitive, affective, and behavioral component.

Verbal aggressiveness A method of winning an argument by attacking the other person's self-concept. Avoid inflicting psychological pain on the other person to win an argument.

Vertical collectivism Cultural orientation where the individual sees the self as an integral part of the in-group but whose members are different from each other.

Vertical individualism Cultural orientation where an autonomous self is valued and the self is seen as different from and perhaps unequal with others.

Walking a narrow ridge Taking both our own and other people's viewpoints into consideration in our dealing with others.

Worldview Underlying assumptions about the nature of reality and human behavior.

W-curve A theory of cultural adaptation suggesting that sojourners experience another U-curve upon returning home.

Xenophilia The feeling that persons and things from abroad must be superior.

Xenophobia The feeling that foreign persons or things are dangerous.

You-messages Messages in which you deny responsibility for your own thoughts and behaviors; messages that attribute your perception to another person; messages of blame. Opposed to I-messages.